THE COMPLETE HANDBOOK OF THE INTERNET

Volume II

The Complete Handbook of the Internet

Volume II

by

W.J. Buchanan

Napier University

KLUWER ACADEMIC PUBLISHERS

BOSTON / DORDRECHT / LONDON

A C.I.P. Catalogue record for this book is available from the Library of Congress.

ISBN 1-4020-7289-9 (Volume II)
ISBN 1-4020-7290-2 (Set)

Published by Kluwer Academic Publishers,
P.O. Box 17, 3300 AA Dordrecht, The Netherlands.

Sold and distributed in North, Central and South America
by Kluwer Academic Publishers,
101 Philip Drive, Norwell, MA 02061, U.S.A.

In all other countries, sold and distributed
by Kluwer Academic Publishers,
P.O. Box 322, 3300 AH Dordrecht, The Netherlands.

Printed on acid-free paper

Printed in the Netherlands.

Contents

Volume 1

G1 Networking operating systems

G1.1 Introduction

A networking operating system is one which allows hosts to intercommunicate using operating system support. Thus, networking is built into the operating system, and not just an add-on. Many early versions of operating systems from Microsoft, including DOS and Microsoft Windows Version 3, had networking as an add-on to the operating system, thus proved un-reliable and difficult to setup. Recent versions of Microsoft Windows have successfully integrated networking, and also support mixed, or hybrid networks. The most successful networking operating systems are:

- **Microsoft Windows.** The de-facto standard PC operating system which supports many applications. It supports a client/server architecture and also peer-to-peer architecture. Windows NT/2000 provides a robust networking technology.
- **Novell NetWare.** A PC-based system which provides an excellent file server support and a print server. It has been enhanced to provide corporate networks using NDS.
- **UNIX.** A robust and well-tested networking operating system which supports most of the industry-standard protocols. UNIX tends to run on high-powered workstations.

G1.2 Microsoft Windows

Windows NT has provided an excellent network operating system. It communicates directly with many different types of networks, protocols and computer architectures. Windows NT and Windows 95/98 have the great advantage over other operating systems that they have integrated network support. Operating systems now use networks to make peer-to-peer connections and also connections to servers for access to file systems and print servers. The three most used operating systems are MS-DOS, Microsoft Windows and UNIX. Microsoft Windows comes in many flavors; the main versions in current use are:

- Microsoft Windows 3.xx – 16-bit PC-based operating system with limited multi-tasking. It runs from MS-DOS and thus still uses MS-DOS functionality and file system structure.
- Microsoft Windows 95/98 – robust 32-bit multi-tasking operating system (although there are some 16-bit parts in it) which can run MS-DOS applications, Microsoft Windows 3.xx applications and 32-bit applications.
- Microsoft Windows NT/2000/XP – robust 32-bit multi-tasking operating systems with integrated networking. Networks are built with NT/2000 servers and clients. As with Microsoft Windows 95/98 they can run MS-DOS, Microsoft Windows 3.x applications and 32-bit applications. In this chapter, Windows NT/2000 will be simply referred to as Microsoft Windows.

G1.2.1 Novell NetWare networking

Novell NetWare is one of the most popular systems for PC LANs and provides file and print server facilities. The protocol used is SPX/IPX. This is also used by Windows NT to communicate with other Windows NT nodes and with NetWare networks. The Internet Packet

Exchange (IPX) protocol is a network layer protocol for transportation of data between computers on a Novell network. IPX is very fast and has a small connectionless datagram protocol. Sequenced Packet Interchange (SPX) provides a communications protocol which supervises the transmission of the packet and ensures its successful delivery.

NetWare uses the Open Data-Link Interface (ODI) standard to simplify network driver development and to provide support for multiple protocols on a single network adapter. It allows Novell NetWare drivers to be written without concern for the protocol that will be used on top of them (similar to NDIS in Microsoft Windows). The link support layer (LSL or LSL.COM) provides a foundation for the MAC layer to communicate with multiple protocols (similar to NDIS in Windows NT). The IPX.COM (or IPXODI.COM) program normally communicates with the LSL and the applications. The MAC driver is a device driver or NIC driver. It provides low-level access to the network adapter by supporting data transmission and some basic adapter management functions. These drivers also pass data from the physical layer to the transport protocols at the network and transport layers.

G1.2.2 Microsoft Windows networking

Networks must use a protocol to transmit data. Typical protocols are:

- IPX/SPX – used with Novell NetWare, it accesses file and printer services.
- TCP/IP – used for Internet access and client/server applications.
- SNA DLC – used mainly by IBM mainframes and minicomputers.
- AppleTalk – used by Macintosh computers.
- NetBEUI – used in some small LANs (stands for NetBIOS Extended User Interface).

Novell NetWare is installed in many organizations to create local area networks of PCs. It uses IPX/SPX for transmitting data and allows access to file servers and network printing services. TCP/IP is the standard protocol used when accessing the Internet and also for client/server applications (such as remote file transfer and remote login).

A major advantage of Microsoft Windows is that networking is built into the operating system. Figure G1.1 shows how it is organized in relation to the OSI model. Microsoft Windows has the great advantage of being protocol-independent and will work with most standard protocols, such as TCP/IP, IPX/SPX, NetBEUI, DLC and AppleTalk. The default protocol is NetBEUI.

There are two main boundaries in Microsoft Windows and NDIS and TDI. The Network Device Interface Standard (NDIS) boundary layer interfaces to several network interface adapters (such as Ethernet, Token Ring, RS-232, modems, and so on) with different protocols. It allows for an unlimited number of network interface cards (NICs) and protocols to be connected to be used with the operating system. In Microsoft Windows, a single software module, NDIS.SYS (the NDIS wrapper), interfaces with the manufacturer-supplied NDIS NIC device driver. The wrapper provides a uniform interface between the protocol drivers (such as TCP/IP or IPX/SPX) and the NDIS device driver.

IPX/SPX and AppleTalk

Novell NetWare networks use SPX/IPX and are supported through Microsoft Windows using the NWLink protocol stack. The AppleTalk protocol allows Windows NT/2000 to share a network with Macintosh clients. It can also act as an AppleShare server.

NetBEUI

NetBEUI (NetBIOS Extended User Interface) has been used with network operating systems, such as Microsoft LAN manager and OS/2 LAN server. In Microsoft Windows, the NetBEUI frame (NBF) protocol stack gives backward compatibility with existing NetBEUI implementations and also provides for enhanced implementations. NetBEUI is the standard technique that NT clients and servers use to intercommunicate.

NBF is similar to TCP/IP and SPX/IPX. It is used to establish a session between a client and a server, and also to provide the reliable transport of the data across the connection-oriented session. Thus NetBEUI tries to provide reliable data transfer through error checking and acknowledgement of each successfully received data packet. In the standard form of NetBEUI each packet must be acknowledged after its delivery. This is wasteful in time. Windows NT uses NBF which improves NetBEUI as it allows several packets to be sent before requiring an acknowledgement (called an adaptive sliding window protocol).

Each NetBEUI is assigned a 1-byte session number and thus allows a maximum of 254 simultaneously active sessions (as two of the connection numbers are reserved). NBF enhances this by allowing 254 connections to computers with 254 sessions for each connection (thus there is a maximum of 254×254 sessions).

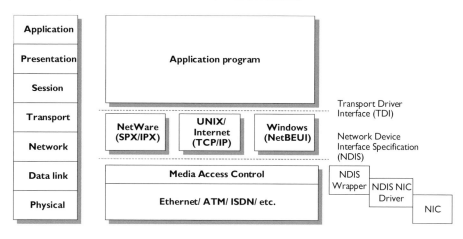

Figure G1.1 Microsoft Windows network interfaces

G1.2.3 Windows sockets

A Windows socket (WinSock) is a standard method that allows nodes over a network to communicate with each other using a standard interface. It supports internetworking protocols such as TCP/IP, IPX/SPX, AppleTalk and NetBEUI. WinSock communicates through the TDI interface and uses the file `WINSOCK.DLL` or `WINSOCK32.DLL`. These DLLs (dynamic link libraries) contain a number of networking functions which are called in order to communicate with the transport and network layers (such as TCP/IP or SPX/IPX). As it communicates with these layers, WinSock is independent of the networking interface (such as Ethernet or FDDI).

G1.2.4 Robust networking

Microsoft Windows servers provide fault tolerance in a number of ways. These are outlined in the following sections.

Disk mirroring

Network servers normally support disk mirroring which protects against hard disk failure. It uses two partitions on different disk drives which are connected to the same controller. Data written to the first (primary) partition is mirrored automatically to the secondary partition. If the primary disk fails then the system uses the partition on the secondary disk. Mirroring also allows unallocated space on the   primary drive to be allocated to the secondary drive. On a disk mirroring system the primary and secondary partitions have the same drive letter (such as C: or D:) and users are unaware that disks are being mirrored.

Disk duplexing

Disk duplexing means that mirrored pairs are controlled by different controllers. This provides for fault tolerance on both disk and controller. Unfortunately, it does not support multiple controllers connected to a single disk drive.

Striping with parity

Network servers normally support disk striping with parity. This technique is based on RAID 5 (Redundant Array of Inexpensive Disks), where a number of partitions on different disks are combined to make one large logical drive. Data is written in stripes across all of the disk drives and additional parity bits. For example, if a system has four disk drives then data is written to the first three disks and the parity is written to the fourth drive. Typically the stripe is 64 KB, thus 64 KB will be written to Drive 1, the same to Drive 2 and Drive 3, then the parity of the other three to the fourth. The following example illustrates the concept of RAID where a system writes the data 110, 000, 111, 100 to the first three drives, which gives parity bits of 1, 1, 0 and 0.

If one of the disk drives fails then the addition of the parity bit allows the bits on the failed disk to be recovered. For example, if disk 3 fails then the bits from the other disk are simply XOR-ed together to generate the bits from the failed drive. If the data on the other disk drives is 111 then the recovered data gives 0, 001 gives 0, and so on.

Disk 1	Disk 2	Disk 3	Disk 4 (Odd parity)
1	1	0	1
0	0	0	1
1	1	1	0
1	0	0	0

The 64 KB stripes of data are also interleaved across the disks. The parity block is written to the first disk drive, then in the next block to the second, and so on. A system with four disk drives would store the following data:

Disk 1	Disk 2	Disk 3	Disk 4
Parity block 1	Data block A	Data block B	Data block C
Data block D	Parity block 2	Data block E	Data block F
Data block G	Data block H	Parity block 3	Data block I

Each of the data blocks will be 64 KB, which is also equal to the parity block. The interlacing of the data ensures that the parity stripes are not all on the same disk. Thus there is no single point of failure for the set.

Striping of data improves reading performance when each of the disk drives has a separate controller, because the data is simultaneously read by each of the controllers and simultaneously passed to the systems. It thus provides fast reading of data but only moderate writing performance (because the system must calculate the parity block).

The main advantages of RAID 5 can be summarized as:

- It recovers data when a single disk drive or controller fails (RAID level 0 does not use a parity block thus it cannot regenerate lost data).
- It allows a number of small partitions to be built into a large partition.
- Several disks can be mounted as a single drive.
- Performance can be improved with multiple disk controllers.

The main disadvantages of RAID 5 are:

- It requires increased memory because of the parity block.
- Performance is reduced when one of the disks fails, because of the need to regenerate the failed data.
- It increases the amount of disk space as it has an overhead due to the parity block (although the overhead is normally less than disk mirroring, which has a 50% overhead).
- It requires at least three disk drives.

UPS services

Microsoft Windows servers provide services to uninterruptable power supplies (UPSs). UPS systems provide power, from batteries, to a computer system when there is a glitch in the supply, power sags or power failure. The operating system detects signals from a UPS unit and performs an orderly shutdown of applications, services and file systems as the stored energy in the UPS is depleted.

G1.2.5 Volumes

A dynamic volume is one which resides on a dynamic disk. Windows allows the following dynamic volumes: simple, spanned, striped, mirrored, and RAID-5, and can be formatted with FAT or NTFS. There are various definitions for volumes, these include:

- **Simple volume**. This is a dynamic volume which uses disk space from a single dynamic disk. It can consist of a single region on a disk or multiple regions of the same disk that are linked together. A simple volume is not fault tolerant, but can be mirror them to create mirrored volumes.
- **Spanned volume**. This is a dynamic volume which uses disk space on more than one physical disk. You can increase the size of a spanned volume by extending it onto additional dynamic disks. You can create spanned volumes only on dynamic disks. Spanned volumes are not fault tolerant and cannot be mirrored.

Windows 2000, and onwards, support dynamic disks. These provide additional features that allow volumes span to span multiple disks. These disks have a hidden database to track information on dynamic volumes.

G1.2.6 Security model

Microsoft Windows treats all its resources as objects that can only be accessed by authorized users and services. Examples of objects are directories, printers, processes, ports,
devices and files. On an NTFS partition the access to an object is controlled by the security
descriptor (SD) structure which contains an access control list (ACL) and security identifier
(SI). The SD contains the user (and group) accounts that have access and permissions to the
object. The system always checks the ACL of an object to determine whether the user is allowed to access it.

The main parts of the SI are:

OWNER	Indicates the user account for the object.
GROUP	Indicates the group the object belongs to.
User ACL	The user-controller ACL.
System ACL	System manager controlled ACL.

The ACL file access rights are:

```
Full control       (All)    Change         (RWXD)
Read               (RX)     Add            (WX)
List               (RX)     Change Permissions  (P)
```

Where R identifies read access, W identifies write access, X identifies execute, D identifies
delete, and P identifies change permissions. There is also another attribute named O, which
is take ownership.

Full control gives all access to all file permissions, and takes ownership of the NTFS volume. The Change rights allows: creation of folders and adding files to them, changing data
in files, appending data to files, changing file attributes, deleting folders and files, and per-
forming all tasks permitted by the Read permission. The Read permission allows the display
of folder and file names, display of the data and attributes of a file, run program files, and
access to other subfolders. For example a directory could have the following permissions:

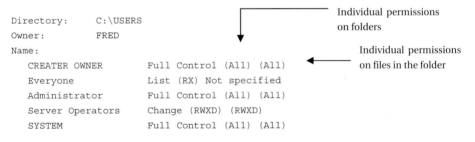

```
Directory:     C:\USERS                              Individual permissions
Owner:         FRED                                  on folders
Name:
    CREATER OWNER      Full Control (All) (All)      Individual permissions
    Everyone           List (RX) Not specified       on files in the folder
    Administrator      Full Control (All) (All)
    Server Operators   Change (RWXD) (RWXD)
    SYSTEM             Full Control (All) (All)
```

It can be seen in this example, that the owner has full control over the directory, but everyone else (apart from the Administrator, Server Operators and SYSTEM) have only List rights
(that is, they can only view or run programs, or get access to subfolders).

G1.2.7 Workgroups and domains

Microsoft Windows assigns users to workgroups, which are collections of users who are
grouped together with a common purpose. This purpose might be to share resources such

as file systems or printers, and each workgroup has its own unique name. With workgroups each Microsoft Windows workstation interacts with a common group of computers on a peer-to-peer level. Each workstation then manages its own resources and user accounts. Workgroups are useful for small groups where a small number of users require to access resources on other computers.

A domain in Microsoft Windows is a logical collection of computers sharing a common user accounts database and security policy. Thus, each domain must have at least one Microsoft Windows server. Each computer in the domain is assigned a unique name.

Microsoft Windows is designed to operate with either workgroups or domains. Figure G1.2 illustrates the difference between domains and workgroups. In this case the name of the domain is my_d (which must be provided when logging into the domain), along with the user name and the associated password. This domain contains a number of computers, such as freds_pc and bills_pc. The top level of the domain is \\, and files can be referred to with *computer_name**directory**filename*.

Domains have the advantages that:

- Each domain forms a single administrative unit with shared security and user account information. This domain has one database containing user and group information and security policy settings.
- They segment the resources of the network so that users, by default, can view all networks for a particular domain.
- User accounts are automatically validated by the domain controller. This stops invalid users from gaining access to network resources. The domain can also be setup so that the server does not validate users, but this is not recommended as it can lead to security problems.

A Microsoft Windows server provides many client services (as illustrated in Figure G1.3), including:

- **User profiles.** The server can store profiles for the user, so that they can be easily changed and stored in a central source. This service can allow a user to get a consistent range of settings, no matter which computer they use (this is known as a roaming user profile). For example, an office may have a number of computers which can be logged into by any of the users within the domain. No matter which computer a user logs into, they will see the same settings, for their desktop, e-mail settings, and so on. User profiles typically related to display settings, regional settings, network connections, printer connections, mouse settings and sounds. A roaming user profile is made up of two parts: roaming personal user profile, which is the part of the profile that the user can change, and the roaming mandatory user profile, which is the part of the profile that cannot be changed by the user. The mandatory user profile is typically used to create a standard desktop configuration.
- **Hardware profiles.** This allows different hardware profiles to be setup.
- **Internet Information Server.** This provides HTTP and FTP access.
- **Directory Services.** Allows for a directory database which allows for network login, and a centralized point of administration and access to resources within the domain.
- **Management Tools.** This includes user and group account management.
- **Additional Network Services.** These include DNS (for domain name resolution), WINS (similar to DCHP and resolves domain names to IP addresses) and DHCP (which dy-

namically assigns IP addresses).

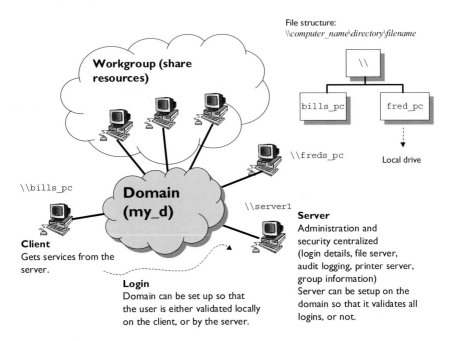

File structure:
\\computer_name\directory\filename

\\freds_pc   Local drive

Workgroup (share resources)

\\bills_pc

Domain (my_d)

\\server1

Client
Gets services from the server.

Login
Domain can be set up so that the user is either validated locally on the client, or by the server.

Server
Administration and security centralized (login details, file server, audit logging, printer server, group information)
Server can be setup on the domain so that it validates all logins, or not.

Figure G1.2 Workgroups and domains

Tools:
- User Manager for Domains. For user and group accounts over the domain.
- User Manager. For local user and group accounts.
- Server Manager. To view and manage computers and domains.
- Event Viewer. Examines events in the domain.

Server can provide:
- User profiles (desktop settings, network connections, printer connections, and so on).
- Roaming user profiles. Made up of Roaming personal user profile and roaming mandatory user profile.
- Hardware profiles.
- Internet Information Server (FTP/ HTTP).
- Security.
- Directory services.
- Management tools (User accounts, groups, and so on).
- Additional networked services (WINs, DHCP, DNS, and so on).

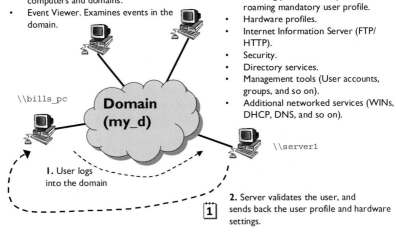

\\bills_pc   **Domain (my_d)**

\\server1

1. User logs into the domain

2. Server validates the user, and sends back the user profile and hardware settings.

Figure G1.3 Services from the server

G1.2.8 Audit policy

Audit policies allow certain events to be monitored, as illustrated in Figure G1.4. Typically this will be related to user login/logout (times that the user logs in and logs out, either successfully, or not), file and object access (files that are being accessed and objectives, such as printers, backup storage devices, and so), use of user rights, user and group management, security policy changes, restart/shutdown (when the computer is started and shutdown) and process tracking (the program which the user runs). These events can be monitored for good events (successful operations) and/or bad events (unsuccessful operations). The audit policy can either be setup on a local computer (for a local audit policy) or over the domain (the domain audit policy). The audit log can then be examined to determine how users have been using the resource within the domain. The system administrator might use the audit log to:

- **Unauthorized logins.** This may point to an external hacker trying to log into a valid account, and the administrator should audit users logging in and out of the domain.
- **Monitor out-of-hours logins.** Security problems typically occur out of normal hours. A system administrator can determine if someone is logging into the domain after normal hours, and possibly trace their operations.
- **Monitor the access to resources.** The administrator can monitor the access to networked resources, such as printers. If a user is using the resource too much, the administrator can limit the access rights to it for that user.
- **Monitoring how file and object permission are changed.** This may point to a breach of security where a user tries to change the permissions on objects and/or files. The administrator can monitor both successful and unsuccessful changes.
- **Monitor the processes that a user is running.** This might be used if it is thought that a user is using a certain package too often, especially if it is not related to their job function. For example, an administrator could monitor the access to a WWW browser, and the times in which it was used. If it was used too much, for non-work-related work, the administrator could either limit the access to it, or ban its usage for that user.
- **Times that the user uses the computer.** This allows the system administrator the chance to monitor how users use their computer and the normal times they use it. Any accesses outside these times can identify a security breach.

Failures in the audit typically identify security breaches, whereas successful accesses can be used to determine the amount of usage of a resource, and can be used for resource planning. An example of audit policies for high-security, medium-security and minimum-security domains are:

High security	Medium security	Minimum security
Successful and unsuccessful user logins	Successful use of key resources	Successful user of resource, for planning purposes
Successful and unsuccessful user of all resources	Successful and unsuccessful administrative and security policy changes	

Successful and unsuccessful administrative and security policy changes	Successful use of sensitive and confidential data, such as accounting information	Successful use of sensitive and confidential data, such as accounting information

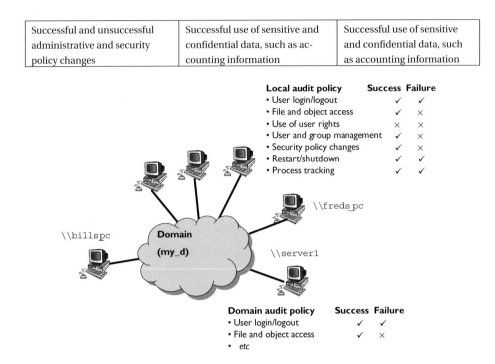

Figure G1.4 Local and domain audit policies

G1.2.9 File systems

Microsoft Windows supports three different types of file system:

- **FAT** (file allocation table) – as used by MS-DOS, OS/2 and Windows NT. A single volume can be up to 2 GB (now increased to over 4 GB). It has no built-in security but can be accessed through Windows 95/98, MS-DOS and Windows NT/2000.
- **HPFS** (high performance file system) – a UNIX-style file system which is used by OS/2 and Windows NT. A single volume can be up to 8 GB. MS-DOS applications cannot access files.
- **NTFS** (NT file system) – as used by Windows NT. A single volume can be up to 64 TB (based on current hardware, but, theoretically, 16 exabytes). It has built-in security and also supports file compression/decompression. MS-DOS applications, themselves, cannot access the file system but they can when run with Windows NT/2000, nor can Windows 95/98.

The FAT file system is widely used and supported by a variety of operating systems, such as MS-DOS, Windows NT and OS/2. If a system is to use MS-DOS it must be installed with a FAT file system.

FAT

The standard MS-DOS FAT file and directory-naming structure allows an 8-character file name and a 3-character file extension with a dot separator (.) between them (the 8.3 file name). It is not case sensitive and the file name and extension cannot contain spaces and other reserved characters, such as:

```
"  /  \  :  ;  |  =  ,  ^  *  ?  .
```

With Windows NT/2000 and Windows 95/98 the FAT file system supports long file names which can be up to 255 characters. The name can also contain multiple spaces and dot separators. File names are not case sensitive, but the case of file names is preserved (a file named `FredDocument.XYz` will be displayed as `FredDocument.XYz` but can be accessed with any of the characters in upper or lower case.

Each file in the FAT table has four attributes (or properties): read-only, archive, system and hidden. The FAT uses a linked list where the file's directory entry contains its beginning FAT entry number. This FAT entry in turn contains the location of the next cluster if the file is larger than one cluster, or a marker that designates this is included in the last cluster. A file which occupies 12 clusters will have 11 FAT entries and 10 FAT links.

HPFS (high-performance file system)

HPFS is supported by OS/2 and is typically used to migrate from OS/2 to Microsoft Windows. It allows long file names of up to 254 characters with multiple extensions. As with Microsoft Windows FAT system the file names are not case sensitive but preserve the case. HPFS uses B-tree format to store the file system directory structure. The B-tree format stores directory entries in an alphabetic tree, and binary searches are used to search for the target file in the directory list.

NTFS (NT file system)

NTFS is the preferred file system for Windows NT/2000 as it makes more efficient usage of the disk and it offers increased security. It allows for file systems up to 16 EB (16 exabytes, or 1 billion gigabytes, or 2^{64} bytes). As with HPFS it uses B-tree format for storing the file system's directory structure. Its main advantages are:

- Increased **reliability**. NTFS automatically logs all directory and file updates which can be used to redo or undo failed operations resulting from system failures such as power losses, hardware faults, and so on.
- Provides sector sparing (or **hot fixing**). When NTFS finds errors in a bad sector, it causes the data in that sector to be moved to a different section and the bad sector to be marked as bad. No other data is then written to that sector. Thus, the disk fixes itself as it is working and there is no need for disk repair programs (FAT only marks bad areas when formatting the disk).
- Increases file system size (up to 16 EB).
- Enhances security permissions.
- Supports POSIX requirements, such as case-sensitive naming, addition of a time stamp to show the time the file was last accessed and hard links from one file (or directory) to another.
- Sparse files. These are very large files that are created by applications which only require portions of the files to be written to part that require to be saved.
- Remote Storage, This is extension to disk space by making use of removable media (such as tapes).
- Recovery logging of meta data. This helps the system restore file system information in

the event of power failure or system problem. This is an automatic system, and does not require any user input.

- Disk quotas. This allows users to be allocated allocated areas of disk space.
- Enhanced scalability to large drives. Some disk formats have a degredation in system performance as the disk size increases, this is not the case for NTFS.
- They can be used with Active Directories to allow fine-tuning of file securities.

NTFS guarantees volume consistency as it uses a transaction logging and recovery techniques. When a system fails, NTFS uses its log file and checkpoint information to restore the file system to a previous point. In Windows 2000/XP, and on, NTFS provides advanced features such as file and folder permissions, encryption, disk quotas, and compression.

A FAT disk can be easily converted into NTFS format using the command:

```
format c: /fs:ntfs
```

G1.3 Active Directories

Windows uses domains (Figure G1.3), which is defined as a group of computers that are part of a network and share a common directory database. These domains are administered as a unit with common rules and procedures. Each domain has a unique name, and users log into specified domains. The standard file structure in a Microsoft domain has a flat structure, and it is often difficult to locate resources on the network (Figure G1.5).

Active Directories is a directory service which enhances the operation of the directory structure by storing information about objects on a network. It then makes this information available to users and network administrators, which allows users of the network access to permitted resources from anywhere on the network using a single logon process. It also provides a hierarchical view of the network and a single point of administration for all network objects (which was the default in Windows NT).

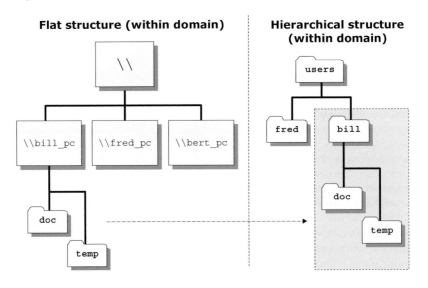

Figure G1.5 Flat v. hierarchical structure

Active Directory domains can be administered as a single entity, with a common directory database, security policies, and security relations with other interconnected domains. A domain administrator maintains all user and group accounts. An Active Directory forest can then be created with more than one physical locality.

Active Directory requires a domain controller which is a host that runs Active Directory, and manages access to the network, such as logging into the domain, authentication, and accesses to directories and shared resources.

In a similar way to NDS, Active Directory has a directory partition, which is a contiguous subtree of a directory that forms a unit of replication. The domain controller stores three partitions for its own domain (and no other domain), these are:

- Schema. This is the object classes and attributes contained in Active Directory.
- Configuration. This identifies the domain controllers, replication topology and other information about the domain controllers within a specific implementation of Active Directory.
- One or more domains that contain the actual directory object data.

Every domain controller within the domain stores the same partition information has the same information (Figure G1.6). This is achieved with replication, which copies data from a data store or file system to multiple computers in order to synchronize their data. Active Directory supports a multimaster replication of the directory between domain controllers within a given domain, and makes the replicas of the directory on each domain controller writable. This facility allows updates to be applied to any replica of a given domain, and the replication service automatically copies of the changes from replica which has been changed to all other replicas. A replica is a folder within a replica set, which is one or more shared folders that are contained within the replication area. The replication topology defines how the physical devices are connected between replicas. DFS only provides for logical descriptions of interconnections.

In an Active Directory, services can be published which allows more control of the domain. Typical services are Security Accounts Manager service, File Replication service, and Routing and Remote Access service.

G1.4   Internet connection sharing

Internet Connection Sharing (ICS) Discovery and Control allows shared Internet connection to be managed from a remote client. On Discovery and Control, the ICS host advertises its shared connection to client computers with a broadcast. Clients then detect these broadcasts, and an icon for the ICS host computer automatically appears in the network connections folder on the client computers. This Discovery and Control allows ICS clients to view statistics on an Internet connection, monitor the status of the connection, and remotely connect and disconnect the shared connection.

Discovery and Control uses a protocol known as Universal Plug and Play (UPnP) which allows control and the sharing of statistics from an ICS host computer and clients. UPnP defines and provides a structure for network device communication, and acts as an enumerator, defining the unique characteristics of each network device. Figure G1.7 shows an example of a shared connection.

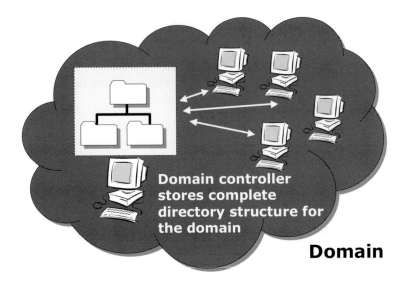

Domain controller stores complete directory structure for the domain

Domain

Figure G1.6 Domain controller

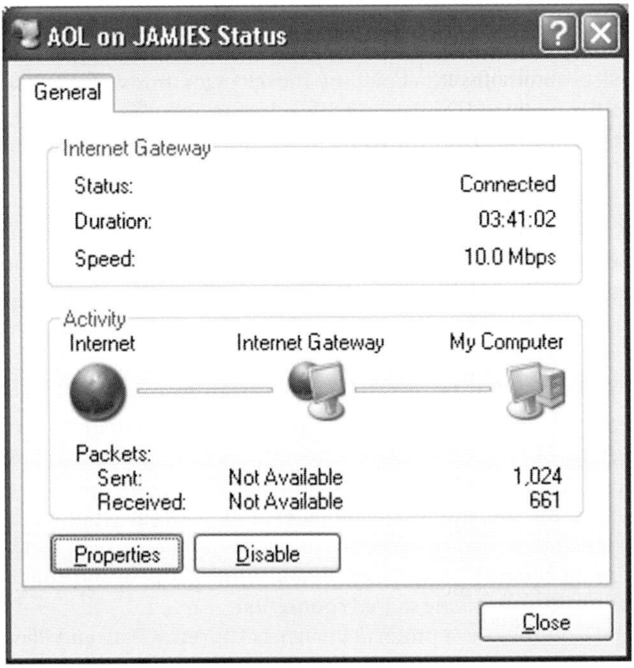

AOL on JAMIES Status

General

Internet Gateway

Status: Connected
Duration: 03:41:02
Speed: 10.0 Mbps

Activity
Internet   Internet Gateway   My Computer

Packets:
  Sent: Not Available   1,024
  Received: Not Available   661

Properties   Disable

Close

Figure G1.7 Statistics on a shared Internet connection

G2   UNIX

G2.1   Introduction

UNIX is an extremely popular operating system and dominates in the high-powered, multi-tasking workstation market. It is relatively simple to use and to administer, and also has a high degree of security. UNIX computers use TCP/IP communications to mount disk resources from one machine onto another. UNIX's main characteristics are:

- **Multi-user.**
- **Memory management with paging** (organizing programs so that the program is loaded into pages of memory) **and swapping** (which involves swapping the contents of memory to disk storage).
- **Pre-emptive multitasking.**
- **Multiprocessing.**
- **Multithreaded applications.**

The two main families of UNIX are UNIX System V and BSD (Berkeley Software Distribution) Version 4.4. System V is the operating system most often used and has descended from a system developed by the Bell Laboratories; it was recently sold to SCO (Santa Cruz Operation).

An initiative by several software vendors has resulted in a common standard for the user interface and the operation of UNIX. The user interface standard is defined by the common desktop environment (**CDE**). This allows software vendors to write calls to a standard CDE API (application program interface). The common UNIX standard has been defined as Spec 1170 APIs. Compliance with the CDE and Spec 1170 API are certified by X/Open, which is a UNIX standard organization.

Another important UNIX-like operating system is Linux, which was developed by Linus Torvalds at the University of Helsinki in Finland. It was first made public in 1991 and most of it is available free-of-charge. The most widely available version was developed by the Free Software Foundation's GNU project. It runs on most Intel-based, SPARC and Alpha-based computers. Modern UNIX-based systems tend to be based around four main components:

- **UNIX operating system.**
- **TCP/IP communications.**
- **Network file system** (NFS). NFS allows disk drives to be linked together to make a global file system.
- **X-Windows interface.** X-Windows presents a machine-independent user interface for client/server applications.

G2.2   File attributes

UNIX provides system security by assigning each file and directory with a set of attributes. These give the privileges on the file usage and the `ls -l` command displays their settings, such as:

- File attributes.
- Owner of the files. Person (user ID) who owns the file.
- Group information. The group name defines the name of the group to which the owner belongs.
- Size of file. The size of the file in bytes.
- Date and time created or last modified. This gives the date and time the file was last modified. If it was modified in a different year then the year and date are given, but no time information is given.
- Filename.

Figure G2.1 defines the format of the extended file listing. The file attributes contain the letters r, w, x which denote read, write and executable. If the attribute exists then the associated letter is placed at a fixed position, else a - appears. The definition of these attributes are as follows:

- Read (r). File can be copied, viewed, and so on, but it cannot be modified.
- Write (w). File can be copied, viewed and changed, if required.
- Executable (x). File can be executed.

The file attributes split into four main sections. The first position identifies if it is a directory or a file. A d character identifies a directory, else it is a file. Positions 2–4 are the owner attributes, positions 5–7 are the group's attributes and positions 8–10 are the rest of the world's attributes. The attributes are:

Owner	Group	Public
r w x	r w x	r w x

The owner is the person who created the file and the group is a collection of several users, such as research, development, production, admin groups, and so on. The public is for everyone else on the system.

The r attribute stands for read privilege and if it is set then the file can be read (that is, listed or copied) by that type of user. The w attribute stands for write privilege and if it is set then the file can be written to (that is, listed, copied or modified) by that type of user. The x attribute stands for execute privilege and if it is set then the file can be executed (that is, it can be run) by that type of user.

For example -rw-r--r-- is a file that the owner can read or write but the group and the public can only read this file. Another example is -r-x--x--x; with these attributes the owner can only read the file. No one else can read the file. No one can change the contents of the file. Everyone can execute the file. The ls -al listing gives the file attributes. Table G2.1 lists some examples.

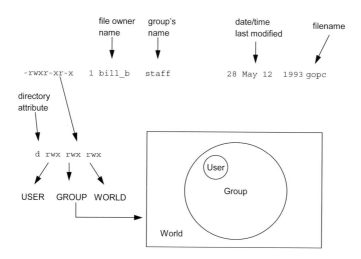

Figure G2.1   Extended file listing

Table G2.1   Example file attributes

Attributes	Description
-r-x--x---	This file can be executed by the owner and his group (e.g. staff, students, admin, research, system, and so on). It can be viewed by the owner but no-one else. No other privileges exist.
drwxr-xr-x	This directory cannot be written to by the members of group and others. All other privileges exist.
-rwxrwxrwx	This file can be read and written to by everyone and it can also be executed by everyone (beware of this).

G2.2.1   Changing attributes of a file

The chmod command can be used by the owner of the file to change any of the attributes. Its general format is:

chmod   *settings filename*

where *settings* define how the attributes are to be changed and the part of the attribute to change. The permission can be set using the octal system. If an attribute exists a 1 is set, if not it is set to a 0. For example, rw-r--r-- translates to 110 100 100, which is 644 in octal. For example:

to set to	rwx--x---	use 710	to set to	r-x------	use 500
to set to	rwxrwxrwx	use 777	to set to	--x------	use 100
to set to	rw-rw-rw-	use 666			

The other method used is symbolic notation. The characters which define which part to modify are u (user), g (group), o (others), or a (all). The characters for the file attributes are a sign (+, - or =) followed by the characters r, w, x. A '+' specifies that the attribute is to   be added, a '-' specifies that the attribute is to be taken away, and the '=' defines the actual attributes. They are defined as:

u	user permission	g	group permission
o	others (public) permission	a	all of user, group and other permissions
=	assign a permission	+	add a permission
-	take away permission	r	read attribute
w	write attribute	x	execute attribute

In sample session G2.1 [2] the owner of the file changes the execute attribute for the user. Sample session G2.2 makes the file file.txt into rw-rw-r--, and the file Run_prog into --x--x---. Some examples of setting and resetting attributes are:

chmod u+x prog1.c	owner has executable rights added
chmod a=rwx prog2.c	sets read, write, execute for all
chmod g-r cprogs	resets read option for group

Sample session G2.1

```
[1:/user/bill_b/shells ] % ls -l
-rw-r--r--   1 bill_b    staff         988 Nov  7 10:20 Cshrc
-rw-r--r--   1 bill_b    staff          43 Nov  7 10:20 Login
-rwxr-xr-x   1 bill_b    staff          28 May 12  2000 gopc
[2:/user/bill_b/shells ] % chmod u+x Login
[3:/user/bill_b/shells ] % ls -l
-rw-r--r--   1 bill_b    10            988 Nov  7 10:20 Cshrc
-rwxr--r--   1 bill_b    10             43 Nov  7 10:20 Login
-rwxr-xr-x   1 bill_b    10             28 May 12  2000 gopc
```

Sample session G2.2

```
[4:/user/bill_b ] %  chmod 664  file.txt
[5:/user/bill_b ] %  chmod 110  Run_prog
[6:/user/bill_b ] % ls -al
---x--x--- 4 bill staff  1102 Jun  4 12:05 Run_prog
drw-r--r-- 2 bill staff    52 Jun  4 14:20 cprogs
-rw-rw-r-- 4 bill staff   102 Jun  1 11:13 file.txt
```

G2.3   TCP/IP protocols

UNIX uses the normal range of TCP/IP protocols, grouped into transport, routing, network addresses, user services, gateway and other protocols.

G2.3.1 Routing

Routing protocols manage the addressing of the packets and provide a route from the source to the destination. Packets may also be split up into smaller fragments and reassembled at the destination. The main routing protocols are:

- **ICMP** (Internet Control Message Protocol) which supports status messages for the IP protocol. These may be errors or network changes that can affect routing.

- **IP** (Internet Protocol) which defines the actual format of the IP packet.
- **RIP** (Routing Information Protocol) which is a route determining protocol.

G2.3.2 Transport

The transport protocols are used by the transport layer to transport a packet around a network. The protocols used are:

- **TCP** (Transport Control Protocol) which is a connection-based protocol where the source and the destination make a connection and maintain the connection for the length of the communications.
- **UDP** (User Datagram Protocol) which is a connectionless service where there is no connection setup between the source and the destination.

G2.3.3 Network and User addresses

The network address protocols resolve IP addresses with their symbolic names, and vice versa. These are:

- **ARP** (Address Resolution Protocol) determines the IP address of nodes on a network.
- **DNS** (Domain Name System) which determines IP addresses from symbolic names (such as `anytown.ac.uk` might be resolved to 112.123.33.22).

User services are applications to which users have direct access.

- **BOOTP** (Boot Protocol) which is typically used to start up a diskless networked node. Thus rather than reading boot information from its local disk it reads the data from a server. Typically it is used by X-Windows terminals.
- **FTP** (File Transfer Protocol) which is used to transfer files from one node to another.
- **TELNET** which is used to remotely log into another node.

G2.3.4 Gateway and other protocols

The gateway protocols provide help for the routing process. These protocols include:

- **EGP** (Exterior Gateway Protocol) which transfers routing information for an external network.
- **GGP** (Gateway-to-Gateway Protocol) which transfers routing information between Internet gateways.
- **IGP** (Interior Gateway Protocol) which transfers routing information for internal networks.

Other important services provide support for networked files systems, electronic mail and time synchronization as well as helping maintain a global network database. The main services are:

- **NFS** (Network File System) which allows disk drives on remote nodes to be mounted on a local node and thus create a global file system.
- **NIS** (Network Information Systems) which maintains a network-wide database for user accounts and thus allows users to log into any computer on the network. Any changes to

a user's account are made over the whole network.

- **NTP** (Network Time Protocol) which is used to synchronize clocks of nodes on the network.
- **RPC** (Remote Procedure Call) which enables programs running on different nodes on a network to communicate with each other using standard function calls.
- **SMTP** (Simple Mail Transfer Protocol) which is a standard protocol for transferring electronic mail messages.
- **SNMP** (Simple Network Management Protocol) which maintains a log of status messages about the network.

G2.4   Directory structure

Files store permanent information, which are used by programs. This information could be schematics, text files, documents, and so on. Directories are then used to arrange the files into a more logical manner. In UNIX the top level of the directory system is the root level and is given the name /. Figure G2.2 shows an example directory structure. In this case there are five sub-directories below the root level (bin, usr, etc, dev and user). Below the usr directory there are three sub-directories (lib, adm and bin). In this case, the users of the system have been assigned to a sub-directory below the users directory, that is, bill_b, fred_a and fred_s.

The full pathname of the bill_b directory is /users/bill_b and the full pathname of the adm directory is /usr/admin. Files can then be stored within a directory structure. Figure G2.3 shows an example structure. In this case, the full pathname of the FORTRAN file prog.ftn is:

```
/user/bill_b/src/fortran/prog.ftn
```

and the full pathname of the c directory is:

```
/user/bill_b/src/c
```

Files and sub-directories can also be referred to in a relative manner, where the directory is not referenced to the top-level (it thus does not have a proceeding /). For example, if the user was in the bill_b directory then the relative path for the C program file1.c is:

```
src/c/file1.c
```

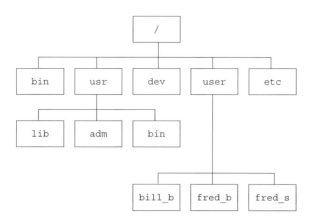

Figure G2.2 Basic directory structure

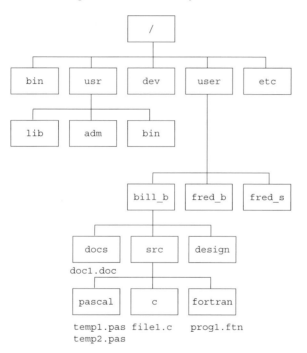

Figure G2.3 Basic directory structure showing files within directories

G2.5   On-line manual

Unix provides an on-line manual to give information on all the UNIX commands. To get information `man` *command-name* is used, such as:

```
man command-name
```

Examples are man `ls` , man `cd` , and so on. Sample session G2.3 shows an example of the help manual for the `ls` command.

💻 Sample session G2.3

```
[7:miranda :/user/bill_b ] % man ls

ls(1)

NAME
     ls, l, ll, lsf, lsr, lsx - list contents of directories

SYNOPSIS
     ls [-abcdfgilmnopqrstuxACFHLR1] [names]
     l [ls_options] [names]
     ll [ls_options] [names]
     lsf [ls_options] [names]
     lsr [ls_options] [names]
     lsx [ls_options] [names]

DESCRIPTION
For each directory argument, ls lists the contents of the directory.
For each file argument, ls repeats its name and any other information
requested.  The output is sorted in ascending collation order by
default (see Environment Variables below).  When no argument is given
the current directory is listed.  When several arguments are given,
the arguments are first sorted appropriately, but file arguments
appear before directories and their contents.
--More--
```

G2.6   Changing directory

The `pwd` command determines the present working directory, and the `cd` command changes the current working directory. When changing directory either the full pathname or the relative pathname is given. If a / precedes the directory name then it is a full pathname, else it is a relative path. Some special character sequences are used to represent other directories, such as the directory above the current directory is specified by a double dot (`. .`).

For example the `cd  . .` command moves to the directory above and if the `cd` command is used on its own then the directory is changed to the user's home directory. Some example command sessions are given next.

`cd . .`	move to the directory above
`cd /`	move to the top-level directory
`cd /user/bill_b/fortran`	move to the directory `/user/bill_b/fortran`
`cd src/c`	move to the sub-directory c which is below the `src` sub-directory
`cd`	move to the user's home directory

G2.7   Listing directories

The `ls` command lists the contents of a directory. If no directory-name is given then it lists the contents of the current directory. In [11] in Sample session G2.4 the user moves to the directory above and in [17] the user moves back to the home directory.

The basic directory listing gives no information about the size of files, if it is a directory, and so on. To list more information the `-l` option is used. In [20] in Sample Session G2.2 the user requests extended information on the files. Other options can be used with `ls` (to get a full list use the on-line manual). In Sample session G2.1 it can be seen that other possible extensions are `abcdfgilmnopqrstuxACFHLR1`.

Examples of usage are:

```
ls  -d  lists only directories
ls  -r  reverse alphabetic order
ls  -t  order in time last modified
```

💻 **Sample session G2.4**

```
[8:miranda :/user/bill_b ] % ls
compress  design    docs      mentor    research  shells    spwfiles
[9:miranda :/user/bill_b ] % cd design
[10:/user/bill_b/design ] % ls
analogue  digital   ic        pcb       vhdl
[11:/user/bill_b/design ] % cd ..
[12:/user/bill_b ] % ls
compress  design    docs      mentor    research  shells    spwfiles
[13:/user/bill_b ] % cd ..
[14:/user ] % ls
bill_b     george_r
[15:/user ] % cd ..
[16:/ ] % ls
bin       etc       usr
etc       lib       user
[17:/ ] % cd
[18:/user/bill_b ] % ls
compress  design    docs      mentor    research  shells    spwfiles
[19:/user/bill_b ] %
[20:/user/bill_b ] % ls -l
total 14
drwxr-xr-x   2 bill_b    10          1024 Nov  1 17:09 compress
drwxr-xr-x   7 bill_b    10          1024 Nov  7 10:11 design
drwxr-xr-x   2 bill_b    10            24 Oct 31 09:52 docs
drwxr-xr-x   3 bill_b    10          1024 Sep 14 13:48 mentor
drwxr-xr-x   3 bill_b    10          1024 Oct 31 09:38 research
drwxr-xr-x   2 bill_b    10          1024 Nov  7 10:21 shells
drwxr-xr-x   2 bill_b    10          1024 Jun 20 18:12 spwfiles
[21:/user/bill_b ] % cd shells
[22:/user/bill_b/shells ] % ls -l
total 6
-rw-r--r--   1 bill_b    10           988 Nov  7 10:20 Cshrc
-rw-r--r--   1 bill_b    10            43 Nov  7 10:20 Login
-rwxr-xr-x   1 bill_b    10            28 May 12  1993 gopc
```

It is also possible to specify more than one extension, such as `ls  -dr` which lists only directories in reverse order. Sample session G2.5 gives some examples. A summary of the various options is given next:

`-a`	lists all entries including files that begin with a . (dot)
`-l`	lists files in the long format. Information given includes size, ownership, group and time last modified.
`-r`	lists in reverse alphabetic order.
`-t`	lists by time last modified (latest first) instead of name.
`-1`	lists one entry per line.
`-F`	marks directories with a trailing slash (/), executables with a trailing star (*).
`-R`	recursively lists subdirectories encountered.

Sample session G2.5

```
% ls -al
-rw-rw----   4 bill   staff   1102 Jun  4 12:05   .temp
drwxr-xr-x   2 bill   staff     52 Jun  4 14:20   cprogs
-r--r--r--   1 fred   staff  10320 Jan 29 15:11   data_file
-rw-rw----   4 bill   staff    102 Jun  1 11:13   file.txt
-rw-rw----   4 bill   staff    102 Jun  1 11:13   file1.f
-rwx--x--x   1 root   staff     20 May 31  9:02   list
-rwxrwx---   4 bill   staff   9102 Feb  4    1988  runfile
dr-xr-xr-x   1 joe    staff    100 Jan 14 13:11   temp
% ls -l
drwxr-xr-x   2 bill   staff     52 Jun  4 14:20   cprogs
-r--r--r--   1 fred   staff  10320 Jan 29 15:11   data_file
-rw-rw----   4 bill   staff    102 Jun  1 11:13   file.txt
-rw-rw----   4 bill   staff    102 Jun  1 11:13   file1.f
-rwx--x--x   1 root   staff     20 May 31  9:02   list
-rwxrwx---   4 bill   staff   9102 Feb  4    1988  runfile
dr-xr-xr-x   1 joe    staff    100 Jan 14 13:11   temp
% ls -r
    temp  runfile  list  file1.f  file.txt  data_file      cprogs
% ls -1
    cprogs
    data_file
    file.txt
    file1.f
    list
    runfile
    temp
% ls -t
    cprogs  file.txt  file1.f  list  runfile  data_file      temp
% ls -F
    cprogs/  data_file  file.txt  file1.f  list*  runfile*  temp/
```

G2.8   File attributes

UNIX provides system security by assigning each file and directory with a set of attributes. These give the privileges on the file usage and the `ls -l` command displays their settings. In the case of [20] in Sample session G2.4, the user uses `ls -l` to get extended information, such as:

- File attributes.
- Owner of the files. Person (user ID) who owns the file.

- Group information. The group name defines the name of the group to which the owner belongs.
- Size of file. The size of the file in bytes.
- Date and time created or last modified. This gives the date and time the file was last modified. If it was modified in a different year then the year and date are given, but no time information is given.
- Filename.

Figure G2.4 defines the format of the extended file listing. The file attributes contain the letters r, w, x which denote read, write and executable. If the attribute exists then the associated letter is placed at a fixed position, else a - appears. The definition of these attributes are as follows:

- Read (r). File can be copied, viewed, and so on, but it cannot be modified.
- Write (w). File can be copied, viewed and changed, if required.
- Executable (x). File can be executed.

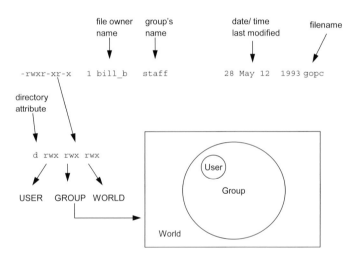

Figure G2.4   Extended file listing

The file attributes split into four main sections. The first position identifies if it is a directory or a file. A d character identifies a directory, else it is a file. Positions 2–4 are the owner attributes, positions 5–7 are the group's attributes and positions 8–10 are the rest of the world's attributes. The attributes are:

	Owner	Group	Public
	r w x	r w x	r w x

The owner is the person who created the file and the group is a collection of several users, such as research, development, production, admin groups, and so on. The public is for everyone else on the system.

The r attribute stands for read privilege and if it is set then the file can be read (that is, listed or copied) by that type of user. The w attribute stands for write privilege and if it is set then the file can be written to (that is, listed, copied or modified) by that type of user. The x attribute stands for execute privilege and if it is set then the file can be executed (that is, it can be run) by that type of user.

For example `-rw-r--r--` is a file that the owner can read or write but the group and the public can only read this file. Another example is `-r-x--x--x`; with these attributes the owner can only read the file. No one else can read the file. No one can change the contents of the file. Everyone can execute the file. The `ls -al` listing gives the file attributes.

Table G2.2 lists some examples.

Table G2.2   Example file attributes

Attributes	Description
`-r-x--x---`	This file can be executed by the owner and his group (e.g. staff, students, admin, research, system, and so on). It can be viewed by the owner but no-one else. No other privileges exist.
`drwxr-xr-x`	This directory can not be written to by the members of group and others. All other privileges exist.
`-rwxrwxrwx`	This file can be read and written to by everyone and it can also be executed by everyone (beware of this).

G2.8.1   Changing attributes of a file

The `chmod` command can be used by the owner of the file to change any of the attributes. Its general format is:

    chmod *settings filename*

where *settings* define how the attributes are to be changed and the part of the attribute to change.

The permission can be set using the octal system. If an attribute exists a 1 is set, if not it is set to a 0. For example, `rw-r--r--` translates to 110 100 100, which is 644 in octal. For example:

to set to	`rwx--x---`	use 710	to set to	`r-x------`	use 500
to set to	`rwxrwxrwx`	use 777	to set to	`--x------`	use 100
to set to	`rw-rw-rw-`	use 666			

The other method used is symbolic notation. The characters which define which part to modify are u (user), g (group), o (others), or a (all). The characters for the file attributes are a sign (+, - or =) followed by the characters r, w, x. A '+' specifies that the attribute is to be added, a '-' specifies that the attribute is to be taken away, and the '=' defines the actual attributes. They are defined as:

u	user permission	g	group permission
o	others (public) permission	a	all of user, group and other permissions
=	assign a permission	+	add a permission
-	take away permission	r	read attribute
w	write attribute	x	execute attribute

In sample session G2.6 [**24**] the owner of the file changes the execute attribute for the user. Sample session G2.7 makes the file `file.txt` into rw-rw-r--, and the file `Run_prog` into --x--x---. Some examples of setting and resetting attributes are:

chmod u+x prog1.c	owner has executable rights added
chmod a=rwx prog2.c	sets read, write, execute for all
chmod g-r cprogs	resets read option for group

Sample session G2.6

```
[23:/user/bill_b/shells ] % ls -l
total 6
-rw-r--r--   1 bill_b   staff        988 Nov  7 10:20 Cshrc
-rw-r--r--   1 bill_b   staff         43 Nov  7 10:20 Login
-rwxr-xr-x   1 bill_b   staff         28 May 12  1993 gopc
[24:/user/bill_b/shells ] % chmod u+x Login
[25:/user/bill_b/shells ] % ls -l
total 6
-rw-r--r--   1 bill_b   10           988 Nov  7 10:20 Cshrc
-rwxr--r--   1 bill_b   10            43 Nov  7 10:20 Login
-rwxr-xr-x   1 bill_b   10            28 May 12  1993 gopc
```

Sample session G2.7

```
[26:/user/bill_b ] %  chmod 664  file.txt
[27:/user/bill_b ] %  chmod 110  Run_prog
[28:/user/bill_b ] % ls -al
---x--x--- 4 bill staff  1102 Jun  4 12:05 Run_prog
drw-r--r-- 2 bill staff    52 Jun  4 14:20 cprogs
-rw-rw-r-- 4 bill staff   102 Jun  1 11:13 file.txt
```

G2.8.2 file (determine file type)

The `file` command tests a file for its type, such as a C program, text file, binary file, and so on. Typical file types include:

- mc68020 demand paged executable.
- ASCII text.
- Archive random library.

C program text.
Empty.
Symbolic link.

Sample session G2.8

```
[29  :/user/bill_b ] % file *
     prog1.c:  C program text
     test :    executable shell script
     fred_dir: symbolic link
     docs:     ascii text
```

G2.9   Special characters (*, ? and ())

There are several special characters which aid access to files, as stated in Table G2.3. Sample session G2.9 shows a few sample uses of wildcards. In [**31**] the user lists all the files which begin with the letter 'm'. In [**33**] all two letter filenames beginning with 'c' are listed. Then in [**34**] the files which begin with the letters 'a', 'b' or 'c' are listed (Note that [a–c] represents

[abc] and [1–9] represents [123456789].).

Table G2.3 Special characters

Char	Description
?	Matches any single character in a filename.
*	Matches zero or more characters in a filename.
[]	Matches one character at a time, these characters are contained in the squared brackets.

Sample session G2.9
```
[30:/user/bill_b ] % cd /bin
[31:/bin ] % ls m*
mail    make    mesg    mkdir   mkfifo  mktemp  model   mstm    mt      mv
[32:/bin ] % ls c*
c89      cd         chmod    cmp      cp       crypt
cat      chacl      chown    cnodes   cpio     csh
cc       chgrp      cksum    command  cps      cstm
[33:/bin ] % ls c?
cc   cd   cp
[34 :/bin ] % ls [a-c]*
alias      basename   cat      chacl    chown    cnodes   cpio   csh
ar         bg         cc       chgrp    cksum    command  cps    cstm
as         c89        cd       chmod    cmp      cp       crypt
[35 :/bin ] % ls [asz]*
alias    as      sh      sleep    strip    su     sync
ar       sed     size    sort     stty     sum    sysdiag
```

G2.10   Listing contents of a file

The command to list the contents of a file is `cat`. Its form is:

> `cat` *filename*

Sample session G2.10 shows how it is used. If a file is larger than one screen full it is possible to stop the text from scrolling by using Cntl-S (^S) to stop the text and Cntl-Q (^Q) to start.

Sample session G2.10
```
[36:/user/bill_b ] % cd shells
[37:/user/bill_b/shells ] % ls
Cshrc   Login   gopc
[38:/user/bill_b/shells ] % cat gopc
setenv DISPLAY pc9:0
xterm
[39:/user/bill_b/shells ] %
```

G2.10.1 cat (concatenate and display)

The `cat` command concatenates, and displays, the specified files to the standard output, which is normally the screen (although this output can be changed using the redirection symbol). Sample session G2.11 [**40**] shows how a file is listed to the screen, and Sample run 13.9 [**41**] shows how two files are concatenated together (`file1.txt` and `file2.txt`) and the result put into a file (`file3.txt`).

If no filename is given then the input is taken from the standard input, normally the keyboard. If a redirect symbol is used then this input (from the keyboard) is sent to the given file. The end of the input is defined by a ^D (a control-D). Sample session G2.11 [42] shows a sample session.

🖳 **Sample session G2.11**

```
[40:/user/bill_b/shells ] cat file.c
     This is the contents of file.c
[41:/user/bill_b/shells ]  cat file1.txt file2.txt  > file3.txt
[42:/user/bill_b/shells ]  cat > newfile.txt
     Mary did not have a little lamb
     She had a fox instead
     ^D
[43:/user/bill_b/shells ]  cat newfile.txt
     Mary did not have a little lamb
     She had a fox instead
```

G2.11   Copying, moving and listing

UNIX is similar to DOS in that it uses `mkdir` and `rmdir` to make and remove a directory, respectively. In both cases the full pathname or relative pathname can be given. The `rm` command removes files or directories. Sample session G2.12 gives some examples. There are various options, such as:

-f   Force mode, remove files without asking questions.

-r   Recursive mode, which deletes the contents of a directory and all its sub-directories.

-i   Interactive mode, where the user is asked to delete each of the files.

🖳 **Sample session G2.12**

```
[44:/user/bill_b/shells ]  ls
   fortran   pascal   text.1   text.2   text.3
[45:/user/bill_b/shells ]  ls fortran
   progs1   progs2
[46:/user/bill_b/shells ]  rm -r fortran/progs2
[47:/user/bill_b/shells ]  ls fortran
    progs1
[48:/user/bill_b/shells ]  rm text.*
[49:/user/bill_b/shells ]  ls
   fortran   pascal
```

G2.11.1 cp (copy files)

The `cp` command copies a given file or directory to a given file or directory. There are several options that can be used:

-i   Interactive mode, where the user is prompted as to whether files are to be overwritten.

-r   Recursive mode, where the files in the subdirectories are copied.

In [50], the file called `file1` is copied into `file2`. Note that if `file2` were a directory then `file1` would be copied into that directory. In [51] a whole directory and all subdirectories are copied, using the `-r` option. It copies the whole directory structure of `/usr/staff/bill` into the directory `/usr/staff/fred`. In [46], a file (`type.c`) is copied into a directory (`cprogs`).

🖳 **Sample session G2.13**

```
[50:/user/bill_b/shells ]   cp file1 file2
[51:/user/bill_b/shells ]   cp -r /usr/staff/bill /usr/staff/fred
[52:/user/bill_b/shells ]   cp type.c  cprogs
```

G2.11.2 mv (move files)

The `mv` command moves files or directories around the file system. The standard formats are:

> mv [-*i*] [-*f*] *filename1 filename2*   mv [-*i*] [-*f*] *directory1 directory2*
> mv [-*i*] [-*f*] *filename directory*

which move a file into another file (similar to renaming the file) or a directory into another directory (similar to directory renaming) and moving a file into another directory. Sample session G2.14 shows examples. The options that can be used are:

`-i`   Interactive mode, where the user is prompted as to whether files are to be moved.

`-f`   Force mode, move files without asking questions.

🖳 **Sample session G2.14**

```
% ls
    fortran  prog1.c  prog2.c  prog3.c  prog.f
% mv prog.f fortran
% ls
    fortran  prog1.c  prog2.c  prog3.c
% ls fortran
    prog.f
% mv fortran fortran_new
% ls
    fortran_new  prog1.c  prog2.c  prog3.c
```

G2.11.3 more (page a file)

The `more` command prints one page of text at a time to the standard output. It pauses at the end of the page with the prompt '--More--'. Sample session G2.15 shows some examples.

🖳 **Sample session G2.15**

```
% more doc.txt
  fsdfsd dfsfs ddfsdfs d
   plpfd fdfsfdf fdfsfpl
       etc
      : :
    --more--
    dfsfsdf dfsfdf dfsffgf
    dfsdf fdfdfhgf
```

```
% cat file | more
   fsdf dfd fghfg fgfg
   lk;lk;l fdf poper
```

G2.12   Standard input and output

The standard input device for a program is the keyboard and the standard output is the monitor. In UNIX, all input/output devices communicate through device files, which are normally stored in the /dev directory. For example, each connected keyboard to the system (including remote computers) has a different device name. Sample session G2.16 shows how the current terminal pathname can be displayed with the tty command.

🖳 **Sample session G2.16**
```
[53  :/user/bill_b ] % tty
/dev/ttys0
```

G2.12.1 Redirection

It is possible to direct the input and/or output from a program to another file or device. The redirection output symbol (>) redirects the output of a program to a given file (or output device). This output will not appear on the monitor (unless it is redirected to it). Sample session G2.17 shows how the output from a directory listing can be sent to a file named dirlist (see [**55**]). The contents of this file is then listed (in [**56**]).

The redirection of output is particularly useful when a process is running and an output to the screen is not required. Another advantage of redirection is that it is possible to keep a permanent copy of a program's execution.

To create a text file the cat command is used with the redirection, as shown next. The file is closed when the user uses the Cntrl-D keystroke (^D), as shown in Sample run 13.18.

If the user does not want the output of a program to appear on the screen then it can be redirected to the file /dev/null (which is the wastepaper basket of the system), and will be automatically deleted.

🖳 **Sample session G2.17**
```
[54  :/user/bill_b ] % ls
compress  design    docs      mentor    research  shells    spwfiles
[55:/user/bill_b ] % ls > dirlist
[56  :/user/bill_b ] % cat dirlist
compress  design    dirlist   docs      mentor    research  shells    spwfiles
[57  :/user/bill_b ] %
```

🖳 **Sample session G2.18**
```
[58  :/user/bill_b ] % cat > file
This is an example of a
file created by cat
^D
[59  :/user/bill_b ] % ls
compress  dirlist   file      research  spwfiles
design    docs      mentor    shells
[60  :/user/bill_b ] % cat file
This is an example of a
```

The input can also be redirected with the redirect symbol (<). The output filename is defined after the input redirect system. For example:

```
% prog1 < inputfile
```

In this case, the program prog1 takes its input from the file inputfile, and not from the keyboard.

G2.12.2 Pipes

Pipes allow the output of one program to be sent to another as its input. The symbol used is the vertical bar (|) and its standard form is:

program_a (*arguments*) | *program_b* (*arguments*)

This notation means that the output of *program_a* is used as the input to *program_b*. The pipe helps in commands where temporary file(s) needs to be created. For example, the who -a command determines who is logged into the system. The sort command can then sort these names alphabetically. Thus to sort the users on the system alphabetically we can use:

Sample session G2.19
```
[61  :/user/bill_b ] % who -a > temp
[62  :/user/bill_b ] % sort temp
aed_9      ttyp8    Nov  9 13:51  old   14496  id=  p8 term=0   exit=0
aed_9      ttyp9    Nov  9 13:51  old   14497  id=  p9 term=0   exit=0
bill_b     ttyp1    Nov  4 16:05  old    6288  id=  p1 term=0   exit=0
bill_b     ttypa    Nov  4 16:02  old    9567  id=  pa term=0   exit=0
bill_b     ttypb    Nov  4 16:05  old    9582  id=  pb term=0   exit=0
bill_b     ttys0    Nov 14 08:57   .    18715  ees10
julian_m ttyp6      Nov  9 13:59  old   14190  id=  p6 term=0   exit=0
peter_t ttyp4       Nov 10 11:10  old   15169  id=  p4 term=0   exit=0
root       ttys1    Nov  8 09:50  old   11292  id=  s1 term=0   exit=0
steve_w ttyp3       Nov  9 10:02  old   13205  id=  p3 term=0   exit=0
steve_w ttyp5       Nov  9 11:17  old   13493  id=  p5 term=0   exit=0
steve_w ttyp7       Nov  9 10:49  old   13570  id=  p7 term=0   exit=0
xia        ttys2    Nov  7 12:07  old    9961  id=  s2 term=0   exit=0
```

It is possible to achieve this with one command line using pipes.

Sample session G2.20
```
[63  :/user/bill_b ] % who -a | sort
aed_9      ttyp8    Nov  9 13:51  old   14496  id=  p8 term=0   exit=0
aed_9      ttyp9    Nov  9 13:51  old   14497  id=  p9 term=0   exit=0
bill_b     ttyp1    Nov  4 16:05  old    6288  id=  p1 term=0   exit=0
bill_b     ttypa    Nov  4 16:02  old    9567  id=  pa term=0   exit=0
bill_b     ttypb    Nov  4 16:05  old    9582  id=  pb term=0   exit=0
bill_b     ttys0    Nov 14 08:57   .    18715  ees10
julian_m ttyp6      Nov  9 13:59  old   14190  id=  p6 term=0   exit=0
peter_t    ttyp4    Nov 10 11:10  old   15169  id=  p4 term=0   exit=0
root       ttys1    Nov  8 09:50  old   11292  id=  s1 term=0   exit=0
steve_w    ttyp3    Nov  9 10:02  old   13205  id=  p3 term=0   exit=0
steve_w    ttyp5    Nov  9 11:17  old   13493  id=  p5 term=0   exit=0
```

```
steve_w   ttyp7     Nov  9 10:49  old   13570  id= p7 term=0   exit=0
xia       ttys2     Nov  7 12:07  old    9961  id= s2 term=0   exit=0
```

G2.13   File manipulation commands

UNIX has a number of file manipulation commands, some of these are defined in this section.

G2.13.1 du (disk usage)

The du command lists the size of a directory and its subdirectories. If no directory name is given the current directory is assumed. Two typical options are:

-a   All file sizes are listed
-s   Summary only

G2.13.2 compress, uncompress (compress and expand files)

The compress command uses the adaptive Lempel-Ziv coding to reduce the size of a file. Compressed files have a .Z added onto their filenames. Sample session G2.21 shows an example.

The contents of the compressed files are in a coded form so that they cannot be viewed by a text editor. The uncompress command can be used to uncompress a compress file. Only files with the extension .Z can be uncompressed.

💻 **Sample session G2.21**
```
[64  :/user/bill_b ] %  ls -al
 -rw-rw----  4 bill   staff    102 Jun  1 11:13 file.c
 -rw-rw----  4 bill   staff   1102 Jun  1 11:15 file.o
 -rw-rw----  3 bill   staff    102 Jun  1 11:13 file1.f
 -rw-rw----  4 bill   staff    102 Jun  1 11:13 file1.o
 -rwxrw----  4 bill   staff  10010 Mar  2 15:23 runfile
[65  :/user/bill_b ] %  compress *
[66  :/user/bill_b ] %  ls -al
 -rw-rw----  4 bill   staff     62 Jun  1 11:13 file.c.Z
 -rw-rw----  4 bill   staff    542 Jun  1 11:15 file.o.Z
 -rw-rw----  3 bill   staff     50 Jun  1 11:13 file1.f.Z
 -rw-rw----  4 bill   staff     50 Jun  1 11:13 file1.o.Z
 -rwxrw----  4 bill   staff   5005 Mar  2 15:23 runfile.Z
[67  :/user/bill_b ] %  uncompress *
```

G2.13.3 df (disk space)

The df command allows you to list the usage of the disk and all other mounted disk drives. Sample session G2.22 gives some examples.

💻 **Sample session G2.22**
```
[68  :/user/bill_b ] %  df
 Filesystem kbytes  used   avail   capacity  Mounted on
 /dev/nst0  200000  50003  159997    25%       /
 /dev/nst1    5000    100   4900      2%      /temp
```

G2.13.4 diff (differences between files)

The diff command shows the difference between two files or two directories. Its format is:

diff *file1 file2*

There are various options, such as:

-i   Ignores the case of letters (such as 'b' is same as 'B').

-w   Ignore all blanks (such as 'fred = 16.2' is same as 'fred=16.2').

Sample session G2.23 gives some examples. In the output listing the < character refers to the first file given and the > character refers to the second file given. A c refers to a change, a d to a line deleted and an a refers to text that has been appended. The line numbers of the first file always appear first.

Sample session G2.23

```
[69 :/user/bill_b ] %  cat oldfile
     This is the contents of the old
     ***
     file. It will be modified and
     a diff will be done.
[70 :/user/bill_b ] %   cat newfile
     This is the contents of the new
     file. It will be modified and
     a diff will be DONE.
[71 :/user/bill_b ] %  diff -i oldfile   newfile
     1c1
     < This is the contents of the old
     - - -
     > This is the contents of the new
     2d1
     < ***
```

G2.13.5 ln (make links)

The ln command makes a soft link to a file or directory. When the *linkname* is used the system will go to the place indicated by the link. Sample session G2.24 shows an example. The general format is:

ln -s *filename* [*linkname*]

Sample session G2.24

```
[72 :/user/bill_b ] %  ls
   fred1   fred2   fred3
[73 :/user/bill_b ] %  ln -s /usr/staff/bill/prog.txt prog
[74 :/user/bill_b ] %  ls
   fred1   fred2   fred3   program
[75 :/user/bill_b ] %  ls -al
 drw-r--r-- 2 bill staff  52 Jun  4 14:20 fred1
 dr--r--r-- 1 fred staff  10 Jan 29 15:11 fred2
 drw-rw---- 4 bill staff 102 Jun  1 11:13 fred3
 lrw-rw---- 4 bill staff 102 Jun  4 13:13 prog->/usr/bill/prog.txt
[76 :/user/bill_b ] %  cat prog
```

```
This is the contents of the
prog.txt file.
```

G2.13.6 find (find file)

The `find` command searches recursively through a directory structure to find files that match certain criteria. It uses a pathname from where to start searching; this is the first argument given after `find`. The name of the file is then specified after the `-name` argument and if the user wants the files found printed to the standard output the `-print` is specified at the end. Sample session G2.25 [77] gives an example of finding a file called `fred.f`, starting from the current directory. In [78], a search of the file `passwd`, starting from the top-level directory.

The wild-card character can be used in the name but this must be inserted in inverted commas (" "). In [79], all '.c' files starting with the `/usr/staff/bill` directory are searched for.

Other extensions can be used such as `-atime` which defines the time of last access. The argument following `-atime` is the number of days since it has been accessed. In [80], '.o' files that have not been used within 10 days are searched for.

Sample session G2.25
```
[77 :/user/bill_b ] %    find . -name fred.f -print
    dir1/fred.f
    fortran/progs/fred.f
[78 :/user/bill_b ] %    find / -name passwd -print
    /etc/passwd
[79 :/user/bill_b ] %    find /usr/staff/bill -name "*.c" -print
    /usr/staff/bill/prog1.c
    /usr/staff/bill/cprogs/prog2.c
    /usr/staff/bill/cprogs/prog3.c
[80 :/user/bill_b ] %    find . -name "*.o" -atime +10 -print
```

G2.13.7 grep (search a file for a pattern)

The `grep` command searches in files for a given string pattern. There are various options, such as:

`-v`	Display lines that do not match.
`-x`	Display only lines that match exactly.
`-c`	Display count of matching lines.
`-i`	Ignore case.

Sample session G2.26 gives some examples and the standard format is:

$$\text{grep } [-v][-c][-x][-i] \text{ } expression \text{ } [file]$$

Sample session G2.26
```
[81 :/user/bill_b ] %    grep function *.c
    prog1.c: function add(a,b)
    prog1.c: function subtract(a,b)
    prog3.c: function xxx
[82 :/user/bill_b ] %    grep -i function *.f
    man.f:          FUNCTION ON_LINE
    man.f:C  This is the function that prints
```

```
[83 :/user/bill_b ] %    grep -v fred listnames
     bert baxter
     sim pointer
     al gutter
```

G2.13.8 head (displays first few lines of a file)

The head command prints the top n lines of a file. The default number is 10 lines and Sample session G2.27 gives examples. The format is as follows:

head -*n filename*

🖥 **Sample session G2.27**
```
[84 :/user/bill_b ] %    head -3 diary.txt
     June 5th 1989
     Dear Diary,
     Today I got my head stuck inside a
[85 :/user/bill_b ] %    head -2 *.doc
 ==>first.doc<==
     This is the first
     document
 ==>second.doc<==
     And this is the
     second document.
```

G2.13.9 tail (display last part of file)

The tail command displays the last part of a file, where the first argument defines the number of lines to be displayed. For example, Sample session G2.28 [86] displays the last four lines of the file file1.txt.

🖥 **Sample session G2.28**
```
[86 :/user/bill_b ] %    tail -4 file1.txt
     and it dropped
     onto the third
     spike on the
     fence.
[87 :/user/bill_b ] %        cat file1
      This is the contents
      of the file to be
      used as an example.
[88 :/user/bill_b ] %    wc -l file1
        3 file1
[89 :/user/bill_b ] %    wc -lc file1
        3   46   file1
[90 :/user/bill_b ] %    wc -w file1
       13   file1
[91 :/user/bill_b ] %    wc file*
       3 13   46   file1
       5 32 103    file2
      10 44 294    file4
      18 89 433    total
```

G2.13.10   wc (word count)

The wc utility counts the words, characters and lines in a file. If several files are given then it gives the sum total of the files. There are three options that can be used; these are c (characters), w (words) and l (letters).

If no filename is given then the keyboard is taken as the input and a Cntrl-D ends the file input. Sample session G2.28 [88]–[91] gives some examples.

G2.14   File locations

UNIX has various default directories which store standard command programs and configuration files. Some of these are defined in the following sections.

G2.14.1 /bin

The /bin directory contains most of the standard commands, such as compilers, UNIX commands, program development tools, and so on. Examples are:

- FORTRAN and C compilers, f77 and cc.
- commands such as ar, cat, man utilities.

G2.14.2 /dev

The /dev directory contains special files for external devices, terminals, consoles, line printers, disk drives, and so on.

- /dev/console Console terminal.
- /dev/null   System wastebasket.
- /dev/tty*   Terminals (such as /dev/tty1 /dev/tty2).

G2.14.3 /etc

The /etc directory contains restricted system data and system utility programs which are normally used by the system manager. These include password file, login, and so on. Examples are:

- /etc/groups   System group tables.
- /etc/hosts   List of system hosts.
- /etc/passwd   List of passwords and users.
- /etc/termcap   Table of terminal devices.
- /etc/ttys   Terminal initialization information.
- /etc/ttytype   Table of connected terminals.
- /etc/utmp   Table of users logged in.

G2.14.4 /lib

The /lib directory contains system utilities and FORTRAN and C run-time support, system calls and input/output routines.

G2.14.5 /tmp

Temporary (scratch) files are used by various utilities, such as editors, compilers, assemblers. These are normally stored in the /tmp directory.

G2.14.6 /usr/adm

The `/usr/adm` stores various administrators files, such as:

`/usr/adm/lastlog`   Table of recent logins

G2.14.7 /usr/bin

The `/usr/bin` contains less used utility programs, such as:

`/usr/bin/at`   `/usr/bin/bc`   `/usr/bin/cal`

G2.14.8 /usr/include

The `/usr/include` directory contains C `#include` header files, such as:

`/usr/include/stdio.h`   `/usr/include/math.h`

G2.14.9 /usr/lib

The `/usr/lib` directory contains library routines and set-up files, such as:

```
/usr/lib/Cshrc          /usr/lib/Login
/usr/lib/Logout         /usr/lib/Exrc
/usr/lib/calendar
```

G2.14.10   /usr/man

The `/usr/man` contains the manual pages, such as

```
/usr/man/cat[1-8]
/usr/man/man[1-8]
```

G2.15   Date

The command to display the date is simply `date`. Sample session G2.29 shows a sample session.

🖥 **Sample session G2.29**
```
[92 :/user/bill_b] % date
Mon Nov 14 11:30:08 GMT 1994
```

G2.16   XDR format

As previously mentioned **XDR** is a standard technique which is used to describe and encode data. This standard form allows for transferring data between different computer architectures. It fits into the presentation layer and uses a language, which is similar to C, to describe data formats. The basic definition of the blocks is this:

• Items are defined in multiples of four bytes (32 bits) of data.

- These bytes are numbered from 0 to n−1.
- Bytes are read (or written) to a byte stream so that byte m always precedes byte m+1.

If the number of bytes (n) in the data is not divisible by 4 then the bytes are followed by enough (0 to 3) residual zero bytes (r) to make the count a multiple of 4.

The basic data types are defined in this section.

G2.16.1   Unsigned Integer and Signed Integer

A signed integer has 32 bits and thus has a range from −2 147 483 648 to +214 7483647. It uses a 2's complement notation with the first byte the most significant and byte 3 the least significant. Integers are declared as follows:

```
int identifier;
```

and can be represented as:

```
(MSB)                     (LSB)
+-------+-------+-------+-------+
|byte 0 |byte 1 |byte 2 |byte 3 |
+-------+-------+-------+-------+
<------------32 bits------------>
```

An unsigned integer has 32 bits and thus has a range from 0 to +4 294 967 295. The most and least significant bytes are 0 and 3, respectively. Unsigned integers are declared as follows:

```
unsigned int identifier;
```

G2.16.2   Enumeration

Enumerations have the same representation as signed integers and are useful in defining subsets of the integers. They are declared as follows:

```
enum { name-identifier = constant, ... } identifier;
```

For example, three menu options (FILE, EDIT and VIEW) could be described by an enumerated type:

```
enum { FILE = 1, EDIT = 2, VIEW = 3 } menu_options
```

G2.16.3   Boolean

Booleans are declared as follows:

```
bool val;
```

which is equivalent to:

```
enum { FALSE = 0, TRUE = 1 } val;
```

G2.16.4 Hyper Integer and Unsigned Hyper Integer

A hyper integer is a 64-bit value and allows greater ranges for integer values. The signed integer format uses 2's completed. In a hyper integer the most significant byte is 0 and the least significant is 7. They are declared as:

```
hyper identifier; unsigned hyper identifier;
```

and can be represented by:

```
  (MSB)                                                          (LSB)
  +-------+-------+-------+-------+-------+-------+-------+-------+
  |byte 0 |byte 1 |byte 2 |byte 3 |byte 4 |byte 5 |byte 6 |byte 7 |
  +-------+-------+-------+-------+-------+-------+-------+-------+
  <--------------------------64 bits-------------------------->
```

G2.16.5 Floating-point

A float data type has 32 bits and uses the standard IEEE standard for normalized single-precision floating-point numbers. It has three fields:

- **S** (sign). A 1-bit value which represents a positive number as a 0 and a negative number as a 1.
- **E** (exponent). An 8-bit value which represents the exponent of the number in base 2, minus 127.
- **F** (fractional part). A 23-bit value which represents the base-2 fractional part of the number's mantissa.

The floating-point value is thus represented by:

$$\text{Value} = -1^S \times 2^{(E-127)} \times 1.F$$

It is declared as follows:

```
float identifier;
```

G2.16.6 Double-precision Floating-point

A double data type has 64 bits and uses the standard IEEE standard for normalized double-precision floating-point numbers. It has three fields:

- **S** (sign). A 1-bit value which represents a positive number as a 0 and a negative number as a 1.
- **E** (exponent). An 11-bit value which represents the exponent of the number in base 2, minus 1023.
- **F** (fractional part). A 52-bit value which represents the base-2 fractional part of the number's mantissa.

The floating-point value is thus represented by:

$$\text{Value} = -1^S \times 2^{(E-1023)} \times 1.F$$

It is declared as follows:

```
double identifier;
```

and can be represented by:

```
+------+------+------+------+------+------+------+------+
|byte 0|byte 1|byte 2|byte 3|byte 4|byte 5|byte 6|byte 7|
S|    E  |                      F                       |
+------+------+------+------+------+------+------+------+
1|<--11-->|<----------------52 bits------------------->|
<----------------------64 bits------------------------>
```

G2.16.7   Fixed-length and Variable-length Opaque Data

Opaque data is uninterpreted data and consists of a number of bytes (either fixed or variable). It is declared as following

```
opaque identifier[n];
```

where the constant n is the (static) number of bytes necessary to contain the opaque data. If n is not divisible by 4 then a number of residual bytes are added. This can be represented as follows:

```
     0        1     ...
+--------+--------+...+--------+--------+...+--------+
| byte 0 | byte 1 |...|byte n-1|   0    |...|   0    |
+--------+--------+...+--------+--------+...+--------+
|<----------n bytes---------->|<------r bytes------>|
|<----------n+r (where (n+r) mod 4 = 0)------------>|
```

Variable-length opaque data is defined as a sequence of n (numbered 0 through n-1) arbitrary bytes. The first four bytes define the number (as an unsigned integer) of encoded bytes in the sequence. If this value is not divisible by 4 then a number of residual bytes are added. It is declared as following:

```
opaque identifier<m>;
```

where the constant m denotes an upper bound of the number of bytes that the sequence may contain. It can be represented by:

```
     0    1    2    3    4    5   ...
+-----+-----+-----+-----+-----+-----+...+-----+-----+...+-----+
|          length n        |byte0|byte1|...| n-1 |  0  |...|  0  |
+-----+-----+-----+-----+-----+-----+...+-----+-----+...+-----+
|<-------4 bytes------->|<------n bytes------>|<---r bytes--->|
```

```
                    |<----n+r (where (n+r) mod 4 = 0)---->|
```

G2.16.8   String

A string contains a number of ASCII bytes (numbered 0 through n-1). The first value is an unsigned 4-byte integer which is the number of bytes in the string. If this value is not divisible by 4 then a number of residual bytes are added. It is declared as following:

```
string object<m>;
```

It can be represented by:

```
       0     1     2     3     4     5   ...
    +-----+-----+-----+-----+-----+-----+...+-----+-----+...+-----+
    |         length n        |byte0|byte1|...| n-1 |  0  |...|  0  |
    +-----+-----+-----+-----+-----+-----+...+-----+-----+...+-----+
    |<-------4 bytes------->|<------n bytes------>|<---r bytes--->|
                            |<----n+r (where (n+r) mod 4 = 0)---->|
```

G2.16.9   Fixed-length Array

Fixed-length arrays of homogeneous elements are declared as follows:

```
type-name identifier[n];
```

where the elements are numbered from 0 to n-1 and each element contains 4 bytes. It can be represented by:

```
    +---+---+---+---+---+---+---+---+...+---+---+---+---+
    |   element 0   |   element 1   |...|  element n-1  |
    +---+---+---+---+---+---+---+---+...+---+---+---+---+
    |<-------------------n elements------------------->|
```

G2.16.10   Variable-length Array

A variable-length array is represented by:

```
type-name identifier<m>;
```

where m specifies the maximum acceptable element count of an array. The first 4 bytes of the array contains the number of elements in the array. It can be represented as:

```
   0  1  2  3
+--+--+--+--+--+--+--+--+--+--+--+--+...+--+--+--+--+
|     n     | element 0 | element 1 |...|element n-1|
+--+--+--+--+--+--+--+--+--+--+--+--+...+--+--+--+--+
|<-4 bytes->|<--------------n elements------------->|
```

G2.16.11   Structure

Structures are declared as follows:

```
struct {
    first-declaration;
    second-declaration;
    ...
} identifier;
```

Each component has four bytes and can be represented as:

```
+-----------------+-----------------+...
| 1st declaration | 2nd declaration |...
+-----------------+-----------------+...
```

G2.16.12   Others

XDR declares several other data types, which include:

- **Void.** This is a 0-byte quantity which can be used for describing operations that take no data as input or no data as output.
- **Constant.** This allows the definition of a constant value. Its syntax is:

```
const name-identifier = n;
```

- **Typedef.** This is used to declared a different data type. Its syntax is:

   typedef declaration;

G3 Novell NetWare and NDS

G3.1 Novell NetWare

Novell NetWare is one of the most popular network operating systems for PC LANs and provides file and print server facilities. Its default network protocol is normally **SPX/IPX**. This can also be used with Windows NT to communicate with other Windows NT nodes and with NetWare networks. The Internet Packet Exchange (**IPX**) protocol is a network layer protocol for transportation of data between computers on a NetWare network. IPX is very fast and has a small connectionless datagram protocol. The Sequenced Packet Interchange (**SPX**) provides a communications protocol which supervises the transmission of the packet and ensures its successful delivery.

NetWare is typically used in organizations and works well on a local network. Network traffic which travels out on the Internet or that communicates with UNIX networks must be in TCP/IP form. IP tunneling encapsulates the IPX packet within the IP packet. This can then be transmitted into the Internet network. When the IP packet is received by the destination NetWare gateway, the IP encapsulation is stripped off. IP tunneling thus relies on a gateway into each IPX-based network that also runs IP. The NetWare gateway is often called an IP tunnel peer.

G3.1.1 NetWare architecture

NetWare provides many services, such as file sharing, printer sharing, security, user administration and network management. The interface between the network interface card (NIC) and the SPX/IPX stack is ODI (Open Data-link Interface). NetWare clients run software which connects them to the server; the supported client operating systems are DOS, Windows, Windows NT, UNIX, OS/2 and Macintosh.

With NetWare Version 3, DOS and Windows 3.*x* clients use a NetWare shell called NETx.COM. This shell is executed when the user wants to log into the network and stay resident. It acts as a command redirector and processes requests which are either generated by application programs or from the keyboard. It then decides whether they should be handled by the NetWare network operating system or passed to the client's local DOS operating system. NETx builds its own tables to keep track of the location of network-attached resources rather than using DOS tables. Figure G3.1 illustrates the relationship between the NetWare shell and DOS, in a DOS-based client. Note that Windows 3.*x* uses the DOS operating system, but Windows NT/2000 and 95 have their own operating systems and only emulate DOS. Thus, Windows NT/2000 and 95 do not need to use the NETx program.

The ODI allows NICs to support multiple transport protocols, such as TCP/IP and IPX/SPX, simultaneously. In addition, in an Ethernet interface card, the ODI allows simultaneous support of multiple Ethernet frame types such as Ethernet 802.3, Ethernet 802.2, Ethernet II, and Ethernet SNAP.

To install NetWare, the server must have a native operating system, such as DOS or Windows NT, and it must be installed on its own disk partition. NetWare then adds a partition in which the NetWare partition is added. This partition is the only area of the disk the NetWare kernel can access.

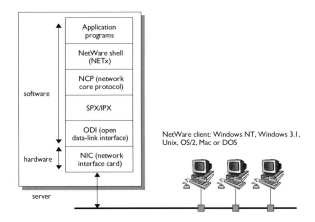

Figure G3.1   NetWare architecture

NetWare loadable modules (NLMs)

NetWare allows enhancements from third-party suppliers using NLMs. The two main categories are:

- **Operating systems enhancements** – these allow extra operating system functions, such as a virus checker and also client hardware specific modules, such as network interface drivers.
- **Application programs** – these programs actually run on the NetWare server rather than on the client machine.

Bindery services

NetWare must keep track of users and their details. Typically, NetWare must keep track of:

- User names and passwords.
- Groups and group rights.
- File and directory rights.
- Print queues and printers.
- User restrictions (such as allowable login times, the number of times a user can simultaneously login to the network).
- User/group administration and charging (such as charging for user login).
- Connection to networked peripherals.

This information is kept in the bindery files. Whenever a user logs into the network their login details are verified against the information in the bindery files.

The bindery is organized with objects, properties and values. Objects are entities that are controlled or managed, such as users, groups, printers (servers and queues), disk drives, and so on. Each object has a set of properties, such as file rights, login restrictions, restrictions to printers, and so on. Each property has a value associated with it. Here are some examples:

Object	Property	Value
User	Login restriction	Wednesday 9 am till 5pm
User	Simultaneous login	2
Group	Access to printer	No

Objects, properties and values are stored in three separate files which are linked by pointers on every NetWare server:

1. NET$OBJ.SYS (contains object information).
2. NET$PROP.SYS (contains property information).
3. NET$VAL.SYS (contains value information).

If multiple NetWare servers exist on a network then bindery information must be exchanged manually between the servers so that the information is the same on each server. In a multiserver NetWare 3.x environment, the servers send SAP (service advertising protocol) information between themselves to advertise available services. Then the bindery services on a particular server update their bindery files with the latest information regarding available services on other reachable servers. This synchronization is difficult when just a few servers exist but is extremely difficult when there are many servers. Luckily, NetWare 4.1 has addressed this problem with NetWare directory services; this will be discussed later.

G3.1.2   NetWare protocols

NetWare uses IPX (Internet Packet Exchange) for the network layer and either SPX (Sequenced Packet Exchange) or **NCP** (NetWare Core Protocols) for the transport layer. The routing information protocol (**RIP**) is also used to transmit information between NetWare gateways. These protocols are illustrated in Figure G3.2.

IPX

IPX performs a network function that is similar to IP. The higher information is passed to the IPX layer which then encapsulates it into IPX envelopes. It is characterized by:

- A connectionless connection – each packet is sent into the network and must find its own way through the network to the final destination (connections are established with SPX).
- It is unreliable – as with IP it only basic error checking and no acknowledgement (acknowledgements are achieved with SPX).

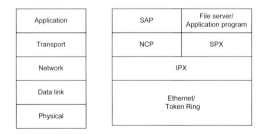

Figure G3.2   NetWare reference model

IPX uses a 12-byte station address (whereas IP uses a 4-byte address). The IPX fields are:

- **Checksum** (2 bytes) – this field is rarely used in IPX, as error checking is achieved in the SPX layer. The lower-level data link layer also provides an error detection scheme (both Ethernet and Token Ring support a frame check sequence).
- **Length** (2 bytes) – this gives the total length of the packet in bytes (i.e. header + DATA). The maximum number of bytes in the DATA field is 546, thus the maximum length will be 576 bytes (2 + 2 + 1 + 1 + 12 + 12 + 546).
- **Transport control** (1 byte) – this field is incremented every time the frame is processed by a router. When it reaches a value of 16 it is deleted. This stops packets from traversing the network for an infinite time. It is also typically known as the time-to-live field or hop counter.
- **Packet type** (1 byte) – this field identifies the upper layer protocol so that the DATA field can be properly processed.
- **Addressing** (12 bytes) – this field identifies the address of the source and destination station. It is made up of three fields: a network address (4 bytes), a host address (6 bytes) and a socket address (2 bytes). The 48-bit host address is the 802 MAC LAN address. NetWare supports a hierarchical addressing structure where the network and host addresses identify the host station and the socket address identifies a process or application and thus supports multiple connections (up to 50 per node).

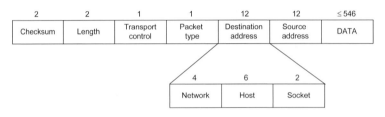

Figure G3.3   IPX packet format

SPX

On a NetWare network the level above IPX is either NCP or SPX. The SPX protocol sets up a virtual circuit between the source and the destination (just like TCP). Then all SPX packets follow the same path and will thus always arrive in the correct order. This type of connection is described as connection-oriented.

SPX also allows for error checking and an acknowledgement to ensure that packets are received correctly. Each SPX packet has flow control and also sequence numbers. Figure G3.4 illustrates the SPX packet.

The fields in the SPX header are:

- **Connection control** (1 byte) – this is a set of flags which assist the flow of data. These flags include an acknowledgement flag and an end-of-message flag.
- **Datastream type** (1 byte) – this byte contains information which can be used to determine the protocol or information contained within the SPX data field.
- **Destination connection ID** (2 bytes) – the destination connection ID allows the routing of the packet through the virtual circuit.

- **Source connection ID** (2 bytes) – the source connection ID identifies the source station when it is transmitted through the virtual circuit.
- **Sequence number** (2 bytes) – this field contains the sequence number of the packet sent. When the receiver receives the packet, the destination error checks the packet and sends back an acknowledgement with the previously received packet number in it.
- **Acknowledgement number** (2 bytes) – this acknowledgement number is incremented by the destination when it receives a packet. It is in this field that the destination station puts the last correctly received packet sequence number.
- **Allocation number** (2 bytes) – this field informs the source station of the number of buffers the destination station can allocate to SPX connections.
- **Data** (up to 534 bytes).

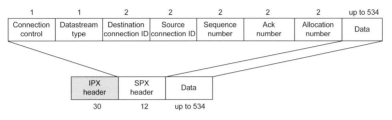

Figure G3.4   SPX packet format

RIP

The NetWare Routing Information Protocol (RIP) is used to keep routers updated on the best routes through the network. RIP information is delivered to routers via IPX packets. Figure G3.5 illustrates the information fields in an RIP packet. The RIP packet is contained in the field which would normally be occupied by the SPX packet.

Routers are used within networks to pass packets from one network to another in an optimal way (and error-free with a minimal time delay). A router reads IPX packets and examines the destination address of the node. If the node is on another network then it routes the packet in the required direction. This routing tends not to be fixed as the best route will depend on network traffic at given times. Thus, the router needs to keep the routing tables up to date; RIP allows routers to exchange their current routing tables with other routers.

The RIP packet allows routers to request or report on multiple reachable networks within a single RIP packet. These routes are listed one after another (Figure G3.5 shows two routing entries). Thus each RIP packet has only one operation field, but has multiple entries of the network number, the number of router hops, and the number of tick fields, up to the length limit of the IPX packet.

The fields are:

- **Operation** (2 bytes) – this field indicates that the RIP packet is either a request or a response.
- **Network number** (4 bytes) – this field defines the assigned network address number to which the routing information applies.
- **Number of router hops** (2 bytes) – this field indicates the number of routers that a packet must go through in order to reach the required destination. Each router adds a single hop.
- **Number of ticks** (2 bytes) – this field indicates the amount of time (in 1/18 second) that it takes a packet to reach the given destination. Note that a route which has the fewest hops may not necessarily be the fastest.

RIP packets add to the general network traffic as each router broadcasts its entire routing table every 60 seconds. This shortcoming has been addressed by NetWare 4/5.

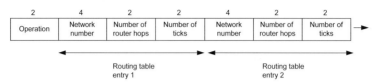

Figure G3.5   RIP packet format

SAP

Every 60 seconds each server transmits a **SAP** (Service Advertising Protocol) packet which gives its address and tells other servers which services it offers. These packets are read by special agent processes running on the routers which then construct a database that defines which servers are operational and where they are located.

When the client node is first booted it transmits a request in the network asking for the location of the nearest server. The agent on the router then reads this request and matches it up to the best server. This choice is then sent back to the client. The client then establishes an **NCP** (NetWare Core Protocol) connection with the server, from which the client and server negotiate the maximum packet size. After this, the client can access the networked file system and other NetWare services.

Figure G3.6 illustrates the contents of a SAP packet. It can be seen that each SAP packet contains a single operation field and data on up to seven servers. The fields are:

- **Operation type** (2 bytes) – defines whether the SAP packet is server information request or a broadcast of server information.
- **Server type** (2 bytes) – defines the type of service offered by a server. These services are identified by a binary pattern, such as:

File server	0000 1000	Job server	0000 1001
Gateway	0000 1010	Print server	0000 0111
Archive server	0000 1001	SNA gateway	0010 0001
Remote bridge server	0010 0100	TCP/IP gateway	0010 0111
NetWare access server	1001 1000		

- **Server name** (48 bytes) – which identifies the actual name of the server or host offering the service defined in the service type field.
- **Network address** (4 bytes) – which defines the address of the network to which the server is attached.
- **Node address** (6 bytes) – which defines the actual MAC address of the server.
- **Socket address** (6 bytes) – which defines the socket address on the server assigned to this particular type of service.
- **Hops to server** (2 bytes) – which indicates the number of hops to reach the particular service.

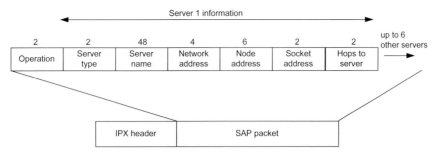

Figure G3.6 SAP packet format

NCP

The clients and servers communicate using the NetWare Core Protocols (NCPs). They have the following operation:

- The NETx shell reads the application program request and decides whether it should direct it to the server.
- If it does redirect, then it sends a message within an NCP packet, which is then encapsulated within an IPX packet and transmitted to the server.

Figure G3.7 illustrates the packet layout and encapsulation of an NCP packet. The fields are:

- **Request type** (2 bytes) – which gives the category of NCP communications. Among the possible types are:

Busy message	1001 1001 1001 1001
Create a service	0001 0001 0001 0001
Service request from workstation	0010 0010 0010 0010
Service response from server	0011 0011 0011 0011
Terminate a service connection	0101 0101 0101 0101

For example the create-a-service request is initiated at login time and a terminate-a-connection request is sent at logout.

- **Sequence number** (1 byte) – which contains a request sequence number. The client reads the sequence number so that it knows the request to which the server is responding.
- **Connection number** (1 byte) – a unique number which is assigned when the user logs into the server.
- **Task number** (1 byte) – which identifies the application program on the client which issued the service request.
- **Function code** (1 byte) – which defines the NCP message or commands. Example codes are:

Close a file	0100 0010	Create a file	0100 1101
Delete a file	0100 0100	Get a directory entry	0001 1111
Get file size	0100 0000	Open a file	0100 1100

Rename a file   0100 0101 Extended functions 0001 0110

Extended functions can be defined after the 0001 0110 field.

- **NCP message** (up to 539 bytes) – the NCP message field contains additional information which is passed between the clients and servers. If the function code contains 0001 0110 then this field will contain subfunction codes.

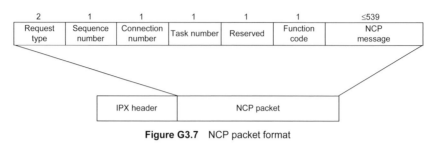

Figure G3.7   NCP packet format

G3.2   NDS

The main disadvantages of NetWare 3.x are:

- It uses SPX/IPX which is incompatible with TCP/IP traffic.
- It is difficult to synchronize servers with user information.
- The file structure is local to individual servers.
- Server architecture is flat and cannot be organized into a hierarchical structure.

These were addressed with NetWare 4/5, in which the bindery was replaced by Novell Directory Services (NDS). NDS is a combination of features from OSI X.500 and Banyan StreeTalk. Its main characteristics are:

- Hierarchical server structure.
- Network-wide users and groups.
- Global objects. NDS integrates users, groups, printers, servers, volumes and other physical resources into a hierarchical tree structure.
- System-wide login with a single password. This allows users to access resources which are connected to remote servers.
- NDS processes logins between NetWare 3.1 and NetWare 4/5 servers, if the login names and passwords are the same.
- Supports distributed file system.
- Synchronization services. NDS allows for directory synchronization, which allows directories to be mirrored on different partitions or different servers. This provides increased reliability in that if a server develops a fault then the files on that server can be replicated by another server.
- Standardized organizational structure for applications, printers, servers and services. This provides a common structure across different organizations.
- It integrates most of the administrative tasks in Windows-based NWADMIN.EXE program.
- It is a truly distributed system where the directory information can be distributed

around the tree.
- Unlimited number of licenses per server. NetWare 3.1 limits the number of licenses to 250 per server.
- Support for NFS server for UNIX resources.
- Multiple login scripts, as opposed to system and user login scripts in NetWare 3.1.
- Windows NT support.

NDS is basically a common, distributed Directory database of logical and physical resources made to look like a single information system. Many other applications have used Directory databases, such as electronic mail and network management. NDS servers within a network access the Directory database for the connected resources and details of how they are accessed. Thus application programs do not need to know the physical location and on which server it is connected, only its logical name.

The main reason to upgrade to NDS is that it better reflects the organizational structure of networked equipment within the organization. NetWare 3.1 is a server-based approach where resources are grouped around servers. This leads to increased maintenance around these servers, thus updates to one server may have to be updated on other servers. NDS allows for a central administration with a structure that reflects organizational structures.

G3.1.3   NetWare directory services (NDS)

One of the major changes between NetWare 3.x and NetWare 4/5 is NDS. A major drawback of the NetWare 3.x bindery files is that they were independently maintained on each server. NDS addresses this by setting up a single logical database, which contains information on all network-attached resources. It is logically a single database, but may be physically located on different servers over the network. As the database is global to the network, a user can log into all authorized network-attached resources, rather than requiring to log into each separate server. Thus, administration is focused on the single database.

As with NetWare 3.x bindery services, NDS organizes network resources by objects, properties, and values. NDS differs from the bindery services in that it defines two types of object:

- **Leaf objects** – which are network resources such as disk volumes, printers, printer queues, and so on.
- **Container objects** – which are cascadable organization units that contain leaf objects. A typical organizational unit might be a company, department or group.

NDS organizes networked resources in a hierarchical or tree structure (as most organizations are structured in this way). The top of the tree is the root object, to which there is only a single root for an entire global NDS database. Servers then use container objects to connect to branches coming off the root object. This structure is similar to the organization of a directory file structure and can be used to represent the hierarchical structure of an organization. Figure G3.8 illustrates a sample NDS database with root, container and leaf objects. In this case, the organization splits into four main containers: Electrical, Mechanical, Production and Administration. Each of these containers has associated leaf objects, such as disk volumes, printer queues, and so on. This is a similar approach to Workgroups in Microsoft Windows.

To improve fault tolerance, NDS allows branches of the tree (or partitions) to be stored on multiple file servers. These mirrors are then synchronized to keep them up to date. Another advantage of replicating partitions is that local copies of files can be stored so that network traffic is reduced.

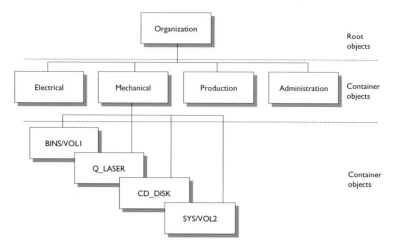

Figure G3.8 NDS structure

The container objects are:

 [ROOT]. This is the top level of the inverted tree and contains all the objects within the organizational structure.

 Organization. This object class defines the organizational name (such as FRED_AND_CO). It is normally the next level after [ROOT] (or below the C=Country object).

 User. This object defines an individual user. The first user created in a NetWare 4 system is the ADMIN user, which is typically the only user with rights to add and delete objects on the whole of the NDS structure.

NCP (NetWare Control Protocol) **Server.** This appears for all NetWare 4 servers.

Volume. This identifies the mounted volume for file services. A network file system data links to the Directory tree through Volume objects.

The most commonly used objects are:

 Bindery. These allow compatibility with existing Bindery-based NetWare 3, NetWare 3 clients and NetWare 4 servers which do not completely implement NDS. They display any object that is not a user, group, queue, profile or print server, which was created using the bindery services.

Organizational unit. This object represents the OU part of the NDS tree. These divide the NDS tree into subdivisions, which can represent different geographical sites, different divisions or workgroups. Different divisions might be PRODUCTION, ACCOUNT, RESEARCH, and so on. Each Organizational Unit has its own login script.

 Organization role. This object represents a defined role within an organization object. It is thus easy to identify users who have an administrative role within the organization.

 Group. This object represents a grouping of users. All users within a group inherit the same access rights.

Directory map. This object points to a file system directory on a mounted volume. It is typically used to create a global file system which has physically separate parts.

 Alias. This identifies an object with another name. For example, a print queue which is called NET_PRINT1 might have an alias name of HP _LASER_JET_6.

 Printer. This can either be connected to the printer port of a PC, or connected to a NetWare server.

Print queue. This object represents the queue of print jobs.

Profile. This object defines a special scripting file. This can be a global login script, a location login script or a special login script.

Print server. This object allows print jobs to be queued, waiting to be serviced by the associated printer.

G3.1.4   NDS tree

Figure G3.9 shows the top levels of the NDS tree. These are:

- **[ROOT].** This is the top level of the tree. The top of the NDS tree is the [ROOT] object.
- **C=Country.** This object can be used, or not, to represent different countries, typically where an organization is distributed over two or more countries. If it is used then it must be placed below the [ROOT] object. NDS normally does not use the Country object and uses the Organization Unit to define the geographically located sites, such as SALES_UK.[ROOT], SALES_USA.[ROOT], and so on.
- **L=Locality.** This object defines locations within other objects, and identifies network portions. The Country and Locality objects are included in the X.500 specification, but they are not normally used, because many NetWare 4 utilities do not recognize it. When used, it must be placed below the [Root] object, Country object, Organization object, or

Organizational Unit object.

- **LP=Licensed Product**. This object is automatically created when a license certificate is installed. When used, it must be placed below the [Root] object, Country object, Organization object, or Organizational Unit object.
- **O=Organization**. This object represents the name of the organization, a company division or a department. Each NDS Directory tree has at least one Organization object, and it must be placed below the [Root] object (unless the tree uses the Country or Locality object).
- **OU=Organization Unit**. This object normally represents the name of the organizational unit within the organization, such as Production, Accounts, and so on. At this level, User objects can be added and a system level login script is created. It is normally placed below the Organizational object.

The structure of the NDS should reflect the organization of the company, for its organizational structure, its locations and the organization of its networks. Normally there is only one Organization object as this makes it easier to merge the NDS tree with other organizations. With every Organization object, there are normally several Organization Units.

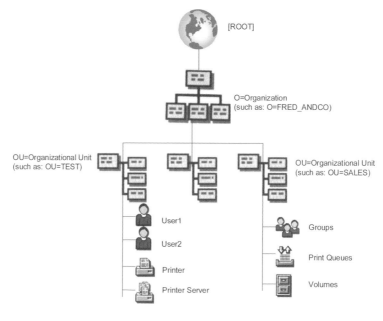

Figure G3.9 NDS structure

Apart from the container objects (C, O, OU, and so on) there are leaf objects. These are assigned a CN (for Common Name). They include:

CN=AFP Server	CN=Bindery	CN=Bindery Queue
CN=Computer	CN=Directory Map	CN=Group
CN=Organizational Role	CN=Print Queue	CN=Print Server
CN=Printer	CN=Profile	CN=Server
CN=User	CN=Volume	

If possible, the NDS tree depth should have between four and eight levels. This makes management easier and allows resources to be easily accessed.

G3.1.5   Typical naming syntax

The NDS tree can use many different naming formats, but a standardized naming structure has been developed. These are:

	Syntax	*Example*
[ROOT]	*company*_TREE	FRED_TREE
Organization	*company_name*	O=FRED
Organization Units	*location* (or *department*)	OU=SALES
Servers	*location-department*-SRV#	SALES-SRV1
Printer Servers	*location-department*-PS#	SALES-LZ5-PS3
Printers	*printer*-P#	HPLJ5-P2
Print Queues	*type*-P#	HPLJ5-P2
Volumes	*server_volume*	SALES-SRV1_DATA

G3.1.6   Object names

The location at which an object is placed is called its context. Two objects which are placed in the same container have the same context. For example, if the user FRED_B works for the Fred & Co. (O=FRED_AND_CO), within the Test Department (OU=TEST), which is within the Engineering Unit (OU=ENGINEERING) then his context will be:

```
OU=TEST.OU=ENGINEERING.O=FRED_AND_CO
```

An object is either identified by its distinguishing name (such as LP_LASER5) or by its complete name (CN). In the name, periods separate the objects (these periods are similar to back slashes or forward slashes, which is common in many operating systems). For a complete name, which is referred to from the [ROOT] object, a leading period is used, whereas a relative name does not have a leading period. For example, a complete name for a User object FRED_B could be:

```
.CN=FRED_B.OU=TEST.OU=ENGINEERING.O=FRED_AND_CO
```

This defines a User, which has an Organization of FRED_AND_CO, which has an Organization Unit called ENGINEERING, there is then a subdivision below this called TEST. It is also poss-ible to define a relative distinguishing name (RDN) which defines the relative path with respect to the current context.

Periods can be added to the start or the end of the context. They have the following definitions:

- Leading period. NDS ignores the current context of the object and resolves the name at the [ROOT] object.
- Trailing period. NDS selects a new context when resolving an object's complete name at the [ROOT] object.

For example, the partial name for the User object FRED_B relative to other objects in

OU=TEST would be:

`.CN=FRED_B.`

The partial name of the User object FRED_B that has a complete name of:

`.CN=FRED_B.OU=TEST.OU=ENGINEERING.O=FRED_AND_CO`

relative to a server object with a complete name of:

`.CN=OU=SALES-SRV1.OU=SALES.O=FRED_AND_CO`

is:

```
CN=FRED_B.OU=TEST.OU=ENGINEERING.
▲
‖------------------------------------------------------  Relative name.
```

The HPLJ5-P2 printer object which has the complete name of:

`.CN=HPLJ5-P2.OU=TEST.OU=ENGINEERING.O=FRED_AND_CO`

would be referred to, within the OU=TEST.OU=ENGINEERING.O=FRED_AND_CO container, as:

`CN=HPLJ5-P2`

Notice that a relative name has a trailing period to identify that it is a partial name. It is also possible not to include the object types (such as CN for common name, OU for Organizational Unit and O for Organization). This is called a **typeless** name, and NDS makes a guess as to the object types. For example:

`FRED_B.TEST.ENGINEERING.FRED_AND_CO`

is the same as one of the previous examples. When guessing NDS uses the following rules:

- The object which is furthest to the left is assumed to be a common name (leaf object).
- The object which is furthest to the right is assumed to be the organization (container object).
- All other objects are assumed to be Organizational Units (container objects).

G3.1.7   CX

The CX (Change conteXt) command is used to display or modify the context, or to view containers and leaf objects in the Directory tree. In a Command Prompt window, the following can be used:

Command	Description
CX	display current context
CX /?	display help manual
CX /CONT	display all containers in the current context
CX /T	display all containers at and below the current context
CX .	move up one level
CX ..	move up two levels
CX /CONT	display containers in the [ROOT]
CX *content*	display context for *content*
CX /R	change current context to [ROOT]
CX /A	display all containers and objects in the current context
CX /R /A /T	display all containers and objects, from the [ROOT] down

For example to set the current context to the TEST.ENGINEERING.FRED_AND_CO container:

CX TEST.ENGINEERING.FRED_AND_CO

Then to change the context to ENGINEERING:

CX ENGINEERING.FRED_AND_CO

or

CX .

G3.1.8   Startup files and scripts

Much of the initialization of a client is done with startup files and scripts. The main startup files are:

- CONFIG.SYS and AUTOEXEC.BAT. These are standard startup files for the PC and normally set up the environment of the computer. The AUTOEXEC.BAT file should include the STARTNET.BAT file.
- STARTNET.BAT. Provides a network connection.
- NET.CFG. Customizes the NetWare setup, such as setting ODI and VLM settings.

The login scripts are:

- Container Login Scripts. These set up the Organization and Organizational Unit properties, and generally replace System login scripts.
- Profile Login Scripts. These set up the environment of User groups.
- User Login Scripts. These customize the User environment. If no User login script exists then a Default Login Script is executed.

The NET.CFG file is similar to NetWare 3 but has extra lines to define the NetWare 4 options. An example file is:

```
Link Driver NE2000
      Int #1 11
      Port #1 320
      Frame Ethernet_II
      Frame Ethernet_802.3
      Protocol IPX 0 Ethernet_802.3

NetWare DOS Requester
      NAME CONTEXT="OU=electrical.OU=engineering.O=napier"
      PREFERRED SERVER = EEE-SRV1
      FIRST NETWORK DRIVE = G
      NETWARE PROTOCOL = NDS, BIND
```

This defines the name context for the user (with NAME CONTEXT) and that the preferred server is EEE-SRV1. The first network drive will be G: and the NetWare protocol is NDS and Bindery.

Drive disks can be mounted by adding lines to the Login Script (such as NETSTART.BAT, which is started from the AUTOEXEC.BAT file). For example, to mount the F:, G: and M: drives then the following could be added:

```
MAP ROOT F:= .EEE-SRV1.ENGINEERING.NAPIER\SYS:APPS
MAP ROOT G:= .CRAIGLOCKHART_1.MAJOR.NAPIER.AC.UK\SYS:APPS
MAP ROOT M:= .CRAIGLOCKHART_3.MAJOR.NAPIER.AC.UK\SYS:MAIL
```

G3.1.9   Volume mapping

Volumes can be mounted as drives using the syntax:

MAP *drive_letter*:=CN=*servername_volumename.context*:

For example, to map the DATA volume of the TEST server to drive letter F: then the following is used:

```
MAP F:=CN=TEST_DATA.OU=TEST.:
```

G3.1.10   Country object

The country object is commonly not used as it fixes the geographical location of objects. It has the advantage, though, that it fits into a common Internet naming structure (such as, www.eece.napier.ac.uk) or X.500 names. Most networks though have the Organizational Unit following the [ROOT] level. For example, an educational organization in the UK will have a country object of UK and the organization object of AC (as defined in the Internet name). The Organization Unit would then be the name of the academic organization (in this case, Napier). Next, the facilities and departments are defined, as follows:

```
[Root]
  c=uk
    o=ac
      ou=napier
        ou=Arts
```

```
   ou=Business
   ou=Engineering
      ou=electrical
      ou=mechanical
      ou=computing
```

Thus, the context name for a printer (LJET5) in the Electrical department would be:

```
CN=LJET5.OU=ELECTRICAL.OU=ENGINEERING.O=NAPIER.C=UK
```

This is obviously similar to the Internet name for the device, which would be:

```
ljet5.electrical.engineering.napier.ac.uk
```

G3.1.11   User class

NDS has an object-oriented database, where each object (such as Users, Printers, and so on) has associated properties. The User object has the following properties:

- **Login Name.** Normally the first character of the first name followed by the last name, such as BBuchanan (for Bill Buchanan). [Required]; **Given Name.** User's first name. [Required]
- **Last Name.** User's last name. [Required]; **Full Name.** User's full name. [Required]
- **Generation Qualification.** [Optional]; **Middle Initial.** [Required]
- **Other Name.** [Optional]; **Title.** Job title. [Required]
- **Description.** [Optional]; **Location.** City or location. [Required]
- **Department.** [Optional]; **Telephone Number.** Full telephone number [Required]; **Fax Number.** Full Fax number [Required]; **Language.** Spoken language. [Optional]
- **Network address.** [System adds this]; **Default server.** Server that the user initially logs into. [Optional]
- **Home Directory.** Volume:subdirectory\user, such as DATA:HOME\BILL_B [Required]; **Required Password.** Force password, or not. [Required]
- **Account Balance.** [Optional]; **Login Script.** [Optional]; **Print Job Configuration.** [Optional]
- **Post Office Box.** [Optional]; **Street.** [Optional]; **City.** [Optional]
- **State or Province.** [Optional]; **Zip Code.** [Optional]; **See also.** [Optional]

G3.1.12   Bindery services

In NetWare 4/5, and further versions, the bindery services have been replaced by NetWare Directory Services (NDS). Many networks take some time to be fully upgraded from bindery to NDS, thus NetWare 4/5 supports bindery. This allows a NetWare 3 server to be upgraded to NetWare 4/5, but still run a bindery. It also allows NetWare 4/5 to integrate with NetWare 3 servers (typically, which run print services).

NetWare 4/5 servers support the following bindery-based resources:

- **Bindery objects class.**   **Bindery programs.**
- **Groups.**   **Print servers.**
- **Profiles.**   **Queues.**

- **Users.** **Bindery-based NetWare client software.**

On a bindery service, NDS supports a flat structure for leaf objects in an Organization or Organizational Unit object. All objects within the specified container can then be accessed by NDS objects and by bindery-based servers and client workstations. On a bindery enabled server, a client gets its login script from that server. The login and script are not automatically transmitted to other servers (as they would be with NDS).

Figure G3.10 shows an example of a bindery-enabled server which is an Organizational Unit object (OU).

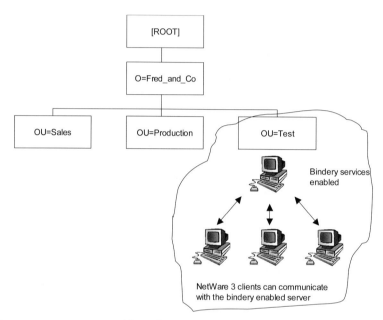

Figure G3.10   Bindery services

G3.1.13   Time synchronization

Time synchronization between servers is important as it allows NDS events and modifications to be accurately time stamped. There are two main options:

- **Single reference configuration.** This provides a single source of time reference and is typically used with networks with less than thirty servers.
- **Time provider group configuration.** This provides a single reference primary server and, at least, two other primary time providers. It is typically used when there are more than thirty servers connected to the network. The other primary time providers allow for a system failure of the reference primary server.

The time synchronization is provided with:

- **SAP.** With SAP the SAP type is 0000 0010 0110 1011 (026Bh). The main disadvantage with this method is that SAP generally adds to network traffic and, as SAP is self configuring, an incorrect set up can cause the incorrect time to be transmitted.

- **Configured List Communication**. This method allows each server to keep a list of servers which it can communicate with. This will generally lead to less network traffic as it does not use an SAP broadcast. It also stops incorrectly setup servers from transmitting incorrect time information (as the server will only communicate with preferred time servers).

NetWare uses the TIMESYNC.NLM (NetWare Loadable Module) module to synchronize their local time. The server then calculates Universal Coordinated Time (UTC) which provides a world standard time. UTC is a machine-independent time standard. It assumes that there are 86 400 seconds each day ($24\times60\times60$) and once every year or two an extra second is added (a 'leap' second). This is normally added on 31 December or 30 June.

Most computer systems define time with GMT (Greenwich Mean Time), which is UT (Universal Time). UTC is based on an atomic clock, whereas GMT is based on astronomical observations. Unfortunately, because of the earth's rotation GMT is not uniform, and is not as accurate as UTC. UTC is calculated by:

UTC = LOCAL TIME + *timezone_offset* + *current_daylight_adjustment*

With TIMESYNC.NLM the system time is not actually changed, the local clock is either speeded up (if the time is behind) or slowed down (if it is ahead). This makes for gradual changes in the system time. This is especially important for server synchronization where directories and files are kept up to date between servers. An incorrectly set time on one server could cause an older file to replace a newer file. Every NDS object and its associated properties have a timestamp associated with them.

NDS timestamp

Particular problems caused with time on computer systems are the Year 2000 bug (where dates are referenced to just the last two digits of the year) and where there is a roll-over in the counter value which stores the system time. The Year 2000 bug was easily eradicated by making sure that all references to time take into account the full year format.

The PC contains a 32-bit counter which is updated every second and is referenced to 1 January 1970 (the starting date for the PC). This provides for 4,294,967,296 seconds (715,827,882 minutes, 11,930,465 hours, 497,103 days and 1361 years). The format of the NDS timestamp uses this format and adds other fields to define the place the event occurred and an indication of events that occur within a single second. It uses 64 bits and its format is:

- **Seconds** (32 bits). This stores the number of seconds since 1/1/1970. This allows for 4 billion seconds, which is approximately 1371 years, before a roll-over occurs.
- **Replica Number** (16 bits). This is a unique number which defines where the event occurred and the timestamp issued.
- **Event ID** (16 bits). Defines each event that occurs within a second a different Event ID. This is required as many events can occur within a single second. This value is reset on every second, and thus allows up to 65,536 events each second.

NDS always uses the most recently time stamped object or properties for any updates. When an object is deleted its property is marked as 'not present'. It will only be deleted once the replica synchronization process propagates the change to all other replicas.

Time server types

NetWare 4/5 servers are set up as time servers when they are installed. They can either be:

- **Primary time servers.** A primary time server provides time information to others, but must contact at least the primary (or reference) server for their own time.
- **Secondary time servers.** These are time consumers, which receive their time from other servers (such as from a primary, reference or single reference time server).
- **Reference time servers.** These servers do not need to contact any other servers, and provide a time source for other primary time servers. This is a good option where there is a large network, as the primary time servers can provide local time information (this is called a time provider group).
- **Single reference time servers.** These servers do not need to contact other time servers to get their own time and are used as a single source of time. This is normally used in a small network, where there is a single reference time server with one or more secondary time servers. The single reference time server and reference time server normally get their local time information from another source, such as Internet time, radio or satellite time. This is the default condition for installation.

G3.1.14 Virtual loadable modules (VLMs)

The NETx redirector shell has been replaced with DOS client software known as the requester. Its main advantage is that it allows NetWare clients to easily add or update their functionality by using VLMs. This is controlled through the DOS-based VLM management program (VLM.EXE). It differs from NETx in that the requester uses DOS tables of network-attached resources rather than creating and maintaining its own. The main difference between NETx and the requester is that it is the DOS system which controls whether the NetWare DOS request is called to handle network requests.

Various VLM modules can be added onto the client, such as:

- **Bindery-based services.**   **File management.**
- **IPX and NCP protocol stacks.**   **NDS services.**
- **NetWare support for multiple protocol stacks** (e.g. TCP/IP, SPX/IPX).
- **NETx shell emulation.**   **Printer redirector to network print queues.**
- **TCP/IP and NCP protocol stacks.**

G3.1.15 Fault tolerance

NetWare 4/5 allows disk mirroring of partitions when a disk drive fails. Thus if one of the disk drives fails, it is possible to switch to the mirror drive. Another major fault occurs when a server becomes inoperative. NetWare 4/5 uses a novel technique, known as SFT III, which allows server duplexing. In this technique, the contents of the disk, memory and CPU are synchronized between primary and duplexed servers. When the primary server fails then the duplexed server takes over transparently. These servers are synchronized using the mirror server link (MSL), a dedicated link between the two servers, as illustrated in Figure G3.11. The MSL is a dedicated link because it prevents general network traffic from swamping the data.

It may seem expensive to have a backup server doing nothing apart from receiving data, but if it is costed with the loss of business or data when the primary server goes down then it is extremely cheap.

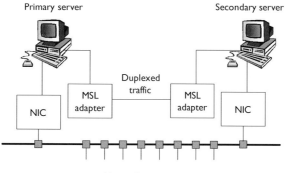

Figure G3.11 Mirror server link

G3.1.16 Communications protocols

NetWare 4/5 has improved existing protocols and added the support for other standard network protocols, especially TCP/IP. These are:

- **TCP/IP.** TCP/IP is supported with NetWare/IP which is included with NetWare 4/5; NetWare/IP servers can support IP, IPX or IP and IPX traffic.
- **Large IPX packets.** Most networks have become less prone to error. Thus larger data packets can be transmitted with a low risk of errors occurring. **LIP** allows NetWare clients to increase the size of their data field by negotiating with routers as to the size of the IPX frame (normally its has a maximum of 576 bytes). Unfortunately, an error in the packet causes the complete packet to be retransmitted (thus causing inefficiencies). In addition, the router must support the use of LIP. The software-based Novell router has a multiprotocol router which supports LIP. Unfortunately, other vendors may not support the LIP protocol.
- **NetWare Link-State Routing Protocol (NLSP).** NLSP overcomes the problems of RIP (File servers transmit their routing table every 60 seconds. This can have a great effect on the network loading, especially for interconnected networks. RIP also only supports 16 hops before an RIP packet is discarded, thus limiting the physical size of the internetwork linking NetWare LAN). With the routing table, NLSP only broadcasts when a change occurs, with a minimum update of once every two hours. This can significantly reduce the router-to-router traffic. As with LIP, Novell routers support NLSP, but other vendors may not necessarily support it. NLSP supports an increased hop size. A great advantage with NLSP is that it can coexist with RIP and is thus backward compatible. This allows a gradual migration of network segments to NLSP.

G3.1.17 NetWare 4.1 SMP

One of the great improvements in computer processing and power will be achievable through the use of parallel processing. This processing can either be realized using multiple local processors or network processors, called symmetrical multiprocessing (SMP). To maintain compatibility with a previous release, NetWare 4.1 **SMP** loads the SMP kernel which works co-operatively with the operating system kernel. The main processor runs the main operating system while the SMP kernel runs the second, third and fourth processors.

H1 Software development

H1.1 Introduction

This chapter has been included to provide a foundation in software development. The following chapters will focus on WWW programs. Some programs provide a framework for a user to manipulate data without the user having to produce their own program. Examples of this include word processors, spreadsheet programs, and so on, where the user writes macro, or script, programs which integrate within the package. With Microsoft products these can be written in Visual Basic. For example, in Microsoft Excel, a macro to select the whole of column A, and then make it bold, and finally to copy and paste it to the D column is achieved with:

```
Sub Macro2()
  Columns("A:A").Select
  Selection.Font.Bold = True
  Selection.Copy
  Columns("D:D").Select
  ActiveSheet.Paste
End Sub
```

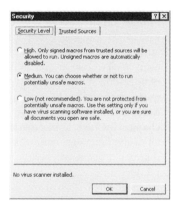

The user can easily call this macro up from a menu, or they can define a hotkey to activate it. In most cases the macro can be written automatically by following the user's actions (such as Tools→Macro→Record New Macro). These can be easily edited and tested, when they are written in Visual Basic, as this comes with an integrated editor and test environment. The Visual Basic scripts can be easily made to react to certain events, such as startup, file saving, and shutdown events.

The technique of generating macros has been popular with users, as it does not require a great deal of programming experience, or for quickly providing a foundation for code development. Unfortunately it has also proved an excellent opportunity for some people to write macro viruses. These are as easy to write for the virus programmer, as they are for the normal user. A typical technique for the virus programmer is to respond to one of the events which occur within a document, and perform some action. Thus, for example, the document could generate an event to copy itself somewhere, when the user opens the document. Normally this is to copy itself into another file (and thus self-replicate itself). A typical action is to copy the macro to the default template, thus all the new documents will have the virus macro. Macro viruses, and script viruses, in general, are one of the greatest causes of viruses, and allow an easy way for viruses to spread quickly, without initial detection. The global Internet has now allowed a fast channel for their spread.

In many cases though users require to customize their programs, and produce a program which will run on its own. This can be done by a programmer writing a program from scratch, or it could be to customize an existing program. Popular programming languages include C++, Visual Basic, Java and Delphi. A programmer can select a software language which is either scripted, interpreted, compiled or assembled. Table H1.1 outlines the main attributes of the different language classifications, which are:

- **Scripted languages**. These are languages which run within a specific environment and they cannot be run without it. Examples include Excel macros and remote access scripts. These scripted languages are often specific to the application package, and cannot be transferred to other similar packages.
- **Interpreted languages**. These are languages that are interpreted by an interpreter when they are run, and the interpreter performs the required operations. The language requires the interpreter to be present when they are run. Examples of interpreted languages are Java (in some cases), HTML and BASIC. Scripted and interpreted languages are the slowest of all the languages, as the interpreter or environment must interpret the language and make a decision on how to implement it on the system. Interpreted languages can also have problems with different versions of the language, as updates to the language can be interpreted by only certain versions of the interpreter. There are many different interpreted languages used on the WWW, including HTML, JavaScript, VBScript, ASP and PHP. These languages are either interpreted by the WWW browser (in the case of HTML, JavaScript and VBScript), or by the WWW server (in the case of ASP and PHP). With interpreted languages it is the interpreter that must be operating system and/or system dependent, and not the program. Thus HTML will work on every WWW browser, but a WWW browser type will only work properly on a certain type of operating system/system type. For example a different WWW browser program is required for an Apple Mac, as one required for a Microsoft Windows-based PC.
- **Compiled languages**. These are languages that are fed through a compiler which changes the high-level program into machine code (object code). The compiler catches all of the language syntax errors (syntax errors), and will typically highlight problems that could occur when running the program (run-time errors). The compiler will not produce an executable program unless all the syntax errors are fixed. Typical compiled languages are C, Pascal and FORTRAN.
- **Assembled languages**. These are languages which use assembly macro commands for equivalent machine code commands. Assembled languages are generally the fastest of all the languages, as they are often optimized to the processor.

Compiled and assembled languages have the advantage over the other types of languages in that they create a single executable program, whereas interpreted and scripted languages require an interpreter or an application environment to run (such as a WWW browser for HTML). Interpreted languages tend to produce smaller programs, as much of the extra code is built into the interpreter (for example, there is no need to add code for interfacing to the keyboard or display, as the interpreter already has this code, for the specific operating system and system specification).

Figure H1.1 shows the sequence of events that occur to generate an executable program from a source code file (the filenames used in this example relate to a PC-based system). With this an editor creates and modifies the source code file; a compiler then converts this into a form which the microprocessor can understand, that is, its own machine code. The file produced by the compiler is named an object code file. This file cannot be executed as it does not have all the required information to run the program. The final stage of the process is linking, which involves adding extra machine code into the program so that it can use devices such as a keyboard, a monitor, and so on. A linker links the object code file with other object code files and with libraries to produce an executable program. These libraries contain other object code modules that are compiled source code.

The complication and linking stages generate either warnings or errors. If they generate errors then the source code must be modified to eliminate them and the process of compilation/linking begins again. A warning in the compile/link stage does not stop the compiler or linker from producing an output, but errors will. All errors in the compilation or linking stage must be eliminated, whereas it is only advisable to eliminate warnings.

The type of programming language is typically defined as either a high-level language or a low-level language. A high-level language uses an almost English-like syntax, so that it is easy to read and write the program. Typical statements are: if; for; while; and so on.

```
if (x> 3) then y=10;
```

which says that: 'if x is greater than 3 then y is equal to 10'. In a high-level language mathematical operations are also defined in a way which is similar to the format which is typically used for mathematical notation, such as:

```
x = 2 * y + 7 * z;
```

A low-level language uses statements which are similar to the machine code of the microprocessor. These are often difficult to remember, and understand, thus it normally takes a great deal of skill to write programs using a low-level language.

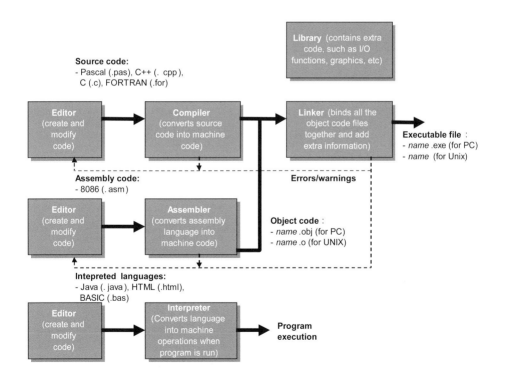

Figure H1.1 Compilation, assembly and interpretation

Table H1.1 Comparison of different types of software languages

	Interpreted languages	Compiled languages	Assembled languages
Examples	Java, BASIC and HTML.	C, C++, Visual Basic, Delphi, FORTRAN, Pascal and COBOL.	8088, 80386, 68000 and 6502.
Speed	**Slowest.** This is because the code must be read by the interpreter, and implemented with the required instructions, as the program is run.	**Medium.** Compiler normally tries to optimize the speed of the program.	**Fastest.** Developed code is exactly engineered for the application and the machine.
Portability	**Excellent.** Can be easily interpreted on another system or on any type of operating system.	**Medium.** Must be recompiled on other system. Problems can happen though on different operating systems, as many programs use different calls for system-dependent system calls, such as calls for windows, or operating system operations. For example a C program typically requires to be modified if it is run on a different system.	**Poor.** Microprocessors produced by different manufacturers tend to use different machine codes (mainly because of historical reasons), thus they tend to be incompatible with each other).
Syntax errors	**Poor.** Interpreter must run the program before errors can be found. It is often difficult to test the whole program for every time of run condition.	**Good.** The compiler should catch most syntax errors.	**Excellent.** The assembler should catch all syntax errors.

	Interpreted languages	Compiled languages	Assembled languages
Run-time errors	**Poor**. Interpreter must run the program before errors can be found. It is often difficult to test the whole program.	**Excellent**. Most errors should be highlighted before the program is run.	**Poor**. Assembly language allows greater control of the system, but can lead to errors because even simple tasks require a great deal of coding, and understanding of the hardware.
Speed of development	**Normally fast**. The programs can be edited with most types of editors, and then easily updated.	**Medium**.	**Slow**. Often one line of a high-level language can be equivalent to many lines of assembly language. The amount of development on assembly language is normally kept to a minimum, and often a high-level to low-level convertor is used to initially generate large amounts of assembly language, which can then be customized for the required functionality.
Producing complex programs	**Medium**. This typically depends on the power of the language.	**Excellent**. Supports most user functions.	**Poor**. A single high-level statement typically requires many assembly language commands, thus it can be extremely difficult to write large and complex programs in assembly language.
Ease of upgrade	**Excellent**. Text files can be easily upgraded. Unfortunately the interpreter may require to be upgraded for changes in the language's specification.	**Medium**. Binary executables, and other binary files typically require to be upgraded.	**Poor**. Binary executables, and other binary files typically require to be upgraded. These may affect other programs.

H1.2　Integrated development environment

At one time programs needed to use a separate editor to create their source code, a separate compiler program to compile the program and a separate linker to bind the compiled code with code from a library, to produce the executable program. Most development systems are now totally integrated, as illustrated in Figure H1.2, where the editor, compiler and linker are all part of the same integrated environment. An important tool is a debugger, which is used for two purposes:

- **To locate and fix errors.** A debugger can be set-up to break the program at given points (known as breakpoints), and then the developer can test any of the variables within the program. This helps to locate errors in the program. The developer can also execute the program one line at a time (known as step-through).
- **To perform a code walk-through.** Even if a program is successfully running, it is important to perform a code walk-through. This involves stepping through the program one line at a time, and watching the route that the code takes, and how the variables change. This is important as there may be something occurring in the program which is unwanted, such as taking more time to conduct an operation, than is necessary.

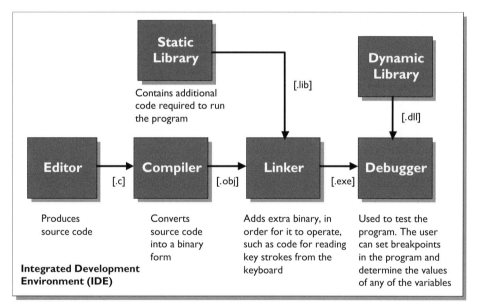

Figure H1.2　Integrated development environment

H1.3　Procedural or modular programming

Modules are identifiable pieces of code with a defined interface. They are called from any part of a program and allow large programs to be split into more manageable tasks, each of which can be independently tested.

A module can be thought of as a 'black box' with a set of inputs and outputs. It has a sole purpose, and processes its inputs in a way dictated by its goal and provides some output. In most cases the actual operation of the 'black box' should be invisible to the rest of the program. This can be likened to an educational programme, where the course is broken down into a series of modules, which the student must undertake. For each module there is an initial specification (the input to the module, along with the students enrolled on the module), and the output are graduated students, with their results. As much as possible these modules should be taken independently from the other modules on the programme, as the teaching and operation of one module should not really have much affect on other modules. The amount that they are inter-related is known as cross-coupling. For example a student on a Computing course may be taking a Java module. The cross-coupling between this module, and the Legal Aspects of Computing module is likely to be zero, as the teaching of one does not affect the other. Some modules will have a strong coupling, such as the Object-Oriented Design Methods (OODM) and the Java module. With this the Java module will typically depend, in some way on the OODM module. If it was totally dependent on the way that it was taught and operated, then it would be 100% dependent. In most cases, lecturers will try and reduce the amount of coupling, so that the module can run without affecting other modules.

A modular program consists of a number of 'black boxes' which, in most cases, work independently of all others, each of which uses variables declared within themselves (local variables) and any parameters sent to it. Figure H1.3 illustrates a function represented by an ideal 'black box' with inputs and outputs, and Figure H1.4 shows a main function calling several subfunctions (or modules). New techniques in software development use components, which are large general-purpose modules, which can be used in a number of ways. For example a networking component could be used in a program. If the component is well designed it could be used in a number of ways, such as supporting different network protocols, or different network types. These have led to the concept of component factories, where large software components are generated, which are general enough so that they can be reused for many different types of applications. These components could be stored around the Internet, and downloaded when a programmer needs to integrate them with their own program.

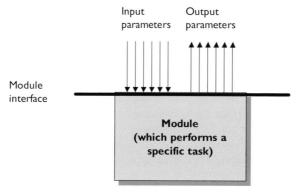

Figure H1.3   An ideal 'black-box' representation of a module

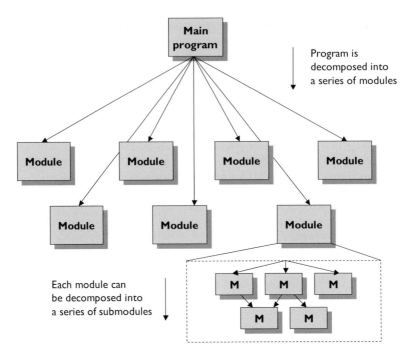

Figure H1.4 Hierarchical decomposition of a program

H1.4 Event-driven programming

Traditional methods of programming involve writing a program which flows from one part to the next in a linear manner. The programs are designed using a top-down structured de-sign, where the task is split into a number of sub-tasks (or submodules) and these are then called when they are required. This means that it is relatively difficult to interrupt the operation of a certain part of a program to do another activity, such as updating the graphics display. It is also an inefficient way of programming, as the pro-gram could be waiting for some other to occur, such as waiting for the user to press a key on the keyboard, because the computer could be doing something else while it is waiting.

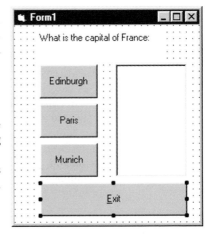

An event-driven program differs from this method, and is written to respond to events, such as:

- When the user clicks the mouse.
- When the user presses a key on the keyboard.
- When a character is received from a modem.
- When the printer becomes busy.

Event-driven programs are typically more responsive to the user, as they can be made to respond to many different types of events. For example, the following are events that can occur when the user has selected a command button:

- MouseOver event. Responding to the mouse cursor moving over the button.
- KeyPress. Responding to a key being press when the mouse cursor is over the button.
- KeyUp event. Responding to a key being released.
- KeyDown event. Responding to a key being pressed.
- DblClick event. Responding to a double-click of a mouse button.
- DragDrop event. Dragging another object on top of the button.
- MouseDown event. Responds to a mouse button down.
- MouseUp event. Responds to a mouse button up.
- LostFocus event. Responds to another object being selected.

H1.5   Object-oriented programming

We live in a world full of objects; so object-oriented programming is a natural technique in developing programs. For example we have an object called a cup, and each cup has a number of parameters, such as its color, its shape, its size, and so on. It is efficient for us to identify it as a cup, as we know that cups should be able to hold liquid, and we will place our cup beside all the other cups that we have. If we were a cup designer then we could list all the possible parameters of a cup, and for each design we could set the parameters. Some of the parameters might not actually be used, but for a general-purpose design we would spe-cific every parameter that a cup might have. So let's design a cup. For a simple case we'll limit the choices for five main parameters:

Parameter	Cup 1	Cup 2	Cup3
Shape (Standard/Square/Mug)	Standard	Square	Mug
Color (Red/Blue/Green)	Blue	Red	Green
Size (Small/Medium/Large)	Small	Large	Small
Transparency (0 to 100%)	100%	50%	25%
Handle type (Small/Large)	Small	Small	Large

Thus we have three choices of shape (square, standard or mug), three choices of color (red, blue or green), three choices in size (small, medium or large) and two choices of handle type (small or large). Also we can choose a level of transparency of the cup from 0 to 100% (in integer steps. In object-oriented programs the collection of parameters is known as a class. Thus we could have a class for our cup which encapsulates all the design parameters for our cup. The instance of our class, such as Cup 1, Cup 2 and Cup 3, is known as an object. We can create many objects from our class.

Many modern programming languages, such as Delphi, C++ and Java, now typically use object-oriented programming. It involves:

- **Classes**. Defines a collection of parameters that can be used to define an object. For example, a class for a car may have the following parameters:
    - Car type.
    - Color.
    - Engine size.

- **Objects**. Objects are created from classes. For example, as illustrated in Figure H1.5, two car objects could be created, as:

  - Car 1 (Object 1). Car type = "Toyota", Color = "Blue", Engine size= "1600".
  - Car 2 (Object 2). Car type = "Ford", Color = "Red", Engine size = "1000"

Object-oriented programming is an excellent programming technique as it involves creating a program around the data, and not, as in modular programming, around the modules. This allows for a much better definition of the problem.

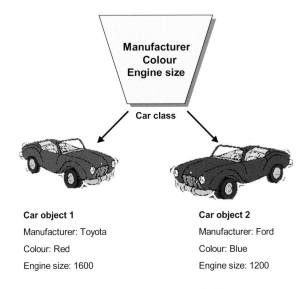

Figure H1.5   Car class and object

Object-oriented design focuses on the data that is used in program, and not on the modules that are used. Objects are operated on functions named methods. These methods define has the object are to be modified. For example, the car object could have the following methods:

- Accelerate(*rate*). Accelerate the car at a rate given by *rate*.
- Brake(*braking*). Brake the car at a rate given by *braking*.
- Change_gear(*mode*). Change the gear of the car, where *mode* can be UP or DOWN. This will move the gear of the car either up or down by one increment. If we are already at the lowest or highest gear, the gear will not be changed.

A new car, such as MyCar can be defined as follows:

```
MyCar = new Car;
```

then properties can be set by:

```
MyCar.colour=Blue;          // It's blue
MyCar.type=SportsCar;       // and it's a sport car
```

```
MyCar.manufacturer=Toyota; // and is a Toyota
```

and methods can be applied by:

```
MyCar.Acceleration(10); // Accelerate at 10 mph/minute
MyCar.ChangeGear(UP);   // Change up gear, if possible
```

H1.6   Interpreted languages

Interpreted languages have several advantages over other types of languages, such as:

- They are extremely portable, compared with compiled and assembled languages, because only the interpreter is required to interface to the hardware and the operating system. Thus, in the case of HTML, only the browser has to be compatible with the system.
- They are small in size, compared to compiled languages.
- They can be easily updated, with a change of the interpreter. An example of an interpreted language is HTML which is interpreted by a WWW browser. Users can easily upgrade their system by downloading a new WWW browser, which may enhance one or more features. Unfortunately the developer of the code must decide on which version of the interpreter they will support.
- They can be easily upgraded and distributed, as all that is required is to distribute a text file. There are typically no binary files, such as library files, to be transported with them.
- Since the program files are text files, they are easily edited. Thus even a BASIC text editor can edit the program. Unfortunately, because they are available in a text form, they can be easily copied and changed. Sometimes, though, as in the case of ASP and PHP, a WWW server processes the code and converts it into another format (such as HTML), so that the requestor is not able to see the original code.

WWW-based languages such as HTML, and languages which integrate into HMTL, such as ASP, PHP, CGI, JavaScript and VBScript will be discussed in the next chapter.

H1.6.1   Java

Java is a totally object-oriented programming language, and has been designed for Internet applications, but can be used for virtually any kind of programming. It has now become the most popular programming language, beating C++ into second place. It can be used as either:

- A **stand-alone** program which is run using a Java interpreter.
- An **applet** which is interpreted by a WWW browser, or can be integrated into a WWW page with JSP (Java Server Page).

The increased power of computers allowed the development of the Java programming language. It was first released in 1995 and was quickly adopted as it fitted well with Internet-based programming. It was followed by several other versions, such as Java 1.4, which gave faster interpretation of Java applets and included many new features. Java is a general-purpose, concurrent, class-based, object-oriented language and has been designed to be relatively simple to build complex applications. Java is developed from C and C++, but some parts of C++ (mainly the most difficult parts, such as pointers and parameter passing) have been dropped and others added.

Java has the great advantage over conventional software languages in that it produces code which is computer hardware independent. This is because the WWW browser interprets the compiled code (called bytecodes). Unfortunately, this leads to slower execution, but, as much of the time in a graphical user interface program is spent updating the graphics display, then the overhead is, as far as the user is concerned, not a great one. Most existing Web browsers are enabled for Java applets (such as Internet Explorer 3.0 and Netscape 2.0 and later versions). Figure H1.6 shows how Java applets are created. First the source code is produced with an editor; next a Java compiler compiles the Java source code into bytecode. An HTML page is then constructed which has the reference to the applet. After this a Java-enabled browser or applet viewer can then be used to run the applet.

The main advantages of Java, over other languages, include:

- **Networking support**. Direct support for the Internet and networking, especially for the transmission of compression image, audio and video formats.
- **Compatibility**. Allows programs to run on any type of system, no matter their operating system or their system type.
- **Threads**. Multitasking involves running several processes at a time. Java allows programs to be split into a number of parts (threads) and each of these is run on the multitasking system (multithreading).
- **RMI** (Remote Method Invocation). This supports the information interchange between the server and client. It uses a distributed object application, where Java objects may be accessed and their methods called remotely to take advantage of a distributed environment and thus spread a workload over a number of network nodes.
- **Object serialization**. This is a process which enables the reading and writing of objects, and has many uses, such as RMI and object persistence. In developing agent applications it is serialization that can provides *mobility*. An object may be serialized (converted to a bit stream), and moved (passed over the socket) to another host where it continues its execution.

The Java Development Kit (JDK) is available, free, from Sun Microsystems. This can be used to compile Java applets and standalone programs. There are versions for Microsoft Windows, Apple Mac and UNIX-based systems with many sample applets.

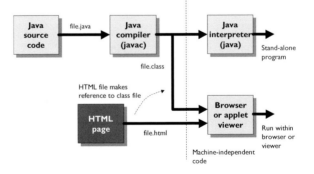

Figure H1.6   Constructing Java applets and standalone programs

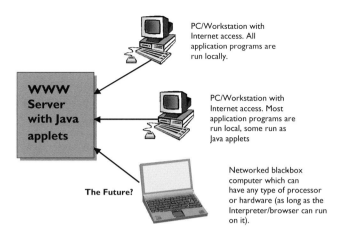

PC/Workstation with Internet access. All application programs are run locally.

WWW Server with Java applets

PC/Workstation with Internet access. Most application programs are run local, some run as Java applets

The Future?

Networked blackbox computer which can have any type of processor or hardware (as long as the Interpreter/browser can run on it).

Figure H1.7   Internet accessing

An example Java applet is given next.

📖 Java applet

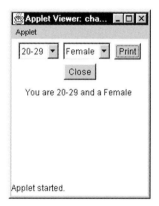

```java
import java.applet.*;
import java.awt.*;
import java.awt.event.*;

public class chap9_15 extends Applet
  implements ItemListener, ActionListener
{
Choice age = new Choice();
Choice gender = new Choice();
Button print= new Button("Print");
Button close= new Button("Close");
String gendertype=null, agetype=null;

String Msg, Options[];
  public void init()
  {
      age.addItem("10-19");
      age.addItem("20-29");
      age.addItem("30-39");
      age.addItem("40-49");
      age.addItem("Other");
      add(age);

      gender.addItem("Male");
      gender.addItem("Female");
      add(gender);
      add(print);
      add(close);

      age.addItemListener(this);
      gender.addItemListener(this);
      print.addActionListener(this);
      close.addActionListener(this);
  }
```

```
public void itemStateChanged(ItemEvent evt)
{
 int i;
 Object obj;

    obj=evt.getItem();

 if (obj.equals("10-19")) agetype="10-19";
 else if (obj.equals("20-29"))
    agetype="20-29";
 else if (obj.equals("30-39"))
    agetype="30-39";
 else if (obj.equals("40-49"))
    agetype="40-49";
 else if (obj.equals("Other"))
    agetype="Other";
 else if (obj.equals("Male"))
    gendertype="Male";
 else if (obj.equals("Female"))
    gendertype="Female";
}
public void actionPerformed(ActionEvent evt)
{
String str;

  str=evt.getActionCommand();
  if (str.equals("Print"))  repaint();
  else if (str.equals("Close")) System.exit(0);
}
public void paint(Graphics g)
{
 if ((agetype!=null) && (gendertype!=null))
  Msg="Your are " + agetype + " and a " + gender-
type;
 else Msg="Please select age and gender";

 if (Msg!=null) g.drawString(Msg,20,80);
}
}
```

JSP, which is a language which integrates the Java programming language with WWW pages, will be discussed in the next chapter.

H7.6.2   BASIC

At the beginning of the 1960s the main programming languages were COBOL and FORTRAN. These languages were not well suited to introducing students to programming languages. Thus, in 1964, John Kemeny and Thomas Kurtz at Dartmouth College developed the BASIC (Beginners All-purpose Symbolic Instruction Code) programming language. It was a great success, although it was never used in many 'serious' applications, until Microsoft adopted it as the basis of their Visual BASIC, which provided an excellent opportunity to develop Microsoft Windows programs. The greatest weakness of many early versions of BASIC was that it was an interpreted language, thus users could actually view the source code, and easily copy it. Newer versions of BASIC included a compiler, and linker, which allowed the BASIC code to be compiled to an executable file.

The golden years for BASIC were when the first microcomputers appeared, and BASIC become a standard programming language on many microcomputer systems. Many of the classic microcomputers, such as the Sinclair ZX Spectrum, used BASIC to develop programs. Unfortunately, at the time, there were no real standards for the language itself, and many compiler developers added their own parts to the language, which made standardization difficult. Thus a BASIC program written on one computer may not run on another computer. Pascal came along and challenged BASIC for a while, but it was the C programming language which then provided the ultimate challenge to BASIC. It was small enough to run on a microcomputer, and was also available on large computers. Along with this it was quickly standardized, so that programs written on one type of computer would have a good chance to run on another type.

H1.7   Compiled languages

Compiled languages are a good compromise between assembled and interpreted languages. The main advantages are:

- They are relatively fast, compared with interpreted languages.
- They are relatively easy to develop compared with assembled languages.
- They are fairly reliable for run-time errors, compared with interpreted and assembled languages.

The main compiled languages are: Visual Basic, C/C++, Pascal and Delphi.

H1.7.1   Visual BASIC

Visual BASIC is one of the best programming languages, and is probably the easiest programming language to actually get something to work, and operating in a Microsoft Windows environment. It uses BASIC programming language for its BASIC language syntax, but adds many new features. It is especially suited to Microsoft Windows programs and integrates well with other Microsoft application programs (such as Word and Excel). Visual BASIC has even been added to many of the Microsoft Office products, where users can develop macro programs in Visual BASIC. In general it is:

- **Object-oriented**. Where the program is designed around a number of ready-made and user-defined objects. Typical objects include buttons, windows and sockets (which are communication ports over a network).
- **Event-driven**. Where the execution of the program is not predefined and its execution is triggered by events, such as a mouse click, a keyboard press, and so on.
- **Designed from the user interface outwards**. The program is typically designed by first developing the user interface and then code is designed to respond to events within the interface.

Figure H1.8 shows an example Visual BASIC desktop, which contains a menu form, controls, main form, project windows and properties window.

An example Visual BASIC program is given next. The module name identifies the name of the object, and the event. For example `Command1_Click()` identifies the command button object named `Command1` which is called on the `Click` event. An additional file is used in Visual BASIC which defines the layout, and types of objects used. This is separate to the Visual BASIC code.

```
Private Sub Command1_Click()
Dim a, b, c As Double
Dim aval, bval, cval As String
    aval = Text1.Text
    bval = Text2.Text
    cval = Text3.Text
    a = CDbl(aval)
    b = CDbl(bval)
    c = CDbl(cval)
    If (Not (IsNumeric(aval)) Or _
        Not (IsNumeric(bval)) Or Not (IsNumeric(cval))) Then
        Text4.Text = ""
        Text5.Text = ""
        Text6.Text = "INVALID"
    ElseIf ((b * b) > (4 * a * c)) Then
        Text4.Text = CStr((-b + Sqr(b * b - 4 * a * c)) / (2 * a))
        Text5.Text = CStr((-b - Sqr(b * b - 4 * a * c)) / (2 * a))
        Text6.Text = "Real"
    ElseIf (b * b < 4 * a * c) Then
        Text4.Text = CStr(-b / (2 * a))
        Text5.Text = "j" + CStr(Sqr(4 * a * c - b * b) / (2 * a))
        Text6.Text = "Complex"
    Else
        Text4.Text = CStr(-b / (2 * a))
        Text5.Text = ""
        Text6.Text = "Singlar"
    End If
End Sub
```

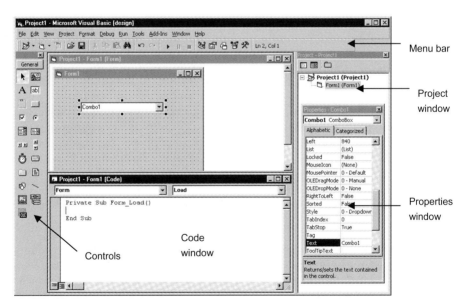

Figure H1.8   Visual Basic desktop

Figure H1.9 shows two sample runs.

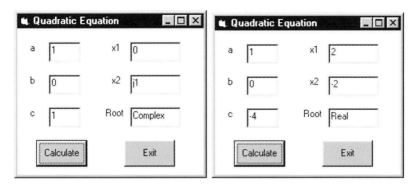

Figure H1.9 Sample runs

H7.7.2   Pascal

Pascal was, at one time, one of the most widely used PC-based programming languages, but its popularity has waned against the strength of C++ and Java. It is an excellent programming language and is typically used to teach good software development techniques. Its popularity is almost solely due to Borland, who developed the excellent Turbo Pascal integrated development environment (IDE), and then enhanced it further, for Microsoft Windows programming, with Borland Delphi.

H7.7.3   Delphi

Visual BASIC has the advantage over the other languages in that it is relatively easy to use and to program, but it suffers when the user needs to achieve complex programming. The greatest weakness of Visual BASIC is that variables do not need to be declared before they are used. Thus variables can be created, but misspelled, which could cause errors in the program. This also causes problems when the programmer performs an operation which is possibly not allowed, or intended. The BASIC compiler does not have a strong method of checking the programs, thus languages such as C++ and Delphi are often preferred for writing large, and complex programs. Figure H1.10 shows a sample Borland Delphi screen.

Delphi uses standard Pascal and can also used object-oriented Pascal (OOP). In general it is:

- **Event-driven**. Where the execution of a program is not predefined and its execution is triggered by events, such as a mouse click, a keyboard press, and so on.
- **Designed from the user interface outwards**. The program is typically designed by first developing the user interface and then coded to respond to events within the interface.
- **Component-based**. Delphi uses standard components which the programming can easily add to the program. These components are typically general-purpose modules which can be used in a number of ways, and in a number of environments. For example a network programming module could be used to transmit either UDP or TCP data packets.

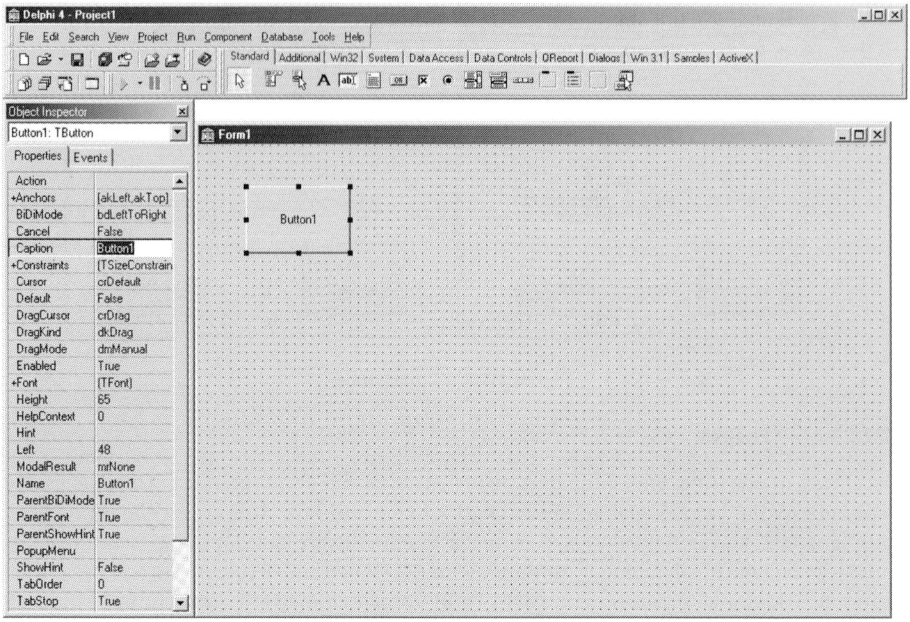

Figure H1.10 Delphi user interface

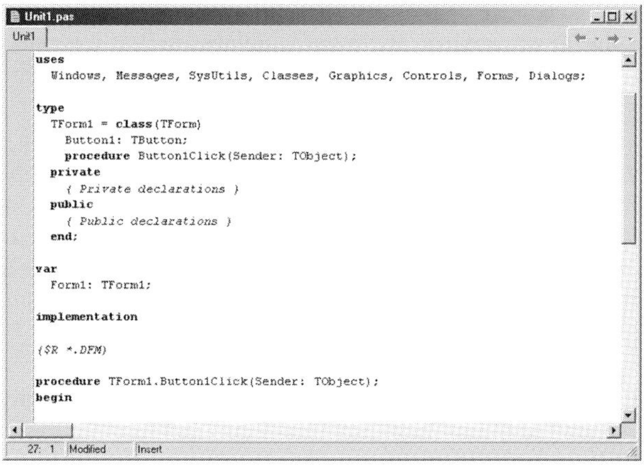

Figure H1.10 Continued

Delphi uses a number of terms to describe design procedures, these are:

- **Components**. The Delphi interface contains a window with component objects which are pasted onto a form. These components can be simple text, menus, spreadsheet grids, radio buttons, and so on. Each component has a set of properties that defines its operation, such as its color, its font size and type, whether it can be resized, and so on. Some components, such as command buttons, menus, and so on, normally have code attached to them, but simple controls, such as text and a graphics image can simply exist on a form with no associated code. Example components are: TRadioButton (Windows radio button), TButton (push button control) and TListBox (Windows list box).

- **Forms**. A form is the anchor for all parts of a Delphi program. Initially it is a blank window and the user pastes controls onto it to create the required user interface. Code is then associated with events on the form, such as responding to a button press or a slider control, although some control elements do not have associated code. A program can have one or more forms, each of which displays and handles data in different ways. When adding components to the form, editing properties, or coding in the form unit, it is the form that is being edited. The following gives an example of some Delphi code, and Figure H1.11 shows a sample run:

```
procedure TForm1.Button1Click(Sender: TObject);
var      outstr,outstr1,outstr2:string;
         a,b,c,x1,x2:real;
         code:integer;
begin
     val(edit1.text,a,code);
     val(edit2.text,b,code);
     val(edit3.text,c,code);
     if (b*b>4*a*c) then
     begin
        edit6.text:='REAL';
        x1:=(-b+sqrt(b*b-4*a*c))/(2*a);
        x2:=(-b-sqrt(b*b-4*a*c))/(2*a);
        str(x1:6:2,outstr);
        edit4.text:=outstr;
        str(x2:6:2,outstr);
        edit5.text:=outstr;
     end
     else if (b*b=4*a*c) then
     begin
        edit6.text:='SINGULAR';
        x1:=-b/(2*a);
        str(x1:6:3,outstr);
        edit4.text:=outstr;
        edit5.text:='';
     end
     else
     begin
         edit6.text:='COMPLEX';
        x1:=-b/(2*a);
        x2:=sqrt(4*a*c-b*b)/(2*a);
        str(x1:6:2,outstr1);
        str(x2:6:2,outstr2);
        outstr:=outstr1+'+j'+outstr2;
        edit4.text:=outstr;
        outstr:=outstr1+'-j'+outstr2;
        edit5.text:=outstr;
     end;
end;
```

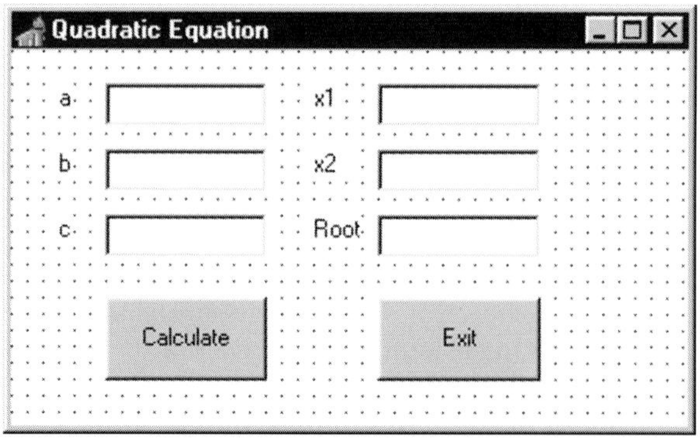

Figure H1.11 Sample run

H1.7.2 C

Up to 1974, most programming languages had been produced either as a teaching language, such as Pascal or BASIC, or had been developed in the early days of computing, such as FORTRAN and COBOL. Both FORTRAN and COBOL had a large hold on the main-frame market, but the emerging microcomputers required much smaller programming languages, that could interface to many different types of hardware. Another factor which called for a new programming language was the increasing influence of operating systems. None of the existing programming languages properly interfaced to the operating system, thus Brian Kernighan and Dennis Ritchie developed the C programming language. Its main advantage was that it was supported in the UNIX operating system. C has since led a charmed existence by software developers for many proven (and unproven) reasons, and quickly took off in a way that Pascal had failed to do. Its main advantages were that: it could be both a high- and a low-level language, it produced small and efficient code, and that it was portable on different systems. Another major advantage was that it was a standardized software language, with ANSI C, that was supported on most operating systems. For this, a program written on one computer system would have a good chance to compile on another system, as long as both compilers conformed to a given standard (typically ANSI C). Pascal always struggled because many compiler developers used non-standard additions to the BASIC language, and thus Pascal programs were difficult to port from one system to another. FORTRAN never really had this problem, as it only had a few standards, mainly FORTRAN 57 and FORTRAN 77. C moved from the UNIX operating system to the PCs, as they became more advanced. It normally requires a relatively large amount of storage space (for all of its standardized libraries), whereas BASIC requires very little storage space.

The following program gives an example of a C program. As can be seen, it is an extremely terse language, which is difficult for non-C programmers to read.

```
/* prog.c          */
#include <stdio.h>

#define    MAX      150
#define    TRUE     1
#define    FALSE    0

void    get_values(int *n,float array[]);
void    print_values(int n,float array_in[]);
void    sort(int n,float input[]);
```

```
void      order(float *val1,float *val2);

int       main(void)
{
float     array[MAX];
int       nvalues;

   get_values(&nvalues,array);
   sort(nvalues,array);
   print_values(nvalues,array);
   return(0);
}

void      get_values(int *n,float array[])
/* *n stores the number of value in the array */
{
int       i,rtn,okay;

   do
   {
      printf("Enter number of values to be processed >>");
      rtn=scanf("%d",n);
      if ((rtn!=1) || (*n<0) || (*n>MAX))
      {
         printf("Max elements is %d, re-enter\n",MAX);
         okay=FALSE;
      }
      else  okay=TRUE;
   } while (!okay);

   for (i=0;i<*n;i++)
   {
      printf("Enter value >>");
      scanf("%f",&array[i]);
   }
}
void      print_values(int n,float array_in[])
{
int       i;
   printf("Ordered values\n");
   for (i=0;i<n;i++)
      printf("%8.3f ",array_in[i]);
}

void      sort(int n,float input[])
/* order array input to give smallest to largest */
{
int       i,j;
   for (i=0;i<n-1;i++)
      for (j=n-1;i<j;j--)
         order(&input[i],&input[j]);
}
void      order(float *val1,float *val2)
/* val1 is the smallest    */
{
float temp;
   if (*val1 > *val2)
   {
      temp = *val1;
      *val1 = *val2;
      *val2 = temp;
   }
}
```

Test run 17. 1 shows a sample run with 10 entered values.

```
Enter number of values be entered >> 10
Enter value >> 3
Enter value >> -2
Enter value >> 4
Enter value >> 10
Enter value >> 3
Enter value >> 2
Enter value >> 1
Enter value >> 0
Enter value >> 19
Enter value >> 14
Ordered values
   -2.000    0.000    1.000    2.000    3.000    3.000    4.000
  10.000   14.000   19.000
```

H1.7.3   C++

C is an excellent software development language for many general-purpose applications. Its approach is that data and associated functions are distinct, where data is declared and the functions are then implemented. Object-oriented programming languages allow the encapsulation of a set of data types and associated functions (called methods) into objects.

C++ is one of the most popular object-oriented languages (alongside Java) and was developed by Bjane Stoustrup at AT&T Bell Laboratories. Its great strength, and also one of its weaknesses, is that it was based on the popular C programming language. Its usage is now widespread and many current applications have been written using C++, whether they be for microcomputers, minicomputers and mainframe computers. The main drawback of C++ is that programmers could still use the C programming language, which, because of its looseness and simplicity, allowed the programmer to produce programs that would compile, but could crash because of a run-time error which was due to badly designed software. Typically errors were running off the end of an array, bad parameter passing into modules, or using memory that was not reserved for other purposes. Object-oriented programming languages are much tighter in their syntax, and the things that are allowed to be done. Thus, the compiler will typically catch more errors, whether they are run-time or syntax errors, before the program is run. Java has since overcome the problems of C++, as it is totally object-oriented, and much tighter in the rules of software coding.

Figure H1.12 shows a Microsoft Visual C++ development environment. C++ has many enhancements over C. These include:

- **I/O stream support**. This facility allows data to be directed to an input and/or an output stream.
- **Objects**. An object incorporates data definitions and the declaration and definitions of functions which operate on that data.
- **Classes**. These are used to implement objects and can be initialized and discarded with constructors and destructors, respectively.
- **Data hiding**. This allows certain data to be hidden from parts of a program which are not allowed access to it.
- **Overloading**. This allows more than one definition and implementation of a function.

- **Virtual functions**. These allow any one of a number of multiple defined functions to be called at run-time.
- **Template classes**. These allow the same class to be used by different data.

```
#include <iostream.h>

class circuit
{
private:
    float r1,r2;
public:
    void  get_res(void);
    float series(void);
    float parallel(void);
};

int    main(void)
{
    circuit   c1;
    float     res;

    c1.get_res();

    res=c1.series();
    cout << "Series resistance is " << res << " ohms\n";

    res=c1.parallel();
    cout << "Parallel resistance is " << res << " ohms\n";
    return(0);
}

void  circuit::get_res(void)
{
    cout << "Enter r1 >> ";
    cin >> r1;
    cout << "Enter r2 >> ";
    cin >> r2;
}

float circuit::parallel(void)
{
    return((r1*r2)/(r1+r2));
}

float circuit::series(void)
{
    return(r1+r2);
}
```

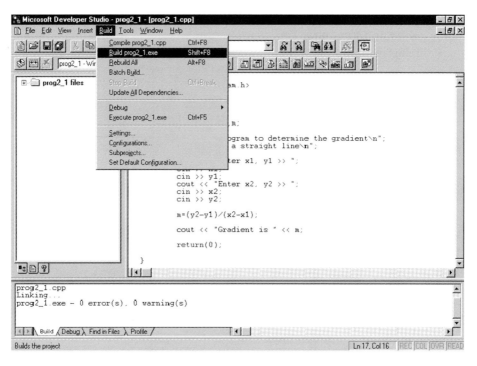

Figure H1.12   Microsoft Visual C++

💻 **Test run 17.2**

```
Enter r1 >> 1000
Enter r2 >> 1000
Series resistance is 2000 ohms
Parallel resistance is 500 ohms
```

H1.7.4   Major problems

BASIC and FORTRAN are similar in their syntax, as BASIC was developed at a time that FORTRAN was the leading programming language. Most programming languages do not allow users to create variables without them first being declared by their data type. For example C declares variables as follows:

```
int     value1, value2;    /* two integers                          */
float   x, y;              /* two real values                       */
char    str1[10], ch;      /* a character string and a character    */
```

FORTRAN, Visual BASIC and BASIC allow variables to be used without them first being declared. It is possible to declare the variables, but it is not statutory. It is thus difficult for the compiler to tell the data type of the variable, and thus reserve enough space in memory for it. In FORTRAN data types are automatically assigned with relation to the first letter of the variable name. For example:

Variable names which start with an I, J, K, L, M or N are integers (for example `Ival`,

`Ndata1` and `Msubt` are all integer values, unless they are declared otherwise).
Variables which start with an H are character strings.
Variables which start with an R, S, T, U, V, W, X and Y are floating-point values.

In BASIC values have implied data types, which are defined in the way they are used. For example if the user does the following:

```
Dim  val as integer
Dim  x, y as double

  z= x * y
```

Then z would automatically be declared to be a double data type.

H1.8   Assembled languages

Assembled languages, such as 8086, 6502, Z80 and 68000 are derived directly from the machine code of the processor. They are thus highly optimized as the programmer can directly control the operation to the program, rather than the compiler making the decisions. They have many major problems, and are hardly ever used to create large programs. An example 8086 assembly language programs is given next.

```
code          SEGMENT
              ASSUME cs:code

BASEADDRESS         EQU     01F0H           ; change this as required
PORTA               EQU     BASEADDRESS
PORTB               EQU     BASEADDRESS+1
CNTRLREG            EQU     BASEADDRESS+3
;   program to output to Port B counts in binary until from 00000000
;   to 11111111 with approximately 1 second delay between changes
start:
          mov dx,CNTRLREG     ; set up PPI with
          mov al,90h          ; Port B as Output
          out dx,al
          mov ax,00h
loop1:
          mov dx,PORTB
          out dx,al           ; output to Port B

          call delay
          inc ax
          cmp ax,100h
          jnz loop1           ; repeat until all 1s

          mov ah,4cH          ; program exit
          int 21h             ;

          ; ROUTINE TO GIVE 1 SECOND DELAY USING THE PC TIMER
DELAY:      push ax
          push bx
          mov ax,18           ; 18.2 clock ticks per second;
          ; Address of system timer on the PC is 0000:046C (low word)
          ; and 0000:046E (high word)
          mov bx,0
          mov es,bx
          ; Add the number of required ticks of the clock (ie 18)
```

```
        add ax,es:[46CH]
        mov bx,es:[46EH]

loop2:      ; Compare current timer count with AX and BX
        ;  if they are equal 1 second has passed
        cmp bx,es:[46EH]
        ja loop2
        jb over
        cmp ax,es:[46CH]
        jg loop2

over:       pop bx
        pop ax
        ret

code    ENDS
    END     start
```

Typically, these days, in-line assembly language is used alongside another programming language. For example, in C:

```
for (ival=0;ival<100;ival++)
{
    cout << "Outputting a value to the port"
    /* Assembly Language statements */
    _asm
    {
    mov dx, 01f0h
    mov al, ival
    out dx, ival
    }
    /******************************/
}
```

As a rule, as little as possible should be done in assembly language, as it is very easy to perform an incorrect operation. These days the major usage of assembly language is to write device drivers. In most cases, it is the operating system which communicates with the hardware, as illustrated in Figure H1.13.

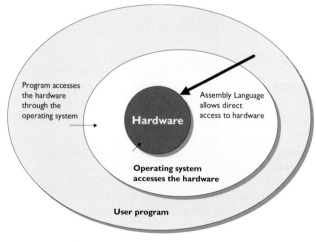

Figure H1.13   Accessing the hardware

H1.9   Cross compiler

Often developers write programs which must be converted so that they can run on another system, possibly with a different processor and/or a different architecture. This requires a cross compiler, which either converts a high-level language to the machine code for the destination computer, or converts a machine code program on one computer to another one that runs on the destination computer. Typical reasons are:

- **Porting programs to other computers**. This can involve recompiling a program for another processor. The cross-compiler must thus know how to convert one type of machine code into another type.
- **Developing programs on a convenient computer**, and using a cross compiler to create the final executable version. This is typically used with game consoles where a programmer can use a PC to develop the code for games console (such as the Sony PlayStation) and then use a cross compiler to convert the code into a form that could run of the required system. Other example include cross compiling for an embedded system.
- **Developing for a prototype system**. Often the hardware is not initially available for software to be developed for a system. Thus often the software will be written for it on another system, and then compiled for the system using a cross compiler.
- **Using a less expensive development system**. Often when developing software for expensive systems it is easier to develop it on a cheaper system (such as a PC) and then port it over to the real system when the software is ready to be tested.
- **Programming microchips**. Typically it is much easier to write programs on a PC and then download the cross-compiled code to the device, rather than directly writing the code for it.
- **Availability of development tools**. Sometimes specific development systems are not available for the required system, thus it is often necessary to use a computer with the required development tools, and then cross compile for the final system.

Figure H1.14 illustrates examples of cross compilation. It should be noted that cross compilation can lead to many problems. This is because the system emulator and the cross compiler are never perfect and it is often difficult to fully test a program.

H1.10   Three layers of programming

Just like in networking and the Internet, with its OSI model, most applications have three logical layers:

- **Data layer**. This manages the data used by the application. An application that stores its data in data files is said to implement the data layer itself. Many applications use a database to manage the storage of data. In these cases, the database itself is considered to be the data layer of the application.
- **Business logic layer**. This layer builds on the data layer, and contains the various rules and operations that the application performs on its data. For example, when an order is placed through an e-commerce Web site, the data layer stores the order details while the business logic layer performs all the required calculations, validates credit card numbers and ensures all the relevant information is present.

- **Presentation layer**. This layer builds on the business logic layer and presents and manages the display which enables the user to interact with the system. Graphical user interfaces (GUI) and web pages are typical examples of a presentation layer.

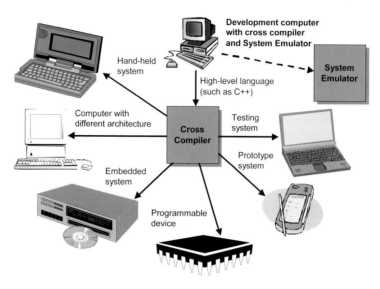

Figure H1.14   Examples of cross compilers

Applications can be categorized by the number of *tiers* they have. A tier is a grouping of the three layers into a single component of the application. Although there are only three sections (data, business logic, and presentation) there are actually four categories for an application.

- **Single-tiered applications**. All three sections combined into a single component, which is usually an executable program. Many PC applications fall into this category such as word processors and spreadsheets, and some simple web based applications.
- **Two-tiered applications**. The data layer is separated out from the presentation and business layers, while the latter are still combined. Although it is possible to separate the presentation layer and leave the business logic and data layers combined, this is not usual as most applications, which separate the presentation layer, will also separate the remaining two as well.
- **Three-tiered applications**. Separate the three layers into separate components. These applications typically use distributed middleware to allow disjoint components of the system to communicate and work together.
- **N-tiered applications.** Similar to three-tiered applications, but more distributed. An N-tiered application has many distributed objects spread across many machines, again using middleware. These objects may have their own individual, separate data layers.

H2 WWW programming

H2.1 Introduction

This section discusses some of the methods which are used to program over the WWW. The WWW was initially conceived in 1989 by CERN, the European particle physics research laboratory in Geneva, Switzerland. Its main objective was to allow various different types of information, such as text, graphics and video, to be integrated together in an easy-to-use manner. It also supports the interlinking of information. The standard language developed is HTML (HyperText Markup Language), which is a text-based language which has certain formatting tags. These tags are identified between a less than (<) and a greater than (>) symbol. Most have an opening and closing version; for example, to highlight bold text the bold opening tag (<B>) is used and the closing tag is </B>. When a greater than or a less than symbol is required then a special character sequence can be used. It is fine for low quality and medium quality documents, but it is difficult to produce any high quality printed material. It is likely that new versions of HTML will support enhanced presentation. Table H2.1 defines some of the tags that are used in HTML. An example HTML is given next, and Figure H2.1 shows how it is interpreted by a WWW browser.

```
<HTML><HEAD><TITLE> Fred Bloggs</TITLE></HEAD>
<BODY TEXT="#000000" BGCOLOR="#FFFFFF">
<H1>Fred Bloggs Home Page</H1>
I'm Fred Bloggs. Below is a table of links.
<HR>
<P>
<TABLE BORDER=10 WIDTH=90% LENGTH=50%>
<TR>
   <TD><B>General</B></TD>
   <TD><A HREF="res.html">Research</TD>
   <TD><A HREF="cv.html">CV</TD>
   <TD><A HREF="paper.html">Papers Published</TD>
   <TD></TD>
</TR>
<TR>
   <TD ROWSPAN=2><B>HTML/Java Tutorials</B></TD>
   <TD><A HREF="intro.html">Tutorial 1</TD>
   <TD COLSPAN=2><A HREF="inter.html">Tutorial 2</TD>
</TR>
<TR>
   <TD><A HREF="java1.html">Tutorial 1</TD>
   <TD><A HREF="java2.html">Tutorial 2</TD>
   <TD><A HREF="java3.html">Tutorial 3</TD>
</TR></TABLE>
</BODY></HTML>
```

Normally WWW designers do not write HTML code, as they can use a WWW page designer, such as Microsoft FrontPage or Macromedia Dreamweaver. Figure H2.2 shows a split between the design view and code view in Dreamweaver and Figure H2.3 shows a screen from FrontPage showing integrated HTML code. In most cases, the designer simply uses the graphical user interface to design the WWW page, and the design package produces the HTML code. If required the designer can edit any part of the HTML code, manually, thus an understanding of HTML is important.

Table H2.1 Example HTML tags

Open tag	Closing tag	Description
<HTML>	</HTML>	Start and end of HTML
<HEAD>	</HEAD>	Defines the HTML header
<BODY>	</BODY>	Defines the main body of the HTML
<TITLE>	</TITLE>	Defines the title of the WWW page
<I>	</I>	Italic text
<B>	</B>	Bold text
<U>	</U>	Underlined text
<BLINK>	</BLINK>	Make text blink
<EM>	</EM>	Emphasize text
<FONT SIZE=+1>	</FONT>	Increase font size by one increment
<FONT SIZE=-1>	</FONT>	Reduce font size by one increment
<CENTER>	</CENTER>	Center text
<H1>	</H1>	Section header, level 1
<H2>	</H2>	Section header, level 2
<H3>	</H3>	Section header, level 3
<P>		Create a new paragraph
 		Create a line break
<!-->	-->	Comments
<SUPER>	</SUPER>	Superscript
_		Subscript

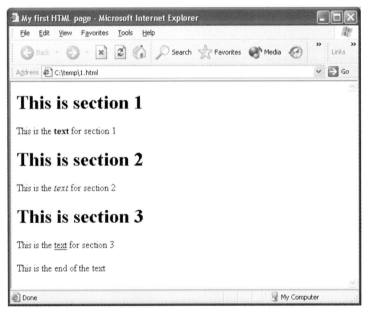

Figure H2.1 Example HTML page

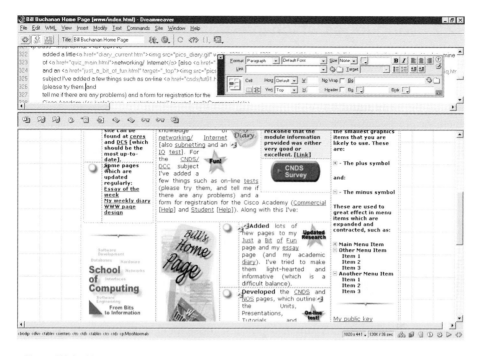

Figure H2.2 Macromedia Dreamweaver showing a split screen for the Code View and Design View

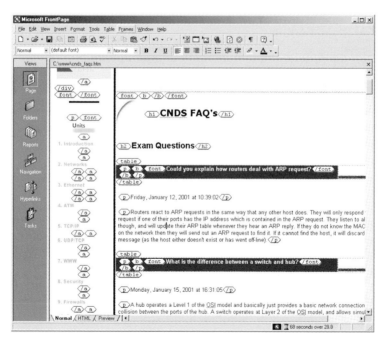

Figure H2.3 Microsoft FrontPage showing HTML tags

H2.2 Languages which integrate with HTML

HTML is the standard language which is used to present WWW pages, and is interpreted by the WWW browser. Unfortunately, HTML is a rather limited language, and can only really present static information. It is also not good at getting user interaction, thus need languages have been added to HTML to enhance it. Typically, this is to process user information, or to respond to user events (such as mouse clicks, or text input). The place where the processing of the additional script defines whether it is a server-side include or a client-side include. If the WWW browser processes the script, then it is a client-side include, otherwise it a server-side include, as illustrated in Figure H2.4. Typical client-side includes are VBScript and JavaScript, and typical server-side includes are PHP and ASP.

A server-side include is better for compatibility with the WWW browser, as it converts the additional script into standard HTML. For example in ASP:

```
<%=time()%>
```

would be processed as an ASP script (as it is contained with <% and %>), and converted to the HTML code:

```
<P>Thur, 5 Oct 2001</P>
```

Thus, it does not depend browser version. Unfortunately, the extra script is dependent on the server, and any problems with this may cause the script to fail. With client-side include the code is processed by the browser, thus it depends if the browser can actually process the script. Fortunately now most browsers are fairly compatible with the client-side includes, but you can never be too sure how different browser versions are going to present the page.

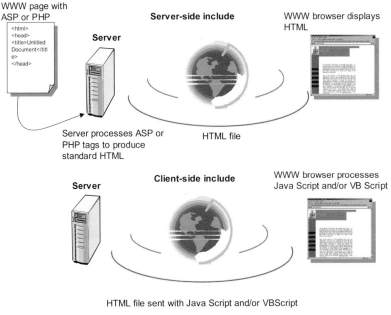

Figure H2.4   Difference between server-side include and client-side include

JSP also uses the <% and %> tags, but the files are named with a JSP extension. These files were initially developed by Sun Microsystems and are typically processed by a UNIX-based server. The basic language used is Java.

H2.3 VBScript

HTML is fine for basic formatting, but it is not so good at getting user interaction, thus VBScript (Visual Basic) is a simplified form of Visual Basic (which is the most popular programming language in the world) and is used to provide some basic functions, such as time() to display the current time. VB script integrates into HTML, and can hide itself from WWW browsers by imbedding it in-between the <SCRIPT LANGUAGE= "VBSCRIPT"> and the </SCRIPT> tags.

```
<SCRIPT LANGUAGE="VBSCRIPT">
sub myheader_onClick
   myheader.Style.Color = "BLACK"
end sub
</SCRIPT>
```

H2.4 JavaScript

JavaScript integrates into the HTML page within the <SCRIPT LANGUAGE= "JAVASCRIPT"> and the </SCRIPT> tags. It has a similar syntax to Java, but is not as strict on the syntax of the code. For example to print the current time (HH:MM) with JavaScript:

```
<p>Current time is
<script language="javascript">
var dat=new Date();
   document.write(dat.getHours() + ":" + dat.getMinutes());
</script>
```

JavaScript will be covered in more detail in Chapter H4.

H2.5 ASP

ASP is similar to VBScript, but rather than the browser processing the script, the WWW server actually does it before it sends the page to the WWW browser. ASP is a Microsoft technology and will typically only run on a Microsoft server (such as with an Microsoft IIS server). ASP pages are named with an asp file extension (such as default.asp), to differentiate them from normal HTML pages. An example is:

<B>Current time is <%=Time()%> </B>

which will display the current time. When this is sent to the WWW browser it will have the Time() function expanded into HTML code, such as:

```
<B>Current time is 10:35pm</B>
```

for which the WWW browser will display as:

```
Current time is 10:35pm
```

JavaScript will be covered in more detail in Chapter H4.

H2.6 JSP

JSP (Java Server Page) allows Java code to be integrated into a WWW page. Like ASP, it uses the <% and %> tags to define Java code and uses the server to process the additional code into HTML. An extract from a JSP page is shown next. The highlighted areas show the JavaScript parts. It can be seen that, in this case, that the JavaScript part hides an if() decision. The server process the Java parts and decides on which parts on the HTML code it sends to the client.

```
<html><body>
<%
  String user = (String)session.getAttribute("user");
  if ((user == null) || (user.equals(""))){
%>
    <p> no user in session</p>
<%
  }
  else{
    session.invalidate();
%>
    <p>User <b><%= user %></b>
      logged out!</p>
<%
  }
%>
    <a href="login.jsp">login</a>
</body></html>
```

In this case, if user is an empty string then the following code will be sent to the client:

```
<html><body>
    <p> no user in session</p>
    <a href="login.jsp">login</a>
</body></html>
```

else the following will be sent:

```
<html><body>
    session.invalidate();
    <p>User <b><%= user %></b> logged out!</p>
    <a href="login.jsp">login</a>
</body></html>
```

As with ASP and PHP, JSP allows an organization to keep their additional code private, so that all that the client sees is pure HTML (possibly also with JavaScript and/or VBScript).

H2.7   PHP

ASP is a Microsoft technology for server-side includes in HTML pages, whereas PHP is a UNIX equivalent, and typically runs on an Apache WWW server. It is one of the oldest scripting languages for WWW pages, but is one of the most useful, as it interfaces with many different types of relational databases, such as Oracle, Sybase, MySQL and ODBC.

In PHP the additional code is added between the <? and ?> tags. For example the following prints a "Hello World" message to the browser:

```
<?php
print("Hello World");
?>
```

PHP will be covered in more detail in Chapter H4.

H2.8   CGI

A CGI program is one that is called from a WWW browser. These can be written in many languages, such as Visual Basic, C++, Java and Perl. Visual Basic, C++ and Java normally require to be compiled into an executable form for it to run on the server. Perl is different in that it is a scripted language, and does not have to be compiled before it is used. Normally Perl programs perform some sore of system function, such as getting information on the current WWW connection, or accessing data in a database. As they have a high level of priority, they must be kept in a secure way, so that external users cannot gain access to the server. This special place is a directory called the cgi-bin. Scripts placed in this place are allowed to gain access to the system. An example Perl program to show the IP address of the user is:

```
#!/usr/local/bin/perl
print "Content-type: text/html","\n\n";
print STDOUT "\n";
$remote_addr = $ENV{'REMOTE_ADDR'};
print STDOUT "<P>Your IP address is: ";
print STDOUT $remote_addr;
```

It operates by sending all of the required commands that a WWW server would normally add to the WWW page. For example "Content-type: text/html","\n\n";" is the string that is sent by the server before the main WWW page is sent, and defines that the page is an HTML page. In the case of Perl the STDOUT is normally sent to the monitor, but in a WWW page the output will be to the connection with the WWW browser. Also the first line of the Perl script defines where the operating system should find the Perl program (in this case it is /usr/local/bin/perl).

Perl, for all its power, is a very difficult language to use, and typically WWW developers use standard cgi scripts, which they can use for their purpose. Typical cgi scripts include page hit counters, form filling, and login user accesses to WWW pages. Perl's strongest feature is its string processing abilities.

H2.9 XML

XML (eXtensible Markup Language) is a markup language which is similar to HTML. Its main application is to produce structured documents. It is much more powerful than HTML, as it is possible to define new tags. XML itself is derived from SGML (Standard Generalized Markup Language), which also defining sets of tags and the relationships among them.

Tags in XML are similar to HTML tags, and they consist of a tag name plus optional attributes, surrounded by angle brackets (< and >). Like HTML, the opening tag has an < followed by the name of the tag, and the closing tag has the tag name is preceded by a slash and then a >. For example we could define our own tags of <PARAGRAPH>, <BOLD> and <ITALICS>, and use them in the following document:

<PARAGRAPH>Some programs provide a <BOLD>framework</BOLD> for a user to manipulate data without the user having to produce their own program. Examples of this include word processors, spreadsheet programs, and so on, where the user writes <ITALIC>macro</ITALIC>, or script, programs which <BOLD>integrate</BOLD> within the package.</PARAGRAPH>

would be formatted (after we had properly defined our tags) as:

Some programs provide a **framework** for a user to manipulate data without the user having to produce their own program. Examples of this include word processors, spreadsheet programs, and so on, where the user writes *macro*, or script, programs which **integrate** within the package.

One difference between HTML and XML is that an empty tag (one that uses only a single tag, such as `<img>`, instead of an opening tag and a closing tag containing text or other material) must end with a slash just before the closing angle bracket. For example, an `<img>` tag in XML might look like this:

```
<img src="mygraphic.gif" />
```

XML, though, is much stricter and less forgiving about its syntax than HTML is; and files, which do not conform to the XML standard, are rejected by XML parsers.

XML will be covered in more detail in Chapter H12.

H2.10 WML

There will be a great increase in the coming years in the usage of mobile computing devices. These devices will typically connect to the Internet through a radio link, and will possibly have a small display area. Thus, the existing WWW pages are not really relevant to this type of system, as they tend to be graphics-intensive, and are designed for a resolution of at least 640 by 480 pixels. Thus a new language has been developed to cope with this: Wireless Markup Language (WML). It is basically a WML is a markup language which is based XML and was developed for specifying content and user interface for devices which have low bandwidth connections, such as cellular phones and pagers.

WML is designed to work with small, wireless devices that have four characteristics:

- **Small display screens with low resolution**. Typically, mobile phones only can support a few lines of text, with only 8–12 characters on each line.
- **Limited capacity.** These devices typically have a limited amount of resources, such as a low-powered processor, limited amount of memory, limited power constraints, and limited storage space.
- **Limited user control**. Typically mobile phones have just a few special keys in which to navigate. It is unlikely that they would have a mouse or other pointing device.
- **Low bandwidth and high latency**. Mobile devices might only have a bandwidth of between 300 bps and 10 kbps network connections, with a delay of over fives seconds.

The characteristics of WML are grouped into four major areas:

- It supports text and images, and has a variety of formatting and layout commands.
- It is created from cards which are grouped into decks. WML decks are similar to HTML pages in that it is identified by an URL, and contain the main content for the page.
- It offers support for managing navigation between cards and decks, and includes commands for event handling. These are typically used to navigate.
- It allows parameters to be set for all the WML decks. Variables can be used in place of strings and are substituted at runtime.

All WML information is arranged as a collection of cards and desks. Cards normally specify one or more units of user interaction. This could be to present a menu, or to enter text in a field. The user then navigates through a number of WML cards, and makes choices before moving onto other cards. A deck is the smallest unit of WML that the server sends to the client. An example WML page is given next. With this the user will receive an ACCEPT option, which, if selected will take them onto the next card in the desk.

```
<?xml version="1.0"?>
<!DOCTYPE wml PUBLIC "-//WAPFORUM//DTD WML 1.1//EN"
"http://www.wapforum.org/DTD/wml_1.1.xml">
<wml>
        <card id="Card1">
                <do type="accept" label="Next">
                        <go href="#Card2"/>
                </do>
                <p> Select <b>Next</b> to go to the next card. </p>
        </card>
        <card id="Card2">
                <p> This is the second card </p>
        </card>
</wml>
```

H2.11 Java and WWW pages

The Java programming language is the natural language for complex Internet and WWW based programming. These are standardized in the J2EE specification.

H2.12 CSS

Another particular problem with HTML is that it is not very good at precisely defining the format of text, especially between different types of browser. Thus the CSS standard has been defined. This involves including a CSS file in the HTML page, which contains definitions for the text styles used in the page. For example to define the first header (H1) style:

```
H1
{font: bold 16pt Verdana, Arial, Helvetica, sans-serif; background:
transparent; color: #000000}
```

which defines the header style (H1) is Verdana font, of 16 points, and black (#000000). Thus

```
<H1>Hello</H1>
```

will become:

Hello

H3   HTML

H3.1   Links

The topology of the WWW is set-up using links where pages link to other related pages. A reference takes the form:

```
<A HREF="url"> Reference Name </A>
```

where *url* defines the URL for the file, *Reference Name* is the name of the reference and `</A>` defines the end of the reference name. HTML script H3.1 shows an example of the uses of references and Figure H3.1 shows a sample browser page. The background color is set using the `<BODY BGCOLOR= "#FFFFFF">` which sets the background color to white. In this case the default text color is black and the link is colored blue.

📖 **HTML script H3.1**

```
<HTML>

<HEAD>
<TITLE>Fred's page</TITLE>
</HEAD>

<BODY BGCOLOR="#FFFFFF">

<H1>Fred's Home Page</H1>

If you want to access information on
this book <A HREF="softbook.html">click here</A>.

<P>A reference to the <A REF="http:www.iee.com/">IEE</A>
</BODY>
</HTML>
```

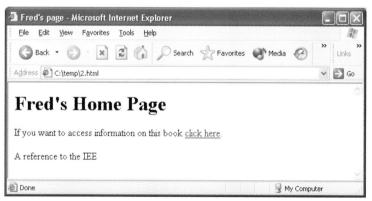

Figure H3.1   Window from example HTML script H3.1

H3.1.1 Other links

Links can be set-up to send to e-mail addresses and newsgroups. For example:

```
<A HREF="news:sport.tennis"> Newsgroups for tennis</A>
```

to link to a tennis newsgroup and

```
<A HREF="mailto:f.bloggs@fredco.co.uk">Send a message to me</A>
```

to send a mail message to the e-mail address: `f.bloggs@ fredco.co.uk`.

H3.2   Lists

HTML allows ordered and unordered lists. Lists can be declared anywhere in the body of the HTML.

H3.2.1 Ordered lists

The start of an ordered list is defined with `<OL>` and the end of the list by `</OL>`. Each part of the list is defined after the `<LI>` tag. Unordered lists are defined between the `<UL>` and `</UL>` tags. HTML script H3.2 gives examples of an ordered and an unordered list. Figure H3.2 shows the output from the browser.

📖 **HTML script H3.2**
```
<HTML><HEAD><TITLE>Fred's page</TITLE></HEAD>
<BODY BGCOLOR="#FFFFFF">
<H1>List 1</H1>
<OL>
<LI>Part 1
<LI>Part 2
<LI>Part 3
</OL>
<H1>List 2</H1>
<UL>
<LI>Section 1
<LI>Section 2
<LI>Section 3
</UL>
</BODY></HTML>
```

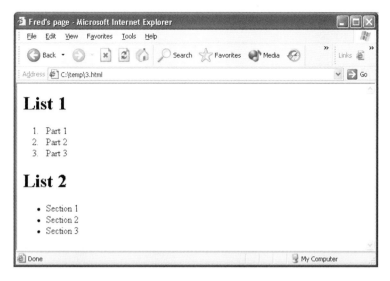

Figure H3.2 WWW browser with an ordered and unordered lists

Some browsers allow the type of numbered list to be defined with the `<OL TYPE=x>`, where *x* can either be:

- A for capital letters (such as A, B, C, and so on).
- a for small letters (such as a, b, c, and so on).
- I for capital roman letters (such as I, II, III, and so on).
- i for small roman letters (such as i, ii, iii, and so on).
- I for numbers (which is the default).

```
<OL Type=I >
<LI> List 1
<LI> List 2
<LI> List 3
</OL>

<OL Type=A>
<LI> List 1
<LI> List 2
<LI> List 3
</OL>
```

would be displayed as:

I.	List 1
II.	List 2
III.	List 3
A.	List 1
B.	List 2
C.	List 3

The starting number of the list can be defined using the `<LI VALUE=`*n*`>` where *n* defines the initial value of the defined item list.

H3.2.2 Unordered lists

Unordered lists are used to list a series of items in no particular order. They are defined between the `<UL>` and `</UL>` tags. Some browsers allow the type of bullet point to be defined with the `<LI TYPE=`*shape*`>`, where *shape* can either be:

- *disc* for round solid bullets (which is the default for first level lists).
- *round* for round hollow bullets (which is the default for second level lists).
- *square* for square bullets (which is the default for third).

HTML script H3.3 gives an example of an unnumbered list and Figure H3.3 shows the WWW page output for this script. It can be seen from this that the default bullets for level 1 lists are discs, for level 2 they are round and for level 3 they are square.

📖 **HTML script H3.3**

```
<HTML><HEAD><TITLE>Example list</TITLE></HEAD>
<H1> Introduction </H1>
<UL>
<LI> OSI Model
<LI> Networks
    <UL>
    <LI> Ethernet
        <UL>
        <LI> MAC addresses
        </UL>
    <LI> Token Ring
    <LI> FDDI
    </UL>
<LI> Conclusion
</UL>
<H1> Wide Area Networks </H1>
<UL>
<LI> Standards
<LI> Examples
    <UL>
    <LI> EastMan
    </UL>
<LI> Conclusion
</UL>
</BODY>
</HTML>
```

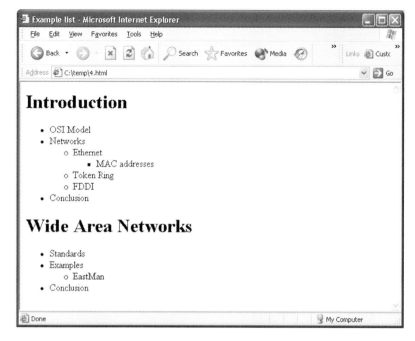

Figure H3.3   WWW page with an unnumbered list

H3.2.3   Definition lists

HTML uses the `<DL>` and `</DL>` tags for definition lists. These are normally used when building glossaries. Each entry in the definition is defined by the `<DT>` tag and the text associated with the item is defined after the `<DD>` tag. The end of the list is defined by `</DL>`. HTML script H3.4 shows an example with a definition list and Figure H3.4 gives a sample output. Note that it uses the `<EM>` tag to emphasize the definition subject.

HTML script H3.4

```
<HTML>
<HEAD>
<TITLE>Example list</TITLE>
</HEAD>
<H1> Glossary </H1>
<DL>
<DT> <EM> Address Resolution Protocol (ARP) </EM>
<DD> A TCP/IP process which maps an IP address to an Ethernet address.
<DT> <EM> American National Standards Institute (ANSI) </EM>
<DD> ANSI is a non-profit organization which is made up of expert committees
that publish standards for national industries.
<DT> <EM> American Standard Code for Information Interchange (ASCII) </EM>
<DD> An ANSI-defined character alphabet which has since been adopted as a stan-
dard international alphabet for the interchange of characters.
</DL>
</BODY></HTML>
```

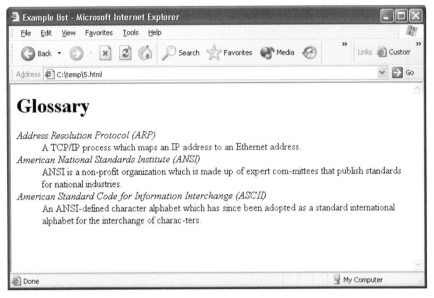

Figure H3.4 WWW page with definition list

H3.3 Colors

Colors in HTML are defined in the RGB (red/green/blue) strength. The format is #rrggbb, where rr is the hexadecimal equivalent for the red component, gg the hexadecimal equivalent for the green component and bb the hexadecimal equivalent for the blue component. Table H3.1 lists some of the codes for certain colors.

Individual hexadecimal numbers use base 16 and range from 0 to F (in decimal this ranges from 0 to 15). A two-digit hexadecimal number ranges from 00 to FF (in decimal this ranges from 0 to 255). Table H3.2 outlines hexadecimal equivalents.

HTML uses percentage strengths for the colors. For example, FF represents full strength (100%) and 00 represent no strength (0%). Thus, white is made from FF (red), FF (green) and FF (blue) and black is made from 00 (red), 00 (green) and 00 (blue). Grey is made from equal weighting of each of the colors, such as 43, 43, 43 for dark grey (#434343) and D4, D4 and D4 for light grey (#D4D4D4). Thus, pure red with be #FF0000, pure green will be #00FF00 and pure blue with be #0000FF.

Table H3.1 Hexadecimal colors

Color	Code	Color	Code
White	#FFFFFF	Dark red	#C91F16
Light red	#DC640D	Orange	#F1A60A
Yellow	#FCE503	Light green	#BED20F
Dark green	#088343	Light blue	#009DBE
Dark blue	#0D3981	Purple	#3A0B59
Pink	#F3D7E3	Nearly black	#434343
Dark gray	#777777	Grey	#A7A7A7
Light gray	#D4D4D4	Black	#000000

Table H3.2 Hexadecimal to decimal conversions

Hex.	Dec.	Hex.	Dec.	Hex.	Dec.	Hex.	Dec.
0	0	1	1	2	2	3	3
4	4	5	5	6	6	7	7
8	8	9	9	A	10	B	11
C	12	D	13	E	14	F	15

Each color is represented by 8 bits, thus the color is defined by 24 bits. This gives a total of $16\,777\,216$ colors (2^{24} different colors). Note that some video displays will not have enough memory to display 16.777 million colors in a certain mode so that colors may differ depending on the WWW browser and the graphics adapter.

The colors of the background, text and the link can be defined with the BODY tag. An example with a background color of white, a text color of orange and a link color of dark red is:

```
<BODY BGCOLOR="#FFFFFF" TEXT="#F1A60A"  LINK="#C91F16">
```

and for a background color of red, a text color of green and a link color of blue:

```
<BODY BGCOLOR="#FF0000" TEXT="#00FF00"  LINK="#0000FF">
```

When a link has been visited its color changes. This color itself can be changed with the VLINK. For example, to set-up a visited link color of yellow:

```
<BODY VLINK="#FCE503" "TEXT=#00FF00"  "LINK=#0000FF">
```

Note that the default link colors are:

Link:	#0000FF	(Blue)
Visited link:	#FF00FF	(Purple)

H3.4   Background images

Images (such as GIF and JPEG) can be used as a background to a WWW page. For this purpose the option BACKGROUND=*'src.gif'* is added to the <BODY> tag. An HTML script with a background of CLOUDS.GIF is given in HTML script H3.5. A sample output from a browser is shown in Figure H3.5.

📖 **HTML script H3.5**

```
<HTML><HEAD>
<TITLE>Fred's page</TITLE></HEAD>
<BODY BACKGROUND="clouds.gif">
<H1>Fred's Home Page</H1>
If you want to access information on
this book <A HREF="gbook.html">click here</A>.<P>
A reference to the <A HREF="http://www.iee.com/">IEE</A>
</BODY>
</HTML>
```

Figure H3.5 WWW page with CLOUDS.GIF as a background

H3.5   Displaying images

WWW pages can support graphics images within a page. The most common sources of images are either JPEG or GIF files, as these types of images normally have a high degree of compression. GIF images, as was previously mentioned, support only 256 colors from a pallet of 16.7 million colors, whereas JPEG supports more than 256 colors.

H3.5.1   Inserting an image

Images can be displayed within a page with the <IMG SRC='*src.gif*'> which inserts the graphic *src.gif*. HTML script H3.6 contains three images: mypic1.jpg, me.gif and mypic2.jpg. These are aligned either to the left or the right using the ALIGN option within the <IMG SRC> tag. The first image (mypic1.jpg) is aligned to the right, while the second image (mypic2.jpg) is aligned to the left. Figure H3.6 shows a sample output from this script. Note that images are left aligned by default.

📖 **HTML script H3.6**

```
<HTML><HEAD>
<TITLE>My first home page</TITLE>
</HEAD>
<BODY BGCOLOR="#ffffff">
<IMG SRC ="mypic1.jpg" width=120 ALIGN=RIGHT>
<H1> Picture gallery </H1>
<P><P>
Here are a few pictures of me and my family. To the right
is a picture of my sons taken in the garden. Below to the
left is a picture of my two youngest sons under an
umbrella and to the right is a picture of me taken in my office.
<P>
<IMG SRC ="mypic2.jpg" ALIGN=LEFT width=200>
```

```
<IMG SRC ="me.gif" ALIGN=RIGHT width=300>
</BODY></HTML>
```

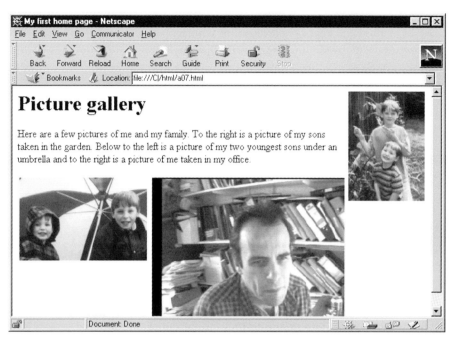

Figure H3.6   WWW page with three images

H3.5.2   Alternative text

Often users choose not to view images in a page and select an option on the viewer which
stops the viewer from displaying any graphic images. If this is the case then the HTML page
can contain substitute text which is shown instead of the image. For example:

```
<IMG SRC ="mypic1.jpg" ALT="In garden" ALIGN=RIGHT>
<IMG SRC ="mypic2.jpg" ALT="Under umbrella" ALIGN=LEFT>
<IMG SRC ="me.gif" ALT="Picture of me" ALIGN=RIGHT>
```

H3.5.3   Other options

Other image options can be added, such as:

- `HSPACE=`x `VSPACE=`y defines the amount of space that should be left around images.
  The x value defines the number of pixels in the x-direction and the y value defines the
  number of pixels in the y-direction.
- `WIDTH=` x `HEIGHT=`y defines the scaling in the x- and y-direction, where x and y are the
  desired pixel width and height, respectively, of the image.
- `ALIGN=`*direction* defines the alignment of the image. This can be used to align an image
  with text. Valid options for aligning with text are *texttop, top, middle, absmiddle, bottom,
  baseline* or *absbottom*. HTML script H3.7 shows an example of image alignment with the
  image `a.gif` (which is just the letter 'A' as a graphic) and Figure H3.7 shows a sample

output. It can be seen that *texttop* aligns the image with highest part of the text on the line, *top* aligns the image with the highest element in the line, *middle* aligns with the middle of the image with the baseline, *absmiddle* aligns the middle of the image with the middle of the largest item, *bottom* aligns the bottom of the image with the bottom of the text and *absbottom* aligns the bottom of the image with the bottom of the largest item.

📖 **HTML script H3.7**

```
<HTML><HEAD><TITLE>My first home page</TITLE></HEAD>
<BODY BGCOLOR="#ffffff">
<IMG SRC ="a.gif" ALIGN=texttop>pple<P>
<IMG SRC ="a.gif" ALIGN=top>pple<P>
<IMG SRC ="a.gif" ALIGN=middle>pple<P>
<IMG SRC ="a.gif" ALIGN=bottom>pple<P>
<IMG SRC ="a.gif" ALIGN=baseline>pple<P>
<IMG SRC ="a.gif" ALIGN=absbottom>pple
</BODY></HTML>
```

H3.6   Horizontal lines

A horizontal line can be added with the <HR> tag. Most browsers allow extra parameters, such as:

SIZE= *n* – which defines that the height of the rule is *n* pixels.
WIDTH=*w* – which defines that the width of the rule is *w* pixels or as a percentage.
ALIGN=*direction* – where direction refers to the alignment of the rule. Valid options for *direction* are *left*, *right* or *center*.
NOSHADE – which defines that the line should be solid with no shading.

HTML script H3.8 gives some example horizontal lines and Figure H3.8 shows an example output.

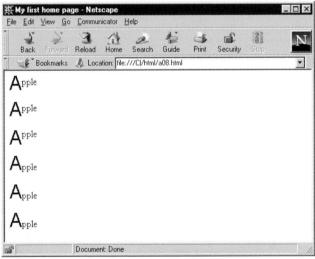

Figure H3.7   WWW page showing image alignment

📖 **HTML script H3.8**

```
<HTML><HEAD><TITLE>My first home page</TITLE></HEAD>
<BODY BGCOLOR="#ffffff">
<IMG SRC ="a.gif">pple<P>
<HR>
<IMG SRC ="a.gif">pple<P>
<HR WIDTH=50% ALIGN=CENTER>
<IMG SRC ="a.gif">pple<P>
<HR SIZE=10 NOSHADE>
</BODY></HTML>
```

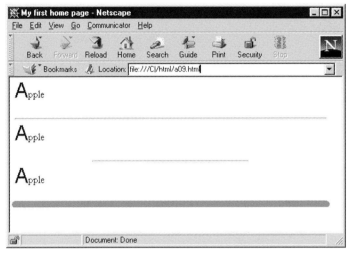

Figure H3.8   WWW page showing horizontal lines

H3.7   Anchors

An anchor allows users to jump from a reference in a WWW page to another anchor point within the page. The standard format is:

`<A NAME="`*anchor name*`">`

where *anchor name* is the name of the section which is referenced. The </A> tag defines the end of an anchor name. A link is specified by:

`<A HREF="#`*anchor name*`">`

followed by the `</A>` tag. HTML script H3.9 shows a sample script with four anchors and Figure H3.9 shows a sample output. When the user selects one of the references, the browser automatically jumps to that anchor. Figure H3.10 shows the output screen when the user selects the `#Token` reference. Anchors are typically used when an HTML page is long or when a backwards or forwards reference occurs (such as a reference within a published paper).

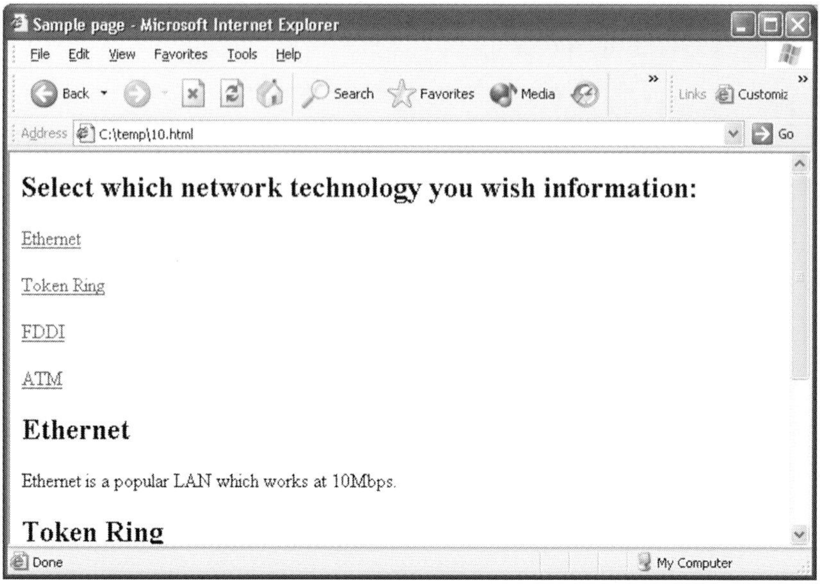

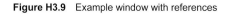

Figure H3.9 Example window with references

📖 **HTML script H3.9**

```
<HTML>
<HEAD>
<TITLE>Sample page</TITLE>
</HEAD>
<BODY BGCOLOR="#FFFFFF">
<H2>Select which network technology you wish information:</H2>
<P><A HREF="#Ethernet">Ethernet</A>
<P><A HREF="#Token">Token Ring</A>
<P><A HREF="#FDDI">FDDI</A>
<P><A HREF="#ATM">ATM</A>
<H2><A NAME="Ethernet">Ethernet</A></H2>
Ethernet is a popular LAN which works at 10Mbps.
<H2><A NAME="Token">Token Ring</A></H2>
Token ring is a ring based network which operates at 4 or 16Mbps.
<H2><A NAME="FDDI">FDDI</A></H2>
FDDI is a popular LAN technology which uses a ring of fibre optic cable and
operates at 100Mbps.
<H2><A NAME="ATM">ATM</A></H2>
ATM is a ring based network which operates at 155Mbps.
</BODY>
</HTML>
```

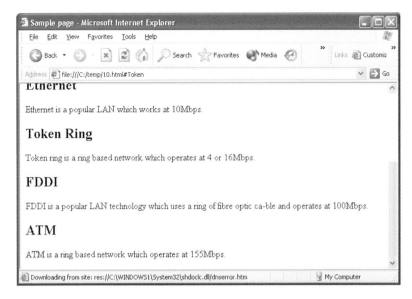

Figure H3.10 Example window with references

H3.8   Tables

Tables are one of the best methods to display complex information in a simple way. Unfortunately, in HTML they are relatively complicated to set up. The start of a table is defined with the <TABLE> tag and the end of a table by </TABLE>. A row is defined between the <TR> and </TR>, while a table header is defined between <TH> and </TH>. A regular table entry is defined between <TD> and </TD>. HTML script H3.10 shows an example of a table with links to other HTML pages. The BORDER=*n* option has been added to the <TABLE> tag to define the thickness of the table border (in pixels). In this case the border size has a thickness of 10 pixels.

📖 **HTML script H3.10**
```
<HTML><HEAD>
<TITLE> Fred Bloggs</TITLE>
</HEAD>
<BODY TEXT="#000000" BGCOLOR="#FFFFFF">
<H1>Fred Bloggs Home Page</H1>
I'm Fred Bloggs. Below is a tables of links.<HR><P>
<TABLE BORDER=10>
<TR>
    <TD><B>General</B></TD>
    <TD><A HREF="res.html">Research</TD>
    <TD><A HREF="cv.html">CV</TD>
    <TD><A HREF="paper.html">Papers Published</TD>
</TR>
<TR>
    <TD><B>HTML Tutorials</B></TD>
    <TD><A HREF="intro.html">Tutorial 1</TD>
    <TD><A HREF="inter.html">Tutorial 2</TD>
    <TD><A HREF="adv.html">Tutorial 3</TD>
</TR>
```

```
<TR>
   <TD><B>Java Tutorials</B></TD>
   <TD><A HREF="java1.html">Tutorial 1</TD>
   <TD><A HREF="java2.html">Tutorial 2</TD>
   <TD><A HREF="java3.html">Tutorial 3</TD>
</TR>
</TABLE>
</BODY></HTML>
```

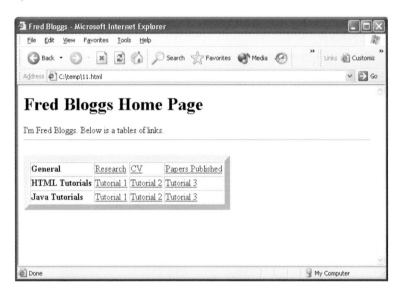

Figure H3.11   Example window from example HTML script H3.10

Other options in the `<TABLE>` tag are:

- `WIDTH=x`, `HEIGHT=y` – defines the size of the table with respect to the full window size. The parameters *x* and *y* are either absolute values in pixels for the height and width of the table or are percentages of the full window size.
- `CELLSPACING=n` – defines the number of pixels desired between each cell where *n* is the number of pixels (note that the default cell spacing is 2 pixels).

An individual cell can be modified by adding options to the `<TH>` or `<TD>` tag. These include:

- `WIDTH=x`, `HEIGHT=y` – defines the size of the table with respect to the table size. The parameters *x* and *y* are either absolute values in pixels for the height and width of the table or are percentages of the table size.
- `COLSPAN=n` – defines the number of columns the cell should span.
- `ROWSPAN=n` – defines the number of rows the cell should span.
- `ALIGN=direction` – defines how the cell's contents are aligned horizontally. Valid options are *left, center* or *right.*
- `VALIGN=direction` – defines how the cell's contents are aligned vertically. Valid options are *top, middle* or *baseline.*
- `NOWRAP` – informs the browser to keep the text on a single line (that is, with no line breaks).

HTML script H3.11 shows an example use of some of the options in the `<TABLE>` and `<TD>` options. In this case the text within each row is center aligned. On the second row the second and third cells are merged using the `COLSPAN=2` option. The first cell of the second and third rows have also been merged using the `ROWSPAN=2` option. Figure H3.12 shows an example output. The table width has been increased to 90% of the full window, with a width of 50%.

📖 **HTML script H3.11**

```
<HTML><HEAD><TITLE> Fred Bloggs</TITLE></HEAD>
<BODY TEXT="#000000" BGCOLOR="#FFFFFF">
<H1>Fred Bloggs Home Page</H1>
I'm Fred Bloggs. Below is a table of links.
<HR>
<P>
<TABLE BORDER=10 WIDTH=90% LENGTH=50%>
<TR>
   <TD><B>General</B></TD>
   <TD><A HREF="res.html">Research</TD>
   <TD><A HREF="cv.html">CV</TD>
   <TD><A HREF="paper.html">Papers Published</TD>
   <TD></TD>
</TR>
<TR>
   <TD ROWSPAN=2><B>HTML/Java Tutorials</B></TD>
   <TD><A HREF="intro.html">Tutorial 1</TD>
   <TD COLSPAN=2><A HREF="inter.html">Tutorial 2</TD>
</TR>
<TR>
   <TD><A HREF="java1.html">Tutorial 1</TD>
   <TD><A HREF="java2.html">Tutorial 2</TD>
   <TD><A HREF="java3.html">Tutorial 3</TD>
</TR>
</TABLE>
</BODY></HTML>
```

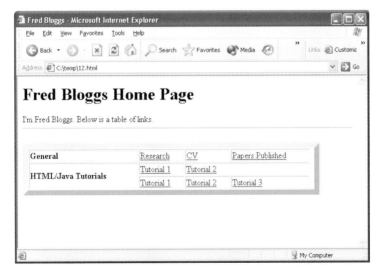

Figure H3.12   Example window from example script H3.12

H3.9   Forms

Forms are excellent methods of gathering data and can be used in conjunction with CGI scripts to collect data for future use. A form is identified between the `<FORM>` and `</FORM>` tags. The method used to get the data from the form is defined with the `METHOD="POST"`. The `ACTION` option defines the URL script to be run when the form is submitted. Data input is specified by the `<INPUT TYPE>` tag. HTML script H3.12 form has the following parts:

- `<form action="/cgi-bin/AnyForm2" method="POST">` – which defines the start of a form and when the `"submit"` option is selected the cgi script `/cgi-bin/AnyForm2` will be automatically run.
- `<input type="submit" value="Send Feedback">` – which causes the program defined in the action option in the `<form>` tag to be run. The button on the form will contain the text `"Send Feedback"`, see Figure H3.13 for a sample output screen.
- `<input type="reset" value="Reset Form">` – which resets the data in the form. The button on the form will contain the text `"Reset Form"`, see Figure H3.14 for a sample output screen.
- `<input type="hidden" name="AnyFormTo" value= "f.bloggs @toytown. ac.uk">` – which passes a value of `f.bloggs@toytown.ac.uk` which has the parameter name of `"AnyFormTo"`. The program `AnyForm2` takes this parameter and automatically sends it to the email address defined in the value (that is, `f.bloggs@toytown.ac.uk`).
- `<input type="hidden" name="AnyFormSubject" value="Feedback form">` – which passes a value of `Feedback form` which has the parameter name of `"AnyFormSubject"`. The program `AnyForm2` takes this parameter and adds the text `"Feedback form"` in the text sent to the email recipient (in this case, `f.bloggs@toytown.ac.uk`).
- `Surname <input name="Surname">` – which defines a text input and assigns this input to the parameter name `Surname`.
- `<textarea name="Address" rows=2 cols=40> </textarea>` – which defines a text input area which has two rows and has a width of 40 characters. The thumb bars appear at the right-hand side of the form if the text area exceeds more than 2 rows, see Figure H3.13.

📖 **HTML script H3.12**

```
<HTML>
<HEAD>
<TITLE>Example form</TITLE>
</HEAD>
<H1><CENTER>Example form</CENTER></H1><P>
<form action="/cgi-bin/AnyForm2" method="POST">
<input type="hidden" name="AnyFormTo" value="f.bloggs@toytown.ac.uk">
<input type="hidden" name="AnyFormSubject" value="Feedback form">
Surname <input name="Surname">
<p>First Name/Names <input name="First Name"><P>
Address (including country)<P>
<textarea name="Address" rows=2 cols=40></textarea><P>
Business Phone <input name="Business Phone">
<P>Place of study (or company) <input name="Study"><P>
E-mail    <input name="E-mail">
Fax Number <input name="Fax Number"><P>
<input type="submit" value="Send Feedback">
<input type="reset" value="Reset Form">
</Form>
<HTML>
```

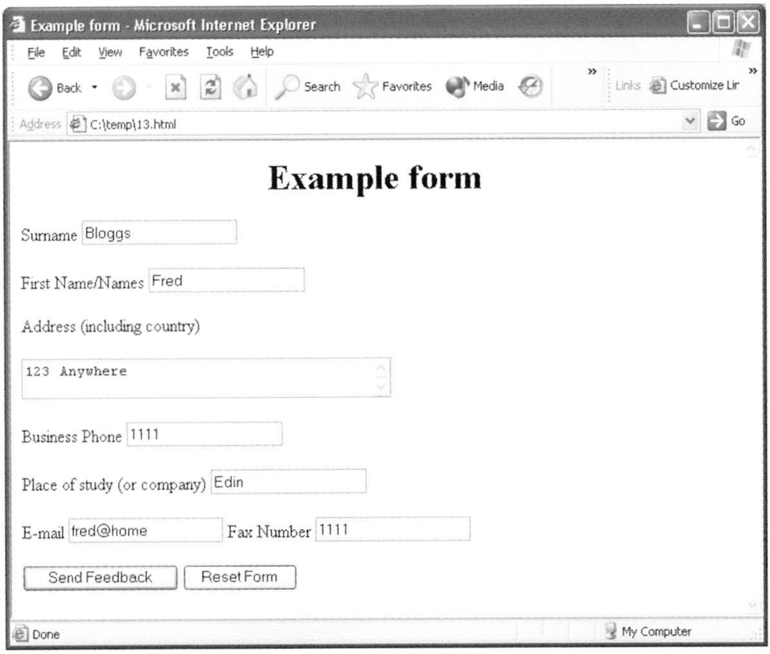

Figure H3.13   Example window showing an example form

In this case the recipient (f.bloggs@toytown.ac.uk) will receive an email with the contents:

```
Anyform Subject=Example form
Surname=Bloggs
First name=Fred
Address=123 Anystreet, Anytown
Business Phone=111-222
Place of study (or company)=Self employed
Email= f.bloggs@nowhere
Fax Number=111-2223
```

The extra options to the <input> tag are size="n", where n is the width of the input box in characters, and maxlength="m", where m is the maximum number of characters that can be entered, in characters. For example:

```
<input type="text"  size="15" maxlength="10">
```

defines that the input type is text, the width of the box is 15 characters and the maximum length of input is 10 characters.

H3.9.1   Input types

The type options to the <input> tag are defined in Table H3.3. HTML script H3.13 gives a few examples of input types and Figure H3.14 shows a sample output.

Table H3.3   Input type options

TYPE=	Description	Options
"text"	The input is normal text.	NAME="*nm*" where *nm* is the name that will be sent to the server when the text is entered. SIZE="*n*" where *n* is the desired box width in characters. SIZE="*m*" where *m* is the maximum number of input characters.
"password"	The input is a password which will be displayed with *s. For example if the user inputs a 4-letter password then only **** will be displayed.	SIZE="*n*" where *n* is the desired box width in characters. SIZE="*m*" where *m* is the maximum number of input characters.
"radio"	The input takes the form of a radio button (such as ⊙ or ○). They are used to allow the user to select a single option from a list of options.	NAME="*radname*" where *radname* defines the name of the button. VALUE="*val*" where *val* is the data that will be sent to the server when the button is selected. CHECKED is used to specify that the button is initially set.
"checkbox"	The input takes the form of a checkbox (such as ☒ or ☐). They are used to allow the user to select several options from a list of options.	NAME="*chkname*" where *chkname* defines the common name for all the checkbox options. VALUE="*defval*" where *defval* defines the name of the option. CHECKED is used to specify that the button is initially set.

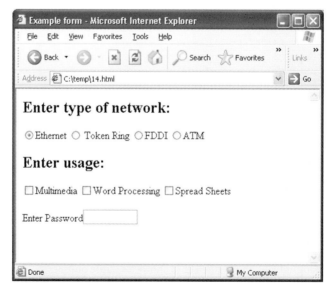

Figure H3.14   Example window with different input options

HTML script H3.13

```
<HTML>
<HEAD>
<TITLE>Example form</TITLE>
</HEAD>
<FORM METHOD="Post" >
<H2>Enter type of network:</H2><P>
<INPUT TYPE="radio" NAME="network" VALUE="ethernet" CHECKED>Ethernet
<INPUT TYPE="radio" NAME="network" VALUE="token"> Token Ring
<INPUT TYPE="radio" NAME="network" VALUE="fddi" >FDDI
<INPUT TYPE="radio" NAME="network" VALUE="atm" >ATM
<H2>Enter usage:</H2><P>
<INPUT TYPE="checkbox" NAME="usage" VALUE="multi" >Multimedia
<INPUT TYPE="checkbox" NAME="usage" VALUE="word" >Word Processing
<INPUT TYPE="checkbox" NAME="usage" VALUE="spread" >Spread Sheets
<P>Enter Password<INPUT TYPE="password" NAME="passwd" SIZE="10">
</FORM>
</HTML>
```

H3.9.2 Menus

Menus are a convenient method of selecting from multiple options. The `<SELECT>` tag is used to define the start of a list of menu options and the `</SELECT>` tag defines the end. Menu elements are then defined with the `<OPTION>` tag. The options defined within the `<SELECT>` are:

- `NAME="`*name*`"` – which defines that *name* is the variable name of the menu. This is used when the data is collected by the server.
- `SIZE="`*n*`"` – which defines the number of options which are displayed in the menu.

HTML script H3.14 shows an example of a menu. The additional options to the `<OPTION>` tag are:
- `SELECTED` – which defines the default selected option.
- `VALUE="`*val*`"` – where *val* defines the name of the data when it is collected by the server.

HTML script H3.14

```
<HTML>
<HEAD><TITLE>Example form</TITLE>
</HEAD>
<FORM METHOD="Post" >
Enter type of network:
<select Name="network" size="1">
<option>Ethernet
<option SELECTED>Token Ring
<option>FDDI
<option>ATM
</select>
</FORM>
</HTML>
```

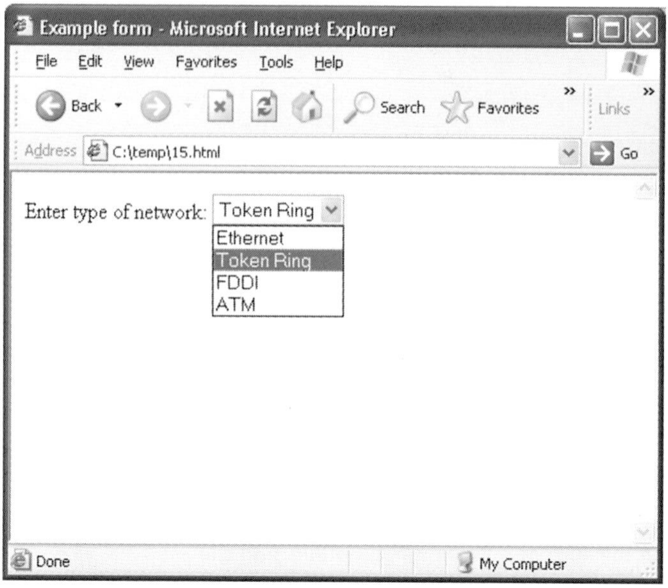

Figure H3.15 Example window showing an example form

H3.10 Multimedia

If the browser cannot handle all the file types it may call on other application helpers to process the file. This allows other 'third-party' programs to integrate into the browser. Figure H3.16 shows an example of the configuration of the helper programs. The options in this case are:

- View in browser.
- Save to disk.
- Unknown: prompt user.
- Launch an application (such as an audio playback program or MPEG viewer).

For certain applications the user can select as to whether the browser processes the file or another application program processes it. Helper programs make upgrades in helper applications relatively simple and also allow new file types to be added with an application helper. Typically when a program is installed which can be used with a browser it will prompt the user to automatically update the helper application list so that it can handle the given file type(s).

Each file type is defined by the file extension, such as `.ps` for postscript files, `.exe` for a binary executable file, and so on. These file extensions have been standardized in MIME (Multipurpose Internet Mail Extensions) specification. Table H3.4 shows some typical file extensions.

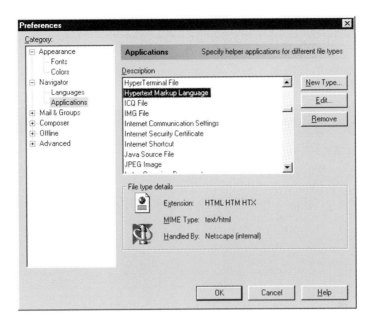

Figure H3.16   Example window showing preferences

Table H3.4   Input type options

Mime type	Extension	Typical action
application/octet-stream	exe, bin	Save
application/postscript	ps, ai, eps	Ask user
application/x-compress	Z	Compress program
application/x-gzip	gz	GZIP compress program
application/x-javascript	js, mocha	Ask user
application/x-msvideo	avi	Audio player
Mime type	*Extension*	*Typical action*
application/x-perl	pl	Save
application/x-tar	tar	Save
application/x-zip-compressed	zip	ZIP program
audio/basic	au, snd	Audio player
image/gif	gif	Browser
image/jpeg	jpeg, jpg, jpe	Browser
image/tiff	tif, tiff	Graphics viewer
image/x-MS-bmp	bmp	Graphics viewer
text/html	htm, html	Browser
text/plain	text, txt	Browser
video/mpeg	mpeg, mpg, mpe, mpv, vbs, mpegv	Video player
video/quicktime	qt, mov, moov	Video player

H4 JavaScript

H4.1 Introduction

JavaScript is a fully object-oriented language which defines a number of terms:

- **Client**. This defines the WWW browser which processes the JavaScript.
- **Event handler**. This associates an object with an event. An example of this is to associate a button with a mouse click by using the onClick event handler.
- **Forms**. These allow the user to gather data from elements of a form, and submit to another WWW page, or to another WWW program (typically to a CGI-script, or a server-side include program).
- **Function**. This defines a software module which can be called from any point on the code. Either they can be written by the designer, or they can be one of the standard JavaScript functions. An example of a predefined function is parseInt(), which allows an integer to be converted from one number base to another.
- **Instance**. An instance is a particular object that has been created. For example, U2 are an instance of a pop group. Thus, U2 are the instance, and *pop group* is the object. In a WWW page, an object may be a date, while current_date can be a particular instance of that date.
- **Method**. Methods are like functions but are applied objects. The range of methods which can be applied to objects is limited by the object itself. For example in a Math object, we can have many mathematical methods which can be applied to it. For example we could have sin(), cos(), sqrt(), and so on. These methods will only apply to the Math object, and cannot be applied to other objects, such as the Date object.
- **Object model**. This defines a group of objects that integrate together to create the required elements. A WWW page might comprise of a WWW page document object, Math objects, and so on.
- **Object**. Objects are an abstract representation of things. This includes the **data** used with the object (data structure), the methods (methods) that can be applied to it, and the properties of the object (properties). The instance of the object is thus constrained by the data structure and the methods. This produces code which is more robust. Many object-oriented languages are script in their implementation of objects.
- **Property:** A property defines an instance of an object. For example, a car is an object. An instance of that object will have various properties, such as Manufacturer= "Toyota", Type= "Corolla", color= "Red", fuel="Petrol", engine size="1600", and so on. These properties could be accessed by mycar.manufacturer= "Toyota", mycar.paint= "Red", mycar.engine.size= "1600", mycar.engine.fuel= "Petrol", and so on.

The main reserved word which are used in JavaScript are:

abstract	else	int	switch
boolean	extends	interface	synchronized

break	false	long	this
byte	final	native	throw
case	finally	new	throws
catch	float	null	transient
char	for	package	true
class	function	private	try
const	goto	protected	typeof
continue	if	public	var
default	implements	return	void
delete	import	short	while
do	in	static	with
double	instanceof	super	

Whenever a WWW page is loaded into a browser, several objects are automatically created. These are created in a hierarchy, which is known as an instance hierarchy, and reflect the structure of the HTML page (Figure H4.1). Every page has the following objects:

- **Window**. This is the top-level object, and defines the properties of the complete window.
- **Document**. *This defines the* properties for the content of the document, such as title, the color of its links, the links, and so on.
- **Location:** This has the properties based on the current URL.
- **History**. This contains properties for the previously required URLs.

For example, window.document.newform.textin.value will define the value property on the textin text field on the form named newform. Normally the window part can be left off, as it relates to the current window. Thus document.newform.textin.value is also valid, for the same property definition.

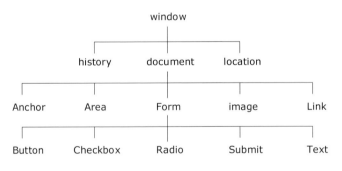

Figure H4.1   JavaScript instance hierarchy

H4.1.1 Document object

The document object has several properties, such as title (show title of the document), bgColor (background color of the document), fgColor (foreground color of the document, linkColor (unvisited hypertext link color), vlinkColor (visited hypertext link color), lastModified (date the document was last modified), URL (the URL of the document), referrer (the referrer for the document) and domain (the domain of the WWW page).

Thus to write these properties:

```
document.write("Title of this page: <B>");
document.write(title + "</B>");
document.write("<BR>Bk color: <B>");
document.write(bgColor + "</B>");
document.write("<BR>Fg color: <B>");
document.write(fgColor + "</B>");
document.write("<BR>Link color: <B>");
document.write(linkColor + "</B>");
document.write("<BR>Visited color: <B>");
document.write(vlinkColor + "</B>");
document.write("<BR>Links: <B>");
document.write(links + "</B>");
document.write("<BR>Modified: <B>");
document.write(lastModified + "</B>");
document.write("<BR>URL: <B>");
document.write(URL+ "</B>");
document.write("<BR>Referrer: <B>");
document.write(referrer + "</B>");
document.write("<BR>Domain: <B>");
document.write(domain + "</B>");
```

A sample run is:

```
Title of this page: JavaScript programming
Bk color: #000066
Fg color: #000000
Link color: #333366
Visited color: #666699
Links: [object]
Modified: 03/17/2002 18:56:54
URL: http://192.168.0.11/jscript_examples.htm
Referrer: http://192.168.0.11/code_snippets.html
Domain: 192.168.0.11
```

H4.1.2   Window object

The window object is the highest-level object, and can be assumed (if it is left off) that it refers to the current document. The main methods are:

- alert(msg) – display an alert message with a message.
- back() – go back one page.
- close(-n) – close the window.
- confirm(msg) – display a confirmation window. The return value is true or false (depending on what the user selects.
- find(searchstr, [matchCase, [searchUpwards]]) – finds a string (searchstr) in the document. The matchcase defines whether the search should be case sensitive, and the searchUpwards option defines whether the search should be upwards in the document.
- forward() – go forward one page.
- home() – go the users home page.
- length() – number of displayed frames.
- name() – the name of the window.
- open(URL, windowname [, options]) – open another window.
- print() – print the current window.

- prompt(msg, default reply) – display a prompt window.
- stop() – stop downloading data.

A few examples are:

```
<a href="javascript:window.close();" class="body">Close window</a>
<a href="javascript:window.print();" class="body">Print window</a>
<script language="JavaScript"> window.alert("Hello World!")</script>
```

H4.1.3   History object

The History object contains several methods, such as:

- back() – go back on page.
- forward() – go forward one page.
- go(-*n*) – go back *n* pages.

A few examples are:

```
<a href="Javascript:history.back()">Back </a>
<a href="Javascript:history.forward()">Forward</a>
<a href="Javascript:history.go(-2)">Go back two pages</a>
```

H4.1.4   Date object

The Date object contains several methods, such as:

- getDate() – get current date. Returns a value between 1 and 31.
- getDay() – get current day. Returns a value of between 0 (Sunday) and 6 (Saturday).
- getFullYear() – get current year.
- getHours() – get current hours. Returns a value between 1 and 23.
- getMilliseconds() – get current milliseconds. Returns a value between 0 and 999.
- getMinutes() – get current minutes. Returns a value between 0 and 59.
- getMonth() – get current month. Return a value between 0 (Jan) and 11 (Dec).
- getSeconds() – get current seconds. Returns a value between 0 and 59.
- getTime() – get current time. Returns a value of the number of seconds since 1 January 1970.
- getTimezoneOffset() – get current time zone. Returns a values between –720 and 720, based on the number of minutes away from GMT.
- getYear() – get the year. Two digit year from between 1900 and 1999, else a four digit year value.
- toString() – convert the number of seconds from 1 January 1970 into a string date format.

A few examples are:

```
<script language="JavaScript">
var dat=new Date();
document.write("<BR>Current date: " +dat.getDate());
document.write("<BR>Current day: " + dat.getDay() );
document.write("<BR>Current year:" + dat.getFullYear() );
document.write("<BR>Current hours: " + dat.getHours() );
```

```
document.write("<BR>Milliseconds: " + dat.getMilliseconds());
document.write("<BR>Minutes: " + dat.getMinutes());
document.write("<BR>Month:" + dat.getMonth());
document.write("<BR>Seconds:" + dat.getSeconds());
document.write("<BR>Seconds since 1/1/70:" + dat.getTime() );
document.write("<BR>Time zone offset: " + dat.getTimezoneOffset() );
document.write("<BR>Year: " + dat.getYear() );
</script>
```

A sample run is:

```
Current date: 17
Current day: 0
Current year:2002
Current hours: 20
Milliseconds: 979
Minutes: 52
Month:2
Seconds:7
Seconds since 1/1/70:1016398327979
Time zone offset: 0
Year: 2002
```

H4.1.5 String object

The Date object contains several methods, such as:

- big(). Make text large.
- blink(). Make text blink.
- charAt(char). Find a character in a string.
- fontcolor(color). Set font color.
- fontsize(size). Set font size.
- italics(). Make italic.
- link(URL). Make a link.
- small(). Make font small.
- sub(). Make font subscript.
- toLowerCase(). Convert to lowercase.
- toUpperCase(). Convert to uppercase.

A few examples are:

```
<script language="JavaScript">
var txt1 = new String("Hello");
var txt2 = new String(" World");
var txt3 = new String(" CNDS page");

document.write("<BR>Large:" + txt1.big() + txt2.big());
document.write("<BR> Small:" + txt1.small() + txt2.small());
document.write("<BR> Lowercase:" + txt1.toLowerCase());
document.write("<BR> Uppercase:" + txt1.toUpperCase());
document.write("<BR> Italic:" + txt1.italics());
document.write("<BR> Size (1):" + txt1.fontsize("1"));
document.write("<BR> Size (2):" + txt1.fontsize("2"));
document.write("<BR> Size (3):" + txt1.fontsize("3"));
document.write("<BR> Size (4):" + txt1.fontsize("4"));
document.write("<BR> Green:" + txt1.fontcolor("green") );
document.write("<BR> Red:" + txt1.fontcolor("red"));
document.write("<BR> Blink:" + txt1.blink());
```

```
document.write("<BR>Subscript:" + txt1 + txt2.sub());
document.write("<BR> Link:" +  txt3.link("cnds.html"));
</script>
```

A sample run is:

```
Large:Hello World
Small:Hello World
Lowercase:hello
Uppercase:HELLO
Italic:Hello
Size (1):Hello
Size (2):Hello
Size (3):Hello
Size (4):Hello
Green:Hello
Red:Hello
Blink:Hello
Subscript:Hello World
Link: CNDS page
```

H4.1.6   Navigator object

The Navigator object contains several properties, which can be usage in determining the system, such as:

- appVersion. Returns the client browser version.
- cookieEnabled. Returns a true if cookies or enabled, else a false.
- cpuClass. Returns the CPU type of the client computer. A PC returns 'x86'.
- onLine. Returns the on-line state.
- userAgent. Returns full browser details, such as operating system, platform and brand.

A few examples are:

```
<script language="JavaScript">
document.write("<BR> Browser version: " + navigator.appVersion);
document.write("<BR>Cookies: " + navigator.cookieEnabled);
document.write("<BR>CPU: " + navigator.cpuClass);
document.write("<BR>Agent: " + navigator.userAgent);
document.write("<BR>Online: " + navigator.onLine);
if (navigator.userAgent.indexOf("MSIE"))
{
document.write("<BR> Browser is IE");
}
else
{
document.write("<BR> Browser is not IE");
}</script>
```

A sample run is:

```
Browser version: 4.0 (compatible; MSIE 6.0; Windows NT 5.1)
Cookies: true
CPU: x86
Agent: Mozilla/4.0 (compatible; MSIE 6.0; Windows NT 5.1)
Online: true
Browser is IE
```

H4.2   Maths operations

An example JavaScript object is **Math**. Typical methods include:

Math.abs()	Absolute value.
Math.acos()	Inverse cosine.
Math.asin()	Inverse sine.
Math.atan()	Inverse tangent.
Math.ceil()	Returns the nearest integer, greater than the number.
Math.cos()	Returns the cosine.
Math.exp()	Return the exponential of a value.
Math.floor()	Returns the nearest integer, less than the number.
Math.min()	Returns the minimum of two values
Math.pow()	Return the value of the first value raised to the power of the second value.
Math.random()	Returns a random number.
Math.round()	Rounds the value of the nearest integer.
Math.sin()	Returns the sine.
Math.sqrt()	Returns the square root.
Math.tan()	Returns the tangent.

The following shows the usage of the sqr() function.

📖 Javascript H4.1

```
<SCRIPT>
function sqr(val)
{ return val * val }
var value=sqr(3);
document.write("Three squared is " + value);
</SCRIPT>
```

> Three squared is 9

JavaScript also contains a function (parseInt()) that will convert from decimal into another number-base. For example to covert in hexadecimal (base-16):

📖 Javascript H4.2

```
53 hex in decimal is
<SCRIPT>
document.write(parseInt("53",16))
</SCRIPT>
```

> 53 hex in decimal is 83

The following show examples of the cos() and sqrt() methods used with the Math object:

📖 Javascript H4.3

```
The cosine of 1.5 radians is
<script>
document.write(Math.cos(1.5))
</script>
The square root of 15 is
<SCRIPT>
document.write(Math.sqrt(15.0));
</SCRIPT>
```

```
The cosine of 1.5
radians is
0.0707372016677029

The square root of 15 is
3.872983346207417
```

H4.2.1 Events

HTML is a static, one-pass, language, where events cannot be reacted. JavaScript extends HTML in that it allows events to occur, which can then be handle. Typical events are when a user presses a button (onClick), or presses a key down (onKeyDown), and so on. The full range of events are:

onAbort()	onBlur()	onChange()
onClick()	onDblClick()	onDragDrop()
onError()	onFocus()	onKeyDown()
onKeyPress()	onKeyUp()	onLoad()
onMouseDown()	onMouseMove()	onMouseOut()
onMouseOver()	onMouseUp()	onMove()
onReset()	onResize()	onSelect()
onSubmit()	onUnload()	

Table H4.1 outlines the main events, and summaries the objects that they react to. In HTML, the JavaScript event handler is defined within the tag, such as:

<TAG *eventHandler*="JavaScript Code">

such as:

```
<a href="" onMouseOver="window.open ( 'message.html',  'Message',
      'scrollbars=yes, width=450, height=250')">
<img src="pics_news.gif"> </a>
```

which will open up a new window when the user moves their mouse cursor over an image. It this case the image is named pics_news.gif, and the page opened is message.html. The open() method is applied to a new window, and creates a windows of width 450 pixels, and a height of 250 pixels, with scrollbars.

Table H4.1 JavaScript events, and event handlers

Event	Objects applied to	Occurance	Event handler
abort	Images	When the user cancels the loading of an image.	onAbort
blur	Windows, frames, and form elements	User moves away from a window, frame or form element.	onBlur

click	Buttons, radio buttons, check-boxes, submit buttons, reset buttons, and links.	User clicks on the object.	onClick
change	Text fields, text areas and select lists	User changes an element.	onChange
error	Images and windows	Document page contains an error.	onError
focus	Windows, frames, and form elements	User moves into a window, frame or form.	onFocus
load	Document body	User loads the page.	onLoad
mouseout	Areas and links	User moves the mouse away from an area or link.	onMouseout
mouseover	Links	User moves the mouse over a link.	onMouseOver
reset	Forms	User resets a form.	onReset
select	Text fields and text areas	User selects a text field or area.	onSelect
submit	Submit button	User submits a form.	onSubmit
unload	Document body	User exits from a page.	onUnload

H4.3   Language basics

The following shows some of the basic elements of JavaScript.

Outputting to browser. The document.write() applies the write() method to the document object, and outputs a processed string to the browser screen. JavaScript has much of the power of a programming language and supports arrays, such as:

```
<script language="javascript">
var dat=new Date(),
mon=["Jan","Feb", "Mar", "Apr", "May", "June", "July", "Aug", "Sept", "Oct",
"Nov", "Dec"];
  document.write("Month is ");
  document.write(dat.getMonth());
  document.write(" and the name of the
  month is ");
  document.write(mon[dat.getMonth()]);
</script>
```

Decisions. As with most programming languages, JavaScript supports decisions with the if() and switch() statements, such as the following which determines if it is morning or afternoon, and greets the user either with a "Good Morning!", or a "Good Afternoon!":

```
<FONT COLOR="GREEN">
<script language="javascript">
var dat=new Date();
   hr=dat.getHours();
   if (hr<12)
   {
```

```
      document.write("Good Morning!");
   }
   else
   {
      document.write("Good Afternoon!");
   }
</script>
</FONT>
```

Repetitive loops. JavaScript supports for() and while() loops. For example, the following loops for values of `fsize` from 1 to 5, which are used to define the font size.

```
<script language="javascript">
var fsize;
for (fsize=1;fsize<=5;fsize++)
{
   document.write("<br> <FONT SIZE = ");
   document.write(fsize + ">");
   document.write("Hello</FONT>");
}
</SCRIPT>
```

User functions. Even user functions can be incorporated into the page. For example, a function call to a square function is as follows:

```
<script language="javascript">
function sqr(val)
{
   return val * val
}
var value=sqr(3);
   document.write("Three squared is " + value);
</SCRIPT>
```

Methods. In object-oriented design, methods are applied to object. Typical objects in JavaScript are Math (which contains mathematical properties and methods), history (which contains lists of the visited URLs), button (which contains the object for buttons) and document (which is the container for the information on the current page). An example JavaScript object is Math. For example, the following determine the square of a value:

```
The square root of 15 is
<script language="javascript">
   document.write(Math.sqrt(15.0));
</SCRIPT>
```

Another example is to determine the cosine of a value, but applying the cos() method to the Math object:

```
<P>The cosine of 1.5 radians is
<script>
document.write(Math.cos(1.5))
</script>
```

The string object has many useful methods, such as toLowerCase(), which converts a string to lowercase, and toUpperCase(), which converts a string to upper, as used in the following example:

```
TYPEwrITer in lowercase is
<SCRIPT>
document.write(("TYPEwrITer").toLowerCase())
document.write("and in uppercase it is");
document.write(("TYPEwrITer").toUpperCase())</SCRIPT>
```

Using events. JavaScript has many useful functions, such as one to open windows of a certain size and with certain conditions, and also to respond to events, such as the onMouseDown() event when the user clicks on a graphic. The following opens a window (with the window.open() function) of width of 310 pixels and height of 200 pixels, when the user clicks on the referred graphic (message.gif). The onMouseDown() is an event which occurs when the user clicks on the graphic.

```
<script language="javascript">
function openWindow(theURL,winName,features) {
   window.open(theURL,winName,features);
}
</script>
<img border="0" src="message.gif" width="159" height="25"
   onMouseDown="openWindow('message.html','', 'toolbar=yes,
   menubar=yes, scrollbars=yes, resizable=yes, width=310, height=200')"
   align="left">
```

H4.4   Examples

The following sections outline some JavaScript examples.

H4.4.1   Displaying date

The Date() object can be operated on to give the current time (HH:MM):

📖 **Javascript H4.4**

```
<script language="javascript">
<p>Current time is
<script language="javascript">
var dat=new Date();
document.write(dat.getHours() + ":" + dat.getMinutes());
</script>
```

```
Current time is 19:36
```

H4.4.2   Outputting to browser

The document.write() applies the write() method to the document object, and outputs a processed string to the browser screen. JavaScript has much of the power of a programming language and supports arrays, such as:

Month is 0 and the name of the month is Jan

Javascript H4.5

```
<script language="javascript">
var dat=new Date(),
mon=["Jan","Feb", "Mar", "Apr", "May", "June", "July", "Aug", "Sept", "Oct",
"Nov", "Dec"];
document.write("Month is ");
document.write(dat.getMonth());
document.write(" and the name of the month is ");
document.write(mon[dat.getMonth()]);
</script>
```

H4.4.3   Decisions

As with most programming languages, JavaScript supports decisions with the if() and switch() statements, such as the following which determines if it is morning or afternoon, and greets the user either with a "Good Morning!", or a "Good Afternoon!":

Javascript H.6

Good Afternoon!

```
<FONT COLOR="GREEN">
<script language="javascript">
var dat=new Date();;
hr=dat.getHours();
if (hr<12)
{
    document.write("Good Morning!");
}
else
{
    document.write("Good Afternoon!");
}
</script>
</FONT>
```

H4.4.4   Repetitive loops

JavaScript supports for() and while() loops. An example of a simple for() loop is:

Javascript H4.7

```
<script>
var int;
for (int=1;int<11;int++)
document.write("Value is " + int + "<BR>");
</script>
```

```
Value is 1
Value is 2
Value is 3
Value is 4
Value is 5
Value is 6
Value is 7
Value is 8
Value is 9
Value is 10
```

The following loops for values of fsize from 1 to 5, which are used to define the font size.

📖 Javascript H4.8

```
<script language="javascript">
var fsize;
for (fsize=1;fsize<=5;fsize++)
{
    document.write("<br> <FONT SIZE = ");
    document.write(fsize + ">");
    document.write("Hello</FONT>");
} </SCRIPT>
```

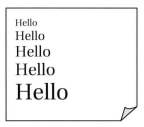

H4.4.5 User functions

Even user functions can be incorporated into the page. For example, a function call to a square function is as follows:

📖 Javascript H4.9

```
<script language="javascript">
function sqr(val)
{
    return val * val
}
var value=sqr(3);
document.write("Three squared is " + value);
</SCRIPT>
```

```
Three squared is 9
```

H4.4.6 Methods

In object-oriented design, methods are applied to object. Typical objects in JavaScript are Math (which contains mathematical properties and methods), history (which contains a lists of the visited URLs), button (which contains the object for buttons) and document (which is the container for the information on the current page). An example JavaScript object is Math. For example the following determine the square of a value:

📖 Javascript H4.10

```
The square root of 15 is
3.872983346207417
```

```
The square root of 15 is
<script language="javascript">
document.write(Math.sqrt(15.0));
</SCRIPT>
```

Another example is to determine the cosine of a value, but applying the cos() method to the Math object:

📖 Javascript H4.11

```
The cosine of 1.5 radians is
0.0707372016677029
```

```
The cosine of 1.5 radians is
<script>
document.write(Math.cos(1.5))
</script>
```

The string object has many useful methods, such as toLowerCase(), which converts a string to lowercase, and toUpperCase(), which converts a string to upper, as used in the following example:

📖 Javascript H4.12

```
TYPEwrITer in lowercase is type-
writer and in uppercase it is
TYPEWRITER
```

```
TYPEwrITer in lowercase is
```

```
<SCRIPT> document.write(("TYPEwrITer")   .toLowerCase())
document.write("and in uppercase it is");
document.write(("TYPEwrITer").toUpperCase()) </SCRIPT>
```

Using events

JavaScript has many useful functions, such as one to open windows of a certain size and with certain conditions, and also to respond to events, such as the onMouseDown() event when the user clicks on a graphic. The following opens a window (with the window.open() function) of width of 310 pixels and height of 200 pixels, when the user clicks on the referred graphic (message.gif). The onMouseDown() is an event which occurs when the user clicks on the graphic.

📖 **Javascript H4.13**

Click here for Message of the day

```
<script language="javascript">
function openWin-
dow(theURL,winName,features) {
window.open(theURL,winName,features);
}
</script>
<img border="0" src="design_new/message.gif" width="159" height="25"
onMouseDown="openWindow('message.html','', 'toolbar=yes,
menubar=yes, scrollbars=yes, resizable=yes, width=310, height=200')"
align="left">
```

H4.5   Various examples

It is also possible to show a window with an alert function using:

📖 **Javascript H4.14**

```
<script type="text/javascript">alert("Hello World!")</script>
```

Often the user requires to go back to a previous page. The following gives an example using the back() method applied to the history object:

Back
Close window
Print window

📖 **Javascript H4.15**

```
<a href="Javascript:history.back()">Back </a>
```

and to close a window:

📖 **Javascript H4.16**

```
<a href="javascript:window.close();"> Close window</a>
```

and to print a window:

📖 **Javascript H4.17**

```
<a href="javascript:window.print();"> Print window </a>
```

The document object has several properties which can be used to display its properties. The with statement allows an object to be specified and the properties referenced to it. For example in the following example, the properties defined are document.title, document.byColor, document.fgColor, and so on.

📖 Javascript H4.18

```
<script>
with (document)
{
document.write("Title of this page: <B>");
document.write(title + "</B>");
document.write("<BR>Bk color: <B>");
document.write(bgColor + "</B>");
document.write("<BR>Fg color: <B>");
document.write(fgColor + "</B>");
document.write("<BR>Links: <B>");
document.write(links + "</B>");
document.write("<BR>Modified: <B>");
document.write(lastModified + "</B>");
}
</script>
```

```
Title of this page:
JavaScript programming
Bk color: #000066
Fg color: #000000
Links: [object]
Modified: 01/14/2002
19:32:06
```

The Date object can be used with several methods to display the data and time, in various formats. The following use the toGMTString(), getMonth(), and getYear() methods:

📖 Javascript H4.19

```
Current date and time is
<script>
var str="" ,dat=new Date();
str=dat.toGMTString();
document.write(str);
</script>
```

```
Current date and time is Mon,
14 Jan 2002 21:42:03 UTC
```

```
Month is 0 and the name of the
month is Jan
```

📖 Javascript H4.20

```
<script>
var dat=new Date(),
mon=["Jan","Feb", "Mar", "Apr",
"May", "June", "July", "Aug", "Sept", "Oct", "Nov", "Dec"];
document.write("Month is ");
document.write(dat.getMonth());
document.write(" and the name of the month is "
document.write(mon[dat.getMonth()]);
</script>
```

📖 Javascript H4.21

```
<script>
var dat=new Date();
document.write("<P>Year is ");
document.write(dat.getYear());
</script>
```

```
Year is 2002
```

H4.6   Functions called from events

An important operation in JavaScript is to call functions from events. In the next example, a pull-down menu is used, with the onChange event. When the user select a different option in the pull down menu, the chback() function is called, with the newly selected option. In this case the background color of the document is changed.

📖 Javascript H4.22

```
<script>
function chback(selObj)
{
    document.bgColor= selObj.options[selObj.selectedIndex].value
}
</script>
<form>
<select name="select" onChange="chback(this)">
<option selected>Bg Color</option>
<option value="Red">Red</option>
<option value="Green">Green</option>
<option value="Yellow">Yellow</option>
<option value="Blue">Blue</option>
<option value="White">White</option>
<option value="Orange">Orange</option>
<option value="Cyan">Cyan</option>
<option value="Magenta">Magenta</option>
</select>
</form>
```

The onClick event can be used when a user click on a hypertext link. In the following example the alert window will be called when the user click on the link.

📖 Javascript H4.23

```
<script>
function chback1()
{
alert("Hello");
}
</script>
```

```
<a href="jscript_examples.htm#t2" onClick= "chback1()">Show alert</A>
```

and the following will open a related window when the related hypertext link is selected:

📖 Javascript H4.24

```
<script>
function chback2(page)
{
winnew=window.open(page,"Test","scrollbars=yes,width=310, height=200");
}
</script>
```

```
<a href="jscript_examples.htm#t1" onClick= "chback2('message.html')"> Message
(Main)</A>
<br><a href="jscript_examples.htm#t1" onClick=" chback2('message_books.html')">
Message (Books)</A>
<br><a href="jscript_examples.htm#t1" onClick= "chback2('message_cnds.html')">
Message (CNDS)</A> <br><a href= "jscript_examples.htm#t1" on-
Click="chback2('message_mypics.html')"> Message (Pics)</A>
<br><a href="jscript_examples.htm#t1" onClick=
"chback2('message_research.html')">Message (Research)</A>
```

while the next example allows the user to click on a graphic file, which calls up a function:

Javascript H4.25

```
<script>
function openWindow(theURL,winName,features) {
window.open(theURL,winName,features);
}
</script>
<img border="0" src="design_files/message.gif"
width="159" height="25" onMouseDown="openWindow('message.html',
'','toolbar=yes,menubar=yes,scrollbars=yes,
resizable=yes, width=310,height=200')" align="left">
```

H4.7   Linking with forms

JavaScript can be linked to forms to dynamic updates. For example, the following script allows a user to enter either a temperature in Celsius or Fahrenheit, and the other equivalent temperature in Fahrenheit or Celsius will be displayed, respectively, without reloading the whole page. In the form, whenever the key is pressed, the onkeyup event is used to update the fields in the form.

Javascript H4.26

```
<script type="text/javascript">
function convert(degree)
{
if (degree=="C")
{
   F=document.myform.celsius.value * 9 / 5 + 32
   document.myform.fahrenheit.value=Math.round(F)
}
else
{
   C=(document.myform.fahrenheit.value -32) * 5 / 9
   document.myform.celsius.value=Math.round(C)
}
}
</script>

<b>Insert a number in either input field, and the number will be converted into
either Celsius or Fahrenheit.</b>
<br>
<form name="myform">
<input name="celsius" onkeyup="convert('C')"> degrees Celsius<br>
equals<br>
<input name="fahrenheit" onkeyup="convert('F')"> degrees Fahrenheit
</form>
```

H4.7.1   JavaScript - Reading, storing and deleting cookies

A cookie is stored in JavaScript by setting the cookie property of the document object (with document.cookie). This then defines the properties of the cookie, such as the date that it expires, and the domain of the WWW page. These are defined in keyword pairs which are separated by semi-colons (;). For example, this cookie produces a text file in the \WINDOWS\COOKIES directory with the name of user@wwwsite.txt:

```
bills
1234
localhost/
```

```
Writing cookie...
(bills= 1234; expires=Thu, 12 Jan 2012
22:19:17 UTC; domain= .napier.ac.uk)
```

```
1088
1553936640
30173035
2771961120
29438780
*
```

📖 Javascript H4.27

```javascript
<script language="Javascript">

function SetCookie (name,value,expires,domain) {
var str;
 document.write("Writing cookie...");
 str=name + "= " + value + "; expires=" +
            expires.toGMTString() + ";domain="+domain;
 document.write("<" + str + ">");
 document.cookie = str;
}
var expdate = new Date ();
 expdate.setTime (expdate.getTime() + (10 * 365 *   24 * 60 * 60 * 1000));
     // 10 years from now
 SetCookie("bills", 1234,expdate , ".napier.ac.uk")
}
</script>
```

When reading the values of a cookie, the cookie is read in keyword pairs, such as:

📖 Javascript H4.28

```javascript
<script language="Javascript">
function getCookieVal (offset) {
var endstr = document.cookie.indexOf (";", offset);
 if (endstr == -1)
  endstr = document.cookie.length;
  return unescape(document.cookie.substring(offset, endstr));
}
</script>
```

The property values in the cookie are defined as name and value. In this case, the cookie is read back and the value is displayed. If a cookie is stored then the value displayed is "1234".

📖 Javascript H4.29

```javascript
<script language="Javascript">
function GetCookie (name) {
var arg = name + "=";
var alen = arg.length;
var clen = document.cookie.length;
var i = 0;
 while (i < clen) {
  var j = i + alen;
  if (document.cookie.substring(i, j) == arg)
    return getCookieVal (j);
  i = document.cookie.indexOf(" ", i) + 1;
  if (i == 0) break;
 }
 return null;
}
 str=GetCookie("bills");
 document.write("Cookie is ", str);
</script>
```

```
Cookie is null
```

A cookie can be deleted by making it expire in a date defined before the current date. In this case the date is set at 1970. The browser automatically deletes any cookies which have expired.

📖 **Javascript H4.30**

```
function DeleteCookie (name,path,domain) {
if (GetCookie(name)) {
 document.cookie = name + "=" +
 ((path) ? "; path=" + path : "") +
 ((domain) ? "; domain=" + domain : "") +
 "; expires=Thu, 01-Jan-70 00:00:01 GMT";
}
}
if ((browser == "ns3") || (browser == "ns4")
    || (browser == "ie4")) {
  popupWin.focus();
}
```

H4.8   JavaScript and Flash

Parameters can be passed into a Flash movie with:

```
window.document.myFlash.SetVariable("debug", sendText);
```

where myFlash is the name and ID of the Flash movie, and debug is one of the variables within it. For example, enter you name here and it should update the text in the movie (enter your name and then click away from the box, or press TAB after you have entered your name):

Enter your name :

The code that is added to allow Javascript to communicate with the Flash movie:

```
<form name="form1" onSubmit="doPassVar(sendText);" action="#">

<p>Enter your name:
<input type="text" name="sendText" maxlength="45" onChange="doPassVar(this);">

<input type="submit" name="Submit" value="Add Name">
</form>

<script language="JAVASCRIPT">
function doPassVar(args){
    var sendText = args.value;
    window.document.myFlash.SetVariable("debug", sendText);
}

</script>
```

H4.9   JavaScript reference

H4.9.1   Conditional statements

if (*condition*) {
      statements1
[} **else** {
      statements2]
}

H4.9.2   Loops statements

for ([*initial-expression*]; [*condition*]; [*increment-expression*]) {
   statements
}

while (*condition*) {
      statements
}

H4.9.3   Color

Color	Red	Green	Blue
aliceblue	F0	F8	FF
antiquewhite	FA	EB	D7
aqua	00	FF	FF
aquamarine	7F	FF	D4
azure	F0	FF	FF
beige	F5	F5	DC
bisque	FF	E4	C4
black	00	00	00
blanchedalmond	FF	EB	CD
blue	00	00	FF
blueviolet	8A	2B	E2
brown	A5	2A	2A
burlywood	DE	B8	87
cadetblue	5F	9E	A0
chartreuse	7F	FF	00
chocolate	D2	69	1E
coral	FF	7F	50
cornflowerblue	64	95	ED
cornsilk	FF	F8	DC
crimson	DC	14	3C
cyan	00	FF	FF
darkblue	00	00	8B
darkcyan	00	8B	8B
darkgoldenrod	B8	86	0B
darkgray	A9	A9	A9
darkgreen	00	64	00
darkkhaki	BD	B7	6B
darkmagenta	8B	00	8B
darkolivegreen	55	6B	2F
darkorange	FF	8C	00

darkorchid	99	32	CC
darkred	8B	00	00
darksalmon	E9	96	7A
darkseagreen	8F	BC	8F
darkslateblue	48	3D	8B
darkslategray	2F	4F	4F
darkturquoise	00	CE	D1
darkviolet	94	00	D3
deeppink	FF	14	93
deepskyblue	00	BF	FF
dimgray	69	69	69
dodgerblue	1E	90	FF
firebrick	B2	22	22
floralwhite	FF	FA	F0
forestgreen	22	8B	22
fuchsia	FF	00	FF
gainsboro	DC	DC	DC
ghostwhite	F8	F8	FF
gold	FF	D7	00
goldenrod	DA	A5	20
gray	80	80	80
green	00	80	00
greenyellow	AD	FF	2F
honeydew	F0	FF	F0
hotpink	FF	69	B4
indianred	CD	5C	5C
indigo	4B	00	82
ivory	FF	FF	F0
khaki	F0	E6	8C
lavender	E6	E6	FA
lavenderblush	FF	F0	F5
lawngreen	7C	FC	00
lemonchiffon	FF	FA	CD
lightblue	AD	D8	E6
lightcoral	F0	80	80
lightcyan	E0	FF	FF
lightgoldenrodyellow	FA	FA	D2
lightgreen	90	EE	90
lightgrey	D3	D3	D3
lightpink	FF	B6	C1
lightsalmon	FF	A0	7A
lightseagreen	20	B2	AA
lightskyblue	87	CE	FA
lightslategray	77	88	99
lightsteelblue	B0	C4	DE
lightyellow	FF	FF	E0
lime	00	FF	00
limegreen	32	CD	32
linen	FA	F0	E6
magenta	FF	00	FF
maroon	80	00	00
mediumaquamarine	66	CD	AA
mediumblue	00	00	CD
mediumorchid	BA	55	D3

mediumpurple	93	70	DB
mediumseagreen	3C	B3	71
mediumslateblue	7B	68	EE
mediumspringgreen	00	FA	9A
mediumturquoise	48	D1	CC
mediumvioletred	C7	15	85
midnightblue	19	19	70
mintcream	F5	FF	FA
mistyrose	FF	E4	E1
moccasin	FF	E4	B5
navajowhite	FF	DE	AD
navy	00	00	80
oldlace	FD	F5	E6
olive	80	80	00
olivedrab	6B	8E	23
orange	FF	A5	00
orangered	FF	45	00
orchid	DA	70	D6
palegoldenrod	EE	E8	AA
palegreen	98	FB	98
paleturquoise	AF	EE	EE
palevioletred	DB	70	93
papayawhip	FF	EF	D5
peachpuff	FF	DA	B9
peru	CD	85	3F
pink	FF	C0	CB
plum	DD	A0	DD
powderblue	B0	E0	E6
purple	80	00	80
red	FF	00	00
rosybrown	BC	8F	8F
royalblue	41	69	E1
saddlebrown	8B	45	13
salmon	FA	80	72
sandybrown	F4	A4	60
seagreen	2E	8B	57
seashell	FF	F5	EE
sienna	A0	52	2D
silver	C0	C0	C0
skyblue	87	CE	EB
slateblue	6A	5A	CD
slategray	70	80	90
snow	FF	FA	FA
springgreen	00	FF	7F
steelblue	46	82	B4
tan	D2	B4	8C
teal	00	80	80
thistle	D8	BF	D8
tomato	FF	63	47
turquoise	40	E0	D0
violet	EE	82	EE
wheat	F5	DE	B3
white	FF	FF	FF
whitesmoke	F5	F5	F5

| yellow | FF | FF | 00 |
| yellowgreen | 9A | CD | 32 |

H4.10   Objects, properties, methods and event handlers

Object	Properties	Methods	Event handlers
Anchor			
anchors array	length		
Applet			
applets array	length		
Area	hash host hostname href pathname port protocol search target		onMouseOut onMouseOver
Array	length prototype	join reverse sort	
Button	form name type value	blur click focus	onBlur onClick onFocus
Checkbox	checked defaultChecked form name type value	blur click focus	onBlur onClick onFocus
Date	prototype	getDate getDay getHours getMinutes getMonth getSeconds getTime getTimezoneOffset getYear parse setDate setHours setMinutes setMonth setSeconds setTime setYear toGMTString toLocaleString toString UTC valueOf	

Object	Properties	Methods	Event handlers
FileUpload	form name type value	blur focus	onBlur onChange onFocus
Form	action Button Checkbox elements encoding FileUpload Hidden length method name Password Radio Reset Select Submit target Text Textarea	reset submit	onReset onSubmit
forms array	length		
Frame	frames name length parent self window	blur clearTimeout focus setTimeout	onBlur onFocus
frames array	length		
Hidden	name type value		
history	current length next previous	back forward go	
history array	length		
Image	border complete height hspace lowsrc name prototype src vspace width		onAbort onError onLoad
images array	length		
Link and Area	hash host hostname href pathname port protocol search target		onClick onMouseOut onMouseOver

Object	Properties	Methods	Event handlers
location	hash host hostname href pathname port protocol search	reload replace	
Math	E LN2 LN10 LOG2E LOG10E PI SQRT1_2 SQRT2	abs acos asin atan atan2 ceil cos exp floor log max min pow random round sin sqrt tan	
MimeType	description enabledPlugin type suffixes		
mimeTypes array	length		
navigator	appCodeName appName appVersion mimeTypes plugins userAgent	javaEnabled taintEnabled	
options array	length		
Password	defaultValue form name type value	blur focus select	onBlur onFocus
Plugin	description filename length name		
plugins array	length	refresh	
Radio	checked defaultChecked form length name type value	blur click focus	onBlur onClick onFocus

Object	Properties	Methods	Event handlers
Select	form length name options selectedIndex text type	blur focus	onBlur onChange onFocus
String	length prototype	anchor big blink bold charAt fixed fontcolor fontsize indexOf italics lastIndexOf link small split strike sub substring sup toLowerCase toUpperCase	
Submit	form name type value	blur click focus	onBlur onClick onFocus
Textarea	defaultValue form name type value	blur focus select	onBlur onChange onFocus onSelect
window	closed defaultStatus document Frame frames history length location name opener parent self status top window	alert blur clearTimeOut close confirm focus open prompt setTimeOut	onBlur onError onFocus onLoad onUnload

H5   PHP

H5.1   Introduction

PHP is a server-side processing language which integrates with HTML to produce HTML code which is browser independent. Its advantages include:

- **Object-oriented**. PHP is not fully object-oriented but supports object-oriented concepts. An object-oriented approach allows for objects to be more easily managed, and controlled.
- **Cross-platform**. The other major server-side include languages, such as ASP and JSP, are focused as a certain WWW platform. ASP is focused on the Windows-based IIS. PHP has been designed to work on many different types of WWW server platforms, and hardware. It can be easily integrated in most types of WWW server.
- **Database integration**. PHP can be integrated with most of the popular database systems, including MySQL, Oracle and Sybase.
- **Version updates**. PHP is continually updated, with new version. It is thus a dynamic language which can be quickly changed by upgrading its component parts. The upgrading of server side components are simpler, than upgrading WWW browsers, as the update of the server only requires a single operation, while the upgrade of WWW browsers requires that every user upgrades their browser.
- **Enhanced security**. PHP hides the original code from the user, as they will only see the processed code, thus more security can be built into the code, such as determining the location of the WWW browser, and determining the rights that the user has in viewing information.
- **Enhanced development tools**. PHP has a whole host of development tools so the creating and testing of PHP code.

The main WWW server platforms include:

- **IIS** (Internet Information Server). This server will run on a Windows NT/2000/XP-server type platform, and directly supports ASP as the server-side include language. By default the Inetpub directory is the home directory for the WWW server. Users accessing the WWW server will not be able to get access to any directories above this. The security of the system is important, thus the Inetpub directory must be created on an NTFS partition.
- **Apache**. This server was originally developed by the Apache Group, and used the UNIX operating system. It has now been converted to support most types of operating systems, and computer types. The full code of the Apache program is available to that it can be modified for certain uses. PHP is the natural server-side language for Apache. The Apache server program reads the httpd.conf file for most of its operating parameters.
- **PWS** (Personal Web Server). This can be used with Workstation-type Windows-based systems, and allows users to setup their own WWW server on their own computer. It supports ASP directly, and can be made to support PHP, with the addition of additional components. As with IIS, the Inetpub directory should be mounted onto an NTFS partition.

PHP is installed onto a Windows-based Apache server by downloading the PHP program from www.php.net (or from the supplied CD), and installing it into a directory such as C:\PHP. It is then added into the server by adding the following lines in the httpd.conf file:

```
LoadModule php4_module c:/php/sapi/php4apache.dll
AddModule mod_php4.c
AddType application/x-httpd-php .php
```

and php4ts.dll file is put into the %WINDOWSROOT%\SYSTEM32 directory. The httpd.conf file can then be modified for the required operating parameters, such as the home directory for the configuration, error and log files with:

```
ServerRoot "C:/Program files/Apache group\Apache"
```

or for the root directory of the WWW site with:

```
DocumentRoot "C:/www"
```

The development system already comes with a PHP.EXE program which can be used as a standalone package to convert from PHP to HTML. For example, a simple PHP file is:

```
<html>
<head>
<title>Untitled Document</title>
<meta http-equiv="Content-Type" content="text/html; charset=iso-8859-1">
</head>

<body bgcolor="#FFFFFF" text="#000000">
<?php
print("Hello World");
?>
</body>
</html>
```

when this is processed by PHP.EXE (php simple.php > simple.html) it gives the following PHP file:

```
X-Powered-By: PHP/4.1.2
Content-type: text/html
<html>
<head>
<title>Untitled Document</title>
<meta http-equiv="Content-Type" content="text/html; charset=iso-8859-1">
</head>

<body bgcolor="#FFFFFF" text="#000000">
Hello World
</body>
</html>
```

This is the form that the WWW browser would expect to see, as it contains the HTTP header information, along with the HTML code.

H5.2 PHP examples

The following sections give a few examples of PHP code.

H5.2.1 Printing to the output

The first example simply uses the PHP print statement to display text to the output screen.

📖 **PHP Code H5.1**

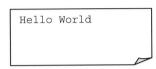

```
<?php
print("Hello World");
?>
```

Strings can support escape sequence characters, such as:

Escape sequence	Description
\n	Start a new line
\r	Carriage return
\t	Tab space
\\	Backslash
\"	Double quote
\$	Dollar sign
\0yy	Octal character (yy)
\x0yy	Hexadecimal character (yy)

PHP Code H5.2 shows a few examples, which included embedded HTML tags within the PHP string (in this case the embedded tag is <br>, which creates a new line).

📖 **PHP Code H5.2**

```
<?php
print("The cost of the subscription is \$10");
print("<br>Please log on with the user name of <i>\"fred\"</i> with a password
of <i>\"bert\"</i>");
print("<br>Your home directory is <b>C:\\docs\\fred</b>");
?>
```

which results in:

```
The cost of the subscription is $10
Please log on with the user name of "fred" with a password of "bert"
Your home directory is C:\docs\fred
```

H5.2.2 Comments

PHP is very much based on C and UNIX-type syntax, thus comments of the form /* and */, and // can be used within the PHP code, and are completely ignored by the PHP processor. The # character can also be used in a similar way to the // sequence. PHP code 5.3 shows a few examples of comments.

📖 **PHP Code H5.3**

```
<?php
echo "Testing ....."; // This shows the C++ type of comment
/* And this is the C type of comment
which is useful for multiple lines */
echo "... 123 ... ";
echo "... 456 ...."; # And an shell style comment
?>
```

H5.2.3 Integrating with HTML

As previously seen, PHP supports the integration of HTML tags with the PHP statements. For example, PHP Code H5.4 shows an example of creating a hypertext link in PHP. If an string is to be defined with the PHP string, then the inverted commas (") and be replaced with a single quote (').

📖 **PHP Code H5.4**

```
<?php
print("<a href='php_test.php'>PHP Test</a>");
print("<br>This is an <b>important</b> example");
?>
```

```
PHP Test
This is an important example
```

H5.2.4 Variables

Variables have a proceeding '$' sign, and are followed by a space or an end of string. If you cannot get a space after a variable then the variable can be enclosed in curly brackets ({ and }). This is useful when there are no spaces between one variable and the next.

📖 **PHP Code H5.5**

```
<?php
$value=100;
$username="eee";
$code=123;
print("<BR>Value is $value");
print("<BR>Your user name will be ${username}$code");
?>
```

```
Value is 100
Your user name will
be eee123
```

H5.2.5 Data types

The main data types are Boolean, integer, float, string, array and object. PHP differs from many other languages in that there is no integer division, thus 1 divided by 2 gives 0.5. PHP is not a strongly typed language, thus a numeric variable is automatically created when a variable is first assigned (using the = character) to a numerical value, after which it can be used as an integer or a floating-point value. Numeric values are assigned to be in decimal, unless they have 0x (for hexadecimal) or 0 (for octal) in front of them.

📖 **PHP Code H5.6**

```
<?php
$a = 24; # decimal number
$b = -24; # a negative number
$c = 024; # octal number
$d = 0x24; # hexadecimal number
print "<P>$a, $b, $c, $d";
$val1=1;
$val2=2;
$result=1/2;
```

```
24, -24, 20, 36

Result of 1/2 is 0.5
```

```
print "<P>Result of 1/2 is $result";
?>
```

H5.2.6   Strings

Strings can be defined in quotes (between ' and ') or double quotes (between " and "). If you want a quote in a string use \", for a new line use \n and a backslash is \\. Also stings are concatenated together using the '.' operator. The other concatenation operator is '.=' which appends the string on the right hand side of the operator, to the string on the left hand side.

📖 PHP Code H5.7

```
<?php
$name1 = "Fred ";
$name2 = "Smith";
print "Hello \"Fred\". How are you?";
print "<br>Your full name is " .
$name1 . " " . $name2;
$name1 .= $name2;
print "<br>Your full name is " . $name1
?>
```

```
Hello "Fred". How are you?
Your full name is Fred Smith
Your full name is Fred Smith
```

H5.2.7   Date

PHP supports a whole host of date operations. These include:

Function	Description	Format
checkdate	Validate a Gregorian date/time	bool **checkdate** (int month, int day, int year)
date	Format a local time/date	string **date** (string format [, int time-stamp])
getdate	Get date/time information	array **getdate** ([int timestamp])
gettimeofday	Get current time	array **gettimeofday** (void)
gmdate	Format a GMT/CUT date/time	string **gmdate** (string format [, int timestamp])
gmmktime	Get UNIX timestamp for a GMT date	int **gmmktime** (int hour, int minute, int second, int month, int day, int year [, int is_dst])
gmstrftime	Format a GMT/CUT time/date according to locale settings	string **gmstrftime** (string format [, int timestamp])
localtime	Get the local time	array **localtime** ([int timestamp [, bool is_associative]])
microtime	Return current UNIX timestamp with microseconds	string **microtime** (void)
mktime	Get UNIX timestamp for a date	int **mktime** (int hour, int minute, int second, int month, int day, int year [, int is_dst])
strftime	Format a local time/date according to locale settings	string **strftime** (string format [, int timestamp])

time	Return current UNIX timestamp	int **time** (void)
strtotime	Parse about any English textual datetime description into a UNIX time-stamp	int **strtotime** (string time [, int now])

PHP Code H5.8 gives a few examples.

📖 **PHP Code H5.8**

```php
<?php
$name1 = "Fred ";
$name2 = "Smith";
print "Hello \"Fred\". How are
you?";
print "<br>Your full name is " . $name1 . " " . $name2;
$name1 .= $name2;
print "<br>Your full name is " . $name1
?>
```

```
Hello "Fred". How are you?
Your full name is Fred Smith
Your full name is Fred Smith
```

The strftime() function can be used to date/time into a given format. The tokens used are:

%a	Abbreviated weekday name according to the current locale
%A	Full weekday name according to the current locale
%b	Abbreviated month name according to the current locale
%B	Full month name according to the current locale
%c	Preferred date and time representation for the current locale
%C	Century number (the year divided by 100 and truncated to an integer, range 00 to 99)
%d	Day of the month as a decimal number (range 01 to 31)
%D	Same as %m/%d/%y
%e	Day of the month as a decimal number, a single digit is preceded by a space (range ' 1' to '31')
%g	Like %G, but without the century.
%G	The 4- digit year corresponding to the ISO week number (see %V). This has the same format and value as %Y, except that if the ISO week number belongs to the previous or next year, that year is used instead.
%h	Same as %b
%H	Hour as a decimal number using a 24-hour clock (range 00 to 23)
%I	Hour as a decimal number using a 12- hour clock (range 01 to 12)
%j	Day of the year as a decimal number (range 001 to 366)
%m	Month as a decimal number (range 01 to 12)
%M	Minute as a decimal number
%n	Newline character
%p	Either `am' or `pm' according to the given time value, or the corresponding strings for the current locale
%r	Time in a.m. and p.m. notation
%R	Time in 24 hour notation
%S	Second as a decimal number
%t	Tab character
%T	Current time, equal to %H:%M:%S

%u	Weekday as a decimal number [1,7], with 1 representing Monday
%U	Week number of the current year as a decimal number, starting with the first Sunday as the first day of the first week
%V	The ISO 8601:1988 week number of the current year as a decimal number, range 01 to 53, where week 1 is the first week that has at least 4 days in the current year, and with Monday as the first day of the week. (Use %G or %g for the year component that corresponds to the week number for the specified timestamp.)
%W	Week number of the current year as a decimal number, starting with the first Monday as the first day of the first week
%w	Day of the week as a decimal, Sunday being 0
%x	Preferred date representation for the current locale without the time
%X	Preferred time representation for the current locale without the date
%y	Year as a decimal number without a century (range 00 to 99)
%Y	Year as a decimal number including the century
%Z	Time zone or name or abbreviation

For example using the %A (to display the current day), %H (to display the current hour), and %M (to display the current minute):

```
Day is Sunday, Date: 24-03-2002
Time zone is GMT Standard Time,
Time: 16:51
```

📖 PHP Code H5.9

```php
<?php
print (strftime("Day is %A, Date: %d-%m-%Y "));
print "<br>";
print (strftime("Time zone is %Z, Time: %H:%M"));
?>
```

H5.2.8 PHP operators

The main **arithmetic** operators are:

Example	Name	Result
$val1 + $val2	Addition	Sum of $val1 and $val2
$val1 - $val2	Subtraction	Difference of $val1 and $val2
$val1 * $val2	Multiplication	Product of $val1 and $val2
$val1 / $val2	Division	Quotient of $val1 and $val2
$val1 % $val2	Modulus	Remainder of $val1 divided by $val2

In the division operation, a division of two integers results in an integer. If one of the operands is a floating-point value, then the result is a floating-point value. PHP Code H5.10 shows that the result of the division of the floating-point values can be converted into an integer using the (int) operator. This changes the data type from a floating-point into an integer. This example also shows that it is possible to use strings as operands in arithmetic operation. The strings are automatically converted into floating-point values.

📖 PHP Code H5.10

```php
<?php
$val1=33;
```

```
$val2=7;
$val3="33";
$val4="7";
print("Division is " . $val1 /
                     $val2);
print("<br>Division is " . $val3 / $val4);
print("<br>Integer division is " . (int) ($val1 / $val2));
print("<br>Modulus is " . $val1 % $val2);
?>
```

```
Division is 4.7142857142857
Division is 4.7142857142857
Integer division is 4
Modulus is 5
```

The main **assignment** operators are:

Operator	Name	Result/equivalent
$val1 = $val2	Assignment	$val1 takes on the value of $val2
$val1 -= $val2	Subtraction and assignment	$val1 = $val1 - $val2
$val1 += $val2	Addition and assignment	$val1 = $val1 + $val2
$val1 *= $val2	Multiplication and assignment	$val1 = $val1 * $val2
$val1 .= $val2	Concatenate and assignment	$val1 = $val1 . $val2

Bitwise operators are useful when bits within integers have to be manipulated. The main bitwise operators are:

Example	Name	Result
$a & $b	And	Bits that are set in both $a and $b are set.
$a | $b	Or	Bits that are set in either $a or $b are set.
$a ^ $b	Xor	Bits that are set in $a or $b but not both are set.
~ $a	Not	Bits that are set in $a are not set, and vice versa.
$a << $b	Shift left	Shift the bits of $a $b steps to the left
$a >> $b	Shift right	Shift the bits of $a $b steps to the right

An example of bitwise operations is given next:

📖 **PHP Code H5.11**
```
<?php
$val1=33;
$val2=9;
print("Values are $val1 and $val2");
print("<br>AND is " . ($val1 & $val2));
print("<br>OR is " . ($val1| $val2));
print("<br>XOR is " . ($val1 ^ $val2));
?>
```

The result of this is:

```
Values are 33 and 9
AND is 1
OR is 41
XOR is 40
```

This is because 33 is 100001, and 9 is 001001. Thus AND operation is:

$$\frac{\begin{array}{r}100001\\001001\end{array}}{000001}$$

which is 1 in decimal. For the OR operation:

$$\frac{\begin{array}{r}100001\\001001\end{array}}{101001}$$

which is 41 in decimal. For the XOR operation:

$$\frac{\begin{array}{r}100001\\001001\end{array}}{101000}$$

which is 40 in decimal.

The main **comparison** operators are:

Example	Name	Result
$val1 == $val2	Equal	TRUE if $val1 is equal to $val2.
$val1 != $val2	Not equal	TRUE if $val1 is not equal to $val2.
$val1 <> $val2	Not equal	TRUE if $val1 is not equal to $val2.
$val1 < $val2	Less than	TRUE if $val1 is strictly less than $val2.
$val1 > $val2	Greater than	TRUE if $val1 is strictly greater than $val2.
$val1 <= $val2	Less than or equal to	TRUE if $val1 is less than or equal to $val2.
$val1 >= $val2	Greater than or equal to	TRUE if $val1 is greater than or equal to $val2.

PHP can run commands that are executed by the system. These operators are named back-ticks (``` `` ```). The output from the command can only be assigned to a variable, and cannot be simply outputted to the screen.

📖 **PHP Code H5.12**

```php
<?php
print "Listing of current directory of all ZIP files";
$output = `ls -al *.zip`;
print "<pre>$output</pre>";
?>
```

A sample listing is given next:

```
Listing of current directory of all ZIP files
total 1742
-rwxrwxrwx  1             90766 Nov  5 11:53 asp.zip
-rwxrwxrwx  1             42845 Nov  5 11:53 asp_examples.zip
-rwxrwxrwx  1              4358 Nov 18 13:53 chap14.zip
: : :
-rwxrwxrwx  1             37271 Jan 20 15:28 vb_rsa.zip
```

This can then be expanded onto other operating system commands. For example the cat command can be used to list the contents of a file. The following PHP code reads the contents of the test1.txt file, and displays it to the WWW page:

📖 **PHP Code H5.13**

```php
<?php
print " Listing of the test1.txt file:";
$output = `cat test1.txt`;
print "<pre>$output</pre>"
?>
```

A sample listing is given next:

```
Listing of the test1.txt file:
This is the contents of the file: test1.txt.
The cat command has been used to list the
contents of it.
```

PHP is based on the C programming language, and thus supports the incrementing/decrementing operators. These can be summarized with:

Example	Name	Effect
++$val	Pre-increment	Increments $val by one, then returns $val.
$val++	Post-increment	Returns $val, then increments $val by one.
--$val	Pre-decrement	Decrements $val by one, then returns $val.
$val--	Post-decrement	Returns $val, then decrements $val by one.

The logical operators are similar to the bitwise operators and are:

Example	Name	Result
$val1 and $val2	And	TRUE if both $val1 and $val2 are TRUE.
$val1 or $val2	Or	TRUE if either $val1 or $val2 is TRUE.
$val1 xor $val2	Xor	TRUE if either $val1 or $val2 is TRUE, but not both.
! $val1	Not	TRUE if $val1 is not TRUE.
$val1 && $val2	And	TRUE if both $val1 and $val2 are TRUE.
$val1 || $val2	Or	TRUE if either $val1 or $val2 is TRUE.

The reason for the two different variations of "and" and "or" operators is that they operate at different precedences. As with most programming languages, PHP supports operator precedence. The following table defines the precedence of the operators:

Association	Operators
left	,
left	or
left	xor
left	and
right	print
left	= += -= *= /= .= %= &= |= ^= ~= <<= >>=
left	? :

left	||
left	&&
left	|
left	^
left	&
non-associative	== != === !==
non-associative	< <= > >=
left	<< >>
left	+ - .
left	* / %
right	! ~ ++ -- (int) (double) (string) (array) (object) @
right	[
non-associative	new

H5.2.9 PHP loops

PHP supports loops which are similar to C, while are while(){}, do{} while(), and for().The while() loop will loop until the condition is **TRUE**. For example:

📖 PHP Code H5.14

```php
<?php
$value=0; //our variable
while($value<=10){
 print(" $value = ".($value*$value));
 print("<br />\n");
 $value=$value+1;
}
?>
```

```
0  =  0
1  =  1
2  =  4
3  =  9
4  =  16
5  =  25
6  =  36
7  =  49
8  =  64
9  =  81
10  =  100
```

The following shows an example of a for(), do {} while (), and while () loops:

📖 PHP Code H5.15

```php
<?php
for ($i=0;$i<11;$i++)
{
$sqr_value=$i*$i;
print "<BR>$i $sqr_value";
}
$i=0;
do
{
$sqr_value=$i*$i;
print "<BR>$i $sqr_value";
$i++;
} while ($i<11);
$i=0;
while ($i<11)
{
$sqr_value=$i*$i;
print "<BR>$i $sqr_value";
```

```
0  0
1  1
:  :
8  64
9  81
10 100
0  0
1  1
:  :
8  64
9  81
10 100
0  0
1  1
8  64
9  81
10 100
```

```
$i++;
}
?>
```

H5.2.10 Arrays

PHP allows numeric and string values to be assigned to numeric elements of an array. For example:

Key	Value
0	red
1	blue
2	green
3	yellow

This could be implemented as follows:

📖 **PHP Code H5.16**

```
<?php
$colors = array('red','blue','green','yellow');
for ($i=0;$i<4;$i++)
{
print "<BR>Color : $colors[$i]";
}
?>
```

```
Color : red
Color : blue
Color : green
Color : yellow
```

In PHP arrays are an ordered map, which maps values to keys. The keys can be numeric of strings. For example an array could be setup with:

Key	Value
Course	CNDS
module	Ethernet
class	D111
year	2001

This would be initialized in PHP with:

```
$val = array('course' => 'CNDS', 'module' => 'Ethernet',
             'class' => 'D111' ,  'year' => '2001'
             , 4 // key will be 0
);
```

and alternative to this is:

```
$val['course'] = 'CNDS';
$val['module'] = 'Ethernet';
$val['class'] = 'D111';
$val['year'] = '2001';
```

The keys can also be numerical values, such as:

```
$val[0] = 'CNDS';
$val[1] = 'Ethernet';
$val[2] = 'D111';
$val[3] = '2001';
```

An example of PHP using arrays is:

📖 PHP Code H5.17

```
// this is how an array can be initialised:
$a = array( 'course'=> 'CNDS'
, 'module' => 'Ethernet'
, 'class' => 'D111'
, 'year' => '2001'
, 4 // key will be 0
);
// is completely equivalent with
$a['course'] = 'CNDS';
$a['module'] = 'Ethernet';
$a['class'] = 'D111';
$a['year'] = '2001';

$val[0] = 'CNDS';
$val[1] = 'Ethernet';
$val[2] = 'D111';
$val[3] = '2001';

print "<p><table border='0' width='247' align='center'>";
print "<tr><td>Course:</td><td>" . $a['course'] . "</td></tr>";
print "<tr><td>Module</td><td>" . $a['module'] . "</td></tr>";
print "<tr><td>Class</td><td>" . $a['class']. "</td></tr>";
print "<tr><td>Year </td><td>" . $a['year']. "</td></tr>";
print "</table>";

print "<p><table border='0' width='247' align='center'>";
print "<tr><td>Course:</td><td>" . $val[0] . "</td></tr>";
print "<tr><td>Module</td><td>" . $val[1] . "</td></tr>";
print "<tr><td>Class</td><td>" . $val[2]. "</td></tr>";
print "<tr><td>Year </td><td>" . $val[3]. "</td></tr>";
print "</table>";

$prime = array(1,2,3,5,7,11,13,17,19,23);
// this sets prime[0] to 1, prime[2] to 2, and so on.

print("<h6>");
for ($i=0;$i<10;$i++)
{
print "<BR>Prime number : $prime[$i]";
}
```

In PHP 4 the foreach construct provides a way to iterate over arrays. The first type of usage is:

```
foreach(arr_expression as $val) statement
```

The first form loops over the array given by arr_expression. For each loop, the current element is assigned to $val and the internal array pointer is incremented by one. An alternative form achieves the same, but that the current element's key is assigned to the variable $key on each loop. The format is:

```
foreach(array_expression as $key => $value) statement
```

An example is given next:

📖 PHP Code H5.18

```php
<?php
foreach ( $colors as $key => $color )
{
// won't work:
//$color = strtoupper($color);
//works:
$colors[$key] = strtoupper($color);
}
print_r($colors);
?>
```

```
Array ( [0] => RED
[1] => BLUE [2] =>
GREEN [3] => YELLOW )
```

The print_r() is a useful function as it can to display the contents of an array. The following shows an example of displaying keys and values:

📖 PHP Code H5.19

```php
<?php
foreach ($val as $key => $value) {
echo "Key: $key; Value: $value<br>\n";
}
?>
```

```
Key: 0; Value: CNDS
Key: 1; Value: Ethernet
Key: 2; Value: D111
Key: 3; Value: 2001
```

In this case, the array to be scanned is $val, and $key takes on the key of each of the elements of the array.

The unset() function can be used to remove a value from the array, such as:

📖 PHP Code H5.20

```php
$arr = array( 1 => 'apple', 2 => 'orange', 3 => 'lemon' );
unset ( $arr[2] );
foreach ($arr as $key => $value) {
   print "Key: $key; Value:
   $value<br>\n";
}
```

```
Key: 1; Value: apple
Key: 3; Value: lemon
```

which uses the unset() function to get rid of the second element of the array.

H5.2.11 Math functions

PHP supports a whole host of functions, and constants. The main constants which are defined are:

Constant	Value	Description
M_PI	3.14159265358979323846	Pi
M_E	2.7182818284590452354	e
M_LOG2E	1.4426950408889634074	$\log_2 e$

M_LOG10E	0.43429448190325182765	log_10 e
M_LN2	0.69314718055994530942	log_e 2
M_LN10	2.30258509299404568402	log_e 10
M_PI_2	1.57079632679489661923	pi/2
M_PI_4	0.78539816339744830962	pi/4
M_1_PI	0.31830988618379067154	1/pi
M_2_PI	0.63661977236758134308	2/pi
M_SQRTPI	1.77245385090551602729	sqrt(pi) [4.0.2]
M_2_SQRTPI	1.12837916709551257390	2/sqrt(pi)
M_SQRT2	1.41421356237309504880	sqrt(2)
M_SQRT3	1.73205080756887729352	sqrt(3) [4.0.2]
M_SQRT1_2	0.70710678118654752440	1/sqrt(2)
M_LNPI	1.14472988584940017414	log_e(pi) [4.0.2]
M_EULER	0.57721566490153286061	Euler constant [4.0.2]

The main math functions include:

Function	Description
abs	Absolute value mixed **abs** (mixed number)
acos	Arc cosine float **acos** (float arg)
acosh	Inverse hyperbolic cosine float **acosh** (float arg)
asin	Arc sine float **asin** (float arg)
asinh	Inverse hyperbolic sine float **asinh** (float arg)
atan	Arc tangent float **atan** (float arg)
atanh	Inverse hyperbolic tangent float **atanh** (float arg)
atan2	arc tangent of two variables float **atan2** (float y, float x)
base_convert	Convert a number between arbitrary bases string **base_convert** (string number, int frombase, int tobase)
bindec	Binary to decimal int **bindec** (string binary_string)
ceil	Round fractions up float **ceil** (float value)
cos	Cosine float **cos** (float arg)
cosh	Hyperbolic cosine float **cosh** (float arg)
decbin	Decimal to binary string **decbin** (int number)
dechex	Decimal to hexadecimal string **dechex** (int number)
decoct	Decimal to octal string **decoct** (int number)
deg2rad	Converts the number in degrees to the radian equivalent float **deg2rad** (float number)
exp	e to the power of ... float **exp** (float arg)
floor	Round fractions down float **floor** (float value)
getrandmax	Show largest possible random value int **getrandmax** (void)
hexdec	Hexadecimal to decimal int **hexdec** (string hex_string)

hypot	Returns sqrt(num1*num1 + num2*num2)
	float **hypot** (float num1, float num2)
is_finite	Is finite?
	bool **is_finite** (float val)
is_infinite	Is infinite?
	bool **is_infinite** (float val)
is_nan	Not a number?
	bool **is_nan** (float val)
log	Natural logarithm
	float **log** (float arg)
log10	Base
	float **log10** (float arg)
max	Find highest value
	mixed **max** (mixed arg1, mixed arg2, mixed argn)
min	Find lowest value
	number **min** (number arg1, number arg2 [, ...])
mt_rand	Generate a better random value
	int **mt_rand** ([int min, int max])
mt_srand	Seed the better random number generator
	void **mt_srand** (int seed)
mt_getrandmax	Show largest possible random value
	int **mt_getrandmax** (void)
number_format	Format a number with grouped thousands
	string **number_format** (float number [, int decimals [, string dec_point [, string thousands_sep]]])
octdec	Octal to decimal
	int **octdec** (string octal_string)
pow	Exponential expression
	number **pow** (number base, number exp)
rad2deg	Converts the radian number to the equivalent number in degrees
	float **rad2deg** (float number)
rand	Generate a random value
	int **rand** ([int min, int max])
round	Rounds a float
	float **round** (float val [, int precision])
sin	Sine
	float **sin** (float arg)
sinh	Hyperbolic sine
	float **sinh** (float arg)
sqrt	Square root
	float **sqrt** (float arg)
srand	Seed the random number generator
	void **srand** (int seed)
tan	Tangent
	float **tan** (float arg)
tanh	Hyperbolic tangent
	float **tanh** (float arg)

The following uses the dechex() and decbin() functions to convert a decimal value into hexademical and binary, respectively.

📖 PHP Code H5.21

```
<?php

print "<table border='1'>";
print "<tr><td>Value</td><td>Hex</td><td>Binary</td></tr>";
for ($val=0; $val<=16; $val++)
{
print "<tr><td>" . $val . "</td><td>" . dechex($val);
print "</td><td>" . decbin($val) . "</td></tr>";
```

```
}
print "</table>";
?>
```

A sample run is as follows:

Value	Hex	Binary
0	0	0
1	1	1
2	2	10
3	3	11
4	4	100
5	5	101
6	6	110
7	7	111
8	8	1000
9	9	1001
10	a	1010
11	b	1011
12	c	1100
13	d	1101
14	e	1110
15	f	1111
16	10	10000

The following gives example code to generate 16 random numbers, in the range from 1 to 20. The microtime() function returns the current time in the number of microseconds followed by the number of microseconds since 1 January 1970. The srand() function starts the random number generator at a unique value for each run.

📖 **PHP Code H5.22**

```php
<?php
print "<table border='1' align='center'>";
list($usec, $sec) = explode(' ',microtime());
srand((float) $sec + ((float) $usec * 100000));
print "<tr><td>Value</td><td>Random number</td></tr>";
for ($val=0; $val<=16; $val++)
{
    print "<tr><td>" . $val . "</td><td>" . rand(1,20) . "</td></tr>";
}
print "</table>";
?>
```

H5.2.12 Functions

Functions are similar in syntax to C, but functions to not have automatic access to global variables, thus the global statement must be used. If in doubt you should always try to pass arguments to your functions.

📖 **PHP Code H5.23**

```php
<?php
$val1 = 11;
```

```
$val2 = 21;

function Add () {
   global $val1, $val2;
   $val2 = $val1 + $val2;
}

function add_with_args($a,$b)
{
return($a+$b);
}

$result=add_with_args($val1,$val2);
print"<BR>Result is $result";

Add ();

print "<BR>Result is $val2";
?>
```

An interesting function is raise(x,y), which will raise x to the power of y. This is achieved using the log (natural logarithm function), and the exp (exponential function). Where x to the power of y is:

x to the power of y = exp (x * log (y));

The PHP function is:

📖 PHP Code H5.24

```
<?php
function raise ($a, $b) {
$val=exp($b*log($a));
return($val);
}
print "<BR>Value of 5 to the power of 6 is " . raise(5,6);
print "<BR>Value of 10.24 to the power of 9 is " . raise(10.24,9);
?>
```

```
Value of 5 to the power of 6 is 15625
Value of 10.24 to the power of 9 is
                      1237940039.2854
```

We could use this to display the binary bit weightings from 0 to 24:

📖 PHP Code H5.25

```
<?php

print "<table>";
for ($i=0 ; $i<=24 ;$i++)
{
    print "<tr><td>" . $i . "</td><td>" . raise(2.0,$i) . "</td></tr>";
}
print "</table>";
?>
```

A sample run gives:

```
0    1
1    2
2    4
3    8
: :
21   2097152
22   4194304
23   8388608
24   16777216
```

H5.2.13 User details

PHP sets up a $_SERVER array which contains information such as headers, paths, and script locations. These can be accessed by $_SERVER['keyname'].

Key	Description
PHP_SELF	Filename of the page, relative to the document root.
GATEWAY_INTERFACE	CGI specification.
SERVER_NAME	Name of the server.
SERVER_SOFTWARE	Name of the server software.
SERVER_PROTOCOL	HTTP server protocol.
REQUEST_METHOD	Request method for the page, such as 'GET', 'HEAD', 'POST', 'PUT'.
QUERY_STRING	Query string for the page (if any).
DOCUMENT_ROOT	Document root
HTTP_ACCEPT	Contents of the Accept/
HTTP_ACCEPT_CHARSET	Contents of the Accept-Charset: header
HTTP_ACCEPT_ENCODING	Contents of the Accept-Encoding: header from the current request, if there is one.
HTTP_ACCEPT_LANGUAGE	Contents of the Accept-Language: header from the current request, if there is one.
HTTP_CONNECTION	Contents of the Connection: header from the current request, if there is one.
HTTP_HOST	Contents of the Host: header from the current request, if there is one.
HTTP_REFERER	The address of the page (if any) which referred the user agent to the current page.
HTTP_USER_AGENT	Displays the contents of the user agent. It can be used to determine the browser type.
REMOTE_ADDR	Define the IP address of the remote host.
REMOTE_PORT	Defines the TCP port of the remote host.
SCRIPT_FILENAME	Absolute pathname of the currently executing script.
SERVER_ADMIN	Location of the web server configuration file.
SERVER_PORT	Server port (normally port 80).
SERVER_SIGNATURE	String containing the server version.

PATH_TRANSLATED	Filesystem for the current script.
SCRIPT_NAME	Contains the current script's path.
REQUEST_URI	URI for the script.

The following shows how PHP can be used to get some basic details on a session.

📖 PHP Code H5.26

```
<?php
print("Browser: $HTTP_USER_AGENT <br />\n");
print("IP: $REMOTE_ADDR <br />\n");
print("Address: ".gethostbyaddr($REMOTE_ADDR));
?>
```

A sample run is as follows:

```
Browser: Mozilla/4.0 (compatible; MSIE 6.0; Windows NT 5.1)
IP: 127.0.0.1
Address: localhost
```

The gethostbyaddr() does a reverse lookup on the IP address, so that the domain name of the host can be displayed. The following gives a more complete coverage of the environment variables:

📖 PHP Code H5.27

```
<?php
print "<BR>CGI: $GATEWAY_INTERFACE";
print "<BR>Server:$SERVER_NAME";
print "<BR>Software:$SERVER_SOFTWARE";
print "<BR>Protocol:$SERVER_PROTOCOL";
print "<BR>Request:$REQUEST_METHOD";
print "<BR>Query:$QUERY_STRING";
print "<BR>Doc:$DOCUMENT_ROOT";
print "<BR>Remote IP:$REMOTE_ADDR";
print "<BR>Remote port:$REMOTE_PORT";
print "<BR>Sever port:$SERVER_PORT";
print "<BR>Remote agent:$HTTP_USER_AGENT";
print "<BR>URI:$REQUEST_URI";
?>
```

A sample run is as follows:

```
CGI:          CGI/1.1
Server:       192.168.0.12
Software:     Apache/1.3.20 (Win32) PHP/4.1.3-dev
Protocol:     HTTP/1.1
Request:      GET
Query:
Doc:          c:/www
Remote IP:    127.0.0.1
Remote port:  3374
Sever port:   80
Remote agent: Mozilla/4.0 (compatible; MSIE 6.0; Windows NT 5.1)
URI:          /php_userdetails.php
```

Next the HTTP variables can be displayed with:

📖 PHP Code H5.28

```php
<?php
print "<BR>HTTP Accept: $HTTP_ACCEPT";
print "<BR>HTTP Charset:$HTTP_ACCEPT_CHARSET";
print "<BR>HTTP Encoding:$HTTP_ACCEPT_ENCODING";
print "<BR>HTTP Language:$HTTP_ACCEPT_LANGUAGE";
print "<BR>HTTP Connection:$HTTP_CONNECTION";
print "<BR>HTTP Host:$HTTP_HOST";
print "<BR>HTTP Referer:$HTTP_REFERER";
?>
```

A sample run is as follows:

```
HTTP Accept: */*
HTTP Charset: iso-8859-1
HTTP Encoding:gzip, deflate
HTTP Language:en-gb
HTTP Connection:Keep-Alive
HTTP Host:localhost
HTTP Referer: temp.html
```

There are also several core constants, such as __FILE__ (which shows the filename of the script being processed), PHP_VERSION (the PHP version) and PHP_OS (the PHP operating system), as given next.

📖 PHP Code H5.29

```php
<?php
print "<BR>File is " . __FILE__;
print "<BR>PHP Version is " . PHP_VERSION;
print "<BR>Operating System is " . PHP_OS;
?>
```

A sample run is as follows:

```
File is c:\www\php_userdetails.php
PHP Version is 4.1.2
Operating System is WINNT
```

H5.2.14 File handling

PHP has a whole host of file handling functions, which are typically based on C/UNIX file accessing.

Function	Description
basename	Returns filename component of path
	string **basename** (string path [, string suffix])
chgrp	Changes file group
	int **chgrp** (string filename, mixed group)
chmod	Changes file mode
	int **chmod** (string filename, int mode)
chown	Changes file owner

	int **chown** (string filename, mixed user)
clearstatcache	Clears file stat cache
	void **clearstatcache** (void)
copy	Copies file
	int **copy** (string source, string dest)
dirname	Returns directory name component of path
	string **dirname** (string path)
disk_free_space	Returns available space in directory
	float **disk_free_space** (string directory)
disk_total_space	Returns the total size of a directory
	float **disk_total_space** (string directory)
fclose	Closes an open file pointer
	bool **fclose** (int fp)
feof	Tests for end of file on a file pointer
	int **feof** (int fp)
fflush	Flushes the output to a file
	int **fflush** (int fp)
fgetc	Gets character from file pointer
	string **fgetc** (int fp)
fgetcsv	Gets line from file pointer and parse for CSV fields
	array **fgetcsv** (int fp, int length [, string delimiter])
fgets	Gets line from file pointer
	string **fgets** (int fp [, int length])
fgetss	Gets line from file pointer and strip HTML tags
	string **fgetss** (int fp, int length [, string allowable_tags])
file_get_contents	Reads entire file into a string
	string **file_get_contents** (string filename [, int use_include_path])
file	Reads entire file into an array
	array **file** (string filename [, int use_include_path])
file_exists	Checks whether a file exists
	bool **file_exists** (string filename)
fileatime	Gets last access time of file
	int **fileatime** (string filename)
filectime	Gets inode change time of file
	int **filectime** (string filename)
filegroup	Gets file group
	int **filegroup** (string filename)
fileinode	Gets file inode
	int **fileinode** (string filename)
filemtime	Gets file modification time
	int **filemtime** (string filename)
fileowner	Gets file owner
	int **fileowner** (string filename)
fileperms	Gets file permissions
	int **fileperms** (string filename)
filesize	Gets file size
	int **filesize** (string filename)

filetype	Gets file type
	string **filetype** (string filename)
flock	Portable advisory file locking
	bool **flock** (int fp, int operation [, int wouldblock])
fgetwrapperdata	Retrieves header/meta data from "wrapped" file pointers
	mixed **fgetwrapperdata** (int fp)
fopen	Opens file or URL
	int **fopen** (string filename, string mode [, int use_include_path])
fpassthru	Output all remaining data on a file pointer
	int **fpassthru** (int fp)
fputs	Writes to a file pointer
	int **fputs** (int fp, string str [, int length])
fread	Binary safe file read
	string **fread** (int fp, int length)
fscanf	Parses input from a file according to a format
	mixed **fscanf** (int handle, string format [, string var1])
fseek	Seeks on a file pointer
	int **fseek** (int fp, int offset [, int whence])
fstat	Gets information about a file using an open file pointer
	array **fstat** (int fp)
ftell	Tells file pointer read/write position
	int **ftell** (int fp)
ftruncate	Truncates a file to a given length.
	int **ftruncate** (int fp, int size)
fwrite	Binary safe file write
	int **fwrite** (int fp, string string [, int length])
set_file_buffer	Sets file buffering on the given file pointer
	int **set_file_buffer** (int fp, int buffer)
is_dir	Tells whether the filename is a directory
	bool **is_dir** (string filename)
is_executable	Tells whether the filename is executable
	bool **is_executable** (string filename)
is_file	Tells whether the filename is a regular file
	bool **is_file** (string filename)
is_link	Tells whether the filename is a symbolic link
	bool **is_link** (string filename)
is_readable	Tells whether the filename is readable
	bool **is_readable** (string filename)
is_writable	Tells whether the filename is writable
	bool **is_writable** (string filename)
is_writeable	Tells whether the filename is writable
	bool **is_writeable** (string filename)
is_uploaded_file	Tells whether the file was uploaded via HTTP POST
	bool **is_uploaded_file** (string filename)
link	Create a hard link
	int **link** (string target, string link)

linkinfo	Gets information about a link
	int **linkinfo** (string path)
mkdir	Makes directory
	mkdir (string pathname, int mode)
move_uploaded_file	Moves an uploaded file to a new location.
	bool **move_uploaded_file** (string filename, string destination)
parse_ini_file	Parse a configuration file
	array **parse_ini_file** (string filename [, bool process_sections])
pathinfo	Returns information about a file path
	array **pathinfo** (string path)
pclose	Closes process file pointer
	int **pclose** (int fp)
popen	Opens process file pointer
	int **popen** (string command, string mode)
readfile	Outputs a file
	int **readfile** (string filename [, int use_include_path])
readlink	Returns the target of a symbolic link
	string **readlink** (string path)
rename	Renames a file
	int **rename** (string oldname, string newname)
rewind	Rewind the position of a file pointer
	int **rewind** (int fp)
rmdir	Removes directory
	int **rmdir** (string dirname)
stat	Gives information about a file
	array **stat** (string filename)
lstat	Gives information about a file or symbolic link
	array **lstat** (string filename)
realpath	Returns canonicalized absolute pathname
	string **realpath** (string path)
symlink	Creates a symbolic link
	int **symlink** (string target, string link)
tempnam	Create file with unique file name
	string **tempnam** (string dir, string prefix)
tmpfile	Creates a temporary file
	int **tmpfile** (void)
touch	Sets access and modification time of file
	int **touch** (string filename [, int time])
umask	Changes the current umask
	int **umask** (int mask)
unlink	Deletes a file
	int **unlink** (string filename)

The following shows how the attributes of a file can be displayed. In this case the name of the file is index.html.

📖 PHP Code H5.30

```php
<?php
$fname = "index.html";
$dname=".";
print "<BR>Real path: " . realpath($fname);
print "<BR>Path name: " . basename($fname);
print "<BR>Dirname: " . dirname($fname);
print "<BR>Disk free space (MB): " .
round(disk_free_space($dname)/1024/1024);
print "<BR>Total disk space (GB): " .
round(disk_total_space($dname)/1024/1024/1024);

print "<BR>File group: " . filegroup($fname);
print "<BR>File mode: " . fileinode($fname);
print "<BR>File owner: " . fileowner($fname);
print "<BR>File permissions: " . decoct(fileperms($fname));
print "<BR>File size (KB): " . round(filesize($fname)/1024);
print "<BR>File type: " . filetype($fname);

$str= strftime("%H:%M, Date: %d-%m-%Y ", fileatime($fname));
print "<BR>File last accessed: " . $str ;
$str= strftime("%H:%M, Date: %d-%m-%Y ", filemtime($fname));
print "<BR>File last modified: " . $str ;
if (is_readable($fname))
{
    print "<BR>File is readable";
}
else
{
    print "<BR>File is not readable";
}
if (is_writeable($fname))
{
    print "<BR>File is writeable";
}
else
{
    print "<BR>File is not writeable";
}
if (is_executable($fname))
{
    print "<BR>File is executable";
}
else
{
    print "<BR>File is not executable";
}
```

A sample run is:

```
Real path: c:\www\index.html
Path name: index.html
Dirname: .
Disk free space (MB): 1459
Total disk space (GB): 19
File group: 0
File mode: 0
File owner: 0
File permissions: 100666
File size (KB): 29
File type: file
```

```
File last accessed: 14:13, Date: 01-04-2002
File last modified: 20:53, Date: 09-03-2002
File is readable
File is writeable
File is not executable
```

The listings will depend on the operating system that the WWW server is reading from. A UNIX server will gives the full user details. The attribute of 100666 can be interpreted by reading the last three octal digits (666), as rw-rw-rw-.

The fopen(fname, attr) function opens up a file named fname with a given set of attributes (either "r" for read access, "w" for write access, and "a" for append). This function, if successful, will return a file pointer to the required location associated with the file. The fgets(fpoint, bmax) function can be used to read a text file, one line at a time, where fpoint is the current file pointer, and bmax defines the maximum number of bytes to read, without encountering a new line. Care must be take when reading a file, as the contents of the file cannot be read after the end of it, thus the feof(fpoint) function is used to determine if the end of file has occurred. This function returns a TRUE when the file pointer has reached the end of the file. The file can then be closed using the fclose(fpoint) function. The following opens a file named text1.txt, and displays the contents:

📖 PHP Code H5.31

```php
<?php
$fname = "test1.txt";
$fp=fopen($fname, "r");

while (!(feof($fp)))
{
    $str=fgets($fp,1024);
    print $str;
}

fclose($fp);
?>
```

A sample run basically just shows the contents of the file. The following shows an example of a file being copied to another file, and then deleted.

📖 PHP Code H5.32
```php
<?php
$file1 = "test1.txt";
$file2 = "test2.txt";

function exists($fname)
{
    if (is_file($fname))
    {
        print "<BR>$fname exists";
    }
    else
    {
        print "<BR>$fname does not exist";
    }
}
```

```
exists($file2);
copy($file1,$file2); // copy $file1 into $file2
exists($file2);
unlink($file2);
exists($file2);
?>
```

A sample run shows that the file does not initially exist, it is then created with the copy()
function, and then deleted with the unlink() function.

```
test2.txt does not exist
test2.txt exists
test2.txt does not exist
```

The following uses some of the UNIX-type commands which allow the PHP code to move
around the file structure and add and remove directories and files. The mkdir(dir, attrib) is
used to create a directory with the required attributes. In this case "777" is used as the attributes (attrib) which equates to rwxrwxrwx. The chdir(dir) function moves into the
required directory (dir), and the system(cmd) function is used to list the contents of a directory. In this example the rmdir(dir) function is used to remove a directory (dir).

📖 **PHP Code H5.33**
```
<?php
$dir = "new";
print "Creating directory: $dir <br>";
mkdir($dir,"777");
print "Changing directory to $dir<br>";
chdir($dir);
print "Copying file test1.txt from above into $dir<br>";
copy ("..\\test1.txt", "test2.txt");
print "List of files in this directory<br>";
system("ls -l");
print "Deleting this file <br>";
unlink("test2.txt");
print "Moving back to home directory<br>";
chdir("..");
print "Deleting directory<br>";
rmdir($dir);
?>
```

A sample run gives:

```
Creating directory: new
Changing directory to new
Copying file test1.txt from above into new
List of files in this directory:

total 0 -rwxrwxrwx 1 106 Apr 1 20:28 test2.txt

Deleting this file
Moving back to home directory
Deleting directory
```

H5.2.15 Including files

With the include() function parsing leaves PHP mode and goes into HTML mode at the beginning of the target file, and resumes again at the end.

```
<?php
include ('infile.php3');
?>
```

H5.2.16 Creating and using objects

PHP is an object-oriented language, and can be used to create objects as an other object-oriented language. These objects tend to make the design of programs simpler, and less prone to errors. Classes are defined within the class construct. In this case the userdetails class has been define. It contains two parameters: name and age, and a method named display() can be applied to it. The methods that can be applied are defined as functions within the class definition. The function which has the name of the class is automatically called when the object is initially created. In this case the name and age are assigned to the object. To call a method the member access operator (->) must be used with the name of the object. The special variable $this is used when calling a private method within the body of another method. It is also used to set the properties within methods in the class.

📖 PHP Code H5.34

```
<?php
class userdetails
{
var $name;
var $age;

    function userdetails($name, $age)
    {
        $this->name = $name;
        $this->age=$age;
    }
    function display()
    {
        print "<BR>Name: " . $this->name;
        print "; Age: " .$this->age;
    }
}

$me = new userdetails("fred","24");
$you = new userdetails("bert","26");
$me->display();
$you->display();
?>
```

A sample run gives:

```
Name: fred; Age: 24
Name: bert; Age: 26
```

H5.3   Strings

PHP supports a whole host of string manipulation functions. These include:

Function	Description
addslashes	Quote string with slashes string **addslashes** (string str)
bin2hex	Convert binary data into hexadecimal representation string **bin2hex** (string str)
chr	Return a specific character string **chr** (int ascii)
chunk_split	Split a string into smaller chunks string **chunk_split** (string body [, int chunklen [, string end]])
convert_cyr_string	Convert from one Cyrillic character set to another string **convert_cyr_string** (string str, string from, string to)
count_chars	Return information about characters used in a string mixed **count_chars** (string string [, int mode])
crc32	Calculates the crc32 polynomial of a string int **crc32** (string str)
crypt	One- way string encryption (hashing) string **crypt** (string str [, string salt])
echo	Output one or more strings **echo** (string arg1 [, string argn...])
explode	Split a string by string array **explode** (string separator, string string [, int limit])
get_html_translation_table	Returns the translation table used by **htmlspecialchars**() and **htmlentities**()
get_meta_tags	Extracts all meta tag content attributes from a file and returns an array array **get_meta_tags** (string filename [, int use_include_path])
htmlentities	Convert all applicable characters to HTML entities string **htmlentities** (string string [, int quote_style [, string charset]])
htmlspecialchars	Convert special characters to HTML entities string **htmlspecialchars** (string string [, int quote_style [, string charset]])
implode	Join array elements with a string string **implode** (string glue, array pieces)
join	Join array elements with a string string **join** (string glue, array pieces)
localeconv	Get numeric formatting information array **localeconv** (void)
ltrim	Strip whitespace from the beginning of a string string **ltrim** (string str [, string charlist])
md5	Calculate the md5 hash of a string string **md5** (string str)

md5_file	Calculates the md5 hash of a given filename string **md5_file** (string filename)	
metaphone	Calculate the metaphone key of a string string **metaphone** (string str)	
nl2br	Inserts HTML line breaks before all newlines in a string string **nl2br** (string string)	
ord	Return ASCII value of character int **ord** (string string)	
parse_str	Parses the string into variables void **parse_str** (string str [, array arr])	
print	Output a string **print** (string arg)	
printf	Output a formatted string void **printf** (string format [, mixed args])	
quoted_printable_ decode	Convert a quoted- printable string to an 8 bit string string **quoted_printable_decode** (string str)	
quotemeta	Quote meta characters string **quotemeta** (string str)	
str_rot13	Perform the rot13 transform on a string string **str_rot13** (string str)	
rtrim	Strip whitespace from the end of a string string **rtrim** (string str [, string charlist])	
sscanf	Parses input from a string according to a format mixed **sscanf** (string str, string format [, string var1])	
setlocale	Set locale information string **setlocale** (mixed category, string locale)	
similar_text	Calculate the similarity between two strings int **similar_text** (string first, string second [, float percent])	
soundex	Calculate the soundex key of a string string **soundex** (string str)	
sprintf	Return a formatted string string **sprintf** (string format [, mixed args])	
strncasecmp	Binary safe case- insensitive string comparison of the first n characters int **strncasecmp** (string str1, string str2, int len)	
strcasecmp	Binary safe case- insensitive string comparison int **strcasecmp** (string str1, string str2)	
strchr	Find the first occurrence of a character string **strchr** (string haystack, string needle)	
strcmp	Binary safe string comparison int **strcmp** (string str1, string str2)	
strcoll	Locale based string comparison int **strcoll** (string str1, string str2)	
strcspn	Find length of initial segment not matching mask int **strcspn** (string str1, string str2)	
strip_tags	Strip HTML and PHP tags from a string string **strip_tags** (string str [, string allowable_tags])	

stripcslashes	Un- quote string quoted with **addcslashes**() string **stripcslashes** (string str)
stripslashes	Un-quote string quoted with **addslashes**() string **stripslashes** (string str)
stristr	Case insensitive **strstr**() string **stristr** (string haystack, string needle)
strlen	Get string length int **strlen** (string str)
strnatcmp	String comparisons using a "natural order" algorithm int **strnatcmp** (string str1, string str2)
strnatcasecmp	Case insensitive string comparisons using a "natural order" algorithm int **strnatcasecmp** (string str1, string str2)
strncmp	Binary safe string comparison of the first n characters int **strncmp** (string str1, string str2, int len)
str_pad	Pad a string to a certain length with another string string **str_pad** (string input, int pad_length [, string pad_string [, int pad_type]])
strpos	Find position of first occurrence of a string int **strpos** (string haystack, string needle [, int offset])
strrchr	Find the last occurrence of a character in a string string **strrchr** (string haystack, string needle)
str_repeat	Repeat a string string **str_repeat** (string input, int multiplier)
strrev	Reverse a string string **strrev** (string string)
strrpos	Find position of last occurrence of a char in a string int **strrpos** (string haystack, char needle)
strspn	Find length of initial segment matching mask int **strspn** (string str1, string str2)
strstr	Find first occurrence of a string string **strstr** (string haystack, string needle)
strtok	Tokenize string string **strtok** (string arg1, string arg2)
strtolower	Make a string lowercase string **strtolower** (string str)
strtoupper	Make a string uppercase string **strtoupper** (string string)
str_replace	Replace all occurrences of the search string with the replacement string mixed **str_replace** (mixed search, mixed replace, mixed subject)
strtr	Translate certain characters string **strtr** (string str, string from, string to)
substr	Return part of a string string **substr** (string string, int start [, int length])
substr_count	Count the number of substring occurrences int **substr_count** (string haystack, string needle)
substr_replace	Replace text within a portion of a string string **substr_replace** (string string, string replacement, int start [, int

	length])
trim	Strip whitespace from the beginning and end of a string
	string **trim** (string str [, string charlist])
ucfirst	Make a string's first character uppercase
	string **ucfirst** (string str)
ucwords	Uppercase the first character of each word in a string
	string **ucwords** (string str)
vprintf	Output a formatted string
	void **vprintf** (string format, array args)
vsprintf	Return a formatted string
	string **vsprintf** (string format, array args)
wordwrap	Wraps a string to a given number of characters using a string break character.
	string **wordwrap** (string str [, int width [, string break [, int cut]]])

PHP has strong character and string conversions. The following PHP script converts from an integer value to an ASCII character, in the range from 32 to 49.

📖 PHP Code H5.35

```php
<?php

print "<table>";
print "<tr><td><B>Dec </td><td><B>Char </td><td><B>Hex</td></tr>";
for ($i=32;$i<50; $i++)
{
    print "<tr><td>$i </td><td>" . chr($i) . "</td> <td>"
            . dechex($i) . "</td><tr>";
}
print "</table>";
?>
```

A sample run gives:

Dec	Char	Hex
32	20	
33	!	21
34	"	22
35	#	23
:::		
48	0	30
49	1	31

The following code uses the sprintf() function to format a string. The formating is in a similar form to the sprintf() function used in C/C++ programming, where %s represents a string, %d represents an integer, and %f represents a floating-point value. For example the %8.3f format displays a value with 8 places reserved for the numeric value, and three decimal places (the WWW browser will crunch any white spaces, though).

📖 PHP Code H5.36

```php
<?php

$user="Fred";
```

```
$userID=24;
$credits=43.354;
$str1=sprintf( "<BR>Hello %s, how are you? Your ID is %d.", $user,$userID);
print $str1;
$str1=sprintf( "<BR>You have %8.1f credits left.", $credits);
print $str1;
print strtolower($str1);
print strtoupper($str1);
print "<BR>There are " . strlen($str1) . " characters in this string.";

?>
```

A sample run gives:

```
Hello Fred, how are you? Your ID is 24.
You have 43.4 credits left.
you have 43.4 credits left.
YOU HAVE 43.4 CREDITS LEFT.
There are 37 characters in this string.
```

PHP has several error detection, encryption and hash functions, these include crc32(), des(), and md5().

📖 PHP Code H5.37

```
<?php
$str1="fred";
$str2="bert";
print "<BR>CRC-32 for $str1 is " . decbin(crc32($str1));
print "<BR>DES encryption for $str1 is " . crypt($str1);
print "<BR>DES encryption for $str2 is " . crypt($str2);
print "<BR>MD5 hash for $str1 is " . md5($str1);
print "<BR>MD5 hash for $str2 is " . md5($str2);
print "<BR>MD5 hash for $str1$str2 is " . md5($str1 . $str2);
?>
```

A sample run shows the formats for each:

```
CRC-32 for fred is 11101000101001111000101011110
DES encryption for fred is d.uBy7Ra2pv4Y
DES encryption for bert is XUgCri2AqLZiQ
MD5 hash for fred is 570a90bfbf8c7eab5dc5d4e26832d5b1
MD5 hash for bert is 3de0746a7d2762a87add40dac2bc95a0
MD5 hash for fredbert is 64a18c7f7307f412daba4e54ddb7ff28
```

Web spiders and search engines often use meta tags to get basic information on the page. These are normally placed in the header of the HTML page. For example:

```
<meta name="keywords" content="PHP, date, time">
```

📖 PHP Code H5.38

```
<?php
$fname="php_strings.php";
$str=get_meta_tags($fname);
print "The meta tags in this document are:";
foreach ($str as $key => $val)
{
   print "<BR><B>$key :</B> $val";
```

```
}
?>
```

H5.3.1 Determining the browser type

📖 **PHP Code H5.39**
```
<?php
if(strstr($HTTP_USER_AGENT,"MSIE")) {
echo "<P>You are using Internet Explorer";
}
if(strstr($HTTP_USER_AGENT,"Windows 98")) {
echo " and Windows 98<br>";
}
elseif(strstr($HTTP_USER_AGENT,"Windows NT")) {
echo "and Windows NT<br>";
}
?>
```

> You are using
> Internet Explorer and
> Windows NT

The full details can be displayed with:

📖 **PHP Code H5.40**
```
<?php
echo "$HTTP_USER_AGENT<hr>\n";
?>
```

An example output is:

```
Mozilla/4.0 (compatible; MSIE 6.0; Windows NT 5.1)
```

H5.4   PHP details

PHP variables:

Variable	Examples
COMSPEC	C:\WINDOWS1\system32\cmd.exe
DOCUMENT_ROOT	c:/www
HTTP_ACCEPT	image/gif, image/x-xbitmap, image/jpeg, image/pjpeg, application/vnd.ms-powerpoint, application/vnd.ms-excel, application/msword, */*
HTTP_ACCEPT_ENCODING	gzip, deflate
HTTP_ACCEPT_LANGUAGE	en-gb
HTTP_CONNECTION	Keep-Alive
HTTP_COOKIE	PHPSESSID=2c363ef09da89cb05657cf9de1fcdb3b
HTTP_HOST	localhost
HTTP_USER_AGENT	Mozilla/4.0 (compatible; MSIE 6.0; Windows NT 5.1)
PATH	C:\WINDOWS1\system32;
REMOTE_ADDR	127.0.0.1
REMOTE_PORT	3067
SCRIPT_FILENAME	c:/www/php_testing.php
SERVER_ADDR	127.0.0.1
SERVER_ADMIN	you@your.address

SERVER_NAME	192.168.1.3
SERVER_PORT	80
SERVER_SIGNATURE	\<ADDRESS>Apache/1.3.20 Server at 192.168.1.3 Port 80\</ADDRESS>
SERVER_SOFTWARE	Apache/1.3.20 (Win32) PHP/4.1.3-dev
SystemRoot	C:\WINDOWS1
WINDIR	C:\WINDOWS1
GATEWAY_INTERFACE	CGI/1.1
SERVER_PROTOCOL	HTTP/1.1
REQUEST_METHOD	GET
QUERY_STRING	
REQUEST_URI	/php_testing.php
SCRIPT_NAME	/php_testing.php

Array definitions

Variable	Value
PHP_SELF	/php_testing.php
_COOKIE["PHPSESSID"]	2c363ef09da89cb05657cf9de1fcdb3b
_SERVER["COMSPEC"]	C:\\WINDOWS1\\system32\\cmd.exe
_SERVER["DOCUMENT_ROOT"]	c:/www
_SERVER["HTTP_ACCEPT"]	image/gif, image/x-xbitmap, image/jpeg, image/pjpeg, application/vnd.ms-powerpoint, application/vnd.ms-excel, application/msword, */*
_SERVER["HTTP_ACCEPT_ENCODING"]	gzip, deflate
_SERVER["HTTP_ACCEPT_LANGUAGE"]	en-gb
_SERVER["HTTP_CONNECTION"]	Keep-Alive
_SERVER["HTTP_COOKIE"]	PHPSESSID=2c363ef09da89cb05657cf9de1fcdb3b
_SERVER["HTTP_HOST"]	localhost
_SERVER["HTTP_USER_AGENT"]	Mozilla/4.0 (compatible; MSIE 6.0; Windows NT 5.1)
_SERVER["PATH"]	C:\\WINDOWS1\\system32;
_SERVER["REMOTE_ADDR"]	127.0.0.1
_SERVER["REMOTE_PORT"]	3067
_SERVER["SCRIPT_FILENAME"]	c:/www/php_testing.php
_SERVER["SERVER_ADDR"]	127.0.0.1
_SERVER["SERVER_ADMIN"]	you@your.address
_SERVER["SERVER_NAME"]	192.168.1.3
_SERVER["SERVER_PORT"]	80
_SERVER["SERVER_SIGNATURE"]	\<ADDRESS>Apache/1.3.20 Server at 192.168.1.3 Port 80\</ADDRESS>
_SERVER["SERVER_SOFTWARE"]	Apache/1.3.20 (Win32) PHP/4.1.3-dev
_SERVER["SystemRoot"]	C:\\WINDOWS1
_SERVER["WINDIR"]	C:\\WINDOWS1
_SERVER["GATEWAY_INTERFACE"]	CGI/1.1
_SERVER["SERVER_PROTOCOL"]	HTTP/1.1
_SERVER["REQUEST_METHOD"]	GET
_SERVER["QUERY_STRING"]	
_SERVER["REQUEST_URI"]	/php_testing.php
_SERVER["SCRIPT_NAME"]	/php_testing.php
_SERVER["PATH_TRANSLATED"]	c:/www/php_testing.php
_SERVER["PHP_SELF"]	/php_testing.php
_SERVER["argv"]	Array
_SERVER["argc"]	0
_ENV["ALLUSERSPROFILE"]	C:\\Documents and Settings\\All Users.WINDOWS1
_ENV["APPDATA"]	C:\\Documents and Settings\\MyUser\\Application Data
_ENV["CLASSPATH"]	C:\\Program Files\\PhotoDeluxe HE 3.0\\AdobeConnectables;
_ENV["CommonProgramFiles"]	C:\\Program Files\\Common Files

_ENV["COMPUTERNAME"]	BILL
_ENV["ComSpec"]	C:\\WINDOWS1\\system32\\cmd.exe
_ENV["HOMEDRIVE"]	C:
_ENV["HOMEPATH"]	\\Documents and Settings\\MyUser
_ENV["LOGONSERVER"]	\\\\BILL
_ENV["NUMBER_OF_PROCESSORS"]	1
_ENV["OS"]	Windows_NT
_ENV["Path"]	C:\\WINDOWS1\\system32;
_ENV["PATHEXT"]	.COM;.EXE;.BAT;.CMD;.VBS;.VBE;.JS;.JSE;.WSF;.WSH
_ENV["PROCESSOR_ARCHITECTURE"]	x86
_ENV["PROCESSOR_IDENTIFIER"]	x86 Family 6 Model 8 Stepping 6, GenuineIntel
_ENV["PROCESSOR_LEVEL"]	6
_ENV["PROCESSOR_REVISION"]	0806
_ENV["ProgramFiles"]	C:\\Program Files
_ENV["PROMPT"]	pg
_ENV["SESSIONNAME"]	Console
_ENV["SystemDrive"]	C:
_ENV["SystemRoot"]	C0B•INDOWS1
_ENV["TEMP"]	C:\\DOCUME~1\\WILLIA~1\\LOCALS~1\\Temp
_ENV["TMP"]	C:\\DOCUME~1\\WILLIA~1\\LOCALS~1\\Temp
_ENV["USERDOMAIN"]	BILL
_ENV["USERNAME"]	MyUser
_ENV["USERPROFILE"]	C:\\Documents and Settings\\MyUser
_ENV["winbootdir"]	C:\\WINDOWS
_ENV["windir"]	C:\\WINDOWS1

H6   PHP (sessions and databases)

H6.1   Cookies

Personalization can be achieved in number of ways, from simple cookies, which are stored on the users computer to logging into a server (in the way which MSN Messenger does). Cookies are simple text files (typically stored as TXT files in the WINDOWS\COOKIES folder on Microsoft Windows), and will contain relevant details on the user, and the any of their preferences. As these are text files, they cannot do any damage to the local computer. Sometimes users delete these cookies, and all the previous information is lost, and must thus re-register for the system to be able to store their details. PHP transparently supports HTTP cookies.

Cookies are defined in the HTTP header, and must thus to specified before the HTML content. The format of the cookie statement in the header is of the form:

```
"Set-Cookie: billCookie=Test expires =Tuesday 10-Apr-2005 00:00:00 GMT;"
```

PHP allows either the header statement to be used, such as:

```
header("Set-Cookie: billCookie=Test expires =Tuesday 10-Apr-2005 00:00:00
GMT;")
```

or with the setcookie function:

```
setcookie("billCookie", "Test", time()+3600)
```

which specifies that the cookie expires in 3600 seconds (which is 1 hour from the current time). The format of the setcookie() function is:

int **setcookie** (string name [, string value [, int expire [, string path
                                     [, string domain [, int secure]]]]])

which **must** be placed before any HTML tags. The path defines the location of the cookie, and the domain defines the domain which can read from the cookie. The domain disallows other WWW servers from reading from the cookie which was created by another domain. The following code can be added to the **top** of an HTML file, and will create a cookie:

📖 **PHP Code H6.1**
```
<?php
setcookie("billsCookie","Test",time()+3600);
/* Expire in 1 hour */
?>
```

To determine if there is a cookie present:

📖 **PHP Code H6.2**
```
<?php
if (isset($billscookie))
```

```
{
    print "<P>A cookie exists on your computer";
}
?>
```

The cookie should contain something like:

```
billscookie
Test
localhost/
1024
142822656
29437464
2805528320
29437455
*
```

To read a cookie:

📖 PHP Code H6.3

```
<?php
if (isset($billscookie))
{
    if ($billscookie == "Yes")
    {
        print "<P>Welcome back";
    }
    else
    {
        print "<P>Nice to see you!";
    }
}
?>
```

A cookie can be deleted by creating a new cookie with the same name as the one which is to be deleted, but setting the expiry time as some time in the past. This will automatically create, and then delete the cookie, such as:

```
<?php
setcookie("billCookie", "Test", time()-60); //delete cookie
?>
```

Note that this statement must be placed at the **top** of the HTML/PHP file, before any HTML statements.

H6.2   Forms

The following shows a simple example of how PHP can get details from a form, and then process this, to give the required functionality. Login screen: PHP is an excellent language to provide security in the accessing of WWW pages. In this example the user must login to get access to certain pages. In this case the user enters the parameters in the form to the variables login and password. These are then passed to the PHP processing file, and authority is given, or not.

In a form the <input> tag is used to define a field in the form. In this case the fields are text fields. The names they are assigned are login and password. The PHP script is called when the user clicks on the submit button (which is defined with the type of "submit"). The login_page.php script will be called, and the login and password variables will be passed to the script.

📖 **PHP Code H6.4**

```
<form action="login_page.php" method="post">


Login: <input type="text" name="login">
<BR>Password <input type="text" name="password">
<input type="submit" value="Login">
</form>
```

The contents of the login_page.php file are:

```php
<?php
if ($login=="fred")
{
   print "<H2>Login name is correct";
}
else
{
   print "<H2>Login name is incorrect<BR>";
}
if ($password=="bert")
{
   print "<H2>Password is correct<BR>";
}
else
{
   print "<H2>Password is incorrect<BR>";
}
if ($name="fred" && $password=="bert")
{
   print "<a href='cnds.html'><H2>Goto CNDS page </a>";
}
else
{
   print "<a href='Javascript:history.back()'><H2>Login again </a>";
}
?>
```

H6.3   Session details

Sessions are useful in storing information on users, and then recalling it. This is especially useful when creating user-specific WWW pages, which are created specially for a specific user. For example a computer-support WWW site might ask a user to enter their unique code for their computer, and their name. This information would then be stored as a cookie on the local machine. When the user went back to the site, the cookie would be read, and the WWW pages could be designed so that the user was presented with specific information on their computer, and all the required updates on that specific computer.

A session is started by inserting the session_start() function at the top of the PHP file:

📖 **PHP Code H6.5**
```
<?php
session_start();
?>
```

The current session ID can then be displayed with:

📖 **PHP Code H6.6**
```
<?php
print "The session ID number is: ";
print $PHPSESSID;
?>
```

A sample run shows:

```
The session ID number is: 6fa022e640f4d606a2bea17c1cd7e1c8
```

Once a session has started, session variables can be registered against the session using the session_register() function. For example, the user may enter their name, which could be stored for future purposes:

📖 **PHP Code H6.7**
```
<?php
session_register("Username");
$Username="Fred";
session_register("Company");
$Company="Home Inc.";
?>
```

Then **another** page can read from these variables, such as:

📖 **PHP Code H6.8**
```
<?php
session_register("Username");
session_register("Company");
print "<BR>Hello $Username";
print "<BR>You are form $Company";
?>
```

The session_start() must be placed at the top of pages which use variables used in the session.

H6.4   Session logging

A common task is to log the accesses to a page. This can be done by inserting a graphics image on a page which is only displayed with one pixel by one pixel. The HTML sends off to the PHP file for the graphic, which logs that it has been called, and then returns the graphic file to the page.

PHP Code H5.9

```
<a href ="http://myserver.co.uk/php_log.php">
<img src="http://myserver.co.uk/php_log.php" border=0 width=1
height=1"></a>
```

Next a log file can be created. This file logs the accesses to the log file, and then returns back the small graphics file. It also tests the log file. If it is greater that 5000 byte, it reads it and sends it to the owner, by email. It then erases the contents of the file (by opening the file with the "w+" attribute).

PHP Code H6.10

```php
<?php
$str = date("F j, Y, g:i a");
$str = "<P>$str Refer: $HTTP_USER_AGENT";
$str = $str . "$REMOTE_ADDR " . gethostbyaddr($REMOTE_ADDR) . "\n";
$filename = "logfile.htt";
$fd = fopen ($filename, "a+");
$size=filesize($filename);
$str = $str . "Size = " . $size;
$contents = fputs ($fd, $str);
if ($size>5000)
{
    $headers = "Content-Type: text/html; charset=iso-8859-1\n";
    fseek($fd,0);
    $contents=fread($fd,filesize($filename));
    mail('fred@myisp.com',"Logfile", $contents, $headers);
    fclose($fd);
    $fd = fopen ($filename, "w+");
    fclose($fd);
}
else
{
    fclose ($fd);
}
print "Location: http://myserver.co.uk/gif_file.gif\n\n";
?>
```

A sample of the file produced is:

```
August 28, 2001, 3:37 pm Refer: Mozilla/4.0 (compatible; MSIE 6.0b; Windows 98;
Win 9x 4.90; L1 IE5.5 December 2000)172.190.50.179 ACBE32B3.ipt.aol.com Size =
0
August 28, 2001, 3:38 pm Refer: Mozilla/4.0 (compatible; MSIE 6.0b; Windows 98;
Win 9x 4.90; L1 IE5.5 December 2000)172.190.50.179 ACBE32B3.ipt.aol.com Size =
163
August 28, 2001, 3:40 pm Refer: Mozilla/4.0 (compatible; MSIE 6.0b; Windows 98;
Win 9x 4.90; L1 IE5.5 December 2000)172.190.50.179 ACBE32B3.ipt.aol.com Size =
328
```

H6.5   COM

COM is a technique which allows programs to call other programs using standard calls (known as APIs). This makes it simpler to write programs, as standard components can be called from the operating system, such as calling up Word as a word processor, or Excel for a spreadsheet. It also separates implementation from interface. The supported classes include:

COM	COM class
VARIANT	VARIANT class
com_load	Creates a new reference to a COM component string **com_load** (string module name [, string server name [, int co-depage]])
com_invoke	Calls a COM component's method. mixed **com_invoke** (resource com_object, string function_name [, mixed function parameters, ...])
com_propget	Gets the value of a COM Component's property mixed **com_propget** (resource com_object, string property)
com_get	Gets the value of a COM Component's property mixed **com_get** (resource com_object, string property)
com_propput	Assigns a value to a COM component's property void **com_propput** (resource com_object, string property, mixed value)
com_propset	Assigns a value to a COM component's property void **com_propset** (resource com_object, string property, mixed value)
com_set	Assigns a value to a COM component's property void **com_set** (resource com_object, string property, mixed value)
com_addref	Increases the components reference counter. void **com_addref** (void)
com_release	Decreases the components reference counter. void **com_release** (void)
com_isenum	Grabs an IEnumVariant void **com_isenum** (object com_module)
com_load_typelib	Loads a Typelib void **com_load_typelib** (string typelib_name [, int case_insensitive])

The format for creating a new object is:

```
$obj = new COM("server.object")
```

For example to call Word, the format is:

```
$word = new COM("word.application")
```

or for an ADODB

```
$conn = new COM("ADODB.Connection")
```

For example to invoke Word and insert some text to the document, and then save it the following code can be used:

📖 PHP Code H6.11

```
<?PHP
// starting word
$word = new COM("word.application") or die("Unable to start Word");
print "Word has been loaded";
```

```
//make it visible
$word->Visible = 1;        // Application property to make visible

//open an empty document
$word->Documents->Add();   // Add method of Documents

//Add some text, and then save
$word->Selection->TypeText("This will add some text to the Word document");
$word->Documents[1]->SaveAs("deleteme.doc");

//closing word
$word->Quit(); // Quit method of Application
//free the object
$word->Release(); // Release method of Application
$word = null;
print "<BR>[<a href='Javascript:history.back()'>Go back to previous page</a>]";
?>
```

This can be called from a form with:

📖 **PHP Code H6.12**

```
<form name="form2" method="post" action="php_startword.php">
<input type="submit" name="Submit" value="Start Word">
</form>
```

The top level object in Microsoft Word is the **Application** object. This object does not need to have the Application object included in the definition. It has several properties which can be set or read. These include:

Property	Example/description
ActiveDocument	
ActivePrinter	$word->ActivePrinter = "HP LaserJet III on \\p_qu\laser"
Browser	
CapsLock	$state=$word.CapsLock;
Visible	$word->Visible = 1;

and several methods, including:

Method	Example/description
Activate	$word.Activate(); // Activate Word
Help	$word.Help(); // Show help
Quit	$word.Quit(); // Quit word

Microsoft Word also has several objects, such as:

Object	Description/Example
Browser	This represents the browser tool used to locate the insertion point to objects in a document. It is comprised of the three buttons at the bottom of the vertical scroll bar. $word.Browser.Next();
Documents	A collection of all the document objects that are currently open in Word. $word->Documents ->Close();

FileConverters	This is a collection of FileConvertor objects, that can be used to open or close files for a given file format.
Selection	This represents the selection in a window pane. $word->Selection->Cut()
System	Contains information about the computer system. $word->System->Msinfo();

The Documents object has several methods which can be applied to it, including:

Method	Example/description
Add	$word->Documents->Add(); // empty document
Close	$word->Documents ->Close(); // close document
Open	$word->Documents ->Open("deleteme.doc");
Save	$word->Documents ->Save //save files, the SaveAs will appear if it has not been saved before

and when there is a collection of documents, the following methods can be used:

Method	Example/description
Add()	$word->Documents[2]->Add();
CheckGrammar()	$word->Documents[1]-> CheckGrammar ();
CheckSpelling()	$word->Documents[1]->CheckSpelling();
Close()	$word->Documents[1]->Close();
PrintPreview()	$word->Documents[1]->PrintPreview();
Reload()	$word->Documents[1]->Reload();
Save()	$word->Documents[1]->Save();
SaveAs()	$word->Documents[1]->SaveAs("deleteme.doc");
Undo()	$word->Documents[1]->Undo();
WebPagePreview()	$word->Documents[1]-> WebPagePreview ();

The **Selection** object has several methods, including:

Method	Example/description
BoldRun()	
Copy()	$word->Selection->Copy()
Cut()	$word->Selection->Cut()
Delete()	$word->Selection->Delete()
InsertAfter()	
InsertBefore()	
InsertCaption()	
InsertDate()	$word->Selection->InsertDate()
InsertFile()	
InsertFormula()	
Paste()	$word->Selection->Paste()
Select()	$word->Selection->Select()
SortAscending()	$word->Selection->SortAscending()
SortDescending()	$word->Selection->SortDescending()

TypeText()	$word->Selection->TypeText("This will add some text to the Word document");

For example to display information on the Word application with the System object, and the MSInfo() method, the following form can be used:

📖 PHP Code H6.13

```
<form name="form2" method="post" action="php_startmsinfo.php">
<input type="submit" name="Submit2" value="Start MSInfo">
</form>
<p>This button will start MSInfo. </p>
```

and the associated PHP code (php_startmsinfo.php) is:

📖 PHP Code H6.14

```
<?php
// starting word
$word = new COM("word.application");
$word->System->Msinfo();
print "MSInfo has been started";

print "<BR>[<a href='Javascript:history.back()'>Go back to previous page</a>]";

?>
```

After the button has been pressed, the MSInfo window will be generated:

The following example shows a form with a textarea named wordtext. When the user clicks on the button on the form, the php_savetext.php file is called, which saves the entered text as part of a Word file. The form code is:

📖 PHP Code H6.15

```
<form name="form2" method="post" action="php_savetext.php">
<textarea name="wordtext" cols="30" rows="10">
<Type over this, then press button></textarea>
<p><input type="submit" name="Submit3" value="Save to Word file">
</form>
```

`<p>This button will save your text into a Word document named deleteme.doc.</p>`
and the PHP file is:

📖 PHP Code H6.16

```php
<?php
// starting word
$word = new COM("word.application") or die("Cannot start Word");
print "Word has been loaded<BR>";

//make Word visible
$word->Visible = 1;

//open an empty document
$word->Documents->Add();

//add some text
$word->Selection->TypeText($wordtext);
$word->Documents[1]->SaveAs("deleteme.doc");

//closing word
$word->Quit();

//free the object
$word->Release();
$word = null;

print "<BR>[<a href='Javascript:history.back()'>Go back to previous page</a>]";
?>
```

H6.6   Databases

The real power of PHP is the way that it supports email, forms and access to databases, in a secure way. CGI was in the past used for this, but it is a complex language that does not integrate into the HTML page. An example of a form in HTML is as following:

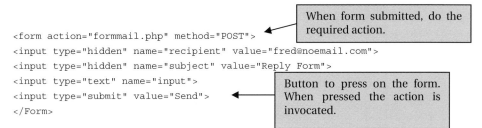

```
<form action="formmail.php" method="POST">
<input type="hidden" name="recipient" value="fred@noemail.com">
<input type="hidden" name="subject" value="Reply Form">
<input type="text" name="input">
<input type="submit" value="Send">
</Form>
```

When form submitted, do the required action.

Button to press on the form. When pressed the action is invoked.

In this form the user can fill-in one of the fields (the type is a "text" field). When the user completes this field, and presses return, or presses the submit button, the action on the form is invoked. In this case the action is to call the PHP file named formmail.php3. The parameters from the form, in this case these are named recipient, subject, and input are then send to the script file (this action is know as posting the parameters). Note that the parameters recipient, and subject are hidden to the user, but are passed to the script file. The contents of formmail.php3 then contain code which e-mail's the message to the recipient, such as:

📖 PHP Code H6.17

```php
<?php
```

```
$fmt_Response=implode("", file("response.htt"));
$fmt_Mail=implode("", file("mail.htt"));
while(list($Key, $Val) = each($HTTP_POST_VARS)) {
    $fmt_Response=str_replace("{$Key}", $Val, $fmt_Response);
    $fmt_Mail=str_replace("{$Key}", $Val, $fmt_Mail);
}
mail($HTTP_POST_VARS["recipient"], $HTTP_POST_VARS["subject"], $fmt_Mail);
echo $fmt_Response;
?>
```

The file response.htt contains a basic message for the user when they have submitted the form, and the mail.htt contains the message which will be added to the e-mail that is sent.

Along with direct e-mail support, PHP supports many different types of databases, which can be accessed directly from the WWW page. To create a table (in this case the table is named datatest) within a database. The variable $server is the name of the SQL server (such as mysqlserver.co.uk); $user is the login name for the user; $password is the password which is associated with the user; and $database is the name of the database. Initially these variables are used with the MYSQL_CONNECT() command to connect to the server, once connected, the database can be accessed with MYSQL_SELECT_DB() command. Next the SQL query: CREATE TABLE is used to create the table within the database. In this case it will create two fields within this table: name and email, each with 25 characters. Finally the SQL_CLOSE() command closes the database.

Some SQL commands

ABORT, ALTER GROUP,
ALTER USER, BEGIN,
CLOSE, CLUSTER,
COMMIT, COPY,
CREATE DATABASE, CREATE GROUP,
CREATE OPERATOR, CREATE TABLE
CREATE USER, CREATE VIEW
DELETE, DROP DATABASE,
DROP TABLE, END,
INSERT, LOAD, LOCK, MOVE
SELECT, SELECT INTO
SET, SHOW, UPDATE

📖 PHP Code H6.18

```
<?php
/* Start of PHP3 Script */
/* Data of SQL-server */
$server= "$$$$";         /* Address of server */
$user= "$$$";            /* FTP-username */
$password= "$$$";        /* FTP-Password */
$database= "$$$";        /* name of database */
$table= "datatest";      /* Name of table, you can select that */

/* Accessing the server and creating the table */
MYSQL_CONNECT($server, $user, $password) or die ( "<H3>Server unreach-
able</H3>");
MYSQL_SELECT_DB($database) or die ( "<H3>database not existent</H3>");
$result=MYSQL_QUERY( "CREATE TABLE $table (name varchar(25),email var-
char(25))");

/* Terminate SQL connection*/

MYSQL_CLOSE();
?>
```

Data can then be written to the database with the INSERT SQL query (as highlight below):

📖 PHP Code H6.19

```php
<?php
$server= "$$$$"; /* Address of database server */
$user= "$$$$"; /* FTP-username */
$password= "$$$$"; /* FTP-Password */
$database= "$$$$"; /* name of database */
$table= "datatest";

/* Accessing SQL-server */
MYSQL_CONNECT($server, $user, $password) or die ( "<H3>Server unreach-
able</H3>");
MYSQL_SELECT_DB($database) or die ( "<H3>Database non existent</H3>");

MYSQL_QUERY( "INSERT INTO $table VALUES('Fred','fred@home.com')");
MYSQL_QUERY( "INSERT INTO $table VALUES('Bert','bert@myplace.com')");

/* Display number of entries */
$query="SELECT * FROM $table";
$result = MYSQL_QUERY($query);

/* How many of these users are there? */
$number = MYSQL_NUMROWS($result);

if ($number==0):
   echo "database empty";
elseif ($number > 0):
   echo "$number rows in database";
endif;
mysql_close();
?>
```

The data can then be read back with an the SELECT query (as highlighted below):

📖 PHP Code H6.20

```php
<?php
$server= "$$$$"; /* Address of database server */
$user= "$$$$"; /* FTP-username */
$password= "$$$$"; /* FTP-Password */
$database= "$$$$"; /* name of database */
$table= "datatest"; /* Name of table, you can select that */
/* Accessing SQL-Server and querying table */
MYSQL_CONNECT($server, $user, $password) or die ( "<H3>Server unreach-
able</H3>");
MYSQL_SELECT_DB($database) or die ( "<H3>Database non existent</H3>");
$result=MYSQL_QUERY( "SELECT * FROM $table order by name");

/* Output data into a HTML table */
echo "<table border=\"1\" align=center width=50%";
echo "<tr>";
echo "<div color=\"#ffff00\">";
while ($field=mysql_fetch_field($result)) {
echo "<th>$field->name</A></th>";
}
echo "</font></tr>";
while($row = mysql_fetch_row($result)) {
   echo "<tr>";
   for($i=0; $i < mysql_num_fields($result); $i++) {
      echo "<td align=center>$row[$i]</td>";
   }
   echo "</tr>\n";
```

```
}
echo "</table><BR><BR>";

/* Close SQL-connection */
MYSQL_CLOSE();
?>
```

And finally, if the table requires to be deleted, the DROP TABLE query can be used (as highlighted below):

📖 **PHP Code H6.21**

```
<?php
/* Accessing the server and deleting the table */
MYSQL_CONNECT($server,  $user,  $password)  or  die  ( "<H3>Server  unreach-
able</H3>");
MYSQL_SELECT_DB($database) or die ( "<H3>database not existent</H3>");
$result=MYSQL_QUERY( "DROP TABLE $table");
print "Result is ";
print $result;
/* Terminate SQL connection*/
MYSQL_CLOSE();
?>
```

As more content becomes database-driven, and more sites use electronic commerce, there will be a great increase in the usage of databases over the WWW, especially in accessing them from WWW pages. Just imagine if you computerized your own home, and you had a database setup which monitored all the conditions in your home, and saved them to a database. If this was interface to a WWW browser you could recall all your data. An excellent usage of database integration with a WWW browser is where users register their details on a database, and are send e-mails are regular intervals to keep them informed of any products that they may be interested in.

H6.7   Getting details from a form

The following shows a simple example of how PHP can read details from a form, write them to a database, and display them to the user:

📖 **PHP Code H6.22**

```
<form method="POST" action= "writedata.php">
First name:
<input type="text" name="name" size="25">
<br>
realname:
<input type="text" name="realname" size="25">
Email:
<input type="text" name="email" size="25">
<input type="submit" name="submit2" value="submit">
</form>
```

The following is a script which will read from the database:

📖 PHP Code H6.23: listing data from a database

```php
<?php
/* Start of PHP3 Script */
/* Data of SQL-server */
$server= "$$$$";       /* Address of database server */
$user= "$$$$$";        /* FTP-username */
$password= "$$$$";    /* FTP-Password */
$database= "$$$";      /* name of database */
$table= "mailing";
/* Accessing the server and creating the table */
MYSQL_CONNECT($server, $user, $password) or die ( "<H3>Server unreach-
able</H3>");
MYSQL_SELECT_DB($database) or die ( "<H3>database not existent</H3>");
$result=MYSQL_QUERY( "CREATE TABLE $table (fname varchar(25),realname var-
char(25),email varchar(25))");
print "Result is $result";
$result=mysql_query("SELECT * from $table");
$rows=mysql_numrows($result);
$i=0;
print "<BR><B>No. First realname Email</B><BR>";

while ($i<$rows) {
    $first=mysql_result($result,$i,'fname');
    $second=mysql_result($result,$i,'realname');
    $third=mysql_result($result,$i,'email');
    print "<BR>$i $first $second $third";
    $i++;
}
?>
```

A sample listing is as follows:

```
Num   First   Surname    Email
---------------------------------
0     fred    smith      fred@home
```

The contents of the file writedata.php is:

📖 PHP Code H6.24 : writing data to a database

```php
<?php
/* Start of PHP3 Script */
/* Data of SQL-server */
$server= "$$$$";       /* Address of database server */
$user= "$$$$";         /* FTP-username */
$password= "$$$$";    /* FTP-Password */
$database= "$$$$";     /* name of database */
$table= "mailing";
/* Accessing the server and creating the table */
MYSQL_CONNECT($server, $user, $password) or die ( "<H3>Server unreach-
able</H3>");
MYSQL_SELECT_DB($database) or die ( "<H3>database not existent</H3>");
$result=MYSQL_QUERY( "CREATE TABLE $table (fname varchar(25),
                          realname varchar(25),email varchar(25))");

MYSQL_QUERY( "INSERT INTO $table VALUES('$name','$realname','$email')");
$result=mysql_query("SELECT * from $table");
$rows=mysql_numrows($result);
$i=0;
print "<BR><B>No. First realname Email</B><BR>";
while ($i<$rows) {
```

```
      $first=mysql_result($result,$i,'fname');
      $second=mysql_result($result,$i,'realname');
      $third=mysql_result($result,$i,'email');
      print "<BR>$i $first $second $email";
      $i++;
}
MYSQL_CLOSE();
print "<P>Data saved to database. Click to go <a
href='Javascript:history.back()' target='_top'>Back </a>";
?>
```

A button could then be added to call a script to delete a table:

📖 PHP Code H6.25

```
<form method="POST" action= "deletetable.php">

<input type="submit" name="submit2" value="Erase table">
</form>
```

The contents of the deletetable.php file is:

📖 PHP Code H6.26

```
<?php
/* Start of PHP3 Script */
/* Data of SQL-server */
$server= "$$$";        /* Address of database server */
$user= "$$$$";         /* FTP-username */
$password= "$$$$";     /* FTP-Password */
$database= "$$$$";     /* name of database */
$table= "mailing";
/* Accessing the server and creating the table */
MYSQL_CONNECT($server, $user, $password) or die ( "<H3>Server unreach-
able</H3>");
MYSQL_SELECT_DB($database) or die ( "<H3>database not existent</H3>");
MYSQL_QUERY( "DROP TABLE $table");
MYSQL_CLOSE();
print "<P>Table deleted. Click to go <a href='Javascript:history.back()' tar-
get='_top'>Back </a>";
?>
```

H6.8   Emailing details from a form

The following shows a simple example of how PHP can email the details from a form, to a remote email address:

📖 PHP Code H6.27

```
Send an email to me. Write your message here:
<form action="formmail.php3" method="POST">
<input type="hidden" name="recipient" value="fred@home">
<input type="hidden" name="subject" value="Reply Form">
<input type="text" name="input">
<input type="submit" value="Send">
</Form>
```

The contents of formmail.php3 are:

PHP Code H6.28

```php
<?php
$fmt_Response=implode("", file("response.htt"));
$fmt_Mail=implode("", file("mail.htt"));
while(list($Key, $Val)= each($HTTP_POST_VARS)) {
    $fmt_Response=str_replace("{$Key}", $Val, $fmt_Response);
    $fmt_Mail=str_replace("{$Key}", $Val, $fmt_Mail);
}
mail($HTTP_POST_VARS["recipient"], $HTTP_POST_VARS["subject"], $fmt_Mail);
echo $fmt_Response;
?>
```

The response.htt file just contains the page which appears after the user has successfully send the email, such as:

📖 **PHP Code H6.29**

```php
<p>Yippee!!! You've just sent an email to me.
<p><a href="Javascript:history.back()">Back</a>
```

📖 **PHP Code H6.30**

```php
<? If(!$submit){ ?>
<form name="test" method="post" action="<? echo $PHP_SELF;?>">
First name:
<input type="text" name="name" size="25">
<br>
realname:
<input type="text" name="realname" size="25">
Email:
<input type="text" name="email" size="25">
<input type="submit" name="submit2" value="submit">
</form>
<? } else { ?>
<? echo "$name
$realname
$email";?>
<? } ?>
```

H6.9   Database creation, addition and recall

The following shows a simple example of how PHP can create a table in a database on a MySQL server, and can create entries in a table, then recalling it, and then finally deleting the table. The table below contains real PHP code on the right-hand side, but you cannot see it because it has been processed by the server.

📖 **PHP Code H6.31**

```php
<?php
/* Start of PHP3 Script */
/* Data of SQL-server */
$server= "$$$$"; /* Address of server */
$user= "$$$"; /* FTP-username */
$password= "$$$"; /* FTP-Password */
$database= "$$$"; /* name of database */
$table= "datatest"; /* Name of table, you can select that */
/* Accessing the server and creating the table */
MYSQL_CONNECT($server, $user, $password) or die ( "<H3>Server unreach-
able</H3>");
MYSQL_SELECT_DB($database) or die ( "<H3>database not existent</H3>");
```

Result is 1

```
$result=MYSQL_QUERY( "CREATE TABLE $table (name varchar(25),email var-
char(25))");
print "Result is $result";
/* Terminate SQL connection*/
MYSQL_CLOSE();
?>
```

and to add data to a database:

📖 PHP Code H6.32

```
* Accessing SQL-server */
MYSQL_CONNECT($server, $user, $password) or die ( "<H3>Server unreach-
able</H3>");
MYSQL_SELECT_DB($database) or die ( "<H3>Database non existent</H3>");

MYSQL_QUERY( "INSERT INTO $table VALUES('Fred','fred@home.com')");
MYSQL_QUERY( "INSERT INTO $table VALUES('Bert','bert@myplace.com')");

/* Display number of entries */
$query="SELECT * FROM $table";
$result = MYSQL_QUERY($query);
/* How many of these users are there? */
$number = MYSQL_NUMROWS($result);
if ($number==0):
   echo "database empty";
   elseif ($number > 0):
   echo "$number rows in database";
endif;
mysql_close();

?>
```

Reading data from a database:

📖 PHP Code H6.33

```
<?php
/* Start of PHP3 Script */
/* Data of SQL-server */
$server= "$$$$"; /* Address of database server */
$user= "$$$$"; /* FTP-username */
$password= "$$$$"; /* FTP-Password */
$database= "$$$$"; /* name of database */
$table= "datatest"; /* Name of table, you can select that */
/* Accessing SQL-Server and querying table */
MYSQL_CONNECT($server, $user, $password) or die ( "<H3>Server unreach-
able</H3>");
MYSQL_SELECT_DB($database) or die ( "<H3>Database non existent</H3>");
$result=MYSQL_QUERY( "SELECT * FROM $table order by name");
/* Output data into a HTML table */
echo "<table border=\"1\" align=center width=50%";
echo "<tr>";
echo "<div color=\"#ffff00\">";
while ($field=mysql_fetch_field($result)) {
   echo "<th>$field->name</A></th>";
}
echo "</font></tr>";
while($row = mysql_fetch_row($result)) {
   echo "<tr>";
   for($i=0; $i < mysql_num_fields($result); $i++) {
      echo "<td align=center>$row[$i]</td>";
   }
```

```
    echo "</tr>\n";
}
echo "</table><BR><BR>";
/* Close SQL-connection */
MYSQL_CLOSE();
?>
```

And deleting a table:

📖 **PHP Code H6.34**

```
<?php
/* Accessing the server and deleting the table */
MYSQL_CONNECT($server, $user, $password) or die ( "<H3>Server unreach-
able</H3>");
MYSQL_SELECT_DB($database) or die ( "<H3>database not existent</H3>");
$result=MYSQL_QUERY( "DROP TABLE $table");
print "Result is ";
print $result;
/* Terminate SQL connection*/
MYSQL_CLOSE();
?>
```

H6.10   Flash

Macromedia Flash can be used with PHP, by setting variables in the Flash movies, and then using the GetURL() action. The following sets on the pressing of a button and assigns the following variables: subject, recipient and env_report, and sends them to the sendmail.php form:

```
On (Release)
Set Variable: "subject" = "Test Flash Form"
Set Variable: "recipient" = "w.buchanan@napier.ac.uk"
Set Variable: "env_report" = "REMOTE_HOST, HTTP_USER_AGENT, REMOTE_ADDRESS"
Get URL ("sendmail.php", vars=POST)
End On
```

The PHP form is then:

```
<?php
// redirect
echo "<H1>Email has been sent</H1>";
echo "<P>To: $recipient ";
echo "<P>Subject: $subject ";
$str = "<P>From: $email ($realname) <p>Question: $question <P>Refer:
$HTTP_USER_AGENT";
$str = $str . " $REMOTE_ADDR " . gethostbyaddr($REMOTE_ADDR);
// format of mail is mail(to, subject, header)
echo $str;
mail($recipient, $subject, $str);
echo "<p>Return to previous <a href='Javascript:history.back()'>page</a>.</p>";
?>
```

The text fields on the Flash form has the names of Recipient, Question, Realname and Subject, so these are sent to the PHP file.

H6.11   Networking

PHP supports a whole host of networking functions. These include:

checkdnsrr	Check DNS records corresponding to a given Internet host name or IP address int **checkdnsrr** (string host [, string type]) *type* may be any one of: A, MX, NS, SOA, PTR, CNAME, or ANY. The default is MX.
closelog	Close connection to system logger int **closelog** (void)
debugger_off	Disable internal PHP debugger int **debugger_off** (void)
debugger_on	Enable internal PHP debugger int **debugger_on** (string address)
define_syslog_variables	Initializes all syslog related constants void **define_syslog_variables** (void)
fsockopen	Open Internet or Unix domain socket connection int **fsockopen** (string hostname, int port [, int errno [, string errstr [, float timeout]]])
gethostbyaddr	Get the Internet host name corresponding to a given IP address string **gethostbyaddr** (string ip_address)
gethostbyname	Get the IP address corresponding to a given Internet host name string **gethostbyname** (string hostname)
gethostbynamel	Get a list of IP addresses corresponding to a given Internet host name array **gethostbynamel** (string hostname)
getmxrr	Get MX records corresponding to a given Internet host name int **getmxrr** (string hostname, array mxhosts [, array weight])
getprotobyname	Get protocol number associated with protocol name int **getprotobyname** (string name)
getprotobynumber	Get protocol name associated with protocol number string **getprotobynumber** (int number)
getservbyname	Get port number associated with an Internet service and protocol int **getservbyname** (string service, string protocol)
getservbyport	Get Internet service which corresponds to port and protocol string **getservbyport** (int port, string protocol)
ip2long	Converts a string containing an (IPv4) Internet Protocol dotted address into a proper address. int **ip2long** (string ip_address)
long2ip	Converts an (IPv4) Internet network address into a string in Internet standard dotted format string **long2ip** (int proper_address)
openlog	Open connection to system logger int **openlog** (string ident, int option, int facility)

`pfsockopen`	Open persistent Internet or Unix domain socket connection int **pfsockopen** (string hostname, int port [, int errno [, string errstr [, int timeout]]])
`socket_get_status`	Returns information about existing socket resource array **socket_get_status** (resource socket_get_status)
`socket_set_blocking`	Set blocking/non- blocking mode on a socket int **socket_set_blocking** (int socket descriptor, int mode)
`socket_set_timeout`	Set timeout period on a socket bool **socket_set_timeout** (int socket descriptor, int seconds, int microseconds)
`syslog`	Generate a system log message int **syslog** (int priority, string message)

The following gives a few examples of networking functions, to determine the host name or a given IP address (using gethostbyaddr), and vice-versa (using gethostbyname):

📖 PHP Code H6.35

```
$ip = gethostbyname ("www.php.net");
$str=sprintf("%u\n", ip2long($ip));
echo "$ip [$str]";

$str = gethostbyaddr ($ip);
print "<BR>DNS is $str";
$str=gethostbyname ($str);
print "<BR>IP address is is $str";
```

A sample run gives:

```
208.210.50.161 [3503436449 ]
DNS is php2.chek.com
IP address is is 208.210.50.161
```

The following shows a simple example of how PHP can open a socket with a remote sever:

📖 PHP Code H6.36

```
<form method="POST" action= "<?PHP echo($PHP_SELF); ?>">
Find an available domain name (for example, try www.php.net):
<P>
<INPUT name="domain" SIZE="20" MAXLENGTH="22">
<P>
<INPUT TYPE="SUBMIT" VALUE="Check name">
<INPUT TYPE="RESET" VALUE="Clear">
</P>
</FORM>
<hr>
<font size="2"><pre>
?>

function whois($domain, $server="www.geektools.com")
{
    $fp = fsockopen ($server, 43, &$errnr, &$errstr) or die("$errno: $errstr");
    fputs($fp, "$domain\n");
    while (!feof($fp))
    echo fgets($fp, 2048);
```

```
    fclose($fp);
}
?>
<?
If (isset ($domain)){
    echo (whois($domain));
}
?>
</pre></font>
```

A sample run gives:

```
Query:      www.php.net
Registry:   whois.opensrs.net
Results:
Registrant:
 PHP Development Team
 104 Shaftsberry Ct
 Cary, NC 27513
 US

 Domain Name: PHP.NET
  Administrative Contact:
     Development Team, PHP   rasmus@lerdorf.on.ca
     104 Shaftsberry Ct
     Cary, NC 27513
```

H7   ASP

H7.1   Introduction

ASP is a server-side include language, which can use VBScript or JavaScript for its server-side language. The server-side includes are enclosed between <% and %> tags, such as:

📖 **ASP Code H7.1**

```
<% for intcounter= 1 to 10 %>
<br>Value is <%=intcounter%>
<% next %>
```

which gives the output of:

```
Value is 1
Value is 2
Value is 3
Value is 4
Value is 5
Value is 6
Value is 7
Value is 8
Value is 9
Value is 10
```

In VBScript there is only one data type: **Variant**. This type can contain several different types of information, such as strings, or numeric values. It is this type that is returned by all the functions using in VBScript. As much as possible VBScript assumes the data type that is being used. For example if it is a numeric operation it will assume that the values are numeric, whereas a string search function would assume the values were strings. Strings, though, can always be defined within quotation marks.

In addition to variant, there are several subtypes, which can be used to convert from one representation to another, these are:

- **Empty**. This is where the variant is uninitialized. In a numeric value, it will be set to zero, in a string format it will be a Null string.
- **Null**. No valid data.
- **Boolean**. This contains a True or False.
- **Byte**. This contains an integer in the range 0 to 255.
- **Integer**. This contains an integer in the range -32,768 to 32,767.
- **Currency**. This contains a range from-922,337,203,685,477.5808 to 922,337,203,685,477. 5807.
- **Long**. This contains an integer in the range -2,147,483,648 to 2,147,483,647.
- **Single**. This contains a single-precision, floating-point number in the range -3.402823E38 to -1.401298E-45 for negative values; 1.401298E-45 to 3.402823E38 for positive values.

- **Double**. This contains a double-precision, floating-point number in the range -1.79769313486232E308 to -4.94065645841247E-324 for negative values; 4.94065645841247E-324 to 1.79769313486232E308 for positive values.
- **Date**. This contains a number that represents a date between January 1, 100 to December 31, 9999.
- **String**. This contains a variable-length string that can be up to approximately 2 billion characters in length.
- **Error**. This contains an error number.

There are several functions which can be used to convert from one format to another. These include:

CBool	Convert expression to a Variant of subtype Boolean.
CByte	Convert expression to a Variant of subtype Byte.
CCur	Convert expression to a Variant of subtype Currency.
CDate	Convert expression to a Variant of subtype Date.
CDbl	Convert expression to a Variant of subtype Double.
CInt	Convert expression to a Variant of subtype Integer.
CLng	Convert expression to a Variant of subtype Long.
CSng	Convert expression to a Variant of subtype Single.
CStr	Convert expression to a Variant of subtype String.

An example of this is given next,

📖 ASP Code H7.2

```
<%
val1 = 10
val2 = 20
result = Cstr(val1) + Cstr(val2)
response.write "<BR>Value is " & result
result = val1 + val2
response.write "<BR>Value is " & result
%>
```

which gives the output of:

```
Value is 1020
Value is 30
```

where it can be seen that the first operation has converted the values into strings and then implemented a string concatenate function, while the second version has implemented an arithmetic addition.

Arrays can be declared with the dim statement, the outline syntax is given next:

📖 ASP Code H7.3

```
<%
dim val1, val2
val1 = 10
val2 = 20
result = Cstr(val1) + Cstr(val2)
response.write "<BR>Value is " & result
```

```
result = val1 + val2
response.write "<BR>Value is " & result
%>
```

H7.2   ASP objects

ASP has six built-in objects. These are:

- **Application**. This can be used to share information among all users of a given application. As applications can be shared, it uses the Lock and Unlock methods to ensure that users do not access the same property, at the same time.
- **ObjectContext**. This can be used to either commit or abort a transaction, managed by Microsoft Transaction Server (MTS).
- **Request**. This can be used to get values from the client browser.
- **Response**. This can be used to send an output to the client.
- **Server**. This can be used to access to methods and properties on the server.
- **Session**. This can be used to store information needed for a particular user-session. In a session, variables are can be used between pages.

A listing of the main methods, and properties in given at the end of this chapter.

H7.3   ASP basics

The response.write() statement is used to output text from within ASP script. For example, from the previous example:

📖 **ASP Code H7.4**
```
<% for intcounter= 1 to 10 %>
<br>Value is <%=intcounter%>
<% next %>
```

could be changed to:

📖 **ASP Code H7.5**
```
<% for intcounter= 1 to 10
response.write "<br>Value is " & intcounter
next %>
```

Just as with PHP, HTML tags can be added to the output, in this case, the <br> tag is included to force a new-line before the values printed. The '&' character operates as the '.' operator in PHP, and appends one string onto another.

H7.3.1   Decisions

ASP uses either JavaScript syntax or VBScript; the following describes the usage of VBScript. The main decision state   ments are:

- **if…then…else** statement. Used to select statements using various conditions.
- **select case** statement. Used to select from one or more of a select of conditions.

The outline syntax of these is given below:

📖 ASP Code H7.6

```
<%
dim mon,da
da = date()
mon=month(da)
response.write "Current month is " & mon
if ((mon<4) or (mon>10)) then
    response.write("<BR>Wintertime")
elseif (mon<6) then
    response.write("<BR>Springtime")
elseif (mon<8) then
    response.write("<BR>Summertime")
else
    response.write("<BR>Autumtime")
end if
%>
```

The equivalent using the select case statement is:

📖 ASP Code H7.7

```
<%
dim mon,da
da = date()
mon=month(da)
response.write "Current month is " & mon
select case mon
    case 1,2,3,11,12
        response.write("<BR>Wintertime")
    case 4,5
        response.write("<BR>Springtime")
    case 6,7
        response.write("<BR>Summertime")
    case 8,9,10
        response.write("<BR>Autumtime")
    end select
%>
```

A sample run is:

```
Current month is 4
Springtime
```

H7.3.2   Loops

The four main loops in VBScript are:

- **For...Next** statement. This statement repeats a group of statements for a given number of times.
- **While...Wend** statement. This statement repeats a group of statements until a given condition is True.
- **Do...Loop while** statement. This statement repeats a group of statements while a given condition is True.
- **Do...Loop until** statement. This statement repeats a group of statements while a given condition is True.

The first example shows the usage of the **for...next** statement:

📖 ASP Code H7.8

```
<%
response.write "<table>"
response.write "<tr><td>Decimal</td><td>Hexadecimal</td><td>Octal</td></tr>"
for i=1 to 10
    response.write "<tr><td>" & i & "</td><td>" & hex(i) & "</td><td>" & oct(i)
    & "</td></tr>"
next
response.write "</table>"
%>
```

The next example shows the same implementation using the **while...wend** statement:

📖 ASP Code H7.9

```
<%
response.write "<table>"
response.write "<tr><td>Decimal</td><td>Hexadecimal</td><td>Octal</td></tr>"
i=0
while (i<10)
    i=i+1
    response.write "<tr><td>" & i & "</td><td>" & hex(i) & "</td><td>" & oct(i)
    & "</td></tr>"
wend
response.write "</table>"
%>
```

The next example shows the same implementation using the **do...loop until** statement:

📖 ASP Code H7.10

```
<%
response.write "<table>"
response.write "<tr><td>Decimal</td><td>Hexadecimal</td><td>Octal</td></tr>"
i=0
do
    i=i+1
    response.write "<tr><td>" & i & "</td><td>" & hex(i) & "</td><td>" & oct(i)
    & "</td></tr>"
loop until i>9
response.write "</table>"
%>
```

A sample run is shown next:

Decimal	Hexadecimal	Octal
1	1	1
2	2	2
3	3	3
4	4	4
5	5	5
6	6	6
7	7	7
8	8	10

9	9	11
10	A	12

It is possible to embed HTML tags within the ASP code. For example the following example shows that the variable fontsize is used to vary the font size in the <font> tag. The tags produced will be:

<font size=1>
<font size=2>
<font size=3>
<font size=4>
<font size=5>

📖 **ASP Code H7.11**

```
<%
for fontsize= 1 to 5
response.write "<font size = " & fontsize & "/>"
response.write "<BR>Hello</font>"
next
%>
```

A sample run is as follows:

Hello
Hello
Hello
Hello
Hello

H7.3.3 Functions

Functions are reusable pieces of code which can be called from several points in a WWW page, or can be reused in different pages. VBScript uses the function...end function statement to implement this. Parameters are passed either as byval, where the value is passed, or byref, where the reference to a parameter is made. Parameters in the function cannot be changed if the byval is used. In this case the byref is used.

📖 **ASP Code H7.12**

```
<%
val1 = 11
val2 = 21

function addfunction(byval a, byval b)
addfunction=(a+b)
end function

result=addfunction(val1,val2)
response.write "<BR>Result is " & result
%>
```

A sample run is as follows:

```
Result is 32
```

Functions only return a single value. If more than one value or none at all, is required to be returned, then the sub...end sub statement can be used. The following shows an example of the sub statement which implements the previous example:

📖 **ASP Code H7.13**

```
<%
val1 = 11
v    al2 = 21
sub addfunction2(byval a, byval b, byref c)
   c=a+b
end sub
call addfunction2(val1,val2,result)
response.write "<BR>Result is " & result

%>
```

H7.3.4 Date and time

VBScript supports several data and time functions, these include:

Function	Return type description
CDate	Convert expression to a Variant of subtype Date.
Date	Current system date.
DateAdd	Date to which a specified time interval has been added. DateAdd(*interval, number, date*)
DateDiff	Number of intervals between two dates. DateDiff(*interval, date1, date2* [*,firstdayofweek*[, *firstweekofyear*]])
DatePart	Specified part of a given date. DatePart(*interval, date*[, *firstdayofweek*[, *firstweekofyear*]])
DateSerial	Variant of subtype Date for a specified year, month, and day. DateSerial(*year, month, day*)
DateValue	Variant of subtype Date. DateValue(*date*)
Day	Whole number between 1 and 31, inclusive, representing the day of the month. Day(*date*)
Hour	Whole number between 0 and 23, inclusive, representing the hour of the day. Hour(*time*)
IsDate	Boolean value indicating whether an expression can be converted to a date. IsDate(*expression*)
Minute	Whole number between 0 and 59, inclusive, representing the minute of the hour. Minute(*time*)
Month	Whole number between 1 and 12, inclusive, representing the month of the year. Month(*date*)
MonthName	String indicating the specified month. MonthName(*month*[, *abbreviate*])

Now	Current date and time according to the setting of your computer's system date and time.
Second	Whole number between 0 and 59, inclusive, representing the second of the minute. Second(*time*)
Time	Variant of subtype Date indicating the current system time.
Timer	Number of seconds that have elapsed since 12:00 AM (midnight).
TimeSerial	Variant of subtype Date containing the time for a specific hour, minute, and second. TimeSerial(*hour, minute, second*)
TimeValue	Variant of subtype Date containing the time. TimeValue(*time*)
Weekday	Whole number representing the day of the week. Weekday(*date*, [*firstdayofweek*])
WeekdayName	String indicating the specified day of the week. WeekdayName(*weekday, abbreviate, firstdayofweek*)
Year	Whole number representing the year. Year(*date*)

The time() function can be used to determine the current time, and the date() function to determine the current date, such as:

📖 ASP Code H7.14

```
<%
response.write "<BR>Current time is : " & Time()
response.write "<BR>Current date is : " & Date()
response.write "<BR>Current date/time is : " & now()
%>
```

A sample run is:

```
Current time is : 16:59:15
Current date is : 06/04/2002
Current date/time is : 06/04/2002 16:59:15
```

The month() function shows the value for the current month and a value. This can then be converted into a month name using the monthname() function. The Year() function can display the current year.

📖 ASP Code H7.15

```
<%
da = date()
day=day()
mon=month()
response.write "Day is " & day(da)
response.write "Month is " & mon
response.write "Name of the month is " & monthname(mon)
```

```
response.write "Year is " & year(da)
%>
```

A sample run is:

```
Day is 6
Month is 4
Name of the month is April
Year is 2002
```

The day of the week can be displayed with the weekday() function, and this can be convered into a name with the weekdayname() function.

📖 ASP Code H7.16

```
<%
da = date()
wkday=weekday(da)
response.write "Today is week day number: " & wkday
response.write "<BR>which is " & weekdayname(wkday,0,vbSunday)
%>
```

A sample run is:

```
Today is week day number: 7
which is Saturday
```

H7.3.5 Cookies

ASP uses the Cookies collection of the Response object to set values in cookies. The properties that can be set are:

- **Expires**. Sets the expiry time and date for the cookie.
- **Domain**. The domain that is allowed to read the cookie.
- **Secure**. Defines whether a secure session is used.
- **Path**. If specified then the cookie is only sent to requests to this path.

If no properties are used, it is assumed that an item value is being set. For example the following defines two items to be stored: freds and berts. The values these are given are Test 01, and Test 02 respectively:

📖 ASP Code H7.17

```
<%
Response.Cookies("freds") = "Test 01"
Response.Cookies("freds").Expires = "July 31, 2010"
Response.Cookies("freds").Secure = FALSE

Response.Cookies("berts") = "Test 02"
Response.Cookies("berts").Expires = "July 31, 2010"
Response.Cookies("berts").Secure = FALSE
Response.write "Cookie values set"
%>
```

These values can be read back using Response.Cookies() to read the cookie and return the value to a variable (in this case, str).

📖 **ASP Code H7.18**

```
<%
str= Request.Cookies("freds")
response.write "Freds=" & str

str= Request.Cookies("berts")
response.write "<BR>Berts=" & str
%>
```

A typical application is to save values from a form to a cookie. The following will write parameters to a cookie, using an external ASP script:

📖 **ASP Code H7.19**

```
<form name="form2" method="post" action="asp_writeasp_to_cookie.asp">
<table border="0" width="395">
<tr>
<td> Name:</td>
<td><input type="text" name="name"></td>
</tr>
<tr>
<td> Email:</td>
<td> <input type="text" name="email"></td>
</tr>
<tr>
<td> Age:</td>
<td><input type="text" name="age"></td>
</tr>
</table>
<input type="submit" name="Submit" value="Submit">
</form>
```

A sample run will give:

Name:	Fred Smith
Email:	fred@home
Age:	32

The ASP file gives:

```
Name:fred smith
Email: fred@home
Age: 32
Values written to cookie
Return
```

The cookie can then be listed with:

📖 **ASP Code H7.20**

```
Value of the cookie is <%= Request.Cookies("myCookie") %>
Name: <%= Request.Cookies("myCookie")("name") %>
Email: <%= Request.Cookies("myCookie")("email") %>
Age: <%= Request.Cookies("myCookie")("age") %>
```

and a run of this gives:

```
Value of the cookie is name=fred+smith&email=fred%40home&age=34
Name: fred smith
Email: fred@home
Age: 34
```

The script for the **asp_writeasp_to_cookie.asp** file is:

```
<%
name=Request.Form("name")
email=Request.Form("email")
age=Request.Form("age")
response.write "Name:" & name
response.write "<BR>Email: " & email
response.write "<BR>Age: " & age

Response.Cookies("mycookie")("name")=name
Response.Cookies("mycookie")("email")=email
Response.Cookies("mycookie")("age")=age

Response.Cookies("mycookie").Expires = "July 31, 2010"

Response.write "<BR>Values written to cookie"
Response.write "<BR><a href='Javascript:history.back()'>Return</A>"
%>
```

In this case the cookie has been saved as a collection of cookies ("mycookie"), and will be saved with the HTTP header of:

```
Set-Cookie:mycookie=name=fred+smith&email=fred%40home&age=34
```

It can be seen that the '&' character delimits the keys set for the cookie. The '@' character is defined with the %40 character (which is the equivalent ASCII character for a '@').

H7.3.6   Application object

The Application object can be used to share information among all users of a given application. As applications can be shared, it uses the Lock and Unlock methods to ensure that users do not access the same property, at the same time. The following example uses an application variable named NumVisits to store the number of access there has been to a particular page. The Lock method makes sure that no other client is accessing the variable while it is being modified. Once it is set, the Unlock method can then be used to allow other users to access the variable.

📖 **ASP Code H7.21**
```
<%
Application.Lock
Application("NumVisits") = Application("NumVisits") + 1
Application.Unlock
str= Application("NumVisits")
response.write "This page has been visited " & str & " times"
%>
```

The Application.Contents collection stores the application variables, and their keys. The following example iterates over all of the application variables, and displays their key names:

📖 ASP Code H7.22

```
<%
Application("MyVar") = "No data"
Application("Var1") = "Hello"
Application("Var2") = "Bill's"
Application("Var3") = "Fred's"
For Each Key in Application.Contents
    Response.Write "<BR>" & Key
Next
%>
```

A sample run gives:

```
NumVisits
MyVar
Var1
Var2
Var3
```

The Application.Contents collection stores the application variables, and their keys. The following example iterates over all of the application variables, and displays their key names:

📖 ASP Code H7.23

```
<%
Application("MyVar") = "No data"
Application("Var1") = "Hello"
Application("Var2") = "Bill's"
Application("Var3") = "Fred's"
For Each Key in Application.Contents
    Response.Write "<BR>" & Key
Next
%>
```

A sample run gives:

```
NumVisits
MyVar
Var1
Var2
Var3
```

and to display the contents of the application variables:

📖 ASP Code H7.24

```
<%
Application("MyVar") = "No data"
Application("Var1") = "Hello"
Application("Var2") = "Bill's"
Application("Var3") = "Fred's"
For Each Key in Application.Contents
Response.Write "<BR>" & Key
Next
%>
```

A sample run gives:

```
NumVisits=3
MyVar=No data
Var1=Hello
Var2=Bill's
Var3=Fred's
```

H7.3.7 Request object

The Request object can be used to determine the values that the client browser passed to the server during an HTTP request. All variables that were passed can be accessed by calling **Request**(*variable*), or with one of the following:

- Response(*variable*).QueryString . This can be used to determine the value of a query string.
- Response(variable).Form. This can be used to determine the parameters set in a form.
- Response(variable).Cookies . This can be used to determine the values of cookie values.
- Response(variable).ClientCertificate . This can be used to access the client certificate.
- Response(variable).ServerVariables . This can be used to access the server variables.

For example the following interrogates the REMOTE_ADDR variable from ServerVariables:

📖 **ASP Code H7.25**

```
<%
response.write "<p>"
for each sv in request.servervariables
response.write "<br>" & "<b>" & sv &"</B>" & "=" & request.servervariables(sv)
& "<br>"
next
%>
```

A sample run gives:

```
ALL_HTTP=HTTP_ACCEPT:*/* HTTP_ACCEPT_LANGUAGE:en-gb HTTP_CONNECTION:Keep-Alive
HTTP_HOST:192.168.0.11 HTTP_USER_AGENT:Mozilla/4.0 (compatible; MSIE 6.0; Win-
dows NT 5.1) HTTP_COOKIE: Freds=Test+01; berts=Test+02; age=23;
email=fred%40home; name=fred; form%5Fname=freddy+boy; form%5Femail=fred%40home;
form%5Fage=freerere; mycookie=age=32&email=fred%40home&name=fred+smith;
ASPSESSIONIDGQQGGEIO=CBMPPBKCCECBHPFOHFOEPBAM;
ASPSESSIONIDQQGQGPAG=HIKJCPLCEDEGPAAJEKDAKEAM HTTP_ACCEPT_ENCODING:gzip, de-
flate
ALL_RAW=Accept: */* Accept-Language: en-gb Connection: Keep-Alive Host:
192.168.0.11 User-Agent: Mozilla/4.0 (compatible; MSIE 6.0; Windows NT 5.1)
Cookie: Freds=Test+01; berts=Test+02; age=23; email=fred%40home; name=fred;
form%5Fname=freddy+boy; form%5Femail=fred%40home; form%5Fage=freerere; my-
cookie=age=32&email=fred%40home&name=fred+smith;
ASPSESSIONIDGQQGGEIO=CBMPPBKCCECBHPFOHFOEPBAM;
ASPSESSIONIDQQGQGPAG=HIKJCPLCEDEGPAAJEKDAKEAM Accept-Encoding: gzip, deflate
APPL_MD_PATH=/LM/W3SVC/1/ROOT
APPL_PHYSICAL_PATH=c:\inetpub\wwwroot\
AUTH_PASSWORD=
AUTH_TYPE=
AUTH_USER=
CERT_COOKIE=
CERT_FLAGS=
CERT_ISSUER=
CERT_KEYSIZE=
```

```
CERT_SECRETKEYSIZE=
CERT_SERIALNUMBER=
CERT_SERVER_ISSUER=
CERT_SERVER_SUBJECT=
CERT_SUBJECT=
CONTENT_LENGTH=0
CONTENT_TYPE=
GATEWAY_INTERFACE=CGI/1.1
HTTPS=off
HTTPS_KEYSIZE=
HTTPS_SECRETKEYSIZE=
HTTPS_SERVER_ISSUER=
HTTPS_SERVER_SUBJECT=
INSTANCE_ID=1
INSTANCE_META_PATH=/LM/W3SVC/1
LOCAL_ADDR=192.168.0.11
LOGON_USER=
PATH_INFO=/www/asp_networking.asp
PATH_TRANSLATED=c:\inetpub\wwwroot\www\asp_networking.asp
QUERY_STRING=
REMOTE_ADDR=192.168.0.12
REMOTE_HOST=192.168.0.12
REMOTE_USER=
REQUEST_METHOD=GET
SCRIPT_NAME=/www/asp_networking.asp
SERVER_NAME=192.168.0.11
SERVER_PORT=80
SERVER_PORT_SECURE=0
SERVER_PROTOCOL=HTTP/1.1
SERVER_SOFTWARE=Microsoft-IIS/5.1
URL=/www/asp_networking.asp
HTTP_ACCEPT=*/*
HTTP_ACCEPT_LANGUAGE=en-gb
HTTP_CONNECTION=Keep-Alive
HTTP_HOST=192.168.0.11
HTTP_USER_AGENT=Mozilla/4.0 (compatible; MSIE 6.0; Windows NT 5.1)
HTTP_COOKIE= Freds=Test+01; berts=Test+02; age=23; email=fred%40home;
name=fred; form%5Fname=freddy+boy; form%5Femail=fred%40home;
form%5Fage=freerere; mycookie=age=32&email=fred%40home&name=fred+smith;
ASPSESSIONIDGQQGGEIO=CBMPPBKCCECBHPFOHFOEPBAM;
ASPSESSIONIDQQGQPAG=HIKJCPLCEDEGPAAJEKDAKEAM
HTTP_ACCEPT_ENCODING=gzip, deflate
```

The HTTP_REFERER variable is useful in determining the previous page that linked to the current page. This can be used as a link to the previous page with:

📖 ASP Code H7.26

```
<a href="<% = Request.ServerVariables("HTTP_REFERER") %>">Previous Page</a>
```

To display the main parameters of a session:

📖 ASP Code H7.27

```
Your web agent is <%=Request.ServerVariables("HTTP_USER_AGENT")%>
<br>Your IP address is <%=Request.ServerVariables("REMOTE_ADDR")%>
<br>Your DNS is
<%=Request.ServerVariables("REMOTE_HOST")%>
<br>Your request method is <%=Request.ServerVariables("REQUEST_METHOD")%>
<br>Your server name is <%=Request.ServerVariables("SERVER_NAME")%>
<br>Your server port is <%=Request.ServerVariables("SERVER_PORT")%>
<br>Your server software is <%=Request.ServerVariables("SERVER_SOFTWARE")%>
```

A sample run gives:

```
Your web agent is Mozilla/4.0 (compatible; MSIE 6.0; Windows NT 5.1)
Your IP address is 192.168.0.12
Your DNS is 192.168.0.12
Your request method is GET
Your server name is 192.168.0.11
Your server port is 80
Your server software is Microsoft-IIS/5.1
```

The REMOTE_ADDR server variable can be used to determine the client's IP address:

📖 ASP Code H7.28

```
<%
addr = Request.ServerVariables("REMOTE_ADDR")
addr1 = Left(addr, 7)
if (addr1 = "146.176") then
%>
You're from Napier (<%=addr1%>)

<% else %>

You're not from Napier (<%=addr1%>)

<% end if %>
```

This script can be enhanced so that the first part of the string is taken. The instr() function can be used to find a token character, and set a string up to the specified token. For example to scan for the first part of the IP address:

📖 ASP Code H7.29

```
<% IPaddress=Request.ServerVariables("REMOTE_ADDR")%>
<% firstpart=instr(IPAddress,".")%>
The first part of your IP address is
<% =left(IPAddress, firstpart-1) %>
```

A sample run gives:

```
The first part of your IP address is 192.
```

Otherwise the split() function can be used to split the IP address into a number of string fragments:

📖 ASP Code H7.30

```
<%IPAddress=Request.ServerVariables("REMOTE_ADDR")%>
Your IP address split into four fields is:
<% ipfield=split(IPAddress, ".") %>
<BR> First part:  <% = ipfield(0) %>
<BR> Second part: <% = ipfield(1) %>
<BR> Third part:  <% = ipfield(2) %>
<BR> Fourth part: <% = ipfield(3) %>
```

A sample run gives:

```
Your IP address split into four fields is:
First part: 192
Second part: 168
Third part: 0
Fourth part: 12
```

H7.4   File system access

ASP can gain accesses to the file system on the WWW server using the FileSystemObject (FSO) object model. The main objects used are FileSystem Object, Drive Object, Textstream Object, File Object and Folder Object. The FSO is programmed using the CreateObject method to create a FileSystemObject object. The methods are that can be applied include:

- GetDrive. Gets the drive object.
- GetFolder. Gets the folder object.
- GetFile. Gets the file object.

For example the following example uses the GetFolder() method to determine the folder element of the file name.

📖 **ASP Code H7.31**

```
<%
Function GetFolderType(filespec)
Dim myfso, f, str
    Set myfso = CreateObject("Scripting.FileSystemObject")
    Set f = myfso.GetFolder(filespec)
    str = UCase(f.Name) & " is a " & f.Type
    GetFolderType = str
End Function

response.write GetFolderType("c:\inetpub")
%>
```

H7.4.1   Filesystem object

The Filesystem object has the following property:

- **Drives**. Returns a Drives collection consisting of all Drive objects available on the local machine

and the following methods:

- BuildPath.
- CopyFile.
- CopyFolder.
- CreateFolder.
- CreateTextFile.
- DeleteFile.
- DeleteFolder.
- DriveExists.
- FileExists.
- FolderExists.

- GetAbsolutePathName.
- GetBaseName.
- GetDrive.
- GetDriveName.
- GetExtensionName.
- GetFile.
- GetFileName.
- GetFolder.
- GetParentFolderName.
- GetSpecialFolder.
- GetTempName.
- MoveFile.
- MoveFolder.
- OpenTextFile.

For example, the following uses the FileExist method to determine if a file exists:

📖 **ASP Code H7.32**

```
<%
Set myfso = CreateObject("Scripting.FileSystemObject")
if (myfso.FileExists("c:\config.sys")) then
   response.write ("Config.sys exists")
else
   response.write("Config.sys does not exist")
end if
%>
```

H7.4.2   Drives object

The main properties of the Drives object are:

- AvailableSpace.
- DriveLetter.
- DriveType.
- FileSystem.
- FreeSpace.
- IsReady.
- Path.
- RootFolder.
- SerialNumber.
- ShareName.
- TotalSize.
- VolumeName.

The following script will test each of the connected drives, and list their main properties. The IsReady property is used to test if the drive is ready to be tested.

📖 **ASP Code H7.33**

```
<%
Dim Drives
Dim Drive
```

```
Dim FSO

Set FSO = CreateObject("Scripting.FileSystemObject")

Set Drives = FSO.Drives

For Each Drive In Drives
    if (Drive.IsReady) then
        response.write "<BR>Drive Letter = " & Drive.DriveLetter
        response.write "<BR>Drive Letter (MB) = " &
                                Drive.AvailableSpace/1024/1024
        response.write "<BR>Drive File System = " & Drive.FileSystem
        response.write "<BR>Drive Free Space = " & Drive.FreeSpace
        response.write "<BR>Drive Path = " & Drive.Path
        response.write "<BR>Drive Root Folder = " & Drive.RootFolder
        response.write "<BR>Drive Serial Number = " & Drive.SerialNumber
        response.write "<BR>Drive Share Name = " & Drive.ShareName
        response.write "<BR>Drive Total Size (MB) = " & Drive.TotalSize/1024/1024
        response.write "<BR>Drive Volume Name = " & Drive.VolumeName
        response.write "<BR>"
        end if
next
%>
```

A sample run gives:

```
Drive Letter = C
Drive Letter (MB) = 4092.40966796875
Drive File System = NTFS
Drive Free Space = 4291202560
Drive Path = C:
Drive Root Folder = C:\
Drive Serial Number = -1139669027
Drive Share Name =
Drive Total Size (MB) = 39079.9638671875
Drive Volume Name =

Drive Letter = D
Drive Letter (MB) = 0
Drive File System = CDFS
Drive Free Space = 0
Drive Path = D:
Drive Root Folder = D:\
Drive Serial Number = -283519743
Drive Share Name =
Drive Total Size (MB) = 645.76171875
Drive Volume Name = PCG101B1001
```

The following shows the drives on the server, and their type. It uses the Drives property of the Filesystem object to determine the drives on the system, and the DriveType property of the disk object to determine the disk type. The DriveType property is set to a 1 if the drive is a removable disk, a 2 for a fixed disk, and so on.

📖 ASP Code H7.34

```
<%
Function GetDriveType(Drive)
Dim Str

    Select Case Drive.DriveType
    Case 1
```

```
      Str= "Removable"
   Case 2
      Str = "Fixed"
   Case 3
      Str = "Network"
   Case 4
      Str = "CD-ROM"
   Case 5
      Str = "RAM Disk"
   Case Else
      Str = "Unknown"
   End Select

   GetDriveType = Str
End Function

Dim Drives
Dim Drive
Dim FSO

   Set FSO = CreateObject("Scripting.FileSystemObject")

   Set Drives = FSO.Drives

   For Each Drive In Drives
      response.write "<BR>Drive = " & Drive & "Type: " & GetDriveType(drive)
   next
%>
```

A sample run gives:

```
Drive = A:Type: Removable
Drive = C:Type: Fixed
Drive = D:Type: CD-ROM
```

H7.4.3   File object

The File object has several properties, such as:

- Attributes.
- DateCreated.
- DateLastAccessed.
- DateLastModified.
- Drive.
- Name.
- ParentFolder.
- Path.
- ShortName.
- ShortPath.
- Size.
- Type.

and the following methods:

- Copy . Used to copy a file.
- Delete . Used to delete a file.

- Move . Used to move a file.
- OpenAsTextSteam. Used to open the file as a text stream.

The following shows how ASP script can be used to display the main properties of a file.

📖 **ASP Code H7.35**
```
<%
Dim S
Dim myfso
Dim file
Dim Attr

Set myfso = CreateObject("Scripting.FileSystemObject")
Set File = myfso.GetFile("c:\config.sys")

response.write    "<BR>Name: "      & file.Name
response.write    "<BR>Type: "      & file.Type
response.write    "<BR>Created: "   & file.DateCreated
response.write    "<BR>Accessed: "  & file.DateLastAccessed
response.write    "<BR>Modified: "  & file.DataLastModified
response.write    "<BR>Size: "      & file.Size
%>
```
A sample run is as follows:

```
Name: CONFIG.SYS
Type: System file
Created: 11/11/2001 12:10:57
Accessed: 27/11/2001 01:00:00
Modified: 27/11/2001 13:22:00
Size: 0
```

The Attributes property of the File object can be used to determine the attributes of a file. It runs an 8-bit value, where the first bit represents that the file is read-only, the next bit represents that the file is hidden, and so on. The script in the following example tests for these using the And bitwise operator. The GetFile() method is used to get the file object.

📖 **ASP Code H7.36**
```
<%
Const FileAttrNormal      =  0
Const FileAttrReadOnly    =  1
Const FileAttrHidden      =  2
Const FileAttrSystem      =  4
Const FileAttrVolume      =  8
Const FileAttrDirectory   =  16
Const FileAttrArchive     =  32
Const FileAttrAlias       =  64
Const FileAttrCompressed  =  128

Function GetFileAttr(fname) ' File can be a file or folder

Dim S
Dim myfso
Dim file
Dim Attr

    Set myfso = CreateObject("Scripting.FileSystemObject")
    Set File = myfso.GetFile(fname)
```

```
   Attr = File.Attributes

   If Attr = 0 Then
      GetFileAttr = "Normal"
      Exit Function
   End If

   If Attr And FileAttrDirectory   Then Str = Str & "Directory "
   If Attr And FileAttrReadOnly    Then Str = Str & "Read-Only "
   If Attr And FileAttrHidden      Then Str = Str & "Hidden "
   If Attr And FileAttrSystem      Then Str = Str & "System "
   If Attr And FileAttrVolume      Then Str = Str & "Volume "
   If Attr And FileAttrArchive     Then Str = Str & "Archive "
   If Attr And FileAttrAlias       Then Str = Str & "Alias "
   If Attr And FileAttrCompressed  Then Str = Str & "Compressed "

   GetFileAttr = Str

End Function

file="c:\config.sys"
response.write "File: " & file " Attributes: " & GetFileAttr(file)
%>
```

A sample run gives:

```
File: c:\config.sys Attributes: Archive
```

H7.4.4 Folders object

The Folders object has several properties, such as:

Attributes.
DateCreated.
DateLastAccessed.
DateLastModified.
Drive Property.
Files.
IsRootFolder.
Name.
ParentFolder.
Path.
ShortName.
ShortPath.
Size.
SubFolders.
Type.

The following shows how ASP script can be used to display the main properties of a folder.

📖 ASP Code H7.37
```
<%
Dim myfso
Dim fold

Set myfso = CreateObject("Scripting.FileSystemObject")
```

```
Set Fold = myfso.GetFolder("c:\inetpub")

response.write "<BR>Name: " & fold.DateCreated
response.write "<BR>Type: " & fold.DateLastAccessed
response.write "<BR>Created: " & fold.DateLastModified
response.write "<BR>Accessed: " & fold.Drive
response.write "<BR>Size: " & fold.IsRootFolder
response.write "<BR>Name: " & fold.Name
response.write "<BR>Parent Folder: " & fold.ParentFolder
response.write "<BR>Path: " & fold.Path
response.write "<BR>ShortName: " & fold.ShortName
response.write "<BR>ShortPath: " & fold.ShortPath
response.write "<BR>Size: " & fold.Size
response.write "<BR>Type: " & fold.Type
%>
```

An example run is given next:

```
Name: 15/03/2002 19:11:47
Type: 12/04/2002 18:09:35
Created: 15/03/2002 19:14:13
Accessed: c:
Size: False
Name: Inetpub
Parent Folder: C:\
Path: C:\Inetpub
ShortName: inetpub
ShortPath: C:\inetpub
Size: 562221815
Type: File Folder
```

The Files and Subfolders properties of the Folder object return one or more names. Thus they must be used in a for each .. in statement. The following shows an example which lists the files and the subfolders within the Inetpub folder.

📖 ASP Code H7.38

```
<%
Dim myfso
Dim fold

Set myfso = CreateObject("Scripting.FileSystemObject")
Set Fold = myfso.GetFolder("c:\inetpub")

response.write "<BR>Name: " & fold.DateCreated
response.write "<BR>Type: " & fold.DateLastAccessed
response.write "<BR>Created: " & fold.DateLastModified
response.write "<BR>Accessed: " & fold.Drive
response.write "<BR>Size: " & fold.IsRootFolder
response.write "<BR>Name: " & fold.Name
response.write "<BR>Parent Folder: " & fold.ParentFolder
response.write "<BR>Path: " & fold.Path
response.write "<BR>ShortName: " & fold.ShortName
response.write "<BR>ShortPath: " & fold.ShortPath
response.write "<BR>Size: " & fold.Size
response.write "<BR>Type: " & fold.Type
%>

Subfolders: C:\Inetpub\AdminScripts
Subfolders: C:\Inetpub\iissamples
Subfolders: C:\Inetpub\mailroot
```

```
Subfolders: C:\Inetpub\Scripts
Subfolders: C:\Inetpub\wwwroot
```

The Folders object has the following methods:

- Copy.
- Delete.
- Move.
- CreateTextFile.

H7.5   ASP reference

H7.5.1   Application object

The collections used are:

Contents	This contains all of the items that have been added to the Application through script commands.
StaticObjects	This contains all of the objects added to the session with the <OBJECT> tag.

and the methods used are:

Lock	This method prevents other clients from modifying **Application** object properties.
Unlock	This method allows other clients to modify **Application** object properties

H7.5.2   Request object

The request object is used to get values from the browser. Its general syntax is:

Request[*.collection|property|method*] (*variable*)

The collections are:

ClientCertificate	Fields stored in the client certificate that is sent in the HTTP request.
Cookies	Cookies sent in the HTTP request.
Form	Form elements in the HTTP request body.
QueryString	Variables in the HTTP query string.
ServerVariables	Predetermined environment variables.

The method is:

BinaryRead	Retrieves data sent to the server from the client as part of a POST request.

The properties are:

TotalBytes	Total number of bytes the client is sending in the body of the request.

H7.5.3 Response object

The response object is used to send values to the output. Its general syntax is:

Response._collection|property|method_
The collection is:

Cookies   This specifies the cookies collection

The properties are:

Buffer	Indicates whether page output is buffered.
CacheControl	Sets whether proxy servers are able to cache the output generated by ASP.
Charset	Appends the name of the character set to the content-type header.
ContentType	Specifies the HTTP content type for the response.
Expires	Specifies the length of time before a page cached on a browser expires.
ExpiresAbsolute	Specifies the date and time on which a page cached on a browser expires.
IsClientConnected	Indicates whether the client has disconnected from the server.
Pics	Adds the value of a PICS label to the pics-label field of the response header.
Status	The value of the status line returned by the server.

The methods are:

AddHeader	Sets the HTML header _name_ to _value._
AppendToLog	Adds a string to the end of the Web server log entry for this request.
BinaryWrite	Writes the given information to the current HTTP output without any character-set conversion.
Clear	Erases any buffered HTML output.
End	Stops processing the .asp file and returns the current result.
Flush	Sends buffered output immediately.
Redirect	Sends a redirect message to the browser, causing it to attempt to connect to a different URL.
Write	Writes a variable to the current HTTP output as a string.

H7.5.4 Server object

The **Server** object allows access to the server. Its syntax is:

Server._property|method_

The methods are:

CreateObject	Creates an instance of a server component.
HTMLEncode	Applies HTML encoding to the specified string.

MapPath	Maps the specified virtual path, either the absolute path on the current server or the path relative to the current page, into a physical path.
URLEncode	Applies URL encoding rules, including escape characters, to the string.

and the property used is:

ScriptTimeout	The time that a script can run before it times out.

H7.5.5   Session object

The session allows access to information on a session. Its syntax is:

Response.*collection|property|method*

The collections are:

Contents	Contains the items that you have added to the session with script commands.
StaticObjects	Contains the objects created with the <OBJECT> tag and given session scope.

The methods is:

Abandon	Destroys a **Session** object and releases its resources.

The properties are:

CodePage	The codepage that will be used for symbol mapping.
LCID	Locale identifier.
SessionID	Session identification for this user.
Timeout	Timeout period for the session state for this application, in minutes

H7.5.6   Function reference

Function	Return type description
Abs	Absolute value of a number.
Array	Variant containing an array.
Asc	ANSI character code corresponding to the first letter in a string.
Atn	Arctangent of a number.
CBool	Convert expression to a Variant of subtype Boolean.
CByte	Convert expression to a Variant of subtype Byte.
CCur	Convert expression to a Variant of subtype Currency.
CDate	Convert expression to a Variant of subtype Date.
CDbl	Convert expression to a Variant of subtype Double.
Chr	Character associated with the specified ANSI character code.
CInt	Convert expression to a Variant of subtype Integer.
CLng	Convert expression to a Variant of subtype Long.
Cos	Cosine of an angle.

CSng	Convert expression to a Variant of subtype Single.
CStr	Convert expression to a Variant of subtype String.
Date	Current system date.
DateAdd	Date to which a specified time interval has been added.
DateDiff	Number of intervals between two dates.
DatePart	Specified part of a given date.
DateSerial	Variant of subtype Date for a specified year, month, and day.
DateValue	Variant of subtype Date.
Day	Whole number between 1 and 31, inclusive, representing the day of the month.
Eval	Expression and returns the result.
Exp	e (the base of natural logarithms) raised to a power.
Filter	Zero-based array containing subset of a string array based on a specified filter criteria.
Fix	Integer portion of a number.
FormatCurrency	Expression formatted as a currency value using the currency symbol defined in the system control panel.
FormatDateTime	Expression formatted as a date or time.
FormatNumber	Expression formatted as a number.
FormatPercent	Expression formatted as a percentage (multiplied by 100) with a trailing % character.
GetObject	Automation object from a file.
GetRef	Procedure that can be bound to an event.
Hex	String representing the hexadecimal value of a number.
Hour	Whole number between 0 and 23, inclusive, representing the hour of the day.
InputBox	Displays a prompt in a dialog box, waits for the user to input text or click a button, and returns the contents of the text box.
InStr	Position of the first occurrence of one string within another.
InStrRev	Position of an occurrence of one string within another, from the end of string.
Int	Integer portion of a number.
IsArray	Boolean value indicating whether a variable is an array.
IsDate	Boolean value indicating whether an expression can be converted to a date.
IsEmpty	Boolean value indicating whether a variable has been initialized.
IsNull	Boolean value that indicates whether an expression contains no valid data (Null).
IsNumeric	Boolean value indicating whether an expression can be evaluated as a number.
IsObject	Boolean value indicating whether an expression references a valid Automation object.
Join	String created by joining a number of substrings contained in an array.
LBound	Smallest available subscript for the indicated dimension of an array.
LCase	String that has been converted to lowercase.
Left	Specified number of characters from the left side of a string.
Len	Number of characters in a string or the number of bytes required to store a variable.
LoadPicture	Picture object.
Log	Natural logarithm of a number.
LTrim	Copy of a string without leading spaces.
Mid	Specified number of characters from a string.

Minute	Whole number between 0 and 59, inclusive, representing the minute of the hour.
Month	Whole number between 1 and 12, inclusive, representing the month of the year.
MonthName	String indicating the specified month.
MsgBox	Message in a dialog box, waits for the user to click a button, and returns a value indicating which button the user clicked.
Now	Current date and time according to the setting of your computer's system date and time.
Oct	String representing the octal value of a number.
Replace	String in which a specified substring has been replaced with another substring a specified number of times.
RGB	Whole number representing an RGB color value.
Right	Specified number of characters from the right side of a string.
Rnd	Random number.
Round	Number rounded to a specified number of decimal places.
RTrim	Copy of a string without trailing spaces.
ScriptEngine	String representing the scripting language in use.
ScriptEngine-BuildVersion	Build version number of the scripting engine in use.
ScriptEngineMa-jorVersion	Major version number of the scripting engine in use.
ScriptEngineMi-norVersion	Minor version number of the scripting engine in use.
Second	Whole number between 0 and 59, inclusive, representing the second of the minute.
Sgn	Integer indicating the sign of a number.
Sin	Sine of an angle.
Space	String consisting of the specified number of spaces.
Split	Zero-based, one-dimensional array containing a specified number of sub-strings.
Sqr	Square root of a number.
StrComp	Value indicating the result of a string comparison.
String	Repeating character string of the length specified.
StrReverse	String in which the character order of a specified string is reversed.
Tan	Tangent of an angle.
Time	Variant of subtype Date indicating the current system time.
Timer	Number of seconds that have elapsed since 12:00 AM (midnight).
TimeSerial	Variant of subtype Date containing the time for a specific hour, minute, and second.
TimeValue	Variant of subtype Date containing the time.
Trim	Copy of a string without leading or trailing spaces.
TypeName	String that provides Variant subtype information about a variable.
UBound	Largest available subscript for the indicated dimension of an array.
UCase	String that has been converted to uppercase.
VarType	Value indicating the subtype of a variable.
Weekday	Whole number representing the day of the week.

WeekdayName	String indicating the specified day of the week.
Year	Whole number representing the year.

H7.5.7 Statements

Language Element	Description
Call Statement	Transfers control to a Sub or Function procedure.
Class Statement	Declares the name of a class.
Const Statement	Declares constants for use in place of literal values.
Dim Statement	Declares variables and allocates storage space.
Do...Loop Statement	Repeats a block of statements while a condition is True or until a condition becomes True.
Erase Statement	Reinitializes the elements of fixed-size arrays and deallocates dynamic-array storage space.
Execute Statement	Executes one or more specified statements.
Exit Statement	Exits a block of Do...Loop, For...Next, Function, or Sub code.
For...Next Statement	Repeats a group of statements a specified number of times.
For Each...Next Statement	Repeats a group of statements for each element in an array or collection.
Function Statement	Declares the name, arguments, and code that form the body of a Function procedure.
If...Then...Else Statement	Conditionally executes a group of statements, depending on the value of an expression.
On Error Statement	Enables error-handling.
Option Explicit Statement	Forces explicit declaration of all variables in a script.
Private Statement	Declares private variables and allocates storage space.
PropertyGet Statement	Declares the name, arguments, and code that form the body of a Property procedure that gets (returns) the value of a property.
PropertyLet Statement	Declares the name, arguments, and code that form the body of a Property procedure that assigns the value of a property.
PropertySet Statement	Declares the name, arguments, and code that form the body of a Property procedure that sets a reference to an object.
Public Statement	Declares public variables and allocates storage space.
Randomize Statement	Initializes the random-number generator.
ReDim Statement	Declares dynamic-array variables and allocates or reallocates storage space at procedure level.
Rem Statement	Includes explanatory remarks in a program.
Select Case Statement	Executes one of several groups of statements, depending on the value of an expression.
Set Statement	Assigns an object reference to a variable or property.
Sub Statement	Declares the name, arguments, and code that form the body of a Sub procedure.
While...Wend Statement	Executes a series of statements as long as a given condition is True.
With Statement	Executes a series of statements on a single object.

H7.5.8 Color constants

Constant	Value	Description
vbBlack	&h00	Black
vbRed	&hFF	Red
vbGreen	&hFF00	Green
vbYellow	&hFFFF	Yellow
vbBlue	&hFF0000	Blue
vbMagenta	&hFF00FF	Magenta
vbCyan	&hFFFF00	Cyan
vbWhite	&hFFFFFF	White

H7.6   FSO Reference

The main methods used for the FSO are:

Method	Description
Add (Dictionary)	Adds a key and item pair to a **Dictionary** object.
Add (Folders)	Adds a new **Folder** to a **Folders** collection.
BuildPath	Appends a name to an existing path.
Close	Closes an open **TextStream** file.
Copy	Copies a specified file or folder from one location to another.
CopyFile	Copies one or more files from one location to another.
CopyFolder	Recursively copies a folder from one location to another.
CreateFolder	Creates a folder.
CreateTextFile	Creates a specified file name and returns a **TextStream** object that can be used to read from or write to the file.
Delete	Deletes a specified file or folder.
DeleteFile	Deletes a specified file.
DeleteFolder	Deletes a specified folder and its contents.
DriveExists	Returns **True** if the specified drive exists; **False** if it does not.
Exists	Returns **True** if a specified key exists in the **Dictionary** object, **False** if it does not.
FileExists	Returns **True** if a specified file exists; **False** if it does not.
FolderExists	Returns **True** if a specified folder exists; **False** if it does not.
GetAbsolutePathName	Returns a complete and unambiguous path from a provided path specification.
GetBaseName	Returns a string containing the base name of the file (less any file extension), or folder in a provided path specification.
GetDrive	Returns a **Drive** object corresponding to the drive in a specified path.
GetDriveName	Returns a string containing the name of the drive for a specified path.
GetExtensionName	Returns a string containing the extension name for the last component in a path.
GetFile	Returns a **File** object corresponding to the file in a specified path.
GetFileName	Returns the last file name or folder of a specified path that is not part of the drive specification.
GetFolder	Returns a **Folder** object corresponding to the folder in a specified path.

GetParentFolderName	Returns a string containing the name of the parent folder of the last file or folder in a specified path.
GetSpecialFolder	Returns the special folder specified.
GetTempName	Returns a randomly generated temporary file or folder name.
Items	Returns an array containing all the items in a **Dictionary** object.
Keys	Returns an array containing all existing keys in a **Dictionary** object.
Move	Moves a specified file or folder from one location to another.
MoveFile	Moves one or more files from one location to another.
MoveFolder	Moves one or more folders from one location to another.
OpenAsTextStream	Opens a specified file and returns a **TextStream** object that can be used to read from, write to, or append to the file.
OpenTextFile	Opens a specified file and returns a **TextStream** object that can be used to read from, write to, or append to the file.
Read	Reads a specified number of characters from a **TextStream** file and returns the resulting string.
ReadAll	Reads an entire **TextStream** file and returns the resulting string.
ReadLine	Reads an entire line (up to, but not including, the newline character) from a **TextStream** file and returns the resulting string.
Remove	Removes a key, item pair from a **Dictionary** object.
RemoveAll	Removes all key, item pairs from a **Dictionary** object.
Skip	Skips a specified number of characters when reading a **TextStream** file.
SkipLine	Skips the next line when reading a **TextStream** file.
Write	Writes a specified string to a **TextStream** file.
WriteBlankLines	Writes a specified number of newline characters to a **TextStream** file.
WriteLine	Writes a specified string and newline character to a **TextStream** file.

The main properties are:

	Description
AtEndOfLine	Returns **True** if the file pointer immediately precedes the end-of-line marker in a **TextStream** file; **False** if it is not.
AtEndOfStream	Returns **True** if the file pointer is at the end of a **TextStream** file; **False** if it is not.
Attributes	Sets or returns the attributes of files or folders.
AvailableSpace	Returns the amount of space available to a user on the specified drive or network share.
Column	Returns the column number of the current character position in a **TextStream** file.
CompareMode	Sets and returns the comparison mode for comparing string keys in a **Dictionary** object.
Count	Returns the number of items in a collection or **Dictionary** object.
DateCreated	Returns the date and time that the specified file or folder was created.
DateLastAccessed	Returns the date and time that the specified file or folder was last accessed.
DateLastModified	Returns the date and time that the specified file or folder was last modified.

Drive	Returns the drive letter of the drive on which the specified file or folder resides.
DriveLetter	Returns the drive letter of a physical local drive or a network share.
Drives	Returns a **Drives** collection consisting of all **Drive** objects available on the local machine.
DriveType	Returns a value indicating the type of a specified drive.
Files	Returns a **Files** collection consisting of all **File** objects contained in the specified folder, including those with hidden and system file attributes set.
FileSystem	Returns the type of file system in use for the specified drive.
FreeSpace	Returns the amount of free space available to a user on the specified drive or network share.
IsReady	Returns **True** if the specified drive is ready; **False** if it is not.
IsRootFolder	Returns **True** if the specified folder is the root folder; **False** if it is not.
Item	Sets or returns an *item* for a specified *key* in a **Dictionary** object.
Key	Sets a *key* in a **Dictionary** object.
Line	Returns the current line number in a **TextStream** file.
Name	Sets or returns the name of a specified file or folder.
Number	Returns or sets a numeric value specifying an error.
ParentFolder	Returns the folder object for the parent of the specified file or folder.
Path	Returns the path for a specified file, folder, or drive.
RootFolder	Returns a **Folder** object representing the root folder of a specified drive.
SerialNumber	Returns the decimal serial number used to uniquely identify a disk volume.
ShareName	Returns the network share name for a specified drive.
ShortName	Returns the short name used by programs that require the earlier 8.3 naming convention.
ShortPath	Returns the short path used by programs that require the earlier 8.3 file naming convention.
Size	Returns the size, in bytes, of the specified file or folder.
SubFolders	Returns a **Folders** collection consisting of all folders contained in a specified folder, including those with Hidden and System file attributes set.
TotalSize	Returns the total space, in bytes, of a drive or network share.
Type	Returns information about the type of a file or folder.
VolumeName	Sets or returns the volume name of the specified drive.

H8 ASP (form, sessions and databases)

H8.1 ASP forms

The Request.Form statement can be used to get information from a form. For example in the next case, the form has variable: name, address, email, gender and country. When the form is submitted the ASP page named in the Action for the form is called (in this case it is asp_form_details.asp). In this file, the variables can be read back with:

```
<% = Request.Form("name") %>
<% = Request.Form("address") %>
<% = Request.Form("email") %>
<% = Request.Form("gender") %>
<% = Request.Form("country") %>
```

📖 **ASP Code H8.1**

```
<form name="form2" method="post" action="asp_form_details.asp">
<table border="0" width="569">
<tr>
<td width="214" bgcolor="#CCFF99">
<p><b>Name:</b></p>
</td>
<td width="345">
<input type="text" name="name">
</td>
</tr>
<tr>
<td width="214" bgcolor="#CCFF99">
<p><b>Address:</b></p>
</td>
<td width="345">
<textarea name="address" wrap="VIRTUAL"> </textarea>
</td>
</tr>
<tr>
<td width="214" bgcolor="#CCFF99">
<p><b>Email:</b></p>
</td>
<td width="345">
<input type="text" name="email">
</td>
</tr>
<tr>
<td width="214" bgcolor="#CCFF99">
<p><b>Gender:</b></p>
</td>
<td width="345">
<p>Male
<input type="radio" name="gender" value="male" checked>
Female
<input type="radio" name="gender" value="female">
</p>
</td>
</tr>
```

```
<tr>
<td width="214" bgcolor="#CCFF99">
<p><b>Country of birth:</b></p>
</td>
<td width="345">
<select name="country">
<option>UK</option>
<option>USA</option>
<option>France</option>
<option>Germany</option>
<option>Japan</option>
<option>Other</option>
</select>
</td>
</tr>
</table>
<input type="submit" name="Submit" value="Submit details">
</form>
```

The asp_form_details.asp page can then display the form variable, such as:

📖 **ASP Code H8.2**

```
<table border="0" width="569">
<tr valign="top">
<td width="214" bgcolor="#CCFF99">
<p><b>Name:</b></p>
</td>
<td width="345">
<% = Request.Form("name") %>
</td>
</tr>
<tr valign="top">
<td width="214" bgcolor="#CCFF99">
<p><b>Address:</b></p>
</td>
<td width="345">
<% = Request.Form("address") %>
</td>
</tr>
<tr valign="top">
<td width="214" bgcolor="#CCFF99">
<p><b>Email:</b></p>
</td>
<td width="345">
<% = Request.Form("email") %>
</td>
</tr>
<tr valign="top">
<td width="214" bgcolor="#CCFF99">
<p><b>Gender:</b></p>
</td>
<td width="345">
<p>
<% = Request.Form("gender") %>
</p>
</td>
</tr>
<tr valign="top">
<td width="214" bgcolor="#CCFF99">
<p><b>Country of birth:</b></p>
</td>
<td width="345">
```

```
<% = Request.Form("country") %>
</td>
</tr>
</table>
<form name="form2" method="post" action="asp_form.asp">
<input type="submit" name="Submit" value="Submit new details">
</form>
```

H8.2   Session object

The Session object store information required for a particular user-session. Any variables which are set are stored for the time of the session, even when the user navigates to different pages. The following shows the setting of two variables:

```
<%
Session("name") = "Fred Smith"
Session("email") = "fred@home"
%>
```

Once the session variables are set, other pages can access them, within the same session. For example another page might have the lines:

```
<p>Hello  <% = Session("name") %>
<p>Your email address is  <% = Session("email") %>
```

The session ID can be displayed using:

```
response.write "Session ID is " & Session.SessionID
```

The TimeOut property can be used to define the amount of time (in minutes) that the session will be open, before it is exited. The default time-out is normally 20 minutes. For example to set the time-out at 5 minutes, the following can be used:

```
<%
Session.Timeout = 5
%>
```

Otherwise the Abandon method can be used to abandon a session, such as:

```
<%
Session.Abandon
%>
```

The Session.Contents collection can be used to display each of the session variables. In the following example each of the session keys are determined:

```
<%
For Each sessitem in Session.Contents
   Response.write(sess_item & " : " & Session.Contents(sess_item) & "<BR>")
Next
%>
```

A sample run of this gives:

```
name : Fred Smith
email : fred@home
Counter1 : 1
```

H8.3   Databases

ASP uses an ActiveX Data Objects (ADO) to access information stored in a database or other tabular data structure. ADO is a set of components that allow access to data through an OLE database provider. Active Data Objects are created used the CreateObject method, such as:

Set *myObj* = Server.CreateObject(*ProgID*)

where

myOby is the name of the object created, and ProgID defines the component that is to be created. These include:

Active Data Object	ProgID
Command	ADODB.Command
Connection	ADODB.Connection
Error	ADODB.Error
Field	ADODB.Field
Parameter	ADODB.Parameter
Property	ADODB.Property
Record	ADODB.Record
Recordset	ADODB.Recordset
Stream	ADODB.Stream

At first, a connection is made with the database server with the ADODB.Connection programmatic identifier, and then a Recordset is initiated. This Recordset is used to interrogate the database. For example, the following scans for the client's IP address, and saves it into a database named log.mdb.

📖 ASP Code H8.3

```
<%
dim ip,day
dim cnn,rst

ip = Request.ServerVariables("REMOTE_ADDR")
day=now

set cnn = Server.CreateObject("ADODB.Connection")
set rst = Server.CreateObject("ADODB.RecordSet")
cnn.Open "driver={Microsoft Access Driver (*.mdb)};;
             DBQ=C:\Inetpub\wwwroot\staff\bill\log.mdb;"

sqltext = "SELECT * FROM log"

rst.Open sqltext,cnn,3,3

rst.AddNew
rst("IpAddr") = ip
rst("Date") = day
```

```
rst.Update
%>
```

In this case, there are two fields in the Log table: IPAddr and Date. The AddNew method is used to add new items to the database. The Open connection method has the syntax of:

connectobj.Open [strConnection], [strUserID], [strPassword]

where

strConnection	is an optional string which defines the type of connection being made.
strUserID	is user ID string that will be sent to the data source.
strPassword	is the password string that will be sent to the data source.

For example:

```
cnn.Open "driver={Microsoft Access Driver
         (*.mdb)};;DBQ=C:\Inetpub\wwwroot\staff\bill\log.mdb;"
```

In this case a connection is made with a Microsoft Access database, which is located in `C:\Inetpub\wwwroot\staff\bill` folder on the server.

H8.3.1 Recordset object

The Recordset object is used to represent the records that are returned from a query on the database. The main methods used are:

- **AddNew**. Adds a new recordset. The basic syntax is Recordset.AddNew [Fieldlist], [Values]
- **Cancel**. Cancels the current execution. The basic syntax is Recordset.Canel.
- **CancelUpdate**. Cancels the update on the current record.
- **Clone**. Clones the current recordset.
- **Close**. Closes the current recordset. The basic syntax is Recordset.Close.
- **Delete**. Deletes a recordset. The basic syntax is Recordset.Delete AffectRecords.
- **Find**. Finds a recordset which matches the search criteria. The basic syntax is Recordset.Find Criteria, [SkipRows], [SearchDirection], [Start].
- **GetRows**. Retrieves multiple rows from a recordset. The basic syntax is Recordset.GetRows([Rows], [Start], [Fields])
- **GetString**. Retrieves a recordset as a string.
- **Move**. Move a recordset.
- **MoveFirst**. Move recordset to the first record.
- **MoveLast**. Move recordset to the last record.
- **MoveNext**. Move recordset to the next record.
- **MovePrevious**. Move recordset to the previous record.
- **NextRecordset**. Move to the next recordset.
- **Open**. Used to open-up the database.
- **Save**. Save the current recordset to a file. The basic syntax is Recordset.Save [Destination], [PersistFormat]
- **Seek**. Searches the current Index in the recordset to locate a particular value. The basic syntax is Recordset.Seek KeyValues, SeekOption.
- **Update**. Save changes to the database.

and the following collections:

- **Fields**. This contains the data in each column of the data in the recordset.

The Open recordset method has the syntax of:

connectobj.Open	vntSource, vntActConnection, _lngCurType, lngLockType, lngOptions

where

vntSource	Command object name or SQL query.
vntActConnection	Name of the Connection object.
lngCurType	Cursor type to be created. Valid cursors include: adOpenForwardOnly (0 - a fast cursor that will only move forward from the current record), adOpenKeySet (1 - cannot see new records that are added by other users), adOpenDynamic (2 - the slowest type, but can see all the changes to the records), adOpenStatic (3 - provides a static snapshot of the database).
lngLockType	Lock on the database. Valid locks include: adLockReadOnly (1 – Records in the cursor are read-only), adLockPessimistic (2 – Records are locked on a record-by-record basis), adLockOptimistic (3 – Records are locked on a record-by-record basis only when changes are to be made).

For example:

```
sqltext = "SELECT * FROM log"

rst.Open sqltext,cnn,3,3
```

which is equivalent to:

```
<% rst.Open "SELECT * FROM log", cnn, adOpenStatic, adLockOptimistic %>
```

In this case, the recordset is opened with a static cursor, and only locks a recordset when there is data to be written to the database. To add records to a table, the following can be used:

```
rst.AddNew
rst("IpAddr") = ip
rst("Date") = day
rst.Update
```

H8.3.2   Reading from a database

The database values can be read back using the *obj*.**Fields**(*recordnum*).Name to determine the name of the field contents, and *obj*.**Fields**(*recordnum*).Value to determine its value.

```
SQLtext = "SELECT * FROM log"
```

```
' -- Execute the query on the data source
rstData.Open SQLtext, cnn

' -- Draw a table
Response.Write "<P><TABLE BORDER=1>" & vbCrLf
Response.Write "<TR>" & vbCrLf

' -- Make a table column for each field in the query
For intFields = 0 to rstData.Fields.Count - 1
Response.Write "<TD BGCOLOR=""#CCCCCC""><B>" & rstData.Fields(intFields).Name &
"</B></TD>" & vbCrLf
Next

Do While Not rstData.EOF
   Response.Write "<TR>" & vbCrLf
' -- Display the value for each field in the query
   For intFields = 0 to rstData.Fields.Count - 1
       Response.Write "<TD>" & rstData.Fields(intFields).Value & "</TD>" &
           vbCrLf
Next
```

The main properties of the **Field** collection are:

- **Name**. The field's name.
- **Type**. The data type of the field's contents.
- **Value**. The value of the field's contents.

The full script to read the contents of the log.mdb file is given next. The *obj*.Fields.Count determines the number of records in a table.

📖 ASP Code H8.4

```
<%
Dim cnn, SQLtext, rstData, intFields

' -- Specify the database to connect to via ODBC
' -- Use an existing data source name
'szDSN = "DSN=email"
' -- OR
' -- You can also use a DSN-less connection by providing the driver and data-
base
cnn = "Driver=Microsoft Access Driver
(*.mdb);DBQ=C:\Inetpub\wwwroot\staff\bill\log.mdb"

' -- Create an ADO Recordset object
Set rstData = Server.CreateObject("ADODB.Recordset")

' -- Supply a SQL statement to query by
SQLtext = "SELECT * FROM log"

' -- Execute the query on the data source
rstData.Open SQLtext, cnn

' -- Draw a table
Response.Write "<P><TABLE BORDER=1>" & vbCrLf
Response.Write "<TR>" & vbCrLf

' -- Make a table column for each field in the query
For intFields = 0 to rstData.Fields.Count - 1
   Response.Write "<TD BGCOLOR=""#CCCCCC""><B>" &
       rstData.Fields(intFields).Name & "</B></TD>" & vbCrLf
```

```
Next

Response.Write "</TR>" & vbCrLf

' -- Loop through the recordset and make a new row for each record
Do While Not rstData.EOF
   Response.Write "<TR>" & vbCrLf
   ' -- Display the value for each field in the query
   For intFields = 0 to rstData.Fields.Count - 1
      Response.Write "<TD>" & rstData.Fields(intFields).Value & "</TD>" &
                                      vbCrLf

   Next

   Response.Write "</TR>" & vbCrLf

   ' -- Go to the next record
   rstData.MoveNext
Loop

Response.Write "</TABLE>" & vbCrLf

' -- Clean up
Set rstData = Nothing

%>
```

H8.3.3 Saving form data to a database

Often entries from a form require to be stored to a database. In this example, a form is submitted, and the contents of the form are added to a database file using an ASP file (xt_mail.asp). The code for producing the form, and to pass variables to the ASP database adding page is:

📖 ASP Code H8.5
```
<% ip = Request.ServerVariables("REMOTE_ADDR") %>
<p>Enter your email address in the database (<%=ip%>)
</p>
<form method="post" action="xt_email.asp">
<input type="text" name="EmailAddr">
<input type="hidden" name="IpAddr" value="<%=ip%>">
<input type="hidden" name="Day" value="<%=now%>">
<input type="submit" value="Submit" name="submit2">
<input type="reset" value="Reset" name="reset">
</form>
<p>Once you add you email address it should appear in
the database listing given <a href="#list_database">below</a>.</p>
```

The following is the file (xt_mail.asp) is called by the form when the submit button is pressed and creates a data entry (for the Access database named email.mdb):

📖 ASP Code H8.6
```
<%
' File name is xt_mail.asp
'Create a connection to our database using a fileless dsn
Response.Buffer = true
dim cnn,rst
set cnn = Server.CreateObject("ADODB.Connection")
set rst = Server.CreateObject("ADODB.RecordSet")
```

```asp
cnn.Open "driver={Microsoft Access Driver
(*.mdb)};;DBQ=C:\Inetpub\wwwroot\staff\bill\email.mdb;"
sqltext = "SELECT * FROM email"
rst.Open sqltext,cnn,3,3

'Server Side form validation to keep our database clean
dim email,ip,day
addr = Request.Form("EmailAddr")
ip = Request.Form("IpAddr")
day = Request.Form("Day")

if addr = "" then
    error = "You have not entered an email address."
    Response.Write error
    Response.End
end if

'If we pass through validation then store the information in the db

rst.AddNew
rst("EmailAddr") = addr
rst("IpAddr") = ip
rst("Date") = day
rst.update

'Lets redirect the user back to where they came from
Response.Redirect "asp_database.asp"
%>
```

The Response.Redirect is a useful statement as it allows the redirection of the browser back to the original page. Next, the database can then be read with the following file:

📖 ASP Code H8.7

```asp
<%
Dim szDSN, szSQL, rstData, intFields

' -- Specify the database to connect to via ODBC
' -- Use an existing data source name
'szDSN = "DSN=email"
' - OR
' - You can also use a DSN-less connection by providing the driver and database
szDSN = "Driver=Microsoft Access Driver (*.mdb);
        DBQ=C:\Inetpub\wwwroot\staff\bill\email.mdb"

' -- Create an ADO Recordset object
Set rstData = Server.CreateObject("ADODB.Recordset")

' -- Supply a SQL statement to query by
szSQL = "SELECT * FROM email"

' -- Execute the query on the data source
rstData.Open szSQL, szDSN

' -- Draw a table
Response.Write "<P><TABLE BORDER=1>" & vbCrLf
Response.Write "<TR>" & vbCrLf

' -- Make a table column for each field in the query
For intFields = 0 to rstData.Fields.Count - 1
    Response.Write "<TD BGCOLOR=""#CCCCCC""><B>" &
                rstData.Fields(intFields).Name & "</B></TD>" & vbCrLf
Next
```

```
Response.Write "</TR>" & vbCrLf

' -- Loop through the recordset and make a new row for each record
Do While Not rstData.EOF
   Response.Write "<TR>" & vbCrLf
   ' -- Display the value for each field in the query
   For intFields = 0 to rstData.Fields.Count - 1
      Response.Write "<TD>" & rstData.Fields(intFields).Value & "</TD>" &
                       vbCrLf
   Next

   Response.Write "</TR>" & vbCrLf

   ' -- Go to the next record
   rstData.MoveNext
Loop

Response.Write "</TABLE>" & vbCrLf

' -- Clean up
Set rstData = Nothing
%>
```

H8.4   ASP installable components

ASP supports a whole host of additional components which can be added on the server. These include:

Ad Rotator	Rotate between advertisements, with a defined schedule.
Browser Capabilities	Determines browser capabilities.
Database Access	Provides access to databases using Active X Data Objects (ADO).
Content Linking	Creates tables of contents for Web pages, and links them together sequentially like pages in a book.
File Access Component	Provides access to file input and output.
Collaboration Data Objects for NTS Component	Sends and receives messages from a Web page.
Tools	Provides utilities that enable additional functionality to web pages.
Status	Determines server status.
MyInfo	Keeps track of personal information, such as the site administrator's name, address, and display choices.
Counters	Creates, stores, increments, and retrieves counters.
Content Rotator	Rotation of HTML content strings on a Web page.
Page Counter	Counts and displays the number of times a Web page has been requested.
Permission Checker	Provides access to the password authentication protocols.

H8.4.1   Browser capabilities

The Browser Capabilities component generates information on the capabilities of the client's Web browser. It gets this information when the browser connects to the Web server, as the client sends a User Agent HTTP header, which has information on the client. The object is created with:

```
Set BrowserType = Server.CreateObject("MSWC.BrowserType")
```

and the properties of the object are:

Description	Property
Available Height	availHeight
Available Width	availWidth
Browser	browser
Buffer Depth	bufferDepth
Color Depth	colorDepth
ConnectionType	connectionType
Cookies	cookies
Cpu Class	cpuClass
Horizontal resolution	width
Is Java installed ?	Java
Is Java enabled?	javaEnabled
Java Applets	javaapplets
JavaScript	JavaScript
Platform	platform
System Language	systemLanguage
User Language	userLanguage
VBScript	VBScript
Version	version
Vertical resolution	height

An example is given next:

📖 ASP Code H8.8

```
<table border width="336">
<tr>
<td>Browser</td>
<td> <% = objBrowsCap.browser %></td>
</tr>
<tr>
<td>Version</td>
<td><% = objBrowsCap.version %></td>
</tr>
<tr>
<td>Cookies</td>
<td> <% = objBrowsCap.cookies %></td>
</tr>
<tr>
<td>Javaapplets</td>
<td> <% = objBrowsCap.javaapplets %></td>
</tr>
<tr>
<td>VBScript</td>
<td> <% = objBrowsCap.VBScript %></td>
</tr>
<tr>
<td>JavaScript</td>
<td><%=objBrowsCap.JavaScript%></td>
</tr>
```

```
<tr>
<td>Platform</td>
<td> <% = objBrowsCap.platform %></td>
</tr>
<% If objBrowsCap.browser = "IE" and objBrowsCap.version >4 then %>
<tr>
<td>Horizontal resolution</td>
<td> <% = objBrowsCap.width %></td>
</tr>
<tr>
<td>Vertical resolution</td>
<td><% = objBrowsCap.height %></td>
</tr>
<tr>
<td>AvailHeight</td>
<td> <% = objBrowsCap.availHeight %></td>
</tr>
<tr>
<td>AvailWidth</td>
<td><% = objBrowsCap.availWidth %></td>
</tr>
<tr>
<td>Buffer Depth</td>
<td> <% = objBrowsCap.bufferDepth %></td>
</tr>
<tr>
<td>Color Depth</td>
<td> <% = objBrowsCap.colorDepth %></td>
</tr>
<tr>
<td>Is Java enabled ?</td>
<td> <% = objBrowsCap.javaEnabled %></td>
</tr>
<tr>
<td>CPU Class</td>
<td> <% = objBrowsCap.cpuClass %></td>
</tr>
<tr>
<td>System Language</td>
<td><% = objBrowsCap.systemLanguage %></td>
</tr>
<tr>
<td>User Language</td>
<td> <% = objBrowsCap.userLanguage %></td>
</tr>
<tr>
<td>connectionType</td>
<td> <% = objBrowsCap.connectionType %></td>
</tr>
<tr>
<td>Is Java installed?</td>
<td> <% = objBrowsCap.Java%></td>
</tr>
<% End if %>

</table>
```

H8.4.2   Ad Rotator

The Ad Rotator component can be used to display an advertisement, as defined in the Rotator Schedule File. The object is created with the following:

```
<% Set advert = Server.CreateObject("MSWC.AdRotator") %>
```

and the Ad Rotator file is set by:

```
<%= ad.GetAdvertisement("adv.txt") %>
```

This file can define the images, size, and general details for the advert. It has two sections (which are separated by an asterisk (*)):

- **Section 1**. This section sets the parameters that apply to all advertisement images in the rotation schedule. It can contain four global parameters, each consisting of a keyword and a value, all of which are optional.
- **Section 2**. This section specifies file and location information for each individual advertisement and the percentage of display time that each advertisement should receive.

The basic syntax is:

```
[REDIRECT URL]
[WIDTH numWidth]
[HEIGHT numHeight]
[BORDER numBorder]
*
adURL
adHomePageURL
Text
impressions
```

where:

URL   This specifies the path to the dynamic-link library (.dll) or application (.asp) file that implements redirection.
numWidth   Specifies the width of the advertisement on the page, in pixels.
numHeight   Specifies the height of the advertisement on the page, in pixels.
numBorder   Specifies the thickness of the hyperlink border around the advertisement, in pixels.
adURL   The location of the advertisement image file.
adHomePageURL
              The location of the advertiser's home page.
Text   Alternate text that is displayed if the browser does not support graphics.
impressions   A number between 0 and 4,294,967,295 that indicates the relative weight of the advertisement.

For example the following gives an example of a rotator schedule file:

```
---ADROT.TXT---
REDIRECT /scripts/myredir.asp
WIDTH 440
HEIGHT 60
BORDER 1
*
http://mygifs/fred.gif
http://www.fred.com
Fred's new WWW site
20
```

```
http://mygifs/bert.gif
http://www.bert.com
Bert's new site
20
http://mygifs/frank.gif
http://www.frank.com
Frank's old site
80
http://mygifs/andy.gif
http://www.andy.com
Andy's site
10
```

H8.4.3   Global.asa file

The gobal.asa file is used to specify event scripts and declare objects that have session or application scope. It is always stored with the name global.asa, and must be stored in the root directory of the application.

H8.4.4   Counters

Many pages require to have their hit count monitored. This can be achieved with the Counter component which allows the creation, storage, and manipulation of any number of individual counters. A counter object is defined as an integer, which is manipulated by the Get, Increment, Set and Remove methods. Note that a counter will not be automatically incremented when an associated page is loaded, thus the Set and Increments are required. Note also that counters are not limited in their scope, and any page can recall them.

A counter can be added to the server by adding the following lines to the GLOBAL.ASA file:

```
<OBJECT RUNAT=Server SCOPE=Application ID=Counter
PROGID="MSWC.Counters">
</OBJECT>
```

The counters object can then be used within an ASP script with the following:

```
Page accesses: <%= Counter.Increment('aspPageHits') %>
```

H9   Java

H9.1   Introduction

Java is a general-purpose, concurrent, class-based, object-oriented language and has been designed to be relatively simple to built complex applications. Java is developed from C and C++, but some parts of C++ have been dropped and others added. The main objective of Java is to produce a software language which would allow programs to run the same on differing types of systems. This might be differing types of hardware, differing operating systems, and differing networking technologies. It will thus produce an intermediate form of an executable, which will not actually run on the processor, and must be interpreted by an interpreter which converts the intermediate form into a form which can be executed on the processor (Figure H9.1).

Java has the great advantage over conventional software languages in that it produces code which is computer hardware independent. This is because the compiled code (called bytecodes) is either interpreted by a WWW browser or run by a stand-alone interpreter. Unfortunately, this leads to slower execution, but, as much of the time in a graphical user interface program is spent updating the graphics display, then the overhead is, as far as the user is concerned, not a great one.

The other advantages that Java has over conventional software languages include:

- It is a more dynamic language than C/C++ and Pascal, and was designed to adapt to an evolving environment. It is extremely easy to add new methods and extra libraries without affecting existing applets and programs. It is also useful in Internet applications as it supports most of the standard compressed image, audio and video formats.
- It has networking facilities built into it. This provides support for TCP/IP sockets, URLs, IP addresses and datagrams.
- While Java is based on C and C++ it avoids some of the difficult areas of C/C++ code (such as pointers and parameter passing).

Table H9.1 shows the main files used in the PC version and Figure H9.2 shows the directory structure of the JDK tools. The Java compiler, Java interpreter and applet viewer programs are stored in the `bin` directory. On the PC, this directory is normally set up in the PATH directory, so that the Java compiler can be called while the user is in another directory. The following is a typical setup (assuming that the home directory is `C:\`*javahome*):

```
PATH=C:\WINDOWS;C:\WINDOWS\COMMAND;C:\javahome\BIN
CLASSPATH=C:\javahome\LIB;.;C:\javahome
```

The `lib` directory contains the `classes.zip` file which is a zipped-up version of the Java class files. These class files are stored in the directories below the `src/java` directory. For example, the `io` classes (such as `File.java` and `InputStream.java`) are used for input/output in Java, the `awt` classes (such as `Panel.java` and `Dialog.java`) are used to create and maintain windows. These and other classes will be discussed later.

The `include` directory contains header files for integrating C/C++ programs with Java applets and the `demo` directory contains some sample Java applets.

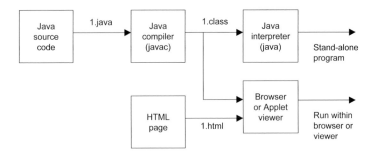

Figure H9.1 Constructing Java applets and standalone programs

Table H9.1 JDK programs

File	Description
javac.exe	Java compiler
java.exe	Java interpreter
appletViewer.exe	Applet viewer for testing and running applets
classes.zip	It is needed by the compiler and interpreter
javap.exe	Java class disassembler
javadoc.exe	Java document generator
javah.exe	C Header and Stub File Generator
jar.exe	Java Archive Tool which combines class files and other resources into a single jar file.
jbd.exe	Java debugger

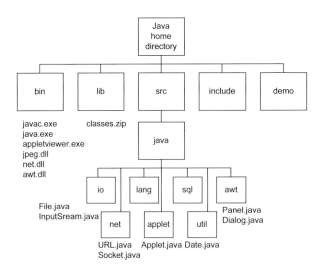

Figure H9.2 Sample directory structure of JDK for a PC-based system

H9.2 Standalone programs

A Java program can be run as a standalone program or as an applet. A standalone program allows the Java program to be run without a browser and is normally used when testing the Java applet. The method of output to the screen is:

```
System.out.println("message");
```

which prints a message (message) to the display. This type of debugging is messy, as these statements need to be manually inserted in the program. It is likely that later versions of the JDK toolkit will contain a run-time debugger which will allow developers to view the execution of the program.

To run a standalone program the java.exe program is used and the user adds output statements with the System.out.println() method. Note that there is no output to the main graphics applet screen with this method.

Java program H9.1 gives a simple example of a standalone program. The public static void main(Strings[] args) defines the main method. Sample run H9.1 shows how the Java program is created (with edit) and then compiled (with javac.exe), and then finally run (with java.exe).

📖 Java program H9.1
```
public class chapH9_01
{
    public static void main(String[] args)
    {
    int i;
       i=10;
       System.out.println("This is an example of the ");
       System.out.println("output from the standalone");
       System.out.println("program");
       System.out.println("The value of i is " + i);
    }
}
```

🖥 Sample run H9.1
```
C:\DOCS\notes\java>edit chapH9_01.java
C:\DOCS\notes\java>javac chapH9_01.java
C:\DOCS\notes\java>java chapH9_01
This is an example of the
output from the standalone
program
The value of i is 10
```

The process of developing a standalone Java program is:

- Create a Java program. This is the main Java program file and is created by a text editor (such as edit in a PC-based system). These files are given the .java file extension. In Sample run H9.1 the file created is chapH9_01.java.
- Compile program to a class file. This is created by the Java compiler (javac.exe) when there is a successful compilation. By default, the file produced has the same filename as the source file and the .class file extension. In Sample run H9.1 the file created is chapH9_01.class.
- Run program with the Java interpreter. The Java interpreter (java.exe) reads from the class file (which contains the bytecode) and gives the required output.

H9.3　Comments

Java supports single line comments with a double slash (//) or multi-line comments which are defined between a /* and a */. The single line comment makes everything on the line after the double slash a comment. A few examples are:

```
PI=3.14157;    // Sets the value of pi
area=PI*r*r    // Area is PI times the square of the radius
/* No more comments */
```

H9.4　Java reserved words

Like any programming language, Java has various reserved words which cannot be used as a variable name. These are given next:

abstract	boolean	break	byte	case	cast
catch	char	class	cons	continue	default
do	double	else	extends	final	finally
float	for	future	generic	goto	if
implements	import	inner	instanceof	in	interface
long	native	new	null	operator	outer
package	private	protected	public	rest	return
short	static	super	switch	synchronized	this
throw	throws	transient	try	var	unsigned
virtual	void	volatile	while		

H9.5　Numbers and representations

H9.5.1　Exponent representation

Relatively large or small numbers can be represented in exponent format. Table H9.2 gives some examples of this format.

Table H9.2　Exponent format conversions

Value (or PHYSICAL CONSTANT)	Exponent format
0.000 000 001	1e-9
1 234 320	1.23432e6
1 000 000 000 000	1e12
0.023	2.3e-2
0.943230	9.4323e-1
CHARGE OF ELECTRON	1.602e-19
MASS OF ELECTRON	9.109e-31
PERMITTIVITY OF FREE SPACE	8.854e-12
SPEED OF LIGHT	2.998e8

H9.5.2　Hexadecimal and octal numbers

Hexadecimal numbers are useful for representing binary values and are represented in Java with a preceding 0x (a zero and an 'x'). To convert a binary value to hexadecimal the value is organized in groups of 4 bits. Then each of the 4-bit groups is represented as a hexadecimal value. For example:

```
0100 1101 1100 1111
```

is represented by:

```
0x4DCF
```

in Java. An octal value has a preceding 0 (zero) value. Program H9.2 shows a simple Java program which has two integer variables (val1 and val2). These are given a value of 34h and 20o. It can be seen in Sample run H9.2 that the output of the program prints the equivalent decimal value.

📖 Java program H9.2
```
public class chapH9_02
{
 public static void main (String args[])
 {
 int val1=0x34,val2=020;
   System.out.println(" Val1 is "+val1+" Val2 is "+val2);
 }
}
```

💻 **Sample run H9.2**
```
C:\java\src\chapH9>edit chapH9_02.java
C:\java\src\chapH9>javac chapH9_02.java
C:\java\src\chapH9>java chapH9_02
 Val1 is 52 Val2 is 16
```

H9.6   Data types

Variables within a program can be stored as either Boolean values, numbers or as characters. For example, the resistance of a copper wire would be stored as a number (a real value), whether it exists or not (as a Boolean value) and the name of a component (such as "R1") would be stored as characters.

An integer is any value without a decimal point. Its range depends on the number of bytes used to store it. A floating-point value is any number and can include a decimal point. This value is always in a signed format. Again, the range depends on the number of bytes used.

Integers either take up 1, 2, 4 or 8 bytes in memory for a byte, short, int and long, respectively. These are all represented in 2's complement notation and thus can store positive and negative integer values. Table H9.3 gives some typical ranges for data types.

Table H9.3 Typical ranges for data types

Type	Storage (bytes)	Range
boolean	1-bit	True or False
byte	1	−128 to 127
short	2	−32 768 to 32 767
int	4	−2 147 483 648 to 2 147 483 647
long	8	2 223 372 036 854 775 808 to −2 223 372 036 854 775 809
char	2	16-bit unsigned integers representing Unicode characters.
float	4	$\pm 3.4 \times 10^{-38}$ to $\pm 3.4 \times 10^{38}$
double	8	$\pm 1.7 \times 10^{-308}$ to $\pm 1.7 \times 10^{308}$

H9.7 Characters and strings

Typically, characters are stored using either ASCII or EBCDIC codes. ASCII is an acronym for American Standard Code for Information Interchange and EBCDIC for Extended Binary Coded Decimal Interchange Code.

ASCII characters from decimal 0 to 32 are non-printing characters that are used either to format the output or to control the hardware. Program H9.3 displays an ASCII character for an entered decimal value. The `print()` method displays the ASCII character. Sample run H9.3 shows a sample run (note that some of the displayed characters are non-printing).

📖 Java program H9.3

```
public class chapH9_03
{
public static void main (String args[])
{
char ch;
    for (ch=0;ch<256;ch++)
        System.out.print(" " + ch); // print from 0 to 255
}
}
```

💻 Sample run H9.3

```
 □ □ □ □ □ □ □ □    □
 □ □ □ □ □ □ □ □ □ □ □ □ □ □ □ -    ! " # $ % & ' ( ) * + , - . / 0 1 2 3 4 5 6
7 8 9 : ; < = > ? @ A B C D E F G H I J K L M N O P Q R S T U V W X Y Z [ \ ] ^
_ ` a b c d e f g h i j k l m n o p q r s t u v w x y z { | } ~ □ □ □ , f „ … †
‡ ^ ‰ Š ‹ Œ □ □ □ □ ' ' " " • – — ~ ™ š › œ □ □ Ÿ  ¡ ¢ £ ¤ ¥ | § " © ª « ¬ - ®
¯ ° ± ² ³ ´ µ ¶ · , ¹ º » ¼ ½ ¾ ¿ À Á Â Ã Ä Å Æ Ç È É Ê Ë Ì Í Î Ï Ð Ñ Ò Ó Ô Õ Ö
× Ø Ù Ú Û Ü Ý Þ ß à á â ã ä å æ ç è é ê ë ì í î ï ð ñ ò ó ô õ ö ÷ ø ù ú û ü ý þ
ÿ
```

Characters of type `char` are stored as 2-byte Unicode characters (0x0000 to 0xFFFF). This allows for internationalization of the character set. The characters from 0 to 255 (0x0000 to 0x00FF) are standard extended ASCII character set (ISO8859-1, or Latin-1), where the characters are stored as the binary digits associated with the character. For example, the ASCII code for the character 'A' is 65 decimal (0x41); the binary storage for this character is thus 0100 0001. Some examples of ASCII codes are given in Table H9.4.

The `println()` method sends a formatted string to the standard output (the display). This string can include special control characters, such as new lines ('\n'), backspaces ('\b') and tabspaces ('\t'); these are listed in Table H9.5.

Table H9.4 Examples of ASCII characters

Decimal	Hex	Binary	Character
32	0x20	0010 0000	SPACE
65	0x41	0100 0001	'A'
66	0x42	0100 0010	'B'
90	0x5A	0101 1010	'Z'
97	0x61	0110 0001	'a'
122	0x7A	0111 1010	'z'
7	0x07	0000 0111	Ring the bell
8	0x08	0000 1000	Perform a backspace

Table H9.5   Special control (or escape sequence) characters

Characters	Function
\"	Double quotes (")
\'	Single quote (')
\\	Backslash (\ )
\u*nnnn*	Unicode character in hexadecimal code, e.g. \u041 gives '!'
\0*nn*	Unicode character in octal code, e.g. \041 gives '!'
\b	Backspace (move back one space)
\f	Form-feed
\n	New line (line-feed)
\r	Carriage return
\t	Horizontal tab spacing

The `println()` method writes a string of text to the standard output and at the end of the text a new line is automatically appended, whereas the `print()` method does not append the output with a new line.

Special control characters use a backslash to inform the program to escape from the way they would be normally be interpreted. The carriage return ('\r') is used to return the current character pointer on the display back to the start of the line (on many displays this is the leftmost side of the screen). A form-feed control character ('\f') is used to feed line printers on a single sheet and the horizontal tab ('\t') feeds the current character position forward one tab space.

Quotes enclose a single character, for example 'a', whereas inverted commas enclose a string of characters, such as "Mastering Java". Java has a special String object (`String`). Java program H9.4 shows an example of declaring two strings (`name1` and `name2`) and Sample run H9.4 shows a sample run. The '\"' character is used to display inverted commas and the backspace character has been used to delete an extra character in the displayed string. The BELL character is displayed with the '\007' and '\u0007' escape sequence characters. Other escape characters used include the horizontal tab ('\t') and the new line character ('\n').

Strings can be easily concatenated using the '+' operator. For example to build a string of two strings (with a space in-between) then following can be implemented:

```
String name1, name2, name3;

    name3=name1+" " + name2;
```

📖 Java program H9.4
```
public class chapH9_04
{
 public static void main (String args[])
 {

 String name1="Bill", name2="Buchanan";
      System.out.println("Ring the bell 3 times \u0007\007\007");
      System.out.print("\"My name is Bill\"\n");
      System.out.println("\t\"Buchh\banan\"");
      System.out.println(name1 + " " + name2);
 }
}
```

H9.8   Declaration of variables

A program uses variables to store data. Before a program can use a variable, its name and its data type must first be declared. A comma groups variables of the same data type. For example, if a program requires integer variables num_steps and bit_mask, floating-point variables resistor1 and resistor2, and two character variables char1 and char2, then the following declarations can be made:

```
int     num_steps,bit_mask;
float   resistor1,resistor2;
char    char1,char2;
```

Program H9.5 is a simple program that determines the equivalent parallel resistance of two resistors of 1000 and 500 Ω connected in parallel. It contains three floating-point declarations for the variables resistor1, resistor2 and eq_resistance.

📖 Java program H9.5
```
public class chapH9_05
{
    public static void main (String args[])
    {
    float resistor1, resistor2, equ_resistance;

        resistor1=1500;
        resistor2=500;
        equ_resistance=1/(1/resistor1+1/resistor2);
        System.out.println("Equ. resistance is "+equ_resistance);
    }
}
```

It is also possible to assign an initial value to a variable at the point in the program at which it is declared. This is known as variable initialisation. Program H9.6 gives an example of this with the declared variables resistor1 and resistor2 initialised with 1000.0 and 500.0, respectively. Sample run H9.5 gives an example run.

📖 Java program H9.6
```
public class chapH9_06
{
    public static void main (String args[])
    {
    float resistor1=1500, resistor2=500, equ_resistance;

        equ_resistance=1/(1/resistor1+1/resistor2);
        System.out.println("Equ. resistance is "+equ_resistance);
    }
}
```

H9.9   Java operators

Java has a rich set of operators, of which there are four main types:

- Arithmetic
- Logical
- Bitwise
- Relational

H9.9.1   Arithmetic

Arithmetic operators operate on numerical values. The basic arithmetic operations are add (+), subtract (-), multiply (*), divide (/) and modulus division (%). Modulus division gives the remainder of an integer division. The following gives the basic syntax of two operands with an arithmetic operator.

operand operator operand

The assignment operator (=) is used when a variable 'takes on the value' of an operation. Other short-handed operators are used with it, including add equals (+=), minus equals (-=), multiplied equals (*=), divide equals (/=) and modulus equals (%=). The following examples illustrate their uses.

Statement	Equivalent
x+=3.0;	x=x+3.0;
voltage/=sqrt(2);	voltage=voltage/sqrt(2);
bit_mask *=2;	bit_mask=bit_mask*2;
screen_val%=22+1;	screen_val=screen_val%22+1;

In many applications, it is necessary to increment or decrement a variable by 1. For this purpose Java has two special operators; ++ for increment and -- for decrement. These can either precede or follow the variable. If they precede, then a pre-increment/decrement is conducted, whereas if they follow it, a post-increment/decrement is conducted. The following examples show their usage.

Statement	Equivalent
no_values--;	no_values=no_values-1;
i--;	i=i-1;
screen_ptr++;	screen_ptr=screen_ptr+1;

When the following example code is executed the values of i, j, k, y and z will be 10, 12, 13, 10 and 10, respectively. The statement z=--i decrements i and assigns this value to z (a pre-increment), while `y=i++` assigns the value of i to y and then increments i (a post-increment).

```
i=10; j=11; k=12;
y=i++;      /*    assign i to y then increment i      */
z=--i;      /*    decrement i then assign it to z      */
j++;        /*    increment j                          */
++k;        /*    increment k                          */
```

Table H9.6 summarizes the arithmetic operators.

Table H9.6 Arithmetic operators

Operator	Operation	Example
-	subtraction or minus	5-4→1
+	addition	4+2→6
*	multiplication	4*3→12
/	division	4/2→2
%	modulus	13%3→1
+=	add equals	x += 2 is equivalent to x=x+2
-=	minus equals	x -= 2 is equivalent to x=x-2
/=	divide equals	x /= y is equivalent to x=x/y
*=	multiplied equals	x *= 32 is equivalent to x=x*32
=	assignment	x = 1
++	increment	Count++ is equivalent to Count=Count+1
--	decrement	Sec-- is equivalent to Sec=Sec-1

H9.9.2 Relationship

The relationship operators determine whether the result of a comparison is TRUE or FALSE. These operators are greater than (>), greater than or equal to (>=), less than (<), less than or equal to (<=), equal to (==) and not equal to (!=). Table H9.7 lists the relationship operators.

Table H9.7 Relationship operators

Operator	Function	Example	TRUE Condition
>	greater than	(b>a)	when b is greater than a
>=	greater than or equal	(a>=4)	when a is greater than or equal to 4
<	less than	(c<f)	when c is less than f
<=	less than or equal	(x<=4)	when x is less than or equal to 4
==	equal to	(x==2)	when x is equal to 2
!=	not equal to	(y!=x)	when y is not equal to x

H9.9.3 Logical (TRUE or FALSE)

A logical operation is one in which a decision is made as to whether the operation performed is TRUE or FALSE. If required, several relationship operations can be grouped together to give the required functionality. Java assumes that a numerical value of 0 (zero) is

FALSE and that any other value is TRUE. Table H9.9 lists the logical operators.

Logical AND operation will only yield a TRUE if all the operands are TRUE. Table H9.9 gives the result of the AND (&&) operator for the operation Operand1 && Operand2. The logical OR operation yields a TRUE if any one of the operands is TRUE. Table H9.9 gives the logical results of the OR (||) operator for the statement Operand1 || Operand2. Table H9.11 gives the logical result of the NOT (!) operator for the statement !Operand.

Table H9.8 Logical operators

Operator	Function	Example	TRUE condition
&&	AND	((x==1) && (y<2))	when x is equal to 1 *and* y is less than 2
||	OR	((a!=b) || (a>0))	when a is not equal to b *or* a is greater than 0
!	NOT	(!(a>0))	when a is *not* greater than 0

Table H9.9 AND and OR logical truth table

Operand1	Operand2	AND	OR
FALSE	FALSE	FALSE	FALSE
FALSE	TRUE	FALSE	TRUE
TRUE	FALSE	FALSE	TRUE
TRUE	TRUE	TRUE	TRUE

Table H9.10 NOT logical truth table

Operand	Result
FALSE	TRUE
TRUE	FALSE

For example, if a has the value 1 and b is also 1, then the following relationship statements would apply:

Statement	Result
(a==1) && (b==1)	TRUE
(a>1) && (b==1)	FALSE
(a==10) || (b==1)	TRUE
!(a==12)	TRUE

Java program H9.7 shows a Java program which proves the above table and Sample run H9.6 shows a sample run.

📖 Java program H9.7

```
public class chapH9_07
{
 public static void main (String args[])
 {
 int a=1,b=1;

        if ((a==1) && (b==1)) System.out.println("TRUE");
        else System.out.println("FALSE");
```

```
    if ((a>1) && (b==1)) System.out.println("TRUE");
    else System.out.println("FALSE");
    if ((a==10) || (b==1)) System.out.println("TRUE");
    else System.out.println("FALSE");
    if (!(a==10)) System.out.println("TRUE");
    else System.out.println("FALSE");
  }
}
```

Sample run H9.6

```
C:\java\src\chapH9>java chapH9_07
TRUE
FALSE
TRUE
TRUE
```

H9.9.4 Bitwise

The bitwise operators are similar to the logical operators but they should not be confused as their operation differs. Bitwise operators operate directly on the individual bits of an operand(s), whereas logical operators determine whether a condition is TRUE or FALSE.

Numerical values are stored as bit patterns in either an unsigned integer format, signed integer (2's complement) or floating-point notation (an exponent and mantissa). Characters are normally stored as ASCII characters.

The basic bitwise operations are AND (&), OR (|), 1's complement or bitwise inversion (~), XOR (^), shift left (<<), shift right with sign (>>) and right shift without sign (>>>). Table H9.11 gives the results of the AND, OR and XOR bitwise operation on two bits $Bit1$ and $Bit2$. Table H9.12 gives the truth table for the NOT (~) bitwise operator on a single bit.

Table H9.11 Bitwise AND truth table

Bit1	Bit2	AND	OR	XOR
0	0	0	0	0
0	1	0	1	1
1	0	0	1	1
1	1	1	1	0

Table H9.12 Bitwise NOT truth table

Bit	Result
0	1
1	0

The bitwise operators operate on each of the individual bits of the operands. For example, if two decimal integers 58 and 41 (assuming 8-bit unsigned binary values) are operated on using the AND, OR and EX-OR bitwise operators, then the following applies.

	AND	OR	EX-OR
58	00111010b	00111010b	00111010b
41	00101001b	00101001b	00101001b
Result	00101000b	00111011b	00010011b

The results of these bitwise operations are as follows:

```
58 & 41 = 40      (that is, 00101000b)
58 | 41 = 59      (that is, 00111011b)
58 ^ 41 = 19      (that is, 00010011b)
```

Java program H9.8 shows a program which tests these operations and Sample run H9.7 shows a test run.

The 1's complement operator operates on a single operand. For example, if an operand has the value of 17 (00010001b) then the 1's complement of this, in binary, will be 11101110b.

📖 Java program H9.8
```
public class chapH9_08
{

 public static void main (String args[])
 {
 int a=58,b=41,val;

        val=a&b; System.out.println("AND "+ val);
        val=a|b; System.out.println("OR "+ val);
        val=a^b; System.out.println("X-OR "+ val);
 }
}
```

💻 **Sample run H9.7**
```
C:\java\src\chapH9>java chapH9_08
AND 40
OR 59
X-OR 19
```

To perform bit shifts, the <<, >> and >>> operators are used. These operators shift the bits in the operand by a given number defined by a value given on the right-hand side of the operation. The left-shift operator (<<) shifts the bits of the operand to the left and zeros fill the result on the right. The right-shift operator (>>) shifts the bits of the operand to the right and zeros fill the result if the integer is positive; otherwise it will fill with 1s. The right shift with sign (>>>) shifts the bits and ignores the sign flag; it thus treats signed integers as unsigned integers. The standard format for the three shift operators is:

```
operand >> no_of_bit_shift_positions
operand << no_of_bit_shift_positions
operand >>> no_of_bit_shift_positions
```

For example, if y = 59 (00111011), then y >> 3 will equate to 7 (00000111) and y<<2 to 236 (11101100). Table H9.13 gives a summary of the basic bitwise operators.

The following examples use shortened forms of the bitwise operators:

`i<<=2`   equivalent to `i=i<<2`   *shift bits of i 2 positions to the left*

`time |= 32`   equivalent to `time=time | 32`   *OR bits of time with 32 decimal*

`bitval^=22`   equivalent to `bitval=bitval^22`   *bitval is EX-ORed with 22*

Table H9.13   Bitwise operators

Operator	Function	Example
`&`	AND	`c = A & B`
`|`	OR	`f = Z	y`
`^`	XOR	`h = 5 ^ f`
`~`	1's complement	`x = ~y`
`>>`	shift right	`x = y >> 1`
`<<`	shift left	`y = y << 2`

H9.10   Precedence

There are several rules for dealing with operators:

- Two operators, apart from the assignment, should never be placed side by side. For example, `x * % 3` is invalid.
- Groupings are formed with parentheses; anything within parentheses will be evaluated first. Nested parentheses can also be used to set priorities.
- A priority level or precedence exists for operators. Operators with a higher precedence are evaluated first; if two operators have the same precedence, then the operator on the left-hand side is evaluated first. The priority levels for operators are as follows:

HIGHEST PRIORITY

`() [] .`	primary
`! ~ ++ -- -`	unary
`* / %`	multiply
`+ -`	additive
`<< >> >>>`	shift
`< > <= >=`	relation
`== !=`	equality
`&`	bitwise
`^`	
`|`	
`&&`	logical
`||`	
`= += -=`	assignment

LOWEST PRIORITY

The assignment operator has the lowest precedence. The following example shows how operators are prioritized in a statement (=> shows the steps in determining the result):

```
23 + 5 % 3 / 2 << 1   =>
23 + 2 / 2 << 1     =>
23 + 1 << 1         =>
23 + 2              => 25
```

H9.11   Data type conversion

A variable's data type can be changed temporarily using a technique known as casting or coercion. The cast modifier precedes the operand and the data type is defined in parentheses. Typical modifiers are (float), (int), (char) and (double). In Program H9.9 two integers b and c are divided and the result is assigned to a. Since b and c are both integers, the operator is an integer division. The result will thus be 1, as an integer division is performed. Sample run H9.8 shows a sample run.

📖 Java program H9.9
```
public class chapH9_09
{
 public static void main (String args[])
 {
 int     b,c;
 float   val;
        b=6; c=11;
        val = c / b;
        System.out.println("Result is "+ val);
 }
}
```

💻 **Sample run H9.8**
```
C:\java\src\chapH9>java chapH9_09
Result is 1
```

Program H9.10 performs a floating-point division as the variable c has been recast or coerced to a float. Sample run H9.9 shows a sample run.

📖 Java program H9.10
```
public class chapH9_10
{
 public static void main (String args[])
 {
 int     b,c;
 float   val;
        b=6; c=11;
        val = (float) c / b;
        System.out.println("Result is "+ val);
 }
}
```

```
C:\java\src\chapH9>java chapH9_10
Result is 1.8333334
```

H9.12   Selection statements

H9.12.1 `if...else`

A decision is made with the `if` statement. It logically determines whether a conditional expression is TRUE or FALSE. For a TRUE, the program executes one block of code; a FALSE causes the execution of another (if any). The keyword `else` identifies the FALSE block. In Java, braces ({ }) are used to define the start and end of the block.

Relationship operators, include:

- Greater than (`>`)
- Less than (`<`)
- Greater than or equal to (`>=`)
- Less than or equal to (`<=`)
- Equal to (`==`)
- Not equal to (`!=`)

These operations yield a TRUE or FALSE from their operation. Logical statements (`&&`, `||`, `!`) can then group these together to give the required functionality. These are:

- AND (`&&`)
- OR (`||`)
- NOT (`!`)

If the operation is not a relationship, such as bitwise or an arithmetic operation, then any non-zero value is TRUE and a zero is FALSE. The following is an example syntax of the `if` statement. If the statement block has only one statement then the braces (`{ }`) can be excluded.

```
if (expression)
{
    statement block
}
```

The following is an example format with an `else` extension.

```
if (expression)
{
    statement block1
}
else
{
    statement block2
}
```

It is possible to nest `if..else` statements to give a required functionality. In the next example, *statement block1* is executed if `expression1` is TRUE. If it is FALSE then the program checks the next expression. If this is TRUE the program executes *statement block2*, else it checks the next expression, and so on. If all expressions are FALSE then the program executes the final `else` statement block, in this case, *statement block4*:

```
if (expression1)
{
    statement block1
}
else if (expression2)
{
    statement block2
}
else if (expression3)
{
    statement block3
}
else
{
    statement block4
}
```

Figure H9.1 shows a diagrammatic representation of this example statement.

Java program H9.11 gives an example of a program which uses the if...else statement. In this case the variable `col` is tested for its value. When it matches a value from 0 to 6 the equivalent colour code is displayed. If it is not between 0 and 6 then the default message is displayed (`"Not Defined Yet!"`). Sample run H9.10 shows a sample run.

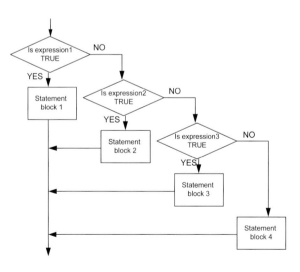

Figure H9.1   Structure of the compound `if` statement

📖 Java program H9.11

```
public class chapH9_11
{
    public static void main (String args[])
    {
    int col;
        col=4;
        if (col==0) System.out.println("BLACK");
        else if (col==1) System.out.println("BROWN");
        else if (col==2) System.out.println("RED");
        else if (col==3) System.out.println("ORANGE");
        else if (col==4) System.out.println("YELLOW");
        else if (col==5) System.out.println("GREEN");
        else System.out.println("Not Defined Yet!");
    }
}
```

Sample run H9.10

```
C:\java\src\chapH9> edit chapH9_01.java
C:\java\src\chapH9> javac chapH9_01.java
C:\java\src\chapH9> java chapH9_01
YELLOW
```

Some mathematical problems require the solution of a quadratic equation. The standard form is:

$$ax^2 + bx + c = 0$$

The solution of x in this equation is given by:

$$x_{1,2} = \frac{-b \pm \sqrt{b^2 - 4ac}}{2a}$$

This can yield three possible types of results:

1. if b^2=4ac, there will be a single real root (x=-b/2a)
2. else, if b^2>4ac, there will be two real roots:

$$x_1 = \frac{-b + \sqrt{b^2 - 4ac}}{2a}, \quad x_2 = \frac{-b - \sqrt{b^2 - 4ac}}{2a}$$

3. else, the roots will be complex:

$$x_1 = \frac{-b}{2a} + j\frac{\sqrt{4ac - b^2}}{2a}, \quad x_2 = \frac{-b}{2a} - j\frac{\sqrt{4ac - b^2}}{2a}$$

Program H9.12 determines the roots of a quadratic equation. In this program the if..else statement is used to determine if the roots are real, complex or singular. The value passed to the square-root function (sqrt ()) should be tested to determine if it is negative. If it is, it may cause the program to terminate as the square root of a negative number cannot be calculated (it is numerically invalid). The program may also terminate if a is zero as this causes a divide by zero. To use the sqrt () method the import java.lang.Math; line must be included in the program (this will be discussed in more detail, later).

📖 Java program H9.12

```java
import java.lang.Math;   // required for the sqrt() method
public class chapH9_02
{
   public static void main (String args[])
   {
   double a,b,c,root1,root2,real,imag;

      a=1; b=2; c=1;
      System.out.println("a, b and c are "+a+ " "+b+" "+c);
      if (b*b==4*a*c)
      {
         root1=-b/(2*a);
         System.out.println("Single root of "+root1);
      }
      else if (b*b>4*a*c)
      {
         root1=(-b+Math.sqrt(b*b-4*a*c))/(2*a);
         root2=(-b-Math.sqrt(b*b-4*a*c))/(2*a);
         System.out.println("Real roots of "+root1+ " " +root2);
      }
      else
      {
         real=-b/(2*a);
         imag=Math.sqrt(4*a*c-b*b)/(2*a);
         System.out.println("Real roots of "+real+ "+/-j "+imag);
      }
   }
}
```

Three sample runs H9.11, H9.12 and H9.13 test each of the three types of roots that occur. In Sample run H9.11 the roots of the equation are real. In Sample run H9.12 the roots are complex, i.e. in the form x+jy. In Sample run H9.13 the result is a singular root.

🖥 **Sample run H9.11**
```
C:\java\src\chapH9>java chapH9_02
a, b and c are 1.0 1.0 -2.0
Real roots of 1.0 -2.0
```

🖥 **Sample run H9.12**
```
C:\java\src\chapH9>java chapH9_02
a, b and c are 2.0 2.0 4.0
Real roots of -0.5+/-j 1.3228756555322954
```

🖥 **Sample run H9.13**
```
C:\java\src\chapH9>java chapH9_02
a, b and c are 1.0 2.0 1.0
Single root of -1.0
```

H9.12.2 switch

The switch statement is used when there is a multiple decision to be made. It is normally used to replace the if statement when there are many routes of execution the program execution can take. The syntax of switch is as follows.

```
switch (expression)
{
```

```
    case const1:    statement(s) : break;
    case const2:    statement(s) ; break;
    :         :
    default:              statement(s) ; break;
}
```

The switch statement checks the expression against each of the constants in sequence (the constant must be an integer or character data type). When a match is found the statement(s) associated with the constant is (are) executed. The execution carries on to all other statements until a break is encountered or to the end of switch, whichever is sooner. If the break is omitted, the execution continues until the end of switch. If none of the constants matches the switch expression a set of statements associated with the default condition (default:) is executed. The data type of the switch constants can be either byte, char, short, int or long.

Java program H9.13 is the equivalent of Java program H9.11 but using a switch statement. Sample run H9.14 shows a sample run.

📖 Java program H9.13

```
import java.lang.Math;
public class chapH9_03
{
    public static void main (String args[])
    {
    int col;
        col=4;
        switch (col)
        {
        case 0:  System.out.println("BLACK");  break;
        case 1:  System.out.println("BROWN");  break;
        case 2:  System.out.println("RED");       break;
        case 3:  System.out.println("ORANGE");    break;
        case 4:  System.out.println("YELLOW");    break;
        case 5:  System.out.println("GREEN");  break;
        default:   System.out.println("Not defined yet!");
        }
    }
}
```

💻 **Sample run H9.14**

```
C:\java\src\chapH9>java chapH9_03
YELLOW
```

H9.13   Loops

H9.13.1 for()

Many tasks within a program are repetitive, such as prompting for data, counting values, and so on. The for loop allows the execution of a block of code for a given control function. The following is an example format; if there is only one statement in the block then the braces can be omitted. Figure H9.2 shows a flow chart representation of this statement.

```
for (starting condition;test condition;operation)
```

```
{
     statement block
}
```

where :

```
starting condition –   the starting value for the loop;
test condition      –   if test condition is TRUE the loop will
                            continue execution;
operation           –   the operation conducted at the end of the loop.
```

Displaying ASCII characters

Program H9.14 displays ASCII characters for entered start and end decimal values. Sample run H9.15 displays the ASCII characters from decimal 40 ('(') to 50 ('2'). The type conversion (char) is used to convert an integer to a char.

📖 Java program H9.14
```
public class chapH9_14
{
    public static void main (String args[])
    {
    int start,end,ch;
       start=40; end=50;
       for (ch=start;ch<=end;ch++)
          System.out.println((int)ch+" "+(char)ch);
    }
}
```

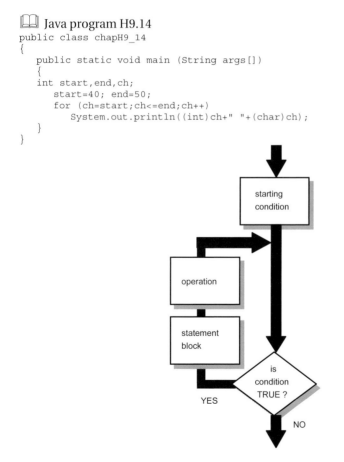

Figure H9.2   Flow chart representation of the for statement

```
C:\java\src\chapH9>java chapH9_01
40 (
41 )
42 *
43 +
44 ,
45 -
46 .
47 /
48 0
49 1
50 2
```

Simulation of a mathematical equation

The program in this section will simulate the results of the equation:

$$y = 3x^2 - 12x - 1$$

for values of x from 0 to 100 in steps of 10. Program H9.15 gives a Java program which implements this. Test run H9.16 shows a sample run of the program. It can be seen that the value of x varies from 0 to 100, in steps of 10.

Java program H9.15

```java
public class chapH9_15
{
    public static void main (String args[])
    {
    double x,y;
        System.out.println("X    Y");
        for (x=0;x<=100;x+=10)
        {
            y=3*(x*x)-12*x-1;
            System.out.println(x+" "+y);
        }
    }
}
```

Sample run H9.16
```
C:\java\src\chapH9>java chapH9_02
X    Y
0.0 -1.0
10.0 179.0
20.0 959.0
30.0 2339.0
40.0 4319.0
50.0 6899.0
60.0 10079.0
70.0 13859.0
80.0 18239.0
90.0 23219.0
100.0 28799.0
```

Boolean logic

Program H9.16 is an example of how a Boolean logic function can be analyzed and a truth table generated. The `for` loop generates all the required binary permutations for a truth table. The Boolean function used is:

$$Z = \overline{(A.B)} + C$$

A schematic of this equation is given in Figure H9.3. Test run H9.17 shows a sample run. The above equation is implemented in Java with:

```
z=~((a & b) | c)          // not ( (a and b) or c)
```

and as `z` is a 16-bit integer then to just show the first bit of the value then the following bit mask is used:

```
z=~((a & b) | c) & 1;   // mask-off least-significant bit
```

which will only display the least-significant bit of the operation.

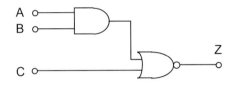

Figure H9.3   Digital circuit

📖 Java program H9.16
```
public class chapH9_16
{
    public static void main (String args[])
    {
    int a,b,c,z;

        System.out.println("A B C Z");

        for (a=0;a<=1;a++)
        for (b=0;b<=1;b++)
        for (c=0;c<=1;c++)
        {
            z=~((a & b) | c) & 1;
            System.out.println(a +  " "+b +" "+ c +" "+ z);
        }
    }
}
```

```
C:\java\src\chapH9>java chapH9_03
A B C Z
0 0 0 1
0 0 1 0
0 1 0 1
0 1 1 0
1 0 0 1
1 0 1 0
1 1 0 0
1 1 1 0
```

H9.13.2 while( )

The `while()` statement allows a block of code to be executed while a specified condition is TRUE. It checks the condition at the start of the block; if this is TRUE the block is executed, else it will exit the loop. The syntax is:

```
while (condition)
{
    :           :
    statement block
    :           :
}
```

If the statement block contains a single statement then the braces may be omitted (although it does no harm to keep them).

H9.13.3 do...while()

The `do...while()` statement is similar in its operation to `while()` except that it tests the condition at the bottom of the loop. This allows *statement block* to be executed at least once. The syntax is:

```
do
{
        statement block
} while (condition);
```

As with `for()` and `while()` loops the braces are optional. The `do...while()` loop requires a semicolon at the end of the loop, whereas the `while()` does not.

Figure H9.4 shows a flow chart representation of the `do...while()` and the `while()` loops. In both loops a TRUE condition will cause the statement block to be repeated.

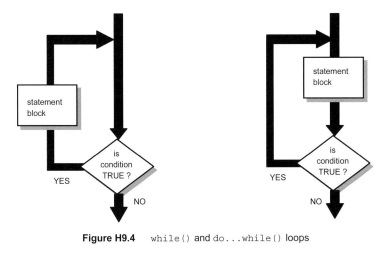

Figure H9.4 `while()` and `do...while()` loops

H9.13.4 Conversion from decimal to octal

Octal numbers uses base eight. To convert a decimal value to an octal number the decimal value is divided by 8 recursively and each remainder noted. The first remainder gives the least significant digit and the final remainder the most significant digit. For example, the following shows the octal equivalent of the decimal number 55:

```
8        55
         6    r 7  <<< LSD (least significant digit)
         0    r 6  <<< MSD (most significant digit)
```

Thus the decimal value 55 is equivalent to 67o (where the o represents octal). Program H9.17 shows a program which determines an octal value for an entered decimal value. Unfortunately, it displays the least significant digit first and the most significant digit last, thus the displayed value must be read in reverse. Test run H9.18 shows a sample run.

📖 Java program H9.17

```java
public class chapH9_17
{
   public static void main (String args[])
   {
   int val,remainder;

      val=55;
      System.out.println("Conversion to octal (in reverse)");
      do
      {
         remainder=val % 8;    // find remainder with modulus
         System.out.print(remainder);
         val=val / 8;
      } while (val>0);
   }
}
```

💻 **Sample run H9.18**

H9.14   Objects and Classes

C++ added object-oriented programming onto C. This allows the language to contain non object-oriented code and object-oriented code. Java differs in that it is completely object-oriented. This chapter discusses the main parts of object-oriented design, that is:

- Classes. This is a collection of data and methods that operate on the data.
- Objects. This is a created instance of a class which contains its own class data.
- Methods. These are used to operate on objects and are equivalent to procedures (in Pascal) and functions (in C).
- Constructors. These are used to initialize an instance of a class.
- Method overloading. These are used to define a method which has different parameters passed to it.
- Garbage collection. This is used to clean-up unused objects.

H9.14.1 Classes

Classes are a general form of structures, which are common in many languages. They basically gather together data members, and in object-oriented design, they also include methods (known as functions in C and procedures in Pascal) which operate on the class. Everything within Java is contained within classes.

In C a program is normally split into modules named functions. Typically these functions have parameters passed to them or from them. In Java these functions are named methods and operate within classes. Java program H9.18 includes a `Circle` class which contains two methods:

- `public float area(double r)`. In which the value of `r` is passed into the method and the return value is equal to πr^2 (`return(3.14159*r*r)`). The preceding `public double` defines that this method can be accessed from another class (`public`) and the `double` defines that the return type is of type `double`.
- `public float circum(double r)`. In which the value of `r` is passed into the method and the return value is equal to $2\pi r$ (`return(2*3.14159*r)`). The preceding `public double` defines that this method can be accessed from another class (`public`) and the `double` defines that the return type is of type `double`.

In defining a new class the program automatically defines a new data type (in Program H9.18 this new data type is named `Circle`). An instance of a class must first be created, thus for the `Circle` it can be achieved with:

```
Circle cir;
```

this does not create a `Circle` object, it only refers to it. Next the object can be created with the `new` keyword with:

```
cir = new Circle();
```

These two lines can be merged together into a single line with:

```
Circle cir = new Circle();
```

which creates an instance of a `Circle` and assigns a variable to it. The methods can then be used to operate on the object. For example to apply the `area()` method:

```
val=cir.area(10);
```

can be used. This passes the value of 10 into the `radius` variable in the `area()` method and the return value will be put into the `val` variable. Sample run H9.19 shows a sample run.

📖 Java program H9.18

```
public class chapH9_18
{
   public static void main(String[] args)
   {
      Circle cir=new Circle();
      System.out.println("Area is "+cir.area(10));
      System.out.println("Circumference is "+cir.circum(10));
   }
}
class Circle             // class is named Circle
{
   public double circum(double radius)
   {
      return(2*3.14159*radius);          // 2πr
   }
   public double area(double radius)
   {
      return(3.14159*radius*radius);     // πr²
   }
}
```

🖥 **Sample run H9.19**
```
C:\java\src\chapH9>java chapH9_01
Area is 314.159
Circumference is 62.8318
```

The data and methods within a class can either be:

- Private. These are variables (or methods) which can only be used within the class and have a preceding `private` keyword. By default variables (the members of the class) and methods are private (restricted).
- Public. These are variables (or methods) which can be accessed from other classes and have a preceding `public` keyword.

It is obvious that all classes must have a public content so that they can be accessed by external functions. In Program H9.19 the `Circle` class has three public parts:

- The methods `area()` and `circum()`, which determine the area and circumference of a circle.

- The Circle class variable `radius`.

Once the `Circle` class has been declared then the class variable `radius` can be accessed from outside the `Circle` class using:

```
cir.radius=10;
```

which sets the class variable (`radius`) to a value of 10. The methods then do not need to be passed the value of radius, as it is now set within the class (and will stay defined until either a new value is set or the class is deleted).

📖 Java program H9.19

```
public class chapH9_19
{
    public static void main(String[] args)
    {
    Circle cir=new Circle();
        cir.radius=10;
        System.out.println("Area is "+c.area());
        System.out.println("Circumference is "+c.circum());
    }
}
class Circle
{
public float radius;

    public double circum()
    {
        return(2*3.14159*radius);
    }
    public double area()
    {
        return(3.14159*radius*radius);
    }
}
```

Many instances of a class can be initiated and each will have their own settings for their class variables. For example, in Program H9.20, two instances of the `Circle` class have been declared (`cir1` and `cir2`). These are circle objects. The first circle object (`cir1`) has a radius of 15 and the second (`cir2`) has a radius of 10. Sample run H9.20 shows a sample run.

📖 Java program H9.20

```
public class chapH9_20
{
    public static void main(String[] args)
    {
    Circle cir1, cir2;

        cir1=new Circle();
        cir2=new Circle();

        cir1.radius=15;
        cir2.radius=10;

        System.out.println("Area1 is "+cir1.area());
        System.out.println("Area2 is "+cir2.area());
```

```
    }
}
class Circle
{
public float radius;

    public double circum()
    {
        return(2*3.14159*radius);
    }
    public double area()
    {
        return(3.14159*radius*radius);
    }
}
```

```
C:\java\src\chapH9>java chapH9_03
Area1 is 706.85775
Area2 is 314.159
```

H9.14.2 Constructors

A constructors allows for the initialization of a class. It is a special initialization function that is automatically called whenever a class is declared. The constructor always has the same name as the class name, and no data types are defined for the argument list or the return type. Normally a constructor is used to initialize a class.

Program H9.21 has a class which is named Circle. The constructor for this class is Circle(). Sample run H9.21 shows a sample run. It can be seen that initially when the program is run the message "Constructing a circle" is displayed when the object is created.

📖 Java program H9.21

```
public class chapH9_21
{
    public static void main(String[] args)
    {
    Circle c1,c2;
    double area1,area2;
        c1=new Circle();   c2=new Circle();

        c1.radius=15;      area1=c1.area();
        c2.radius=10;         area2=c2.area();
        System.out.println("Area1 is "+area1);
        System.out.println("Area2 is "+area2);
    }
}
class Circle
{
public float radius;

    public Circle()      // constructor called when object created
    {
        System.out.println("Constructing a circle");
    }
    public double circum()
    {
        return(2*3.14159*radius);
    }
    public double area()
```

```
    {
        return(3.14159*radius*radius);
    }
}
```

🖥 **Sample run H9.21**
```
C:\java\src\chapH9>java chapH9_04
Constructing a circle
Constructing a circle
Area1 is 706.85775
Area2 is 314.159
```

C++ has also a destructor which is a member of a function and is automatically called when the class is destroyed. It has the same name as the class name but is preceded by a tilde (~). Normally a destructor is used to clean-up when the class is destroyed. Java normally has no need for destructors as it implements a technique known as garbage collection which gets rids of objects which are no longer needed. If a final clear-up is required then the finalize() method can be used. This is called just before the garbage collection. For example:

```
class Circle
{

    public Circle()      // constructor called when object created
    {
        System.out.println("Constructing a circle");
    }
    public finalize()    // called when object deleted
    {
        System.out.println("Goodbye. I'm out with the trash");
    }

    public double circum()
    {
        return(2*3.14159*radius);
    }
    public double area()
    {
        return(3.14159*radius*radius);
    }
}
```

H9.14.3 Method overloading

Often the programmer requires to call a method in a number of ways but wants the same name for the different implementations. Java allows this with method overloading. With overloading the programmer defines a number of methods, each of which has the same name but which are called with a different argument list or return type. The compiler then automatically decides which one should be called. For example in Java Program H9.22 the programmer has defined two square methods named sqr() and two for max(), which is a maximum method. The data type of the argument passed is of a different type for each of the methods, that is, either an int or a double. The return type is also different. The data type of the parameters passed to these methods is tested by the compiler and it then determines which of the methods it requires to use. Sample run H9.22 shows a sample run.

📖 Java program H9.22

```
public class chapH9_22
{
    public static void main(String[] args)
    {
    MyMath m;
    int val1=4;
    double val2=4.1;

        m=new MyMath();

        System.out.println("Sqr(4)="+m.sqr(val1));
        System.out.println("Sqr(4.1)="+m.sqr(val2));
        System.out.println("Maximum (3,4)="+m.max(3,4));
        System.out.println("Maximum (3.0,4.0)="+m.max(3.0,4.0));
    }
}
class MyMath
{
    public int sqr(int val)
    {
        return(val*val);
    }
    public double sqr(double val)
    {
        return(val*val);
    }
    public int max(int a, int b)
    {
        if (a>b) return(a);
        else return(b);
    }
    public double max(double a, double b)
    {
        if (a>b) return(a);
        else return(b);
    }
}
```

🖥 Sample run H9.22

```
C:\java\src\chap9>java chapH9_22
Sqr(4)=16
Sqr(4.1)=16.81
Maximum (3,4)=4
Maximum (3.0,4.0)=4.0
```

The argument list of the overloaded function does not have to have the same number of arguments for each of the overloaded functions. Program H9.23 shows an example of an overloaded method which has a different number of arguments for each of the function calls. In this case the max() function can either be called with two integer values or by passing an array to it. Arrays will be covered later.

📖 Java program H9.23

```
public class chapH9_23
{
    public static void main(String[] args)
    {
    MyMath   m;
    int      val1=4, arr[]={1,5,-3,10,4}; // array has 5 elements
    double   val2=4.1;
```

```
        m=new MyMath();

        System.out.println("Sqr(4)="+m.sqr(val1));
        System.out.println("Sqr(4.1)="+m.sqr(val2));
        System.out.println("Maximum (3,4)="+m.max(3,4));
        System.out.println("Maximum (array)="+m.max(arr));
    }
}

class MyMath
{
    public int sqr(int val)
    {
        return(val*val);
    }
    public double sqr(double val)
    {
        return(val*val);
    }
    public int max(int a, int b)
    {
        if (a>b) return(a);
        else return(b);
    }
    public int max(int a[])
    {
    int i,max;
        max=a[0];                       // set max to first element
        for (i=1;i<a.length;i++)    //a.length returns array size
            if (max<a[i]) max=a[i];
        return(max);
    }
}
```

🖥 **Sample run H9.23**
```
C:\java\src\chapH9>java chapH9_06
Sqr(4)=16
Sqr(4.1)=16.81
Maximum (3,4)=4
Maximum (array)=10
```

H9.14.4 Static methods

Declaring an object to get access to the methods in the MyMath class is obviously not efficient as every declaration creates a new object. If we just want access to the methods in a class then the methods within the class are declared as static methods. The methods are then accessed by preceding the method with the class name. Static methods are associated with a class and not an object, thus there is no need to create an object with them. Thus in Program H9.24 the methods are accessed by:

```
val=MyMath.sqr(val1);    val=MyMath.max(3,4);
val=MyMath.max(arr);
```

Sample run H9.24 shows a sample run.

```
public class chapH9_24
{
    public static void main(String[] args)
    {
    int     val1=4, arr[]={1,5,-3,10,4};     // array has 5 elements
    double  val2=4.1;
        System.out.println("Sqr(val1) "+MyMath.sqr(val1));
        System.out.println("Sqr(arr) "+MyMath.sqr(val2));
        System.out.println("Max(3.0,4.0) "+MyMath.max(3,4));
        System.out.println("Max(arr) "+MyMath.max(arr));
    }
}
class MyMath
{
    public static int sqr(int val)
    {
        return(val*val);
    }
    public static double sqr(double val)
    {
        return(val*val);
    }
    public static int max(int a, int b)
    {
        if (a>b) return(a);
        else return(b);
    }
    public static int max(int a[])
    {
    int i,max;
        max=a[0];                          // set max to first element
        for (i=1;i<a.length;i++)   //a.length returns array size
           if (max<a[i]) max=a[i];
        return(max);
    }
}
```

💻 **Sample run H9.24**

```
C:\java\src\chapH9>java chapH9_06
Sqr(val1) 16
Sqr(arr) 16.81
Max(3.0,4.0) 4
Max(arr) 10
```

H9.14.5 Constants

Classes can contain constants which are defined as `public static` class variables. Such as:

```
class MyMath
{
    public static final double E = 2.7182818284590452354;
    public static final double PI = 3.14159265358979323846;
    public int sqr(int val)
    {
        return(val*val);
    }
    public double sqr(double val)
    {
        return(val*val);
    }
```

}

In this case the value of π is referenced by:

```
omega=2*MyMath.PI*f
```

The static class variables are declared as final so that they cannot be modified when an object is declared. Thus the following is INVALID:

```
MyMath.PI=10.1;
```

Program H9.25 shows a sample program and Sample run H9.25 shows a sample run.

📖 Java program H9.25

```
public class chapH9_25
{
    public static void main(String[] args)
    {
        System.out.println("PI is "+m.PI);
        System.out.println("E is ="+m.E);
    }
}
class MyMath
{
    public static final double E = 2.7182818284590452354;
    public static final double PI = 3.14159265358979323846;
    public static int sqr(int val)
    {
        return(val*val);
    }
    public static double sqr(double val)
    {
        return(val*val);
    }
    public static int max(int a, int b)
    {
        if (a>b) return(a);
        else return(b);
    }
    public static int max(int a[])
    {
    int i,max;

        max=a[0];                       // set max to first element
        for (i=1;i<a.length;i++)     //a.length returns array size
            if (max<a[i]) max=a[i];
        return(max);
    }
}
```

🖥 Sample run H9.25

```
C:\java\src\chapH9>java chap_08
PI is 3.141592653589793
E is =2.718281828459045
```

H9.14.6 Garbage collection

Most programming languages have a technique which allows memory to be freed once a variable or an object is not being used any more. C++ uses the `free` function to free the memory allocated to a variable or object. This is a very efficient technique but many programmers forget to free up memory once an object is not required. This leads to programs which tend to eat up memory.

Java does not have a method to release memory, but instead uses a garbage collection process which gets rid of objects which are no longer needed. The Java interpreter keeps a track of the objects that have been allocated and which variables are used with which objects. Then when an object is not used the interpreter deletes the object. The garbage collector runs as a low-priority process and picks up objects which need to be deleted. Thus it allows the programmer to develop programs which do not need to worry about the deletion of objects.

H9.15 Java Class Libraries and Arrays

H9.15.1 Package statements

The `package` statement defines that the classes within a Java file are part of a given package. The full name of a class is:

package . classFilename

The fully qualified name for a method is:

package . classFilename . method_name ()

Each class file with the same package name is stored in the same directory. For example, the `java.applet` package contains several files, such as:

```
applet.java            appletcontent.java
appletstub.java        audioclip.java
```

Each has a first line of:

```
package java.applet;
```

and the fully classified names of the class files are:

```
java.applet.applet          java.applet.appletcontent
java.applet.appletstub      java.applet.audioclip
```

These can be interpreted as in the `java/applet` directory. An example listing from the class library given in Sample run H9.26.

Normally when a Java class is being developed it is not part of a package as it is contained in the current directory.

```
java/
java/lang/
java/lang/Object.class
java/lang/Exception.class
java/lang/Integer.class
```

The main packages are:

java.applet	java.awt	java.awt.datatransfer
java.awt.event	java.awt.image	java.awt.peer
java.beans	java.io	java.lang
java.lang	java.lang.reflect	java.math
java.net	java.rmi	java.rmi.dgc
java.rmi.registry	java.rmi.server	java.security
java.security.acl	java.security.interfaces	java.sql
java.text	java.util	java.utils.zip

H9.15.2 Import statements

The `import` statement allows previously written code to be included in the applet. This code is stored in class libraries (or packages), which are compiled Java code. For the JDK tools, the Java source code for these libraries is stored in the `src/java` directory.

For example a Java program which uses maths methods will begin with:

```
import java.lang.Math;
```

This includes the `math` class libraries (which is in the `java.lang` package). The default Java class libraries are stored in the `classes.zip` file in the `lib` directory. This file is in a compressed form and should not be unzipped before it is used. The following is an outline of the file.

```
Searching ZIP: CLASSES.ZIP
Testing: java/
Testing: java/lang/
Testing: java/lang/Object.class
Testing: java/lang/Exception.class
Testing: java/lang/Integer.class
    ::          ::
Testing: java/lang/Win32Process.class
Testing: java/io/
Testing: java/io/FilterOutputStream.class
Testing: java/io/OutputStream.class
    ::          ::
Testing: java/io/StreamTenizer.class
Testing: java/util/
Testing: java/util/Hashtable.class
Testing: java/util/Enumeration.class
    ::          ::
Testing: java/util/Stack.class
Testing: java/awt/
Testing: java/awt/Toolkit.class
Testing: java/awt/peer/
Testing: java/awt/peer/WindowPeer.class
    ::          ::
```

```
Testing: java/awt/peer/DialogPeer.class
Testing: java/awt/Image.class
Testing: java/awt/MenuItem.class

Testing: java/awt/MenuComponent.class
Testing: java/awt/image/
   ::              ::
Testing: java/awt/ImageMediaEntry.class
Testing: java/awt/AWTException.class
Testing: java/net/
Testing: java/net/URL.class
Testing: java/net/URLStreamHandlerFactory.class
   ::              ::
Testing: java/net/URLEncoder.class
Testing: java/applet/
Testing: java/applet/Applet.class
Testing: java/applet/AppletContext.class
Testing: java/applet/AudioClip.class
```

The other form of the import statement is:

```
import package.*;
```

which will import all the classes within the specified package. Table 9.14 lists the main class libraries and some sample libraries.

It can be seen that upgrading the Java compiler is simple, as all that is required is to replace the class libraries with new ones. For example, if the basic language is upgraded then java.lang.* files is simply replaced with a new version. The user can also easily add new class libraries to the standard ones.

Table H9.14   Class libraries

Class libraries	Description	Example libraries
java.lang.*	Java language	java.lang.Class
		java.lang.Number
		java.lang.Process
		java.lang.String
java.io.*	I/O routines	java.io.InputStream
		java.io.OutputStream
java.util.*	Utilities	java.util.BitSet
		java.util.Dictionary
java.awt.*	Windows, menus and graphics	java.awt.Point
		java.awt.Polygon
		java.awt.MenuComponent
		java.awt.MenuBar
		java.awt.MenuItem
java.net.*	Networking (such as sockets, URLs, ftp, telnet and HTTP)	java.net.ServerSocket
		java.net.Socket
		java.net.SocketImpl
java.applet.*	Code required to run an applet	java.applet.AppletContext
		java.applet.AppletStub
		java.applet.AudioClip

H9.15.3 Mathematical operations

Java has a basic set of mathematics methods which are defined in the `java.lang.Math` class library. Table H9.15 outlines these methods. An example of a method in this library is `abs()` which can be used to return the absolute value of either a `double`, an `int` or a `long` value. Java automatically picks the required format and the return data type will be of the same data type of the value to be operated on.

As the functions are part of the `Math` class they are preceded with the `Math.` class method. For example:

```
val2=Math.sqrt(val1);
val3=Math.abs(val2);
z=Math.min(x,y);
```

Java stand-alone program H9.26 shows a few examples of mathematical operations and Sample run H9.27 shows a sample compilation and run session.

Table H9.15   Methods defined in `java.lang.Math`

Method	Description
double **abs**(double a)	Returns the absolute double value of a.
float **abs**(float a)	Returns the absolute float value of a.
int **abs**(int a)	Returns the absolute integer value of a.
long **abs**(long a)	Returns the absolute long value of a.
double **acos**(double a)	Returns the arc cosine of a, in the range of 0.0 through `Pi`.
double **asin**(double a)	Returns the arc sine of a, in the range of `Pi/2` through `Pi/2`.
double **atan**(double a)	Returns the arc tangent of a, in the range of –`Pi/2` through `Pi/2`.
double **atan2**(double a, double b)	Converts rectangular co-ordinates (a, b) to polar (r, theta).
double **ceil**(double a)	Returns the 'ceiling' or smallest whole number greater than or equal to a.
double **cos**(double a)	Returns the trigonometric cosine of an angle.
double **exp**(double a)	Returns the exponential number e (2.718…) raised to the power of a.

Table H9.15 Methods defined in `java.lang.Math` (continued)

`double floor( double a)`	Returns the 'floor' or largest whole number less than or equal to a.
`double IEEEremainder(` `double f1, double f2)`	Returns the remainder of f1 divided by f2 as defined by IEEE 754.
`double log(double a)`	Returns the natural logarithm (base e) of a.
`double max(double a,` `double b)`	Takes two double values, a and b, and returns the greater.
`double max(float a,` `float b)`	Takes two float values, a and b, and returns the greater number of the two.
`int max(int a, int b)`	Takes two int values, a and b, and returns the greater number.
`long max(long a,long b)`	Takes two long values, a and b, and returns the greater.
`double min(double a,` `double b)`	Takes two double values, a and b, and returns the smallest.
`float min(float a,` `float b)`	Takes two float values, a and b, and returns the smallest.
`int min(int a, int b)`	Takes two integer values, a and b, and returns the smallest number.
`long min(long a,` `long b)`	Takes two long values, a and b, and returns the smallest number of the two.
`double pow(double a,` `double b)`	Returns the number a raised to the power of b.
`double random()`	Generates a random number between 0.0 and 1.0.
`double rint(double b)`	Converts a double value into an integral value in double format.
`long round(double a)`	Rounds off a double value by first adding 0.5 to it and then returning the largest integer that is less than or equal to this new value.

Table H9.15	Methods defined in `java.lang.Math` (continued)
`int round(float a)`	Rounds off a float value by first adding 0.5 to it and then returning the largest integer that is less than or equal to this new value.
`double sin(double a)`	Returns the trigonometric sine of a.
`double sqrt(double a)`	Returns the square root of a.
`double tan(double a)`	Returns the trigonometric tangent of an angle.

📖 Java program H9.26

```
import java.lang.Math;
public class chapH9_26
{
    public static void main(String[] args)
    {
    double x,y,z;
    int i;
        i=10;
        y=Math.log(10.0);
        x=Math.pow(3.0,4.0);
        z=Math.random(); // random number from 0 to 1
        System.out.println("Value of i is " + i);
        System.out.println("Value of log(10) is " + y);
        System.out.println("Value of 3^4 is " + x);
        System.out.println("A random number is " + z);
        System.out.println("Square root of 2 is " + Math.sqrt(2));
    }
}
```

💻 Sample run H9.27

```
C:\DOCS\notes\INTER\java>javac chap05_1.java
C:\DOCS\notes\INTER\java>java chap05_1
Value of i is 10
Value of log(10) is 2.30259
Value of 3^4 is 81
A random number is 0.0810851
Square root of 2 is 1.41421
```

Java has also two predefined mathematical constants. These are:

- Pi is equivalent to 3.14159265358979323846
- E is equivalent to 2.7182818284590452354

H9.15.4 Arrays

An array stores more than one value, of a common data type, under a collective name. Each value has a unique slot and is referenced using an indexing technique. For example, a circuit with five resistor components could be declared within a program with five simple float declarations. If these resistor variables were required to be passed into a method then all five values would have to be passed through the parameter list. A neater way uses arrays to store all of the values under a common name (in this case R). Then a single array variable can then be passed into any method that uses it.

The declaration of an array specifies the data type, the array name and the number of elements in the array in brackets ([]). The following gives the standard format for an array declaration.

data_type array_name [] ;

The array is then created using the new keyword. For example, to declare an integer array named new_arr with 200 elements then the following is used:

```
int new_arr[];

new_arr=new int[200];
```

or, in a single statement, with:

```
int new_arr[]=new int[200];
```

Java program H9.27 gives an example of this type of declaration where an array (arr) is filled with 20 random numbers.

Figure H9.3 shows that the first element of the array is indexed 0 and the last element as size-1. The compiler allocates memory for the first element array_name[0] to the last array element array_name[size-1]. The number of bytes allocated in memory will be the number of elements in the array multiplied by the number of bytes used to store the data type of the array.

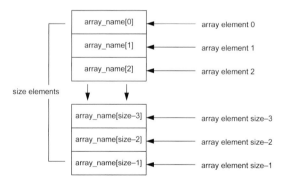

Figure H9.3 Array elements

📖 Java program H9.27
```
public class chapH9_27
{
   public static void main(String[] args)
   {
      double arr[]=new double[20];
      int   i;

      for (i=0;i<20;i++)   arr[i]=Math.random();
      for (i=0;i<20;i++)   System.out.println(arr[i]);
```

```
        }
}
```

```
C:\java\src\chapH9>java chapH9_02
0.6075765411193292
0.7524300612559963
0.8100796233691735
0.45045015538577704
0.32390753542869755
0.34033464565015836
0.5079716192482706
0.6426253967106341
0.7691175624480434
0.6475110502592946
0.1416366173783874
0.21181433233783153
0.21758072702009412
0.24203490620407764
0.7587570097412505
0.4470154908107362
0.19823448357551965
0.7340429664182364
0.7402367706819387
0.8975606689180567
```

Another way to create and initialize an array is to define the elements within the array within curly brackets ({ }). A comma separates each element in the array. The size of the array is then equal to the number of elements in the array. For example:

```
int     arr1[]={-3, 4, 10, 100, 30, 22};
String  menus[]={"File", "Edit", "View", "Insert", "Help"};
```

A particular problem in most programming languages (such as C and Pascal) exists when accessing array elements which do not exist, especially by accessing an array element which is greater than the maximum size of the array. Java overcomes this by being able to determine the size of the array. This is done with the `length` field. For example, the previous example can be modified with:

```
for (i=0;i<arr.length;i++)    arr[i]=Math.random();
for (i=0;i<arr.length;i++)    System.out.println(arr[i]);
```

Java program H9.28 gives an example of an array of strings. In this case, the array contains the names of playing cards. When run the program displays five random playing cards. Sample run H9.29 shows a sample run.

📖 **Java program H9.28**
```
public class chapH9_28
{
    public static void main(String[] args)
    {
    int cards,pick;
    String   Card[]={"Ace","King","Queen","Jack","10",
                "9", "8", "7", "6", "5", "4", "3", "2"};
```

```
        for (cards=0;cards<5;cards++)
        {
            pick=(int)Math.round((Card.length)*Math.random());
            System.out.print(Card[pick] + " ");
        }
    }
}
```

🖥 **Sample run H9.29**
Ace   10   King   2   3

Multi-dimensional arrays are declared in a similar manner. For example, an array with 3 rows and 4 columns is declared with either of the following:

```
int arr[][]=new int[3][4];
```

or if the initial values are known with:

```
int arr[][]= { {1,2,3,4}, {5,6,7,8}, {9,10,11,12} } ;
```

where `arr[0][0]` is equal to 1, `arr[1][0]` is equal to 5, `arr[2][3]` is equal to 12, and so on. This is proved with Java program H9.29 and Sample runH9.30.

📖 **Java program H9.29**
```
public class chapH9_29
{
    public static void main(String[] args)
    {
    int    row,col;
    int    arr[][]={ {1,2,3,4},{5,6,7,8}, {9,10,11,12} };

    for (row=0;row<3;row++)
        for (col=0;col<4;col++)
            System.out.println("Arr["+row+"]["+col+"]="+arr[row][col]);
    }
}
```

🖥 **Sample run H9.30**
```
C:\java\src\chapH9>java chapH9_05
Arr[0][0]=1
Arr[0][1]=2
Arr[0][2]=3
Arr[0][3]=4
Arr[1][0]=5
Arr[1][1]=6
Arr[1][2]=7
Arr[1][3]=8
Arr[2][0]=9
Arr[2][1]=10
Arr[2][2]=11
Arr[2][3]=12
```

H10 Java (applets and events)

H10.1 Java applets

As has been previously discussed a Java program can either be run as an applet with a WWW Browser (such as Internet Explorer or Netscape Communicator) or can be interpreted as a stand-alone program. The basic code within each program is almost the same and they can be easily converted from one to the other (typically a Java program will be run through an interpreter to test its results and then converted to run as an applet).

H10.1.1 applet tag

An applet is called from within an HTML script with the APPLET tag, such as:

```
<applet code="Test.class" width=200 height=300></applet>
```

which loads an applet called `Test.class` and sets the applet size to 200 pixels wide and 300 pixels high. Table H10.1 discusses some optional parameters.

Applet viewer

A useful part of the JDK tools is an applet viewer which is used to test applets before they are run within the browse. The applet viewer on the PC version is `AppletViewer.exe` and the supplied argument is the HTML file that contains the applet tag(s). It then runs all the associated applets in separate windows.

Table H10.1 Other applet HTML parameters

applet parameters	Description
CODEBASE=*codebaseURL*	Specifies the directory (*codebaseURL*) that contains the applet's code.
CODE=*appletFile*	Specifies the name of the file (*appletFile*) of the compiled applet.
ALT=*alternateText*	Specifies the alternative text that is displayed if the browser cannot run the Java applet.
NAME=*appletInstanceName*	Specifies a name for the applet instance (*appletInstanceName*). This makes it possible for applets on the same page to find each other.
WIDTH=*pixels* HEIGHT=*pixels*	Specifies the initial width and height (in *pixels*) of the applet.
ALIGN=*alignment*	Specifies the *alignment* of the applet. Possible values are: `left`, `right`, `top`, `texttop`, `middle`, `absmiddle`, `baseline`, `bottom` and `absbottom`.
VSPACE=*pixels* HSPACE=*pixels*	Specifies the number of *pixels* above and below the applet (VSPACE) and on each side of the applet (HSPACE).

H10.1.2 Creating an applet

Java applet H10.1 shows a simple Java applet which displays two lines of text and HTML script H10.1 shows how the applet integrates into an HTML script.

First, the Java applet (chapH10_01.java) is created. In this case, the edit program is used. The directory listing below shows that the files created are chapH10_01.java and chapH10_01.html.

📖 Java applet H10.1 (chapH10_01.java)

```java
import java.awt.*;
import java.applet.*;

public class chapH10_01 extends Applet
{
  public void paint(Graphics g)
  {
    g.drawString("This is my first Java",5,25);
    g.drawString("applet.....",5,45);
  }
}
```

📖 HTML script H10.1 (chapH10_01.html)

```html
<HTML>
<TITLE>First Applet</TITLE>
<APPLET CODE=chapH10_01.class WIDTH=200
HEIGHT=200></APPLET></HTML>
```

🖥 **Sample run H10.1**

```
C:\java\src\chapH10>edit chapH10_01.java
C:\java\src\chapH10>edit chapH10_01.html
C:\java\src\chapH10>dir
.              <DIR>        13/05/98   22:39  .
..             <DIR>        13/05/98   22:39  ..
CHAPH10_~1 HTM      111   14/05/98   18:40  chapH10_01.html
CHAPH10_~1 JAV      228   13/05/98   22:35  chapH10_01.java
           2 file(s)           339 bytes
           2 dir(s)     30,703,616 bytes free
```

Next, the Java applet is compiled using the javac.exe program. It can be seen from the listing that, if there are no errors, the compiled file is named chapH10_01.class. This can then be used, with the HTML file, to run as an applet.

🖥 **Sample run H10.2**

```
C:\java\src\chapH10>javac chapH10_01.java
C:\java\src\chapH10>dir
CHAPH10_~1 HTM      111   14/05/98   18:40  chapH10_01.html
CHAPH10_~1 JAV      228   14/05/98   18:43  chapH10_01.java
CHAPH10_~1 CLA      460   14/05/98   18:43  chapH10_01.class
C:\DOCS\notes\INTER\java>appletviewer ch6_01.html
```

H10.1.3 Applet basics

Java applet H10.1 recaps the previous Java applet. This section analyses the main parts of this Java applet.

📖 Java applet H10.1 (chapH10_01.java)

```java
import java.awt.*;
import java.applet.*;
public class chapH10_01 extends Applet
{
  public void paint(Graphics g)
  {
   g.drawString("This is my first Java",5,25);
   g.drawString("applet.....",5,45);
  }
}
```

Applet class

The start of the applet code is defined in the form:

```java
public class chapH10_01 extends Applet
```

which informs the Java compiler to create an applet named `chapH10_01` that extends the existing Applet class. The `public` keyword at the start of the statement allows the Java browser to run the applet, while if it is omitted the browser cannot access your applet.

The `class` keyword is used to creating a class object named `chapH10_01` that extends the applet class. After this, the applet is defined between the left and right braces (grouping symbols).

Applet functions

Functions allow Java applets to be split into smaller sub-tasks called functions. These functions have the advantage that:

- They allow code to be reused.
- They allow for top-level design.
- They make applet debugging easier as each function can be tested in isolation to the rest of the applet.

A function has the `public` keyword, followed by the return value (if any) and the name of the function. After this the parameters passed to the function are defined within rounded brackets. Recapping from the previous example:

```java
public void paint(Graphics g)
{
   g.drawString("This is my first Java",5,25);
   g.drawString("applet.....",5,45);
}
```

This function has the `public` keyword which allows any user to execute the function. The `void` type defines that there is nothing returned from this function and the name of the function is `paint()`. The parameter passed into the function is g which has the data type of `Graphics`. Within the `paint()` function the `drawString()` function is called. This function is defined in `java.awt.Graphics` class library (this library has been included with the `import java.awt.*` statement. The definition for this function is:

```java
   public abstract void drawString(String str, int x, int y)
```

which draws a string of characters using the current font and color. The x,y position is the starting point of the baseline of the string (str).

It should be noted that Java is case sensitive and the names given must be referred to in the case that they are defined as.

H10.1.4 The paint() object

The paint() object is the object that is called whenever the applet is redrawn. It will thus be called whenever the applet is run and then it is called whenever the applet is redisplayed.

Java applet H10.2 shows how a for() loop can be used to display the square and cube of the values from 0 to 9. Notice that the final value of i within the for() loop is 9 because the end condition is i<10 (while i is less than 10).

📖 Java applet H10.2 (chapH10_02.java)

```
import java.awt.*;
import java.applet.*;

public class chapH10_02 extends Applet
{
  public void paint(Graphics g)
  {
  int      i;

    g.drawString("Value Square Cube",5,10);
    for (i=0;i<10;i++)
    {
      g.drawString(""+ i,5,20+10*i);
      g.drawString(""+ i*i ,45,20+10*i);
      g.drawString(""+ i*i*i,85,20+10*i);
    }
  }
}
```

```
Applet Viewer: cha...  _ □ ×
Applet
Value Square Cube
0     0      0
1     1      1
2     4      8
3     9      27
4     16     64
5     25     125
6     36     216
7     49     343
8     64     512
9     81     729


Applet started.
```

📖 HTML script H10.2 (chapH10_02.html)

```
<HTML>
<TITLE>First Applet</TITLE>
<APPLET CODE=chapH10_02.class WIDTH=200
HEIGHT=200>
</APPLET>
</HTML>
```

Java applet H10.3 uses a for() loop and the if() statement to test if a value is less than, equal to or greater than 5. The loop is used to repeat the test 10 times.

The random() function is used to generate a value between 0 and 1, the returned value is then multiplied by 10 so as to convert to into a value between 0 and 10. Then it is converted to an integer using the data type modifier (int). The if() statement is then used to test the value.

📖 Java applet H10.3 (chapH10_03.java)

```java
import java.awt.*;
import java.applet.*;
import java.lang.Math;

public class chapH10_03 extends Applet
{
  public void paint(Graphics g)
  {
    int      i,x;
    double   val;
    for (i=0;i<10;i++)
    {
      val=Math.random();

      x=(int)(val*10.0);
  // Convert value between 0 and 10

      if (x<5)
        g.drawString("Less than 5",
                        5,20+i*10);
      else if (x==5)
        g.drawString("Equal to 5",
                        5,20+i*10);
      else
        g.drawString("Greater than 5",
                        5,20+i*10);
    }
  }
}
```

Applet Viewer: j5.cl...

Applet

```
Less than 5
Less than 5
Greater than 5
Greater than 5
Greater than 5
Equal to 5
Less than 5
Greater than 5
Less than 5
Less than 5
```

Applet started.

📖 HTML script H10.3 (chapH10_03.html)

```html
<HTML>
<TITLE>First Applet</TITLE>

<APPLET CODE=chapH10_03.class WIDTH=200
HEIGHT=200>

</APPLET>
</HTML>
```

H10.2   Java mouse and Keyboard methods

This chapter investigates event-driven programs. Traditional methods of programming involve writing a program which flows from one part to the next in a linear manner. Most programs are designed using a top-down structured design, where the task is split into a number of sub-modules, these are then called when they are required. This means that it is relatively difficult to interrupt the operation of a certain part of a program to do another activity, such as updating the graphics display.

In general, Java is event-driven where the execution of a program is not predefined and its execution is triggered by events, such as a mouse click, a keyboard press, and so on. The main events are:

- Initialization and exit methods (init(), start(), stop() and destroy()).
- Repainting and resizing (paint()).

- Mouse events (`mouseUp()`, `mouseDown()` and `mouseDrag()` for Java 1.0, and `mouse-Pressed()`, `mouseReleased()` and `mouseDragged()` for Java 1.1).
- Keyboard events (`keyUp()` and `keyDown()` for Java 1.0, and `keyPressed()` and `keyReleased()` for Java 1.1).

H10.2.1 Java 1.0 and Java 1.1

There was been a big change between Java 1.0 and Java 1.1. The main change is to greatly improve the architecture of the AWT, which helps in compatibility. Java 1.0 programs will work with most browsers, but only upgraded browsers will work with Java 1.1. The main reasons to upgrade though are:

- Java 1.1 adds new features.
- Faster architecture with more robust implementations of the AWT.
- Support for older facilities will be phased out.

Deprecation

Older facilitates which are contained with Java 1.0 and are still supported Java 1.1, but the Java compiler gives a deprecation warning. This warning means that the facility will eventually be phased-out. The warning is in the form of:

```
C:\jdk\src\chapH10>javac chapH10_01.java
Note: chapH10_01.java uses a deprecated API.  Recompile with "-deprecation" for
details.
1 warning
```

The full details on the deprecation can be found by using the –deprecation flag. For example:

```
C:\jdk\src\chapH10>javac -deprecation chapH10_01.java
chapH10_01.java:9: Note: The method boolean mouseUp(java.awt. Event, int, int)
in class java.awt.Component has been deprecated, and class chapH10_01 (which is
not deprecated) overrides it.

    public boolean mouseUp(Event event,
                   ^
Note: chapH10_01.java uses a deprecated API.  Please consult the documentation
for a better alternative.
1 warning
```

H10.2.2 Initialization and exit methods

Java applets have various reserved methods which are called when various events occur. Table H10.2 shows typical initialization methods and their events, and Figure H10.1 illustrates how they are called.

Java applet H10.4 gives an example using the `init()` and `start()` methods. The variable i is declared within the applet and it is set to a value of 5 in the `init()` method. The `start()` method then adds 6 onto this value. After this the `paint()` method is called so that it displays the value of i (which should equal 11).

Table H10.2 Java initialisation and exit methods

Method	Description
public void **init**()	This method is called each time the applet is started. It is typically used to add user-interface components.
public void **stop**()	This method is called when the user moves away from the page on which the applet resides. It is thus typically used to stop processing while the user is not accessing the applet. Typically, it is used to stop animation or audio files, or mathematical processing. The start() method normally restarts the processing.
public void **paint**(Graphics g)	This method is called when the applet is first called and whenever the user resizes or moves the windows.
public void **destroy**()	This method is called when the applet is stopped and is normally used to release associated resources, such as freeing memory, closing files, and so on.

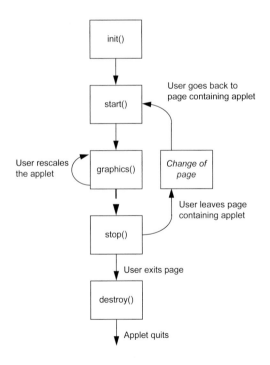

Figure H10.1   Java initialisation and exit methods

📖 Java applet H10.4 (`chapH10_04.java`)

```java
import java.awt.*;
import java.applet.*;

public class chapH10_04 extends Applet
{
int     i;

  public void init()
  {
     i=5;
  }
  public void start()
  {
     i=i+6;
  }
  public void paint(Graphics g)
  {
    g.drawString("The value of i is "
           + i,5,25);
  }
}
```

📖 HTML script H10.4 (`chapH10_01.html`)

```html
<HTML>
<TITLE>Applet</TITLE>
<APPLET CODE=chapH10_04.class WIDTH=200
HEIGHT=200>
</APPLET></HTML>
```

H10.2.3 Mouse events in Java 1.0

Most Java applets require some user interaction, normally with the mouse or from the keyboard. A mouse operation causes mouse events. The six basic mouse events which are supported in Java 1.0 are:

- `mouseUp(Event evt, int x, int y)`
- `mouseDown(Event evt, int x, int y)`
- `mouseDrag(Event evt, int x, int y)`
- `mouseEnter(Event evt, int x, int y)`
- `mouseExit(Event evt, int x, int y)`
- `mouseMove(Event evt, int x, int y)`

Java applet H10.5 uses three mouse events to display the current mouse cursor. Each of the methods must return a true value to identify that the event has been handled successfully (the return type is of data type boolean thus the return could only be a true or a false). In the example applet, on moving the mouse cursor with the left mouse key pressed down the `mouseDrag()` method is automatically called. The x and y co-ordinate of the cursor is stored in the x and y variable when the event occurs. This is used in the methods to build a message string (in the case of the drag event the string name is `MouseDragMsg`).

The `mouseEnter()` method is called when the mouse enters the component, `mouseExit()` is called when the mouse exits the component and `mouseMove()` when the mouse moves (the mouse button is up).

📖   Java applet H10.5 (chapH10_05.java)

```
import java.awt.*;
import java.applet.*;
public class chapH10_05 extends Applet
{
String  MouseDownMsg=null;
String  MouseUpMsg=null;
String  MouseDragMsg=null;

  public boolean mouseUp(Event event,
   int x, int y)
  {
    MouseUpMsg = "UP>" +x + "," + y;
    repaint();   // call paint()
    return(true);
  }
  public boolean mouseDown(Event event,
   int x, int y)
  {
    MouseDownMsg = "DOWN>" +x + "," + y;
    repaint();   // call paint()
    return(true);
  }

  public boolean mouseDrag(Event event,
   int x, int y)
  {
    MouseDragMsg = "DRAG>" +x + "," + y;
    repaint();   // call paint()
    return(true);
  }

  public void paint(Graphics g)
  {
    if (MouseUpMsg !=null)
      g.drawString(MouseUpMsg,5,20);
    if (MouseDownMsg !=null)
      g.drawString(MouseDownMsg,5,40);
    if (MouseDragMsg !=null)
      g.drawString(MouseDragMsg,5,60);
  }
}
```

Applet Viewer: cha...

Applet

UP>34,117
DOWN>171,94
DRAG>171,94

Applet started.

📖   HTML script H10.5 (chapH10_05.html)

```
<HTML>
<TITLE>Applet</TITLE>
<APPLET CODE=chapH10_05.class WIDTH=200
HEIGHT=200>
</APPLET></HTML>
```

H10.2.4 Mouse event handling in Java 1.1

Java 1.1 has changed the event handling. In its place is the concept of listeners. Each listener receives notification about the types of events that it is interested in. For mouse handling the two listeners are:

- MouseListener. This has the associated methods of:
  - mousePressed() which is equivalent to mouseDown() in Java 1.0
  - mouseReleased() which is equivalent to mouseUp() in Java 1.0
  - mouseEntered() which is equivalent to mouseEnter() in Java 1.0

- mouseExited() which is equivalent to mouseExit() in Java 1.0
- mouseClicked()
- MouseMotionListener. This has the associated methods of:
  - mouseDragged() which is equivalent to mouseDrag() in Java 1.0
  - mouseMoved() which is equivalent to mouseMove() in Java 1.0

Mouse methods

The arguments passed to the methods have also changed, in that there are no x and y integers passed, and there is no return from them. Their syntax is as follows:

```
public void mousePressed(MouseEvent event) {};
public void mouseReleased(MouseEvent event) {};
public void mouseClicked(MouseEvent event) {};
public void mouseExited(MouseEvent event) {};
public void mouseEntered(MouseEvent event) {};
public void mouseDragged(MouseEvent event) {};
public void mouseMoved(MouseEvent event) {};
```

The x and y co-ordinates of the mouse event can be found by accessing the getX() and getY() methods of the event, such as:

```
x=event.getX();    y=event.getY();
```

Event class

The other main change to the Java program is to add the java.awt.event package, with:

```
import java.awt.event.*;
```

Class declaration

The class declaration is changed so that the appropriate listener is defined. If both mouse listeners are required then the class declaration is as follows:

```
public class class_name extends Applet
    implements MouseListener, MouseMotionListener
```

Defining components that generate events

The components which generate events must be defined. In the case of a mouse event these are added as:

```
        this.addMouseListener(this);
        this.addMouseMotionListener(this);
```

Updated Java program

Java applet H10.6 gives the updated Java program with Java 1.1 updates.

📖 Java applet H10.6 (`chapH10_06.java`)

```
import java.awt.*;
import java.applet.*;
import java.awt.event.*;

public class chapH10_02 extends Applet
implements MouseListener, MouseMotionListener
{
String  MouseDownMsg=null;
String  MouseUpMsg=null;
String  MouseDragMsg=null;

  public void init()
  {
        this.addMouseListener(this);
        this.addMouseMotionListener(this);
  }

  public void paint(Graphics g)
  {
    if (MouseUpMsg !=null)  g.drawString(MouseUpMsg,5,20);
    if (MouseDownMsg !=null) g.drawString(MouseDownMsg,5,40);
    if (MouseDragMsg !=null) g.drawString(MouseDragMsg,5,60);
  }

  public void mousePressed(MouseEvent event)
  {
    MouseUpMsg = "UP>" +event.getX() + "," + event.getY();
    repaint();    // call paint()
  }
  public void mouseReleased(MouseEvent event)
  {
    MouseDownMsg = "DOWN>" +event.getX() + "," + event.getY();
    repaint();    // call paint()
  }
  public void mouseClicked(MouseEvent event) {};
  public void mouseExited(MouseEvent event) {};
  public void mouseEntered(MouseEvent event) {};

   public void mouseDragged(MouseEvent event)
  {
    MouseDragMsg = "DRAG>" +event.getX() + "," + event.getY();
    repaint();    // call paint()
  }
  public void mouseMoved(MouseEvent event) {};
}
```

H10.2.5 Mouse selection in Java 1.0

In many applets, the user is prompted to select an object using the mouse. To achieve this x and y position of the event is tested to determine if the cursor is within the defined area. Java applet H10.7 is a program which allows the user to press the mouse button on the applet screen. The applet then uses the mouse events to determine if the cursor is within a given area of the screen (in this case between 10,10 and 100,50). If the user is within this defined area then the message displayed is HIT, else it is MISS. The graphics method `g.drawRect(x1,y1,x2,y2)` draws a rectangle from (x1,y1) to (x2,y2).

📖 Java applet H10.7 (chapH10_07.java)

```java
import java.awt.*;
import java.applet.*;
public class chapH10_07 extends Applet
{
String  Msg=null;
int     x_start,y_start,x_end,y_end;

  public void init()
  {
    x_start=10;   y_start=10;
    x_end=100;    y_end=50;
  }

  public boolean mouseUp(Event event,
   int x, int y)
  {
    if ((x>x_start) && (x<x_end) &&
            (y>y_start) && (y<y_end))
              Msg = "HIT";
    else Msg="MISS";
    repaint();   // call paint()
    return(true);
  }

  public boolean mouseDown(Event event,
   int x, int y)
  {
    if ((x>x_start) && (x<x_end) &&
            (y>y_start) && (y<y_end))
              Msg = "HIT";
    else Msg="MISS";
    repaint();   // call paint()
    return(true);
  }

  public void paint(Graphics g)
  {

  g.drawRect(x_start,y_start,x_end,y_end);
    g.drawString("Hit",30,30);
    if (Msg !=null)
     g.drawString("HIT OR MISS: "
         + Msg,5,80);
  }
}
```

📖 HTML script H10.6 (chapH10_06.html)

```html
<HTML>
<TITLE>Applet</TITLE>
<APPLET CODE=chapH10_07.class WIDTH=200
HEIGHT=200>
</APPLET></HTML>
```

Java applet H10.8 gives the updated Java program with Java 1.1 updates.

📖 Java applet H10.8 (chapH10_08.java)

```java
import java.awt.*;
import java.applet.*;
import java.awt.event.*;
```

```
public class chapH10_08 extends Applet implements MouseListener
{
String  Msg=null;
int     x_start,y_start,x_end,y_end;

  public void init()
  {
    x_start=10;    y_start=10;
    x_end=100;     y_end=50;
    this.addMouseListener(this);
  }

  public void mousePressed(MouseEvent event)
  {
    int x,y;
    x=event.getX(); y=event.getY();

    if ((x>x_start) && (x<x_end) && (y>y_start) && (y<y_end))
              Msg = "HIT";
    else Msg="MISS";
    repaint();   // call paint()
  }

  public void mouseReleased(MouseEvent event)
  {
    int x,y;
    x=event.getX();   y=event.getY();
    if ((x>x_start) && (x<x_end) && (y>y_start) && (y<y_end))
              Msg = "HIT";
    else Msg="MISS";
    repaint();   // call paint()
  }
  public void mouseEntered(MouseEvent event) {};
  public void mouseExited(MouseEvent event) {};
  public void mouseClicked(MouseEvent event) {};

  public void paint(Graphics g)
  {

  g.drawRect(x_start,y_start,x_end,y_end);
    g.drawString("Hit",30,30);
    if (Msg !=null)
     g.drawString("HIT OR MISS: "
         + Msg,5,80);
  }
}
```

H10.2.6 Keyboard input in Java 1.0

Java 1.0 provides for two keyboard events, these are:

- keyUp(Event evt, int key). Called when a key has been released
- keyDown(Event evt, int key). Called when a key has been pressed

The parameters passed into these methods are event (which defines the keyboard state) and an integer Keypressed which describes the key pressed.

Java applet H10.9 (`chapH10_0H10.java`)

```
import java.awt.*;
import java.applet.*;

public class chapH10_09 extends Applet
{
String  Msg=null;

 public boolean keyUp(Event event,
  int KeyPress)
 {
   Msg="Key pressed="+(char)KeyPress;
   repaint();   // call paint()
   return(true);
 }
 public void paint(Graphics g)
 {
  if (Msg !=null)
       g.drawString(Msg,5,80);
 }
}
```

HTML script H10.7 (`chapH10_09.html`)

```
<HTML><TITLE>Applet</TITLE>
<APPLET CODE=chapH10_09.class WIDTH=200
HEIGHT=200></APPLET></HTML>
```

The event contains an identification as to the type of event it is. When one of the function keys is pressed then the variable `event.id` is set to the macro `Event.KEY_ACTION` (as shown in Java applet H10.10). Other keys, such as the Ctrl, Alt and Shift keys, set bits in the `event.modifier` variable. The test for the Ctrl key is:

```
if ((event.modifiers & Event.CTRL_MASK)!=0)
    Msg="CONTROL KEY "+KeyPress;
```

This tests the `CTRL_MASK` bit; if it is a 1 then the CTRL key has been pressed. Java applet H10.7 shows its uses.

Java applet H10.10 (`chapH10_10.java`)

```
import java.awt.*;
import java.applet.*;

public class chapH10_10 extends Applet
{
String  Msg=null;

 public boolean keyDown(Event event,
                   int KeyPress)
 {
 if (event.id == Event.KEY_ACTION)
   Msg="FUNCTION KEY "+KeyPress;
 else if ((event.modifiers & Event.SHIFT_MASK)!=0)
   Msg="SHIFT KEY "+KeyPress;
 else if ((event.modifiers & Event.CTRL_MASK)!=0)
   Msg="CONTROL KEY "+KeyPress;
 else if ((event.modifiers & Event.ALT_MASK)!=0)
   Msg="ALT KEY "+KeyPress;
 else Msg=""+(char)KeyPress;
 repaint();   // call paint()
```

```
 return(true);
 }
 public void paint(Graphics g)
 {
  if (Msg!=null)
    g.drawString(Msg,5,80);
 }
}
```

📖　HTML script H10.8 (chapH10_10.html)

```
<HTML>
<TITLE>Applet</TITLE>
<APPLET CODE= chapH10_10.class WIDTH=200 HEIGHT=200>
</APPLET></HTML>
```

For function keys, the KeyPress variable has the following values:

Key	Value	Key	Value	Key	Value	Key	Value	Key	Value
F1	1008	F2	1009	F3	1010	F4	1011	F5	1012
F7	1014	F8	1015	F9	1016	F10	1017	F11	1018

Thus, to test for the function keys the following routine can be used:

```
if (event.id == Event.KEY_ACTION)
        if (KeyPress==1008) Msg="F1";
        else if (KeyPress==1009) Msg="F2";
        else if (KeyPress==1010) Msg="F3";
        else if (KeyPress==1011) Msg="F4";
        else if (KeyPress==1012) Msg="F5";
        else if (KeyPress==1013) Msg="F6";
        else if (KeyPress==1014) Msg="F7";
        else if (KeyPress==1015) Msg="F8";
        else if (KeyPress==1016) Msg="F9";
        else if (KeyPress==1017) Msg="F10";
```

The function keys have constant definitions for each of the keys. These are F1, F2, F3, and so. Thus the following is equivalent to the previous example:

```
if (event.id == Event.KEY_ACTION)
        if (KeyPress==F1) Msg="F1";
        else if (KeyPress==F2) Msg="F2";
        else if (KeyPress==F3) Msg="F3";
        else if (KeyPress==F4) Msg="F4";
        else if (KeyPress==F5) Msg="F5";
        else if (KeyPress==F6) Msg="F6";
        else if (KeyPress==F7) Msg="F7";
        else if (KeyPress==F8) Msg="F8";
        else if (KeyPress==F9) Msg="F9";
        else if (KeyPress==F10) Msg="F10";
```

For control keys the KeyPress variable has the following values:

Key	Value	Key	Value	Key	Value	Key	Value
Cntrl-A	1	Cntrl-B	2	Cntrl-C	3	Cntrl-D	4
Cntrl-E	5	Cntrl-F	6	Cntrl-G	7	Cntrl-H	8

Thus, to test for the control keys the following routine can be used:

```
if ((event.modifiers & Event.CTRL_MASK)!=0)
   if (KeyPress==1) Msg="Cntrl-A";
   else if (KeyPress==2) Msg="Cntrl-B";
   else if (KeyPress==3) Msg="Cntrl-C";
   else if (KeyPress==4) Msg="Cntrl-D";
```

The complete list of the keys defined by the `KeyPress` variable are:

Key	Value	Key	Value	Key	Value	Key	Value	Key	Value
HOME	1000	END	1001	PGUP	1002	PGDN	1003	UP	1004
DOWN	1005	LEFT	1006	RIGHT	1007	F1	1008	F2	1009
F3	1010	F4	1011	F5	1012	F7	1014	F8	1015
F9	1016	F10	1017	F11	1018	F12	1019		

H10.2.7 Keyboard events in Java 1.1

Java 1.1 has changed the event handling. In its place is the concept of listeners. Each listener receives notification about the types of events that it is interested in. For keyboard handling the two listeners are:

- `KeyListener`. This has the associated methods of:
  - `keyPressed()` which is equivalent to `keyDown()` in Java 1.0
  - `keyReleased()` which is equivalent to `keyUp()` in Java 1.0
  - `keyTyped()`

Key methods

The arguments passed to the methods have also changed. Their syntax is as follows:

```
public void keyPressed(KeyEvent event) {}
public void keyReleased(KeyEvent event) {}
public void keyTyped(KeyEvent event) {}
```

Event class

Another change to the Java program is to add the `java.awt.event` package, with:

```
import java.awt.event.*;
```

Class declaration

The class declaration is changed so that the appropriate listener is defined. If the key listener is required then the class declaration is as follows:

```
public class class_name extends Applet implements KeyListener
```

Defining components that generate events

The components which generate events must be defined. In the case of a key event these are added as:

```
compname.addKeyListener(this);
```

Updated Java program

Java applet H10.11 gives the updated Java program with Java 1.1 updates. In this case a TextField component is added to the applet (text). The TextField component will be discussed in a later section. When a key is pressed on this component then the keyPressed event listener is called, when one is released the keyReleased is called.

The getKeyCode() method is used to determine the key that has been activated. In the event method the KeyEvent defines a number of VK_ constants, such as:

VK_F1	Function Key F1	VK_A	Character 'A'	VK_ALT	Alt key
VK_CONTROL	Control Key	VK_0	Character '0'	VK_SHIFT	Shift key

📖 Java applet H10.11 (chapH10_11.java)

```java
import java.awt.*;
import java.applet.*;
import java.awt.event.*;

public class chapH10_11 extends Applet implements KeyListener
{
String  Msg=null;
TextField text;

    public void init()
    {
        text=new TextField(20);
        add(text);
        text.addKeyListener(this);
    }

    public void keyPressed(KeyEvent event)
    {
    int KeyPress;

        KeyPress=event.getKeyCode();

        if (KeyPress == KeyEvent.VK_ALT)  Msg="ALT KEY";
        else if (KeyPress == KeyEvent.VK_CONTROL)  Msg="CNTRL KEY ";
        else if (KeyPress == KeyEvent.VK_SHIFT) Msg="SHIFT KEY ";
        else if (KeyPress == KeyEvent.VK_RIGHT) Msg="RIGHT KEY ";
        else if (KeyPress == KeyEvent.VK_LEFT)  Msg="LEFT KEY ";
        else if (KeyPress == KeyEvent.VK_F1)    Msg="Function key F1";
        else Msg="Key:"+(char)KeyPress;

        text.setText(Msg);
    }
    public void keyReleased(KeyEvent event) { }
    public void keyTyped(KeyEvent event)    { }
}
```

Figure H10.2 Sample run

H10.3 Java graphics and sound

Java has excellent support for images and sound. For graphics files it supports GIF (`.gif`) and JPEG (`.jpg`) files, each of which is in a compressed form. The image object is declared with:

```
Image mypic;
```

Next the graphics image is associated with the image object with the `getImage()` method:

```
mypic=getImage(getCodeBase(),"myson.gif");
```

where the `getCodeBase()` method returns the applet's URL (such as `www.eece.napier.ac.uk`) and the second argument is the name of the graphics file (in this case, `myson.gif`). After this, the image can be displayed with:

```
g.drawImage(mypic,x,y,this);
```

where `mypic` is the name of the image object, and the `x` and `y` values are the co-ordinates of the upper-left hand corner of the image. The `this` keyword associates the current object (in this case it is the graphics image) and the current applet. Java applet 8.1 gives an applet which displays an image.

H10.3.1 Graphics

The `java.awt.Graphics` class contains a great deal of graphics-based methods; these are stated in Table H10.3.

Java applet H10.12

```
import java.awt.*;
import java.applet.*;

public class chap10_12 extends Applet
{
Image    mypic;
  public void init()
  {
   mypic = getImage(getCodeBase(),
            "myson.gif");
  }
  public void paint(Graphics g)
  {
    g.drawImage(mypic,0,0,this);
  }
}
```

HTML script H10.9

```
<HTML><TITLE>Applet</TITLE>
<APPLET CODE=chapH10_12.class WIDTH=200
HEIGHT=200></APPLET></HTML>
```

Table H10.3   Java graphics methods

Graphics method	Description
`public abstract void translate(` `  int x,int y)`	Translates the specified parameters into the origin of the graphics context. All subsequent operations on this graphics context will be relative to this origin. Parameters: x - the x co-ordinate y - the y co-ordinate.
`public abstract Color getColor()`	Gets the current color.
`public abstract void setColor(` `  Color c)`	Set current drawing color.
`public abstract Font getFont()`	Gets the current font.
`public abstract void setFont(Font font)`	Set the current font.
`public FontMetrics getFontMetrics()`	Gets the current font metrics.
`public abstract FontMetrics` `  getFontMetrics(Font f)`	Gets the current font metrics for the specified font.

`public abstract void copyArea(`
`  int x, int y, int width,`
`  int height, int dx,int dy)`
	Copies an area of the screen where (x,y) is the co-ordinate of the top left-hand corner, width and height, and dx is the horizontal distance and dy the vertical distance.

`public abstract void drawLine(` `  int x1,int y1,int x2,  int y2)`	Draws a line between the (x1,y1) and (x2,y2).

`public abstract void fillRect(`
`  int x, int y, int width,`
`  int height)`
	Fills the specified rectangle with the current color.

`public void drawRect(int x,int y,` `  int width,  int height)`	Draws the outline of the specified rectangle using the current color.

```
public abstract void clearRect(
   int x, int y, int width,
   int height)
```
Clears the specified rectangle by filling it with the current background color of the current drawing surface.

```
public void draw3DRect(
   int x, int y, int width,
   int height,boolean raised)
```
Draws a highlighted 3-D rectangle where raised is a boolean value that defines whether the rectangle is raised or not.

```
public void fill3DRect(int x,
   int y,int width,
   int height,boolean raised)
```
Paints a highlighted 3-D rectangle using the current color.

```
public abstract void drawOval(
   int x,int y, int width,
   int height)
```
Draws an oval inside the specified rectangle using the current color.

```
public abstract void fillOval(
   int x,int y, int width,
   int height)
```
Fills an oval inside the specified rectangle using the current color.

```
public abstract void drawArc(
   int x, int y, int width,
   int height, int startAngle,
   int arcAngle)
```
Draws an arc bounded by the specified rectangle starting. Zero degrees for startAngle is at the 3-o'clock position and arcAngle specifies the extent of the arc. A positive value for arcAngle indicates a counter-clockwise rotation while a negative value indicates a clockwise rotation. The parameter (x,y) specifies the centre point, and width and height specifies the width and height of a rectangle

```
public abstract void fillArc(
   int x, int y, int width,
   int height, int startAngle,
   int arcAngle)
```
Fills a pie-shaped arc using the current color.

```
public abstract void drawPolygon(
   int xPoints[],int yPoints[],
   int nPoints)
```
Draws a polygon using an array of x and y points (xPoints[] and yPoints[]). The number of points within the array is specified by nPoints.

```
public abstract void fillPolygon(
   int xPoints[],
   int yPoints[],int nPoints)
```
Fills a polygon with the current color.

```
public abstract void drawString(
   String str, int x, int y)
```
Draws the specified String using the current font and color.

```
public abstract boolean drawImage(
   Image img,int x, int y)
```
Draws the specified image at the specified co-ordinate (x, y).

```
public abstract void dispose()
```
Disposes of this graphics context.

Setting the color

The current drawing color is set using the setColor() method. It is used as follows:

```
g.setColor(Color.yellow);
```

Colors are defined in the `java.awt.Color` class and valid colors are:

```
Color.black     Color.blue      Color.cyan          Color.darkGray
Color.gray      Color.green     Color.lightGray     Color.magenta
Color.orange    Color.pink  Color.red               Color.white
Color.yellow
```

Any other 24-bit color can be generated with the method `Color` which has the format:

```
public Color(int r, int g, int b);
```

where `r`, `g` and `b` are values of strength from 0 to 255. For example:

```
Color(255,0,0)      gives red;          Color(255,255,255) gives white;
Color(0,128,128)    gives blue/green;   Color(0,0,0) gives black.
```

Drawing lines and circles

Normally to draw a graphics object the user must plan its layout for the dimension within the object. Figure H10.3 shows an example graphic with the required dimensions. The `drawOval()` method uses the top level hand point for the x and y parameters in the method and the width and height define the width and height of the oval shape. Thus the `drawOval()` method can be used to draw circles (if the width is equal to the height) or ovals (if the width is not equal to the height). Java applet H10.13 shows the Java code to draw the object. This applet uses the `setColor()` method to make the circle red and the other shapes blue.

Drawing polygons

The `drawPolygon()` method can be used to draw complex objects where the object is defined as a group of (x,y) co-ordinates. Java applet H10.14 draws a basic picture of a car and the `xpoints` array holds the x co-ordinates and `ypoints` hold the y co-ordinates. Figure H10.4 illustrates the object.

📖 Java applet H10.13

```
import java.awt.*;
import java.applet.*;
public class chapH10_13 extends Applet
{
  public void paint(Graphics g)
  {
    g.setColor(Color.red);
    g.fillOval(50,30,50,50);
    g.setColor(Color.blue);
    g.fillOval(30,80,90,100);
    g.fillRect(15,130,15,10);
    g.fillRect(120,130,15,10);
  }
}
```

📖 HTML script H10.10

```
<HTML>
```

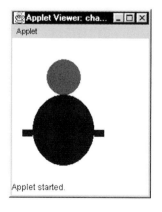

```
<TITLE>Applet</TITLE>
<APPLET CODE= chapH10_13.class WIDTH=200
HEIGHT=200>
</APPLET>
</HTML>
```

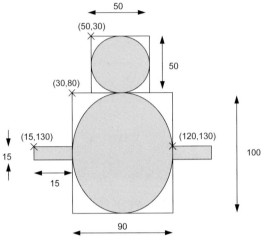

Figure H10.3 Dimensions for graphic

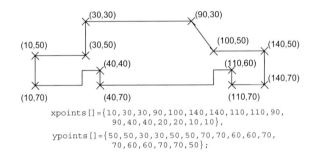

```
xpoints[]={10,30,30,90,100,140,140,110,110,90,
           90,40,40,20,20,10,10},

ypoints[]={50,50,30,30,50,50,70,70,60,60,70,
           70,60,60,70,70,50};
```

Figure H10.4 Co-ordinates of graphic

📖 Java applet H10.14

```
import java.awt.*;
import java.applet.*;
public class chapH10_14 extends Applet
{
int    xpoints[]={10,30,30,90,100,140,
       140,110,110,90,90,40,40,20,20,10,10},
       ypoints[]={50,50,30,30,50,50,70,
       70,60,60, 70, 70,60,60,70,70,50};
 public void paint(Graphics g)
 {
   g.drawPolygon(xpoints,ypoints,17);
 }
}
```

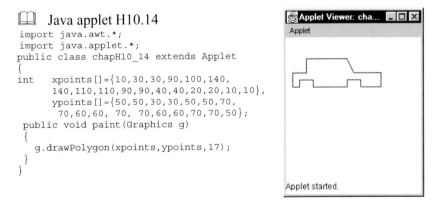

```
<HTML>
<TITLE>Applet</TITLE>
<APPLET CODE= chapH10_14.class WIDTH=200
HEIGHT=200>
</APPLET></HTML>
```

H10.3.2 Moving objects with the arrow keys

A graphic object can appear to move if it is drawn in a color which is not the same as the background color. The image can then be erased by re-drawing the image with the background color. Next, the image can be made to appear to move by changing the co-ordinates of the image and then re-drawing it with a color which is not the same as the background color. The movements can be controlled easily in Java with the arrow keys.

The arrow keys (UP, DOWN, LEFT and RIGHT) have defined values of 1004 (UP), 1005 (DOWN), 1006 (LEFT) and 1007 (RIGHT). These can be used to move graphics objects around the screen. The code is:

```
g.fillOval(x,y,10,10);
g.fillOval(x+30,y,10,10);
g.fillOval(x,y+30,40,20);
g.drawLine(x+5,y+10,x+5,y+35);
g.drawLine(x+35,y+10,x+35,y+35);
```

which draws an object at a position referenced to x and y. This can be made to move with the following:

```
public boolean keyDown(Event evt, int key)
{
        if (key==1006) { x-=5; repaint(); } // LEFT key
        else if (key==1007) { x+=5; repaint(); } // RIGHT key
        else if (key==1004) { y-=5; repaint(); } // UP key
        else if (key==1005) { y+=5; repaint(); } // DOWN key
        return true;
}
```

which when the RIGHT button is pressed it increments the x co-ordinate by 5, if the LEFT button is pressed then the x co-ordinate is decremented by 5. When the UP key is pressed the y co-ordinate is decremented by 5, if the DOWN key is pressed then the y co-ordinate is incremented by 5. Within each of these key presses, paint() is called.

Applet H10.15 shows a sample code which displays an object (alien()) which starts at the co-ordinates (100, 100) and is then moved with arrow keys.

Java applet H10.15 (≠Java 1.0)

```
import java.awt.*;
import java.applet.*;

public class chapH10_15 extends Applet
{
int x=100,y=100;
 public void paint(Graphics g)
 {
    g.setColor(getBackground());
    alien(g);

    if ( x>100) x=200;
    if ( y>200) y=200;
    if ( x<0 )  x=0;
    if ( y<0 )  y=0;
    g.setColor(Color.black);
    alien(g);
 }

 public void alien(Graphics g)
 {
    g.fillOval(x,y,10,10);
    g.fillOval(x+30,y,10,10);
    g.fillOval(x,y+30,40,20);
    g.drawLine(x+5,y+10,x+5,y+35);
    g.drawLine(x+35,y+10,x+35,y+35);
 }
 public boolean keyDown(Event evt, int key)
 {
   if (key==1006) { x-=5; repaint(); }
   else if (key==1007) { x+=5; repaint(); }
   else if (key==1004) { y-=5; repaint(); }
   else if (key==1005) { y+=5; repaint(); }
   return true;
 }
}
```

HTML script H10.12

```
<HTML><TITLE>Applet</TITLE>
<APPLET CODE= chap8_04.class WIDTH=200
HEIGHT=200>
</APPLET></HTML>
```

Modified Java 1.1 program

Java applet H10.16 (≠Java 1.1)

```
import java.awt.*;
import java.awt.event.*;
import java.applet.*;

public class chapH10_16 extends Applet implements KeyListener
{
int x=100,y=100;
     public void init()
     {
     TextField text;
        text = new TextField(1);
        add(text);
        text.addKeyListener(this);
     }
```

```
    public void paint(Graphics g)
    {
       g.setColor(getBackground());
       alien(g);

       if ( x>100) x=200;
       if ( y>200) y=200;
       if ( x<0 )  x=0;
       if ( y<0 )  y=0;

  g.setColor(Color.black);
  alien(g);
    }

    public void alien(Graphics g)
    {
       g.fillOval(x,y,10,10);
       g.fillOval(x+30,y,10,10);
       g.fillOval(x,y+30,40,20);
       g.drawLine(x+5,y+10,x+5,y+35);
       g.drawLine(x+35,y+10,x+35,y+35);
    }

    public void keyPressed(KeyEvent evt)
    {
    int key;

       key=evt.getKeyCode();
       if (key==KeyEvent.VK_RIGHT) { x-=5; repaint(); }
       else if (key==KeyEvent.VK_LEFT) { x+=5; repaint(); }
       else if (key==KeyEvent.VK_DOWN) { y-=5; repaint(); }
       else if (key==KeyEvent.VK_UP) { y+=5; repaint(); }
    }

    public void keyReleased(KeyEvent evt) {  }
    public void keyTyped(KeyEvent evt) {  }
}
```

H10.3.3 Sound

The playing of sound files is similar to displaying graphics files. Java applet H10.17 shows a sample applet which plays an audio file (in this case, test.au). Unfortunately, the current version of the Java compiler only supports the AU format, thus WAV files need to be converted into AU format.

The initialization process uses the getAudioClip() method and the audio file is played with the loop() method. This method is contained in the java.applet. AudioClip class, these methods are:

public abstract void play()	Plays the audio file and finishes at the end
public abstract void loop()	Starts playing the clip in a loop
public abstract void stop()	Stops playing the clip

📖 Java applet H10.17

```
import java.awt.*;
import java.applet.*;

public class chap10_17 extends Applet
{
```

```
AudioClip     audClip;
  public void paint(Graphics g)
  {
    audClip=getAudioClip(getCodeBase(),"hello.au");
    audClip.loop();
  }
}
```

📖 HTML script H10.13

```
<HTML><TITLE>Applet</TITLE>
<APPLET CODE=chapH10_17.class WIDTH=200 HEIGHT=200>
</APPLET></HTML>
```

H10.4   Java buttons and menus

One of the features of Java is that it supports many different types of menus items, these are:

- Buttons. Simple buttons which are pressed to select an item.
- Pop-up menus (or pull-down menus). Used to select from a number of items. The se-
  lected item is displayed in the pop-up menu window.
- List boxes.
- Dialog boxes. Used to either load or save files.
- Checkboxes. Used to select/deselect an item.
- Radio buttons. Used to select from one or several items.
- Menu bars. Used to display horizontal menus with pull-down menus.

These are used with event handlers to produce event-driven options.

H10.4.1 Buttons and events

Java applet H10.18 creates three Button objects. These are created with the add() method
which displays the button in the applet window. An alternative approach to creating buttons is to declare them using the Button type. For example the following applet is
equivalent to Java applet H10.18. The names of the button objects, in this case, are but-
ton1, button2 and button3.

```
import java.applet.*;
import java.awt.*;

public class chapH10_18 extends Applet
{
Button button1, button2, button3;

    public void init()
    {
        button1= new Button("Help");
        button2= new Button("Show");
        button3= new Button("Exit");
        add(button1);
        add(button2);
        add(button3);
    }
}
```

Java applet H10.18

```
import java.awt.*;
import java.applet.*;

public class chapH10_18 extends Applet
{
  public void init()
  {
    add(new Button("Help"));
    add(new Button("Show"));
    add(new Button("Exit"));
  }
}
```

H10.4.2 Action with Java 1.0

In Java 1.0, the `action` method is called when an event occurs, such as a keypress, button press, and so on. The information on the event is stored in the `Event` parameter. Its format is:

```
public boolean action(Event evt, Object obj)
```

where `evt` is made with the specified target component, time stamp, event type, x and y coordinates, keyboard key, state of the modifier keys and argument. These are:

- `evt.target` is the target component
- `evt.when` is the time stamp
- `evt.id` is the event type
- `evt.x` is the x coordinate
- `evt.y` is the y coordinate
- `evt.key` is the key pressed in a keyboard event
- `evt.modifiers` is the state of the modifier keys
- `evt.arg` is the specified argument

Java applet H10.19 contains an example of the `action` method. It has two buttons (named `New1` and `New2`). When any of the buttons is pressed the `action` method is called. Figure H10.5 shows the display when either of the buttons are pressed. In the left hand side of Figure 10.5 the `New1` button is pressed and the right-hand side shows the display after the `New2` button is pressed. It can be seen that differences are in the `target`, `arg` parameter and the x, y co-ordinate parameters.

Java applet H10.19 (✠Java 1.0)

```
import java.applet.*;
import java.awt.*;

public class chapH10_19 extends Applet
{
String Msg1=null, Msg2, Msg3, Msg4;
Button new1,new2;

    public void init()
    {
```

```
        new1=new Button("New 1");
        new2=new Button("New 2");
        add (new1); add(new2);
    }

    public boolean action(Event evt, Object obj)
    {
        Msg1= "Target= "+evt.target;
        Msg2= "When= " + evt.when + " id=" + evt.id +
               " x= "+ evt.x + " y= " + evt.y;
        Msg3= "Arg= " + evt.arg + " Key= " + evt.key;
        Msg4= "Click= " + evt.clickCount;
        repaint();
        return true;
    }

    public void paint(Graphics g)
    {
        if (Msg1!=null)
        {
            g.drawString(Msg1,30,80);
            g.drawString(Msg2,30,100);
            g.drawString(Msg3,30,120);
            g.drawString(Msg4,30,140);
        }
    }
}
```

Figure H10.5   Sample runs

Thus to determine the button that has been pressed the `evt.arg` string can be tested. Java applet H10.20 shows an example where the `evt.arg` parameter is tested for its string content.

📖   Java applet H10.20 (⇐Java 1.0)

```
import java.applet.*;
import java.awt.*;

public class chapH10_20 extends Applet
{
String   Msg=null;
Button   new1, new2;
    public void init()
    {
        new1=new Button("New 1");      new2=new Button("New 2");
        add (new1); add(new2);
    }
```

```
   public boolean action(Event evt, Object obj)
   {
      if (evt.arg=="New 1") Msg= "New 1 pressed";
      else if (evt.arg=="New 2") Msg= "New 2 pressed";
      repaint();
      return true;
   }

   public void paint(Graphics g)
   {
      if (Msg!=null)
         g.drawString(Msg,30,80);
   }
}
```

Java applet H10.21 uses the `action` method which is called when an event occurs. Within this method the `event` variable is tested to see if one of the buttons caused the event. This is achieved with:

```
if (event.target instanceof Button)
```

If this test is true then the `Msg` string takes on the value of the object, which holds the name of the button that caused the event.

📖 Java applet H10.21 (⚡Java 1.0)

```
import java.awt.*;
import java.applet.*;

public class chapH10_21 extends Applet
{
String  Msg=null;

   public void init()
   {
    add(new Button("Help"));
    add(new Button("Show"));
    add(new Button("Exit"));
   }

   public boolean action(Event event,
     Object object)
   {
    if (event.target instanceof Button)
    {
      Msg = (String) object;
      repaint();
    }
    return(true);
   }

   public void paint(Graphics g)
   {
    if (Msg!=null)
    g.drawString("Button:" + Msg,30,80);
   }
}
```

H10.4.3 Action Listener in Java 1.1

As with mouse events, buttons, menus and textfields are associated with an action listener (named `ActionListener`). When an event associated with these occurs then the `action-Performed` method is called. Its format is:

```
public void actionPerformed(ActionEvent evt)
```

where `evt` defines the event. The associated methods are:

- `getActionCommand()` is the action command
- `evt.getModifiers()` is the state of the modifier keys
- `evt.paramString()` is the parameter string

Java applet H10.22 contains an example of the `action` method. It has two buttons (named `New1` and `New2`). When any of the buttons is pressed the action method is called. Each of the buttons has an associated listener which is initiated with:

```
button1.addActionListener(this);
button2.addActionListener(this);
```

Figure H10.6 shows the display when either of the buttons are pressed. In the left-hand side of Figure H10.6 the `New1` button is pressed and the right-hand side shows the display after the `New2` button is pressed.

📖 Java applet H10.22 (⇔Java 1.1)

```
import java.applet.*;
import java.awt.*;
import java.awt.event.*;

public class chapH10_22 extends Applet implements ActionListener
{
Button    button1, button2;
String    Msg1=null, Msg2, Msg3;

    public void init()
    {

        button1 = new Button("New 1");
        button2 = new Button("New 2");
        add(button1);  add(button2);
        button1.addActionListener(this);
        button2.addActionListener(this);
    }

    public void actionPerformed(ActionEvent evt)
    {
        Msg1= "Command= "+evt.getActionCommand();
        Msg2= "Modifiers= " + evt.getModifiers();
        Msg3= "String= " + evt.paramString();
        repaint();
    }

    public void paint(Graphics g)
    {
        if (Msg1!=null)
```

```
        {
           g.drawString(Msg1,30,80);
           g.drawString(Msg2,30,100);
           g.drawString(Msg3,30,120);
        }
    }
}
```

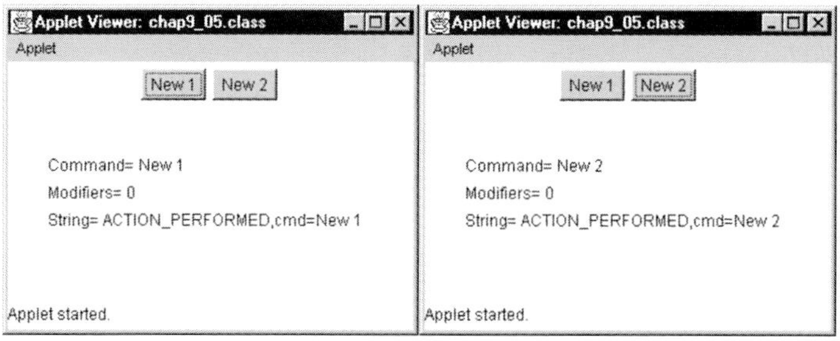

Figure H10.6   Sample run

Thus to determine the button that has been pressed the getActionCommand() method is used. Java applet H10.23 shows an example where the getActionCommand() method is tested for its string content. Figure H10.7 shows a sample run.

Java applet H10.23 (≉Java 1.1)

```
import java.applet.*;
import java.awt.*;
import java.awt.event.*;

public class chapH10_23 extends Applet implements ActionListener
{
Button button1, button2;
String Msg=null;

    public void init()
    {

        button1 = new Button("New 1");
        button2 = new Button("New 2");
        add(button1); add(button2);
        button1.addActionListener(this);
        button2.addActionListener(this);
    }

    public void actionPerformed(ActionEvent evt)
    {
    String command;

        command=evt.getActionCommand();

        if (command.equals("New 1")) Msg="New 1 pressed";
        if (command.equals("New 2")) Msg="New 2 pressed";

        repaint();
    }

    public void paint(Graphics g)
    {
```

```
        if (Msg!=null)
        {
                g.drawString(Msg,30,80);
        }
    }
}
```

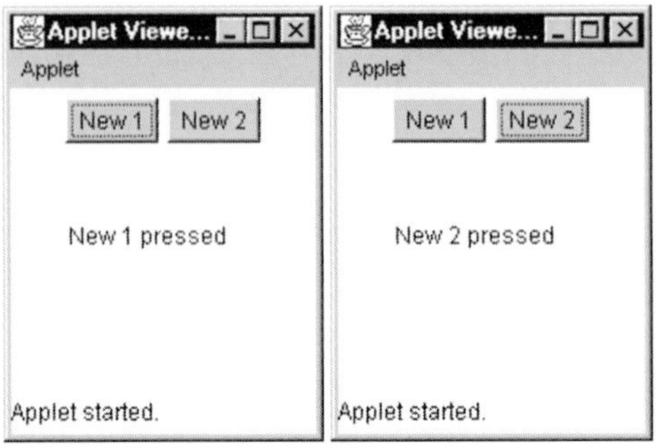

Figure H10.7   Sample run

H10.4.4 Checkboxes

Typically checkboxes are used to select from a number of options. Java applet H10.24 shows
how an applet can use checkboxes. As before, the `action` method is called when a
checkbox changes its state and within the method the `event.target` parameter is tested
for the checkbox with:

```
if (event.target instanceof Checkbox)
```

If this is true, then the method `DetermineCheckState()` is called which tests
`event.target` for the checkbox value and its state (true or false).

📖   Java applet H10.24 (✓Java 1.0)

```
import java.awt.*;
import java.applet.*;
public class chapH10_24 extends Applet
{
String  Msg=null;
Checkbox fax, telephone, email, post;

 public void init()
  {
  fax=new Checkbox("FAX");
  telephone=new Checkbox("Telephone");
  email=new Checkbox("Email");
  post=new Checkbox("Post",null,true);
  add(fax); add(telephone);
  add(email); add(post);
 }

 public void DetermineCheckState(
     Checkbox Cbox)
  {
  Msg=Cbox.getLabel()+" "+ Cbox.getState();
  repaint();
 }
```

```
public boolean action(Event event,
    Object object)
{
  if (event.target instanceof Checkbox)
    DetermineCheckState(
      (Checkbox)event.target);
  return(true);
}
public void paint(Graphics g)
{
  if (Msg!=null)
    g.drawString("Check box:" + Msg,30,80);
}
}
```

H10.4.5 Item listener in Java 1.1

As with mouse events, checkboxes and lists are associated with an item listener (named
`ItemListener`). When an event associated with these occur then the `itemStateChanged`
method is called. Its format is:

```
public void itemStateChanged(ItemEvent event)
```

where `event` defines the event. The associated methods are:

- `getItem()` is the item selected
- `getStateChange()` is the state of the checkbox
- `paramString()` is the parameter string

Java applet H10.25 contains an example of checkboxes and Figure H10.8 shows a sample
run. Each of the checkboxes has an associated listener which is initiated in the form:

> *chbox*.addItemListener(this);

📖 Java applet H10.25 (⟵Java 1.1)
```
import java.awt.*;
import java.applet.*;
import java.awt.event.*;

public class chapH10_25 extends Applet implements ItemListener
{
String      Msg1=null,Msg2,Msg3;
Checkbox    fax, telephone, email,post;

    public void init()
    {
      fax=new Checkbox("FAX");
      telephone=new Checkbox("Telephone");
      email=new Checkbox("Email");
      post=new Checkbox("Post",null,true);
      add(fax);
      add(telephone);
      add(email);
      add(post);

      fax.addItemListener(this);
```

```
      email.addItemListener(this);
      telephone.addItemListener(this);
      post.addItemListener(this);
   }

   public void itemStateChanged(ItemEvent event)
   {
      Msg1=""+event.getItem();
      Msg2=""+event.getStateChange();
      Msg3=event.paramString();
      repaint();
   }

   public void paint(Graphics g)
   {
      if (Msg1!=null)
      {
         g.drawString(Msg1,30,80);
         g.drawString(Msg2,30,110);
         g.drawString(Msg3,30,150);
      }
   }
}
```

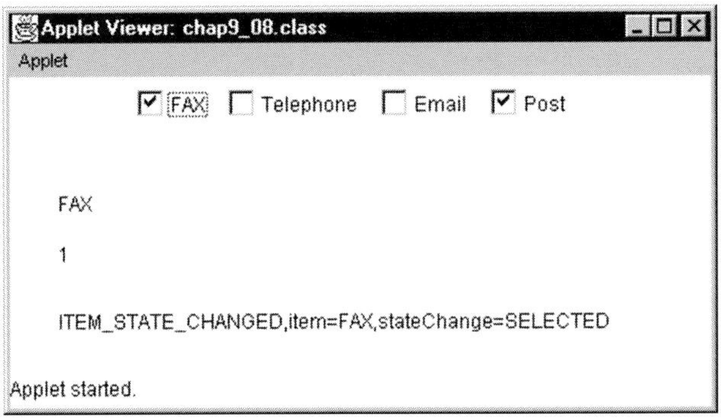

Figure H10.8   Sample run

H10.4.6 Radio buttons

The standard checkboxes allow any number of options to be selected. A radio button allows only one option to be selected at a time. The program is changed by:

- Adding checkbox names (such as fax, tele, email and post).
- Initializing the checkbox with CheckboxGroup() to a checkbox group identifier.
- Add the identifier of the checkbox group to the Checkbox() method.
- Testing the target property of the event to see if it equals a checkbox name.

Java applet H10.26 shows how this is achieved.

    Java applet H10.26 (⇔Java 1.0)

```
import java.awt.*;
import java.applet.*;

public class chapH10_26 extends Applet
```

```
{
String      Msg=null;
Checkbox    fax, tele, email, post;

  public void init()
  {

  CheckboxGroup RadioGroup = new CheckboxGroup();

      add(fax=new Checkbox("FAX",RadioGroup,false));
      add(tele=new Checkbox("Telephone",RadioGroup,false));
      add (email=new Checkbox("Email",RadioGroup,false));
      add (post=new Checkbox("Post",RadioGroup,true));
  }

  public boolean action(Event event, Object object)
  {
      if (event.target.equals(fax)) Msg="FAX";
      else if (event.target.equals(tele)) Msg="Telephone";
      else if (event.target.equals(email)) Msg="Email";
      else if (event.target.equals(fax)) Msg="FAX";
      repaint();
      return(true);
  }

  public void paint(Graphics g)
  {

      if (Msg!=null) g.drawString("Check box:" + Msg,30,80);
  }
}
```

Java applet H10.27 show the Java 1.1 equivalent.

📖   Java applet H10.27 (⇐Java 1.1)

```
import java.awt.*;
import java.awt.event.*;
import java.applet.*;

public class chapH10_27 extends Applet implements ItemListener
{
String  Msg=null;
Checkbox fax, tele, email, post;

 public void init()
  {

   CheckboxGroup RadioGroup = new CheckboxGroup();

      add(fax=new Checkbox("FAX",RadioGroup,true));
      add(tele=new Checkbox("Telephone",RadioGroup,false));
      add (email=new Checkbox("Email",RadioGroup,false));
      add (post=new Checkbox("Post",RadioGroup,false));
      fax.addItemListener(this);
      tele.addItemListener(this);
      email.addItemListener(this);
      post.addItemListener(this);
  }

  public void itemStateChanged(ItemEvent event)
  {
  Object obj;
```

```
        obj=event.getItem();

        if (obj.equals("FAX")) Msg="FAX";
        else if (obj.equals("Telephone")) Msg="Telephone";
        else if (obj.equals("Email")) Msg="Email";
        else if (obj.equals("Post")) Msg="Post";
        repaint();
    }

    public void paint(Graphics g)
    {
        if (Msg!=null)    g.drawString("Check box:" + Msg,30,80);
    }
}
```

This sets the checkbox type to `RadioGroup` and it can be seen that only one of the checkboxes is initially set (that is, 'FAX'). Figure H10.9 shows a sample run. It should be noted that grouped checkboxes use a round circle with a dot (⊙), whereas ungrouped checkboxes use a square box with a check mark (☑).

Figure H10.9 Sample run

H10.4.7 Pop-up menu choices

To create a pop-up menu the `Choice` object is initially created with:

```
Choice mymenu = new Choice();
```

After this, the menu options are defined using the `addItem` method. Java applet H10.28 shows an example usage of a pop-up menu.

As before the `arg` property of the event can also be tested as shown in Java applet H10.29. Java applet H10.30 gives the Java 1.1 equivalent.

Java applet H10.28 (≠Java 1.0)

```java
import java.awt.*;
import java.applet.*;

public class chapH10_28 extends Applet
{
String  Msg=null;
Choice  mymenu= new Choice();

  public void init()
  {
    mymenu.addItem("FAX");
    mymenu.addItem("Telephone");
    mymenu.addItem("Email");
    mymenu.addItem("Post");
    add(mymenu);
  }
  public void DetermineCheckState(
     Choice mymenu)
  {
    Msg=mymenu.getItem(
       mymenu.getSelectedIndex());
    repaint();
  }
  public boolean action(Event event,
     Object object)
  {
   if (event.target instanceof Choice)
    DetermineCheckState(
       (Choice)event.target);
   return(true);
  }

  public void paint(Graphics g)
  {
  if (Msg!=null)
   g.drawString("Menu select:"+Msg,30,120);
  }
}
```

Java applet H10.29 (≠Java 1.0)

```java
import java.awt.*;
import java.applet.*;

public class chapH10_29 extends Applet
{
String  Msg=null;
Choice  mymenu= new Choice();

  public void init()
  {
    mymenu.addItem("FAX");
    mymenu.addItem("Telephone");
    mymenu.addItem("Email");
    mymenu.addItem("Post");
    add(mymenu);
  }
  public boolean action(Event event, Object object)
  {
   if (event.arg=="FAX") Msg="FAX";
    else if (event.arg=="Telephone") Msg="Telephone";
```

```
  else if (event.arg=="Email") Msg="Email";
  else if (event.arg == "Post") Msg="Post";
  repaint();
  return(true);
  }
  public void paint(Graphics g)
  {
    if (Msg!=null)
      g.drawString("Menu select:" + Msg,30,120);
  }
}
```

📖 Java applet H10.30 (⇐Java 1.1)

```
import java.awt.*;
import java.awt.event.*;
import java.applet.*;

public class chapH10_30 extends Applet implements ItemListener
{
String  Msg=null;
Choice  mymenu= new Choice();

  public void init()
  {
    mymenu.addItem("FAX");
    mymenu.addItem("Telephone");
    mymenu.addItem("Email");
    mymenu.addItem("Post");
    add(mymenu);
    mymenu.addItemListener(this);
  }
  public void itemStateChanged(ItemEvent event)
  {
  Object obj;
   obj=event.getItem();

   if (obj.equals("FAX")) Msg="FAX";
   else if (obj.equals("Telephone")) Msg="Telephone";
   else if (obj.equals("Email")) Msg="Email";
   else if (obj.equals("Post")) Msg="Post";
   repaint();
  }
  public void paint(Graphics g)
  {
    if (Msg!=null)
      g.drawString("Menu select:" + Msg,30,120);
  }
}
```

H10.4.8 Other pop-up menu options

The java.awt.Choice class allows for a pop-up menu. It includes the following methods:

public void **addItem**(String item);
  Adds a menu item to the end.

public void **addNotify**();
  Allows the modification of a list's appearance without changing its functionality.

public int **countItems**();
  Returns the number of items in the menu.

```
public String getItem(int index);
```
Returns the string of the menu item at that index value.

```
public int getSelectedIndex();
```
Returns the index value of the selected item.

```
public String getSelectedItem();
```
Returns the string of the selected item.

```
protected String paramString();
```
Returns the parameter String of the list.

```
public void select(int pos);
```
Select the menu item at a given index.

```
public void select(String str);
```
Select the menu item with a given string name.

The `countItems` method is used to determine the number of items in a pop-up menu, for example:

```
Msg= "Number of items is " + mymenu.countItems()
```

The `getItem(int index)` returns the string associated with the menu item, where the first item has a value of zero. For example:

```
Msg= "Menu item number 2 is " + mymenu.getItem(2);
```

Java applet H10.31 uses the `select` method to display the second menu option as the default and the `getItem` method to display the name of the option.

📖 Java applet H10.31 (≠Java 1.1)

```
import java.awt.*;
import java.awt.event.*;
import java.applet.*;

public class chap10_31 extends Applet
     implements ItemListener
{
String  Msg=null;
Choice  mymenu= new Choice();

  public void init()
  {
    mymenu.addItem("FAX");
    mymenu.addItem("Telephone");
    mymenu.addItem("Email");
    mymenu.addItem("Post");
    add(mymenu);
    mymenu.addItemListener(this);
    mymenu.select(1);
        // Select item 1 (Telephone)
}

public void itemStateChanged(ItemEvent evt)
{
Object obj;

  obj=evt.getItem();
```

```
 if (obj.equals("FAX"))
     Msg=mymenu.getItem(0);
 else if (obj.equals("Telephone"))
     Msg=mymenu.getItem(1);
 else if (obj.equals("Email"))
     Msg=mymenu.getItem(2);
 else if (obj.equals("Post"))
     Msg=mymenu.getItem(3);
 repaint();
}
public void paint(Graphics g)
{
 if (Msg!=null)
   g.drawString("Menu select:"+Msg,30,120);
}
}
```

H10.4.9 Multiple menus

Multiple menus can be created in a Java applet and the `action` event can be used to differ-entiate between the menus. Java applet H10.32 has two pull-down menus and two buttons (age, gender, print and close). The event method getItem is then used to determine which of the menus was selected. In this case the print button is used to display the op-tions of the two pull-down menus and close is used to exit from the applet.

Java applet H10.32 (Java 1.1)

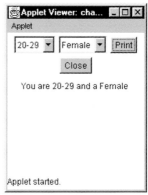

```
import java.applet.*;
import java.awt.*;
import java.awt.event.*;

public class chapH10_32 extends Applet
  implements ItemListener, ActionListener
{
Choice age = new Choice();
Choice gender = new Choice();
Button print= new Button("Print");
Button close= new Button("Close");
String gendertype=null, agetype=null;

String Msg, Options[];

  public void init()
  {
      age.addItem("10-19");
      age.addItem("20-29");
      age.addItem("30-39");
      age.addItem("40-49");
      age.addItem("Other");
      add(age);

      gender.addItem("Male");
      gender.addItem("Female");
      add(gender);
      add(print);
      add(close);

      age.addItemListener(this);
      gender.addItemListener(this);
      print.addActionListener(this);
      close.addActionListener(this);
```

```
  }

  public void itemStateChanged(ItemEvent evt)
  {
    int i;
    Object obj;

       obj=evt.getItem();

    if (obj.equals("10-19")) agetype="10-19";
    else if (obj.equals("20-29"))
       agetype="20-29";
    else if (obj.equals("30-39"))
      agetype="30-39";
    else if (obj.equals("40-49"))
      agetype="40-49";
    else if (obj.equals("Other"))
      agetype="Other";
    else if (obj.equals("Male"))
      gendertype="Male";
    else if (obj.equals("Female"))
      gendertype="Female";
    }

  public void actionPerformed(ActionEvent evt)
  {
  String str;

    str=evt.getActionCommand();
    if (str.equals("Print"))  repaint();
    else if (str.equals("Close"))
      System.exit(0);
  }

  public void paint(Graphics g)
  {
   if ((agetype!=null) && (gendertype!=null))
    Msg="Your are " + agetype + " and a "
                    + gendertype;
   else Msg="Please select age and gender";

   if (Msg!=null) g.drawString(Msg,20,80);
  }
  }
```

H10.4.10   Menu bar

Menu bars are now familiar in most GUIs (such as Microsoft Windows and Motif). They consist of a horizontal menu bar with pull-down submenus. The `java.awt.MenuBar` class contains a constructor for a menu bar. Its format is:

```
       public MenuBar();
```

and the methods which can be applied to it are:

`public Menu add(Menu m);`   Adds the specified menu to the menu bar.

`public void addNotify();`   Allows a change of appearance of the menu bar without changing any of the menu bar's functionality.

```
public int countMenus();                    Counts the number of menus on the menu bar.

public Menu getHelpMenu();                  Gets the help menu on the menu bar.

public Menu getMenu(int i);                 Gets the specified menu.

public void remove(                         Removes the menu located at the specified index from the
    int index);                             menu bar.

public void remove(                         Removes the specified menu from the menu bar.
        MenuComponent m);

public void removeNotify();                 Removes notify.

public void setHelpMenu(                    Sets the help menu to the specified menu on the menu bar.
    Menu m);
```

Java program H10.33 gives an example of using a menu bar. Initially the menu bar is created with the `MenuBar()` constructor, and submenus with the `Menu` constructors (in this case, `mfile`, `medit` and `mhelp`). Items are added to the submenus with the `MenuItem` constructor (such as New, Open, and so on). A `handleEvent()` method has been added to catch a close window operation. The `addSeparator()` method has been added to add a line between menu items. Note that this program is not an applet so that it can be run directly with the Java interpreter (such as `java.exe`).

📖 Java standalone program H10.33 (Java 1.0)

```java
import java.awt.*;

public class gomenu extends Frame
{
MenuBar mainmenu = new MenuBar();
Menu mfile = new Menu("File");
Menu medit = new Menu("Edit");
Menu mhelp = new Menu("Help");

    public gomenu()
    {
        mfile.add(new MenuItem("New"));
        mfile.add(new MenuItem("Open"));
        mfile.add(new MenuItem("Save"));
        mfile.add(new MenuItem("Save As"));
        mfile.add(new MenuItem("Close"));
        mfile.addSeparator();
        mfile.add(new MenuItem("Print"));
        mfile.addSeparator();
        mfile.add(new MenuItem("Exit"));

        mainmenu.add(mfile);

        medit.add(new MenuItem("Cut"));
        medit.add(new MenuItem("Copy"));
        medit.add(new MenuItem("Paste"));
        mainmenu.add(medit);

        mhelp.add(new MenuItem("Commands"));
        mhelp.add(new MenuItem("About"));
        mainmenu.add(mhelp);
```

```
        setMenuBar(mainmenu);
    }

    public boolean action(Event evt, Object obj)
    {
        if (evt.target instanceof MenuItem)
        {
            if (evt.arg=="Exit") System.exit(0);
        }
        return true;
    }

    public boolean handleEvent(Event evt)
    {
        if (evt.id == Event.WINDOW_DESTROY)
                System.exit(0);
        return true;
    }

    public static void main(String args[])
    {
        Frame f = new gomenu();
        f.resize(400,400);
        f.show();
    }
}
```

H10.4.11   List box

A List component creates a scrolling list of options (where in a pull-down menu only one option can be viewed at a time). The java.awt.List class contains the List constructor which can be used to display a list component., which is in the form:

```
public List();
public List(int rows, boolean multipleSelections);
```

where row defines the number of rows in a list and multipleSelections is true when the user can select a number of selections, else it is false. The methods that can be applied are:

public void **addItem**(String item);	Adds a menu item at the end.
public void **addItem**(String item, int index);	Add a menu item at the end.
public void **addNotify**();	Allows the modification of a list's appearance without changing its functionality.
public boolean **allowsMultipleSelections**();	Allows the selection of multiple selections.
public void **clear**();	Clears the list.
public int **countItems**();	Returns the number of items in the list.
public void **delItem**(int position);	Deletes an item from the list.
public void **delItems**(int start, int end);	Deletes items from the list.

`Public void deselect(int index);`	Deselects the item at the specified index.
`Public String getItem(int index);`	Gets the item associated with the specified index.
`public int getRows();`	Returns the number of visible lines in this list.
`public int getSelectedIndex();`	Gets the selected item on the list.
`public int[] getSelectedIndexes();`	Gets selected items on the list.
`public String getSelectedItem();`	Returns the selected item on the list as a string.
`public String[] getSelectedItems();`	Returns the selected items on the list as an array of strings.
`public int getVisibleIndex();`	Gets the index of the item that was last made visible by the method `makeVisible`.
`public boolean isSelected(` `  int index);`	Returns true if the item at the specified index has been selected.
`public void makeVisible(int index);`	Makes a menu item visible.
`public Dimension minimumSize();`	Returns the minimum dimensions needed for the list.
`public Dimension minimumSize` `  (int rows);`	Returns the minimum dimensions needed for the amount of rows in the list.
`protected String paramString();`	Returns the parameter String of the list.
`public Dimension preferredSize();`	Returns the preferred size of the list.
`public Dimension` `  preferredSize(int rows);`	Returns the preferred size of the list.
`public void removeNotify();`	Removes notify.
`public void replaceItem(` `  String newValue, int index);`	Replaces the item at the given index.
`Public void select(int index);`	Selects the item at the specified index.
`public void` `  setMultipleSelections(boolean v);`	Allows multiple selections.

Java program H10.34 shows an example of a program with a list component. Intially the list is created with the `List` constructor. The `addItem` method is then used to add the four items ("Pop", "Rock", "Classical" and "Jazz"). Within `actionPerformed` the program uses the `Options` array of strings to build up a message string (`Msg`). The `Options.length` parameter is used to determine the number of items in the array.

📖 Java program H10.34 (⁴Java 1.1)

```java
import java.awt.*;
import java.awt.event.*;
import java.applet.*;

public class chapH10_34 extends Applet
                    implements ActionListener
{
List lmenu = new List(4,true);
String Msg, Options[];
    public void init()
    {
        lmenu.addItem("Pop");
        lmenu.addItem("Rock");
        lmenu.addItem("Classical");
        lmenu.addItem("Jazz");
        add(lmenu);
        lmenu.addActionListener(this);
    }

  public void actionPerformed(
                        ActionEvent evt)
  {
    int i;
    String str;

    str=evt.getActionCommand();
    Options=lmenu.getSelectedItems();
    Msg="";
    for (i=0;i<Options.length;i++)
          Msg=Msg+Options[i] + " ";
    repaint();
  }

  public void paint(Graphics g)
  {
    if (Msg!=null) g.drawString(Msg,20,80);
  }
}
```

H10.4.12   File dialog

The `java.awt.Filedialog` class contains the `FileDialog` constructor which can be used to display a dialog window. To create a dialog window the following can be used:

```java
public FileDialog(Frame parent, String title);
public FileDialog(Frame parent, String title, int mode);
```

where the `parent` is the owner of the dialog, `title` is the title of the dialog window and the `mode` is defined as whether the file is to be loaded or save. Two fields are defined for the mode, these are:

```java
public final static int LOAD;
```

```
      public final static int SAVE;
```

The methods that can be applied are:

`public void addNotify();`	Allows applications to change the look of a file dialog window without changing its functionality.
`public String getDirectory();`	Gets the initial directory.
`public String getFile();`	Gets the file that the user specified.
`public FilenameFilter getFilenameFilter();`	Sets the default file filter.
`public int getMode();`	Indicates whether the file dialog box is for file loading from or file saving.
`protected String paramString();`	Returns the parameter string representing the state of the file dialog window.
`public void setDirectory(String dir);`	Gets the initial directory.
`public void setFile(String file);`	Sets the selected file for this file dialog window to be the specified file.
`public void setFilenameFilter( FilenameFilter filter);`	Sets the filename filter for the file dialog window to the specified filter.

H11   Java (date, strings and multithreading)

H11.1   Java text and date

H11.1.1 Text input

Single-line text can be entered into a Java applet using the `TextField` action, which is contained in the `java.awt.TextField` class. Its format can be one of the following:

```
public TextField();
public TextField(int cols);
public TextField(String text);
public TextField(String text, int cols);
```

with the following methods:

```
public void addActionListener(ActionListener l)    // Java 1.1
public void addNotify();
public boolean echoCharIsSet();
public int getColumns();
public char getEchoChar();
public char getMinimumSize(int cols);              // Java 1.1
public char getMinimumSize ();                     // Java 1.1
public char getPreferredSize(int cols);            // Java 1.1
public char getPreferredSize();                    // Java 1.1
public Dimension minimumSize();                    // Java 1.0
public Dimension minimumSize(int cols);            // Java 1.0
protected String paramString();
public Dimension preferredSize();                  // Java 1.0
public Dimension preferredSize(int cols);          // Java 1.0
public void setEchoCharacter(char c);              // Java 1.0
public void setEchoChar(char c);                   // Java 1.1
```

Where the methods with the Java 1.0 comment are deprecated. The `java.awt. TextComponent` class contains a number of methods that can be used to get the entered text. The following methods can be applied:

```
public void addTextListener(Listener l);           // Java 1.1
public int getCaretPosition();                     // Java 1.1
public String getSelectedText();
public int getSelectionEnd();
public int getSelectionStart();
public String getText();
public boolean isEditable();
protected String paramString();
public void removeNotify();
public void removeTextListener();
public void select(int selStart, int selEnd);
public void selectAll();
public int setCaretPosition();                     // Java 1.1
public void setEditable(boolean t);
```

```
      public void setSelectionEnd(int selEnd);         // Java 1.1
      public void setSelectionStart(int selStart);      // Java 1.1
      public void setText(String t);
```

In Java applet H11.1 the `TextField(20)` defines a 20-character input field. The `get-Text()` method is used within `action()` to get the entered text string. Java applet H11.2 shows the Java 1.1 equivalent.

📖 Java applet H11.1 (Java 1.0)

```
import java.awt.*;
import java.applet.*;

public class chapH11_01 extends Applet
{
String     Msg=null;
TextField  tfield = new TextField(20);

 public void init()
 {
   add(new Label("Enter your name"));
   add(tfield);
 }

 public boolean action(Event event,
   Object object)
 {
   if (event.target.equals(tfield))
       Msg=tfield.getText();
   repaint();
   return(true);
 }

  public void paint(Graphics g)
  {
    if (Msg!=null)
     g.drawString("Your name is:"+
                           Msg,30,120);
  }
}
```

Applet Viewer: cha...

Applet

Enter your name

| fred smith |

Your name is:fred smith

Applet started.

📖 Java applet 11.2 (Java 1.1)

```
import java.awt.*;
import java.applet.*;
import java.awt.event.*;

public class chapH11_02 extends Applet implements ActionListener
{
String     Msg=null;
TextField  tfield = new TextField(20);

   public void init()
   {
     add(new Label("Enter your name"));
     add(tfield);
     tfield.addActionListener(this);
   }
   public void actionPerformed(ActionEvent event)
   {
     Msg=tfield.getText();
     repaint();
```

```
        }
    public void paint(Graphics g)
    {
        if (Msg!=null)
        g.drawString("Your name is:" + Msg,30,120);
    }
}
```

Setting text

In Java applet H11.3 the `TextField(20)` defines a 20-character input field. The `get-Text()` method is used within `actionPerformed()` to get the entered text string and the `setText()` method to put the text to a text field (`tfield2`).

📖 Java applet H11.3 (≠Java 1.1)

```
import java.awt.*;
import java.awt.event.*;
import java.applet.*;

public class chapH11_03 extends Applet
        implements ActionListener
{
String     Msg=null;
TextField tfield1 = new TextField(20);
TextField tfield2 = new TextField(20);
 public void init()
 {
    add(new Label("Enter your name"));
    add(tfield1);
    add(tfield2);
    tfield1.addActionListener(this);
    tfield2.addActionListener(this);
 }

 public void actionPerformed(
                      ActionEvent event)
 {
    Msg=tfield1.getText();
    tfield2.setText(Msg);
 }
 }
```

Applet Viewer: cha...
Applet

Enter your name

| fred smith |

| fred smith |

Applet started.

Password entry

Many programs require the user to enter a password before they can execute a certain part of the program. Normally this password should be displayed in a manner in which no other user can view. Thus Java has the `setEchoChar()` method (in Java 1.0 this is `setEcho-Character()`) to define which character is displayed in the given text field. Java applet H11.4 is an example applet where the user enters their name and it is displayed with the '*' character. When the user presses the Enter key the entered name is displayed in the second text field.

📖   Java applet H11.4 (✦Java 1.1)

```
import java.awt.*;
import java.awt.event.*;
import java.applet.*;

public class chapH11_04 extends Applet
                  implements ActionListener
{
String     Msg=null;
TextField  tfield1 = new TextField(20);
TextField  tfield2 = new TextField(20);

 public void init()
 {
   add(new Label("Enter your name"));
   add(tfield1);
   tfield1.setEchoChar('*');
    // this is setEchoCharacter() in Java 1.0
   add(tfield2);
   tfield1.addActionListener(this);
   tfield2.addActionListener(this);
 }

public void actionPerformed(ActionEvent event)
{
    Msg=tfield1.getText();
    tfield2.setText(Msg);
}
}
```

Multiple-line text input

Multiple-line text can be entered into a Java applet using the `TextArea` action, which is contained in the `java.awt.TextArea` class. Its format can be one of the following:

```
public TextArea();
public TextArea(int rows, int cols);
public TextArea(String text);
public TextArea(String text, int rows, int cols);
```

with the following methods:

```
public void addNotify();
public void append(String str);                      // Java 1.1
public void appendText(String str);                  // Java 1.0
public int getColumns();
public char getMinimumSize(int cols);                // Java 1.1
public char getMinimumSize ();                       // Java 1.1
public char getPreferredSize(int cols);              // Java 1.1
public char getPreferredSize();                      // Java 1.1
public int getRows();
public void insertText(String str, int pos);
public Dimension minimumSize();                      // Java 1.0
public Dimension minimumSize(int rows, int cols);    // Java 1.0
protected String paramString();                      // Java 1.0
public Dimension preferredSize();                    // Java 1.0
public Dimension preferredSize(int rows, int cols);  // Java 1.0
public void replaceText(String str, int start, int end);
                                                     // Java 1.0
public int setColumns(int cols);                     // Java 1.1
```

```
    public int setRows(int rows);                              // Java 1.1
```

H11.1.2 Fonts

Java is well supported with different fonts. The class library `java.awt.Font` defines the Font class and the general format for defining the font is:

Font *font* = new **Font** (*font_type*, *font_attrib*, *font_size*)

and the methods are:

```
        public Font decode(String str);
        public boolean equals(Object obj);
        public String getFamily();
        public static Font getFont(String nm);
        public static Font getFont(String nm, Font font);
        public String getName();
        public FontPeer getPeer();                             // Java 1.1
        public int getSize();
        public int getStyle();
        public int hashCode();
        public boolean isBold();
        public boolean isItalic();
        public boolean isPlain();
        public String toString();
```

The font class has various fields, these are:

```
        protected String name;
        protected int size;
        protected int style;
```

and the defined bit masks are:

```
        public final static int BOLD;
        public final static int ITALIC;
        public final static int PLAIN;
```

The `java.awt.Graphics` class also contains a number of methods related to fonts, these include:

```
        public abstract Font getFont();
        public FontMetrics getFontMetrics();
        public abstract FontMetrics getFontMetrics(Font f);
        public abstract void setColor(Color c);
        public abstract void setFont(Font font);
```

In Java 1.0, the main font types are:

"TimesRoman"   "Helvetica"   "Courier"   "Symbol"

In Java 1.1 the font names "Serif", "SanSerif" and "Monospaced" should be used instead of the ones given above. This book is written in Times Roman. Helvetica looks good as a header, such as Header 1. Courier produces a mono-space font where all of the characters have the same width. The Java applets in this chapter use the Courier font. Symbol is normally used when special symbols are required. The *font_attrib* can either be BOLD (Value of 1), ITALIC (Value of 2) or NORMAL (Value of 0) and the font_size is an integer value which is supported by the compiler. The font size of this text is 11 and most normal text varies between 8 and 12.

Java applet H11.5 shows an example applet using different fonts.

📖 Java applet H11.5

```
import java.awt.*;
import java.applet.*;

public class chapH11_05 extends Applet
{
Font  TimesRoman= new
          Font("TimesRoman",Font.BOLD,24);
Font  Courier= new
Font("Courier",Font.BOLD,24);
Font  Helvetica= new
             Font("Helvetica",Font.BOLD,24);
Font  Symbol= new Font("Symbol",Font.BOLD,24);

  public void paint(Graphics g)
  {
    g.setFont(TimesRoman);
    g.drawString("Sample text",10,40);
    g.setFont(Courier);
    g.drawString("Sample text",10,60);
    g.setFont(Helvetica);
    g.drawString("Sample text",10,80);
    g.setFont(Symbol);
    g.drawString("Sample text",10,100);
  }
}
```

Java applet H11.6 shows an example applet using a pull-down menu to select from a number of different fonts.

📖 Java applet H11.6 (✦Java 1.1)

```
import java.applet.*;
import java.awt.event.*;
import java.awt.*;
public class chapH11_06 extends Applet
                    implements ItemListener
{
Choice font= new Choice();

 public void init()
 {
   font.addItem("Courier");
   font.addItem("Times");
   font.addItem("Helvetica");
   add(font);
   font.addItemListener(this);
 }
 public void itemStateChanged(ItemEvent evt)
 {
 Object obj;

   obj=evt.getItem();
```

```
  if (obj.equals("Courier"))
    setFont(new Font("Courier",Font.PLAIN,12));
  else if (obj.equals("Times"))
    setFont(new Font("Times",Font.PLAIN,12));
  else if (obj.equals("Helvetica"))
    setFont(new
Font("Helvetica",Font.PLAIN,12));
  repaint();
 }
 public void paint(Graphics g)
 {
   g.drawString("Test message",40,100);
 }
}
```

H11.1.3 Date

Java has a wide range of date constructors and methods. They are defined in the java.util.Date class. The constructors for a date are:

```
    public Date();
    public Date(int year, int month, int date);          //Java 1.0
    public Date(int year, int month, int date, int hrs, int min);
                                                         //Java 1.0
    public Date(int year, int month, int date, int hrs, int min,
                    int sec);                            //Java 1.0
    public Date(long date);
    public Date(String s);                               // Java 1.0
```

and the methods are as follows:

```
    public boolean after(Date  when);
    public boolean before(Date  when);
    public boolean equals(Object  obj);
    public int getDate();                                // Java 1.0
    public int getDay();                                 // Java 1.0
    public int getHours();                               // Java 1.0
    public int getMinutes();                             // Java 1.0
    public int getMonth();                               // Java 1.0
    public int getSeconds();                             // Java 1.0
    public long getTime();
    public int getTimezoneOffset();                      // Java 1.0
    public int getYear();                                // Java 1.0
    public int hashCode();
    public static long parse(String  s);
    public void setDate(int  date);                      // Java 1.0
    public void setHours(int  hours);                    // Java 1.0
    public void setMinutes(int  minutes);                // Java 1.0
    public void setMonth(int  month);                    // Java 1.0
    public void setSeconds(int  seconds);                // Java 1.0
    public void setTime(long  time);
    public void setYear(int  year);                      // Java 1.0
    public String toGMTString();                         // Java 1.0
    public String toLocaleString();                      // Java 1.0
    public String toString();
    public static long UTC(int  year, int  month, int  date, int  hrs,
                    int  min, int  sec);
```

In Java 1.1, many of the date methods have been deprecated. The Calendar class has thus been favoured. Java applet H11.7 shows an applet which displays the date in two different formats. The first ("Date 1") displays it using the `toString()` method and the second ("Date 2") displays it by building up a string using the `getMinutes()`, `getHours()`, `get-Day()`, `getMonth()` and `getYear()` methods.

📖 Java applet H11.7 (¶Java 1.0)

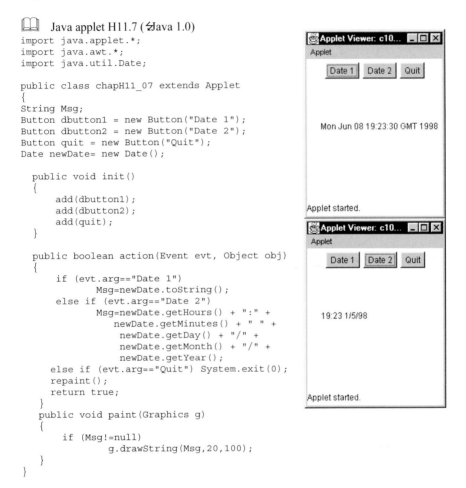

```
import java.applet.*;
import java.awt.*;
import java.util.Date;

public class chapH11_07 extends Applet
{
String Msg;
Button dbutton1 = new Button("Date 1");
Button dbutton2 = new Button("Date 2");
Button quit = new Button("Quit");
Date newDate= new Date();

    public void init()
    {
        add(dbutton1);
        add(dbutton2);
        add(quit);
    }

    public boolean action(Event evt, Object obj)
    {
        if (evt.arg=="Date 1")
                Msg=newDate.toString();
        else if (evt.arg=="Date 2")
                Msg=newDate.getHours() + ":" +
                    newDate.getMinutes() + " " +
                    newDate.getDay() + "/" +
                    newDate.getMonth() + "/" +
                    newDate.getYear();
        else if (evt.arg=="Quit") System.exit(0);
        repaint();
        return true;
    }
    public void paint(Graphics g)
    {
        if (Msg!=null)
                g.drawString(Msg,20,100);
    }
}
```

The date format is specified with the following:

- Year. The year value of the date is the year minus 1990. Thus the year 1998 is specified with the year value of 98, and the year 2000 by 100.
- Day. The day value of the date is the day number, from 1 to 31.
- Month. The month value of the date is the month number minus 1. Thus January is represented by 0, February by 1, and so on.
- Hour. The hour value of the date is the hour number, from 0 to 23.
- Minute. The minute value of the date is the minute number, from 0 to 59.
- Second. The second value of the date is the second number, from 0 to 59.

Java applet H11.8 shows an applet which displays the day of the week for a certain entered date (note that the day array is incomplete as it only ranges from day 1 to day 12). Three arrays of strings are setup for the day ("1", "2", and so on), month ("Jan", "Feb", and so on) and year (such as "1998", "1999" and "2000"). These arrays are named Days[], Months[] and Years[], and are used to set the text on the pull-down menu.

It can be seen from the sample run that the 3 May 1998 was on a Sunday.

Java applet H11.8 (☞Java 1.0)

```
import java.applet.*;
import java.awt.*;
import java.util.Date;

public class chapH11_08 extends Applet
{
String Msg;
Choice day = new Choice();
Choice year = new Choice();
Choice month = new Choice();
Button quit = new Button("Quit");
Date    newDate= new Date(98,0,1);
                // 1 Jan 1998
String Days[]={"1", "2", "3", "4","5","6",
       "7","8","9","10","11","12"}; // TBC

String Month[]={"Jan","Feb","Mar","Apr","May",
   "Jun","Jul","Aug","Sep","Oct","Nov","Dec"};
String Years[]={"1998", "1999", "2000"};
int i,inday=1,inmonth=0,inyear=98;
TextField tfield = new TextField(20);

  public void init()
  {
    for (i=0;i<12;i++) day.addItem(Days[i]);
    add(day);
    for (i=0;i<12;i++) month.addItem(Month[i]);
    add(month);
    for (i=0;i<3;i++) year.addItem(Years[i]);
    add(year);

    add(quit);
    add(tfield);

    Msg=newDate.toString();
    tfield.setText(Msg);
  }
  public boolean action(Event evt, Object obj)
  {
    if (evt.target.equals(day))
      inday=day.getSelectedIndex()+1;
    if (evt.target.equals(month))
      inmonth=month.getSelectedIndex();
    if (evt.target.equals(year))
      inyear=year.getSelectedIndex()+98;
    if (evt.target.equals(quit))
      System.exit(0);
    newDate= new Date(inyear,inmonth,inday);
    Msg=newDate.toString();
    tfield.setText(Msg);
    return true;
  }
}
```

Java time

Java keeps time by incrementing a long value every 1ms. Java applet H11.9 shows an applet which determines the amount of time that a program has been running. It uses the get-Time() method to initially get a value for the current time and puts it into oldtime. Then when the user presses the "Show Time" button the number of seconds is calculated by subtracting the new time (newtime) from oldtime, and dividing by 1000 (so that it can be displayed in seconds).

📖   Java applet H11.9 (✪Java 1.0)

```
import java.applet.*;
import java.awt.*;
import java.util.Date;

public class chapH11_09 extends Applet
{
String Msg;
Button dbutton1 = new Button("Show Time");
Button quit = new Button("Quit");
long    newtime,oldtime;
TextField tfield = new TextField(20);

  public void init()
  {
      add(dbutton1);
      add(quit);
      add(tfield);
      Date newDate= new Date();
      oldtime=newDate.getTime();
      tfield.setText("Press Show Time");
  }

  public boolean action(Event evt, Object obj)
  {
      if (evt.arg=="Show Time")
      {
        Date newDate= new Date();
        newtime=newDate.getTime();
        Msg=" " + (newtime-oldtime)/1000 +
              " seconds";
      }
      else if (evt.arg=="Quit") System.exit(0);
      tfield.setText(Msg);
      return true;

  }
}
```

UTC format

UTC (Co-ordinated Universal Time) is a machine-independent method of representing time. It assumes that there are 86 400 seconds each day (24×60×60) and once every year or two an extra second is added (a "leap" second). This is normally added on 31 December or 30 June.

Most computer systems define time with GMT (Greenwich Mean Time) which is UT (Universal Time). UTC is based on an atomic clock whereas GMT is based on astronomical observations. Unfortunately, because the earth rotation is not uniform, it is not as accurate as UTC.

H11.2 Strings

C has strong support for strings, Java greatly enhances the use of strings and makes it easy to initialise and copy strings. A string is declared with:

```
String Msg;
```

There is no need to declare the size of the string as it is automatically allocated. The methods that can be used with strings are:

```
public char charAt(int index);
public int compareTo(String anotherString);
public String concat(String str);
public static String copyValueOf(char data[]);
public static String copyValueOf(char data[], int offset,  int count);
public boolean endsWith(String suffix);
public boolean equals(Object anObject);
public boolean equalsIgnoreCase(String anotherString);
public void getBytes(int srcBegin, int srcEnd, byte dst[], int dstBegin);
                                                // Java 1.0
public void getBytes();                         // Java 1.1
public void getChars(int srcBegin, int srcEnd, char dst[], int dstBegin);
public int hashCode();
public int indexOf(int ch);
public int indexOf(int ch, int fromIndex);
public int indexOf(String str);
public int indexOf(String str, int fromIndex);
public String intern();
public int lastIndexOf(int ch);
public int lastIndexOf(int ch, int fromIndex);
public int lastIndexOf(String str);
public int lastIndexOf(String str, int fromIndex);
public int length();
public boolean regionMatches(boolean ignoreCase,
        int toffset, String other, int ooffset, int len);
public boolean regionMatches(int toffset, String other,
        int ooffset, int len);
public String replace(char oldChar,   char newChar);
public boolean startsWith(String prefix);
public boolean startsWith(String prefix, int toffset);
public String substring(int beginIndex);
public String substring(int beginIndex, int endIndex);
public char[] toCharArray();
public String toLowerCase();
public String toLowerCase(Local locale);       // Java 1.1
public String toString();
public String toUpperCase();
public String toUpperCase(Local locale);       // Java 1.1
public String trim();
public static String valueOf(boolean b);
public static String valueOf(char c);
public static String valueOf(char data[]);
public static String valueOf(char data[], int offset, int count);
public static String valueOf(double d);
public static String valueOf(float f);
public static String valueOf(int i);
public static String valueOf(long l);
public static String valueOf(Object obj);
```

Java applet H11.10 compares two entered strings and uses the equal() method to compare them. A compare button (comp) is used to initiate the comparison.

```java
import java.applet.*;
import java.awt.*;
import java.lang.String;

public class chapH11_10 extends Applet
{
String str1,str2;
TextField tfield1 = new TextField(20);
TextField tfield2 = new TextField(20);
TextField tfield3 = new TextField(20);
Button comp = new Button("Compare");
Button quit = new Button("Quit");

 public void init()
 {
    add(new Label("Enter two strings"));
    add(tfield1); add(tfield2);
    add(new Label("Comparison:"));
    add(tfield3);
    add(comp); add(quit);
 }
 public boolean action(Event evt, Object obj)
 {
    if (evt.target.equals(comp))
    {
       str1=tfield1.getText();
       str2=tfield2.getText();
       if (str1.equals(str2))
          tfield3.setText("Same");
       else tfield3.setText("Different");
    }
    else if (evt.target.equals(quit))
          System.exit(0);
    return true;
 }
}
```

Java applet H11.11 shows the Java 1.1 equivalent.

Java applet H11.11 (≰Java 1.1)

```java
import java.applet.*;
import java.awt.*;
import java.awt.event.*;
import java.lang.String;

public class chapH11_12 extends Applet implements ActionListener
{
TextField   tfield1 = new TextField(20);
TextField   tfield2 = new TextField(20);
TextField   tfield3 = new TextField(20);
Button      comp = new Button("Compare");
Button      quit = new Button("Quit");

  public void init()
  {
     add(new Label("Enter two strings"));
     add(tfield1); add(tfield2);
     add(new Label("Comparison:"));
     add(tfield3);
```

```
        add(comp); add(quit);
        comp.addActionListener(this);
        quit.addActionListener(this);
    }
    public void actionPerformed(ActionEvent evt)
    {
    String str, str1, str2;

        str=evt.getActionCommand();
        if (str.equals("Compare"))
        {
            str1=tfield1.getText();
            str2=tfield2.getText();
            if (str1.equals(str2)) tfield3.setText("Same");
            else tfield3.setText("Different");
        }
        else if (str.equals("quit")) System.exit(0);
    }
}
```

Applet H11.10 compares the characters in two strings and will display that the strings differ when the letters are the same but their case differs. Java applet H11.12 uses a checkbox (ccase) to define whether the case of the entered strings should be ignored, or not. If the checkbox is checked then the entered strings are converted into lowercase with the toLow-erCase() method.

📖 Java applet H11.12 (⌘Java 1.1)

```
import java.applet.*;
import java.awt.*;
import java.awt.event.*;
import java.lang.String;

public class chapH12_12 extends Applet implements ActionListener,ItemListener
{
String      str1,str2;
TextField   tfield1 = new TextField(20);
TextField   tfield2 = new TextField(20);
TextField   tfield3 = new TextField(20);
Button      comp = new Button("Compare");
Button      quit = new Button("Quit");
Checkbox    ccase = new Checkbox("Case");
boolean     case_show=false;

    public void init()
    {
        add(new Label("Enter two strings"));
        add(tfield1); add(tfield2);
        add(new Label("Comparison:"));
        add(tfield3);
        add(comp); add(quit);
        add(ccase);
        comp.addActionListener(this);
        quit.addActionListener(this);
        ccase.addItemListener(this);
    }

    public void actionPerformed(ActionEvent evt)
    {
    String str;
        str=evt.getActionCommand();
        if (str.equals("Compare"))
```

```
        {
            str1=tfield1.getText();
            str2=tfield2.getText();
            if (case_show)
            {
                str1=str1.toLowerCase();
                str2=str2.toLowerCase();
            }
            if (str1.equals(str2)) tfield3.setText("Same");
            else tfield3.setText("Different");
        }
        else if (str.equals("Quit")) System.exit(0);
    }
    public void itemStateChanged(ItemEvent evt)
    {
    Object obj;
        obj=evt.getItem();
        if (obj.equals("Case")) case_show=ccase.getState();
    }
}
```

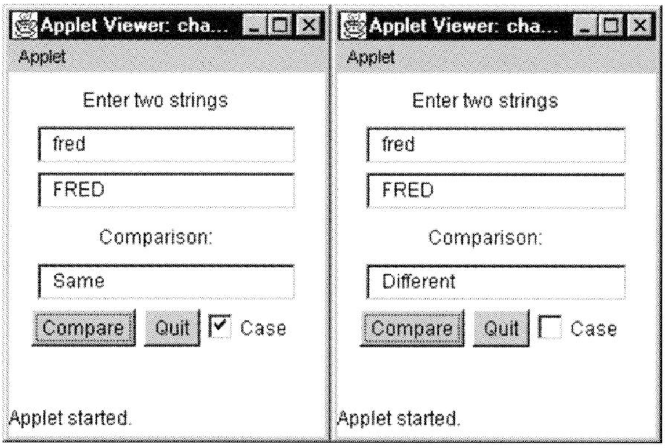

Figure H11.1   Sample runs

Note that the `equalsIgnoreCase()` method could have also been used. For example the lines:

```
if (case_show)
{
        str1=str1.toLowerCase();        str2=str2.toLowerCase();
}
if (str1.equals(str2))
    tfield3.setText("Same");
else    tfield3.setText("Different");
```

could be replaced with:

```
if (case_show)
{
    if (str1.equalsIgnoreCase(str2)) tfield3.setText("Same");
    else tfield3.setText("Different");
}
```

```
            else
            {
                if (str1.equals(str2)) tfield3.setText("Same");
                else tfield3.setText("Different");
            }
```

Applet H11.13 uses the indexOf() method to find a given character in an entered string. It can be seen in the sample runs, in Figure 11.2, that a run value of –1 identifies that the character has not been found in the string. As with C, the first indexed value of a string is a 0, the second at 1, and so on.

📖 Java applet H11.13 (⊀Java 1.1)
```java
import java.applet.*;
import java.awt.*;
import java.awt.event.*;
import java.lang.String;

public class chapH11_13 extends Applet implements ActionListener
{
String    str1,str2;
TextField tfield1 = new TextField(20);
TextField tfield2 = new TextField(2);
TextField tfield3 = new TextField(20);
Button    find = new Button("Find");
Button    quit = new Button("Quit");

    public void init()
    {
        add(new Label("Enter a string"));
        add(tfield1);
        add(new Label("Character to find:"));
        add(tfield2);
        add(new Label("Dialog"));
        add(tfield3);
        add(find); add(quit);
        find.addActionListener(this);
        quit.addActionListener(this);
    }

    public void actionPerformed(ActionEvent evt)
    {
    int index;
    String Msg,str;
        str=evt.getActionCommand();
        if (str.equals("Find"))
        {
                str1=tfield1.getText();
                str2=tfield2.getText();
                index=str1.indexOf(str2);
                Msg="Found at " + index;
                tfield3.setText(Msg);
        }
        else if (str.equals("Quit"))  System.exit(0);
    }
}
```

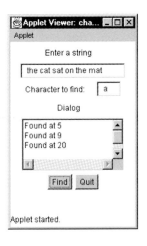

Figure H11.2 Sample run

Applet H11.13 only displays the first occurrence of a character in a string. Applet 11.14 adds an index term to the `indexOf()` method to find multiple occurrences of a character in the string. A loop is set up to test the value of index and will quit from the loop when the index term is –1.

📖 Java applet H11.14 (⇔Java 1.1)

```java
import java.applet.*;
import java.awt.*;
import java.awt.event.*;
import java.lang.String;

public class chapH11_14 extends Applet
        implements ActionListener
{
TextField  tfield1 = new TextField(20);
TextField  tfield2 = new TextField(2);
TextArea   tarea = new TextArea(4,20);
Button     find = new Button("Find");
Button     quit = new Button("Quit");

  public void init()
  {
    add(new Label("Enter a string"));
    add(tfield1);
    add(new Label("Character to find:"));
    add(tfield2);
    add(new Label("Dialog"));
    add(tarea);
    add(find); add(quit);
    find.addActionListener(this);
    quit.addActionListener(this);
  }

  public void actionPerformed(ActionEvent evt)
  {
  int index,curr;
    String Msg=null, str1, str2, str;
    str=evt.getActionCommand();

    if (str.equals("Find"))
    {
```

```
      str1=tfield1.getText();
      str2=tfield2.getText();
      curr=0;
      do
      {
        index=str1.indexOf(str2,curr);
        curr=index+1;
        if (Msg!=null)
            Msg=Msg+"Found at "+index + "\n";
        else Msg="Found at "+index + "\n";

        if (index!=-1) tarea.setText(Msg);
      } while (index!=-1);
    }
    else if (str.equals("Quit"))
              System.exit(0);
  }
}
```

Java applet H11.15 allows a user to enter a string and then replace a given character with another given character. The `replace()` method is used to replace the characters in the string, while the `charAt(0)` is used to determine the first character in the entered character replacement strings (`str2` and `str3`).

Java applet H11.15 (↩Java 1.1)

```
import java.applet.*;
import java.awt.*;
import java.awt.event.*;
import java.lang.String;

public class chapH11_15 extends Applet
       implements ActionListener
{
TextField tfield1 = new TextField(20);
TextField tfield2 = new TextField(2);
TextField tfield3 = new TextField(2);
TextField tfield4 = new TextField(20);
Button convert = new Button("Convert");
Button quit = new Button("Quit");
```

```
  public void init()
  {
    add(new Label("Enter a string"));
    add(tfield1);
    add(new Label("Character to replace"));
    add(tfield2);
    add(new Label("with"));
    add(tfield3);
    add(new Label("Substituted text:"));
    add(tfield4);

    add(convert); add(quit);
    convert.addActionListener(this);
    quit.addActionListener(this);
  }

  public void actionPerformed(ActionEvent
evt)
  {
```

```
   int index,curr;
   String str1,str2,str3,str4,str;

     str=evt.getActionCommand();

     if (str.equals("Convert"))
     {
       str1=tfield1.getText();
       str2=tfield2.getText();
       str3=tfield3.getText();
       str4=str1.replace(str2.charAt(0),
               str3.charAt(0));
       tfield4.setText(str4);
     }
     else if (str.equals("Quit"))
           System.exit(0);
   }
}
```

Java applet H11.16 converts an entered string (`str`) into a character array (`c`). It uses the `length()` method to determine the number of characters in the string.

📖   Java applet H11.16 (⇐Java 1.1)

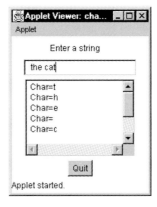

```
import java.applet.*;
import java.awt.*;
import java.awt.event.*;
import java.lang.String;

public class chapH11_16 extends Applet
    implements ActionListener
{
TextField  tfield1 = new TextField(20);
TextArea   tarea = new TextArea(6,20);
Button     quit = new Button("Quit");

  public void init()
  {
    add(new Label("Enter a string"));
    add(tfield1);
    tfield1.addActionListener(this);
    add(tarea);
    add(quit);  quit.addActionListener(this);
  }

public void actionPerformed(ActionEvent evt)
{
char c[];
String Msg=null,str;
  int i=0;

    str=evt.getActionCommand();
    if (str.equals("Quit")) System.exit(0);
    else
    {
      str=tfield1.getText();
      c=str.toCharArray();
      for (i=0;i<str.length();i++)
      {
        if (Msg!=null) Msg=Msg + " Char=" +
                   c[i] + "\n";
        else Msg= " Char=" + c[i] + "\n";
      }
```

```
        tarea.setText(Msg);
      }
   }
  }
```

H11.3 Exceptions

Many errors can occur in a program. In most programming languages they can cause a program to crash or act unpredictably. For example C and Pascal can cause a run-time error when the program accesses an array element which does not correspond with the number of elements which have been declared. In Java an error causes an exception, which can be tested and handled in the required mode. The format is:

```
try
{
     // statements to catch if an exception occurs
}
catch
{
   // the catch is called when an exception occurs
}
```

When an exception occurs the rest of the statements are not executed and the program goes to the `catch` statements. After completing the exception the program does not return to the `try` statement. Multiple catch statements can also be inserted after a `try` statement, such as:

```
try
{
   // statements which might cause an exception
}
catch NumberFormatException()
{
     // exception caused when a numeric value conversion has an
     // invalid format
}
catch NegativeArraySizeException()
{
   // exception caused when there is a negative array size
}
```

The constructors are:

public **Exception**()
> Constructs an exception with no specified detail message.

public **Exception**(String s)
> Constructs a exception with the specified detail message (s).

Java applet H11.17 shows an example of an exception in a program which accesses an array element which has not been declared. It can be seen in Test run 12.1 that the exception message is:

```
java.lang.ArrayIndexOutOfBoundsException: 4.
```

📖 Java applet H11.17

```
import java.net.*;
import java.awt.*;
import java.applet.*;
public class chapH11_17 extends Applet
{
    public void paint(Graphics g)
    {
    float arr[]=new float[4];
    int i;
        arr[0]=1; arr[1]=2; arr[2]=3; arr[3]=4;
        try
        {
            for (i=0;i<100;i++)
                System.out.println(" " + arr[i]);
        }
        catch (Exception e)
        {
            System.out.println("Error :" + e);
        }
    }
}
```

🖥 **Test run H11.1**

```
C:\java\temp>appletviewer chap12_01.html
 1
 2
 3
 4
Error :java.lang.ArrayIndexOutOfBoundsException: 4
```

H11.3.1 Typical exceptions

The java.lang package contains a number of exceptions, these include:

public **ArithmeticException**()
> Thrown when an exceptional arithmetic condition has occurred, such as a division-by-zero or a square root of a negative number.

public **ArrayIndexOutOfBoundsException**()
> Thrown when an illegal index term in an array has been accessed.

public **ArrayStoreException**()
> Thrown when the wrong type of object is stored in an array of objects.

public **ClassCastException**()
> Exception that is thrown when an object is casted to a subclass which it is not an instance.

public **Exception**()
> Exception that indicates conditions that a reasonable application might want to catch.

```
public IllegalArgumentException()
```
Thrown when a method has been passed an illegal or inappropriate argument.
```
public IllegalThreadStateException()
```
Thrown to indicate that a thread is not in an appropriate state for the requested operation.
```
public IndexOutOfBoundsException()
```
Thrown to indicate that an index term is out of range.
```
public InterruptedException()
```
Thrown when a thread is waiting, sleeping, or otherwise paused for a long time and another thread interrupts it using the interrupt method in class `Thread`.
```
public NegativeArraySizeException()
```
Thrown when an array is created with a negative size.
```
public NullPointerException()
```
Thrown when an application attempts to use a null pointer.
```
public NumberFormatException()
```
Thrown when an application attempts to convert a string to one of the numeric types, but that the string does not have the appropriate format.

```
public StringIndexOutOfBoundsException()
```
Thrown when a string is indexed with a negative value or a value which is greater than or equal to the size of the string.

Other exceptions will be discussed in the following chapters.

H11.3.2 Math exceptions

Java applet H11.18 shows a simple applet which determines the value of a division between two integer numbers. It uses the `ArithmeticException` exception which will be thrown when there is a divide-by-zero error (or any other exceptional arithmetic condition). The second sample run shows a divide-by-zero error.

The statement:

```
val1=Integer.valueOf(str);
```

converts a string (`str`) in an `Integer`. To convert it to an `int` type (in order to perform a calculation) the following is used:

```
val1.intValue();
```

Note that `val3` could also have been calculated directly with the following line:

```
val3=Integer.valueOf(str).intValue();
```

Java applet H11.19 calculates the square root of an entered floating point value. If the entered value is a negative then an exception is thrown when the applet tries to determine the square root of the negative value.

Java applet H11.18 (Java 1.1)

```java
import java.applet.*;
import java.awt.*;
import java.awt.event.*;

public class H11_18 extends Applet
        implements ActionListener
{
TextField tfield1 = new TextField(5);
TextField tfield2 = new TextField(5);
TextField tfield3 = new TextField(15);
Button calc = new Button("Calc");
Button quit = new Button("Quit");

 public void init()
 {
   add(new Label("Enter value 1"));
   add(tfield1);
   add(new Label("Enter value 2"));
   add(tfield2);
   add(new Label("Result"));
    add(tfield3);
    add(calc); calc.addActionListener(this);
    add(quit); quit.addActionListener(this);
 }
public void actionPerformed(ActionEvent evt)
{
String    str,str1;
Integer   val1,val2;
int       val3;

   str=evt.getActionCommand();
   if (str.equals("Calc"))
   {
    str1=tfield1.getText();
    val1=Integer.valueOf(str1);
    str1=tfield2.getText();
    val2=Integer.valueOf(str1);
    try
    {
     val3=val1.intValue()/val2.intValue();
     tfield3.setText(""+val3);
    }
    catch (ArithmeticException err)
    {
     tfield3.setText("Divide-by-0");
    }
   }
   else if (str.equals("Quit"))
              System.exit(0);
 }
}
```

📖 Java applet H11.19 (≠Java 1.1)

```java
import java.applet.*;
import java.awt.*;
import java.awt.event.*;

public class chapH11_19 extends Applet
    implements ActionListener
{
TextField tfield1 = new TextField(5);
TextField tfield2 = new TextField(5);
Button    quit = new Button("Quit");

    public void init()
    {
        add(new Label("Value:"));
        add(tfield1);
        add(new Label("Result:"));
        add(tfield2);
        add(quit);
        quit.addActionListener(this);
        tfield1.addActionListener(this);
    }

    public void actionPerformed(
                      ActionEvent evt)
    {
    String str=null;
    Double val1;
    double val,res;

    str=evt.getActionCommand();

    if (str.equals("Quit"))
        System.exit(0);
    else
    {
     val1=Double.valueOf(tfield1.getText());
     try
     {
        val=val1.floatValue();
        res=Math.sqrt(val);
        tfield2.setText(""+res);
     }
     catch (ArithmeticException err)
     {
        tfield2.setText("Exception");
     }
    }
  }
 }
}
```

Note that `val1` could also have been calculated directly with the following line:

```java
val1= Double.valueOf(tfield1.getText()).doubleValue();
```

Java applet H11.20 calculates the square root of an entered floating point value. It uses the `NumberFormatException` exception to determine if the entered value is not in the correct format.

Java applet H11.20 (☐Java 1.1)

```java
import java.applet.*;
import java.awt.*;
import java.awt.event.*;
import java.lang.*;

public class chapH11_20 extends Applet
        implements ActionListener
{
TextField tfield1 = new TextField(5);
TextField tfield2 = new TextField(10);
Button    quit = new Button("Quit");
   public void init()
   {
      add(new Label("Value:"));
      add(tfield1);
      add(new Label("Result:"));
      add(tfield2);      add(quit);
      quit.addActionListener(this);
      tfield1.addActionListener(this);
   }
   public void actionPerformed(
                        ActionEvent evt)
   {
String str=null;
Double val1;
double val,res;

      str=evt.getActionCommand();

      if (str.equals("Quit"))
         System.exit(0);
      else
      {
         try
         {
            val1=Double.valueOf(
              tfield1.getText());
            val=val1.floatValue();
            res=Math.sqrt(val);
            tfield2.setText(""+res);
         }
         catch (NumberFormatException err)
         {
            tfield2.setText("INVALID");
         }
      }
   }
}
```

H11.4   Multithreading

Multitasking involves running several tasks at the same time. It normally involves each task running on a process for a given amount of time, before it is released and another process is given some time. There are two forms of multitasking, these are:

- Pre-emptive multitasking. This type involves the operating system controlling how long a process stays on the processor. This allows for smooth multitasking and is used in Microsoft Windows 32-bit programs.

- Co-operative multitasking. This type of multitasking relies on a process giving up the processor. It is used with Windows 3.1 programs and suffers from processor hogging, where a process can stay on a processor and the operating system cannot kick it off.

The logical extension to multitasking programs is to split programs into a number a parts (threads) and running each of these on the multitasking system (multithreading). A program which is running more than one thread at a time is known as a multithreaded program. Multithreaded programs have many advantages over non-multithreaded programs, including:

- They make better use of the processor, where different threads can be run when one or more threads are waiting for data. For example a thread could be waiting for keyboard input, while another thread could be searching the Internet for information.
- They are easier to test, where each thread can be tested independently of other threads.
- They can use standard threads, which are optimized for a given hardware.

They also have disadvantages, including:

- The program has to be planned properly so that threads must know on which threads they depend on.
- A thread may wait indefinitely for another thread has which crashed.

The main difference between multiple processes and multiple threads is that each process has independent variables and data, while multiple threads share data from the main program.

H11.4.1 Threads class

The `java.lang.Thread` class implements one or more threads. A thread is typically constructed with:

```
Thread proc=null;

    proc = new Thread(this);
```

where *proc* defines the name of the thread. The main methods that can be applied to the thread are:

```
public void destroy();
public void interrupt();
public static boolean interrupted();
public final boolean isAlive();
public final boolean isDaemon();
public boolean isInterrupted();
public final void resume();
public void run();
public final void setDaemon(boolean on);
public static void sleep(long millis);
public void start();
public final void stop();
public final void stop(Throwable obj);
public final void suspend();
public static void yield();
```

The start() method starts the thread and the stop() method stops it. The sleep() method suspends the thread for a number of milliseconds. For example to suspend a thread of 0.5 seconds and then stop it, the following can be used:

```
Thread proc = null;

    proc = new Thread(this);
    proc.start();
    proc.sleep(500);
    proc.stop();
```

Java applet H15.21 implements a basic time and date display. The thread is initially started with:

```
mytimer = new Thread(this);
mytimer.start();
```

The timer routine is contained within run(), with:

```
try {    mytimer.sleep(1000); }
catch (InterruptedException e) {}
repaint();
```

The sleep(1000) method causes the thread to suspend for 1 second (1000 milliseconds). After this paint() is called, which implements:

```
g.setColor(getBackground());

if (lastdate!=null)
        g.drawString(lastdate, 5, 40);

g.setColor(Color.darkGray);
g.drawString(today, 5, 40);
lastdate = today;
```

This sets the drawing color to the background color (typically either white or grey). The previous time and date string is then erased from the screen. Next the text color is changed to dark grey and the new date and time is then re-drawn.

📖 Java applet H11.21

```
import java.util.*;
import java.awt.*;
import java.applet.*;

public class chapH11_21 extends Applet
                        implements Runnable
{
Thread mytimer = null;
String lastdate = null;

    public void paint(Graphics g)
    {
    String today;
    Date ddd = new Date();

     today = ddd.toLocaleString();

     g.setFont(new Font("TimesRoman",
               Font.BOLD, 22));

     // Erase and redraw time
     g.setColor(getBackground());

    if (lastdate!=null)
      g.drawString(lastdate, 5, 40);

     g.setColor(Color.darkGray);
     g.drawString(today, 5, 40);
     lastdate = today;
    }

    public void start()
    {
      if(mytimer == null)
      {
         mytimer = new Thread(this);
         mytimer.start();
      }
    }

    public void stop()
    {
        mytimer = null;
    }

    public void run()
    {
      while (mytimer != null)
      {
         try {mytimer.sleep(1000);}
         catch (InterruptedException e){}
         repaint();
      }
      mytimer = null;
    }
}
```

Applet Viewer: cha... ▪️◻️✖️
Applet

06-Jun-98 22:53:41

Applet started.

Java applet H11.22 uses the suspend(), resume() and stop() methods to suspend, re-
sume (after a suspend) and stop a thread, respectively.

Java applet H11.22

```java
import java.util.*;
import java.awt.*;
import java.applet.*;

public class chapH11_22 extends Applet
        implements Runnable
{
Thread mytimer = null;
String lastdate = null;
Button dstart= new Button("Start");
Button dsus=new Button("Suspend");
Button dend=new Button("Stop");
Button quit=new Button("Quit");

  public void init()
  {
      add(dstart);
      add(dsus);
      add(dend);
      add(quit);
  }

  public boolean action(Event evt,
        Object obj)
  {
      if (evt.target.equals(dstart))
          mytimer.resume();
      else if (evt.target.equals(dsus))
          mytimer.suspend();
      else if (evt.target.equals(dend))
          mytimer.stop();
       else if (evt.target.equals(quit))
       {
                  mytimer=null;
                  System.exit(0);
       }
       return true;
  }

  public void paint(Graphics g)
  {
   String today;
   Date ddd = new Date();

      today = ddd.toLocaleString();

      g.setFont(new Font("TimesRoman",
            Font.BOLD, 22));

       // Erase and redraw time
      g.setColor(getBackground());

      if (lastdate!=null)
        g.drawString(lastdate, 5, 40);

      g.setColor(Color.darkGray);
      g.drawString(today, 5, 80);
      lastdate = today;
  }

  public void start()
  {
```

```
    if (mytimer == null)
    {
      mytimer = new Thread(this);
      mytimer.start();
    }
  }
  public void stop()
  {
    mytimer = null;
  }
  public void run()
  {
    while (mytimer != null)
    {
      try {mytimer.sleep(1000);}
      catch (InterruptedException e){}
      repaint();
    }
    mytimer = null;
  }
}
```

Note that a general-purpose delay method can be constructed as follows:

```
public void delay(int ms)
{
    try {mytimer.sleep(ms);}
    catch (InterruptedException e){}
}
```

which will delay the thread by a number of milliseconds (ms). This could be used as follows:

```
public void run()
{
  while (mytimer != null)
  {
    delay(2000);   // Delay for 2 seconds (2000 ms)
    repaint();
  }
  mytimer = null;
}
```

H11.4.2 Simple animation

The previous Java applet can be modified so that it can display an animated object. In Java applet H15.23 an oval graphic is randomly moved around the screen. Each update is 100 ms and the object will be constrained with a (0, 0) to (200, 200) window. The 100 ms delay is set up with:

```
    delay(100);   // try {mytimer.sleep(100);}
```

and the graphic is constrained with:

```
  if ( x>200) x=200;        if ( y>200) y=200;
```

```
          if ( x<0 )   x=0;              if ( y<0 )   y=0;
```

As before the graphic is erased from the window by drawing it with the background color of
the window, then redrawing it with a blue color.

📖   Java applet H11.23

```
import java.util.*;
import java.awt.*;
import java.applet.*;

public class chapH11_23 extends Applet
           implements Runnable
{
Thread timer = null;
int x=0,y=0;

  public void paint(Graphics g)
  {
    g.setColor(getBackground());
    g.fillOval(x,y,20,10);

    x+=(Math.random()*10)-5;
    y+=(Math.random()*10)-5;

    if ( x>200) x=200;
    if ( y>200) y=200;
    if ( x<0 )   x=0;
    if ( y<0 )   y=0;

    g.setColor(Color.blue);
    g.fillOval(x,y,20,10);
  }

  public void start()
  {
   if(timer == null)
   {
      timer = new Thread(this);
      timer.start();
   }
  }
  public void stop()
  {
     timer = null;
  }

  public void run()
  {
     while (timer != null)
     {
        delay(100); // wait 100 ms
        repaint();
     }
     timer = null;
  }

  public void delay(int ms)
  {
    try {timer.sleep(ms);}
    catch (InterruptedException e){}
  }
}
```

Java applet H11.24 is similar to the previous applet but the image now has three ovals and two lines. The oval and line drawing have also been put into `alien()`. This is called when the image is erased (with the background color set) and then to draw it again in blue.

Java applet H11.24

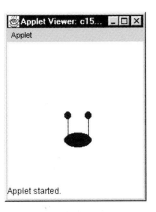

```
import java.util.*;
import java.awt.*;
import java.applet.*;

public class chapH11_24 extends Applet
        implements Runnable
{
Thread   timer = null;
int      x=100,y=100;//put alien in middle of
                       //screen

  public void paint(Graphics g)
  {
    g.setColor(getBackground());
    alien(g);

    x+=(Math.random()*10)-5;
    y+=(Math.random()*10)-5;

    if ( x>200) x=200;   if ( y>200) y=200;
    if ( x<0 )  x=0;     if ( y<0 )  y=0;

    g.setColor(Color.blue);
    alien(g);
  }

  public void alien(Graphics g)
  {
     g.fillOval(x,y,10,10);
     g.fillOval(x+30,y,10,10);
     g.fillOval(x,y+30,40,20);
     g.drawLine(x+5,y+10,x+5,y+35);
     g.drawLine(x+35,y+10,x+35,y+35);
  }

  public void start()
  {
    if(timer == null)
    {
      timer = new Thread(this);
      timer.start();
    }
  }

  public void stop()
  {
     timer = null;
  }
  public void run()
  {
    while (timer != null)
    {
       delay(100); // wait 100 ms
       repaint();
    }
    timer = null;
```

```
    }

  public void delay(int ms)
  {
    try {timer.sleep(ms);}
    catch (InterruptedException e){}
  }
}
```

H12 XML

H12.1 Introduction

WWW languages of the past, especially HTML, have been fixed in their tags. A new format named XML (eXtensible Markup Language) can be used to create new tags, and provide a common platform for transferring information between different systems and packages. The first line of an XML file typically contains an optional *xml* processing instruction (known as the XML declaration). This can contain pseudo-attributes that indicate the XML language version, the character set, and whether it can be used as a standalone entity. An example is the XML declaration that begins every valid XML file:

```
<?xml version="1.0" standalone="yes" ?>
```

The XML document conforms to the XML recommendations, and has a logical structure that is composed of declarations, elements, comments, character references, and processing instructions. It also has a physical structure which is composed of entities, starting with the root, or document entity.

XML uses a document type definition (DTD) which defines the rules of the document, such as the elements which are present and the structural relationship between all the elements. It thus defines the tags that can be used and the tags that can contain other tags, the number and sequence of the tags, the attributes of the tags and, optionally, their values. DTDs allow documents to be properly validated, and is used within the production of an XML file. A **schema** is functionally equivalent to a DTD, but is written in XML. It extends the basic DTD, providing data typing, inheritance, and presentation rules.

The vocabulary of XML is a set of actual elements and the structure for a specific document type used in particular data formats. These are defined in a DTD that is the rulebook for the vocabulary. One of the first of these languages is the Channel Definition Format which is used to define Web pages that automatically send their contents to users (known as "push" technologies).

The XML object model defines a standard way in which the elements of the XML structured tree are defined. It is fully object-oriented and uses properties, methods, and the actual content (data) contained in an object. This model controls how users interpret the trees, and exposes all tree elements as objects, which can be accessed without any return trips to the server. The XML object model uses the W3C standard know as **Document Object Model**.

XML-Data Reduced (XDR) is one of the first languages defined which uses a schema (that is one that is defined in an XML form. It defines the:

- Form of elements that are child elements of others.
- Sequence in which the child elements can appear.
- Number of child elements.

It also defines whether an element is empty or can include text. XDR is now well established and uses XML as its basic language. A new standard known as **XSD** (XML Schema Definition) has been standardized by the W3C XML Schema Working Group.

An XML-based system typically uses an XML engine, which contains an **XML parser**, an XSL processor, and **schema** support. The XML parse reads the XML document and provide access to its content and structure. For this, it generates a hierarchically structured tree, and passes the data to viewers and other applications for processing. A major function of the XML parser is in checking the XML syntax and report any errors.

H12.1.1 XML Pointer Language

The XML pointer language (XPointer) is a W3C-led scheme which specifies the constructs which are used in addressing the internal structures of XML documents. Its main aim is to provide references to elements, character strings, and other parts of XML documents, whether or not they bear an explicit ID attribute. An XPointer consists of a series of location terms, each of which specifies a location, usually relative to the location specified by the prior location term. Each location term has a keyword (such as id, child, ancestor, and so on) and can have arguments, such as an instance number, element type, or attribute. For example, the XPointer:

```
child(3,precocious)
```

which refers to the to third child element whose type is *precocious*.

H12.1.2 XML Query Language (XQL)

XQL is a set of extensions to XSL Patterns that have been proposed to the W3C. It extends XSL in that it also includes searching/data retrieval in/from XML documents. XQL defines ways to manipulate XML in order to create new documents, and to control the content of existing documents.

H12.1.3 XML Schema Definition (XSD)

XSD is a language which has been proposed by the W3C XML Schema Working Group and is used to defining schemas, which is hoped to become the standard method of defining XML schemas. XSD uses XML as its source language.

H12.1.4 Extensible Stylesheet Language (XSL)

XSL is an XML-based language which transforms XML-based data into HTML or other presentation formats, which can be displayed in a Web browser. This is achieved in a declarative way, which makes it easier to implement that a scripting language. It creates an XML tree with formatting properties, which is transformed into a new tree (such as HTML). This allows extensive reordering, generated text, and calculations. It contains two parts:

- **XSL formatting objects**. This is a set of formatting semantics of the form of a tree, defined in XML. These define typographic elements such as page, paragraph, rule, and so forth. Finer control over the presentation of these elements is provided by a set of formatting properties, such as indent measures; word- and letter-spacing; and widow, orphan, and hyphenation control.
- **XSL Patterns**. This is a simple query language which identify nodes in an XML document. These are based on their type, name, and values, as well as the relationship of the node to other nodes in the document.

An example of an XSL file is:

```
<xsl:stylesheet language="javascript" xmlns:xsl="http://www.w3.org/TR/WD-xsl">
   <xsl:template match="/">
      <xsl:for-each select="Root/ContentItem">
      <xsl:element name="div">
         <xsl:attribute name="name">Node</xsl:attribute>
         <xsl:attribute name="Href">
               <xsl:value-of select="@Href" /></xsl:attribute>
         <xsl:attribute name="NOWRAP">NOWRAP</xsl:attribute>
         <xsl:attribute name="id"><xsl:value-of select="@ID" /></xsl:attribute>

         <xsl:attribute name="HasChildren">
               <xsl:value-of select="@HasChildren" /></xsl:attribute>
         <xsl:attribute name="ParentID">
               <xsl:value-of select="@ParentID" /></xsl:attribute>
      <xsl:element name="div">
            <xsl:attribute name="name">Parent</xsl:attribute>
            <xsl:attribute name="id">__idParent</xsl:attribute>
            <xsl:attribute name="style">
         margin-bottom:5px;position:relative;cursor:hand</xsl:attribute>
            <xsl:choose>
                <xsl:when test="@CloseIcon">
                   <xsl:element name="img">
                      <xsl:attribute name="name">Item_Img</xsl:attribute>
                      <xsl:attribute name="id">__idItem_Img</xsl:attribute>
                      <xsl:attribute name="align">absmiddle</xsl:attribute>
                      <xsl:attribute name="src">
                         <xsl:value-of select="@CloseIcon"/></xsl:attribute>
                      <xsl:attribute name="img_collapse">
                         <xsl:value-of select="@CloseIcon"/></xsl:attribute>
                      <xsl:attribute name="img_expand">
                         <xsl:value-of select="@OpenIcon"/></xsl:attribute>
                   </xsl:element>
                </xsl:when>
                <xsl:otherwise>
                   <xsl:element name="img">
                      <xsl:attribute name="name">Item_Img</xsl:attribute>
                      <xsl:attribute name="id">__idItem_Img</xsl:attribute>
                      <xsl:attribute name="align">absmiddle</xsl:attribute>
                      <xsl:attribute name="src">
                         <xsl:value-of select="@LeafIcon"/></xsl:attribute>
                   </xsl:element>
                </xsl:otherwise>
             </xsl:choose>
             <xsl:element name="img">
                <xsl:attribute name="name">__idItemStatusImg</xsl:attribute>
                <xsl:attribute name="id">__idItemStatusImg</xsl:attribute>
                <xsl:attribute name="align">absmiddle</xsl:attribute>
                <xsl:choose>
                   <xsl:when test="LessonStatus">
                      <xsl:attribute name="src">
                   <xsl:value-of select="LessonStatus"/>.gif</xsl:attribute>
                   </xsl:when>
                   <xsl:otherwise>
                      <xsl:attribute name="src">1px.gif</xsl:attribute>
                   </xsl:otherwise>
                </xsl:choose>
             </xsl:element>

             <xsl:element name='a'>
                <xsl:attribute name="name">link</xsl:attribute>
```

```
            <xsl:attribute name="id">__idLinkCaption</xsl:attribute>
            <xsl:attribute name="href"></xsl:attribute>
            <xsl:value-of select="@Name" />
         </xsl:element>

      </xsl:element>
      <xsl:element name="div">
         <xsl:attribute name="id">__idChildrenContainer</xsl:attribute>
         <xsl:attribute name="style">margin-top:5px;
            position:relative;margin-left:18px; </xsl:attribute>

      </xsl:element>
   </xsl:element>
   </xsl:for-each>

</xsl:template>
</xsl:stylesheet>
```

H12.2   XML syntax

XML, as HTML, uses <, >, and & to create element and attribute structures. Most HTML browsers either accept or ignore incorrectly formatted markup language. XML parsers, though, are most formal and are more strict on the syntax used. An incorrectly formatted, or structure XML document will give an error to the user. The basic rules include:

- **An XML document can only have one document element**. In XML a document element is a single element that contains all the content that is to be considered as past of the document itself. The document root is the first element that appears in the XML document.
- **All XML elements must have end tags**. In HTML, some tags do not require an end tag, such as <P>, whereas XML requires that every tag has an end tag.
- **XML elements cannot overlap**. The XML tags must be properly structured so that they do not overlap. For example the following is not allow:

```
<tag1>Blah blah <tag2>Blah</tag1> Blah</tag2>
```

In this case the XML parser will stop after </tag1> as the parser expects to find the </tag1> next.

- **Attribute values must contain quotes, whether or not they contain spaces**. These quotes can either be a single invert comma, or a double one.
- **<, >, or & cannot be used within the text the document**. For these characters the entities of <, > and & can be used.

H12.2.1 Attributes

An attribute is an XML structural construct. It has a name-value pair, separated by an equals sign, and is included inside a tagged element that modifies the features of an element. Thus, all attributes are string values. The following shows an example of an attribute were id_value is set to "disk001".

```
<?xml version="1.0"?>
<software>
```

```
<disk id_value="disk001">
    <author>Smith, Fred</author>
    <title>XML Developer's Guide</title>
    <function>Disk tools</function>
    <price>100</price>
    <version>1.02</version>
    <description>Windows XP version </description>
  </disk>
</software>
```

H12.2.2 Entity

An entity is an XML structural construct. It can be a file, a database record, or any other item that contains data. Its main aim is to hold content, and not structure, rules, or grammar. In the XML document, each entity is has a unique name and contains its own content.

H12.2.3 XML format

The XML document is formed in two parts:

- **Prolog**. This part is at the start of the document (or root element). It contains information on the document as a whole. Typical references are to the character encoding, document structure, and style sheets. An example is:

```
<?xml version="1.0" encoding="UTF-8"?>
<?xml-stylesheet type="text/xsl" href="my_style.xsl"?>
<!DOCTYPE catalog SYSTEM "mycatalog.dtd">
<!--This file was last updated 2002-12-10-->
```

    The prolog can include processing instructions, such as the xml-stylesheet processing instruction (as shown in the about example). The <!-- .... --> statement contains a comment.

- **Document elements**. The form the backbone of the XML documents, and creates the required structure. Within it there the elements identify named sections of information, and use markup tags that identify the name, start, and end of the element.

All elements have names, and are case-sensitive and must start with a letter or an underscore.

Tags establish boundaries around content. The start tags has the following format:

<elementName attrib1="attrib1Value" attrib2="attrib2Value"...>

If an element name does not have any attributes then its format is:

<elementName >

and the end tag has the following format (which cannot have any attributes):

</elementName>

Elements are contained between a start and an end tag. For example:

```
<pet>
   <type>Cat</type>
   <name>Honey</name>
</pet>
```

where the pet element contains two other elements: <type> and <name>. The <type> tags contains the text 'Cat', and the <name> element contains 'Honey'. An empty tag can be used when there is no textual content. An empty tags contains a slash (/) before the closing character, such as:

```
<help/>
```

which is the same as:

```
<help></help>
```

H12.2.4 Element relationships

Family and tree metaphors are used to describe the relationship between elements. All XML documents must contain a root element (which is also know as a document). In the following XML document, <pet> is the root document:

```
<pet>
   <type>Cat</type>
   <name>Honey</name>
</pet>
```

The following cannot be an XML document, as it has no root document:

```
<type>Cat</type>
<name>Honey</name>
```

With a tree structure, the leaves refer to elements that do not contain any other elements (such as in a real tree, where leaves are ends of branches. These leaf elements generally contain simple text or no textural information.

The terms used in a family metaphors are such as parent, child, ancestor, descendant, and sibling. These are used to describe relationship between elements relative to each other (and not to the entire document). The following abstract sample document illustrates the relationships between elements.

```
<tag1>
 <tag2>
   <tag3>
     <tag4/>
   </tag3>
 </tag2>
</tag1>
```

The <tag1> element contains the <tag2> which, in turn, contains the <tag3> element. This then contains the <tag4> element. With a tree metaphor, <tag1> and <tag4> is a leaf element. The tags <tag2> and <tag3> can be considered as trunks or branches.

With a family metaphor, the sibling in this document is <tag4>, which is contained by the <tag3> element. Thus <tag3> is the parent of <tag4>, and <tag4> is the child of <tag3>. In the same way, <tag3> is a child of <tag2>, and so on. Ancestors and descendants are defined in a similar way but they do not have to contain or be contained directly. For example the <tag1> element is the parent of <tag2> and the ancestor of every element in the document. The element <tag4> is a descendants of the <tag1>, <tag2> and <tag4> elements.

H12.3   XML/Flash

XML is similar to HTML, but XML allows for tags to be defined by the user. A good example of an XML file is one which defines questions for a quiz. For example, a simple XML-based file for multiple-choice questions could be:

```
<?xml version="1.0" encoding="iso-8859-1"?>
<!DOCTYPE questions SYSTEM "http://www.dcs.napier.ac.uk/~bill/flash.xml">
<questions>
<quest id="000001">
    <title>This is the first question</title>
    <q1>Answer a1</q1>
    <q2>Answer a2</q2>
    <q3>Answer a3</q3>
    <q4>Answer a4</q4>
    <q5>Answer a5</q5>
    <correct>q1</correct>
    <level>1</level>
    </quest>
<quest id="000002">
    <title>This is the second question</title>
    <q1>Answer b1</q1>
    <q2>Answer b2</q2>
    <q3>Answer b3</q3>
    <q4>Answer b4</q4>
    <q5>Answer b5</q5>
    <correct>q1</correct>
    <level>2</level>
    </quest>
<quest id="000003">
    <title>This is the third question</title>
    <q1>Answer c1</q1>
    <q2>Answer c2</q2>
    <q3>Answer c3</q3>
    <q4>Answer c4</q4>
    <q5>Answer c5</q5>
    <correct>q1</correct>
    <level>3</level>
    </quest>
<quest id="000004">
    <title>This is the forth question</title>
    <q1>Answer d1</q1>
    <q2>Answer d2</q2>
    <q3>Answer d3</q3>
    <q4>Answer d4</q4>
    <q5>Answer d5</q5>
    <correct>q1</correct>
    <level>4</level>
</quest>
<quest id="000005">
```

```
        <title>This is the fifth question</title>
        <q1>Answer e1</q1>
        <q2>Answer e2</q2>
        <q3>Answer e3</q3>
        <q4>Answer e4</q4>
        <q5>Answer e5</q5>
        <correct>q1</correct>
        <level>5</level>
</quest>
</questions>
```

This defines a <questions> tag, which contains a number of nested questions. Each of these questions has a title (<title>); up to five answers (<q1> to <q6>); a level (<level>) and a correct answer (<connect>). This can be read into Flash 5 with the load action, as given below:

```
// define the main arrays which will be populated with questions
var question_titles = new Array();
var question_q1 = new Array();
var question_q2 = new Array();
var question_q3 = new Array();
var question_q4 = new Array();
var question_level = new Array();
var question_ans = new Array();
var no_q=0;

urlXML = new XML();
urlXML.onLoad = convertXML;
output1 = "Loading data...";
urlXML.load("questions.xml");

function convertXML () {

    mainTag = new XML();
    elementTag = new XML();
    questionList = new Array();

    mainTag = this.firstChild.nextSibling;

    no_q=0; // no of questions in file

    if (mainTag.nodeName.toLowerCase() == "questions") {
    // if we have a match, collect all of the questions beneath it as
    // an array of xml objects

        questionList = mainTag.childNodes;

        // get tags
        for (i=0; i<=questionList.length; i++) {

            if (questionList[i].nodeName.toLowerCase() == "quest") {

            // we get the child node array beneath the questions
                elementList = questionList[i].childNodes;
                no_questions=elementList.length;

            // and loop through that looking for the data we need
                for (j=0; j<=elementList.length; j++) {
                    elementTag = elementList[j];

                    elementType = elementTag.nodeName.toLowerCase();
                    if (elementType == "title") {
                        question_titles[no_q]=elementTag.firstChild.nodeValue ;
```

```
            no_q++;
        }
        if (elementType == "q1") {
            question_q1[no_q-1]=elementTag.firstChild.nodeValue ;
        }
        if (elementType == "q2") {
            question_q2[no_q-1]=elementTag.firstChild.nodeValue ;
        }
        if (elementType == "q3") {
            question_q3[no_q-1]=elementTag.firstChild.nodeValue ;
        }
        if (elementType == "q4") {
            question_q4[no_q-1]=elementTag.firstChild.nodeValue ;
        }
        if (elementType == "correct") {
            question_ans[no_q-1]=elementTag.firstChild.nodeValue ;
        }
        if (elementType == "level") {
            question_level[no_q-1]=elementTag.firstChild.nodeValue ;
        }
      }
    }
  }
 }
}
```

This will load the XML file locally (such as using it from a CD-ROM or when not connected to the Internet). It is also possible to load the file from a WWW server. For example, the load action can be changed to:

urlXML.load("http://*mywebser*/questions.xml");

In Flash, the populated arrays can then be viewed by add the following action to a button:

```
on (release) {
    output1 = "<BR><B>Question </B>"+(i+1)+" "+question_titles[i];
    output1 = output1+"<BR>"+question_q1[i];
    output1 = output1+"<BR>"+question_q2[i];
    output1 = output1+"<BR>"+question_q3[i];
    output1 = output1+"<BR>"+question_q4[i];
    output1 = output1+"<BR>"+question_q5[i];
    if (i==no_q-1) { stop(); i=0; }
    else {i++; }
}
```

When testing the program it is much easier to be able to read the XML locally, and then when it is on the WWW, the XML file is read from a WWW site. This can be achieved by testing to see if the XML object has been loaded. This is achieved with:

```
urlXML = new XML();
urlXML.onLoad = convertXML;
urlXML.load("questions.xml");

if (!XML.loaded)
    urlXML.load("http://myserver/questions.xml");
```

The application can be then enhanced by creating a symbol for the multiple choice question. In this a symbol is created and is named question. The text boxes created are named title, q1, q2, q3 and q4. A button on the main page will then have the action of:

```
on (release) {
    i=random(no_q-1);
    question.title=question_titles[i];
    question.q1=question_q1[i];
    question.q2=question_q2[i];
    question.q3=question_q3[i];
    question.q4=question_q4[i];
    stop();
}
```

The random() function selects a random number, with the maximum of the number of questions in the XML file. The symbol is then loaded with the values from the arrays. The computing.xml file is defined as:

```
<?xml version="1.0" encoding="iso-8859-1"?><!DOCTYPE questions>
<questions>
    <quest id="000001">
        <title> How many bits are in a nibble:</title>
        <q1>4</q1>
        <q2>8</q2>
        <q3>16</q3>
        <q4>32</q4>
        <q5>Answer a5</q5>
        <correct>q1</correct>
        <level>1</level>
    </quest>
    <quest id="000002">
        <title>Which unit represents 1024 bytes:</title>
        <q1>B</q1>
        <q2>KB</q2>
        <q3>MB</q3>
        <q4>GB</q4>
        <q5>Answer b5</q5>
        <correct>q1</correct>
        <level>2</level>
    </quest>
    <quest id="000003">
        <title>Which unit represents bits per second:</title>
        <q1>bps</q1>
        <q2>bs</q2>
        <q3>bit</q3>
        <q4>bsec</q4>
        <q5>Answer c5</q5>
        <correct>bps</correct>
        <level>3</level>
    </quest>
</questionS>
```

Next we can add actions on the green buttons, so that they set variables when they are pressed. This can be achieved with the following action code:

```
on (press, release) {
    ../:question_select="q1";
}
```

which sets the questions_select variable on the parent movie. Each of the buttons then set the question_select variable. Next, we can add two new functions to the main action script. The get_question() function sets the question for the array of questions, and the answered()

function is called when an answer is select. These are given next:

```
function get_question()
{
    i = random(no_q-1);
    question_text = correct;
    question.title = question_titles[i];
    question.q1 = question_q1[i];
    question.q2 = question_q2[i];
    question.q3 = question_q3[i];
    question.q4 = question_q4[i];
}

function answered()
{
    if (question_select == question_ans[i]) {
        correct++;
    }
    question_text = correct;
    question_select = "";
}
```

These functions can be called from an action script with:

```
if (question_select<>"")
{
    answered();
    get_question();
}
```

which selects if an answer has been selected. If it has the answered() function is called, followed by the get_question() function. After this we need to determine the maximum number of questions to ask, and the user should be shown their score after it. The get_question() and the answered() functions can be modified with:

```
function get_question () {
    i = random(no_q);
    question_text = correct;

    question.title = (correct+incorrect+1) + "." + question_titles[i];
    question.q1 = question_q1[i];
    question.q2 = question_q2[i];
    question.q3 = question_q3[i];
    question.q4 = question_q4[i];
    debug = "Question "+(i+1)+" from "+no_q+"[Level:"+question_level[i]+"]";
}
function answered () {
    if (question_select == question_ans[i]) {
        correct++;
    }
    else incorrect++;
    question_text = correct;
    question_select = "";
    if ((correct+incorrect)==no_questions_taken)
    {
        final_score=correct + " out of " + no_questions_taken;
        gotoAndPlay ( 8 );
    }
}
```

H12.4 Reusable component

XML provides an excellent method of creating reusable media content, where the XML provides a method for changing the operation of the media component. For example, let's say we have a condition where we either want to show the running score or not. Thus we could set a value in the XML of:

```
<score>1</score>
```

If this is included in the XML file, the score box will not be displayed. Thus we could set a binary variable of show_score, so that the score box will only be seen as a background object. This is achieved by setting the alpha property of the score box to 20%:

```
if (elementType == "score") {
    show_score=false;
    trace("Score found");
    setProperty("/correctbox", _alpha,20);
}
```

Then where the current score is to be displayed, the show_score value is tested. If it is still true, the score is displayed, else it will not.

```
if (show_score==true) correctbox.question_text = correct;
```

H12.5 XML-based component

A good example of a reusable component is to read and display SWF files. For this the SWF can be specified in an XML file format:

```
<?xml version="1.0"?>
<flash>
<files>top_cnds.swf</files>
<files>top_nos.swf</files>
<files>agent01.swf</files>
<files>agent02.swf</files>
<files>agents01.swf</files>
<files>agents02.swf</files>
<files>agents_movie.swf</files>
<files>agents_moview.swf</files>
<files>agent_movie.swf</files>

::: etc :::
</flash>
```

This can be read in using the ActionScript:

```
var str = new Array();
var movie_number=0, max_movie_number=0;

urlXML = new XML();
urlXML.onLoad = convertXML;
urlXML.load("flash.xml");

function convertXML () {
    mainTag = new XML();
    elementTag = new XML();
```

```
    mainTag = this.firstChild.nextSibling;

    if (mainTag.nodeName.toLowerCase() == "flash") {

        flist = mainTag.childNodes;

        // get tags
        for (i=0; i<=flist.length; i++) {
            if (flist[i].nodeName.toLowerCase() == "files") {
            // we get the child node array beneath the questions
                elementList = flist[i].childNodes;
                str[max_movie_number]=elementList;

                max_movie_number++;
            }
        }
    }
}
```

The convertXML function reads in the XML and inserts the file names into the str[] array. The buttons can then contain the following code (for the forward button):

```
on (press) {
    loadMovie (str[movie_number], "bg");
    fname=str[movie_number];

    movie_number = movie_number+1;
    if (movie_number>max_movie_number) movie_number=1;
    gotoAndPlay (2);
}
```

and (for the back button):

```
on (press) {
    loadMovie (str[movie_number], "bg");
    fname=str[movie_number];

    movie_number = movie_number-1;
    if (movie_number<0) movie_number=0;
    gotoAndPlay (2);
}
```

The SWF file is loaded in the movie clip, which is named "bg". Thus, we can spend more time on creating a solid, and reconfigurable component, and less time on creating new content for each design.

Is it reusable? The short answer is yes, but it would have to be considerably enhanced to make it truly reuseable. Many other options would have to be added to make it reusable in other application. A good example would be to define the graphic content at the top of the movie within the XML file, such as:

```
<?xml version="1.0"?>
<flash>
    <banner>
        <graphic>
        <file>top.swf</file>
        <x_pos>34</x_pos>
        <y_pos>40</y_pos>
        </graphic>
    </banner>
```

```
      <files>top_cnds.swf</files>
      <files>top_nos.swf</files>
      <files>agent01.swf</files>
      <files>agent02.swf</files>
      <files>agents01.swf</files>
      <files>agents02.swf</files>
::: etc :::
</flash>
```

Is it reconfigurable? Well. It provides a foundation for further reconfigurability. For it to be more reconfigurable we would have to add lots of other options that allowed the graphics to be manipulated, such as scaling, movement, alpha processing, and so on.

So let's try and reuse it. In this case, the XML file has been changed to contain the names of the pictures, and also a description of the picture. The file used is:

```
<?xml version="1.0"?>
<flash>
<files>skye_pics\0001.swf</files>
<description>This is a picture taken from my car, in the High-
lands.</description>
<files>skye_pics\0002.swf</files>
<description>Another picture of the Highlands, showing the beautiful mirror
image on the loch.</description>
<files>skye_pics\0003.swf</files>
<description>I took this from the side of the road on the way up to Skye. It
shows how still the loch was.</description>
<files>skye_pics\0004.swf</files>
<description>A picture of the Ragamuffin shop, on Skye. I had an excellent cof-
fee in the little cafe beside this.</description>
<files>skye_pics\0005.swf</files>
<description>A picture of the ferry which travels to the South of the is-
land.</description>
<files>skye_pics\0006.swf</files>
<description>Another picture of the bay.</description>
<files>skye_pics\0007.swf</files>
<description>A picture of the Scottish mainland taken from Skye. It was warm
and the sky was a beautiful blue color.</description>
<files>skye_pics\0008.swf</files>
<description>And again...</description>
</flash>
```

For this, the Actionscript on the button can be changed to:

```
on (press) {
   loadMovie (str[movie_number], "bg");
   bg._xscale=90; // 90% scaling of the picture
   bg._yscale=90; // 90% scaling of the picture
   fname=str[movie_number];
   descript=description[movie_number];
   movie_number = movie_number+1;
   if (movie_number>max_movie_number-1) movie_number=0;
   gotoAndPlay (2);
}
```

The reading of the XML file has also been changed so that the description is added:

```
function convertXML () {
   mainTag = new XML();
   elementTag = new XML();
   mainTag = this.firstChild.nextSibling;
```

```
    trace("Tag " + mainTag);

    if (mainTag.nodeName.toLowerCase() == "flash") {

        flist = mainTag.childNodes;

        // get tags
        for (i=0; i<=flist.length; i++) {
            if (flist[i].nodeName.toLowerCase() == "files") {
            // we get the child node array beneath the questions
                elementList = flist[i].childNodes;
                trace("Element list: " + elementList);
                str[max_movie_number]=elementList;

                max_movie_number++;
            }
            if (flist[i].nodeName.toLowerCase() == "description") {
                elementList = flist[i].childNodes;
                description[max_movie_number-1]=elementList;

            }
        }
    }
}
```

H12.6   DOM

The Document Object Model (DOM) is a standardized method that can access and manipulate XML documents. DOM thus provides an interface between applications and XML documents. It allows XML documents to be loaded, and processed. Initially this object is created with the form:

```
xmldoc = new ActiveXObject("Msxml2.DOMDocument.3.0");
```

and the XML file is loaded with the load() method:

```
xmldoc.load("myxml.xml");
```

The XML parser will read the document from start to finish, and creates a logical model for it. As previously mentioned the document itself is the root element, which in turn contains other elements. The following VBScript reads from a document, and displays all the child nodes from the root document, in a message box:

```
<script language="VBScript">
Dim root
Dim child
Dim my_xmlDoc

Set my_xmlDoc = CreateObject("Msxml2.DOMDocument.4.0")
my_xmlDoc.async = False
my_xmlDoc.load("cnds01.xml")
'Define the root
Set root = my_xmlDoc.documentElement
'Show the children
For Each child In root.childNodes
  MsgBox child.text
Next
</script>
```

The following ASP script reads the XML file, and shows its structure.

```
<%@LANGUAGE=VBScript%>
<html> <head> <title>Display tree</title></head><body>
<%

function show_structure(find_node)

  For i=1 to indent_measure
    Response.Write(" ")
  Next
  For Each attr In find_node.attributes
   Response.Write("|--")
   Response.Write(attr.nodeTypeString)
   Response.Write(":")
   Response.Write(attr.name)
   Response.Write("--")
   Response.Write(attr.nodeValue)
   Response.Write("<br />")
  Next
end function

function span_tree(node)
dim nodeName
dim child

indent_measure=indent_measure+2

For Each child In node.childNodes
  For i=1 to indent_measure
    Response.Write(" ")
  Next

  Response.Write("|--")
  Response.Write(child.nodeTypeString)
  Response.Write("--")
  If child.nodeType<3 Then
    Response.Write(child.nodeName)
    Response.Write("<br />")
  End If
  If (child.nodeType=1) Then
    If (child.attributes.length>0) Then
      indent_measure=indent_measure+2
      show_structure(child)
      indent_measure=indent_measure-2
    End If
  End If
  If (child.hasChildNodes) Then
    span_tree(child)
  Else
    Response.Write child.text
    Response.Write("<br />")
  End If
Next

  indent_measure=indent_measure-2

end function

Dim my_xmlDoc
Dim indent_measure
```

```
indent_measure=0

Set my_xmlDoc = CreateObject("Msxml2.DOMDocument.4.0")
my_xmlDoc.async = False
' By default XML is loaded asynchronously, to use synchronous load the
' asnyc property is set to False
' This allows the entire loading of the XML document before
' processing continues.
my_xmlDoc.validateOnParse=False
' Set so that there is no validation when parsed
my_xmlDoc.load("file.xml")

If my_xmlDoc.parseError.errorcode = 0 Then
  Response.Write("<pre>")
  span_tree(xmlDoc)
  Response.Write("</pre>")
endif
%>
```

The span_tree function is a recursive function which expands the tree, and the
show_structure function is used to show the attributes of the content. XML documents are
loaded using the load or loadXML methods, and the save method and xml property are used
to convert the DOM back in an XML format. To save an XML file, in ASP, the following format can be used:

```
<%
  dim my_xmldoc
  set my_xmldoc = Server.CreateObject("Msxml2.DOMDocument.4.0")
  my_xmldoc.async = false
  my_xmldoc.load("sample.xml")
  my_xmldoc.save(Server.MapPath("test.xml"))
%>
```

Errors in loading the XML can be found by testing the parseError property. If it set to
IXMLDOMParseError object, then there has been an error. The properties of the object are:

- errorCode. Defines the code number of an error. A zero value identifies that there is no
  error.
- filepos. Defines the absolute file position where the error occurred.
- line. Defines the line number of the error.
- linepos. Defines the character position of the error.
- reason. Gives a basic reason for the error.
- srcText. Gives the text of the line where the error occurred.
- url. Defines the URL of the XML file which caused the error.

The following gives an example of code which can be used to display the error:

```
var my_xmldoc;
my_xmldoc = new ActiveXObject("Msxml2.DOMDocument.3.0");
my_xmldoc.async = false;
my_xmldoc.load("test.xml");
if (my_xmldoc.parseError.errorCode != 0) {
  alert("errorCode: " +  my_xmldoc.parseError.errorCode  + "\n" +
         "filepos: "  +  my_xmldoc.parseError.filepos   + "\n" +
         "line: "     +  my_xmldoc.parseError.line      + "\n" +
         "linepos: "  +  my_xmldoc.parseError.linepos   + "\n" +
         "reason: "   +  my_xmldoc.parseError.reason    + "\n" +
```

```
            "srcText: "   +   my_xmldoc.parseError.srcText   + "\n" +
            "url: "        +   my_xmldoc.parseError.url);
   } else {
      alert(my_xmldoc.documentElement.xml);
      }
}
```

H13   DHTML

H13.1   Introduction

Dynamic HTML (DHTML) is an enhancement to HTML version 4.0, and can be used to create enhanced visual effects on a WWW page. It works with Microsoft Internet Explorer 4.0
and Netscape Navigator 4.0, and later. The simplest way to reference an element In DHTML
is to use the elements id tag. For example:

```
<html><head><title>ID referencing</title></head>

<script type = "text/javascript">
function go()
{
   alert(mytext.innerText);
   mytext.innerText = "Goodbye";
}
</script>

<body onload="go()">
<p id="mytext">Hello, how are you?</p>
</body>
</html>
```

which will cause the message Hello, how are you? to be set within the browser. An alert
box will then be displayed with the same text. Once the user accepts it, the text in the
browser will change to Goodbye.

The following defines the main objects used in Dynamic HTML:

!DOCTYPE	A	ACRONYM	ADDRESS
APPLET	AREA	Attribute	B
BASE	BASEFONT	BDO	BGSOUND
BIG	BLOCKQUOTE	BODY	BR
BUTTON	CAPTION	CENTER	CITE
clientInformation	clipboardData	CODE	COL
COLGROUP	COMMENT	currentStyle	custom
dataTransfer	DD	DEL	DFN
DIR	DIV	DL	document
DT	EM	EMBED	event
external	FIELDSET	FONT	FORM
FRAME	FRAMESET	HEAD	history
Hn	HR	HTML	I
IFRAME	IMG	INPUT	INS
ISINDEX	KBD	LABEL	LEGEND
LI	LINK	LISTING	location

MAP	MARQUEE	MENU	META
navigator	NEXTID	NOBR	NOFRAMES
NOSCRIPT	OBJECT	OL	OPTION
P	PARAM	PLAINTEXT	PRE
Q	RT	RUBY	rule
runtimeStyle	S	SAMP	screen
SCRIPT	SELECT	selection	SMALL
SPAN	STRIKE	STRONG	style
STYLE	styleSheet	SUB	SUP
TABLE	TBODY	TD	TEXTAREA
TextNode	TextRange	TextRectangle	TFOOT
TH	THEAD	TITLE	TR
TT	U	UL	userProfile
VAR	WBR	window	XML
XMP			

With the following properties:

!important	@charset	@font-face
@import	@media	accessKey
action	activeElement	align
align	align	align
aLink	aLinkColor	alt
altHTML	altKey	appCodeName
appMinorVersion	appNameapp	Version
autocomplete	availHeight	availWidth
background	background	background
backgroundAttachment	backgroundColor	backgroundImage
backgroundPosition	backgroundPositionX	backgroundPositionY
backgroundRepeat	balance	behavior
behavior	bgColor	bgProperties
border	borderBottom	borderBottomColor
borderBottomStyle	borderBottomWidth	borderCollapse
borderColor	borderColor	borderColorDark
borderColorLight	borderLeft	borderLeftColor
borderLeftStyle	borderLeftWidth	borderRight
borderRightColor	borderRightStyle	borderRightWidth
borderStyle	borderTop	borderTopColor
borderTopStyle	borderTopWidth	borderWidth
bottom	bottomMargin	boundingHeight
boundingLeft	boundingTop	boundingWidth
browserLanguage	bufferDepth	button
cancelBubble	canHaveChildren	caption
cellIndex	cellPadding	cellSpacing
checked	classid	className
clear	clientHeight	clientLeft
clientTop	clientWidth	clientX
clientY	clip	clipBottom

clipLeft	clipRight	
clipTop	closed	code
codeBase	codeType	color
color	colorDepth	cols
cols	cols	colSpan
compact	complete	content
cookie	cookieEnabled	coords
cpuClass	cssText	ctrlKey
cursor	data	data
dataFld	dataFld	dataFormatAs
dataPageSize	dataSrc	defaultCharset
defaultChecked	defaultSelected	defaultStatus
defaultValue	defer	designMode
dialogArguments	dialogHeight	dialogLeft
dialogTop	dialogWidth	dir
direction	direction	disabled
disabled	display	documentElement
domain	dropEffect	dnsrc
effectAllowed	encoding	event
expando	face	fgColor
fileCreatedDate	fileModifiedDate	fileSize
fileUpdatedDate	filter	firstChild
font	fontFamily	fontSize
fontSmoothingEnabled	fontStyle	fontVariant
fontWeight	form	frame
frameBorder	frameSpacing	fromElement
hash	height	height
height	hidden	host
hostname	href	href
href	href	hspace
htmlFor	htmlFor	htmlText
httpEquiv	id	imeMode
indeterminate	index	innerText
isMap	isTextEditkeyCode	lang
language	lastChild	lastModified
layoutGrid	layoutGridChar	layoutGridCharSpacing
layoutGridMode	layoutGridType	left
left	leftMargin	length
length	letterSpacing	lineBreak
lineHeight	link	linkColor
listStyle	listStyleImage	listStylePosition
listStyleType	loop	loop
lowsrc	margin	marginBottom
marginHeight	marginLeft	marginRight
marginTop	marginWidth	maxLength
media	menuArguments	method
Methods	multiple	name
name	name	nameProp

nextSibling	nodeName	nodeType
nodeValue	noHref	noResize
noShade	noWrap	object
offscreenBuffering	offsetHeight	offsetLeft
offsetParent	offsetTop	offsetWidth
offsetX	offsetY	onLine
opener	outerHTML	outerText
overflow	overflowX	overflowY
owningElement	padding	paddingBottom
paddingLeft	paddingRight	paddingTop
pageBreakAfter	pageBreakBefore	palette
parent	parentElement	parentNode
parentStyleSheet	parentTextEdit	parentWindow
pathname	pixelBottom	pixelHeight
pixelLeft	pixelRight	pixelTop
pixelWidth	platform	pluginspage
port	posBottom	posHeight
position	posLeft	posRight
posTop	posWidth	previousSibling
propertyName	protocol	qualifier
readOnly	readOnly	readyState
reason	recordNumber	recordset
referrer	rel	repeat
returnValue	returnValue	rev
right	right	rightMargin
rowIndex	rows	rows
rowSpan	rubyAlign	rubyOverhang
rubyPosition	rules	scopeName
screenLeft	screenTop	screenX
screenY	scroll	scrollAmount
scrollDelay	scrollHeight	scrolling
scrollLeft	scrollTop	scrollWidth
search	sectionRowIndex	selected
selectedIndex	selectorText	self
shape	shiftKey	size
size	size	sourceIndex
span	specified	src
src	src	srcElement
srcFilter	srcUrn	start
start	status	status
styleFloat	systemLanguage	tabIndex
tableLayout	tagName	tagUrn
target	text	text
text	text	textAlign
textAutospace	textDecoration	textDecorationLineThrough
textDecorationNone	textDecorationOverline	textDecorationUnderline
textIndent	textJustify	textTransform
tFoot	tHead	title

title	toElement	top
top	top	topMargin
trueSpeed	type	type
type	type	type
type	type	type
type	unicodeBidi	uniqueID
units	updateInterval	URL
urn	useMap	userAgent
userLanguage	vAlign	vAlign
value	value	value
vcard_name	verticalAlign	visibility
vLink	vlinkColor	volume
vspace	whiteSpace	width
width	width	wordBreak
wordSpacing	wrap	x
XMLDocument	y	zIndex

The following is a list of the methods in the Dynamic HTML Object Model:

add	addBehavior	AddChannel
AddDesktopComponent	AddFavorite	addImport
addReadRequest	addRule	alert
appendChild	applyElement	assign
attachEvent	AutoCompleteSaveForm	AutoScan
back	blur	clear
clear	clearAttributes	clearData
clearInterval	clearRequest	clearTimeout
click	cloneNode	close
close	collapse	compareEndPoints
componentFromPoint	confirm	contains
createCaption	createControlRange	createElement
createRange	createStyleSheet	createTextNode
createTextRange	createTFoot	createTHead
deleteCaption	deleteCell	deleteRow
deleteTFoot	deleteTHead	detachEvent
doReadRequest	doScroll	duplicate
elementFromPoint	empty	execCommand
execScript	expand	findText
firstPage	focus	forward
getAdjacentText	getAttribute	getAttribute
getBookmark	getBoundingClientRect	getClientRects
getData	getElementById	getElementsByName
getElementsByTagName	getExpression	go
hasChildNodes	ImportExportFavorites	inRange
insertAdjacentElement	insertAdjacentHTML	insertAdjacentText
insertBefore	insertCell	insertRow
isEqual	IsSubscribed	item
javaEnabled	lastPage	mergeAttributes

move	moveBy	moveEnd
moveRow	moveStart	moveTo
moveToBookmark	moveToElementText	moveToPoint
namedRecordset	navigate	NavigateAndFind
nextPage	open	open
parentElement	pasteHTML	previousPage
print	prompt	queryCommandEnabled
queryCommandIndeterm	queryCommandState	queryCommandSupported
queryCommandValue	recalc	refresh
releaseCapture	reload	remove
removeAttribute	removeBehavior	removeChild
removeExpression	removeNode	removeRule
replace	replaceAdjacentText	replaceChild
replaceNode	reset	resizeBy
resizeTo	scroll	scrollBy
scrollIntoView	scrollTo	select
select	setAttribute	setCapture
setData	setEndPoint	setExpression
setInterval	setTimeout	ShowBrowserUI
showHelp	showModalDialog	showModelessDialog
splitText	start	stop
submit	swapNode	tags
taintEnabled	urns	write
writeln		

The following events are used in DHTML:

onabort	onafterprint	onafterupdate
onbeforecopy	onbeforecut	onbeforeeditfocus
onbeforepaste	onbeforeprint	onbeforeunload
onbeforeupdate	onblur	onbounce
oncellchange	onchange	onclick
oncontextmenu	oncopy	oncut
ondataavailable	ondatasetchanged	ondatasetcomplete
ondblclick	ondrag	ondragend
ondragenter	ondragleave	ondragover
ondragstart	ondrop	onerror
onerrorupdate	onfilterchange	onfinish
onfocus	onhelp	onkeydown
onkeypress	onkeyup	onload
onlosecapture	onmousedown	onmousemove
onmouseout	onmouseover	onmouseup
onpaste	onpropertychange	onreadystatechange
onreset	onresize	onrowenter
onrowexit	onrowsdelete	onrowsinserted
onscroll	onselect	onselectstart
onstart	onstop	onsubmit
onunload		

and the following collections:

all	anchors	applets
areas	attributes	behaviorUrns
bookmarks	boundElements	cells
childNodes	children	controlRange
elements	embeds	filters
forms	frames	images
imports	links	mimeTypes
options	plugins	rows
rules	scripts	styleSheets
tBodies	TextRectangle	

H13.2   Filters

DHTML supports a range of filters using the filters property, which sets the filters on an object or gets them from an object. Its basic format is:

object.**style.filter** [= sFilter]

where sFilter are in the form:

filtertype (parameter1, parameter2,...)

H13.2.1 Alpha()

The alpha filter sets the opacity for the object. Its syntax is:

object.style.filter = "alpha(sProperties)"

or as HTML with:

<ELEMENT STYLE = "filter: alpha(sProperties)" ... >

The properties include:

- enabled. Defines whether the filter is currently enabled.
- finishOpacity. Defines the opacity level.
- finishX. Defines the x-coordinate of the point at which the opacity gradient ends.
- finishY. Defines the y-coordinate of the point at which the opacity gradient ends.
- Opacity. Defines the opacity level.
- startX. Defines the x-coordinate of the point at which the opacity gradient starts.
- startY. Defines the y-coordinate of the point at which the opacity gradient starts.
- Style. Defines the shape characteristics of the opacity gradient.

The following gives an example of changing the opacity property on a graphic:

```
<div id = "pic"
```

```
    style = "position: absolute; filter: alpha( style = 2,
    opacity = 100, finishopacity = 0 );
    z-index: 2; left: 160px; top: 149px">
<img src="pics_cookie.jpg" width="600" height="450">
</div>
```

H13.2.2 blendTrans Filter

The blendTrans filter fades an object. Its syntax is:

object.style.filter = "blendTrans(sProperties)"

or as HTML:

<ELEMENT STYLE = "filter: blendTrans(sProperties)" ... >

The properties include:

- apply. Applies a transition to the designated object.
- duration. Defines the length of time the transition takes to complete.
- enabled. Defines whether the filter is currently enabled.
- play. Plays transition.
- status. Gets the current state of the transition.
- stop. Stops transition playback.

The following example fades text out when the FadeOut button is pressed, otherwise the FadeIn button fades in the text. The <DIV> tag is used to define the name of the text object (in this case it is named myText), and this is then operated on by the blendTrans filter.

```
<SCRIPT>
function filterFadeOut() {
   myText.style.filter="blendTrans(duration=2)";
   if (myText.filters.blendTrans.status != 2) {
      myText.filters.blendTrans.apply();
      myText.style.visibility="hidden";
      myText.filters.blendTrans.play();
   }
}
function filterFadeIn() {
   myText.style.filter="blendTrans(duration=2)";
   if (myText.filters.blendTrans.status != 2) {
      myText.filters.blendTrans.apply();
      myText.style.visibility="visible";
      myText.filters.blendTrans.play();
   }
}
</SCRIPT>
</HEAD>

<BODY>
<DIV ID="myText" STYLE="width: 200">
This text can be faded in and out.
</DIV>
<P>
<BUTTON onclick="filterFadeOut()">Fade Text Out</BUTTON>
```

```
<BUTTON onclick="filterFadeIn()">Fade Text In</BUTTON>
</P>
```

H13.2.3 Blur()

The blur() filter causes the object to appear to be in motion. Its syntax is:

object.style.filter = "blur(sProperties)"

or as HTML:

<ELEMENT STYLE = "filter: blur(sProperties)" ... >

where:

- **Direction**. Defines a directional offset of the filter. This is defined in 45° increments, from the vertical alignment of the object.
- **Strength**. Sets or gets the intensity of the filter.

For example the following applies a 45° blur on an image:

```
<img style="filter:blur(strength=100, Direction=45)" src="pics_cookie.jpg">
```

H13.2.4 Chroma

The chroma filter renders a defined color as being transparent. Its syntax is:

object.style.filter = "chroma(sProperties)"

or as HTML:

<ELEMENT STYLE = "filter: chroma(sProperties)" ... >

where sProperties can be defined with:

- color. Set/gets the color to be made transparent.
- enabled. Set/get the state.

The following changes of the black colors into transparent ones:

```
<img style="filter:chroma(color=#000000)" src="pics_research_poster01.gif">
```

H13.2.5 Dropshadow

The dropshadow filter projects a shadow of the object. Its syntax is:

object.style.filter = "dropshadow(sProperties)"

or as HTML:

```
<ELEMENT STYLE = "filter: dropshadow(sProperties)" ... >
```

where sProperties can be defined with:

- color. Defines color applied with the filter.
- enabled. Defines if the filter is enabled.
- offX. Defines x-axis offset of the drop shadow.
- offY. Defines y-axis offset of the drop shadow.
- Positive. Defines if drop shadow has nontransparent pixels of the object.

H13.2.6 Fliph

The fliph() filter creates a mirror image of an object, whereas the flipv() filter creates a vertical flip. Their syntax is:

```
object.style.filter = "fliph(sProperties)"
object.style.filter = "flipv(sProperties)"
```

or as HTML:

```
<ELEMENT STYLE = "filter: fliph(sProperties)" ... >
<ELEMENT STYLE = "filter: flipv(sProperties)" ... >
```

The only parameter is enabled, which sets/get whether the filter is enabled. For example the following shows examples of the flip filters:

```
<img style="filter:fliph()" src="pics_cookie.jpg" width="600" height="450">
<img style="filter:flipv()" src="pics_cookie.jpg" width="600" height="450">
```

H13.2.7 Glow

The glow filter adds a radiance around an object. Its syntax are:

```
object.style.filter = "glow(sProperties)"
```

or as HTML:

```
<ELEMENT STYLE = "filter: glow(sProperties)" ... >
```

where sProperties can be defined with:

- color. The color of the filter.
- enabled. Defines whether filter is enabled.
- strength. Set/gets the strength of the filter.

The following gives an example of a blue glow, with a strength of 10:

```
<img style="filter:glow(color=blue,strength=10)" src="top_nos.gif"
                                    width="441" height="63">
```

H13.2.8 gray

The gray filter converts the object to a grayscale. Its syntax is:

object.style.filter = "gray(sProperties)"

or as HTML:

<ELEMENT STYLE = "filter: gray(sProperties)" ... >

The only parameter is enabled, which sets/get whether the filter is enabled. The following gives an example of the filter:

```
<img style="filter:gray()" src="pics_cookie.jpg" width="600" height="450">
```

H13.2.9 Invert

The invert filter creates the inverse of an object. Its syntax is:

object.style.filter = "invert(sProperties)"

or as HTML:

<ELEMENT STYLE = "filter: invert(sProperties)" ... >

The only parameter is enabled, which sets/get whether the filter is enabled. The following gives an example of the filter:

```
<img style="filter:invert()" src="pics_cookie.jpg" width="600" height="450">
```

H13.2.10   Light

The light filter allows light to be projected onto an object. Its syntax is:

object.style.filter = "light(sProperties)"

or as HTML:

<ELEMENT STYLE = "filter: light(sProperties)" ... >

The parameters are:

- **addAmbient** Applies an ambient light to the filter.
- **addCone** Applies cone light to the filter.
- **addPoint**. Applies a pinpoint of light that shines in all directions.
- **changeColor**. Changes the light color.
- **changeStrength** Changes light intensity.
- **clear**. Clears all the applied lights.
- **enabled**. Sets or gets whether the filter is currently enabled.

- **moveLight**. Moves the light effect on the page.

The following gives an example of moving a light source with the mouse. Initially, on the page load event (onload) a point source of light is added to (150,150), with while light (255,255,255). This is then moved around on the mouse event (onMouseMove).

```
<body onload = "setlight()">
<script language="JavaScript">
function setlight( )
{

      myImg.filters( "light" ).addPoint( 150, 150,125, 255, 255, 255, 100 );
}

function movelight()
{

   eX = event.offsetX;
   eY = event.offsetY;
   xCoordinate = Math.round( eX-event.srcElement.width / 2, 0 );
   yCoordinate = Math.round( eY-event.srcElement.height / 2, 0 );
   myImg.filters( "light" ).moveLight( 0, eX, eY, 125, 1 );
}
</script>
</p>

<p align="center"> <img id = "myImg" src = "pics_cookie.jpg"
style = "top: 100; left: 100; filter: light()"
onMouseMove = "movelight()" width="400" height="300" />
</body>
```

H13.2.11   mask

The mask filters creates a transparent mask, from its non-transparent pixels. Its syntax is:

object.style.filter = "mask(sProperties)"

or as HTML:

<ELEMENT STYLE = "filter: mask(sProperties)" ... >

The two parameters are enabled, which defines it the mask is enabled and color, which defines the value of the color applied with the filter. The following gives an example of the filter:

<img src = "pics_code_snippets.gif" filter:mask(color=#000000) align="middle" />

H13.2.12   revealTrans

The revealTrans filter either hides or shows objects, and applies a transition to it. Its syntax are:

object.style.filter = "revealTrans(sProperties)"

or as HTML:

<ELEMENT STYLE = "filter: revealTrans(sProperties)" ... >

where sProperties can be defined with:

- apply. Applies the transition
- duration. Defines the transition time.
- enabled. Defines if the transition is enabled.
- play. Play the transition.
- status. Gets current status.
- stop. Stops transition.
- transition.Defines transition type. These are can set to:

0	Box in.	1	Box out.
2	Circle in.	3	Circle out.
4	Wipe up.	5	Wipe down.
6	Wipe right.	7	Wipe left.
8	Vertical blinds.	9	Horizontal blinds.
10	Checkerboard across.	11	Checkerboard down.
12	Random dissolve.	13	Split vertical in.
14	Split vertical out.	15	Split horizontal in.
16	Split horizontal out.	17	Strips left down.
18	Strips left up.	19	Strips right down.
20	Strips right up.	21	Random bars horizontal.
22	Random bars vertical.	23	Random.

The following uses a transition setting of two, which defines a circle in, and for a transition setting of three, for a circle out:

```
<input type=BUTTON value="Circle In " onClick="do_in();" name="BUTTON">
<input type=BUTTON value="Circle Out " onClick="do_out();" name="BUTTON2">

<p><span id=cat style="Filter:revealTrans (duration=4, transition=4);
    background-image: url(pics_cookie.jpg);>
</span> </p>

<script>
function do_in() {
    cat.filters[0].Apply();
    cat.style.visibility = "hidden";
    cat.filters.revealTrans.transition=2;
    cat.filters[0].Play();
}
function do_out() {
    cat.filters[0].Apply();
    cat.style.visibility = "visible";
    cat.filters.revealTrans.transition=3;
    cat.filters[0].Play();
}
</script>
```

H13.2.13   shadow

The shadow filter creates a shadow behind the object. Its syntax are:

object.style.filter = "shadow(sProperties)"

or as HTML:

<ELEMENT STYLE = "filter: shadow(sProperties)" ... >

where sProperties can be defined with:

- enable. Defines whether the filter is active.
- color. Defines the color of the filter.
- direction. Defines the direction of the filter.

The follow defines a style named myshadow, which has a shadow of Red, that has a direction of 60°:

```
<style>
DIV.myshadow
{filter: shadow(color=#FF0000,direction=60); width: 400; color: black;
font-weight: bold}
</style>

<div class="myshadow">This is how you create fiery looking text </div>
```

H13.2.14   wave

The wave filter allows a sine wave distortion to an object. Its syntax are:

object.style.filter = "wave(sProperties)"

or as HTML:

<ELEMENT STYLE = "filter: wave(sProperties)" ... >

where sProperties can be defined with:

- enable. Defines whether the filter is active.
- add. Defines whether the image is added to.
- freq. Defines the number of waves.
- lightstrength. Defines the light intensity.
- phase. Defines the phase of the wave.
- strength. Defines the strength of the wave.

The following gives an example:

```
<style>
DIV.mywave {filter: wave(freq=1, add=0,
phase=0, strength=6, lightstrength=10);
width: 400; color: black;font-weight: bold}
</style>
<div class="mywave">This is how you create wavy looking
text </div>
```

H13.2.15　xray

The xray filter allows takes an x-ray of an object. Its syntax is:

object.style.filter = "xray(sProperties)"

or as HTML:

<ELEMENT STYLE = "filter: xray(sProperties)" ... >

The only parameter is enabled, which sets/get whether the filter is enabled. The following gives an example of the filter:

```
<img id = "myImg" src = "pics_cookie.jpg" style = "top: 100; left: 100; filter:
xray()" width="400" height="300" align="middle" />
```

H13.3　z-index

The z-index attribute/property is used to define the stacking order of objects. Larger values will be placed in front of smaller values. The following defines two objects on Layer 1 and Layer2. The first layer has a graphic pics_man_graphic.gif, and the other layer has a graphic of pics_agent.gif. The graphic on Layer2 will be shown above Layer1, as its z-index value is larger than the other layer:

```
<div id="Layer1" style="position:absolute;
   width:200px; height:115px; z-index:1">
   <img src=" pics_man_graphic.gif" width="100" height="142">
</div>
<div id="Layer2" style="position:absolute;
   width:200px; height:115px; z-index:2; left: 77px; top: 65px">
   <img src="pics_agent.gif" width="50" height="104">
</div>
```

H13.4　<DIV> tag

The <DIV> tag defines a block element, which is defined between the <DIV> and </DIV> tag. Its syntax is:

```
<DIV
    ALIGN=CENTER | LEFT | RIGHT | JUSTIFY
    CLASS=class_name
    DATAFLD=datafield_name
    DATAFORMATAS=HTML | TEXT
    DATASRC=#ID
    ID=value
    LANG=language
    LANGUAGE=JAVASCRIPT | JSCRIPT | VBSCRIPT
    STYLE=css1-properties
    TITLE=text
    event = script
  >
```

<DIV> is typically used for defining an in-line style, such as:

```
<DIV STYLE='border:none;border-bottom:solid'>
  <H1>Test</H1>
</DIV>
```

which will draw a line beneath the material defined between the <DIV> and </DIV> tags. The line styles are thus:

- border-bottom-style
- border-top-style
- border-left-style
- border-right-style

of which the line styles can be dotted, dashed, double, groove, ridge, inset, outset, and none. For example, the following defines a solid red line on the right-hand side, a dashed green line on the top, a dotted blue line on the bottom, and the double black line on the left.

```
<DIV  STYLE='border:none;
border-right-style:solid;      border-right-color:red;
border-top-style:dashed;       border-top-color:green;
border-bottom-style:dotted;    border-bottom-color:blue;
border-left-style:double;      border-left-color:black; '>
<h1>Test</h1>
</div>
```

It is also possible to vary the thickness of the line with the width parameter, such as:

```
<DIV STYLE='border:none;
border-bottom-style:solid; border-bottom-color:red;  border-bottom-width:10; '>
```

A typical <DIV> tag is also typically used to provide alignment. For example, the following defines a center alignment:

```
<div align="center">This is some text </div>
```

Its basic attributes are:

ACCESSKEY	Defines accelerator key.
ALIGN	Defines the alignment relative to the display or table.
CLASS	Defines the class.
DATAFLD	Defines a given data source.
DATAFORMATAS	Defines rendering of the data.
DATASRC	Defines source of the data.
DIR	Defines reading order.
ID	Defines ID.
LANG	Defines language.
LANGUAGE	Defines scripting language.
NOWRAP	Defines word wrap, or not.
STYLE	Defines an inline style.
TABINDEX	Defines the index for the tab selection.

| TITLE | Defines advisory information. |

It has certain properties, such as:

accessKey	Defines accelerator key.
align	Defines alignment.
className	Defines class.
clientHeight	Defines height.
clientLeft	Defines left-hand spacing.
clientTop	Defines top spacing.
clientWidth	Defines width.
currentStyle	Defines style.
dataFld	Defines data source.
dataFormatAs	Defines data rendering.
dataSrc	Defines source of the data.
dir	Defines reading order.
firstChild	Defines first child in a collection of childNodes.
id	Defines the ID.
innerHTML	Defines HTML.
lang	Defines language.
language	Defines scripting language.
lastChild	Defines the last child in a collection of childNodes.
nextSibling	Defines next child of the parent.
nodeName	Defines name of a node.
nodeType	Defines type of node.
nodeValue	Defines value of node.
noWrap	Defines word wrap, or not.
offsetHeight	Defines offset height.
offsetLeft	Defines offset left.
offsetParent	Defines parent offset.
offsetTop	Defines top offset.
offsetWidth	Defines width offset.
outerHTML	Defines a <DIV> with HTML.
outerText	Defines text.
parentElement	Defines parent object of an object hierarchy.
parentNode	Defines parent object of a document hierarchy.
previousSibling	Defines previous child of the parent.
readyState	Defines current download state.
runtimeStyle	Defines cascaded format.
scopeName	Defines namespace of an element.
scrollHeight	Defines scrolling height.
scrollLeft	Defines scrolling left.
scrollTop	Defines scrolling top.
scrollWidth	Defines scrolling width.
sourceIndex	Defines source index.
style	Defines a new style.
tabIndex	Defines an index value for the tab order.
tagName	Defines tag name.

tagUrn	Defines Uniform Resource Name (URN).
tool	Defines advisory data .
uniqueID	Defines an automatically generated identifier.

An example of properties is:

```
<DIV ID=text_area>
  <textarea name="textfield" rows="5">Test</textarea>
</DIV>
<script language=javascript>
   document.write(text_area.offsetHeight, ", ", text_area.offsetWidth);
</script>
```

The method are:

addBehavior	Assigns a behavior.
appendChild	Appends an element as a child .
applyElement	Defines if <DIV> is a child or parent.
attachEvent	Defines an event.
blur	Defines a blur event.
clearAttributes	Removes all attributes.
click	Defines a click event.
cloneNode	Clone a node.
detachEvent	Detaches an event.
doScroll	Define a scroll event.
getAdjacentText	Gets an adjacent character.
getAttribute	Defines a specified attribute.
getExpression	Defines the expression for the given property.
hasChildNodes	Returns whether there are children.
insertAdjacentElement	Inserts an element.
insertAdjacentHTML	Inserts the given HTML text.
insertAdjacentText	Inserts text.
insertBefore	Inserts an element into the hierarchy.
releaseCapture	Removes mouse capture .
removeAttribute	Removes an attribute.
removeBehavior	Detaches a behavior.
removeChild	Removes a child node.
removeExpression	Removes an expression.
removeNode	Removes a <DIV> from the hierarchy.
replaceChild	Replaces an existing child element.
replaceNode	Replaces a <DIV> by an element.
scrollIntoView	Defines scrolling, or not.
setAttribute	Defines an attribute.
setCapture	Defines the mouse capture .
setExpression	Defines an expression.
swapNode	Swaps two nodes.

The behaviours are:

| clientCaps | Determines browser capabilities.. |

download	Downloads a file.
homePage	Determines information on home page.
httpFolder	Determines scripting features.
saveFavorite	Adds a Favorite.
saveHistory	Adds to the browser history.
saveSnapshot	Saves the WWW page.
time	Defines a timeline for the element.
userData	Enables user data.

H14 CSS (Cascadable Style Sheet)

H14.1 Introduction

HTML has been widely accepted. It initial objectives were to present text and graphic with integrated hypertext links, which allowed users to move easily between pages which were stored either locally or on different page servers. For this, it created simple style tags for paragraphs and section headings. These included:

- <P>. Defines a new paragraph.
- <H1>, <H2>, ... <H6>. Header 1, Header 2, ... Header 6.

Along with this the <A> tag allowed support for hypertext links, and images can be incorporated with the <IMG> tag. This worked well for the basic layout of text and graphics, but fails to properly present objects in a precise form. This is mainly due to the lack of re-definition of the standard styles, thus the designer had very little control over the actual presentation of the HTML page in the browser. With standard HTML, the designer cannot change the actual format of the standard styles, or define new ones, which could be reused in either page elements.

CSS tries to overcome these problems by defining a language which can be used to define font and text layout styles. World Wide Web Consortium (W3C) has standardized the format, so that most browsers support it. The CSS has not only defined a standard for WWW browsers, but one which can be used in any print layout system.

An example of a CSS definition is:

```
<style type="text/css">
H3
{
font: 14pt Courier New, Courier, mono;
margin-right: 8px; margin-left: 8px;
left: auto; text-align: justify
}
</style>
<h3>Some text</h3>
```

This changes the style of the <H3> tag to a font size of 14 point, with a font of either Courier New, Courier or any other mono spaced font. The margins have been set at 8 pixels on the left and right hand side, and the text align is set to justify.

Often there is a requirement to change a style of a small amount of text. In CSS this is possible where the change to a style is defined using the style modifier. For example the following changes the style for <H1> for all the text up to the end of the closing </H2> tag:

```
<h1 style='font: 14pt Courier New, Courier, mono; margin-left:0cm;
text-indent:0cm;tab-stops:54.0pt'>
Some text</h1>
```

```
<h1>Some more text</h1>
```

Typically, also, it is required to modify a standard style with the addition of additional styles definition, or to change defined ones. This can be done by defining a new class style onto the standard one. For example the following modify the <P> style and defines a new class (NewFormat):

```
<style type="text/css">
p.NewFormat
{
    margin:0.5cm;
    margin-bottom:.0.5cm;
    text-align:left;
    line-height:12.0pt;
    tab-stops:14.2pt 1.0cm 42.55pt 2.0cm
    punctuation-wrap:simple;
    text-autospace:none;
    font-size:12.0pt;
    font-family:Times New Roman;
}
</style>

<p class=NewFormat> This is the new text
```

This will change the <P> style for the new class named NewFormat, and modify the font type to Times New Roman, of a font size of 12 points. In this case the <P> will not be modified with this changed. In general, custom styles (class) must begin with a period.

H14.2   CSS file definitions

One of the strengths of CSS file definition is to reuse styles across several pages. This allows styles to be referenced in a single place, and a change in the definition will immediately be reflected in all the referenced pages. The CSS is included using the <LINK> tag. This uses the HREF attributed of the <LINK> tag, but unlike the <A> tag it is included in the <HEAD> element of the page.

```
<LINK href="styles.css" type=text/css  rel=stylesheet>
```

An example of a style sheet is:

```
/* description for custom style */
BODY
{margin-left: 12px;
font-family: Arial, Helvetica, sans-serif;
font-size: 9pt;}

P
{font: 10pt Verdana, Arial, Helvetica, sans-serif; clip:    rect(   );
margin-right: 12px; margin-left: 12px;
left: auto; text-align: justify}


H1
{font: bold 16pt Verdana, Arial, Helvetica, sans-serif;
background: transparent;
color: #000000; margin-right: 6px; margin-left: 6px; clip:    rect(   )}
```

```
H2
{font: bold 14px Verdana, Arial, Helvetica, sans-serif;
background: transparent;
margin-right: 6px; margin-left: 6px;
color: #000000; left: 8px; clip:   rect(    )}

B, STRONG {font-weight: bold}

I, CITE, EM, VAR, ADDRESS
{font-style: italic}

PRE, TT, CODE, KBD, SAMP
{font-family: monospace}

A:link {color: #006699;
font-family: Verdana, Arial, Helvetica, sans-serif;
font-size: 11px; text-decoration: none; font-weight: normal}

A:visited {color: #0066AA;
text-decoration: none; font-family: Verdana, Arial, Helvetica, sans-serif;
font-size: 11px; font-weight: normal;}

a:hover {  color: #FF0000;
font-family: Verdana, Arial, Helvetica, sans-serif;
font-size: 11px; font-weight: normal; text-decoration: underline}
```

H14.3   Link attributes

The CSS style can define attributes to a style. An important style is the link style (<A>). This style has several different types of definitions. These include:

- Unvisited link. This can be defined with the A:link style.
- Visited link. This can be defined with the A:visited style.
- Hover over a link. This can be defined with the A:hover style.

The following defines an unvisited link color of #006699, a visited link color of #0066AA, and a hover color of #FF0000:

```
A:link {color: #006699;
font-family: Verdana, Arial, Helvetica, sans-serif;
font-size: 11px; font-weight: normal}

A:visited {color: #0066AA;
font-family: Verdana, Arial, Helvetica, sans-serif;
font-size: 11px; font-weight: normal;}

A:hover {  color: #FF0000;
font-family: Verdana, Arial, Helvetica, sans-serif;
font-size: 11px; font-weight: normal; text-decoration: underline}
```

The main difference in this case is that the hover action will provide an underline beneath the hypertext link, and that different colors are used for the different type of links.

H14.4   Redefining standard styles

Along with modifying the paragraph and heading styles, it is also possible to redefine other styles. These include tag which are used to define bold areas, such as <B> and <STRONG>, citation and emphasis tags, such as <I>, <CITE>, <EM>, <VAR> and <ADDRESS>, and monospaced-type tags, such as <PRE>, <TT>, <CODE>, <KBD> and <SAMP>. Examples of these include:

```
B, STRONG {font-weight: bold}

I, CITE, EM, VAR, ADDRESS
{font-style: italic}

PRE, TT, CODE, KBD, SAMP
{font-family: monospace}
```

It is unlikely that these styles would require to be changed, but there is scope to change them in the CSS definitions, especially to refine their format.

H14.5   CSS Properties

CSS has defined a number of properties. These include:

H14.5.1 Lists and displaying

The classification properties define how objects are rendered. They include:

```
list-style              list-style-image
list-style-position     list-style-type
```

The list-type property is an important as it fixes some of the properties of lists that occur in HTML. An example of modifying the un-numbered list tag (<UL>) is:

```
<style>
   ul { list-style:square outside none}
</style>
<ul>
   <li>test 1</li>
   <li>test 2</li>
</ul>
```

The same thing can be applied to the other list objects, such as DD, DT, LI, OL and UL. The parameters which can be defined with the list-style properties are:

list-style-type:	disc | circle | square | decimal | lower-roman | upper-roman | lower-alpha | upper-alpha | none.
list-style-image:	(URL) | none
list-style-type:	inside | outside

For example to define a graphic for the bullet:

```
LI

{
    display: list-item;
    margin-left: 0px;
    list-style-position: inside;
    list-style-image: url(aro_blue.gif);
    list-style-type: none;
}

<ul>
    <li>test 1</li>
    <li>test 2</li>
</ul>
```

H14.5.2 Background

The color/background properties are useful for setting background images.

background	background-attachment
background-color	background-image
background-position	background-repeat

An example of setting a background graphic for a modified form of the <P> tag is:

```
<style>
p.mystyle1
{   background-color: #EEEEEE;
    background-image: url(pics_mobile_agents07_alpha.gif);
    background-repeat: no-repeat; font-weight: bold}
p.mystyle2
{   background-color: #EEEEEE;
    background-image: url(pics_mobile_agents07_alpha.gif);
    background-repeat: repeat; font-weight: bold}
p.mystyle3
{   background-color: #EEEEEE;
    background-image: url(pics_mobile_agents07_alpha.gif);
    background-repeat: repeat-x; font-weight: bold}
p.mystyle4
{   background-color: #EEEEEE;
    background-image: url(pics_mobile_agents07_alpha.gif);
    background-repeat: repeat-y; font-weight: bold}
</style>
<p class="mystyle"><b>Mobile Agents</b>.
```

which sets a non-repeated graphic (pics_mobile_agents07_alpha.gif) on the mystyle1 style. Also, the mystyle2 style will have a repeated graphic on the text, while the mystyle3 and mystyle4 styles will have repeated background images on the x-direction and y-direction, respectively.

The parameters for the background properties are:

background-repeat: no-repeat, repeat, repeat-x, repeat-y.
background-attachment: fixed, scrolled.
background-position: left, center, right, top, center, bottom

For example:

{ background-attachment: fixed ; background-repeat: repeat; background-position: center center}

H14.5.3 Type

The main type options include:

font	@font-face
font-family	font-size
font-style	font-variant
font-weight	line-height
letter-spacing	text-align
text-decoration	text-indent
text-transform	vertical-align

An example of font properties is given next:

```
<style>
p.mystyle1 { font: Arial; font-size: large;
font-weight: normal}
</style>
```

The main parameters for the types properties are:

font-size:	9 | 10 | 12 | 14 | 16 | 18 | 24 | 36 | x-large | xx-large | x-small | xx-small | small | medium | large | smaller
font-style:	italic | normal | oblique
line-height:	normal | (size)
font-variant:	normal | small-caps
font-weight:	normal | bold | bolder | lighter | 100 | 200 | 300 | 400 | 500 | 600 | 700 | 800 | 900.
text-transform:	capitalize | uppercase | lowercase

H14.5.4 Borders and margins

The border/margin properties define parameters for a border and/or margins. The main properties are:

border	border-bottom
border-bottom-color	border-bottom-style
border-bottom-width	border-color
border-left	border-left-color
border-left-style	border-left-width
border-right	border-right-color
border-right-style	border-right-width
border-style	border-top
border-top-color	border-top-style
border-top-width	border-width
clear	float
margin	margin-bottom

margin-left	margin-right
margin-top	padding
padding-bottom	padding-left
padding-right	padding-top

The following show some examples of solid lines on the top, bottom, left and right of text:

```
<h1 style='border:none;border-bottom-style:solid;'>Test</h1>
<h1 style='border:none;border-top-style:solid; >Test</h1>
<h1 style='border:none;border-left-style:solid;'> Test</h1>
<h1 style='border:none;border-right-style:solid;'>Test</h1>
```

The options for the styles are:

border-*pos*-style	none | dotted | dashed | solid | double | groove | ridge | inset | outset
border-*pos*-width	thin | medium | thick | auto | (value)

An example of using a mixture of border styles and colors is:

```
<h1 style='border:none;border-right-style:solid; border-right-color:red;
border-top-style:dashed; border-top-color:green;
border-bottom-style:dotted; border-bottom-color:blue;
border-left-style:double; border-left-color:black; '>
Test</h1>
```

The margin property is important for creating the precise layout of text and other objects. The following shows a few examples of changing the width of the margin on the left hand side:

```
<p style='margin-left:10px'>This is some text (10-pixel margin)</p>
<p style='margin-left:20px'>This is some text (20-pixel  margin)</p>
<p style='margin-left:30px'>This is some text (30-pixel margin)</p>
<p style='margin-left:40px'>This is some text (40-pixel  margin)</p>
```

H14.5.5 Positioning

The positioning attributes allow objects to be properly positioned, these include:

bottom	clip
height	left
overflow	position
right	top
visibility	width
z-index	

Most of these are defined in screen sizes. Other parameters include:

overflow:	visible | hidden | scroll | auto
position:	absolute | relative | static
visibility:	inherit | visible | hidden

The clip property uses a shape to clip to. In the following example a rectangle is used:

clip: rect(20px 20px 20px 20px)

An example is:

```
ADDRESS
 { overflow: hidden; position: absolute; visibility: visible; z-index: 2;
height: 2px; width: 2px; left: 2px; top: 2px; clip:  rect(20px 20px 20px 20px)}
```

The following creates a scrolling window, where text that cannot fit into the text area (which is defined with a 100-pixel height, and a 200-pixel width:

```
<p overflow: scroll;
position: relative; visibility: visible; z-index: 2;
height: 100px; width: 200px; left: 0px; top: 0px;
clip: rect(200px 200px 200px 200px)'>This is a test. Em blonko
de poli em aco. This is a test. Em blonko de poli </P>
```

H14.5.6 Printing

The following are the main printing properties, and are used to control how WWW pages are printed:

page-break-after   page-break-before

The settings for these are auto, always, left or right.

H14.5.7 Others

Other formatting properties include:

active   cursor
hover   @import
!important   link
visited   color
display

The cursor property can be set to:

cursor: hand | crosshair | text | wait | default | help | e-resize | n-resize | s-resize | w-resize | ne-resize | nw-resize | se-resize | sw-resize | auto

The following gives examples of differing cursors:

```
<p style='cursor:hand'>This is an example of the <b>hand cursor</b>. Please
move your mouse cursor over this text.</p>
<p style='cursor:crosshair'>This is an example of the <b>crosshair cursor</b>.
Please move your mouse cursor over this text.</p>
<p style='cursor:text'>This is an example of the <b>text cursor</b>. Please
move your mouse cursor over this text.</p>
```

```
<p style='cursor:help'>This is an example of the <b>help cursor</b>. Please
move your mouse cursor over this text.</p>
<p style='cursor:wait'>This is an example of the <b>wait cursor</b>. Please
move your mouse cursor over this text.</p>
<p style='cursor:e-resize'>This is an example of the <b>e-resize cursor</b>.
Please move your mouse cursor over this text.</p>
```

The hover property defines the event which is called when the user moves their cursor over the referenced object. For example, the following changes the hover style for a link, so that the colour of the link is red, and in uppercase:

```
<style>
A:hover { color:red; text-transform:uppercase; }
</style>
<a href="css_others.htm">This is a link</a>
```

We can set the color of the visited and unvisited links with:

```
<style>
A:link      { color:green; }
A:visited   { color:red; }
</style>
```

H14.6   CSS length units

CSS allows text layout rules that are used in the publishing industry, and can use either relative or absolute units. The relative units are defined in terms of another unit, and are:

em	Height of the letter 'm'
ex	Height of the letter 'x'
px	Pixels
%	Percentage

and the absolute units are:

in	Inches, where 1 inch is 2.54 cm
cm	Centimeters.
mm	Millimeters.
pt	Points, where 1 point is 1/72 inch
pc	Picas, where 1 pica is 12 points

Relative length units are useful when objects are scaled, whereas absolute are typically used when the actual dimensions of an object are know. The following gives a few examples of different units:

```
<p style='font-size=20px;'>
<p style='font-size=2em;'>This is a sample text
<p style='font-size=2ex;'>This is a sample text
<p style='font-size=0.2in;'>This is a sample text
<p style='font-size=0.5cm;'>This is a sample text
```

H15 WAP

H15.1 Introduction

Wireless Application Protocol (WAP) provides a standard for the presentation and delivery of wireless information and telephony services on mobile phones and other mobile terminals. It was fully specified in 1997 using many of the existing standards from telephony manufacturers, such as Ericsson, Nokia or Motorola (who joined the WAP Forum). This group has since defined global wireless protocol specifications, based on existing Internet standards such as XML and IP, for all wireless networks. It has the following objectives:

- Integrate Internet content and advanced data services for wireless phones and other wireless terminals.
- Define a global wireless protocol specification which supports existing wireless network technologies.
- Define and extend existing standards.
- Support the creation of content and applications that can be scaled across a wide range of wireless networks and devices types.

WAP has a similar architecture to the global Internet. Like the HTTP protocol, WAP uses the concept of a browser, which is included inside the mobile phone. This delivers the content and is adapted to support the special environment with a mobile phone. The main difference between common WWW technology and WAP is a gateway (sometimes called proxy), which bridges the GSM network and Internet.

Mobile devices are typically grouped into three main classifications:

- Mobile phones.
- PDA (Personal Data Assistant).
- HPC (Hand-held PC).

As these devices typically have limited resources, in terms of memory, processing power and graphical displays, the browser supports two types of simplified mark-up languages: WML and WMLScript Given that the terminals have small resources (CPU or memory). Typically the micro browser is either initially installed or, with a PDA and HPC, can downloaded on the terminal. The mobile client is an important key element in the WAP environment as it allows interacting directly with the user and keeps the data transferred confidential.

An important part of the WAP framework is the link between the WML content server and the GSM operator. This is illustrated in Figure H15.1. The WML page typical resides on a standard WWW server. This makes it easy to setup WML pages.

When mobile terminal makes a request for a page, the request is sent through the GSM network to a gateway. This then transforms the request into a standard HTTP request, and passes it onto the content server (in the same way that a normal HTTP request would). The gateway is thus responsible for checking the integrity of the content format, for its WML content, and to compress the data before to send it back to the mobile terminal.

The gateway thus makes the WAP device look like any other WWW-access device. It can thus use most of the standard protocols, such as HTTP and SSL, and standard WWW servers (Figure H15.2).

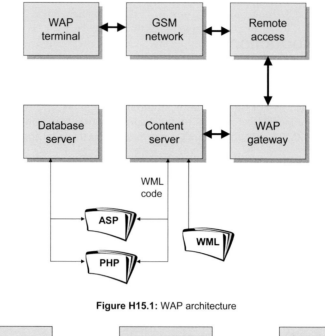

Figure H15.1: WAP architecture

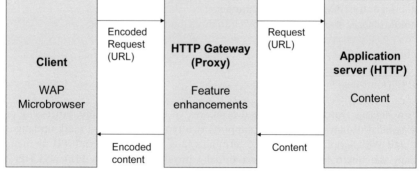

Figure H15.2: WAP gateway

WAP uses a layer approach to its protocols. These are:

- Wireless Application Environment (WAE).
- **Wireless Session Protocol** (WSP). This layer defines the services which can be used by the micro browser. There are two main modes: connected or non-connected. WSP is mainly responsible for data confirmation.
- **Wireless Transaction Protocol** (WTP). This layer is transaction oriented, and has the following functions: transaction services classes; asynchronous transaction; and concatenation and acknowledgement of data.

- **Wireless Transport Layer Security** (WTLS). This is based on SSL (Secure Sockets Layer). It is designed to support networks with limited bandwidth, and provides the following functions: data integrity; private channel; and authentication.
- **Wireless Datagram Protocol** (WDP). This is responsible for the transport process between a mobile terminal and the gateway. It is independent from the speed of data transfer, so that it can support any type of network, such as SMS, GSM, and GPDbase. Its main function is to provide the upper layers with a network independent access to a network.

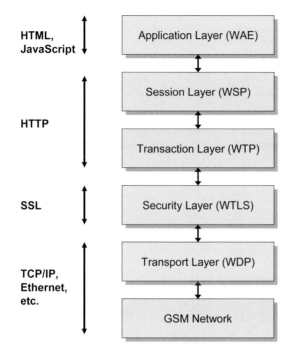

Figure H15.3: Protocols model

The WAE supports several services, these include:

- WML. This is a standard layout description language, which is similar to XML/HTML.
- WMLScript. This provides access to a scripting language, in the same way that JavaScript integrates with HTML.
- Wireless Telephony Application. This is an API providing access to functions on the mobile.
- WBMP. This provides a basic graphical format.
- vCard and vCalendar support, transmission of addresses and meetings.

H15.1.1 WML (Wireless Markup Language)

WML information arranges content in terms of cards and decks. A deck is the smallest unit of WML that the server sends to the client, and can contain one or more cards. The advantage of cards is that it is more efficiency in data transfer as the cards are downloaded in the same transmission. The following WML page will move from Card 1 to Card 2 when the user selects an ACCEPT option.

```
<?xml version="1.0" encoding="ISO-8859-1"?>
<!DOCTYPE wml PUBLIC "-//WAPFORUM//DTD WML 1.1//EN"
"http://www.wapforum.org/DTD/wml_1.1.xml">
<wml>
        <card id="Card1">
                <do type="accept" label="Next">
                        <go href="#Card2"/>
                </do>
                <p> Select <b>Next</b> to go to the next card. </p>
        </card>
        <card id="Card2">
                <p> This is the second card </p>
        </card>
</wml>
```

H15.1.2 WMLScript

As with HTML, WML defines the layout of pages. Also as HTML, it does not support local control and processing, thus WMLScript has been added to provide a scripting language. It is based on ECMAScript (defined by ECMA European Computer Manufacturers Association), and supports low bandwidth terminals with limited resources.

WMLScript is procedural in its approach and supports a large number of libraries. Typically it is used to:

- Check the validity of data filled by the user before transmission.
- Access to additional functionalities, such as to generate a phone call from a script.
- Provide enhanced user interaction.

H15.1.3 Telephony extensions (WTA)

WTA (Wireless Telephony Application) provides a number of specifications which allow interaction between data services (like the WML pages) and voice services (calls). Thus a call can be made from a WML tag. WTA is an agent which is integrated into the mobile device and allows three main kinds of services:

- **Public services**. These can be accessed by everyone, but can only initiate a call.
- **Common network services**. These are network independent and define functions such as answering a call, or write or read into the memory of the mobile device.
- **Specific network services**. This is available for certain types of networks, such as GSM, and gives the possibility to reject an unanswered call.

H15.2   WML reference

The main WML tags are defined in this section.

H15.2.1 Deck / Card Elements

These tags are used to define card elements:

Tag	Description	Attribute	Example
`<access>`	Defines information	**domain**. URL of other decks that can access cards in the deck path.	`<head>` `<access`

	about the access control of a deck .	**path**. Defines a path for access control
		class. Sets a case sensitive class name for the element. The class name is case sensitive.
		id. Sets a unique name for the element.
			```domain="billweb.net"```
			```path="home"/>```
			```</head>```

`<card>`	Defines a card in a deck	**newcontext**. Initializes browser context. True | False.
		ordered. Specifies the order of card content. A True specifies that the browser will display the content in a fixed order, otherwise the user decides the order as they navigate between content. True | False.
		title Card title [*cdata*]
		xml:lang Define language used in [*language_code*]
		onenterbackward Arises when user enters a card using a *prev* task [*url*]
		onenterforward *url* Arises when user enters a card using a *go* task
		ontimer *url* Arises when a *timer* expires
		class Defines a class name [*cdata*]
		id Defines a unique name [*id*]
			```<card id="card1"```
			```title="First card">```
			```<p>Hello</p>```
			```</card>```
			```<card id="card2"```
			```title="Second card">```
			```<p>Hello, again</p>```
			```</card>```

`<head>`	Information on the document	**class** Defines a class name [*cdata*]
		id Defines a unique name [*id*]
			```<head>```
			```<access```
			```domain="billweb.net"/>```
			```<meta name="keyword"```
			```content="WML"/>```
			```</head>```

`<meta>`	Meta information	**content**. Define a description of the name attribute.
		class. Sets a case sensitive class name for the element. The class name is case sensitive. [*cdata*]
		id. Sets a unique name for the element. [*id*]
		name. Defines the name of a tag (keyword, author, and so on).
			```<head>```
			```<access```
			```domain="billweb.net"/>```
			```<meta name="author"```
			```content="fred"/>```
			```</head>```

`<template>`	Defines code template	**onenterbackward** Arises when user enters a card using a *prev* task [*url*]
		onenterforward *url* Arises when user enters a card using a *go* task
		ontimer *url* Arises when a *timer* expires
		class Defines a class name [*cdata*]
		id Defines a unique name [*id*]
			```<template>```
			```<do type="Bk"```
			```label="GoBack">```
			```<Bk/>```
			```</do>```
			```</template>```

`<!-->`	Comment		`<!-- This is a comment -->`

`<wml>`	WML deck (WML root)	**xml:lang** Define language used in [*language_code*]
		class Defines a class name [*cdata*]
		id Defines a unique name [*id*]
			`<wml>`
			`<card id="card1"`
			`title="First card">`
			`<p>How are you?</p>`
			`</card>`
			`</wml>`

H15.2.2 Text and graphical elements

These tags are used to define the layout of text and graphical elements:

Tag	Description	Attribute	Example

`<a>`	Hypertext link	**href** Defines a hypertext link [*url*]
		title Defines title for the link [*cdata*]
			`<wml>`
			`<card title="Lnk">`
			`<p>`
			` <a href="fred.wml"> Fred</a>`
			`</p>`
			`</card>`
			`</wml>`

`<anchor>`	Anchor	**title** Defines title for the anchor [*cdata*]	`<wml>`
			`<card title="Anchor1">`
			`<p>`
			`<anchor>Fred`
			`<go href="fred.wml"/>`
			`</anchor>`
			`</p>`
			`</card>`
			`</wml>`

`<img>`	Image	**align** Aligns the image. Top | Middle | Bottom
		alt Defines the alternative text.
		height Defines the height of the image.
		hspace Sets horizontal white space.
		src Defines the image source.
		vspace Sets vertical white space.
		width Defines the width of the image.
			`<wml>`
			`<card title="Image">`
			`<p>`
			`<img src="logo.wbmp" alt="Logo WBMP"/>`
			`</p>`
			`</card>`
			`</wml>`

`<b>`	Bold text. If possible use `<strong>` and `<em>` before the use of `<b>`, `<i>` and `<u>`.		`<wml>`
			`<card title="Test">`
			`<p>This is a <b>WAP</b> page</p>`
			`</card>`
			`</wml>`

`<big>`	Large text	**Test**
		This is a **WAP**page
			`<wml>`
			`<card title="Test">`
			`<p>This is a <big>WAP</big> page`
			`</p>`
			`</card>`
			`</wml>`

`<em>`	Emphasized text	**Test**
		This is a *WAF*page
			`<wml>`
			`<card title="Test">`
			`<p>This is a <em>WAP</em> page</p>`
			`</card>`
			`</wml>`

`<small>`	Small text		`<wml>`
			`<card title="Test">`
			`<p>This is a <small>WAP</small>`
			`page</p>`
			`</card>`
			`</wml>`

`<strong>`	Strong text		`<wml>`
			`<card title="Test">`
			`<p>This is a <strong>WAP</strong>`
			`page</p>`
			`</card>`
			`</wml>`

`<u>`	Underline		
` `	Line break		
`<p>`	Paragraph		

`<table>`	Table	**title** Specifies the title.
		column Specifies the number of columns.
		align Specifies the alignment of the columns. "L" specifies left alignment, "R" specifies right, "C" specifies center, and "D" for default.
			`<card>`
			`<p>`
			`<table columns="2" align="LL">`
			`<tr><td>R1C1</td><td>R1C2</td></tr>`
			`<tr><td>R2C1</td><td>R2C2</td></tr>`
			`<tr><td>R3C1</td><td>R3C2</td></tr>`
			`</table>`
			`</p>`
			`</card>`

`<td>`	Table cell		
`<tr>`	Table row		

H15.2.3 Event Elements

These tags are used to define the events that occur in a page:

Tag	Description	Attribute	Example

`<do>`	Runs a task when the user selects a link.	See below.	`<do name="Home" type="accept" la-`
			`bel="Home" optional="false">`
			`<go href="index.wml" method="get" sen-`
			`dreferer="false"/>`
			`</do>`

`<onevent>`	Defines the code to be executed on the following events: onenterbackward, nenterforward, onpick and ontimer		`<onevent type="onenterforward">`
			`<go href="next.wml"/>`
			`</onevent>`

\<postfield\>	Contains the information to be sent to the WWW server, from the \<go\> tag.		See example

The do element allows the user to act on the current card. It has the form:

\<do name="Name" type="accept" label="Label" optional="false"\>

where:

- **Label**. Defines a new label.
- Name. Defines the name of the do event. When two do elements are defined, and have the same name, they refer to the same binding.
- Type. This provides a hint to the user agent on the usage of the element. These include:

  - Accept. Positive acknowledgement (acceptance)
  - Prev. Backward history navigation.
  - Help. Request for help.
  - Reset. Clearing or resetting state.
  - Options. Context-sensitive request for options.
  - Delete. Delete item.

The Do element is typically used to provide a response for click on buttons for the Go href, Previous, Refresh and Noop tasks. For example, the following creates two buttons which will either link to another card (#card2), or to another deck (index.wml):

```
<do name="next" type="accept" label="next" optional="false">
   <go href="#card2" method="get" sendreferer="false"/>
</do>
<do name="Link" type="accept" label="Link" optional="false">
   <go href="index.wml" method="get" sendreferer="false"/>
</do>
```

The onenterforward event occurs on the user agent entering a card with the go task (or similar method), whereas the onenterbackward event occurs on the user agent entering a card with the prev task. The onenterbackward event thus occurs when the user navigates back to a card from a history stack.

The postfield tag is used to send information to a WWW server. For example, the following has three fields where the user enters (email, realname and message). Once these are entered the parameters taken from these fields will be submitted to the wapmail.php file. The parameters taken from the fields are send using $(*varname*).

```
<?xml version="1.0" encoding="ISO-8859-1"?><!DOCTYPE wml PUBLIC "-
//WAPFORUM//DTD WML 1.1//EN" "http://www.wapforum.org//DTD//wml_1.1.xml">
<wml>
<card id="email" title="Email" ordered="true" newcontext="false">
<p align="left">
Send me an email
</p>
```

```
<p align="left">
Your name:
</p>
<p align="left">
   <input name="realname" type="text" emptyok="false"/>
</p>
<p align="left">
Your email address:
</p>
<p align="left">
   <input name="email" type="text" emptyok="false"/>
</p>
<p align="left">
Message:
</p>
<p align="left">
   <input name="message" type="text" emptyok="false"/>
</p>

<do type="accept" label="Send" optional="false">
   <go href="wapmail.php" method="get" sendreferer="false">
                        <postfield name="message" value="$(message)"/>
                        <postfield name="realname" value="$(realname)"/>
                        <postfield name="email" value="$(email)"/>
                        <postfield name="subject" value="WAP message"/>
   </go>
</do>
</card>
</wml>
```

H15.2.4 Task Elements

The task elements include four tags:

Tag	Description	Attribute	Example
`<go>`	Defines the action of moving to another card.	**Href**. This specifies the destination URI. **Sendreferer**. If set to true, the user agent must specify the URI of the deck containing this task. True | False **Method**. This specifies the HTTP submission method. POST | GET.	`<do type='option' label='Send'>` `<go href='check.asp? Password= $(password)' />` `</do>`
`<noop>`	No operation.		
`<prev>`	Goes back to the previous card.		`<do name="Prev" type="previous" label="Prev">` `<prev/>` `</do>`
`<refresh>`	Refresh screen.		`<do name="Refresh" type="accept" label="Refresh">` `<refresh/>` `</do>`

H15.3   Input Elements

The input elements allow the user to enter information into the WML page. The tags are:

Tag	Description	Attribute	Example
<fieldset>	Used to group together related elements in a card		``` <wml> <card title="Lnk"> <p> <a href="fred.wml"> Fred</a> </p> </card> </wml> ```
<input>	Defines an input field (a text field where the user can enter some text)	**Type**. Defines type. Text | password **Format**. Defines the format (see below). *cdata* **Size**. Defines the width of the input. *number* **Maxlength**. Defines the maximum number of characters for the input. Title. Defines a title. *vdata*	
<optgroup>	Defines an option group in a selectable list		
<option>	Defines an option in a selectable list	**Value**. Define the value to be set. *vdata* **Title**. Defines the title. *vdata* **Onpick**. Define an event. *Href*	See example.
<select>	Defines a selectable list	**Title**. Defines a title. *vdata*; **Name**. Define the name. *vdata*; **Multiple**. Defines if there are multiple values selected. True | False **Tabindex**. Define tab index value. *number*	See example.

The default format for input is "*M". The format codes are:

- *A. Defines uppercase non-numeric characters.
- *a. Defines lowercase non-numeric characters.
- *N. Defines any numeric character.
- *n. Defines any numeric, symbol, or punctuation character.
- *X. Defines any uppercase letter, numeric character, symbol, or punctuation character.
- *x. Defines any lowercase letter, numeric character, symbol, or punctuation character.

For example:

```
<p align='left'>
Password:<input name='password' type='password' maxlength='10'
title='password' />
</p>
```

The option tag can be used to define a number of options, from the <select> tag. For example the following allows the user to select the current day, and is displayed, once it has been selected:

```
<?xml version="1.0" encoding="ISO-8859-1"?><!DOCTYPE wml PUBLIC "-
//WAPFORUM//DTD WML 1.1//EN" "http://www.wapforum.org//DTD//wml_1.1.xml">
<wml>
<card id="card1" ordered="true" newcontext="false">
<p align="left">
Enter the day:</p>
<p align="left">
<select name="day" multiple="false">
    <option value="Monday">Monday</option>
    <option value="Tuesday">Tuesday</option>
    <option value="Wednesday">Wednesday</option>
    <option value="Thursday">Thursday</option>
    <option value="Friday">Friday</option>
</select>
</p>
<do type="accept" optional="false">
    <go href="#card2" method="get" sendreferer="false"/>
</do>

</card>
<card id="card2" title="Card 2" ordered="true" newcontext="false">
<p align="left">
    Today is $(day)</p>
</card>
</wml>
```

H15.3.1 Variable Elements

The variable elements are used to select variables, and are:

Tag	Description	Attribute	Example
<setvar>	Sets a variable to a specified value in a <go>, <prev>, or <re-fresh> task	**Name.** Defines the name of the variable. *vdata* **Value.** Defines the value of a variable. *vdata*	
<timer>	Defines a card timer	**Name.** Define the name of the timer. **Value.** Defines the value of the time (in 100 milliseconds intervals). vdata	

The following will display a message for 5 seconds and then go to

```
<wml>
<card ontimer="homepage.wml">
<timer value="50"/>
<p>
You will be redirected in 5 seconds ...
</p>
</card>
</wml>
```

H15.4   ASP/PHP interfaces with WML

Often it is easier to generate WML code from server-side scripts, such as PHP or ASP. This allows for easier integration with databases. As with HTTP, the content must be set correctly. This is defined as *text/vnd.wap.wml*. In ASP the property Content-Type of the Response object defines the correct format, and is achieved with;

```
Response.ContentType = "text/vnd.wap.wml"
```

Next the CharSet property of the Response component is set, in order to define the set of characters:

```
Response.CharSet = "ISO-8859-1"
```

After this the main headers can be sent, to define the WML content:

```
Response.Write "<?xml version='1.0'?>"
Response.Write  "<!DOCTYPE  wml  PUBLIC  '-//WAPFORUM//DTD  WML  1.1//EN'
'http://www.wapforum.org/DTD/wml_1.1.xml'>"
```

This gives the following format:

```
Response.ContentType = "text/vnd.wap.wml"
Response.CharSet = "ISO-8859-1"
Response.Write "<?xml version='1.0'?>"
Response.Write  "<!DOCTYPE  wml  PUBLIC  '-//WAPFORUM//DTD  WML  1.1//EN'
'http://www.wapforum.org/DTD/wml_1.1.xml'>"
Response.Write "<wml>"
Response.Write "<card id='default' title='Card 1'>"
Response.Write "<p align='center'>"
Response.Write "This is my first ASP-generated card"
Response.Write "</p>"
Response.Write "</card>"
Response.Write "</wml>"
```

In PHP this is defined as:

```
<?php
headers("Content-Type:text/vnd.wap.wml");
print "<?xml version='1.0'?>";
print "<!DOCTYPE wml PUBLIC '-//WAPFORUM//DTD WML 1.1//EN'
'http://www.wapforum.org/DTD/wml_1.1.xml'>";
print "<wml>";
print "<card id='default' title='Card 1'>";
print "<p align='center'>";
print "This is my first PHP-generated card";
print "</p>";
print "</card>";
print "</wml>";
?>
```

A database-driven WAP system using ASP will require initially to test the status of the database. This can be achieved by testing the State attribute on the System Properties table:

```
Set Dbase = Server.CreateObject("ADODB.Recordset")
str = "SELECT * FROM SystemProperties"
Set Dbase = DatabaseObjConnect.Execute(str)
```

```
If Dbase.Fields("State")=0 Then
    error = 1
' Error exists
Else
    error = 0
' Everything is fine
End If
```

A value of zero identifies that the database system is currently operating. Next, the access rights for the user can be tested with the following:

```
If Dbase("AccessRights")=1 Then
                            Response.Write "<go href='link1.asp'
method='get'/>"
    End If
    If Dbase("AccessRights")=2 Then
                            Response.Write "<go href='link2.asp'
method='get'/>"
    End If
    If Dbase("AccessRights")=3 Then
                            Response.Write "<go href='link3.asp'
method='get'/>"
    End If
End If
```

For example, if the user has entered

```
<%@ Language=VBScript %>
<% Option Explicit %>
'Based on code by B.Colas

'Define the variables
Dim databaseConnect, DatabaseObjConnect, Dbase, str, parameter
parameter = Request.QueryString("parameter")

'Get database connection
databaseConnect = "Driver={Microsoft Access Driver (*.mdb)};DBQ=" &
Server.MapPath("../database.mdb")
Set DatabaseObjConnect = Server.CreateObject("ADODB.Connection")
DatabaseObjConnect.Open databaseConnect

' Create a recordset
Set Dbase = Server.CreateObject("ADODB.Recordset")
Set Dbase = DatabaseObjConnect.Execute("SELECT * FROM SystemProperties")

'Send WML code
Response.ContentType = "text/vnd.wap.wml"
Response.CharSet = "ISO-8859-1"
Response.Write "<?xml version='1.0'?>"
Response.Write "<!DOCTYPE wml PUBLIC '-//WAPFORUM//DTD WML 1.1//EN'
'http://www.wapforum.org/DTD/wml_1.1.xml'>"
Response.Write "<wml>"
Response.Write "<card id='Logon' title='" & Dbase.Fields("Title") & "'>"
If parameter=0 Then
    Response.Write "<p align='center'>    Please logon, first</p>"
Else
    Response.Write "<p align='center'>Invalid</p>"
End If
Response.Write "<p align='left'>"
Response.Write "Login:<input name='login' maxlength='10' title='login' />"
```

```
Response.Write "</p>"
Response.Write "<p align='left'>"
Response.Write "Password:<input name='password' type='password' max-
length='10' title='password' />"
Response.Write "</p>"
Response.Write "<do type='option' label='Send'>"
Response.Write "<go href='logon.asp' method='get'>"
Response.Write "<postfield name='parameter' value='0'/>"
Response.Write "<postfield name='login' value='$(login)'/>"
Response.Write "<postfield name='password' value='$(password)'/>"
Response.Write "</go>"
Response.Write "</do>"
Response.Write "<do type='option' label='Back'>"
Response.Write "<go href='index.asp'/>"
Response.Write "</do>"
Response.Write "</card>"
Response.Write "</wml>"

'Close database
Dbase.Close
DatabaseObjConnect.Close
Set Dbase = Nothing
Set DatabaseObjConnect = Nothing
%>
```

WML can integrate well with either ASP or PHP. The following example shows how it is possible to send an email from a WAP page. It uses three text fields: realname, eadd and message. Once these are entered, the PHP page to email the variables is called (wapmail.php). The postfield tag passes these variables:

```
<?xml version="1.0" encoding="ISO-8859-1"?><!DOCTYPE wml PUBLIC "-
//WAPFORUM//DTD WML 1.1//EN" "http://www.wapforum.org//DTD//wml_1.1.xml">
<wml>
<card id="mail" title="Email" ordered="true" newcontext="false">
<p align="left">
<b>
<big>
Send me an email
</big>
</b>
</p>
<p align="left">
Your name:
</p>
<p align="left">
<input name="realname" type="text" emptyok="false"/>
</p>
<p align="left">
Your email address:
</p>
<p align="left">
<input name="eadd" type="text" emptyok="false"/>
</p>
<p align="left">
Message:
</p>
<p align="left">
 
<input name="message" type="text" emptyok="false"/>
</p>
<p align="left"> 
```

```
</p>
<do type="accept" label="Send" optional="false">
<go href="wapmail.php" method="get" sendreferer="false">
<postfield name="message" value="$(message)"/>
<postfield name="realname" value="$(realname)"/>
<postfield name="email" value="$(eadd)"/>
<postfield name="subject" value="WAP message"/>
</go>
</do>

</card>
</wml>
```

The PHP script will then send the email, and generate the resultant page:

```
<?php
$headers = "From: $email\n";

$headers = $headers . "Content-Type: text/html; charset=iso-8859-1\n";

reset ($HTTP_POST_VARS);
while (list ($key, $val) = each ($HTTP_POST_VARS)) {
$str = $str . "<BR>$key = $val ##";
}
$str = $str . "</tr></table>";
$str = $str . "<P>From: $email ($realname) <P>Refer: $HTTP_USER_AGENT";
$str = $str . " $REMOTE_ADDR " . gethostbyaddr($REMOTE_ADDR);

// format of mail is mail(to, subject, message, headers)

mail('fred@home', $subject, $str, $headers);


header("Content-Type:text/vnd.wap.wml\n\n");
' Generate new page
print "<?xml version='1.0'?>";
print "<!DOCTYPE wml PUBLIC '-//WAPFORUM//DTD WML 1.1//EN'
'http://www.wapforum.org/DTD/wml_1.1.xml'>";
print "<wml>";
print "<card id='default' title='Email'>";
print "<p align='center'>";
print "Your message has been set successfully. Thank you.";
print "</p>";
print "<do name='Bills' type='accept' label='Bills' optional='false'>";
print "<go href='index.wml' method='get' sendreferer='false'/>";
print "</do>";
print "</card>";
print "</wml>";
?>
```

H15.5   References

Some of the source code is based on a project by Bertrand Colas conducted at Napier University, 2001/2002.

I1   Multimedia

I1.1   Introduction

Human history has developed through the storage and distribution of information. Initially this involved writing and distributing material in a printed form such as with books, newspapers, leaflets and posters. One of the first changes to this type of distribution came when Ted Nelson, in 1960, published 'As We May Think', which was basically a description of a global document system, based on the **hypertext** principle. This paper inspired many people including Tim Bernes-Lee at CERN who, in the 1980s, actually developed the first prototype of the WWW. A major change has thus occurred over the last century where computers were used to distribute, store and present information.

Up until the end of the 1970s, computers systems could only really support text-based information, and were large, and difficult-to-use systems. The great change in computer systems came in 1981, when IBM released the PC. This was followed, in 1984, by the Apple Macintosh and in 1985 by the Commodore Amiga. The Macintosh and Amiga were based around GUIs and their applications used **WIMPs** (Windows, Icons, Menus and Pointers). These concepts allowed for proper multimedia. The PC would eventually catch up with the usage of Microsoft Windows, a GUI for the PC. Slowly the PC has supported multimedia, with the addition of graphical cards, audio cards and high-speed CD-ROM drives.

Before the integration of multimedia on computers, the media tended to be delivered in a non-computer-based way, such as through video, or audiotape delivery, or even over TV systems (such as used by the Open University). These systems did not provide much interaction between the trainer and the user. The new integrated multimedia systems supported the integration of audio, video, graphics and text. Initially the production of this material was difficult as there were very few development packages available, but over the 1990s, several companies, especially Macromedia and Adobe, produced development packages, which successfully integrated all the media into a single form.

Multimedia is the integration of many different media types into a single integrated unit. This normally involves converting the original media source, such as images, audio, video, text, and so on, into a digital form, so that it can be integrated into a digital package. This can then be delivered as a single entity. Figure I1.1 illustrates this. The text, video, sound and images are typically produced in a raw format. For example, video is normally available in either an NSTC, PAL or SECAM format. This can then be digitized into a digital form. This will give RGB and pixel data, arranged in frames. Next, the video can be compressed into a standard format, such as MPEG or AVI. Sound can be converted into MP-3, and images are typically converted into JPEG, GIF or PNG. The output from the media integration package depends on how the media will be delivered. The main forms are:

- **Stand-alone package**. This is where the media can be run without requiring any additional software viewer. Typically, it is compiled for the specific computer and operating system that it will run on.
- **Media player integration**. This involves converting the media into a form which can be played in a media player. Typical media players include Macromedia Shockwave Player (which plays DCR files), Macromedia Flash Player (which plays SWF files). The forms can also be integrated into a WWW browser (using the required browser plug-in).

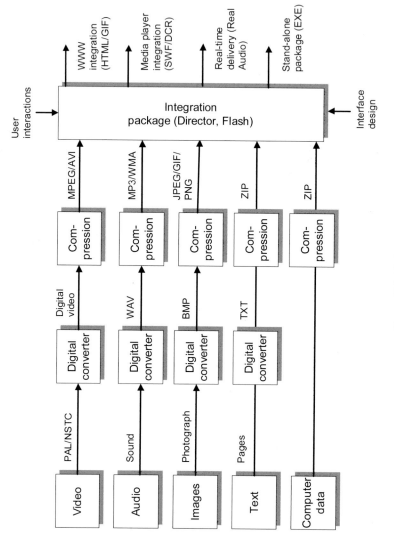

Figure I1.1 Media integration

- **WWW integration**. This involves converting the media into a form which can be viewed by a WWW browser. For this the media is converted into a number of HTML pages, which contain media content, such as AVI, MPEG, GIF, JPG and PNG files. Note that additional plug-ins are required for the delivery of AVI and MPEG movies. A typical player is Quicktime, which is available from Apple Computers.
- **Real-time delivery**. This involves delivering the media, in real time over a network connection. Sometimes this can involve the synchronization of images or video with sound. Typical real-time formats include the Real Audio (RA) format, and Windows Media Audio (WMA).

I1.1.1 Applications areas

The use of multimedia systems has increased over the past decade and the main developments are: education, tourism, retail and entertainment, corporate markets, will increase over the next few years. With education, there can be no replacement for the teacher, but multimedia has enhanced education with:

- Increased availability to information, especially over the Internet.
- Access to material produced by the best professionals. This can be backed-up by the teacher.
- Access to video conferencing and chat facilities which allows for remote conversations.
- Delivery of material in many different forms, such as video, audio, graphical and text. Multimedia allows for much richer content than traditional systems, and also provides faster linking of additional material.

A great increase of multimedia will come in the next few years, as more courses are delivered, and taken, on-line. This will provide for the delivery of educational material over the Internet, and will allow instant access to tutors. It will also support exams to be taken on-line, and instantly marked. Students will thus be able to pace their own training to the speed at which they learn best, rather than having to conform to college/university timetables.

Multimedia in tourism

In the past tourists relied on brochures, videotapes and books. Multimedia enhances this by providing a much richer form of presentation. Currently it is possible to view places around the world and sample them before traveling. For example, it is possible to get a 3D-view of the Coliseum in Rome, and to view in real time with web cameras. Tourists can also access information via kiosks in city streets, to get information, e.g. live shows to area maps. It is also possible to arrange bookings for travel and accommodation over the Internet.

Multimedia in retail

With retail, multimedia has allowed goods to be sampled remotely. This is especially useful if the media is already in a digital format. Areas, which have been successfully developed include the selling of books over the Internet (with Amazon.com), and the sale of music CDs (with Cdpoint.com). These have allowed users to view and review the content before they buy them. Also, as they do not need a shop to view the goods, and as there is no sale person involved, the supplier can ship the material at a much reduce cost. Over the next few years multimedia and WWW integration will allow for many more goods to be purchased over the Internet. For example, it is now possible to view a new car over the Internet, and then change its color, and view how it would look. It is even possible, to drive a simulator of the car, and get a feel of how it would drive, without ever visiting a showroom. In the past consumers would have had to visit shops or use mail order catalogues to sample material.

Corporate use

In the corporate market, the use of electronic mail has considerably increased commercial activities. Electronic mail now supports full multimedia with text, images, video and audio. There is also an increased amount of training conducted using multimedia. This saves time in travel, and in training costs. Video conferencing has allowed for remote meetings, but this still is not as widely used as the telephone.

Entertainment

The largest increase in the use of multimedia will come in the entertainment market. This will be in many forms. In TV, there is now a great amount of digital information sent along with the main content. This has even been expanded to support user interaction (especially in sports matches). Once TV is fully integrated with the Internet there will be scope for linking extra information from many sources. For cinema it is now possible to review films, and sample them before you book tickets, which can also be done on-line. Radio stations are also going on-line, and their content is being transmitted over the Internet. This allows radio stations to provide extra content, such as providing information on the songs, with their lyrics. Multimedia has improved many traditional forms of entertainment, such as:

- **Encyclopedias**. These are now fully interactive with video and sound.
- **DVDs**. Analogue videos are being replaced with DVDs for movies, as DVD supports improved graphics quality and also enhanced sound, such as surround sound and a special effects channel. They also allow users to view different scenes and angles, and support the integration of text and graphical data, alongside the video data.
- **Console games**. These have become more sophisticated, and it is even possible to play interactive games, over the Internet, with music and video.

I1.1.2 Conclusions

A key to the future will be the integration of multimedia with all forms for current delivery. This will include its integration into traditional systems, such as TV, radio and telephone. The future is likely to involve the integration of many different content sources into a single system, which is likely to be delivered over a single transmission source: the Internet. The WWW is now a global database of knowledge, and search engines make it easy to locate information, in a way that was never possible before. Unlike libraries, which tended to support printed material, this material is now available in many different forms, and can be easily integrated to produce a single entity.

I1.2   Multimedia development

Multimedia is not really a very good term for the creation, production and delivery of media content. Unfortunately, it has become a standard part of the IT vocabulary. Also many people still view it to be a single activity, but it actually involves many different skills from content design and media design, to software engineering and content delivery skills. For example many find it difficult to differentiate the creation of the content from its development as an integrated system. Many also cannot differentiate this development from the delivery of the material. Each of these stages is a definitive part of the process, and requires different skills at each stage. The stages might be:

- **Content creation**. At the creation phase there are normally expert users, who know how the system should operate, and who it is aimed at. For example, a French language teacher will know how to present a structured course in the teaching of French, for a certain level of knowledge. They may not know how the material would operate in a multimedia environment, but they can produce material in a form that could be used in this.
- **Content integration**. This is where IT skills are important, and normally involves integrating the content into a single package. As much as possible the developer must have communications with the content creators, and the delivery specialists.
- **Delivery**. This is an important stage as it involves delivering the content to the user's computer. Typically these days the delivery is over the Internet, or over a network, thus bandwidth is a major consideration. It is important that delivery issues are taken into account, before the decisions are taken on the design and development of the package.
- **Maintenance**. The material, once produced, must be kept up to date, and bugs fixed, and new material generated.

Just like software development, there is no defined way to develop multimedia. Each developed system will have its own aims; its own target audience; its own method of delivery, and its own special problems. The factors that typically affect the develop cycle include:

- **Aims of the content**. Different subject areas have differing requirements for the way that the content needs to be delivered. For example, a PhD student might require just a basic text-based document with simple line drawings for their research, but pre-school children would need a more graphically rich user interface, where text was replaced by pictures. The navigation would also be simpler.
- **Source content**. The source content can be available in a number of different formats, and it may have to be generated before the system was developed, or it may have to be produced after the system has been designed. Another major factor is the protection of the content against it being copied by others.
- **User system requirements**. This can have a great effect on the type of multimedia used, because it is no good at all to develop a totally graphical-based, animated system for a mobile computing device which has limited processing and memory capabilities. The operating system can also have a great effect on how the content is presented. It is extremely difficult to aim the requirements at every user, but market research will show the typical systems that the target user uses.
- **Compatibility**. This can be a major factor, for many reasons. If possible, the amount of development for different types of delivery should be minimized. Thus it is a great advantage to a developer if they can develop the same material for both CD-ROM delivery and for Internet delivery.
- **Delivery**. This is a major factor, and the delivery type should be defined by both the user, and the type of material. A multimedia system which has a great deal of video content will typically not cope well with a modem connection to the Internet. Thus CD-ROM would probably give better delivery. In addition, it is difficult to deliver ex-

ecutable programs over the Internet (and, in some case, they should not be trusted), and CD-ROM distribution makes this easier.

- **Maintainability**. This is an important factor for the long-term development of a multimedia product. It is unlikely that the product will ever be completely finished, as new material is often added to it, or bugs fixed. Thus, maintainability is an important factor. It does little good to develop a system, which is extremely difficult to add to, or to change in any way. A good example of this is in the Adobe PDF format. In this, a package known as Abode Acrobat can be used to convert from many types of documents, such as Word documents, to the PDF format. Acrobat can then be used to add navigation, movies, sound, menus, and so on. Unfortunately it is difficult to update the original material without starting from the beginning again (although there is a basic touch-up tool to make small changes). Thus, it is often better to choose a system which can easily update the material and reproduce the product. It is thus an advantage to make the media elements as small as possible, as a change in these will not have a great effect on the rest of the material.

- **Reusability**. This is important, especially when parts of the multimedia system can be used in other systems. If possible, content should be developed in a generic way, so that it can be easily modified so that it can be used again in another system. For example, a developer could develop a range of buttons, with associated interactions. If possible, the developer should design them so that they could be easily used in another system. This might involve creating a way of changing the color of the button, or the text, or the way that events occur on the buttons.

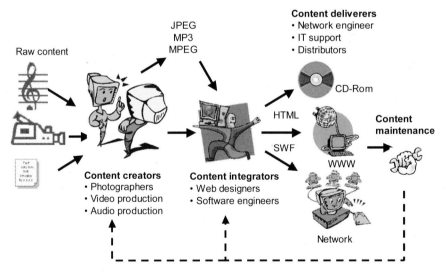

Figure I1.2 Content stages

I1.3 Content design and delivery

The stages of content development involve different types of people, with different skills. As much as possible the creators of the content should be kept up-to-date in the development of the project, as many software project fail, as the software designers have not received continual feedback from the actual people who have initiated the idea for the project, or how they use the product.

A good approach in the development of the multimedia is to setup two design teams. These should be small enough to be efficient (as often the larger the committee, the slower that the work will proceed). These would be:

- **Instructional design team**. The objectives of this team are to analyze, to design, to build and to evaluate the product. Typically, this team would be made up of content creators, such as graphics designers, and the idea generators. This is the main design team, and will feed ideas to the software design team. Representatives from the software design team should be part of this team, and should give the instructional team technical support for their ideas. This team will initially ask the software design team to produce prototypes which will be presented to the instructional design team, so that the instructional team can generate a design.

- **Software design team**. The objectives of this team are to prototype, to generate new ideas, to construct and code, and to test and evaluate the product. This team will be led by the instructional design team, and must report back to this team, as technical requirements should never overrule the aims of the product (unless the instructional team were to approve these). After the generation of initial prototypes, the instructional team will give outline designs for the product. These would be turned into a formal design specification by the software design team, which would be presented back to the instructional team, for their acceptance, or not. Once accepted the software design team can start to properly code and integrate the media. After this is complete they can feed differing versions to the instructional team, who would give feedback on their developments. Finally, the product would enter the test and evaluate phase.

Any failure in the project is likely to be shared by the two teams, rather than resting on an individual. A good approach is to formalize meetings of the two teams. For example, let us imagine that we have a language tool for primary school children. Initially the teams would be defined, and the list distributed to everyone. For example the instruction team could be:

Ms J. Goodie, French Teacher (Instructional Group Leader).
Mr M. Plode, Teacher, Design Department.
Mr R.Headingly, School Head.
Ms A. Bigwig, Legal Department, Local Authority.
Ms I.S. Techno, Multimedia Developer (Software Group Leader).
Ms A.N. Pupil, Senior Year Pupil.

This team should involve the main content creators (the teachers), and representatives of users of the system (the pupil). It also includes the School Head, who is likely to be able to make discussions on finance and resources. The representative from the Legal Department will help with copyright issues. In addition, the technical person (Ms Techno) is there to represent the Software Design team. Initially they would meet and define the main designs for the project; these would be fed to the software team, so that they can work on prototypes and the main design specifications. The software design team could be made up of:

Ms I.S. Techno, Multimedia Developer (Software Group Leader).
Ms J. Goodie, French Teacher (Instructional Group Leader).

Mr C. Plus, Software Developer.
Mr E.Ternet, IT Support.

This team includes someone from the instructional team, and will meet to discuss the ideas and the requirements from that team. The number of meetings of the teams depends on the project, but, in this case we could define:

- Formal instructional team meets every two weeks, to discuss documents and things like design details and content creation. An informal agenda is created for each meeting, and each meeting focuses on a specific aim.
- Software design team meets every two weeks, to discuss technical development. An informal agenda is created for each meeting, and each meeting focuses on a specific aim.
- Representatives from both teams meet every four weeks to discuss the progress. This meeting should have a formal agenda with documents and presentations tabled before the meeting, which are open to discussion. This meeting is fully minuted, and actions are put on people. Any major changes in the project are discussed at this meeting.

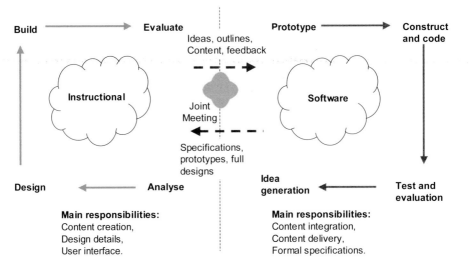

Figure I1.3 Content development teams

In most cases, the copyright of the original material should be preserved as much as possible. There does seem to be a focusing of multimedia material on integrating it with the WWW. Figure I1.4 shows an example of a possible flow of content in developing multimedia. If a WWW page is required the developer can simply use a WWW design package, such as Macromedia Dreamweaver or Microsoft FrontPage. The content, though, may have to be generated by another package such as Adobe Photoshop or Macromedia Flash. In many cases though the content must be protect against copying of the original source, thus packages such as Macromedia Flash and Macromedia Director can be used to protect this against copying. These packages also support enhanced user interaction, and excellent animation facilities. As the diagram shows the designer uses Flash and/or Director to produce SWF or DCR files, respectively. These can then either be integrated in a WWW page, or they can produce a stand-alone package, using Director. Flash is an excellent package in that it allows media to be broken into small parts, which can then be integrated in the whole system. Flash content is often known as a Flash movie. The actual design files for Flash and Director are stored with FLA and DIR extensions, respectively. These files are typically not distributed, and should be kept in a secure way, as they contain much of the original source content.

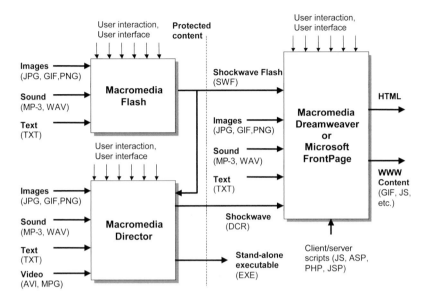

Figure I1.4 Typical media development

Macromedia Flash has many advantages, including:

- **Scaleable graphics**. Flash produces graphics which can be expanded or contracted without losing the definition of the graphics content. It does this by making the content vector based, rather than in a bitmapped format. Vector graphics are much more scaleable than bitmaps.
- **Streamed content**. Flash allows the content to be delivered in required stages. For example it is possible to transmit the parts of the content which the user needs to see first, and then load the rest in the background.
- **Timeline-based**. Each Flash movie is created along a timeline. This allows events within the animation to be synchronized. This is especially important when audio needs to be synchronized with video/images. This timeline-based system allows different movies to run at different speeds.
- **Optimized for the WWW**. Flash content is highly optimized for producing excellent graphics with the minimum amount of bandwidth required. This is because much of the graphics capabilities is available in the player, which plugs into the browser.
- **Scripted actions**. Flash content can contain actions on the elements of the content, such as mouse over events on graphics, or mouse down events on buttons.

Apart from Flash and Shockwave, the other main document format for protecting content is

Multimedia 1325

Acrobat PDF (Portable Document Format). With this, documents are converted into a form which can be protected against copying (such as from a copy-and-paste action), or protected against printing. As the document cannot be printed, it has better protection than a document in a paper form, as the document can be scanned, and then converted to text with an OCR (Optical Character Recognition) package. Many packages can now produce PDF documents, especially Adobe packages, and many have a plug-in to support it. The documents can either be displayed within the PDF Reader, or can be viewed within a browser with the required PDF Reader plug-in. PDF also has the advantage that it supports scaleable graphics, where the graphics (or text) can be zoomed-into without loosing any of the definition of the graphic (or text).

11.4   CD-ROMs

Apart from distribution over the Internet, CD-ROM technology is one of the most used technologies for distributing multimedia. The first use of CD-ROMs was in the distributed of audio, and has largely replaced phonograph distribution. This application provided a foundation for the development of CD-ROM technology into other areas, such as the distribution of computer data, and also in images and video. CD-ROM technology thus is now used to distribute virtually all types of digital data, such as computer data, video and audio.

11.4.1   CD-ROM technology

Analogue information can take on any value. Typical analogue values are the temperature of the room, air pressure, and so on. These analogue values can be difficult to store, and can be affected by noise. An improved method of storage is to covert the analogue information into a digital form, which is in the binary form of a '0' or a '1'. These binary digits can be easily stored on a CD-ROM with series of pits to represent the binary digits. For example a pit on the disk could represent a '0' and the lack of a pit could represent a '1'. To maximize the amount of storage a laser beam directed into the pit, and if the pit does not **exist**, it is **reflected** back. If a pit **exists**, the laser beam is absorbed into the pit, and **does not reflect** back.

The basic specification of CD-ROM is:

Diameter	120 mm (4.7 inch)
Thickness	1.2 mm[1]
Reflective coating	Aluminum
Reflective coating thickness	30μm[2]
Pit length	0.1μm
Pit depth	0.1μm
Track width	1.6μm
Protective coating	1.2 mm (this helps to focus the laser beam on the disk)

In audio CDs, one side contains the digital audio, the other side is typically used to print the CD label, and the aluminum coating gives the disk a silvered appearance.

---

[1] 1 mm is one thousandth of a meter

[2] 1 μm is one millionth of a meter

I1.4.2 CD-ROM specifications

The basic specification of CD's gives a data storage capacity of 650MB[3]. As the rate of stereo audio is transferred at a rate of approximately 150KB/sec, thus gives a maximum storage of about 72 minutes of stereo audio (650M÷150K÷60). The transfer rate for a standard CD-ROM is based on the transfer of audio data, which is around 150KB/sec[4]. This gives us our basic specification for a CD-ROM:

Storage capacity: 650MB
Stereo storage: 72 minutes
Standard transfer rate: 150KB/sec

After this standard was developed, it was then expanded to store computer data. In order for it to properly support video, the speed of the interface has gradually been increased, as a multiple of the basic rate. For example ×2 CD-ROM drive transfers at 300KB/sec, a ×8 CD-ROM drive transfers at 1200KB/sec, and a ×24 CD-ROM drive transfers at 3600KB/sec (3.6MB/sec).

On a PC, the IDE interface is typically used to connect an internal CD-ROM drive and the USB or printer port is used to connect an external CD-ROM drive. On an Apple Mac, the SCSI interface can be used to connect a CD-ROM drive, either internally or externally.

I1.4.3 CD-ROM standards

The standards for CD-ROM have been defined in a series of standards books. These define the media, the hardware, the operating system, file system and the software, and been developed mainly by Philips and Sony. The main standards books are:

Red book   World standard for audio CDs (**CD-DA**[5])
Yellow book Physical standard for CD-ROM[6] and **CD-ROM-XA** data formats
Green book   **CD-I**[7] data formats and operating systems (photographs)
White book   CD form for video
Orange book **CD-R/CD-E** for recordable and erasable disks
Blue book   These allow for multisessions (**CD-Enhanced, CD Extra, CD Plus**)

I1.4.4 DVD

The capacity of the standard CD-ROM is 650MB, which cannot properly support high-quality movies (which are typically over 2 hours long, and have five channels of high-quality audio). Thus a new format has been developed to support this: DVD (Digital Versatile Disks). These support the MPEG-2 video and audio formats, and give a capacity of several GBs of video and audio data. DVDs can also support computer data, and WWW links.

---

[3] MB is one million bytes

[4] KB/sec is one thousand bytes per second

[5] Compact Disc Digital Audio. Jointly developed by Philips and Sony and launched in October, 1982.

[6] Compact Disc-Read Only Memory. A standard for compact disc to be used as digital memory media for personal computers

[7] Compact Disk Interactive. Developed by Philips, designed to allow interactive multimedia applications to be run on a player attached to a television.

I1.4.5   CD-R/CD-RW

A CD-R (CD-Recordable) disk allows for data to be written to a CD disk. This data is written in the form of a session. Unfortunately, each session can take up to 14MB of data. CD-R's are now extremely popular, and are inexpensive to buy.

A CD-RW (CD-ReWriteable) allows a disk to be written many times, but it has a file format which is incompatible with standard CD-ROMs (ISO 9660). The formatting of a CD-RW can take hours, and it only leaves a data capacity of 430MB. These disks are not very popular, and are relatively expensive to purchase.

I1.4.6   File formats

On a CD, data is created in the form of sectors, which contain a number of bytes of data. The file system translates the physical (sector) view of a CD into a logical (files, directories) structure, and helps both computers and users locate files. The two main standards for file systems are ISO9660 and UDF. ISO9660 supports two different types of file names:

- **ISO9660.** This is the format which can be used on different platforms including DOS, Macintosh, OS/2, Windows and UNIX. Files and directories recorded to CD based on the ISO 9660 standard must meet the following (8+3) requirements:

    - o A file name may not contain more than eight alphanumeric characters and the underscore symbol [_].
    - o A file name extension may not contain more than three alphanumeric characters.
    - o A directory name may not contain more than eight alphanumeric characters and the underscore symbol [_].

- **Joliet.** This format allows file names which are up to 64 characters in length, including spaces. This is the default option and is used to record most CDs. Joliet also records the associated DOS-standard name (8+3 characters) for each file so that the CD may be read on DOS systems or earlier versions of Windows.

For example the filename:

```
Julies new file.psd
```

will appear as:

```
Julie~1.psd
```

in ISO9660 format. In an ISO 9960 format there are also a number of volume descriptors defined, such as:

- *System Name*: The operating system under which the application runs.
- *Volume Name*: This is the CD name that is displayed by your operating system when the CD is mounted.
- *Volume Set Name*: If the CD you are preparing is part of a set of CDs, every CD in the set may have an identical Volume Set Name, recorded in this field.

- *Publisher's Name*: Identifies the publisher of the CD.
- *Data Preparer's Name*: Records the name of author of the content of the CD.
- *Application Name*: Records the name of a particular application needed to access the data on the CD, if any.
- *Copyright File Name*: Authors can protect their work with a copyright notice stored in a file that must be placed in the root directory.
- *Abstract File Name*: This field records the name of a file stored in the root directory that describes the contents of the CD.
- *Bibliographic File Name*: This field stores the name of a file (which may be recorded in any directory) containing bibliographic information such as an ISBN number.
- *Date Fields*: There is a Volume Descriptor field for each of four dates (Creation, Modification, Expiration, Effective), in the format: year, month, day; hour, minute, second.

CD file formats for recordable CDs

Recordable CDs can either be written in a single session or as a multisession. The basic modes are:

- **Mode 1 (CDROM).** Used to write a single session disk. After writing, the disk cannot be written to again.
- **Mode 2 (CDROM XA).** This mode is used to write a multisession, and the disk can be written too many times, and are defined in the Blue Book. This type of disk cannot be read by a standard CD-ROM drive.

The method of storing ISO9660 data on a recordable is very efficient, thus a new standard has been developed to make the storage more efficient. This is Universal Disc Format (**UDF**). Which is endorsed by OSTA (the Optical Storage Technology Association) and is used with packet writing and other recordable optical disc technologies, such as DVD. The format of this can only be read with computer systems which can read UDF.

I1.4.7   CD-ROM applications

The two main classifications of CD-ROMs are:

- **Permanent**. With this type a disk is initially mastered, which is the process of creating a glass master from which CDs are reproduced in quantity. One mastered, many copies can then be made. These copies will be permanent, and cannot be re-written. Typically applications for this type of technology are music CDs, movie DVDs, and so on. The cost of creating the master is expensive, thus permanent CD-ROMs are typically only used for medium-scale to large-scale distributions of media. For large-scale distributions, the cost per disk is extremely inexpensive, typically just a few pence per disk.
- **Recordable**. These types of disks allow data to be written from a recordable drive. Typically applications of this are: data backup and small-scale distributions of media. The cost can be relatively expensive for medium and large-scale distributions, but in small-scale distribution the advantage of being able to create and update the CD within an organization overweigh the advantage of producing a master CD.

A major problem in the past has been that CD-ROM can be easily copied, either for music CD and with computer CDs. This is now being overcome with new encrypted CD-ROMs, which are almost impossible to copy.

I1.5   Audio components for multimedia

Speech and audio are normally in an analogue format. In order for them to be stored, analyzed or transmitted by a computer they must be digitized also, the analogue waveform must be sampled at a fixed rate. Typically, speech quality audio is sampled at 8,000 times per second and high quality audio is sampled at 44,100 samples per second. Each of these samples is converted into a digital form, with a given number of bits to define an analogue intensity. The greater the number of bits, the more accurate the digitized sample. CD audio uses 16 bits per sample; telephone uses 8 bits per sample. The output from the digitization process gives results in a raw file format such as WAV, this file format can be inefficient in its storage, such as that CD quality audio requires 10MB for every minute of stereo. Compact disks use the following parameters:

Sample rate:	44.1 kHz
Channels:	2 (stereo)
Bits per sample, per channel:	16
Levels per sample:	65,536
Total data rate (Mb/s):	1.4112

I1.5.1   Compressed audio

A more efficient method of storing or transmitting audio is to use an audio compression algorithm such as:

MP3   This format was developed by the Motion Picture Experts Group (MPEG). Almost all MPEG files are recorded in MPEG 1 or MPEG 3. This format is well known for its excellent compression and good sound quality. The quality of the conversion is normally defined by the converted bit rate. A rate of 128 kbps gives almost CD-like sound quality.

WAV   This was developed by Microsoft for the PC. It has become a standard on the Microsoft Windows operating systems. Many of the sounds produced by the Microsoft operating system are generated from WAV files. In general, WAV files support either 8-bit or 16-bit samples with either a stereo or mono format. It also supports a wide range of sampling rates.

AU   This format was developed by Sun Microsystems, and is comparable to the WAV format. It is mainly used with NeXT and SUN UNIX systems, and uses a format called the Sun u-law, which is an international compression standard. Like WAV files, it supports many sampling rates, of which the 8 kHz sampling rate is most common.

AIFF   This format is Audio Interchange File Format, and was developed by Apple. It is mainly used for Macintosh and cross-platform applications. AIFF can files can support 8-bit or 16-bit using mono or stereo sound. It is also capable of many different sampling rates.

A logical extension to the delivery of audio content is to use the Internet, and deliver the audio when required. This technology is named **streaming** audio. With this, a server sends out compressed audio data in a continuous steam, and the receive stores the incoming samples and plays them when required. If the rate of playing the audio is faster than the rate that it is being received, then the player will play the audio without any interruptions. Typically, an audio player will try to store (buffer) as many audio samples as possible before it starts, so that they can be used if the received rate becomes too slow. Thus, the concept of only ever listening to a radio station at the same time, as everyone else will disappear in the future. With streaming technology it is possible for each user to listen to the audio (and video) when they require.

Typical formats for streaming audio over the Internet are WMA (Windows Media Audio) and:

RA The Real Audio file format by Real Networks is used for streaming audio in real time over the Internet and is a popular audio format for streaming audio. This format is optimized for compression over low data bandwidth such as a standard 56 k modem.

The two main applications, which are used to receive streaming audio, are Windows media player and RealNetworks Realplayer.

I1.5.2 MIDI files

The MIDI (musical instrument digital interface) format is a standard interface between electronic instruments and music synthesizers. Software designed to compose and edit music usually provides input and output in the MIDI format. The MIDI format has several advantages over full digital sound files, in that it is much more compact, and can be easily edited. It allows for musical tracks to be easily combined. MIDI files can also be played in a Web browser. The main disadvantage of MIDI files is that some servers do not recognize them.

I1.5.3 File formats

Audio files have various file extensions, these include:

AU (UNIX)	.au and .snd
Audio Interchange File Format (AIFF)	.aif, .aifc, and .aiff
CD audio	.cda
DVD video	.vob
Intel Indeo video technology	.ivf
Moving Picture Experts Group (MPEG)	.mpeg, .mpg, .m1v, .mp2, .mpa, .mpe, .mp2v*, and .mpv2
MP3	.mp3 and .m3u
MIDI	.mid, .midi, and .rmi
Windows audio and video files	.avi and .wav
Windows Media audio and video files	.asf, .asx, .wax, .wm, .wma, .wmd, .wmv, .wvx, .wmp, and .wmx
Windows Media Player skins	.wmz and .wms

12 Databases and data storage

12.1 Introduction

Databases store information in an easy-to-access format. They have an increasing role in virtually every area of computing. Many WWW pages are now generated from a database, where content is added to the database, and the WWW page reads it to generate the WWW page. This allows for more dynamic content within WWW pages. For example, a database could contain a list of recommended WWW links, which were updated every hour. There may be many pages which use these links. Thus, a good approach is to design so that the links are generated from the database, which is updated hourly.

We have a great deal of information on us already in databases. For example, now it is possible to receive approval for a loan request in a matter of seconds. This is because there are databases around the Internet which contain much of your financial details, such as the number of times your have been late with your payments, your monthly salary, your current loan commitments, and so on. The loan application program thus goes and gathers the information on you and quickly generates a score which relates to your ability to pay back the loan. This type of approach is known as data mining where programs gather data on the user from several different sources. In the future, with data mining, it should be possible to determine many other things about a user, apart from their financial details. For example if a user purchases movie tickets on-line that a data-mining agent might determine the type of movie that the person preferred, and use this information for advertising new movie releases. This may lead to an increasing amount of personalization on WWW pages. For example if a person accessed amazon.com then, if the WWW browser knew the user, they would be greeted with a page which displayed the books that were recommended for that user, based on their interests. At one time, the user would have to enter these preferences, but in the future they may be generated automatically. A typical technique, these days, is to store user details on a database, such as their credit card number, bank details, and so on, so that when the user purchases something on-line, these details are automatically entered. This makes shopping on-line easier.

Databases can be organized in a flat format where everything was added as a record in the complete database. For example, a college could have a single database that contained staff details (**Lecturer**), then another database which contained all the modules on the courses (**Modules**), and another which had a database which contained the modules on a course (**Programme**). If would be inefficient to create a database for each of these, as the Programme database could use the modules defined in the Modules database. A relational database has the advantage that tables with records can be setup, and then the relationship between them can be defined. Figure 12.1 shows an example of a relational database with tables for Lecturer, Modules and Programme. The window below the main database window shows the relationship between the tables (this will be defined in more detail in the following sections).

The basic elements of a relational database are:

- **Record**. Databases are made up with a number of records which are a collection of data. For example the personal record for an individual could be that they are 42 years old (age), 2.2 meters tall (height), 57 kg heavy (weight) and that they're male (sex). This would constitute a personal record for an individual. A record can also be known as a row in a database.

- **Table**. In relational databases the table is one of the most fundamental elements of the database, and defines a particular category within the database (such as employees or sales stock). Figure I2.2 illustrates a Lecturer Table which is made up of a number of records (in rows), and a number of fields (in columns).
- **Field**. These are specific items of elements within a table. For example, in a table of personal details the fields could be age, height, weight and sex. An instance of these would constitute a record. Fields are represented in a database by a column within a table, as illustrated in Figure I2.2.
- **Item**. An item is the basic element that holds information in a database.

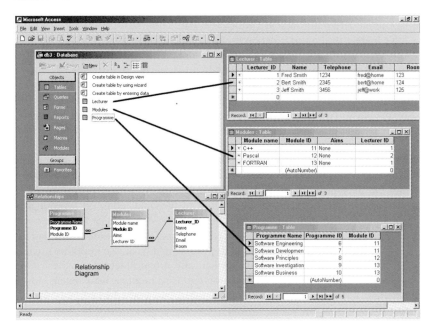

Figure I2.1 Example database

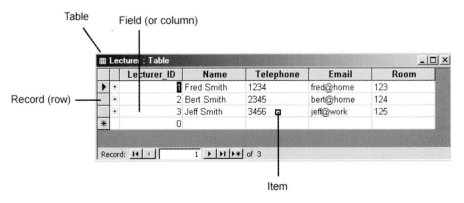

Figure I2.2 Database definitions

Relational databases bring information from different tables and use queries, forms and reports to present the information. These can be defined as follows:

- **Query**. This is a question about the data stored in multiple tables, or a request to perform an action on the data. This can provide the source of data for a form or report. Typically an SQL request is made to the database. Structured Query Language (SQL) is a language used in querying, updating, and managing relational databases.
- **Form**. This allows for taking actions or for entering, displaying, and editing data in fields.
- **Report**. This produces formatted information for displaying the results of database queries. Examples might be to produce monthly sales figures, or a weekly stock control report.

In order to use a relational database, each table must contain a primary key which uniquely identifies each record stored in the table. For example in Figure I2.2 the Lecturer_ID code is defined as the primary key for the Lecturers table.

I2.2   Database creation steps

The steps in designing a database should include:

- **Define the aims**. To be able to produce a well-designed database it is important to properly define the main purpose of the database. If possible, gather as much information on the required subject areas which will define the tables, and the information to be stored in each of the tables (the fields). If possible, determine the data types of the information to be stored in the fields (such as numeric, text, currency, and so on).
- **Determine tables**. In this step the main subjects should be defined a tables. These should not relate to the information that is required for reports, but should be a structured approach to the data. There should be no duplication of information in a table, and between tables. A table should thus be a flat-file structure. When one piece of information is stored, it should only be stored in the one table, and other tables can refer to this. Each table should only contain information on the things that are required to store in that table. For example, personal data on an individual would be stored in one table, and their scores for their sporting activities would be stored in another table. This would allow the sports scores to be easily deleted without affecting the personal details.
- **Determine fields**. After each of the tables have been determined, the next task is to define the fields in the table. For example, a customer table might have fields for company name (name), company address (address), company city (city), company telephone number (telephone), and so on. If possible, store the data in the smallest logical part as this makes it easier to differential data. For example, the address field could be split into: number of street (street_no), street name (street_name), street area (street_area). This would allow someone to search for just a street name, and ignore the street number.
- **Define primary keys**. This involves identifying the field or fields with unique values in each record. This is important as they provide connections between separate tables, as uniquely identifies each individual record in the table.
- **Define relationships between tables**. Once the tables and primary keys have been defined, it is then necessary to define who the tables are inter-related, in order to build the

data in a meaningful way.

- **Enter data and create database objects**. This involves actually entering the data in the records, and creating the objects which might be required (such as queries, forms, reports, and so on).

Of course, at every stage the design should be refined, so that errors can be minimized. If possible prototypes of part of the database should be created in order to determine if the database achieves the required aims.

I2.3   Relationships

After building tables, relationships allow the data to build back into a meaningful form. In the previous example, there were three tables: Lecturer, Module and Programme. Each module has a module leader which is defined in the Lecturer database, and each Programme has modules which are defined in the Module database. Thus, there is a relationship between the Module table and the Lecturer table, and one between the Programme table and the Module table. A relationship works by matching data in key fields. Two things are common:

- Fields normally have the **same name** in both tables.
- Fields are typically a **primary key** from one table, which provides a unique identifier for each record, and a **foreign key** in the other table. For example, in the Module database the Module ID is the primary key as this is the place that stores the module ID data, while the Module ID field in the Programme table will be the foreign key, as it links to the primary key, which is in the Module table.

There are three main types of relationships between tables:

- **One-to-many relationship**. This is the most common type of relationship, and relates to when there is one matching record in one table, which can link to another table with many matching records. For example Table A can have many matching records with Table B, but there is only one matching from a record in Table B to Table A. For example there is a one-to-many relationship from the Module database to the Lecturer database, as each module can link to many possible lecturers, but there will only be one actually link from a lecturer to a module. A one-to-many relationship is created if only one of the related fields is a primary key.
- **Many-to-many relationship**. In this case, a record in Table A can have many matching records in Table B, and a record in Table B can have many matching records in Table A. A many-to-many relationship uses a third table (called a junction table) whose primary key consists of two fields, which are the foreign keys from both Tables A and B. Thus a any-to-many relationship is constructed with two one-to-many relationships with a third table.
- **One-to-one relationship**. This is the least common case, and relates to when a record in Table A can only have one matching record in Table B, and each record in Table B can only have one matching record in Table A. A one-to-one relationship is created if both of the related fields are primary keys.

I2.4   SQL query

An SQL queries allow for the database to be interrogated with a with an SQL statement. Typical SQL queries are:

- SELECT. Select fields from a table or several tables.
- WHERE. Criteria for selection that determine the rows to be retrieved.
- FROM. Tables from which to field
- GROUP BY. Groups records.
- HAVING. Used by GROUP BY to define how the groups are grouped.
- ORDER BY. Criteria for ordering.

I2.4.1   SELECT

A typical SQL query is to select information from several tables. For example to select all the fields from the Modules table:

```
SELECT *
FROM [Module marks]
```

The * represents the wildcard, where all the fields are read, and the square brackets are used if there is a space between words in a field (or table). To just retrieve one field the following could be used:

```
SELECT [Module results] FROM Modules
```

Name	Module result
Buchanan, Bill	99
Fair, Alan	54
Greig, Sam	21
Martin, Bill	62
Smith, Bert	46
Smith, Fred	50
	0

I2.4.2   WHERE clause

The WHERE clause is used to locate records which match a certain criteria, and is added to the end of a SELECT query. For example, to find all the modules with a mark of over 50 (from the Mark field of the Module marks table):

```
SELECT *
FROM [Module marks]
WHERE [Module result]>=50;
```

Name	Module result
Smith, Fred	50
Buchanan, Bill	99
Martin, Bill	62
Fair, Alan	54
	0

The operators that can be used with WHERE are < (less than), > (greater than), <= (less than or equal to), >= (greater than or equal to), = (equal to), <> (not equal to), or Like. The Like operator can be used to match string patterns. Typical examples are:

```
SELECT *
FROM [Module marks]
WHERE [Name] Like 'S*';
```

Which will list all the names in the Name field which start with the letter 'S', and followed

Name	Module result
Smith, Bert	46
Smith, Fred	50
	0

and any other character sequence. The '?' character is used to signify any single character. A range of characters is signified by a hyphen, and enclosed within square brackets. For example:

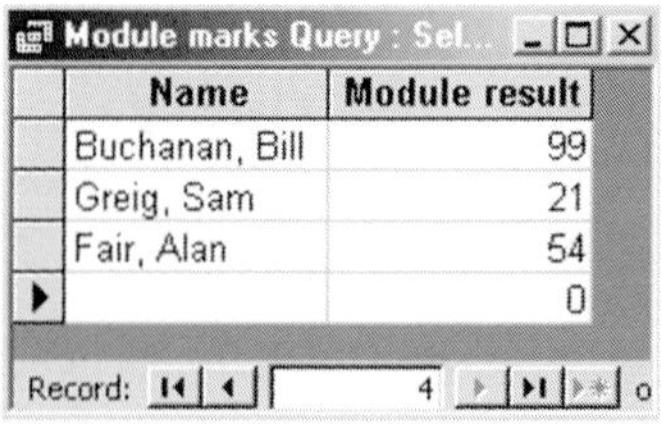

```
SELECT *
FROM [Module marks]
WHERE ((([Module marks].Name) Like '[A-G]*');
```

Which will find all the names beginning with characters from 'A' to 'G' in the Names field.

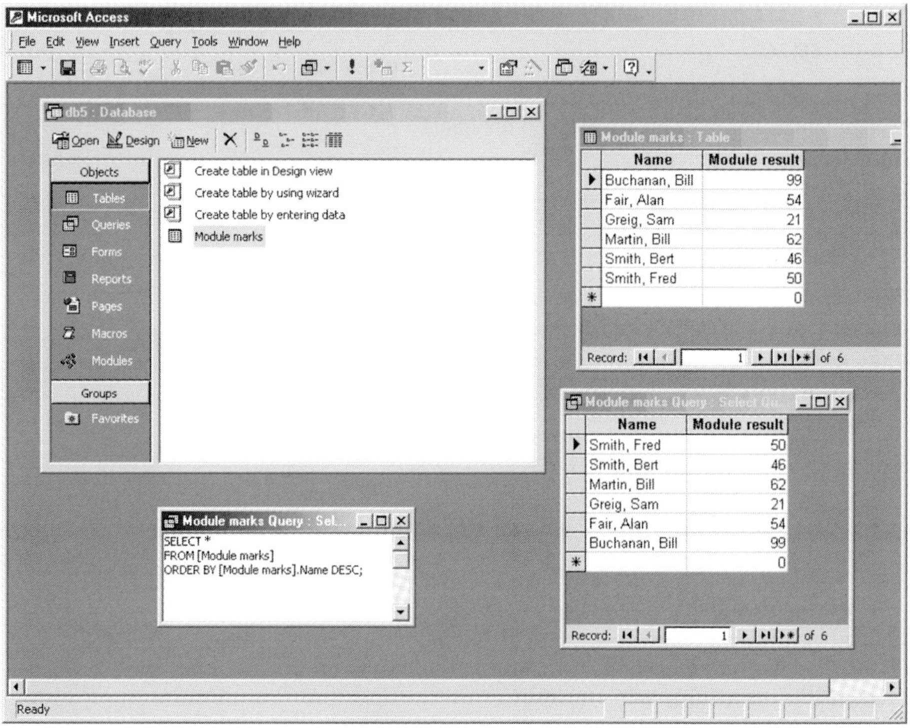

Figure I2.3 Example query

I2.4.3 ORDER BY clause

The ORDER BY clause is used to arrange the results of a query. The typical format is:

```
SELECT * FROM TableName ORDER BY field ASC
SELECT * FROM TableName ORDER BY field DESC
```

Where ASC is to order in ascending order, and DESC is for descending order. So, for example, if we wanted to order the marks from the database in descending order of name (where Name is a field of Module marks), then:

```
SELECT * FROM  [Module marks] ORDER BY Name DESC
```

Figure I2.3 shows an example of a query in Microsoft Access. The table for the marks table [Module marks] is shown in the top left hand window, and the query is shown in the bottom left hand window. In this case the query is:

```
SELECT *
FROM [Module marks]
ORDER BY [name] DESC;
```

The result of the query is shown in the bottom right-hand window. It can be seen that it has put Smith, Fred at the top of the list, followed by Smith, Bert.

I2.4.4 INNER JOIN

This `INNER JOIN` is used to merge multiple tables together so that the merged tables can be searched. The standard format is:

`SELECT * FROM` *Table1* `INNER JOIN` *Table2* `ON` *Table1.field* = *Table2.field*

Where the `ON` part specifies the fields from each table that should be compared to determine which records will be selected. For example, if we add a new table named Details to the previous example, and then add the following records:

Name	Matriculation Number
Buchanan, Bill	1
Martin, Bill	2

Then to merge the search for the Module marks and Details database, we could do the following:

```
SELECT *
FROM [Module marks] INNER JOIN Details ON [Module marks].Name =
Details.Name;
```

The result is shown in Figure I2.4.

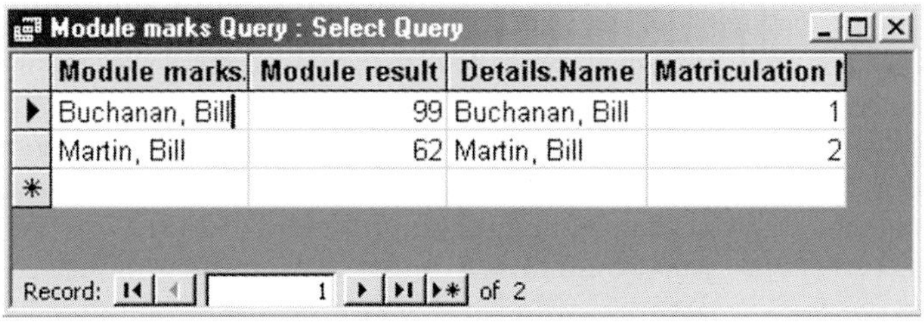
Module marks Query : Select Query

Module marks.	Module result	Details.Name	Matriculation N
Buchanan, Bill	99	Buchanan, Bill	1
Martin, Bill	62	Martin, Bill	2

Record: 1 of 2

Figure I2.4 Example query

12.5 Data Protection

The increasing usage of databases causes a great deal of worry for individuals. For example, what is someone typed in your zip/code and house number instead of someone else who was on a credit black list. What could you do once the data was on the database, as this data could be sent around the world in seconds? Fortunately, there are laws on what can be done with databases, such as the from the European Data Protection and Telecoms Protection Directives, which states:

- That the data is processed fairly and lawfully.
- That the data is collected for specific, explicit and legitimate purposes.
- That the data is adequate, relevant and not excessive in relation to the processes for which they are collected and/or processed.
- That the data is accurate and, where necessary, kept up-to-date.
- That the data is kept in a form which permits identification of data subjects for no longer than is necessary.
- That appropriate technical and organizational measures are taken by the data controller to protect personal data against accidental or unlawful destruction or loss, etc.
- That where the data controller chooses a data processor to process personal data for him, he must take appropriate measures to ensure that the data processor complies with the obligations of data controller.
- That the transfer of personal data to a country outside the EEA (the 15 member states of the EU plus Iceland, Norway and Liechtenstein) may take place only if the country in question ensures an adequate level of protection or there are appropriate contractual arrangements in place or the data subjects have given consent.

And individuals have the following rights:

- The right to information concerning the personal data held about them by a data controller.
- The alteration of personal data held by controllers where such personal data is incorrect.

In addition, special conditions are made for personal data which on racial or ethnic origin, political options, religious or philosophical beliefs, trade union membership, and information concerning the health of those still alive. For these areas individual must give explicit permission for the data to be used for other purposes. Thus, a company who wants to view the medical records of an individual would have to get the permission of the individual before they could do this.

Of course, at one time this was easy to control, as request for data were made via the postal service. These days, data can be transferred from one place to another within a fraction of a second, and transferring around the world in seconds. Thus, it is important that electronic data is kept in a secure form, which cannot be tampered with, especially personal data. As much as possible databases with personal data should be protected by passwords, firewalls, and all the other secure methods that were discussed in a previous chapter. When the data is transmitted over the Internet, it must be encrypted, as TCP/IP allows any listener to view the data. Any breaches in security can leave the organization responsible, and they could receive a heavy fine.

Any organization which does business in the EU must adhere to the following:

- Provide clear and concise notice for the purpose for which the data is being collected, and any third parties which may share the data.
- Offer the opportunity to choose whether and how personal information is used or disclosed to third parties.
- Enforce mechanisms that allow, at a minimum, independent complaint procedures.

The seven rules of providing safe data can be summarized as:

- **Notice**. This should be given about the reasons for the data collect.
- **Choice**. This gives individuals the choice as to whether they want their data collected, or not.
- **Onward transfer**. This gives individuals the choice as to whether they want the data to be forwarded to third parties, or not.
- **Access**. This gives individuals the right to access any data which the organization has on them.
- **Security**. The data must be kept securely.
- **Data integrity**. The data must be correct, and up-to-date.
- **Enforcement**. There must be enforcement procedures for complaints.

12.6 Personalization and Data Mining

An increasing concept is personalization, where the WWW pages are designed especially for the user. The information to generate these is contained in databases. This personalization can either be:

- **Implicit personalization**. With this the pages are designed using the user's personal preferences. A good example of this is My Yahoo and MSN which allow the user to design the WWW page for their preferences, such as the news articles that they would like on the page, the stocks that they would like to view, and so on.
- **Explicit personalization**. With this the pages are designed using data from the user's behaviors, and occurs automatically without the user have any direct influence on the choices. A good example of this is Amazon's book recommendation service which offers customers books based on the books that they have purchased in the past.

This personalization has many advantages. A good example is Amazon's One Click service which allows the user's credit card details to be held in a secure manner, and used every time that the user requires to purchase a book. Users could also benefit from being offered products that another user with a similar profile has bought.

For organizations, there is also an increased amount of targeted marketing, where complimentary services can be offered, such as a company which gives a holiday book, might also provide travel insurance to the user. In addition, marketing can be targeted at specific users, rather than, at present, with blanket marketing. Most users now ignore the advertising banners which appear at the top of many WWW pages. This database approach also leads to savings in WWW development, as template pages are produced, and the content for these are generated from the database. With a non-database driven system, the pages must be coded for every different type of page. Changes in products can also be quickly updated, as it only requires a single change to the database, rather than over many pages.

Examples of personalization include:

- **Customized user interface**. This could be with fonts, colors, layout, and structure.
- **Stimuli**. This could be related to the way that the content is delivered, such as differing ways of delivering content using images, video or audio.
- **Personalized content**. This allows the user to select the types of content they wish to receive (such as My Yahoo), such as which providing content on news, sports, events, and so on.
- **Personalized services**. This would allow registered users more access to services than a guest user.
- **Remembering details**. This allows the details of the user to be stored. Many sites now remember the name of the person who is accessing the site. These details are typically stored as a text file, called a cookie, on the users computer. When the user goes back to the site, the cookie is loaded back, and the details of the site can be remembered. Secure information, such as credit card details will be stored on a secure database.
- **Match services or products**. Services can be exactly matched to the user's preferences.
- **Pre-emptive customer service**. With this organizations can predict the requirements of the user, such as providing a graduation gown service in the month of June in the year that they graduate from college.
- **Product suggestions**. This is based on products that the user has bought in the past, or ones that similar users have purchased.
- **Cater for individual needs**. This caters for special needs that only apply for a few customers.

A good example of personalization is on the Dell.com WWW site (see Figure I2.4). With this the user enters the system service tag (or express service code) of their computer and the WWW site generates pages which relate specifically to the product. This allows Dell to provide details of software downloads, hardware updates, and so on, specifically for the computer. This overcomes one of the most annoying features when trying to find the correct documentation and software downloads for a specific product. It also allows Dell to quickly target specific products for bug fixes, and product updates.

The Dell database also keeps track of the complete history of a product, as the service tag is a unique code. This is shown as a text code, and also as a bar code, from which the servicing department can easily update and retrieve data on the system. The database knows the specification of the computer, and when it was shipped from Dell. It will also track the product and stores details of its operating system, its specification, and so on. These provide important information for the Dell Support team, and make it easier for them to make the correct decisions in providing help. Database systems are even used to track a product that is being fixed, as the user can contact Dell, and they are able to track the actually location of the system, and its current status.

An example of a Dell cookie is (stored as user@dell.txt):

```
SITESERVER
ID=e4f7cb198cb4880753345da5a68f6d37
dell.com/
642859008
31887777
2953433472
29419968
*
```

WELCOME TO SUPPORT.EURO.D**⊄**LL.COM

Your System Information

Model: **Inspiron 7000**
Processor: PENTIUM II 400 NB DIX MMC2

System Service Tag: **N7TF3**
Express Service Code: **38995887**

System Ship Date: **28/7/1999**

Support News & Highlights

▷ **Dell Hints & Tips** **NEW!**

Quick hints and tips for all your
computing and technology needs.

▷ **Dell Inspiron Newsletters**

▷ **Enhanced OnLine Order Status**

Please try out the new version of
OnLine Order Status. You will find
many changes and new features that
should help you to locate and receive
your order status more easily. If you
would like to receive further
information about these things
please click on new features.

▷ **Online Support Press & Reviews**

Dell was recently named
one of the winners of
the **1999 Ten Best Web
Support Sites** from **The
Association of Support
Professionals**.

This national
organization focuses on
support trends in the
industry and hosts
ongoing regional

Support Tools

Fix-It

Resolve hardware and software issues
with your Dell system.

▷ **Ask Dudley!**
▷ **Dell Knowledge Base Documents**
▷ **Your System Documentation**
▷ **more . . .**

Downloads

Download files to update the software
on your Dell system.

▷ **All Files For Your System**
▷ **Advanced Search**
▷ **FTP**
▷ **Y2K (Year 2000) Compliance**

Communicate

Interact with Dell technicians or other
Dell customers.

▷ **DellTalk**
▷ **E-Mail Dell**
▷ **more . . .**

Customer Services

Get non-technical assistance with your
order or account.

▷ **Order Status**
▷ **OrderWatch**
▷ **Factory Phases**
▷ **more . . .**

Figure I2.4 Dell.com personalized site

I2.6.1 Cookies or remote storage of details

The personalization can be achieved in number of ways, from simple cookies, which are stored on the users computer. Cookies are simple text files
(typically stored as TXT files in the WINDOWS\COOKIES folder on Microsoft Windows), and will contain relevant details on the user, and the any of
their preferences. As these are text files, they cannot do any damage to the
local computer. Sometimes users delete these cookies, and all the previous information is lost, and must thus re-register for the system to be
able to store their details. Other system store details of the user on the
server, and this allows the user to move around the Internet and still get
access to their logged data. A good example of this is MSN Messenger
which allows the user to login with a passport, and their contacts, and

other data is downloaded from the server. This allows the user to read their e-mail or contact the buddies from any location
on the Internet. As the users details
and preferences (such as where
they live, and their favorite links)
are stored on a server, they can't be deleted when they erase the cookies on the own computer. Unfortunately the logon process can be quite time consuming, as the program must
contact the server, which is likely to be processing many other logins. Problems can also
occur when the server goes down, as users will not be able to login. These types of servers

Databases and data storage 1343

are targets for DOS (denial-of-service) attacks, and can be made to slow down their processing, if they have to respond to too many logins, at a time.

With cookies the data stored can involve:

- **User profile**. This would typically store details of the user, such as their common name, date of birth, and so on. This could also store the user's login name and password (obviously this would not be shown in the cookie in a text form, and will be encoded in some way, so that the user's login and password details cannot be viewed from their cookies.
- **Session details**. This would store the date and time that the user last accessed the site, and the time they have spent there.
- **Customer identification**. This might contain a unique customer identification, which can be used to match-up with the organization's database entry.
- **Advertising profiles**. This typically defines the adverts that have already been displayed. For example many sites show an initial 'flash' screen which is useful initially to present a good image for the organization, but should not be displayed again, the user has already seen it. If the user has viewed it, then the cookie stores this information, so that it will not be displayed again (obviously if they were to delete the cookie, it would appear again).

As cookies are just simple text files, they cannot pass information on a user's computer, other than the information contained within the cookie. In addition, the cookie generated by a WWW site cannot be used by another other WWW, as they can only be used by the WWW site that created it. Thus, cookies cannot be used to track users around the Internet. The greatest drawback with cookies is that users typically do not get the opportunity as to whether they want the cookie stored to their local disk, or not.

An example of the usage of centralized market information is DoubleClick, who specialize in generating banner advertisements which are aimed at specific users. With this companies who subscribe to DoubleClick, have a cookie request from DoubleClick on their page. If the user has an existing one it is read for the user's details (otherwise a new one is generated). As DoubleClick has many organizations subscribing to it, they can search for the types of sites that the user has most frequently accessed. The user will then receive a targeted banner advertisement which is most relevant to them. Over time the advertising will become more focused as DoubleClick learn more about the user. Note all the cookies will be sent and received by DoubleClick, and not by the organization that subscribed to them.

12.6.2   Data warehousing

Data warehousing is a method which stored vast quantities of raw data, such as one generated from logs files. This data can then be prepared and reformatting for data mining process, which will try to create meaningful information from the raw data. This is similar to traditional paper-based storage, but it is obviously easier to stored large amounts of electronic data in a small physical space. For example, exam papers could be marked to get the final exam mark. The raw data for this would be the actual exam papers. This data could be analyzed for the average number of words per question, or the average mark for each question, or the number of pages used, and so on. With the raw data, it is possible to analyze the data in many different ways, and find new insights on it. Without the raw data, it is often difficult to run different analyses. Another example relates to car sales. With the raw data on car sales, it would be possible to determine the percentage of people within a certain street that bought red cars, or the number of people in a city that bought a blue, 2000cc car, or the number of people with a surname that begun with a letter 'C', that bought a Ford van. All this data in warehouses will make marketing more refined in the future.

There is obviously a very fine line between personalization and personal intrusion, and the collection of data must comply with current laws. Unfortunately, many data collection programs confuse the user by displaying great deals of text, for which the user is asked to read, and then agree to. Most users now, typically, just click the accept button without even bothering to read the agreement statement. For example, when was the last time that someone actually read the license agreement for a software program that they had just bought?

Data mining methods include:

- **Anonymous profile data**. This is generated whenever a user contacts a site, and might contain the network address (IP address), domain name, ISP provider, WWW browser version, and so on.
- **Cookies**. This provides information on the user.
- **Monitoring newsgroups and chat rooms**. This can used to determine information on the user. For example if the user subscribes to many job related newsgroups, then there is a good chance that the user is actively looking for another job.
- **Self-divulgence of information for a purchase**. This is data that is completed when purchasing a product.
- **Self-divulgence of information for free merchandise**. This typically related to on-line prize draws, where the user completes a form, in order to win a prize or receive a free gift.
- **Self-divulgence of information to access a web site**. This is where the user subscribes to a WWW site, and fills-in a form.

A registration form is an excellent method for an organization to get user data, and is an opportunity for the organization to ask questions about the user, in which they could use for marketing purposes. For example, how many times have you been asked if you where male or female when you registered for a WWW site? It should not matter to the registration if you were male or female. So why do they ask? For marketing and data mining purposes. This form of data mining is **explicit**, where the user actually knows that there data is being stored. Many users do not like this form of data mining, as they feel that it is obtrusive. In newer form of data mining is implicit, where the user does not know that they are being monitored for their usage patterns. These include cookies, but WWW sites can also monitor how the user moves through a site, and the pages that they are most likely to spend time with. For example if the user on a bank site spends more time looking at the corporate page, then the may possibly be interested either in buying stocks in the company, or they are looking for a job with them.

Future technologies may include **spyware**. With these WWW pages code contains graphics files which are invisible to the user (as they may only contain a few pixels), but are resident on a data mining server. When the page is loaded the data mining server is contacted, and the details of the access can be logged. This will give details of where the user is located, their network address, their browser details, and so on. This could also be applied to e-mails, which contain graphics which are contained on data mining services. The server can then log the accesses to the graphics, and thus log when the e-mail was read, and from which location.

12.7 Examples

12.7.1 ASP interface to a Microsoft Access database

The first part of the code reads the IP address of the user, and then asks for their e-mail address. After they submit their details through a submit button, the xt_mail.asp file is called.

```
<% ip = Request.ServerVariables("REMOTE_ADDR") %>
<p>Enter your email address in the database (<%=ip%>) </p>
<form method="post" action="xt_email.asp">
<input type="text" name="EmailAddr">
<input type="hidden" name="IpAddr" value="<%=ip%>">
<input type="hidden" name="Day" value="<%=now%>">
<input type="submit" value="Submit" name="submit2">
<input type="reset" value="Reset" name="reset">
</form>
```

The xt_mail.asp file is given next. It opens the database with a full pathname, and then adds the e-mail address, IP address, and the current day.

```
<%
' File name is xt_mail.asp
'Create a connection to our database using a fileless dsn
Response.Buffer = true
dim cnn,rst
set cnn = Server.CreateObject("ADODB.Connection")
set rst = Server.CreateObject("ADODB.RecordSet")
cnn.Open "driver={Microsoft Access Driver
(*.mdb)};;DBQ=C:\Inetpub\wwwroot\staff\bill\email.mdb;"
sqltext = "SELECT * FROM email"
rst.Open sqltext,cnn,3,3

'Server Side form validation to keep our database clean
dim email,ip,day
addr = Request.Form("EmailAddr")
ip = Request.Form("IpAddr")
day = Request.Form("Day")

if addr = "" then
error = "You have not entered an email address."
Response.Write error
Response.End
end if

'If we pass through validation then store the information in the db
rst.AddNew
rst("EmailAddr") = addr
rst("IpAddr") = ip
rst("Date") = day
rst.update
'Lets redirect the user back to where they came from
Response.Redirect "user_details"
%>
```

Finally the database can be read back with the following:

```
<%
Dim szDSN, szSQL, rstData, intFields
' -- Specify the database to connect to via ODBC
' -- Use an existing data source name
```

```
'szDSN = "DSN=email"
' -- OR
' -- You can also use a DSN-less connection by providing the driver and data-
base
szDSN = "Driver=Microsoft Access Driver
(*.mdb);DBQ=C:\Inetpub\wwwroot\staff\bill\email.mdb"

' -- Create an ADO Recordset object
Set rstData = Server.CreateObject("ADODB.Recordset")

' -- Supply a SQL statement to query by
szSQL = "SELECT * FROM email"

' -- Execute the query on the data source
rstData.Open szSQL, szDSN

' -- Draw a table
Response.Write "<P><TABLE BORDER=1>" & vbCrLf
Response.Write "<TR>" & vbCrLf

' -- Make a table column for each field in the query
For intFields = 0 to rstData.Fields.Count - 1
Response.Write "<TD BGCOLOR=""#CCCCCC""><B>" & rstData.Fields(intFields).Name &
"</B></TD>" & vbCrLf
Next

Response.Write "</TR>" & vbCrLf

' -- Loop through the recordset and make a new row for each record
Do While Not rstData.EOF
Response.Write "<TR>" & vbCrLf
' -- Display the value for each field in the query
For intFields = 0 to rstData.Fields.Count - 1
Response.Write "<TD>" & rstData.Fields(intFields).Value & "</TD>" & vbCrLf
Next

Response.Write "</TR>" & vbCrLf
' -- Go to the next record
rstData.MoveNext
Loop
Response.Write "</TABLE>" & vbCrLf
' -- Clean up
Set rstData = Nothing

%>
```

12.8   SQL reference

The following gives a basic outline of the main SQL statements:

CREATE TABLE

The CREATE TABLE is used to create a new table in the database. The name of the table is defined after the CREATE TABLE part, followed by the fields in the table, separated by commas. For example to create a table named mytab in the database, with fields from matriculation (8 digits), name (up to 255 characters) and fees (a floating-point value with 2 decimal places):
 	
`CREATE TABLE mytab`
`(`
`    matriculation INT(8),`

```
      name CHAR(255),
      fees FLOAT(9,2)
)
```

INSERT

The INSERT statement allows records to be added to a table. It uses the INTO clause to define the table that the records are to be added to, and the VALUES cause to define their values. An example is:

```
INSERT INTO mytab (matriculation, fees) VALUES (12345678, 1200.10)
```

UPDATE

The UPDATE statement modifies data in the database. The name of the table is defined after UPDATE, followed by the SET clause which indicates the field to be updated, and the WHERE cause which defines the data to be modified. An example is:

```
UPDATE mytab SET fees = 2200.00 WHERE matriculation = 12345678
```

SELECT

The SELECT statement allows data to be retrieved from the data. The names of the fields which the data is required from are specified, the FROM clause defines the table that the data is taken from, and the WHERE clause specifies where the data to be taken from. It returns data in a table format (which is often called a result set). An example is:

```
SELECT matriculation,name FROM mytab WHERE fees>100.00
```

DELETE

The DELETE statement removes data from a database. It uses the FROM clause to define the table and the WHERE clause to define the conditions for the data to be deleted. An example is:

```
DELETE FROM mytab WHERE fees<100.00
```

12.8.1   PHP interface to a MySQL database

The first part creates a table in an existing database:

```
<?php
/* Data of SQL-server */
$server= "db.myserver.co.uk"; /* Address of server */
$user= "myuser";               /* FTP-username */
$password= "mypassword";       /* FTP-Password */
$database= "dbname";           /* name of database */
$table= "datatest";            /* Name of table, you can select that */

/* Accessing the server and creating the table */
MYSQL_CONNECT($server, $user, $password) or die (
        "<H3>Server unreachable</H3>");
MYSQL_SELECT_DB($database) or die ( "<H3>database not existent</H3>");
$result=MYSQL_QUERY( "CREATE TABLE $table (
name varchar(25),email varchar(25))");

print "Result is $result";
/* Terminate SQL connection*/
MYSQL_CLOSE();
```

```
?>
```

To add a record:

```php
<?
/* Data of SQL-server */
$server= "db.myserver.co.uk"; /* Address of server */
$user= "myuser";              /* FTP-username */
$password= "mypassword";      /* FTP-Password */
$database= "dbname";          /* name of database */
$table= "datatest";           /* Name of table, you can select that */

/* Accessing SQL-server */
MYSQL_CONNECT($server, $user, $password) or die (
    "<H3>Server unreachable</H3>");
MYSQL_SELECT_DB($database) or die ( "<H3>Database non existent</H3>");

MYSQL_QUERY( "INSERT INTO $table VALUES('Fred','fred@home.com')");
MYSQL_QUERY( "INSERT INTO $table VALUES('Bert','bert@myplace.com')");

/* Display number of entries */
$query="SELECT * FROM $table";
$result = MYSQL_QUERY($query);

/* How many of these users are there? */
$number = MYSQL_NUMROWS($result);

if ($number==0):
   echo "database empty";
elseif ($number > 0):
   echo "$number rows in database";
endif;
mysql_close();
?>
```

To read data from the database:

```php
<?php
$server= "db.myserver.co.uk"; /* Address of server */
$user= "myuser";              /* FTP-username */
$password= "mypassword";      /* FTP-Password */
$database= "dbname";          /* name of database */
$table= "datatest";           /* Name of table, you can select that */
/* Accessing SQL-Server and querying table */
MYSQL_CONNECT($server, $user, $password) or die (
      "<H3>Server unreachable</H3>");
MYSQL_SELECT_DB($database) or die ( "<H3>Database non existent</H3>");
$result=MYSQL_QUERY( "SELECT * FROM $table order by name");

/* Output data into a HTMl table */
echo "<table border=\"1\" align=center width=50%";
echo "<tr>";
echo "<div color=\"#ffff00\">";
while ($field=mysql_fetch_field($result)) {
   echo "<th>$field->name</A></th>";
}
echo "</font></tr>";
while($row = mysql_fetch_row($result)) {
   echo "<tr>";
   for($i=0; $i < mysql_num_fields($result); $i++) {
      echo "<td align=center>$row[$i]</td>";
   }
   echo "</tr>\n";
```

```
}
echo "</table><BR><BR>";

/* Close SQL-connection */
MYSQL_CLOSE();
?>
```

and to delete a table:

```
<?php
/* Accessing the server and deleting the table */
MYSQL_CONNECT($server, $user, $password) or die (
    "<H3>Server unreachable</H3>");
MYSQL_SELECT_DB($database) or die ( "<H3>database not existent</H3>");
$result=MYSQL_QUERY( "DROP TABLE $table");
print "Result is ";
print $result;
/* Terminate SQL connection*/
MYSQL_CLOSE();
?>
```

12.9   Database Management Systems (DBMS)

- **MySQL**. A common database program which is used on many sites. It is suitable for small to medium sized databases, and is free of charge. It is also excellent to learn how to use databases.
- **PostgreSQL**. A popular DBMS, and is available free of charge. It is more advanced than MySQL, and supports virtually all of the SQL features. Unfortunately, it is only available for UNIX and Linux systems.
- **Oracle**. A high-powered database system, which is used on many of the high-end WWW servers, especially in on-line shopping sites. It is reliable, highly scaleable, and has a great deal of tools to manage the databases. Oracle is available for both Windows and UNIX.
- **Microsoft SQL**. This is a powerful DBMS which is comparable to the power of Oracle. It uses many advanced features, such as OnLine Analytical Processing (OLAP), and data mining. Unfortunately, it is only available on Windows systems.
- **Microsoft Access**. This is a popular database program which is used in small to medium sized database applications.

13 Design tips (part 1)

13.1 Introduction

This chapter contains some design tips which may be useful in WWW page design. The full color versions can be viewed on the supplied CD.

13.2 Paint strokes

A nice effect is to put a paint stoke as a background and then superimpose text onto it. The text can then be changed so it has a good contrast against the paint stoke. For example for the CNDS, NOS and Code Snippets graphics:

The NOS graphic is built from a simple brush stroke:

and the text (Verdana, font size of 50 points):

$$\textbf{N} \bigcirc \textbf{S}$$

and combined them together. The white text should cover the brush stroke, while the dark text is outwith the stroke.

13.3 Focal point graphics

A good design tip is to add a nice graphic, with a shadow behind it, onto a WWW page. Figure I3.1 shows examples of graphics that could integrate into WWW pages, and Figure I3.3 shows an example of how these graphics could be integrated into a page.

13.4 Xmas, and seasonal graphics

The seasons of the year allow you to add a little bit of character to your pages. The best time is to add Christmas graphics. If possible, you should avoid tacky looking graphics, Figure I3.2 shows a few examples of graphics which might be used over a Christmas period.

Figure I3.1 Using focal point graphics

Figure I3.2 Christmas graphics

The great advantage of using a snowman, as opposed to Father Christmas, is that you can use a snowman for a longer time, as it will still be relevant in March. Notice that the snowman in the page in Figure I3.3 gives the page an up-to-date feel (of course, it is only up-to-date when it is Christmas time). As soon as Christmas is over the graphic can be replaced.

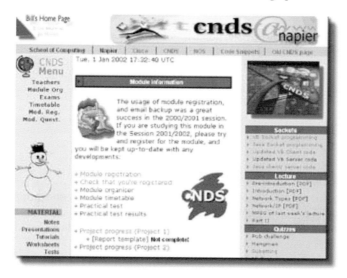

Figure I3.3 Integrating a Christmas graphic into a WWW page

I3.5 Producing sharp graphics

Many users design their graphics using Microsoft PowerPoint, as it is one of the easiest packages to use, and has lots of good clipart. Unfortunately, it does not produce good-quality graphics. Figure I3.4 shows an example of a graphic produced in PowerPoint, and Figure I3.5 shows that the graphic can be easily imported into Fireworks (or Photoshop), and gives a much sharper looking graphic.

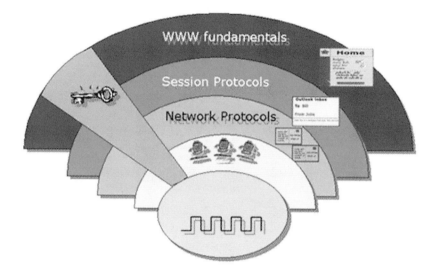

Figure I3.4 Graphic generated in Microsoft PowerPoint

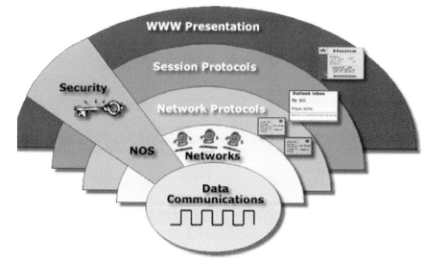

Figure I3.5 Graphic imported into Macromedia Fireworks

To highlight the difference, the zoomed version of the PowerPoint graphic gives:

and with the Firework's graphic:

I can be seen that the text is much smoother in Fireworks, and the shadow is also more realistic. Another big difference is in the display of graphics. For example, the key looks much smoother in Fireworks:

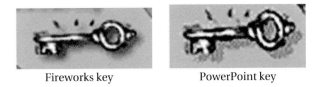

Fireworks key   PowerPoint key

Thus, a good method of producing graphics is to use PowerPoint to import and draw graphics. Finally, the graphic can be exported into Fireworks (using cut-and-paste, or exporting to PNG format).

13.6   Distorting graphics and transparency

A good trick to add interest to a graphic is to distort it, so that it appears to be viewed from a different angle. Most graphics are scanned-in, in a 2D space, thus distorting can give the effect of an image taken at a different angle. For example:

In Fireworks, this can be distorted with the Modify→Transform→Distort menu option, to give:

Then the image can be faded into the background with the transparency option on the Layers window:

I3.7   Mouse-over events and layers

A great trick with layers is to make the layer invisible by default, and then use a graphic roll-over to make it appear. The JavaScript events which can produce this are:

- **onMouseOver()** - which is used to make the layer visible. In Dreamweaver this is achieved by selecting the graphic, and then selecting the Show-Hide Layers in the Behaviours window. After this, the layer is defined as Show.
- **onMouseOut()** - which is used to make the layer invisible again. In Dreamweaver this is achieved by selecting the graphic, and then selecting the Show-Hide Layers in the Behaviours window. After this, the layer is defined as Hide.

The JavaScript produced is:

```
<a href="javascript:;"
onMouseOver="MM_showHideLayers ('Layer1','','show')"
onMouseOut="MM_showHideLayers ('Layer1','','hide')">
<img src="pics_bulb.gif" width="60" height="80" border="0"> </a>
```

The window in Macromedia which shows the events is given in Figure I3.6.

Figure I3.6 Mouse behaviours in Dreamweaver

I3.8   Enhancing metafiles

If you have clip art images in a metafile format (such as WMF), they can be enhanced by putting a small drop shadow behind them (it only requires about seven pixels, or so). For example:

and the unshadowed version:

Remember to **scale** the image down before you add your shadow. In this case the graphic was scaled from 200 pixel width to a 100 pixel width, and then the shadow was applied.

13.9   Bullets

There is a whole range of bullets you can select from. Here's a few that I have used (if you want to use them, just right-click on the bullet and Save As to your local drive):

Pinboard pin

Copper nail

Blurry-blue thing

Cross

Squiggle

Spiral

Arrow

Diamond

Square, squirrel

Colorful

Target

Square

Square, but blurry

It is important to be consistent with the usage of bullets in WWW pages, where only a certain type is used on a single page.

13.10   Graphic file formats

Where bandwidth is limited, it is sometimes a good idea to make images as small as possible, and still be able to portray the required information. Two of the main techniques are:

• To reduce the number of pixels in the graphic, as this wastes bandwidth to display a graphic which is scaled down. For example, never use a width and height tag in an im-

age insert which is not equal to the graphics' size.
- Reduce the number of colors in the image.

For example, the following shows four pictures taken with 16.7 million colors, 32 colors, 8 colors and 4 colors, respectively:

16.7 million colors

32 colors

8 colors

4 colors

Even when the colors have been reduced, you can still see that the image is of a cat. The sizes of the files produced are 3.62KB, 2.42KB, 1.10KB and 562B. It can be seen that reducing the number of colors in the image has a considerable effect on the file size (and the bandwidth used, of course, if the image is being sent over a communications channel). The reason that the file sizes reduce is that the file are compressed using an algorithm which detects long sequences of the same color, and replaces it with a special code. Thus the fewer the colors, the more likely these sequences will occur, thus the smaller the file size will be.

I3.11   Adding opacity to a background image

A great technique in adding interest to a graphic is to add opacity to a background image. If the graphic has been built-up in layers, it is then possible in Photoshop or Fireworks to change the opacity of the background image. Figure I3.7 shows an example in Fireworks.

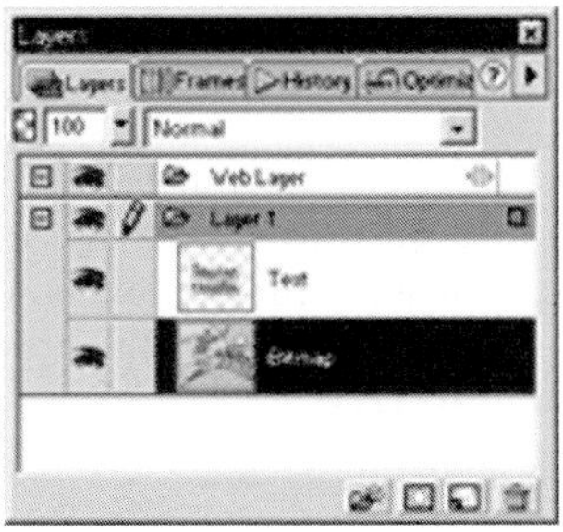

Figure I3.7 Example of layers

The following gives a 100% opacity:

The following gives a 50% opacity:

Next 25% opacity:

And finally 10% opacity:

In this case, possibly 25% gives the best contrast between the text, and the background image. If you're saving images with transparency always remember to store them as PNG files, as this preserves all the layers and meta information. If possible, export the file to a GIF file, as GIF files tend to give a much smaller file size, and they are supported by more browsers.

I3.12   Column corners

Often WWW pages have a very square look, with very little smoothness around the columns. A simple technique which can be used to enhance the look of a page is to use a smooth corner. This corner should like from one column into another with the same color as the corner. This gets rid of the sharp edges that are produced when a column uses a background color. Here are two of the corners produced for left and right columns, respectively

You can see that they are half-transparent, and half colored the same color as the column. The other little trick is to smooth the edges of the end of a row. This can be achieved with a curved corner which is white on the top right-hand side, and transparent on the bottom left-hand side. Thus, as the background is white, it looks as if there is a smooth corner at the end.

l3.13   Transparent backgrounds

The GIF and PNG formats support transparent colors, which allows graphics to have a transparent element which will take on the color of the background. This is useful in WWW design when a graphic is included on differing backgrounds. For example, the two graphics are my design for a School of Computing graphic. The first has been saved with a transparent background, and the other does not have a transparent background:

Thus, whenever possible, save your graphics with a transparent background. The following shows the options for saving a graphic. If the **No Transparency** is selected there will be no transparent colors in the GIF file. The **Index Transparency** allows for transparency for a certain color (by default this is normally white, but the eye dropper can be used to select the transparent color). Unfortunately Index Transparency can make elements within the graphic to be transparent, thus **Alpha Transparency** can be used to define transparency up to the edge of an image, and not within it.

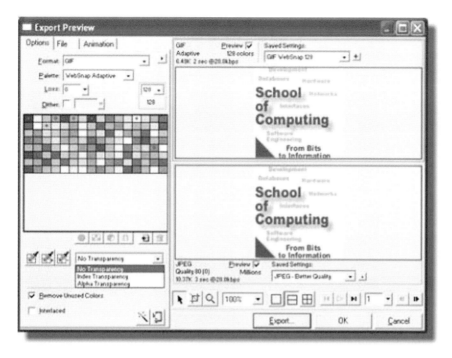

Figure I3.8 Adding transparency

To see the difference between Index and Alpha Transparency, observe the following graphics:

| Alpha Transparency | Index transparency |

You can see that the Index Transparency has changed some of the white fills to the transparent colors, whereas the Alpha Transparency has only made the background transparent.

I3.14   Lines in tables

The following shows a menu item with lines between the groups of items:

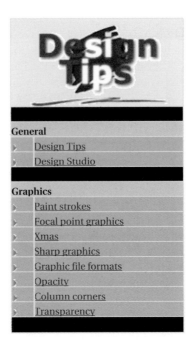

These are produced by inserting a row in the table (such as above the menu title, and then inserting a GIF file which doesn't have any content. The graphic can then be set-up with a certain height, such as with a 3-pixel height:

```
<td bgcolor=#000000 colspan=2><img height=3 src="nothing.gif"
width=170 border=0></td>
```

The background to the row is also set to be the required color, which, in this case, is BLACK (#000000). For a vertical line, we do the same, but a column is created, and the width is varied:

The code for the column is thus:

```
<td rowspan="12" bgcolor="#000000" width=2><img
src="nothing.gif" width=2 border=0></td>
```

1362   Handbook of the Internet

I3.15   Animating objects

Dynamic HTML (DHTML) is a powerful tool, but should be used sparingly. Often users en-
joy a moving element on a WWW page the first few times that they access the page, but it
can become annoying, so the technique has to be used sparingly.

   The great thing about DHTML is that it is extremely easy to design moving content in
Dreamweaver. Basically you create a new layer for the HTML that you wish to move, then
select it, and select Window→Timelines (if the timeline is not already shown). Next right
click on the point on the timeline that you want to add a keyframe, and then select Add Keyframe. Move to the next keyframe, and add another keyframe, and so on. Each time move
the object to where you want it to move. The timeline below gives an example for the menu
item which moves in from the right-hand side on this page. Notice that it moves at 10
frames per second, and it has 35 frames, thus it will take a total of 3.5 seconds to move in
from the left. The keyframe at Frame 19 defines the lowest point of the movement.

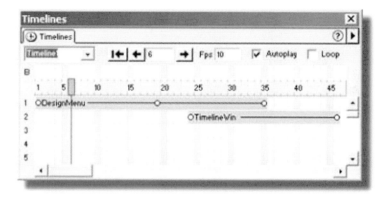

Figure I3.9 Defining a timeline

I3.16   Creating pop-up message boxes

Pop-up boxes are useful methods of spawning pages from a main page, but they must be
kept to minimum. The events which cause these pop-ups are important, and must be care-
fully design for. Typical events would be:

- **Pop-up on page load**. This event should be used sparely, as the user may become irri-
  tated by the pop-up window, every time that they load the page.
- **Pop-up on a mouse over event**. This is a good event to catch, as it does not require the
  user to click their mouse on anything, but it can get a little irritating if the use keeps
  catching the event when navigating around the page.
- **Pop-up on a mouse down event**   This is the best event to catch, once the user knows
  where to click.

In Dreamweaver this can be easy added by adding a behavior (Window→Behaviors, or press
Shift-F3), as shown next:

and the properties for the Open Browser Window:

There are many events which can be selected, such as OnClick, onKeyPress:

The associated code is:

```
<a href="javascript:;"
onMouseOver="window.open('message_home.html',
'Message' , 'scrollbars=yes, width=450, height=250')">
<img src="pics_news.gif" width="56" height="55"
border="0" align="left"></a>
```

which creates a fixed window of 450 pixels width, and 250 pixels high. It also has scrollbars, but no navigation and location toolbars (as we only want the user to close this window, and go back to the main content).

If you want the message to load on the page:

```
<body onload="Javascript: window.open(
'message_example.html','Message' , 'scrollbars=yes, width=450,
height=250')" bgcolor="#ffffff" marginheight="0" marginwidth="0"
topmargin="0" leftmargin="0" rightmargin="0" bottommargin="0">
```

If you want to stop someone from printing page, then you can disable the right-click menu, which will display a print option:

```
<script type="text/javascript">
var message="Sorry, you are not allow to print this message box";
function click(e) {
if (document.all) {
if (event.button==2||event.button==3) {
alert(message);
return false;
}
}
}
if (document.layers) {
document.captureEvents(Event.MOUSEDOWN);
}
document.onmousedown=click;
//-->
</SCRIPT>
```

This produces the following when the user tries to print a graphic:

The lack of a menu bar, and the redirection of the right-click menu, stops the user from viewing the HTML source code, from selecting any of the content, and from printing. The same thing happens when they try to copy any part of the page. A typical right-click menu bar is shown next:

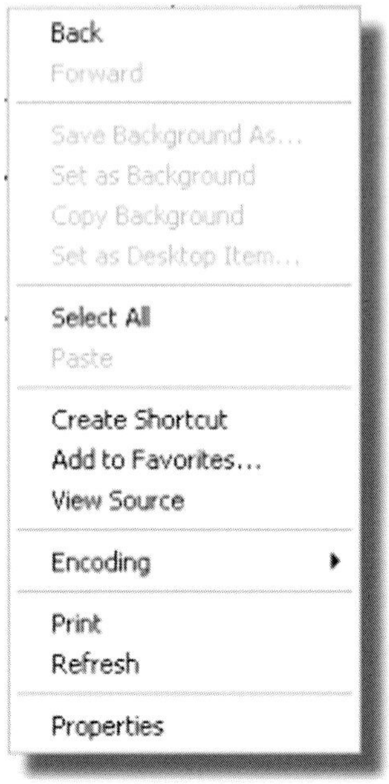

| Back |
| Forward |
| Save Background As... |
| Set as Background |
| Copy Background |
| Set as Desktop Item... |
| Select All |
| Paste |
| Create Shortcut |
| Add to Favorites... |
| View Source |
| Encoding ▸ |
| Print |
| Refresh |
| Properties |

Of course, it is still in the local cache, so the user can still view it (or print it), but it is a useful method for protecting content from being stolen, with the authors permission.

I3.17   Drawing lines in diagrams

Diagrams can considerably enhance the presentation, and understanding of a subject. As much as possible these diagrams should have shapes and lines which symmetric. This typically involves creating simple shapes and then pasting them at even intervals. For example in the graphic below (of a routing protocol) the nodes are first laid out (these are the blue circles). Next, the lines are drawn through the nodes with single **continuous** lines. This creates a smooth flow from one place to the next (rather than with broken lines as these can look disjointed). Notice that the centre of the circle is the **focal point** for the lines. This line which start or end should start or end at the centre point. In addition, any lines which flow through the circles will also go through the circle.

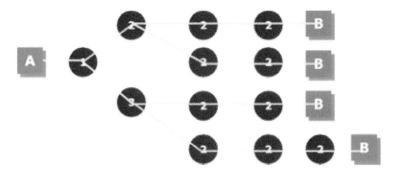

Next the lines can be moved to the background (typically by selecting the complete line, and selecting **Send to Background**).

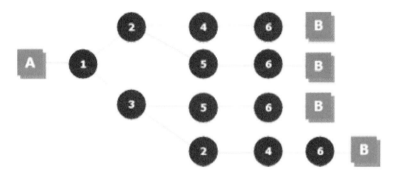

Finally, the nodes can be given more depth with a shadow, and the lines between the nodes can also be thickened, to give:

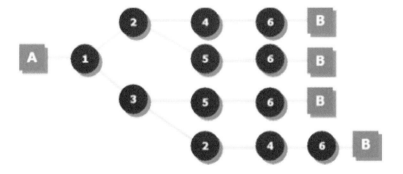

A final check to see if all the nodes are spaced evenly apart gives (and changing the color of the lines to black, which gives a better contrast with the background):

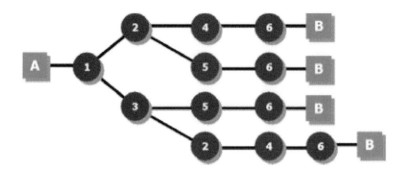

I3.18   Scaling graphics for text

When a graphic is scaled down, the resolution of the text is often reduced so that it cannot be read. For example, the following graphic was created with a width of 900 pixels, and has been reduced to have a width of 200 pixels.

You can see that the text cannot be properly viewed. Next the image can be stored with a width of 300 pixels, but forced (in HTML) to viewed with a width of 200 pixels with:

```
<img src="study_at_napier.gif" width="200" height="161">
```

This then gives the following image:

You can see that the *Studying @ napier* text is now readable. The only problem with this method is that the file size increases for the larger version. A file listing gives:

```
21,476   study_at_napier.gif
12,763   study_at_napier_200pixels.gif
```

which shows that the 200-pixel version has a file size of around 10KB, and the larger version has a file size of around 20KB. Thus, we have doubled the file size, but we have considerably improved the readability of the text. In these days of fast Internet connections, the size of the files is not as major a problem as it was a one time. In addition, it can be said that the increase in file size is well worth it, as it presents the graphic as it was meant to be shown.

Here is the graphic in its 300-pixel format:

It is even better in a 400-pixel format:

and then if we show this version with 200-pixels:

Thus summarizing with the different versions:

Graphic with a 200-pixel width, displayed with a 200-pixel width (10KB file size)

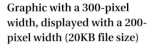

Graphic with a 300-pixel width, displayed with a 200-pixel width (20KB file size)

Graphic with a 400-pixel width, displayed with a 200-pixel width (30KB file size)

13.19 Designing for easy configuration

A key element in any content design is to try to allow new content to be easily integrated into the existing structure. If possible, the pages should be structured into sub-WWW domains. These are described as parent pages, and a new page becomes a child of the parent. The overall index page is the Master, and integrates with the parents.

Each child page has a template which is borrowed from the parent, and often contains navigation elements which either lead back to the parent or have an integrated child menu structure, so that it is possible to move to any one of the children. This page, itself, is like this structure, as it is possible to navigate to any one of the children from this page.

So how is it possible to create a dynamic menu structure? One of the best ways is to use JavaScript which creates the basic elements of the navigation, and then put it in a file. All the documents can then refer to this, so that any new additions will be automatically updated in all of the pages which reference the JavaScript file. An example pull down menu is:

```
document.write("<form>");
document.write("<select name='menu1' onChange=MM_jumpMenu('parent',this,
0)>");
document.write("<option value='design_tips.html' selected>Home</option>");
document.write("<option value='design_tips01.html'>Paint Strokes</option>");
document.write("<option value='design_tips02.html'>Focal point graph-
ics</option>");
document.write("<option value='design_tips03.html'>Xmas</option>");
document.write("<option value='design_tips04.html'>Sharp graphics</option>");
document.write("<option value='design_tips05.html'>Distorting graph-
ics</option>");
document.write("<option value='design_tips06.html'>Mouse-over
events</option>");
document.write("<option value='design_tips07.html'>Enhancing meta-
files</option>");
document.write("<option value='design_tips08.html'>Bullets</option>");
document.write("<option value='design_tips09.html'>Graphic file for-
mats</option>");
document.write("<option value='design_tips10.html'>Opacity</option>");
document.write("<option value='design_tips11.html'>Column corners</option>");
document.write("<option value='design_tips12.html'>Transparency</option>");
document.write("<option value='design_tips13.html'>Lines in ta-
bles</option>");
document.write("<option value='design_tips14.html'>Cut-out graph-
ics</option>");
document.write("<option value='design_tips15.html'>Dynamic HTML</option>");
document.write("<option value='design_tips16.html'>Message boxes</option>");
document.write("<option value='design_tips17.html'>Lines in
diagrams</option>");
document.write("<option value='design_tips18.html'>Scaling graphics for
text</option>");
document.write("</select>");
document.write("</form>");
```

It can then be referred to in the page with:

```
<script language=JavaScript src="design_tips.js"></script>
```

To add another page in the menu a line is added to the JS file, such as:

```
document.write("<option value='design_tips19.html'>Designing for easy configura-
tion</option>");
```

The MM_Jumpmenu code is:

```
function MM_jumpMenu(targ,selObj,restore){ //v3.0
  eval(targ+".location='"+selObj.options[selObj.selectedIndex].value+"'");
  if (restore) selObj.selectedIndex=0;
}
```

I3.20   Creating icons for program files

There is an art to creating icons, and in many cases they can add a little bit of polish to the programs/media content that you've created. Typically these files are only 32 pixels by 32 pixels with 256 colors. Thus we must select a graphic which does not loose too much of its content when it has been reduced. Let's say that we want to create a program icon for the following graphic:

Figure I3.10 Sample graphic

The original graphic is 100 pixels by 141 pixels, so there is not too much scaling involved. First the graphic is scaled so that it is square (100 pixels by 100 pixels) and then is reduced to a 32-by-32 pixel format (this is achieved in Fireworks with Modify→Image Size and selecting the width as 100 pixels). Finally, the image is saved as a BMP-8 format to give the graphic in Figure I3.11.

The file format is now small enough to be imported into an icon editor (in this case I've named it lock.bmp). Next, you must use an icon editor, which allows you to import the BMP file, and then paste it into the icon file. In this case, in Figure I3.12, the icon editor in Microsoft Visual C++.

With a little bit of scaling, the final ICO file can be created. Finally, the icon can then be easily associated with a program, to give the graphic in Figure I3.13. It is important that you keep your icons simple, as complex images will loose their resolution when they are reduced in size.

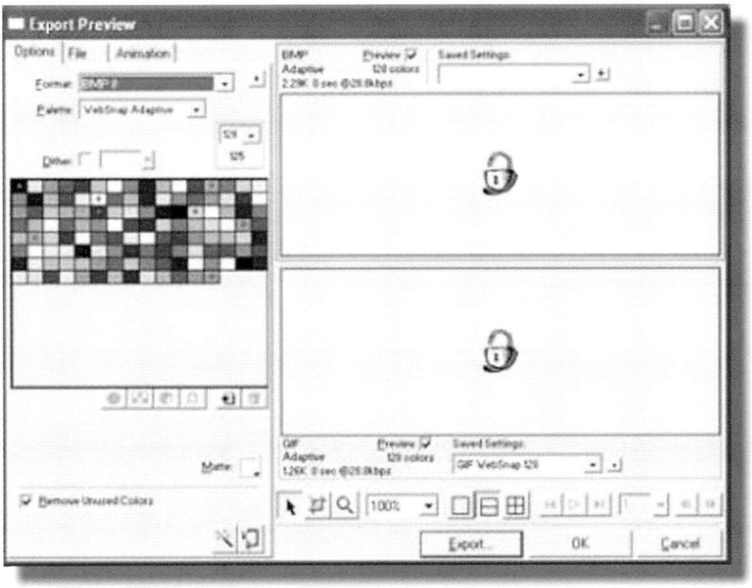

Figure I3.11 Icon graphic

Figure I3.12 Icon editor in Visual C++

Figure I3.13 Icon editor in Visual C++

I3.21 Pencil first, package later

The key to design is not the package, but the content. Unfortunately, there has never been a computer package that can properly encapsulate design ideas. The best tool of this is a pencil and paper. If you start with a package, you are never going to properly investigate your ideas, and find out which one works. It is really the same argument as reading a book against reading text from a computer screen. Books are one of the most portable devices ever created, and you can virtually move from any part of the content to any other part, in a matter of seconds.

Example of the sketches might be as given in Figure I3.14. The scan of the page can be quickly enhanced by selecting Adjust Color→Autolevels to give the graphic in Figure I3.15.

You can see that the newspaper graphic sort of works, especially with the abstraction of the man. Unfortunately the initial graphic of the book does not work. Here's the three versions:

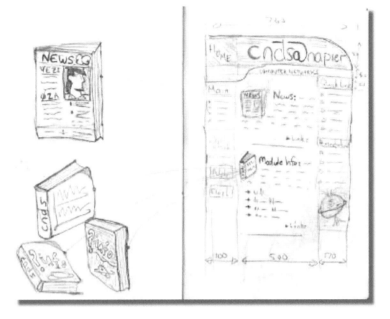

Figure I3.14 Example sketches

Figure I3.15 Example sketches after applying AutoLevels

For the book design, that the final one works best (the one where the book is standing up). Once the design has been selected, it can be enhanced and integrated into the final design.

You can see that it would have been difficult to enhance the graphic, and try out ideas, using a computer package.

A clever trick is to add a little bit of color to the scanned images of pencil sketches. This is achieved, in Photoshop, with Image→Adjust-Variations. So does it work when it is reduced in size? Well there is only one way to find out. Here are three different versions using the green version of the graphic (remember the graphic is still in a very rough form, but it will allow us to try different layouts):

A key in design, though, is to **observe** your content over **time**, and see if your eye becomes tired of the design. If so, do not use it. Over time, you should learn the good and bad tips, but there is no real definitive techniques that will work for every type of presentation. In fact if you do not experiment with your graphic elements you designs may start to look a little too much everyone else's work, which might be fine if your trying to sell soap powder, but not very good if you're trying to innovate your work.

I3.22   From sketch to graphic

A key element of producing graphics is to be able to draft them on paper, and then convert them into a digital form. For example, let us try and make a logo graphic. First a few ideas are sketched as in Figure I3.16. The bottom graphic looks okay, so let us cut it out. Next, we can start to fill the image in, paying particular attention to the bits that the fill tool does not fill as shown in Figure I3.17, followed by the background colors. Next we fill-in some of the back areas, the text and a border are added.

Finally, we need to reduce the size of the graphic, so that it can be properly integrated into a page. To assess the right size, we reduce the graphic to 200 pixel width, 150 pixel width, 100-pixel width, and then finally to 50 pixels:

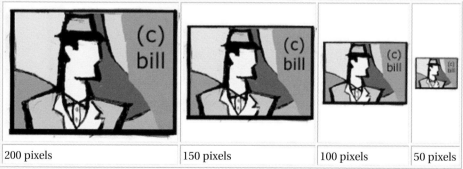

200 pixels   150 pixels   100 pixels   50 pixels

Figure I3.16 Example sketches

Figure I3.17 Example sketch

You can see that 100 pixels seems to work best, as the 50-pixel version is too small. Each of the graphic elements can be used, though, in different situations, as the user will become accustomed to the graphic element, and will know that what it is intended to present (in this case it is the copyright graphic).

So does it work? Let us try it with some text:

 No paragraph of this publication may be reproduced, copied or transmitted save with written permission or in accordance with the provision of the Copyright, Designs and Patents Act 1988, or under the terms of any license permitting limited copying issued by the Copyright Licensing Agency, 90 Tottenham Court Road, London W1P 0LP.
Any person who does any unauthorized act in relation to this WWW site may be liable to criminal prosecution and civil claims for damages.

The rough edges, and lack of preciseness, really appeals to me, as it makes a nice difference from the clean edges of clip-art, and metafile graphics.

I4 Design tips (part 2)

I4.1 From photo to graphic

Often it is difficult to get the exact images that you want from standard clip-art and image files. A key skill is to be able to convert a photograph into a graphic. For example, Figure I4.1 shows a photograph of a guitar. It is difficult to select the outline with the magic wand, thus it is a good idea to cut around the guitar, and copy and paste it into another file, as illustrated in Figure I4.2.

Figure I4.1 Photograph of a guitar

Figure I4.2 Guitar cut-out

Often it is possible to select the rest of the outline with the magic wand; otherwise, the outline is deleted using a large air brush, followed by smaller air-brushes around the edges of the guitar, as illustrated in Figure I4.3. Some of the edges can be cleaned up by adding straight lines, as shown in Figure I4.4.

Figure I4.3 Guitar

Figure I4.4 Guitar

Next we can reduce the image, and put a drop shadow on it. In Figure I4.5 some text has been added, along with a straight line, so that it gives the user something to focus on. Figure I4.6 gives an alternative design. Next, we can fill the white space beside the text with a simple image, to give Figure I4.7. Figure I4.8 shows how the graphic scales.

Figure I4.5 Guitar in a graphic

Figure I4.6 Guitar in a graphic

Figure I4.7 Guitar in a graphic

| 300-pixel width | 200-pixel width |

Figure I4.8 Scaling graphic

So let us try the 200-pixel graphic in a mock WWW page:

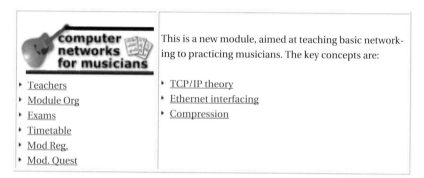

| **Main**
• Teachers
• Module Org
• Exams
• Timetable
• Mod Reg.
• Mod. Quest | (graphic) computer networks for musicians

This is a new module, aimed at teaching basic net-working to practicing musicians. The key concepts are:

• TCP/IP theory
• Ethernet interfacing
• Compression |

or if we use a 150-pixel image, and put it into the menu option:

or using the large graphic across two columns:

I4.2   To matte or not to matte

Transparent graphics often do not blend into the background, as they do not have a transition color between the graphic and the background. A matte color tries to approximate of the background, and inserts a thin line around the graphic of the matte color, and then leaves the rest as a transparent background. Figure I4.9 shows an example of a banner with a matte.

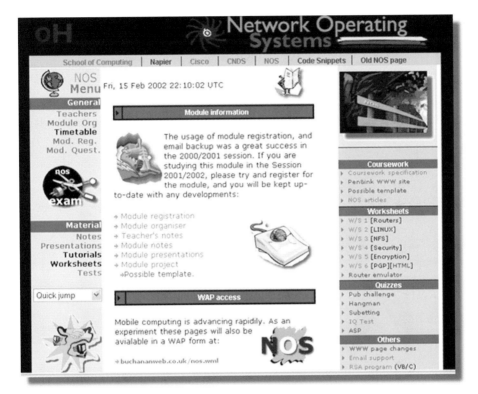

Figure I4.9 Example WWW design

The banner graphic created is:

As you can see, there is matte of blue around the graphic, and the graphic has a transparent background. When the blue background is added it gives:

The advantage of using the matte and transparent background is that the matte will always nearly match the background color, even it is has a limited color palate.

I4.3   From vector to graphic

This tip uses a simple graphic that can be used as an abstract graphic. First, we create layers with the pen tool, and add elements, as illustrated Figure I4.10. You can see that the main elements of the graphic are made from simple shapes, and the shading is achieved with a paint brush with around 50% transparency. Text has also been added to the graphic. In Figure I4.11 the layers have been merged, and blur the background graphic. The graphic on the right-hand side has a 50% transparency added to the background graphic.

Figure I4.10 Example graphic

Figure I4.11 Example graphic

Finally the graphic can be reduced in size to give:

 **cnds@napier**

This is the cnds@napier page. You will be guided through the page by **CNDS Sam**. who will show you the main concepts of the subject.

If you would like to subscribe to this module, please select the graphic given below.

I4.4   Animation

Animation adds interest to a page, but should not be overdone. It provides a natural focus, if it is designed correctly. As much as possible the graphics in the animation should be smooth, and fade in and out, so that they are gentle on the eye. First, we could give a quick introduction to the animation with some text. This is achieved by inserting text at Frame 1, and then a key from at another frame, then the Create Motion Tweening between the frame, such as:

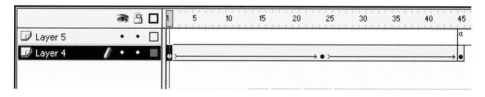

The first frame is then scaled down, and Frame 24 has the expanded version:

An agent can be animated by inserting the graphic for the agent, and then scaling it down, and adding a 0% alpha transparency to it. The agent will then appear on the screen, and expand to show the correct size. Finally, the agent is faded away.

I4.5   Tracing designs

As a child, we were introduced to the joys of tracing drawings. In the digital world, we can do the same, but the one thing that you should avoid is allowing a drawing package to trace an image for you. In most cases, it will either over elaborate the image or under elaborate it. Figure I4.12 shows an example sketch. The network link graphic looks promising, so let us create a new layer on top of the original sketch, and draw lines on top of it, as shown in Figure I4.13.

Figure I4.12 Example sketch

Figure I4.13 Example sketch

The color, style and thickness of the lines do not really matter at this stage. The contrast of the yellow against the black works well. So let us now go back to our design, and use yellow as the in-fill, and a darker yellow for the hair. The left-hand side of Figure I4.14 shows that a textured brush stroke has been added to accentuate the shadows around the figure. This gives it a 3D feel, and lifts it off the page. In addition, the background has been given an Alpha setting of around 50%. The right-hand side of Figure I4.15 adds some text, with a drop shadow. In the left-hand side of Figure I4.15 added some text to the background, while the right-hand side has a cloud to the background.

Figure I4.14 Example sketch

Figure I4.15 Example sketch

I4.6   Logo mania

Humans are extremely visually driven, and the human brain is automatically drawn towards images. Unfortunately, there is a fine line between the things that are attractive to the eye, and things that are not. In addition, some people are attracted by one thing, while others to another. So let us experiment with a few basic ideas, and try to determine things that look good in graphics. First, we will start with the graphic shown in Figure I4.16. The first one uses the Object→Compound Path option to cut text out from the background. This gives the graphic in Figure I4.17. A liquid silver effect is used in Figure I4.18, which doesn't quite work, as the silver text needs to be contrasted with a dark background. Therefore, Figure I4.19 shows the original image, with a drop shadow on the background shape. This gives the image a little bit of depth.

Now, let's make it more interesting by adding text, that will allow the eye to move from the main text in the centre, around the shapes. Figure I4.21 has some smaller text items. Next we can add a drop shadow onto the main text, and scale the '@' symbol up. In addition, we can add a border so that the image stands-out more against the white background (Figure I4.22).

Figure I4.16 Example graphic

Figure I4.17 Example graphic

Figure I4.18 Example graphic

Figure I4.19 Example graphic

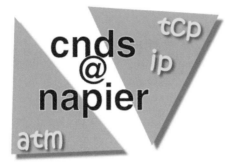

Figure I4.20 Example graphic

Figure I4.21 Example graphic

This looks nice and modern, and has many clean edges. The orange gives the graphic a vibrant feeling, and the typefaces used are modern. Next, we must see how well the graphic will scale. As much as possible the text has been set in this resolution with large font faces, which use sans-serif fonts (which scale well).

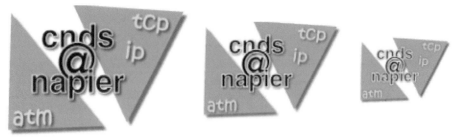

| 200-pixel width | 150 pixel width | 100-pixel width |

In conclusion, simple images, with clean edges, bright colors, and a modern looking font can make an excellent basis for a graphic.

I4.7   Animating the alien

Macromedia Flash is one of the most amazing packages ever produced, and has carved out a particular niche in the market. There isn't any package which come near it for its ease-of-use, and its integration with the WWW. Thus, let us see how easy it is to create a basic animation with our alien. First, we can cutout its eyes and hands (or suction pads), as shown in Figure I4.22.

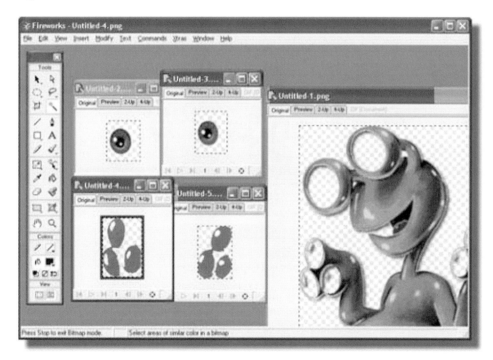

Figure I4.22 Example design

We can then add each of these elements onto their own layers, and generate Figure I4.22.

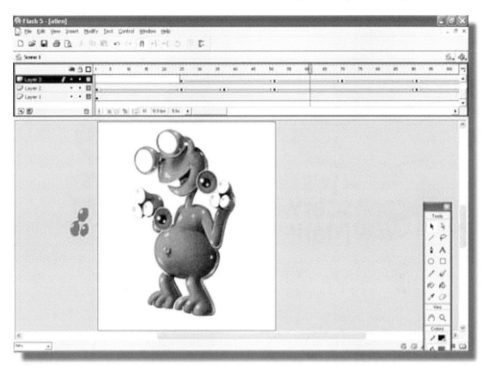

Figure I4.23 Example animation

I4.8   Experimenting with designs

It is impossible to ever get a design correct with the first draft. That is why a pencil and rubber are much better tools than a pen and correction fluid. Therefore, it is important when designing digital graphics that you can easily try out different colours, textures and ideas. So let us try with a scary skeleton graphic. First, in Figure I4.24, we have two basic designs. The changes that have been made are to put a glow around the main text in the first graphic, but a drop-shadow in the second one. The arrow at the bottom of the graphic has also been changed.

The one with the text that glows helps to blend the text into the skull, but the arrows are not quite right. In Figure I4.25 there are two updated arrow graphics. These have been embossed, and have a drop-shadow behind. In Figure I4.26 the skull has been embossed, and gives a 3D feel, which contrasts against the 2D feel of the text.

Figure I4.24 Example graphics

Figure I4.25 Example graphics

Figure I4.26 Example graphics

I4.9   XML and reuse

The future for reuse and reconfigurability on the WWW is XML, which will provide the plat-form for the creation of generic components which can be configured using XML In this design, a Flash component will be designed which will uses an XML to define the SWF files to read in.

The XML can be setup with the following:

```
<?xml version="1.0"?>
<flash>
<files>top_cnds.swf</files>
<files>top_nos.swf</files>
<files>agent01.swf</files>
<files>agent02.swf</files>
<files>agents01.swf</files>
<files>agents02.swf</files>
<files>agents_movie.swf</files>
<files>agents_moview.swf</files>
<files>agent_movie.swf</files>
::: etc :::
</flash>
```

This can be read in using the ActionScript:

```
var str = new Array();
var movie_number=0, max_movie_number=0;
urlXML = new XML();
urlXML.onLoad = convertXML;
urlXML.load("flash.xml");
function convertXML () {
  mainTag = new XML();
  elementTag = new XML();
```

```
mainTag = this.firstChild.nextSibling;
if (mainTag.nodeName.toLowerCase() == "flash") {
 flist = mainTag.childNodes;
 // get tags
 for (i=0; i<=flist.length; i++) {
  if (flist[i].nodeName.toLowerCase() == "files") {
  // we get the child node array beneath the questions
   elementList = flist[i].childNodes;
   str[max_movie_number]=elementList;
   max_movie_number++;
  }
 }
 }
}
```

The convertXML function reads in the XML and inserts the file names into the str[] array. The buttons can then contain the following code (for the forward button):

```
on (press) {
 loadMovie (str[movie_number], "bg");
 fname=str[movie_number];
 movie_number = movie_number+1;
 if (movie_number>max_movie_number) movie_number=1;
 gotoAndPlay (2);
}
```

and (for the back button):

```
on (press) {
 loadMovie (str[movie_number], "bg");
 fname=str[movie_number];
 movie_number = movie_number-1;
 if (movie_number<0) movie_number=0;
 gotoAndPlay (2);
}
```

The SWF file is loaded in the movie clip, which is named "bg". Thus, we can spend more time on creating a solid, and reconfigurable component, and less time on creating new content for each design.

To make it more reusable, many other options would have to be added to make it reusable in other application. A good example would be to define the graphic content at the top of the movie within the XML file, such as:

```
<?xml version="1.0"?>
<flash>
<banner>
<graphic>
<file>top.swf</file>
<x_pos>34</x_pos>
<y_pos>40</y_pos>
</file>
</banner>
<files>top_cnds.swf</files>
<files>top_nos.swf</files>
<files>agent01.swf</files>
<files>agent02.swf</files>
<files>agents01.swf</files>
```

```
<files>agents02.swf</files>
<files>agents_movie.swf</files>
<files>agents_moview.swf</files>
<files>agent_movie.swf</files>
::: etc :::
</flash>
```

For it to be more reconfigurable we would have to add lots of other options that allowed the graphics to be manipulated, such as scaling, movement, alpha processing, and so on. In this case the XML file is changed to contain the names of the pictures, and also a description of the picture. The file used is:

```
<?xml version="1.0"?>
<flash>
<files>skye_pics\0001.swf</files>
<description>This is a picture taken from my car, in the Highlands.</description>
<files>skye_pics\0002.swf</files>
<description>Another picture of the Highlands, showing the beautiful mirror image
on the loch.</description>
<files>skye_pics\0003.swf</files>
<description>I took this from the side of the road on the way up to Skye. It shows
how still the loch was.</description>
<files>skye_pics\0004.swf</files>
<description>A picture of the Ragamuffin shop, on Skye. I had an excellent coffee
in the little cafe beside this.</description>
<files>skye_pics\0005.swf</files>
<description>A picture of the ferry which travels to the South of the is-
land.</description>
<files>skye_pics\0006.swf</files>
<description>Another picture of the bay.</description>
<files>skye_pics\0007.swf</files>
<description>A picture of the Scottish mainland taken from Skye. It was warm and
the sky was a beautiful blue colour.</description>
<files>skye_pics\0008.swf</files>
<description>And again...</description>
</flash>
```

For this, the Actionscript for the button is changed to:

```
on (press) {
  loadMovie (str[movie_number], "bg");
  bg._xscale=90; // 90% scaling of the picture
  bg._yscale=90; // 90% scaling of the picture
  fname=str[movie_number];
  descript=description[movie_number];
  movie_number = movie_number+1;
  if (movie_number>max_movie_number-1) movie_number=0;
  gotoAndPlay (2);
}
```

The reading of the XML file has also been changed so that the description is added:

```
function convertXML () {
  mainTag = new XML();
  elementTag = new XML();
  mainTag = this.firstChild.nextSibling;
  trace("Tag " + mainTag);
  if (mainTag.nodeName.toLowerCase() == "flash") {
```

```
flist = mainTag.childNodes;
trace("Number of elements: " + questionList.length);
// get tags
 for (i=0; i<=flist.length; i++) {
 if (flist[i].nodeName.toLowerCase() == "files") {
 // we get the child node array beneath the questions
  elementList = flist[i].childNodes;
   trace("Element list: " + elementList);
   str[max_movie_number]=elementList;
  max_movie_number++;
}
if (flist[i].nodeName.toLowerCase() == "description") {
elementList = flist[i].childNodes;
description[max_movie_number-1]=elementList;
}
}
}
}
}
```

14.10   Showing text where to go

The human eye is well used to viewing horizontal and vertical text, but when placed against a curved graphic it can often seem a little disconnected. Thus, a good design technique is to be able to place text around a set path. So let us take a mobile agent graphic:

The line is drawn with the pen tool which will be used to define the path for the text. Next, we can use Text→Attach to Path to attach the text. This then gives:

This is fine but it does not follow the line of the branch, so let us undo the path, and redo the path so that it follows the line of the branch:

which is a definite improvement as the eye can now flow over the smooth lines of the branch. Now we can modify the path for the upper text, with:

When we apply the text to the path, it gives:

which compresses the text into the single area. This is because the default alignment is for centre-aligned text. We can enhance this by selecting the stretch option for the object. This gives:

This does not look quite right, and is a bit painful on the eye. So let us try to mould the text around the branch. This is done this by simply splitting the 'o' and the 'bile' and moving the 'o' below the 'bile', and gives:

14.11 Fade-in, fade-out

Macromedia Flash has very few rivals. It is one of the best packages for quickly creating a fade-in, and fade-out animated graphic. This can be achieved by created an initial image with a 100% alpha, and then created a motion tweening effect with a 0% alpha at the end. This will create a fade-out. The other image can be faded-in using the opposite effect.

14.12 Programming with Flash

It often takes software developers a while to get used to Macromedia Flash or Director. The reason for this is that the package was initially developed around stages, movies, and lots of other acting terms. This makes the environment difficult as the terms are new to software developers. Another problem is that software developers are used to creating code, which is executed, and run on the system. In Macromedia there has, in the past, been a great reliance on tweening, and scripting, which differs from code writing. These problems were overcome in Flash 5 which allows proper code to be written. Let us take a simple example of a Flash file with four movies: right, left, eyes and mouth (see CD). This is simply setup by inserting the code (on Frame 2):

```
mouth._alpha=i;
```

and on Frame 5 the following can be setup:

```
i=i+5;
if (i>100) i=0;
gotoAndPlay ( 2 );
```

which add a value of 5 onto the alpha setting, until it gets over 100, where it will be set back to zero again. The first frame contains the initialization of the i variable with:

```
var i=0;
```

The _alpha property of the movie is one of many properties which can be set, including: _x (x position), _y (y position), _height (the height of the movie), _scale (scaling of the movie), _url (URL of the movie), _xscale, _yscale, _visible (make it visible), and _rotation (rotate the movie).

So let us try modifying the rotation properties of two of the elements. This was simply setup by inserting the code (on Frame 2):

```
right._rotation=angle;
left._rotation=angle;
```

and on Frame 5 the following can be setup:

```
angle=angle+10;
if (angle>0) angle=-90;
gotoAndPlay ( 2 );
```

which add a value of 10 degrees onto the rotation setting, until it gets over 0, where it will be set back to -90 again. The first frame contains the initialization of the i variable with:

```
var angle=-90;
```

Now let us see if we can take a value from a pull-down menu, and add it as a property to the rotation. In the following example, we can increment the angle of rotation by 1, 2, 5, 10 or 30 degrees. The pull-down menu is taken from one of the standard libraries. This was simply setup by inserting the code (on Frame 2):

```
right._rotation=angle;
left._rotation=angle;
```

and on Frame 5 the following can be setup:

```
angle=angle+speed.currentvalue;
trace(speed.currentvalue);
if (angle>0) angle=-90;
gotoAndPlay ( 2 );
```

The speed object is the name of the movie for the pull-down menu (from the Smart Clips library). It sets the currentvalue for the increment in the angle. Next, let us use the pull-down menu to set the alpha factor for the whole movie: This was simply setup by inserting the code (on Frame 2):

```
right._alpha=alpha.currentvalue;
left._alpha=alpha.currentvalue;
eyes._alpha=alpha.currentvalue;
mouth._alpha=alpha.currentvalue;
```

where alpha is the name of the pull-down menu instance.

14.13 Dragging events in Flash

There is a great move towards interactive exercises which are rich in graphical content. Thus a good skill is to be able to pick up objects with the mouse and place them at other points in the content. Flash easily achieves this with its mouse events. For example the following allows the three elements on the left-hand side to be picked up and moved around on the movie (see CD).This was achieved by adding an invisible button in each of the graphics to be dragged with the event of:

```
on (press) {
 startDrag ("");
}
on (release) {
 stopDrag ();
}
```

This causes the movie to be dragged when the mouse is pressed over the movie. It stays dragable until the mouse is released.

Next a text box named layer can be added to the movie, so that it displays the _droptarget property. This displays the name of the instance that has received the dragged movie:

```
on (press) {
 startDrag ("");
}
on (release) {
 stopDrag ();
 _level0.layer = this._droptarget;
}
```

Next we can detect where the movies are dragged to, and make them disappear if they are placed on the correct location. This is achieved by interrogating the _droptarget property. This displays the name of the instance that has received the dragged movie:

```
on (press) {
 startDrag ("");
}
on (release) {
 stopDrag ();
 trace (this._droptarget);
 if (this._droptarget=="/network_layer")
 {
  _level0.ip._visible=false;
  _level0.layer = "Correct";
```

```
    }
    else _level0.layer = "INCORRECT";
}
```

This is the case for the IP instance. If it is dragged to the /network_layer instance, it will become invisible using the _visible property. Next, we can add a reset button which restarts the games and makes everything visible again.

This is achieved by adding the following action script to the button:

```
on (release) {
_level0.ip._visible = true;
_level0.ip._x = 80;
_level0.ip._y = 100;
_level0.tcp._visible = true;
_level0.tcp._x = 80;
_level0.tcp._y = 150;
_level0.ethernet._visible = true;
_level0.ethernet._x = 80;
_level0.ethernet._y = 200;
}
```

Next we can add a little challenge to the movie, but updating a clock, which is reset at the start of the task. The score can also be displayed. This was achieved by modifying the action on the dragable objects to.

```
on (press) {
startDrag ("");
}
on (release) {
stopDrag ();
trace (this._droptarget);
if (this._droptarget=="/network_layer")
{
_level0.ip._visible=false;
_level0.correct++;
_level0.layer = _level0.correct;
if (_level0.correct==3) _level0.stop_timer=true;
}
else _level0.layer = "INCORRECT";
}
```

The main variables are initialised at Frame 1 with:

```
var t;
var stop_timer;
var correct=0;
t= new Date();
start_time=t.getTime();
stop_timer=false;
```

and at Frame 5 the time can be updated with:

```
if (stop_timer==false)
{
t= new Date();
end_time=t.getTime();
```

```
trace(end_time);
trace(start_time);
showtime=int((end_time-start_time)/1000);
}
gotoAndPlay (2);
```

The getTime() method returns the number of milliseconds since 1 January 1970 (the start time for the PC). The start_time is set at the start of the movie, or when the Restart button is pressed. The end_time is the current time, which along with the start_time is used to determine the number of seconds passed.

14.14   Reusing forms

Obviously, WWW pages can be designed using PHP or ASP, so that content can be repeated across several pages, but this makes the pages dependent on the WWW server software. It also makes it dependent on the server being present, which sometimes make proper testing difficult. Thus good old JavaScript is one the best ways to create reusable content which server independent. For example you'll notice that many of the pages on this site have forms which can be filled-in with a response.

For this I designed the form, and copied the HTML from the form to Microsoft Word. I then used Microsoft Word to find and replace every new line (or paragraph marker) with nothing (well I know it's bad grammar, but it's better than saying not anything). This gets rid of the new lines. Next I crunched the white-spaces by replacing two whitespaces with one, and then repeated this until all the multiple whitespaces were gone. This leaves a crunched version of the HTML code:

```
<table width="600" border="0" cellspacing="0" cellpadding="0" vspace="1"
align="center"><tr valign="top" bgcolor="#003300"> <td height="40" colspan="3"
<h2><b><font color="#FFFFFF">Design files, and help </font></b></h2> </td>
</tr> <tr valign="middle" bgcolor="#99FF66"> <td height="50" colspan="3"> <p>I
you would like the design files, or further help on this topic, or perhaps
you've got a certain viewpoint on this area, please submit the following
form:</p> </td> </tr> <tr valign="top" bgcolor="#99FF66"> <td height="40"
width="80"> <div align="right"><font color="#000000" face="Verdana, Arial, Hel
vetica, sans-serif" size="2"><b>Name:</b></font></div> </td> <td height="40"
width="150"> <input name="realname" size="25"> </td> <td height="120"
rowspan="3" valign="bottom"><font face="Verdana, Arial, Helvetica, sans-serif"
size="2"><b>Comments:</b></font><font face="Arial" size="2"> <br> <textarea
name="comment" rows="6" cols="30" wrap="VIRTUAL"></textarea> </font></td> </tr
<tr valign="top" bgcolor="#99FF66"> <td height="40" width="80"> <div
align="right"><font color="#000000" face="Verdana, Arial, Helvetica, sans-
serif" size="2"><b>E-mail:</b></font></div> </td> <td height="40" width="150">
<input type=text name="email" size="25"> <br> </td> </tr> <tr valign="top"
bgcolor="#99FF66"> <td colspan="2"> <div align="center"><font face="Arial"
size="2"> <input type="submit" value="Send Request" name="submit"> </font>
</div> </td> </tr> <tr valign="middle" bgcolor="#99FF66"> <td height="50" col-
span="3"> <div align="right"><font face="Arial" size="2"> </font></div> </td>
</tr> </table>
```

Next Word is used to replace the instances of a double quote (") with a single quote to give:

```
<table width='600' border='0' cellspacing='0' cellpadding='0' vspace='1'
align='center'><tr valign='top' bgcolor='#003300'> <td height='40' colspan='3'
```

```
<h2><b><font color='#FFFFFF'>Design files, and help </font></b></h2> </td>
</tr> <tr valign='middle' bgcolor='#99FF66'> <td height='50' colspan='3'> <p>I:
you would like the design files, or further help on this topic, or perhaps
you've got a certain viewpoint on this area, please submit the following
form:</p> </td> </tr> <tr valign='top' bgcolor='#99FF66'> <td height='40'
width='80'> <div align='right'><font color='#000000' face='Verdana, Arial, Hel
vetica, sans-serif' size='2'><b>Name:</b></font></div> </td> <td height='40'
width='150'> <input name='realname' size='25'> </td> <td height='120'
rowspan='3' valign='bottom'><font face='Verdana, Arial, Helvetica, sans-serif'
size='2'><b>Comments:</b></font><font face='Arial' size='2'> <br> <textarea
name='comment' rows='6' cols='30' wrap='VIRTUAL'></textarea> </font></td> </tr
<tr valign='top' bgcolor='#99FF66'> <td height='40' width='80'> <div
align='right'><font color='#000000' face='Verdana, Arial, Helvetica, sans-
serif' size='2'><b>E-mail:</b></font></div> </td> <td height='40' width='150'>
<input type=text name='email' size='25'> <br> </td> </tr> <tr valign='top'
bgcolor='#99FF66'> <td colspan='2'> <div align='center'><font face='Arial'
size='2'> <input type='submit' value='Send Request' name='submit'> </font>
</div> </td> </tr> <tr valign='middle' bgcolor='#99FF66'> <td height='50' col-
span='3'> <div align='right'><font face='Arial' size='2'> </font></div> </td>
</tr> </table>
```

Next we can paste this into Dreamweaver (or FrontPage, or even a text editor), and we can add the JavaScript code with:

```
document.write("<table width='600' border='0' cellspacing='0' cellpadding='0'
vspace='1' align='center'><tr valign='top' bgcolor='#003300'> <td height='40'
colspan='3'> <h2><b><font color='#FFFFFF'>Design files, and help
</font></b></h2> </td> </tr> <tr valign='middle' bgcolor='#99FF66'> <td
height='50' colspan='3'> <p>If you would like the design files, or further hel
on this topic, or perhaps you've got a certain viewpoint on this area, please
submit the following form:</p> </td> </tr> <tr valign='top' bgcolor='#99FF66'>
<td height='40' width='80'> <div align='right'><font color='#000000'
face='Verdana, Arial, Helvetica, sans-serif' size='2'><b>Name:</b></font></div
</td> <td height='40' width='150'> <input name='realname' size='25'> </td> <td
height='120' rowspan='3' valign='bottom'><font face='Verdana, Arial, Helvetica
sans-serif' size='2'><b>Comments:</b></font><font face='Arial' size='2'> <br>
<textarea name='comment' rows='6' cols='30' wrap='VIRTUAL'></textarea>
</font></td> </tr> <tr valign='top' bgcolor='#99FF66'> <td height='40'
width='80'> <div align='right'><font color='#000000' face='Verdana, Arial,
Helvetica, sans-serif' size='2'><b>E-mail:</b></font></div> </td> <td
height='40' width='150'> <input type=text name='email' size='25'> <br> </td>
</tr> <tr valign='top' bgcolor='#99FF66'> <td colspan='2'> <div
align='center'><font face='Arial' size='2'> <input type='submit' value='Send
Request' name='submit'> </font> </div> </td> </tr> <tr valign='middle'
bgcolor='#99FF66'> <td height='50' colspan='3'> <div align='right'><font
face='Arial' size='2'> </font></div> </td> </tr> </table>");
```

and the file is saved with a .js extension (such as form.js). This can then be included in any WWW page with:

```
<script language=JavaScript src="form.js"></script>
```

14.15   Other examples

There are many other examples of design tips on the CD.

Ap1 Modem codes

Ap1.1 AT commands

The AT commands are preceded by the attention code AT. They are:

A   **Go on-line in answer mode**
Instructs the modem to go off-hook immediately and then make a connection with a remote modem

Bn   **Select protocol to 300 bps to 1200 bps**
B0   Selects CCITT operation at 300 bps or 1200 bps
B1   Selects BELL operation at 300 bps or 1200 bps

D   **Go on-line in originate mode**
Instructs the modem to go off-hook and automatically dials the number contained in the dial string which follows the D command

En   **Command echo**
E0   Disable command echo   E1   Enables command echo (default)

Fn   **Select line modulation**
F0   Select auto-detect mode
F1   Select V.21 or Bell 103
F4   Select V.22 or Bell 212A 1200 bps
F5   Select V.22bis line modulation.
F6   Select V.32bis or V.32 4800 bps line modulation
F7   Select V.32bis or V.32 7200 bps line modulation
F8   Select V.32bis or V.32 9600 bps line modulation
F9   Select V.32bis 12000 line modulation
F10 Select V.32bis 14400 line modulation

Hn   **Hang-up**
H0   Go on-hook (hang-up connection)
H1   Goes off-hook

In   **Request product code or ROM checksum**
I0   Reports the product code
I1/I2   Reports the hardware ROM checksum
I3   Reports the product revision code
I4   Reports response programmed by an OEM
I5   Reports the country code number

Ln   **Control speaker volume**
L0   Low volume   L1   Low volume
L2   Medium volume (default)   L3   High volume

Mn   **Monitor speaker on/off**
M0/M   Speaker is always off   M1 Speaker is off while receiving carrier (default)
M2 Speaker is always on   M3 Speaker is on when dialing but is off at any other time

Nn   **Automode enable**
N0   Automode detection is disabled   N1   Automode detection is enabled

On   **Return to the on-line state**

O0 Enters on-line data mode with a retrain

O1 Enters on-line data mode without a retrain

P   **Set pulse dial as default**

Q   **Result code display**

Q0 Send result codes to the computer

Q1 No return codes

Sn   **Reading and writing to S registers**

Sn? Reads the Sn register

Sn=val Writes the value of val to the Sn register

T   **Set tone dial as default**

Vn   **Select word or digit result code**

V0 Display result codes in a numeric form

V1 Display result code in a long form (default)

Wn   **Error correction message control**

W0 When connected report computer connection speed

W1 When connected report computer connection speed, error correcting protocol and line speed

W2 When connected report modem connection speed

Xn   **Select result code**

X0 Partial connect message, dial-tone monitor off, busy tone monitor off

X1 Full connect message, dial-tone monitor off, busy tone monitor off

X2 Full connect message, dial-tone monitor on, busy tone monitor off

X3 Full connect message, dial-tone monitor off, busy tone monitor on

X4 Full connect message, dial-tone monitor on, busy tone monitor on

Yn   **Enables or disables long space disconnection**

Y0 Disables long space disconnect (default)

Y1 Enables long space disconnect

Zn   **Reset**

Z0 Resets modem and load stored profile 0

Z1 Resets modem and load stored profile 1

&Cn   **Select DCD options**

&C0   Sets DCD permanently on

&C1   Use state of carrier to set DCD (default)

&Dn   **DTR option**

This is used with the &Qn setting to determine the operation of the DTR signal

	&D0	&D1	&D2	&D3
&Q0	a	c	d	e
&Q1	b	c	d	e
&Q2	d	d	d	d
&Q3	d	d	d	d
&Q4	b	c	d	e
&Q5	a	c	d	e
&Q6	a	c	d	e

where

a – modem ignore DTR signal

b – modem disconnects and sends OK result code

c – modem goes into command mode and sends OK result code

d – modem disconnects and sends OK result code.

&F   **Restore factory configuration**

&Gn   **Set guard tone**

    &G0   Disables guard tone (default)

    &G1   Disables guard tone

    &G2   Selects 1800 Hz guard tone

&Kn   **DTE/modem flow control**

    &K0   Disables DTE/DCE flow control

    &K3   Enables RTS/CTS handshaking flow control (default)

    &K4   Enables XON/XOFF flow control

    &K5   Enables transparent XON/XOFF flow control

    &K6   Enables RTS/CTS and XON/XOFF flow control

&L   **Line selection**

    &L0   Selects dial-up line operation (default)

    &L1   Selects leased line operation

&Mn   **Communications mode**

&Pn   **Select pulse dialing make/break ratio**

    &P0   Sets a 39/61 make-break ratio at 10 pps (default)

    &P1   Sets a 33/67 make-break ratio at 10 pps (default)

    &P2   Sets a 39/61 make-break ratio at 20 pps (default)

    &P3   Sets a 33/67 make-break ratio at 20 pps (default)

&Qn   **Asynchronous/synchronous mode selection**

    &Q0   Set direct asynchronous operation

    &Q1   Set synchronous operation with asynchronous off-line

    &Q2   Set synchronous connect mode with asynchronous off-line

    &Q3   Set synchronous connect mode

    &Q5   Modem negotiation for error-corrected link

    &Q6   Set asynchronous operation in normal mode

&Rn   **RTS/CTS option**

    &R0   In synchronous mode, CTS changes with RTS (the delay is defined by the S26 register)

    &R1   In synchronous mode, CTS is always ON

&Sn   **DSR option**

    &S0   DSR is always ON (default)

    &S1   DSR is active after the answer tone has been detected

&Tn   **Testing and diagnostics**

    &T0   Terminates any current test

    &T1   Local analogue loopback test

    &T2   Local digital loopback test

&V   **View configuration profiles**

&Wn   **Store the current configuration in non-volatile RAM**

    &W0   Writes current settings to profile 0 in nonvolatile RAM

    &W1   Writes current settings to profile 1 in nonvolatile RAM

&Xn   **Clock source selection**

    &X0   Selects internal timing, where the modem uses its own clock for transmitted data

    &X1   Selects external timing, where the modem gets its timing from the DTE (computer)

&X2	Selects slave receive timing, where the modem gets its timing from the received signal		
&Yn	**Select default profile**		
&Y0	Use profile 0 on power-up (default)		
&Y1	Use profile 1 on power-up		
&Zn	**Store telephone numbers**		
&Z0	Store telephone number 1	&Z1	Store telephone number 2
&Z2	Store telephone number 3	&Z3	Store telephone number 4
\An	**Maximum MNP block size**		
\A0	64 characters	\A1	128 characters
\A2	192 characters	\A3	256 characters
\Bn	**Transmit break**		
\B1	Break length 100 ms	\B2	Break length 200 ms
\B3	Break length 300 ms (Default)		*and so on.*
\Gn	**Modem/modem flow control**		
\G0	Disable (Default)	\G1	Enable
\Jn	**Enable/disable DTE auto rate adjustment**		
\J0	Disable	\J1	Enable
\Kn	**Break control**		
\K0	Enter on-line command mode with no break signal		
\K1	Clear data buffers and send a break to the remote modem		
\K3	Send a break to the remote modem immediately		
\K5	Send a break to the remote modem with transmitted data		
\Ln	**MNP block transfer control**		
\L0	Use stream mode for MNP connection (default)		
\L1	Use interactive MNP block mode.		

Ap1.2 Result codes

After the modem has received an AT command it responds with a return code. A complete set of return codes are given in Table Ap1.1.

Table Ap1.1 Modem return codes

Message	Digit	Description
OK	0	Command executed without errors
CONNECT	1	A connection has been made
RING	2	An incoming call has been detected
NO CARRIER	3	No carrier detected
ERROR	4	Invalid command
CONNECT 1200	5	Connected to a 1200 bps modem
NO DIAL-TONE	6	Dial-tone not detected
BUSY	7	Remote line is busy
NO ANSWER	8	No answer from remote line
CONNECT 600	9	Connected to a 600 bps modem
CONNECT 2400	10	Connected to a 2400 bps modem
CONNECT 4800	11	Connected to a 4800 bps modem
CONNECT 9600	13	Connected to a 9600 bps modem
CONNECT 14400	15	Connected to a 14 400 bps modem

CONNECT 19200	16	Connected to a 19200 bps modem
CONNECT 28400	17	Connected to a 28400 bps modem
CONNECT 38400	18	Connected to a 38400 bps modem
CONNECT 115200	19	Connected to a 115200 bps modem
FAX	33	Connected to a FAX modem in FAX mode
DATA	35	Connected to a data modem in FAX mode
CARRIER 300	40	Connected to V.21 or Bell 103 modem
CARRIER 1200/75	44	Connected to V.23 backward channel carrier modem
CARRIER 75/1200	45	Connected to V.23 forwards channel carrier modem
CARRIER 1200	46	Connected to V.22 or Bell 212 modem
CARRIER 2400	47	Connected to V.22 modem
CARRIER 4800	48	Connected to V.32bis 4800 bps modem
CONNECT 7200	49	Connected to V.32bis 7200 bps modem
CONNECT 9600	50	Connected to V.32bis 9600 bps modem
CONNECT 12000	51	Connected to V.32bis 12000 bps modem
CONNECT 14400	52	Connected to V.32bis 14400 bps modem
CONNECT 19200	61	Connected to a 19 200 bps modem
CONNECT 28800	65	Connected to a 28 800 bps modem
COMPRESSION: CLASS 5	66	Connected to modem with MNP Class 5 compression
COMPRESSION: V.42bis	67	Connected to a V.42bis modem with compression
COMPRESSION: NONE	69	Connection to a modem with no data compression
PROTOCOL: NONE	70	
PROTOCOL: LAPM	77	
PROTOCOL: ALT	80	

Ap1.3   S-registers

The modem contains various status registers called the S-registers which store modem settings. Table Ap1.2 lists these registers.

S14	**Bitmapped options**		
	0		1
	Bit 1	E0	**E1**
	Bit 2	**Q0**	Q1
	Bit 3	V0	**V1**
	Bit 4	Reserved	
	Bit 5	**T** (tone dial)	P (pulse dial)
	Bit 6	Reserved	
	Bit 7	Answer mode	**Originate mode**
S16	**Modem test mode register**		
		0	1
	Bit 0	Local analogue loopback terminated	Local analogue loopback test in progress

Bit 2	Local digital loopback terminated	Local digital loopback test in progress
Bit 3	Remote modem analogue loopback test terminated	Remote modem analogue loopback test in progress
Bit 4	Remote modem digital loopback test terminated	Remote modem digital loopback test in progress
Bit 5	Remote modem digital self-test terminated	Remote modem digital self-test in progress
Bit 6	Remote modem analogue self-test terminated	Remote modem analogue self-test in progress
Bit 7	Unused	

S21   Bitmapped options

	0	1
Bit 0	**&J0**	&J1
Bit 1		
Bit 2	&R0	**&R1**
Bit 5	&C0	**&C1**
Bit 6	**&S0**	&S1
Bit 7	**Y0**	Y1

Bit 4, 3 = 00 &D0
Bit 4, 3 = 01 &D1
Bit 4, 3 = 10 **&D2**
Bit 4, 3 = 11 &D3

S22   Speaker/results bitmapped options

Bit 1, 0 = 00 L0
Bit 1, 0 = 01 **L1**
Bit 1, 0 = 10 L2
Bit 1, 0 = 11 L3
Bit 3, 2 = 00 M0
Bit 3, 2 = 01 **M1**
Bit 3, 2 = 10 M2
Bit 3, 2 = 11 M3
Bit 6, 5, 4 = 000 X0
Bit 6, 5, 4 = 001 Reserved
Bit 6, 5, 4 = 010 Reserved
Bit 6, 5, 4 = 011 Reserved
Bit 6, 5, 4 = 100 X1
Bit 6, 5, 4 = 101 X2
Bit 6, 5, 4 = 110 X3
Bit 6, 5, 4 = 111 **X4**
Bit 7 Reserved

S23   Bitmapped options

	0	1
Bit 0	&T5	**&T4**

Bit 3, 2, 1 = 000 300 bps communications rate
Bit 3, 2, 1 = 001 600 bps communications rate
Bit 3, 2, 1 = 010 1200 bps communications rate
Bit 3, 2, 1 = 011 **2400 bps communications rate**

Bit 3, 2, 1 = 100	4800 bps communications rate
Bit 3, 2, 1 = 101	9600 bps communications rate
Bit 3, 2, 1 = 110	19 200 bps communications rate
Bit 3, 2, 1 = 111	Reserved
Bit 5, 4 = 00	Even parity
Bit 5, 4 = 01	**Not used**
Bit 5, 4 = 10	Odd parity
Bit 5, 4 = 11	No parity
Bit 7, 6 = 00	**G0**
Bit 7, 6 = 01	G1
Bit 7, 6 = 10	G2
Bit 7, 6 = 11	G3

S23   Bitmapped options

Bit 3, 1, 0 = 000	&M0 or &Q0
Bit 3, 1, 0 = 001	&M1 or &Q1
Bit 3, 1, 0 = 010	&M2 or &Q2
Bit 3, 1, 0 = 011	&M3 or &Q3
Bit 3, 1, 0 = 100	&Q3
Bit 3, 1, 0 = 101	&Q4
Bit 3, 1, 0 = 110	**&Q5**
Bit 3, 1, 0 = 111	&Q6

	0	1
Bit 2	**&L0**	&L1
Bit 6	B0	**B1**

Bit 5, 4 = 00	**X0**
Bit 5, 4 = 01	X1
Bit 5, 4 = 10	X2

S28   Bitmapped options

Bit 4, 3 = 00	**&P0**
Bit 4, 3 = 01	&P1
Bit 4, 3 = 10	&P2
Bit 4, 3 = 11	&P3

S31   Bitmapped options

	0	1
Bit 1	**N0**	N1

Bit 3, 2 = 00	**W0**
Bit 3, 2 = 01	W1
Bit 3, 2 = 10	W2

S36   LAPM failure control

Bit 2, 1, 0 = 000	Modem disconnect
Bit 2, 1, 0 = 001	Modem stays on line and a direct mode connection
Bit 2, 1, 0 = 010	Reserved
Bit 2, 1, 0 = 011	Modem stays on line and normal mode connection is established
Bit 2, 1, 0 = 100	An MNP connection is made, if it fails then the modem disconnects
Bit 2, 1, 0 = 101	An MNP connection is made, if it fails then the modem makes a direct connection
Bit 2, 1, 0 = 110	Reserved
Bit 2, 1, 0 = 111	An MNP connection is made, if it fails then the modem makes a normal

mode connection

S37 Desired line connection speed

Bit 3, 2, 1, 0 = 0000 **Auto mode connection (F0)**

Bit 3, 2, 1, 0 = 0001 Modem connects at 300 bps (F1)

Bit 3, 2, 1, 0 = 0010 Modem connects at 300 bps (F1)

Bit 3, 2, 1, 0 = 0011 Modem connects at 300 bps (F1)

Bit 3, 2, 1, 0 = 0100 Reserved

Bit 3, 2, 1, 0 = 0101 Modem connects at 1200 bps (F4)

Bit 3, 2, 1, 0 = 0110 Modem connects at 2400 bps (F5)

Bit 3, 2, 1, 0 = 0111 Modem connects at V.23 (F3)

Bit 3, 2, 1, 0 = 1000 Modem connects at 4800 bps (F6)

Bit 3, 2, 1, 0 = 1001 Modem connects at 9600 bps (F8)

Bit 3, 2, 1, 0 = 1010 Modem connects at 12 000 bps (F9)

Bit 3, 2, 1, 0 = 1011 Modem connects at 144 000 bps (F10)

Bit 3, 2, 1, 0 = 1100 Modem connects at 7200 bps (F7)

S39 Flow control

Bit 2, 1, 0 = 000 No flow control

Bit 2, 1, 0 = 011 **RTS/CTS (&K3)**

Bit 2, 1, 0 = 100 XON/XOFF (&K4)

Bit 2, 1, 0 = 101 Transparent XON (&K5)

Bit 2, 1, 0 = 110 RTS/CTS and XON/XOFF (&K6)

S39 General bitmapped options

Bit 5, 4, 3 = 000 \K0

Bit 5, 4, 3 = 001 \K1

Bit 5, 4, 3 = 010 \K2

Bit 5, 4, 3 = 011 \K3

Bit 5, 4, 3 = 100 \K4

Bit 5, 4, 3 = 101 **\K5**

Bit 7, 6 = 00 MNP 64 character block size (\A0)

Bit 7, 6 = 01 **MNP 128 character block size (\A1)**

Bit 7, 6 = 10 MNP 192 character block size (\A2)

Bit 7, 6 = 11 MNP 256 character block size (\A3)

Table Ap1.2 Modem registers

Register	Function	Range [typical default]
S0	Rings to Auto-answer	0–255 rings [0 rings]
S1	Ring counter	0–255 rings [0 rings]
S2	Escape character	[43]
S3	Carriage return character	[13]
S6	Wait time for dial-tone	2–255 s [2 s]
S7	Wait time for carrier	1–255 s [50 s]
S8	Pause time for automatic dialing	0–255 s [2 s]
S9	Carrier detect response time	1–255 in 0.1 s units [6]
S10	Carrier loss disconnection time	1–255 in 0.1 s units [14]
S11	DTMF tone duration	50–255 in 0.001 s units [95]
S12	Escape code guard time	0–255 in 0.02 s units [50]
S13	Reserved	
S14	General bitmapped options	[8Ah (1000 1010b)]

S15	Reserved	
S16	Test mode bitmapped options (&T)	[0]
S17	Reserved	
S18	Test timer	0–255 s [0]
S19–S20	Reserved	
S21	V.24/General bitmapped options	[04h (0000 0100b)]
S22	Speak/results bitmapped options	[75h (0111 0101b)]
S23	General bitmapped options	[37h (0011 0111b)]
S24	Sleep activity timer	0–255 s [0]
S25	Delay to DSR off	0–255 s [5]
S26	RTS–CTS delay	0–255 in 0.01 s [1]
S27	General bitmapped options	[49h (0100 1001b)]
S28	General bitmapped options	[00h]
S29	Flash dial modifier time	0–255 in 10 ms [0]
S30	Disconnect inactivity timer	0–255 in 10 s [0]
S31	General bitmapped options	[02h (0000 0010b)]
S32	XON character	[Cntrl–Q, 11h (0001 0001b)]
S33	XOFF character	[Cntrl–S, 13h (0001 0011b)]
S34–S35	Reserved	
S36	LAMP failure control	[7]
S37	Line connection speed	[0]
S38	Delay before forced hang-up	0–255 s [20]
S39	Flow control	[3]
S40	General bitmapped options	[69h (0110 1001b)]
S41	General bitmapped options	[3]
S42–S45	Reserved	
S46	Data compression control	[8Ah (1000 1010b)]
S48	V.42 negotiation control	[07h (0000 0111b)]
S80	Soft-switch functions	[0]
S82	LAPM break control	[40h (0100 0000b)]
S86	Call failure reason code	0–255
S91	PSTN transmit attenuation level	0–15 dBm [10]
S92	Fax transmit attenuation level	0–15 dBm [10]
S95	Result code message control	[0]
S99	Leased line transmit level	0–15 dBm [10]

Ap2   HTML Reference

Ap2.1   Introduction

Ap2.1.1   Data Characters

Characters which are not markup text are mapped directly to strings of data characters. An ampersand followed by a character reference or a number value can be used to define a character. Table Ap2.1 defines these characters (the equivalent ampersand character reference is given in brackets). For example:

```
Fred&#174&ampBert&iquest
```

will be displayed as:

```
Fred®&Bert¿
```

An ampersand is only recognized as markup when it is followed by a letter or a '#' and a digit:

```
Fred & Bert
```

will be displayed as:

```
Fred & Bert
```

In the HTML document character set only three control characters are allowed: Horizontal Tab, Carriage Return, and Line Feed (code positions 9, 13, and 10).

Table Ap2.1   Character mappings

&#00-&#08	Unused	&#09	Horizontal tab
&#10	Line feed	&#11,&#12	Unused
&#13	Carriage Return	&#14-&#31	Unused
&#32	Space	&#33	Exclamation mark
&#34	Quotation mark (&quot)	&#35	Number sign
&#36	Dollar sign	&#37	Percent sign
&#38	Ampersand (&amp)	&#39	Apostrophe
&#40	Left parenthesis	&#41	Right parenthesis
&#42	Asterisk	&#43	Plus sign
&#44	Comma	&#45	Hyphen
&#46	Period (full stop)	&#47	Solidus
&#48-&#57	Digits 0-9	&#58	Colon
&#59	Semi-colon	&#60	Less than (&lt)
&#61	Equals sign	&#62	Greater than (&gt)
&#63	Question mark	&#64	Commercial at

&#65-&#90	Letters A-Z	&#91	Left square bracket
&#92	Reverse solidus (\)	&#93	Right square bracket
&#94	Caret	&#95	Underscore
&#96	Acute accent	&#97-&#122	Letters a-z
&#123	Left curly brace	&#124	Vertical bar
&#125	Right curly brace	&#126	Tilde

&#127-&#159 Unused

	Non-breaking Space ( )
&#161	Inverted exclamation, ¡ (&iexcl)
&#162	Cent sign ¢ (&cent)
&#163	Pound sterling £ (&pound)
&#164	General currency sign, ¤ (&curren)
&#165	Yen sign, ¥ (&yen)
&#166	Broken vertical bar, ¦ (&brvbar)
&#167	Section sign, § (&sect)
&#168	Umlaut, ¨ (&uml)
&#169	Copyright, © (&copy)
&#170	Feminine ordinal, ª (&ordf)
&#171	Left angle quote, « (&laquo)
&#172	Not sign, ¬ (&not)
&#173	Soft hyphen, - (&shy)
&#174	Registered trademark, ® (&reg)
&#175	Macron accent, ¯ (&macr)
&#176	Degree sign, ° (&deg)
&#177	Plus or minus, ± (&plusmn)
&#178	Superscript two, ² (&sup2)
&#179	Superscript three, ³ (&sup3)
&#180	Acute accent, ´ (&acute)
&#181	Micro sign, µ (&micro)
&#182	Paragraph sign, ¶ (&para)
&#183	Middle dot, · (&middot)
&#184	Cedilla, ¸ (&cedil)
&#185	Superscript one, ¹ (&sup1)
&#186	Masculine ordinal, º (&ordm)
&#187	Right angle quote, » (&raquo)
&#188	Fraction one-fourth, ¼ (&frac14)
&#189	Fraction one-half, ½ (&frac12)
&#190	Fraction three-fourths, ¾ (&frac34)
&#191	Inverted question mark, ¿ (&iquest)
&#192	Capital A, grave accent, À (&Agrave)
&#193	Capital A, acute accent, Á (&Aacute)
&#194	Capital A, circumflex accent, Â (&Acirc)
&#195	Capital A, tilde, Ã (&Atilde)
&#196	Capital A, dieresis, Ä (&Auml)
&#197	Capital A, ring, Å (&Aring)
&#198	Capital AE dipthong, Æ (&AElig)
&#199	Capital C, cedilla, Ç (&Ccedil)
&#200	Capital E, grave accent, È (&Egrave)

&#201	Capital E, acute accent, É	(&Eacute)
&#202	Capital E, circumflex accent, Ê	(&Ecirc)
&#203	Capital E, dieresis, Ë	(&Euml)
&#204	Capital I, grave accent, Ì	(&Igrave)
&#205	Capital I, acute accent, Í	(&Iacute)
&#206	Capital I, circumflex accent, Î	(&Icirc)
&#207	Capital I, dieresis, Ï	(&Iuml)
&#208	Capital Eth, Icelandic, Ð	(&ETH)
&#209	Capital N, tilde, Ñ	(&Ntilde)
&#210	Capital O, grave accent, Ò	(&Ograve)
&#211	Capital O, acute accent, Ó	(&Oacute)
&#212	Capital O, circumflex accent, Ô	(&Ocirc)
&#213	Capital O, tilde, Õ	(&Otilde)
&#214	Capital O, dieresis, Ö	(&Ouml)
&#215	Multiply sign, ×	(&times)
&#216	Capital O, slash, Ø	(&Oslash)
&#217	Capital U, grave accent, Ù	(&Ugrave)
&#218	Capital U, acute accent, Ú	(&Uacute)
&#219	Capital U, circumflex accent, Û	(&Ucirc)
&#220	Capital U, dieresis or umlaut mark, Ü	(&Uuml)
&#221	Capital Y, acute accent, Ý	(&Yacute)
&#222	Capital THORN, Icelandic, Þ	(&THORN)
&#223	Small sharp s, German, ß	(&szlig)
&#224	Small a, grave accent, à	(&agrave)
&#225	Small a, acute accent, á	(&aacute)
&#226	Small a, circumflex accent, â	(&acirc)
&#227	Small a, tilde, ã	(&atilde)
&#228	Small a, dieresis or umlaut mark, ä	(&auml)
&#229	Small a, ring, å	(&aring)
&#230	Small ae dipthong, æ	(&aelig)
&#231	Small c, cedilla, ç	(&ccedil)
&#232	Small e, grave accent, è	(&egrave)
&#233	Small e, acute accent, é	(&eacute)
&#234	Small e, circumflex accent, ê	(&ecirc)
&#235	Small e, dieresis or umlaut mark, ë	(&euml)
&#236	Small i, grave accent, ì	(&igrave)
&#237	Small i, acute accent, í	(&iacute)
&#238	Small i, circumflex accent, î	(&icirc)
&#239	Small i, dieresis or umlaut mark, ï	(&iuml)
&#240	Small eth, Icelandic, ð	(&eth)
&#241	Small n, tilde, ñ	(&ntilde)
&#242	Small o, grave accent, ò	(&ograve)
&#243	Small o, acute accent, ó	(&oacute)
&#244	Small o, circumflex accent, ô	(&ocirc)
&#245	Small o, tilde, õ	(&otilde)
&#246	Small o, dieresis or umlaut mark, ö	(&ouml)
&#247	Division sign, ÷	(&divide)
&#248	Small o, slash, ø	(&oslash)

&#249;	Small u, grave accent, ù (&ugrave)
&#250;	Small u, acute accent, ú (&uacute)
&#251;	Small u, circumflex accent, û (&ucirc)
&#252;	Small u, dieresis or umlaut mark, ü (&uuml)
&#253;	Small y, acute accent, ý (&yacute)
&#254;	Small thorn, Icelandic, þ (&thorn),
&#255;	Small y, dieresis or umlaut mark, ÿ (&yuml)

The following gives a script which generates the range of the characters:

```
<script>
  var i;
  for (i=1;i<256;i++)
  document.write("&#" + i);
</script>
```

and a sample run is:

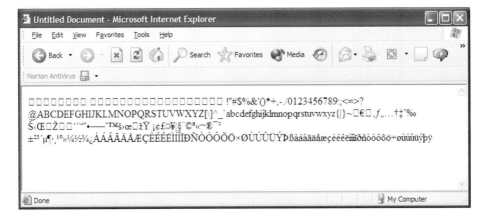

Ap2.1.2 Tags

Tags are used to delimit elements such as headings, paragraphs, lists, character highlighting and links. Normally an HTML element consists of a start-tag, which gives the element name and attributes, followed by the content and then the end tag. A start-tags is defined between a '<' and '>', and end tags between a '</' and '>'. For example to display text as bold:

```
<B>Header Level 1</B>
```

Some of the HTML only require a single start tag, these include:

</BR>	Line break.	</P>	Paragraph.
</LI>	List Item.	</DT>	Definition term.
</DD>	Definition Description.		

Element content is a sequence of data character strings and nested elements. Some elements, such as anchors, cannot be nested.

Ap2.1.3 Names

Names consist of a letter followed by letters, digits, periods or hyphens (normally limited to 72 characters). Entity names are case sensitive, but element and attribute names are not. For example:

'`<FONT>`', '`<Font>`', and '`<font>`'

are equivalent, but

'`&lt`' is different from '`&LT`'.

Start-tags always begin directly after the opening delimiter ('`<`').

Ap2.1.4 Attributes

In a start-tag, white space and attributes are allowed between the element name and the closing delimiter. Attributes typically consist of an attribute name, an equal sign, and a value, which can be:

- A string literal, delimited by single quotes or double quotes and not containing any occurrences of the delimiting character.
- A name token (a sequence of letters, digits, periods, or hyphens). Name tokens are not case sensitive.

Ap2.1.5 Comments

Comments are defined with a '`<!`' and ends with a '`>`'. Each comment starts with `--' and includes all text up to and including the next occurrence of '`--`'. When defining a comment, white space is allowed after each comment, but not before the first comment. The entire comment declaration is ignored.

```
<!DOCTYPE HTML PUBLIC "-//IETF//DTD HTML 2.0//EN">
<HEAD>
<TITLE>Comment Document</TITLE>
<!-- Comment field 1 -->
<!-- Comment field 2 -->
<!>
</HEAD> <BODY>
```

Ap2.1.6 HTML Public Text Identifiers

Documents that conform to the HTML 2.0 specification can include the following line at the start of the document:

```
<!DOCTYPE HTML PUBLIC "-//IETF//DTD HTML 2.0//EN">
```

Ap2.2 Document structure and block structuring

An HTML document is a tree of elements, including a head and body, headings, paragraphs, lists, and so on. These include:

<HTML>	Document element. Consists of a head and a body. The head contains the title and optional elements, and the body is the main text consisting of paragraphs, lists and other elements.
<HEAD>	Head element. An unordered collection of information about the document.
<TITLE>	Title. Identifies the contents of the document in a global context.
<BASE>	Base address. Provides a base address for interpreting relative URLs when the document is read out of context.
<ISINDEX>	Keyword index. Indicates that the user agent should allow the user to search an index by giving keywords.
<LINK>	Link. Represents a hyperlink (see Hyperlinks) and has the same attributes as the <A> element.
<META>	Associated meta-information. A container for identifying specialized document meta-information.
<BODY>	Body element. Contains the text flow of the document, including headings, paragraphs, lists, etc.
<H1>...<H6>	Headings. The six heading elements, <H1> to <H6> identify section headings. Typical renderings are:

H1   Bold, very-large centered font. One or two blank lines above and below.

H2   Bold, large flush-left font. One or two blank lines above and below.

H3   Italic, large font, slightly indented from the left margin. One or two blank lines above and below.

H4   Bold, normal font, indented more than H3. One blank line above and below.

H5   Italic, normal font, indented as H4. One blank line above.

H6   Bold, indented same as normal text, more than H5. One blank line above.

<P>	Paragraph. Indicates a paragraph. Typically, paragraphs are surrounded by a vertical space of one line or half a line. The first line in a paragraph is indented in some cases.
<PRE>	Preformatted text. Represents a character cell block of text and can be used to define monospaced font. It may be used with the optional WIDTH attribute, which specifies the maximum number of characters for a line.
<ADDRESS>	Address. Contains information such as address, signature and authorship. It is often used at the beginning or end of the body of a document.
<BLOCKQUOTE>	
	Block quote. Contains text quoted from another source. A typical rendering is a slight extra left and right indent, and/or italic font, and typically provides space above and below the quote.
<UL>, <LI>	Unordered List. <UL> represents a list of items and is typically rendered as a bulleted list. The content of a <UL> element is a sequence of <LI> elements.
<OL>	Ordered List. <OL> represents an ordered list of items which are sorted by sequence or order of importance and is typically rendered as a numbered list. The content of a <OL> element is a sequence of <LI> elements.
<DIR>	Directory List. <DIR> is similar to the <UL> element and represents a list of short items. The content of a <DIR> element is a sequence of <LI> elements.
<MENU>	Menu List. <MENU> is a list of items with typically one line per item. It is typically a more compact than an unordered list. The content of a <MENU> element is a sequence of <LI> elements.
<DL>, <DT>, <DD>	
	Definition list. Lists terms and corresponding definitions. Definition lists are typically formatted with the term flush-left and the definition, format-

	ted paragraph style, indented after the term. The content of a <DL> element is a sequence of <DT> elements and/or <DD> elements, usually in pairs.
<CITE>	Citation. <CITE> is used to indicate the title of a book or other citation. It is typically rendered as italics.
<CODE>	Code. <CODE> indicates an example of code and is typically rendered in a mono-spaced font. It is intended for short words or phrases of code.
<EM>	Emphasis. <EM> indicates an emphasized phrase and is typically rendered as italics.
<KBD>	Typed text. <KBD> indicates text typed by a user and is typically rendered in a mono-spaced font.
<SAMP>	Literal characters. <SAMP> indicates a sequence of literal characters and is typically rendered in a mono-spaced font.
<STRONG>	Strong emphasis. <STRONG> indicates strong emphasis and is typically rendered in bold.
<VAR>	Placeholder variable. <VAR> indicates a placeholder variable and is typically rendered as italic.
<B>	Bold. <B> indicates bold text.
<I>	Italic. <I> indicates italic text.
<TT>	Teletype. <TT> indicates teletype (monospaced) text.
<A>	Anchor. The <A> element indicates a hyperlink . Attributes of the <A> element are:

HREF	URI of the head anchor of a hyperlink.
NAME	Name of the anchor.
TITLE	AdvISOry title of the destination resource.
REL	The REL attribute gives the relationship(s) described by the hyperlink.
REV	Same as the REL attribute, but the semantics of the relationship are in the reverse direction.
URN	Specifies a preferred, more persistent identifier for the head anchor of the hyperlink.
METHODS	
	Specifies methods to be used in accessing the destination, as a whitespace-separated list of names.

 	Line Break. specifies a line break between words.
<HR>	Horizontal Rule. <HR> is a divider between sections of text and is typically a full width horizontal rule.
<IMG>	Image. <IMG> refers to an image or icon. Attributes are:
ALIGN	alignment of the image with respect to the text baseline:

- 'TOP' specifies that the top of the image aligns with the tallest item on the line containing the image.
- 'MIDDLE' specifies that the center of the image aligns with the baseline of the line containing the image.
- 'BOTTOM' specifies that the bottom of the image aligns with the baseline of the line containing the image.

ALT	Text to use in place of the referenced image resource.
ISMAP	Indicates an image map.
SRC	Specifies the URI of the image resource.

Ap2.3   Elements

!DOCTYPE	A	ACRONYM	ADDRESS	APPLET	AREA

B	BASE	BASEFONT	BDO	BGSOUND	BIG
BLOCKQUOTE	BODY	BR	BUTTON	CAPTION	CENTER
CITE	CODE	COL	COLGROUP	COMMENT	custom
DD	DEL	DFN	DIR	DIV	DL
DT	EM	EMBED	FIELDSET	FONT	FORM
FRAME	FRAMESET	HEAD	Hn	HR	HTML
HTML	Comment	I	IFRAME	IMG	INPUT

INPUT type=button INPUT type=checkbox
INPUT type=file INPUT type=hidden
INPUT type=image INPUT type=password
INPUT type=radio INPUT type=reset
INPUT type=submit INPUT type=text

INS	ISINDEX	KBD			
LABEL	LEGEND	LI	LINK	LISTING	MAP
MARQUEE	MENU	META	NOBR	NOFRAMES	NOSCRIPT
OBJECT	OL	OPTION	P	PARAM	PLAINTEXT
PRE	Q	RT	RUBY	S	SAMP
SCRIPT	SELECT	SMALL	SPAN	STRIKE	STRONG
STYLE	SUB	SUP	TABLE	TBODY	TD
TEXTAREA	TFOOT	TH	THEAD	TITLE	TR
TT	U	UL	VAR	WBR	XML
XMP					

Ap2.4   ISO Latin-1 Character Set

The following defines the ISO Latin-1 character set, which corresponds to the first 256 characters of Unicode.

Character	Decimal code	Named entity	Description
-	&#00;	-	Unused
-	&#01;	-	Unused
-	&#02;	-	Unused
-	&#03;	-	Unused
-	&#04;	-	Unused
-	&#05;	-	Unused
-	&#06;	-	Unused
-	&#07;	-	Unused
-	&#08;	-	Unused
-	&#09;	-	Horizontal tab
-	&#10;	-	Line feed
-	&#11;	-	Unused
-	&#12;	-	Unused
-	&#13;	-	Carriage Return

-	&#14;	-	Unused
-	&#15;	-	Unused
-	&#16;	-	Unused
-	&#17;	-	Unused
-	&#18;	-	Unused
-	&#19;	-	Unused
-	&#20;	-	Unused
-	&#21;	-	Unused
-	&#22;	-	Unused
-	&#23;	-	Unused
-	&#24;	-	Unused
-	&#25;	-	Unused
-	&#26;	-	Unused
-	&#27;	-	Unused
-	&#28;	-	Unused
-	&#29;	-	Unused
-	&#30;	-	Unused
-	&#31;	-	Unused
	&#32;	-	Space
!	&#33;	-	Exclamation mark
"	&#34;	&quot;	Quotation mark
#	&#35;	-	Number sign
$	&#36;	-	Dollar sign
%	&#37;	-	Percent sign
&	&#38;	&amp;	Ampersand
'	&#39;	-	Apostrophe
(	&#40;	-	Left parenthesis
)	&#41;	-	Right parenthesis
*	&#42;	-	Asterisk
+	&#43;	-	Plus sign
,	&#44;	-	Comma
-	&#45;	-	Hyphen
.	&#46;	-	Period (fullstop)
/	&#47;	-	Solidus (slash)
0	&#48;	-	Digit 0
1	&#49;	-	Digit 1
2	&#50;	-	Digit 2
3	&#51;	-	Digit 3
4	&#52;	-	Digit 4

5	&#53;	-	Digit 5
6	&#54;	-	Digit 6
7	&#55;	-	Digit 7
8	&#56;	-	Digit 8
9	&#57;	-	Digit 9
:	&#58;	-	Colon
;	&#59;	-	Semicolon
<	&#60;	&lt;	Less than
=	&#61;	-	Equals sign
>	&#62;	&gt;	Greater than
?	&#63;	-	Question mark
@	&#64;	-	Commercial at
A	&#65;	-	Capital A
B	&#66;	-	Capital B
C	&#67;	-	Capital C
D	&#68;	-	Capital D
E	&#69;	-	Capital E
F	&#70;	-	Capital F
G	&#71;	-	Capital G
H	&#72;	-	Capital H
I	&#73;	-	Capital I
J	&#74;	-	Capital J
K	&#75;	-	Capital K
L	&#76;	-	Capital L
M	&#77;	-	Capital M
N	&#78;	-	Capital N
O	&#79;	-	Capital O
P	&#80;	-	Capital P
Q	&#81;	-	Capital Q
R	&#82;	-	Capital R
S	&#83;	-	Capital S
T	&#84;	-	Capital T
U	&#85;	-	Capital U
V	&#86;	-	Capital V
W	&#87;	-	Capital W
X	&#88;	-	Capital X
Y	&#89;	-	Capital Y
Z	&#90;	-	Capital Z
[	&#91;	-	Left square bracket

\	&#92;	-	Reverse solidus (backslash)
]	&#93;	-	Right square bracket
^	&#94;	-	Caret
_	&#95;	-	Horizontal bar (underscore)
`	&#96;	-	Acute accent
a	&#97;	-	Small a
b	&#98;	-	Small b
c	&#99;	-	Small c
d	&#100;	-	Small d
e	&#101;	-	Small e
f	&#102;	-	Small f
g	&#103;	-	Small g
h	&#104;	-	Small h
i	&#105;	-	Small i
j	&#106;	-	Small j
k	&#107;	-	Small k
l	&#108;	-	Small l
m	&#109;	-	Small m
n	&#110;	-	Small n
o	&#111;	-	Small o
p	&#112;	-	Small p
q	&#113;	-	Small q
r	&#114;	-	Small r
s	&#115;	-	Small s
t	&#116;	-	Small t
u	&#117;	-	Small u
v	&#118;	-	Small v
w	&#119;	-	Small w
x	&#120;	-	Small x
y	&#121;	-	Small y
z	&#122;	-	Small z
{	&#123;	-	Left curly brace
|	|	-	Vertical bar
}	&#125;	-	Right curly brace
~	&#126;	-	Tilde
-	&#127;	-	Unused
			Nonbreaking space
¡	&#161;	&iexcl;	Inverted exclamation
¢	&#162;	&cent;	Cent sign

£	&#163;	&pound;	Pound sterling
¤	&#164;	&curren;	General currency sign
¥	&#165;	&yen;	Yen sign
¦	&#166;	¦ or &brkbar;	Broken vertical bar
§	&#167;	&sect;	Section sign
¨	&#168;	¨ or ¨	Diæresis / Umlaut
©	&#169;	&copy;	Copyright
ª	&#170;	&ordf;	Feminine ordinal
«	&#171;	&laquo;	Left angle quote, guillemot left
¬	&#172;	&not	Not sign
	&#173;	&shy;	Soft hyphen
®	&#174;	&reg;	Registered trademark
¯	&#175;	¯ or &hibar;	Macron accent
°	&#176;	&deg;	Degree sign
±	&#177;	&plusmn;	Plus or minus
²	&#178;	&sup2;	Superscript two
³	&#179;	&sup3;	Superscript three
´	&#180;	&acute;	Acute accent
µ	&#181;	&micro;	Micro sign
¶	&#182;	&para;	Paragraph sign
·	&#183;	&middot;	Middle dot
¸	&#184;	&cedil;	Cedilla
¹	&#185;	&sup1;	Superscript one
º	&#186;	&ordm;	Masculine ordinal
»	&#187;	&raquo;	Right angle quote, guillemot right
¼	&#188;	&frac14;	Fraction one-fourth
½	&#189;	&frac12;	Fraction one-half
¾	&#190;	&frac34;	Fraction three-fourths
¿	&#191;	&iquest;	Inverted question mark
À	&#192;	&Agrave;	Capital A, grave accent
Á	&#193;	&Aacute;	Capital A, acute accent
Â	&#194;	&Acirc;	Capital A, circumflex
Ã	&#195;	&Atilde;	Capital A, tilde
Ä	&#196;	&Auml;	Capital A, diæresis / umlaut
Å	&#197;	&Aring;	Capital A, ring
Æ	&#198;	&AElig;	Capital AE ligature
Ç	&#199;	&Ccedil;	Capital C, cedilla
È	&#200;	&Egrave;	Capital E, grave accent
É	&#201;	&Eacute;	Capital E, acute accent

Ê	&#202;	&Ecirc;	Capital E, circumflex
Ë	&#203;	&Euml;	Capital E, diæresis / umlaut
Ì	&#204;	&Igrave;	Capital I, grave accent
Í	&#205;	&Iacute;	Capital I, acute accent
Î	&#206;	&Icirc;	Capital I, circumflex
Ï	&#207;	&Iuml;	Capital I, diæresis / umlaut
Ð	&#208;	&ETH;	Capital Eth, Icelandic
Ñ	&#209;	&Ntilde;	Capital N, tilde
Ò	&#210;	&Ograve;	Capital O, grave accent
Ó	&#211;	&Oacute;	Capital O, acute accent
Ô	&#212;	&Ocirc;	Capital O, circumflex
Õ	&#213;	&Otilde;	Capital O, tilde
Ö	&#214;	&Ouml;	Capital O, diæresis / umlaut
×	&#215;	&times	Multiply sign
Ø	&#216;	&Oslash;	Capital O, slash
Ù	&#217;	&Ugrave;	Capital U, grave accent
Ú	&#218;	&Uacute;	Capital U, acute accent
Û	&#219;	&Ucirc;	Capital U, circumflex
Ü	&#220;	&Uuml;	Capital U, diæresis / umlaut
Ý	&#221;	&Yacute;	Capital Y, acute accent
Þ	&#222;	&THORN;	Capital Thorn, Icelandic
ß	&#223;	&szlig;	Small sharp s, German sz
à	&#224;	&agrave;	Small a, grave accent
á	&#225;	&aacute;	Small a, acute accent
â	&#226;	&acirc;	Small a, circumflex
ã	&#227;	&atilde;	Small a, tilde
ä	&#228;	&auml;	Small a, diæresis / umlaut
å	&#229;	&aring;	Small a, ring
æ	&#230;	&aelig;	Small ae ligature
ç	&#231;	&ccedil;	Small c, cedilla
è	&#232;	&egrave;	Small e, grave accent
é	&#233;	&eacute;	Small e, acute accent
ê	&#234;	&ecirc;	Small e, circumflex
ë	&#235;	&euml;	Small e, diæresis / umlaut
ì	&#236;	&igrave;	Small i, grave accent
í	&#237;	&iacute;	Small i, acute accent
î	&#238;	&icirc;	Small i, circumflex
ï	&#239;	&iuml;	Small i, diæresis / umlaut
ð	&#240;	&eth;	Small eth, Icelandic

ñ	&#241;	&ntilde;	Small n, tilde
ò	&#242;	&ograve;	Small o, grave accent
ó	&#243;	&oacute;	Small o, acute accent
ô	&#244;	&ocirc;	Small o, circumflex
õ	&#245;	&otilde;	Small o, tilde
ö	&#246;	&ouml;	Small o, diæresis / umlaut
÷	&#247;	&divide;	Division sign
ø	&#248;	&oslash;	Small o, slash
ù	&#249;	&ugrave;	Small u, grave accent
ú	&#250;	&uacute;	Small u, acute accent
û	&#251;	&ucirc;	Small u, circumflex
ü	&#252;	&uuml;	Small u, diæresis / umlaut
ý	&#253;	&yacute;	Small y, acute accent
þ	&#254;	&thorn;	Small thorn, Icelandic
ÿ	&#255;	&yuml;	Small y, diæresis / umlaut

Ap2.5 Additional Named Entities for HTML

The following gives additional names for entities.

Character	Named entity	Numeric character reference	Description
Greek			
Α	&Alpha;	&#913;	Greek capital letter alpha, U0391
Β	&Beta;	&#914;	Greek capital letter beta, U0392
Γ	&Gamma;	&#915;	Greek capital letter gamma, U0393 ISOgrk3
Δ	&Delta;	&#916;	Greek capital letter delta, U0394 ISOgrk3
Ε	&Epsilon;	&#917;	Greek capital letter epsilon, U0395
Ζ	&Zeta;	&#918;	Greek capital letter zeta, U0396
Η	&Eta;	&#919;	Greek capital letter eta, U0397
Θ	&Theta;	&#920;	Greek capital letter theta, U0398 ISOgrk3
Ι	&Iota;	&#921;	Greek capital letter iota, U0399
Κ	&Kappa;	&#922;	Greek capital letter kappa, U039A
Λ	&Lambda;	&#923;	Greek capital letter lambda, U039B ISOgrk3
Μ	&Mu;	&#924;	Greek capital letter mu, U039C
Ν	&Nu;	&#925;	Greek capital letter nu, U039D
Ξ	&Xi;	&#926;	Greek capital letter xi, U039E ISOgrk3
Ο	&Omicron;	&#927;	Greek capital letter omicron, U039F
Π	&Pi;	&#928;	Greek capital letter pi, U03A0 ISOgrk3
Ρ	&Rho;	&#929;	Greek capital letter rho, U03A1

Σ	&Sigma;	&#931;	Greek capital letter sigma, U03A3 ISOgrk3
Τ	&Tau;	&#932;	Greek capital letter tau, U03A4
Υ	&Upsilon;	&#933;	Greek capital letter upsilon, U03A5 ISOgrk3
Φ	&Phi;	&#934;	Greek capital letter phi, U03A6 ISOgrk3
Χ	&Chi;	&#935;	Greek capital letter chi, U03A7
Ψ	&Psi;	&#936;	Greek capital letter psi, U03A8 ISOgrk3
Ω	&Omega;	&#937;	Greek capital letter omega, U03A9 ISOgrk3
α	&alpha;	&#945;	Greek small letter alpha, U03B1 ISOgrk3
β	&beta;	&#946;	Greek small letter beta, U03B2 ISOgrk3
γ	&gamma;	&#947;	Greek small letter gamma, U03B3 ISOgrk3
δ	&delta;	&#948;	Greek small letter delta, U03B4 ISOgrk3
ε	&epsilon;	&#949;	Greek small letter epsilon, U03B5 ISOgrk3
ζ	&zeta;	&#950;	Greek small letter zeta, U03B6 ISOgrk3
η	&eta;	&#951;	Greek small letter eta, U03B7 ISOgrk3
θ	&theta;	&#952;	Greek small letter theta, U03B8 ISOgrk3
ι	&iota;	&#953;	Greek small letter iota, U03B9 ISOgrk3
κ	&kappa;	&#954;	Greek small letter kappa, U03BA ISOgrk3
λ	&lambda;	&#955;	Greek small letter lambda, U03BB ISOgrk3
μ	&mu;	&#956;	Greek small letter mu, U03BC ISOgrk3
ν	&nu;	&#957;	Greek small letter nu, U03BD ISOgrk3
ξ	&xi;	&#958;	Greek small letter xi, U03BE ISOgrk3
ο	&omicron;	&#959;	Greek small letter omicron, U03BF NEW
π	&pi;	&#960;	Greek small letter pi, U03C0 ISOgrk3
ρ	&rho;	&#961;	Greek small letter rho, U03C1 ISOgrk3
ς	&sigmaf;	&#962;	Greek small letter final sigma, U03C2 ISOgrk3
σ	&sigma;	&#963;	Greek small letter sigma, U03C3 ISOgrk3
τ	&tau;	&#964;	Greek small letter tau, U03C4 ISOgrk3
υ	&upsilon;	&#965;	Greek small letter upsilon, U03C5 ISOgrk3
φ	&phi;	&#966;	Greek small letter phi, U03C6 ISOgrk3
χ	&chi;	&#967;	Greek small letter chi, U03C7 ISOgrk3
ψ	&psi;	&#968;	Greek small letter psi, U03C8 ISOgrk3
ω	&omega;	&#969;	Greek small letter omega, U03C9 ISOgrk3
ϑ	&thetasym;	&#977;	Greek small letter theta symbol, U03D1 NEW
ϒ	&upsih;	&#978;	Greek upsilon with hook symbol, U03D2 NEW
ϖ	&piv;	&#982;	Greek pi symbol, U03D6 ISOgrk3
General Punctuation			
·	&bull;	&#8226;	bullet, =black small circle, U2022 ISOpub
…	&hellip;	&#8230;	horizontal ellipsis, =three dot leader, U2026 ISOpub

'	&prime;	&#8242;	prime, =minutes, =feet, U2032 ISOtech
"	&Prime;	&#8243;	double prime, =seconds, =inches, U2033 ISOtech
‾	&oline;	&#8254;	overline, =spacing overscore, U203E NEW
/	&frasl;	&#8260;	fraction slash, U2044 NEW

Letterlike Symbols

℘	&weierp;	&#8472;	script capital P, =power set, =Weierstrass p, U2118 ISOamso
ℑ	&image;	&#8465;	blackletter capital I, =imaginary part, U2111 ISOamso
ℜ	&real;	&#8476;	blackletter capital R, =real part symbol, U211C ISOamso
™	&trade;	&#8482;	trade mark sign, U2122 ISOnum
ℵ	&alefsym;	&#8501;	alef symbol, =first transfinite cardinal, U2135 NEW

Arrows

←	&larr;	&#8592;	leftward arrow, U2190 ISOnum
↑	&uarr;	&#8593;	upward arrow, U2191 ISOnum
→	&rarr;	&#8594;	rightward arrow, U2192 ISOnum
↓	&darr;	&#8595;	downward arrow, U2193 ISOnum
↔	&harr;	&#8596;	left right arrow, U2194 ISOamsa
↵	&crarr;	&#8629;	downward arrow with corner leftward, =carriage return, U21B5 NEW
⇐	&lArr;	&#8656;	leftward double arrow, U21D0 ISOtech
⇑	&uArr;	&#8657;	upward double arrow, U21D1 ISOamsa
⇒	&rArr;	&#8658;	rightward double arrow, U21D2 ISOtech
⇓	&dArr;	&#8659;	downward double arrow, U21D3 ISOamsa
⇔	&hArr;	&#8660;	left right double arrow, U21D4 ISOamsa

Mathematical Operators

∀	&forall;	&#8704;	for all, U2200 ISOtech
∂	&part;	&#8706;	partial differential, U2202 ISOtech
∃	&exist;	&#8707;	there exists, U2203 ISOtech
∅	&empty;	&#8709;	empty set, =null set, =diameter, U2205 ISOamso
∇	&nabla;	&#8711;	nabla, =backward difference, U2207 ISOtech
∈	&isin;	&#8712;	element of, U2208 ISOtech
∉	&notin;	&#8713;	not an element of, U2209 ISOtech
∋	&ni;	&#8715;	contains as member, U220B ISOtech
∏	&prod;	&#8719;	n-ary product, =product sign, U220F ISOamsb
−	&sum;	&#8722;	n-ary sumation, U2211 ISOamsb
−	&minus;	&#8722;	minus sign, U2212 ISOtech
∗	&lowast;	&#8727;	asterisk operator, U2217 ISOtech
√	&radic;	&#8730;	square root, =radical sign, U221A ISOtech
∝	&prop;	&#8733;	proportional to, U221D ISOtech

∞	&infin;	&#8734;	infinity, U221E ISOtech
∠	&ang;	&#8736;	angle, U2220 ISOamso
⊥	&and;	&#8869;	logical and, =wedge, U2227 ISOtech
⊢	&or;	&#8870;	logical or, =vee, U2228 ISOtech
∩	&cap;	&#8745;	intersection, =cap, U2229 ISOtech
∪	&cup;	&#8746;	union, =cup, U222A ISOtech
∫	&int;	&#8747;	integral, U222B ISOtech
∴	&there4;	&#8756;	therefore, U2234 ISOtech
~	&sim;	&#8764;	tilde operator, =varies with, =similar to, U223C ISOtech
≅	&cong;	&#8773;	approximately equal to, U2245 ISOtech
≅	&asymp;	&#8773;	almost equal to, =asymptotic to, U2248 ISOamsr
≠	&ne;	&#8800;	not equal to, U2260 ISOtech
≡	&equiv;	&#8801;	identical to, U2261 ISOtech
≤	&le;	&#8804;	less-than or equal to, U2264 ISOtech
≥	&ge;	&#8805;	greater-than or equal to, U2265 ISOtech
⊂	&sub;	&#8834;	subset of, U2282 ISOtech
⊃	&sup;	&#8835;	superset of, U2283 ISOtech
⊄	&nsub;	&#8836;	not a subset of, U2284 ISOamsn
⊆	&sube;	&#8838;	subset of or equal to, U2286 ISOtech
⊇	&supe;	&#8839;	superset of or equal to, U2287 ISOtech
⊕	&oplus;	&#8853;	circled plus, =direct sum, U2295 ISOamsb
⊗	&otimes;	&#8855;	circled times, =vector product, U2297 ISOamsb
⊥	&perp;	&#8869;	up tack, =orthogonal to, =perpendicular, U22A5 ISOtech
·	&sdot;	&#8901;	dot operator, U22C5 ISOamsb

Miscellaneous Technical

⌈	&lceil;	&#8968;	left ceiling, =apl upstile, U2308, ISOamsc
⌉	&rceil;	&#8969;	right ceiling, U2309, ISOamsc
⌊	&lfloor;	&#8970;	left floor, =apl downstile, U230A, ISOamsc
⌋	&rfloor;	&#8971;	right floor, U230B, ISOamsc
⟨	&lang;	&#9001;	left-pointing angle bracket, =bra, U2329 ISOtech
⟩	&rang;	&#9002;	right-pointing angle bracket, =ket, U232A ISOtech

Geometric Shapes

◊	&loz;	&#9674;	lozenge, U25CA ISOpub

Miscellaneous Symbols

♠	&spades;	&#9824;	black spade suit, U2660 ISOpub
♣	&clubs;	&#9827;	black club suit, =shamrock, U2663 ISOpub
♥	&hearts;	&#9829;	black heart suit, =valentine, U2665 ISOpub
♦	&diams;	&#9830;	black diamond suit, U2666 ISOpub

Ap2.6 Character Entities for Special Symbols

Using NE	NE	NCR	Using NCR
C0 Controls and Basic Latin			
"	&quot	&#34;	quotation mark, =apl quote, U0022 ISOnum
&	&amp	&#38;	ampersand, U0026 ISOnum
<	&lt	&#60;	less-than sign, U003C ISOnum
>	&gt	&#62;	greater-than sign, U003E ISOnum
Latin Extended-A			
Œ	&OElig	&#338;	Latin capital ligature oe, U0152 ISOlat2
œ	&oelig	&#339;	Latin small ligature oe, U0153 ISOlat2
Š	&Scaron	&#352;	Latin capital letter s with caron, U0160 ISOlat2
š	&scaron	&#353;	Latin small letter s with caron, U0161 ISOlat2
Ÿ	&Yuml	&#376;	Latin capital letter y with diaeresis, U0178 ISOlat2
Spacing Modifier Letters			
ˆ	&circ	&#710;	modifier letter circumflex accent, U02C6 ISOpub
˜	&tilde	&#732;	small tilde, U02DC ISOdia
General Punctuation			
			en space, U2002 ISOpub
			em space, U2003 ISOpub
•			thin space, U2009 ISOpub
	&zwnj	&#8204;	zero width non-joiner, U200C NEW RFC 2070
	&zwj	&#8205;	zero width joiner, U200D NEW RFC 2070
	&lrm	&#8206;	left-to-right mark, U200E NEW RFC 2070
	&rlm	&#8207;	right-to-left mark, U200F NEW RFC 2070
–	&ndash	&#8211;	en dash, U2013 ISOpub
—	&mdash	&#151;	em dash, U2014 ISOpub
'	&lsquo	&#8216;	left single quotation mark, U2018 ISOnum
'	&rsquo	&#8217;	right single quotation mark, U2019 ISOnum
‚	&sbquo	&#8218;	single low-9 quotation mark, U201A NEW
"	&ldquo	&#8220;	left double quotation mark, U201C ISOnum
"	&rdquo	&#8221;	right double quotation mark, U201D ISOnum
„	&bdquo	&#8222;	double low-9 quotation mark, U201E NEW
†	&dagger	&#8224;	dagger, U2020 ISOpub
‡	&Dagger	&#8225;	double dagger, U2021 ISOpub
‰	&permil	&#8240;	per mille sign, U2030 ISOtech
‹	&lsaquo	&#8249;	single left-pointing angle quotation mark, U2039 ISO proposed
›	&rsaquo	&#8250;	single right-pointing angle quotation mark, U203A ISO proposed

Ap2.7　Character Set Recognition

The **META** element can be used to define the character set for a document. The HTTP-EQUIV attribute is set to "Content-Type" and CONTENT attribute defines the content type. A character set is defined with the CHARSET= attribute. For example, the following defines the Windows-1251 character set:

```
<META HTTP-EQUIV="Content-Type"
  CONTENT="text/html; CHARSET=windows-1251">
```

If the META element is inserted before the BODY element, it affects the whole document. Example character sets are:

Display Name	Preferred Charset ID	Additional Aliases	MLang Code Page	Supported by Versions
Arabic ASMO-708	ASMO-708		708	4CS, 5
Arabic (DOS)	DOS-720		720	4CS, 5
Arabic (ISO)	ISO-8859-6	ISO_8859-6:1987, ISO-ir-127, ISO_8859-6, ECMA-114, arabic, csISOLatinArabic	28596	4CS, 5
Arabic (Windows)	Windows-1256		1256	4CS, 5
Baltic (ISO)	ISO-8859-4	csISOLatin4, ISO-ir-110, ISO_8859-4, ISO_8859-4:1988, l4, latin4	28594	4, 5
Baltic (Windows)	Windows-1257		1257	4, 5
Central European (DOS)	IBM852	cp852	852	4, 5
Central European (ISO)	ISO-8859-2	csISOLatin2, ISO-ir-101, ISO8859-2, ISO_8859-2, ISO_8859-2:1987, l2, latin2	28592	3, 4, 5
Central European (Windows)	Windows-1250	x-cp1250	1250	3, 4, 5
Chinese Simplified (GB2312)	Gb2312	chinese, csGB2312, csISO58GB23128, GB2312, GBK, GB_2312-80, ISO-ir-58	936	3, 4, 5
Chinese Simplified (HZ)	Hz-gb-2312		52936	4, 5
Chinese Traditional	big5	csbig5, x-x-big5	950	3, 4, 5
Cyrillic (DOS)	Cp866	IBM866	866	4, 5

Cyrillic (ISO)	ISO-8859-5	csISOLatinCyrillic, cyrillic, ISO-ir-144, ISO_8859-5, ISO_8859-5:1988	28595	4, 5
Cyrillic (KOI8-R)	koi8-r	csKOI8R, koi	20866	3, 4, 5
Cyrillic (Windows)	windows-1251	x-cp1251	1251	3, 4, 5
Greek (ISO)	ISO-8859-7	csISOLatinGreek, ECMA-118, ELOT_928, greek, greek8, ISO-ir-126, ISO_8859-7, ISO_8859-7:1987	28597	3, 4, 5
Greek (Windows)	Windows-1253	windows-1253	1253	5
Hebrew (DOS)	DOS-862		862	4CS, 5
Hebrew (ISO)	ISO-8859-8	csISOLatinHebrew, hebrew, ISO-ir-138, ISO_8859-8, visual, ISO-8859-8 Visual	28598	4CS, 5
Hebrew (Windows)	windows-1255	logical, ISO_8859-8:1988, ISO-ir-138	1255	3CS, 4CS, 5
Japanese (JIS)	ISO-2022-jp	csISO2022JP	50220	4, 5
Japanese (JIS-Allow 1-byte Kana)	csISO2022JP	ISO-2022-jp	50221	4, 5
Japanese (JIS-Allow 1-byte Kana - SO/SI)	ISO-2022-jp	csISO2022JP	50222	3, 4, 5
Japanese (EUC)	euc-jp	csEUCPkdFmtJapanese, Extended_UNIX_Code_Packed_Format_for_Japanese, x-euc, x-euc-jp	51932	3, 4, 5
Japanese (Shift-JIS)	shift_jis	csShiftJIS, csWindows31J, ms_Kanji, shift-jis, x-ms-cp932, x-sjis	932	3, 4, 5
Korean	ks_c_5601-1987	csKSC56011987, euc-kr, korean, ks_c_5601	949	3, 4, 5
Korean (ISO)	ISO-2022-kr	csISO2022KR	50225	3, 4, 5
Latin 3 (ISO)	ISO-8859-3		28593	4, 5
Thai (Windows)	ISO-8859-11	windows-874	874	3, 4, 5
Turkish (Windows)	Windows-1254	windows-1254	1254	3, 4, 5
Turkish (ISO)	ISO-8859-9	csISOLatin5, ISO_8859-9, ISO_8859-9:1989, ISO-ir-148, l5, latin5	28599	3, 4, 5
Ukrainian (KOI8-U)	koi8-u		21866	4, 5
Unicode (UTF-7)	utf-7	csUnicode11UTF7, unicode-1-1-utf-7, x-unicode-2-0-utf-7	65000	4, 5

Unicode (UFT-8)	utf-8	unicode-1-1-utf-8, unicode-2-0-utf-8, x-unicode-2-0-utf-8	65001	4, 5
Vietnamese (Windows)	windows-1258		1258	3, 4, 5
Western European (Windows)	Windows-1252		1252	5
Western European (ISO)	ISO-8859-1	ANSI_X3.4-1968, ANSI_X3.4-1986, ascii, cp367, cp819, csASCII, IBM367, IBM819, ISO-ir-100, ISO-ir-6, ISO646-US, ISO8859-1, ISO_646.irv:1991, ISO_8859-1, ISO_8859-1:1987, latin1, us, us-ascii, x-ansi	1252	3, 4, 5

Ap3 ASCII Reference

Ap3.1 Standard ASCII

ANSI defined a standard alphabet known as ASCII. This has since been adopted by the CCITT as a standard, known as IA5 (International Alphabet No. 5). The following tables define this alphabet in binary, as a decimal value, as a hexadecimal value and as a character.

Binary	Decimal	Hex	Character	Binary	Decimal	Hex	Character
00000000	0	00	NUL	00010000	16	10	DLE
00000001	1	01	SOH	00010001	17	11	DC1
00000010	2	02	STX	00010010	18	12	DC2
00000011	3	03	ETX	00010011	19	13	DC3
00000100	4	04	EOT	00010100	20	14	DC4
00000101	5	05	ENQ	00010101	21	15	NAK
00000110	6	06	ACK	00010110	22	16	SYN
00000111	7	07	BEL	00010111	23	17	ETB
00001000	8	08	BS	00011000	24	18	CAN
00001001	9	09	HT	00011001	25	19	EM
00001010	10	0A	LF	00011010	26	1A	SUB
00001011	11	0B	VT	00011011	27	1B	ESC
00001100	12	0C	FF	00011100	28	1C	FS
00001101	13	0D	CR	00011101	29	1D	GS
00001110	14	0E	SO	00011110	30	1E	RS
00001111	15	0F	SI	00011111	31	1F	US

Binary	Decimal	Hex	Character	Binary	Decimal	Hex	Character
00100000	32	20	SPACE	00110000	48	30	0
00100001	33	21	!	00110001	49	31	1
00100010	34	22	"	00110010	50	32	2
00100011	35	23	#	00110011	51	33	3
00100100	36	24	$	00110100	52	34	4
00100101	37	25	%	00110101	53	35	5
00100110	38	26	&	00110110	54	36	6
00100111	39	27	/	00110111	55	37	7
00101000	40	28	(	00111000	56	38	8
00101001	41	29	)	00111001	57	39	9
00101010	42	2A	*	00111010	58	3A	:
00101011	43	2B	+	00111011	59	3B	;
00101100	44	2C	,	00111100	60	3C	<
00101101	45	2D	–	00111101	61	3D	=
00101110	46	2E	.	00111110	62	3E	>
00101111	47	2F	/	00111111	63	3F	?

Binary	Decimal	Hex	Character	Binary	Decimal	Hex	Character
01000000	64	40	@	01010000	80	50	P
01000001	65	41	A	01010001	81	51	Q
01000010	66	42	B	01010010	82	52	R
01000011	67	43	C	01010011	83	53	S
01000100	68	44	D	01010100	84	54	T
01000101	69	45	E	01010101	85	55	U
01000110	70	46	F	01010110	86	56	V
01000111	71	47	G	01010111	87	57	W
01001000	72	48	H	01011000	88	58	X
01001001	73	49	I	01011001	89	59	Y
01001010	74	4A	J	01011010	90	5A	Z
01001011	75	4B	K	01011011	91	5B	[
01001100	76	4C	L	01011100	92	5C	\
01001101	77	4D	M	01011101	93	5D	]
01001110	78	4E	N	01011110	94	5E	`
01001111	79	4F	O	01011111	95	5F	_

Binary	Decimal	Hex	Character	Binary	Decimal	Hex	Character
01100000	96	60		01110000	112	70	p
01100001	97	61	a	01110001	113	71	q
01100010	98	62	b	01110010	114	72	r
01100011	99	63	c	01110011	115	73	s
01100100	100	64	d	01110100	116	74	t
01100101	101	65	e	01110101	117	75	u
01100110	102	66	f	01110110	118	76	v
01100111	103	67	g	01110111	119	77	w
01101000	104	68	h	01111000	120	78	x
01101001	105	69	i	01111001	121	79	y
01101010	106	6A	j	01111010	122	7A	z
01101011	107	6B	k	01111011	123	7B	{
01101100	108	6C	l	01111100	124	7C	:
01101101	109	6D	m	01111101	125	7D	}
01101110	110	6E	n	01111110	126	7E	~
01101111	111	6F	o	01111111	127	7F	DEL

Ap3.2   Extended ASCII code

The standard ASCII character has 7 bits and the basic set ranges from 0 to 127. This code is rather limited as it does not contain symbols such as Greek letters, lines, and so on. For this purpose the extended ASCII code has been defined. This fits into character numbers 128 to 255. The following four tables define a typical extended ASCII character set.

Binary	Decimal	Hex	Character	Binary	Decimal	Hex	Character
10000000	128	80	Ç	10010000	144	90	É
10000001	129	81	ü	10010001	145	91	æ
10000010	130	82	é	10010010	146	92	Æ
10000011	131	83	â	10010011	147	93	ô
10000100	132	84	ä	10010100	148	94	ö
10000101	133	85	à	10010101	149	95	ò
10000110	134	86	å	10010110	150	96	û
10000111	135	87	ç	10010111	151	97	ù
10001000	136	88	ê	10011000	152	98	ÿ
10001001	137	89	ë	10011001	153	99	Ö
10001010	138	8A	è	10011010	154	9A	Ü
10001011	139	8B	ï	10011011	155	9B	¢
10001100	140	8C	î	10011100	156	9C	£
10001101	141	8D	ì	10011101	157	9D	¥
10001110	142	8E	Ä	10011110	158	9E	₧
10001111	143	8F	Å	10011111	159	9F	ƒ

Binary	Decimal	Hex	Character	Binary	Decimal	Hex	Character
10100000	160	A0	á	10110000	176	B0	░
10100001	161	A1	í	10110001	177	B1	▒
10100010	162	A2	ó	10110010	178	B2	▓
10100011	163	A3	ú	10110011	179	B3	│
10100100	164	A4	ñ	10110100	180	B4	┤
10100101	165	A5	Ñ	10110101	181	B5	╡
10100110	166	A6	ª	10110110	182	B6	╢
10100111	167	A7	º	10110111	183	B7	╖
10101000	168	A8	¿	10111000	184	B8	╕
10101001	169	A9	⌐	10111001	185	B9	╣
10101010	170	AA	¬	10111010	186	BA	║
10101011	171	AB	½	10111011	187	BB	╗
10101100	172	AC	¼	10111100	188	BC	╝
10101101	173	AD	¡	10111101	189	BD	╜
10101110	174	AE	«	10111110	190	BE	╛
10101111	175	AF	»	10111111	191	BF	┐

Binary	Decimal	Hex	Character	Binary	Decimal	Hex	Character
11000000	192	C0	└	11010000	208	D0	╨
11000001	193	C1	┴	11010001	209	D1	╤
11000010	194	C2	┬	11010010	210	D2	╥
11000011	195	C3	├	11010011	211	D3	╙
11000100	196	C4	─	11010100	212	D4	╘
11000101	197	C5	┼	11010101	213	D5	╒
11000110	198	C6	╞	11010110	214	D6	╓
11000111	199	C7	╟	11010111	215	D7	╫
11001000	200	C8	╚	11011000	216	D8	╪
11001001	201	C9	╔	11011001	217	D9	┘
11001010	202	CA	╩	11011010	218	DA	┌
11001011	203	CB	╦	11011011	219	DB	█
11001100	204	CC	╠	11011100	220	DC	▄
11001101	205	CD	═	11011101	221	DD	▌
11001110	206	CE	╬	11011110	222	DE	▐
11001111	207	CF	╧	11011111	223	DF	▀

Binary	Decimal	Hex	Character	Binary	Decimal	Hex	Character
11100000	224	E0	α	11110000	240	F0	Ξ
11100001	225	E1	ß	11110001	241	F1	±
11100010	226	E2	Γ	11110010	242	F2	≥
11100011	227	E3	π	11110011	243	F3	≤
11100100	228	E4	Σ	11110100	244	F4	⌠
11100101	229	E5	σ	11110101	245	F5	⌡
11100110	230	E6	µ	11110110	246	F6	÷
11100111	231	E7	τ	11110111	247	F7	≈
11101000	232	E8	Φ	11111000	248	F8	°
11101001	233	E9	Θ	11111001	249	F9	·
11101010	234	EA	Ω	11111010	250	FA	·
11101011	235	EB	δ	11111011	251	FB	√
11101100	236	EC	φ	11111100	252	FC	^{n}
11101101	237	ED	φ	11111101	253	FD	^{2}
11101110	238	EE	ε	11111110	254	FE	■
11101111	239	EF	Λ	11111111	255	FF	

Ap4   Glossary

100Base-FX   IEEE-defined standard for 100 Mbps Ethernet using multimode fiber-optic cable.

100Base-TX (802.3u)   IEEE-defined standard for 100 Mbps Ethernet using two pairs of Cat-5 twisted-pair cable.

100VG-AnyLAN   HP-derived network architecture based on the IEEE 802.12 standard that uses 100 Mbps transmission rates. It uses a centrally controlled access method referred to as the Demand Priority Protocol (DPP), where the end node requests permission to transmit and the hub determines which node may do so, depending on the priority of the traffic.

10BASE-T   IEEE-defined standard for 10 Mbps Ethernet using twisted-pair cables.

802.10   IEEE-defined standard for LAN security. It is sometimes used by network switches as a VLAN protocol and uses a technique where frames on any LAN carry a virtual LAN identification. For large networks this can be modified to provided security over the Internet.

802.12 Demand Priority Protocol

IEEE-defined standard of transmitting 100 Mbps over voice grade (telephone) twisted-pair cabling. *See* 100VG-AnyLAN.

802.1d   IEEE-defined bridging standard for Spanning Tree protocol that is used to determine factors on how bridges (or switches) forward packets and avoid networking loops. Networks which use redundant loops (for alternative routes) need to implement the IEEE 802.1d standard to stop packets from looping forever.

802.2   A set of IEEE-defined specifications for Logical Link Control (LLC) layer. It provides some network functions and interfaces the IEEE 802.5, or IEEE 802.3, standards to the transport layer.

802.3   IEEE-defined standard for CSMA/CD networks. IEEE 802.3 is the most popular implementation of Ethernet.

802.3u   IEEE-defined standard for 100 Mbps Fast Ethernet. It also covers a technique called auto sensing which allows 100 Mbps devices to connecting to 10 Mbps devices.

802.4   IEEE-defined token bus specifications.

802.5   IEEE-defined standard for token ring networks.

AAL   ATM adaptation layer. A service-dependent sublayer of the data link layer, which accepts data from different applications and presents it to the ATM layer as a 48-byte ATM payload segment. AALs have two sublayers: CS and SAR. There are four types of AAL, recommended by the ITU-T, these are: AAL1, AAL2, AAL3/4, and AAL5.

AAL1	ATM adaptation layer 1. Connection-oriented, delay-sensitive services requiring constant bit rates, such as uncompressed video and other isochronous traffic.
AAL2	ATM adaptation layer 2. Connection-oriented services that support a variable bit rate, such as some isochronous video and voice traffic.
AAL3/4	ATM adaptation layer 3/4. Connectionless and connection-oriented links, but is primarily used for the transmission of SMDS packets over ATM networks.
AAL5	ATM adaptation layer 5. Connection-oriented, VBR services, and is used predominantly for the transfer of classical IP over ATM and LANE traffic.
AARP	AppleTalk Address Resolution Protocol. An AppleTalk protocol which maps the data-link address to a network address.
AARP	AppleTalk probe packets. Data packets which determine if a node ID is being used by another node in a AppleTalk network. If the node determines that the node ID is not being used, the node will use it. If not, it will send out more AARP packets.
ABM	Asynchronous Balanced Mode. An HDLC communication mode supporting peer-oriented, point-to-point communications between two nodes, where either station can initiate transmission.
ABR	Available bit rate. A QoS class defined by the ATM Forum for ATM networks. ABR is used for connections that do not require a timing relationships between source and destination. It also provides no guarantees in terms of cell loss or delay, providing only best-effort service.
Access list	A list which is kept by Cisco routers which define the control access for the router.
Access method	The method that network devices use to access the network medium.
Access server	A communications device that allows the connection of asynchronous devices, such as serial port terminals, to a LAN. It thus converts an asynchronous protocol to a synchronous one.
Acknowledgment	Notification sent from one network device to another to acknowledge an event.
ACR	Allowed cell rate. This is used in ATM and is used for traffic management.
ACSE	Association control service element. This has been defined by the OSI and is used to establish, maintain, or terminate a connection between two applications.
Active hub	Multiported device that amplifies LAN transmission signals.
Active monitor	A device which is responsible for managing a Token Ring. A node becomes the active monitor if it has the highest MAC address on the ring, and is responsible for such management tasks, such as ensuring that tokens are not lost, or that frames

do not circulate indefinitely.

Adapter Device which usually connects a node onto a network, normally called a network interface adapter (NIC).

Adaptive cut-through switching

A forwarding technique on a switch which determines when the error count on frames received has exceeded the pre-configured limits. When this count is exceeded, it modifies its own operating state so that it no longer performs cut-through switching and goes into a store-and-forward mode. The cut-through method is extremely fast but suffers from the inability to check the CRC field. Thus if incorrect frames are transmitted they could have severe effects on the network segment. This is overcome with an adaptive cut-through switch by checking the CRC as the frame moves through the switch. When errors become too great the switch implements a store-and-forward method.

Adaptive delta modulation PCM

Similar to delta modulation PCM, but uses a number of bits to code the slope of the signal.

Adaptive Huffman coding Uses a variable Huffman coding technique which responds to local changes in probabilities.

ADCCP Advanced Data Communications Control Protocol. An ANSI-defined standard for a bit-oriented data link control protocol.

Address aging The time that a dynamic address stays in the address routing table of a bridge or switch.

Addressed call mode A mode that uses control signals and commands to establish and terminate calls in V.25bis.

Address resolution Resolves the data link layer address from the network layer address.

Address tables These are used by routers, switches and hubs to store either physical (such as MAC addresses) or higher-level addresses (such as IP addresses). The tables map node addresses to network addresses or physical domains. These address tables are dynamic and change due to nodes moving around the network.

Address A unique label for the location of data or the identity of a communications device. This address can either be numeric or alphanumeric.

Administrative distance Rating of the trustworthiness of a routing information source (typically between 0 and 255). The higher the value, the lower the trustworthiness rating.

Address mask A combination of bits which define the address part and the host part.

Address resolution A method which resolves differences in addressing schemes, typically between data link and network addresses.

Administrative distance Used on Cisco routers to define the trustworthiness of a routing

	information source. It varies between 0 and 255, where 255 gives the lowest trustworthiness rating.
Advertising	Method used by routers where routing or service updates are sent at specified intervals so that other routers on the network can maintain lists of usable routes.
AEP	AppleTalk Echo Protocol. This is used to test the connectivity between two AppleTalk nodes.
Agent	A program which allows users to configure or fault-find nodes on a network, and also a program that processes queries and returns replies on behalf of an application.
Aging	The removal of an address from the address table of a router or switch that is no longer referenced to forward a packet.
A-law	The ITU-T companding standard used in the conversion between analog and digital signals in PCM systems. Used mainly in European telephone networks.
Alignment error	In Ethernet, an error that occurs when the total number of bits of a received frame is not divisible by eight.
AM	Amplitude modulation. Modulation technique which represents the data as the amplitude of a carrier signal.
ANSI	American National Standards Institute. ANSI is a non-profit making organization which is made up of expert committees that publish standards for national industries.
ASCII	American Standard Code for Information Interchange. An ANSI-defined character alphabet which has since been adopted as a standard international alphabet for the interchange of characters.
AM	Amplitude modulation. Information is contained in the amplitude of a carrier.
ASK	Amplitude-Shift Keying. Uses two, or more, amplitudes to represent binary digits. Typically used to transmit binary over speech-limited channels.
AppleTalk	Series of communications protocols designed by Apple Computer.
Application layer	The highest layer of the OSI model.
ARP	Address Resolution Protocol. Internet protocol used to map an IP address to a MAC address.
ARPA	Advanced Research Projects Agency. Research and development organization that is part of DoD. ARPA evolved into DARPA, but have since changed back to ARPA.
ARPANET	Advanced Research Projects Agency Network, which was developed in the 1970s (funded by ARPA, then DARPA).
ASN.1	Abstract Syntax Notation One. OSI language for describing data types independent of particular computer structures and representation techniques.

Asynchronous transmission

Transmission where individual characters are sent one-by-one. Normally each character is delimited by a start and a stop bit. With asynchronous communications the transmitter and receiver only have to be roughly synchronized.

Asynchronous

Communication which does not depend on a clock.

ATM

Asynchronous Transfer Mode. Networking technology which involves sending 53-byte fast packets (ATM cell), as specified by the ANSI T1S1 subcommittee. The first 5 bytes are the header and the remaining bytes are the information field which can hold 48 bytes of data. Optionally the data can contain a 4-byte ATM adaptation layer and 44 bytes of actual data. The ATM adaptation layer field allows for fragmentation and reassembly of cells into larger packets at the source and destination respectively. The control field also contains bits which specify whether this is a flow control cell or an ordinary data cell, a bit to indicate whether this packet can be deleted in a congested network, and so on.

ATM Forum

Promotes standards-based implementation agreements for ATM technology.

ATM layer

Service-independent sublayer of the data link layer in an ATM network. The ATM layer receives the 48-byte payload segments from the AAL and attaches a 5-byte header to each, producing standard 53-byte ATM cells.

Attenuation

Loss of communication signal energy.

AUI

Attachment unit interface. In Ethernet, it is the interface between an MAU and a NIC (network interface card).

Automatic broadcast control

Technique which minimizes broadcast and multicast traffic flooding through a switch. A switch acts as a proxy server and screens previously resolved ARP. This eliminates broadcasts associated with them.

Autonegotiation

Technique used by an IEEE 802.3u node which determines whether a device that it is receiving or transmitting data in one of a number of Ethernet modes (100Base-TX, 100Base-TX Full Duplex, 10Base-T, 10Base-T Full Duplex or 100Base-T4). When the mode is learned, the device then adjusts to the required transmission speed.

Autonomous system

A collection of networks which have a common administration and share a common routing strategy. Each autonomous system is assigned a unique 16-bit number by the IANA.

Autosensing

Used by a 100Base-TX device to determine if the incoming data is transmitted at 10 Mbps or 100 Mbps.

Back pressure

Technique which slows the incoming data rate into the buffer of a 802.3 port preventing it from receiving too much data.

	Switches which implement back pressure will transmit a jam signal to stop data input.
Backbone cabling	Cabling interconnects wiring closets, wiring closets, and between buildings.
Backbone	The primary path for networked traffic.
Backoff	The retransmission delay enforced when a collision occurs.
BACP	Bandwidth allocation control protocol. Protocol which monitors network traffic and allows or disallows access to users, depending on their needs. It is awaiting approval by the IETF.
Bandwidth	In an analogue system it is defined as the range of frequencies contained in a signal. As an approximation it is the difference between the highest and lowest frequency in the signal. In a digital transmission system it is normally quoted as bits per second.
Baseband	Data transmission using unmodulated signals.
BRI	Basic rate interface. Connection between ISDN and the user. It has three separate channels, one D-channel (which carries control information) and two B channels (which carry data).
Baud rate	The number of signaling elements sent per second with RS-232, or modem, communications. In RS-232 the baud rate is equal to the bit-rate. With modems, two or more bits can be encoded as a single signaling element, such as 2 bits being represented by four different phase shifts (or one signaling element). The signaling element could change its amplitude, frequency or phase-shift to increase the bit-rate. Thus the bit-rate is a better measure of information transfer.
BER	Bit error rate. The ratio of received bits that contain errors.
BGP	Border Gateway Protocol. Interdomain routing protocol that replaces EGP.
Big-endian	Method of storing or transmitting data in which the most significant bit or byte is presented first.
Bit stuffing	The insertion of extra bits to prevent the appearance of a defined sequence. In HDLC the bit sequence 01111110 delimits the start and end of a frame. Bit stuffing stops this bit sequence from occurring anywhere in the frame by the receiver inserting a 0 whenever there are five consecutive 1's transmitted. At the receiver if five consecutive 1's are followed by a 0 then the 0 is deleted.
BNC	A commonly used connector for coaxial cable.
BOOTP	A standard TCP/IP protocol which allows nodes to be dynamically allocated an IP address from an Ethernet MAC address.
Border gateway	Router that communicates with routers in other autonomous systems.
Bridge	A device which physically links two or more networks using the

	same communications protocols, such as Ethernet/Ethernet or token ring/token ring. It allows for the filtering of data between network segments.
Broadband	Data transmission using multiplexed data using an analogue signal or high-frequency electromagnetic waves.
Broadcast address	Special address reserved for sending a message to all stations. Generally, a broadcast address is a MAC destination address of all ones.
Broadcast domain	Network where broadcasts can be reported to all nodes on the network bounded by routers. Broadcast packets cannot traverse a router.
Broadcast storm	Flood of broadcast packets generated by a broadcast transmission where high numbers of receivers are targeted for a long period of time.
Broadcast	Data packet that will be sent to all nodes on a network. Broadcasts are identified by a broadcast address.
BSD	Berkeley Standard Distribution. Term used to describe any of a variety of UNIX-type operating systems.
Buffer	A temporary-storage space in memory.
Bus	A network topology where all nodes share a common transmission medium.
Byte	A group of eight bits.
Capacity	The maximum data rate in Mbps.
Cat-1 cable	Used for telephone communications and is not suitable for transmitting data.
Cat-2 cable	Used for transmitting data at speeds up to 4 Mbps.
Cat-3 cable	An EIA/TIA-568 wiring standard for unshielded or shielded twisted pair cables. Up to 10 Mbps.
Cat-4 cable	Used in Token Ring networks and can transmit data at speeds up to 16 Mbps.
Cat-5 cable	An EIA/TIA-568 wiring standard for unshielded or shielded twisted-pair cables for the transmission of over 100 Mbps.
CBR `	Constant bit rate. QOS class defined by the ATM Forum for ATM networks and is used for connections that depend on precise clocking to ensure undistorted delivery.
CCITT	Consultative Committee for International Telegraph and Telephone. International organization responsible for the development of communications standards. Now named ITU-T.
CDP	Cisco Discovery Protocol. Used in Cisco routers, bridges and switches to pass information on the connected networks.
Cell relay	Networking technology based on the use of small, fixed-size packets, or cells.

Cell	The basic unit for ATM switching and multiplexing. Cells contain identifiers that specify the data stream to which they belong. Each cell consists of a 5-byte header and 48 bytes of payload.
CEPT	Conférence Européenne des Postes et des Télécommunications. Association
CHAP	Challenge-handshake authentication protocol. Identification method used by PPP to determine the originator of a connection.
Cheapernet	IEEE 802.3 10Base2 standard.
Checksum	An error-detection scheme in which bits are grouped to form integer values which are then summated. Normally, the negative of this value is then added as a checksum. At the receiver, all the grouped values and the checksum are summated and, in the absence of errors, the result should be zero.
Circuit switching	Switching system in which a dedicated physical circuit path must exist between sender and receiver for the call duration
Cisco IOS software	Cisco Internetwork Operating System software. Provides an operating system for a Cisco router.
Client	Node or program that connects to a server node or program.
CLP	Cell loss priority. Field in the ATM cell header that determines the probability of a cell being dropped if the network becomes congested.
Coaxial cable	A transmission medium consisting of one or more central wire conductors surrounded by an insulating layer and encased in either a wire mesh or extruded metal sheathing. It supports RF frequencies from 50 to about 500 MHz. It comes in either a 10-mm diameter (thick coax) or a 5-mm diameter (thin coax).
Collapsed backbone	Non-distributed backbone in which all network segments are interconnected by way of an internetworking device.
Collision domain	The network area within which frames that have collided are propagated. Repeaters and hubs propagate collisions, but switches, bridges and routers do not.
Collision	Occurs when one or more devices try to transmit over an Ethernet network simultaneously.
Connectionless	Describes data transfer without the existence of a virtual circuit.
Connection-oriented	Describes data transfer that requires the establishment of a virtual circuit. See also connectionless.
Contention	Access method in which network devices compete to get access the physical medium.
Convergence	The speed and ability of a group of internetworking devices running a specific routing protocol to agree on the topology of an internetwork after a change in that topology.
CDDI	Copper distributed data interface. FDDI over copper.

Cost	An arbitrary value used by routers to compare different routes. Typically it is measured by hop counts, typical time delays or bandwidth.
Count to infinity	Occurs in routing algorithms that are slow to converge, where routers continuously increment the hop count to particular networks. It is typically overcome by setting an arbitrary hop-count limit.
CRC	Cyclic Redundancy Check. An error-detection scheme.
Cross-talk	Interference noise caused by conductors radiating electromagnetic radiation to couple into other conductors.
CSMA/CD	Carrier sense multiple access collision detect. Media-access method in which nodes contend to get access to the common bus. If the bus is free of traffic (Carrier Sense) any of the nodes can transmit (Multiple Access). If two nodes gain access at the same time then a collision occurs (Collision Detection). A collision then occurs, and the nodes causing the collision then wait for a random period of time before they retransmit. CSMA/CD access is used by Ethernet and IEEE 802.3.
Cut sheet	Rough diagram indicating where cable runs are located and the numbers of rooms they lead to.
Cut-through switching	Technique where a switching device directs a packet to the destination port(s) as soon as it receives the destination and source address scanned from the packet header.
DARPA	Defense Advanced Research Projects Agency. US government agency that funded research for and experimentation with the Internet.
Data link layer	Second layer of the OSI model which is responsible for link, error and flow control. It normally covers the framing of data packets, error control and physical addressing. Typical data link layers includes Ethernet and FDDI.
Data stream	All data transmitted through a communications line in a single read or write operation.
Datagram	Logical grouping of information sent as a network layer unit over a transmission medium without prior establishment of a virtual circuit. IP datagrams are the primary information units in the Internet.
DCE	Data communications equipment. These are devices and connections of a communications network that comprise the network end of the user-to-network interface, such as modems and cables.
Decorative raceway	Wall-mounted channel with removable cover used to support horizontal cabling.
Delta modulation PCM	Uses a single-bit code to represent the analogue signal. A 1 is transmission when the current sample increases its level, else a 0 is transmitted. Delta modulation PCM requires a higher sam-

	pling rate that the Nyquist rate, but the actual bit rate is normally lower.
Destination MAC address	A 6-byte data unique of the destination MAC address. It is normally quoted as a 12-digit hexadecimal number (such as A5:B2:10:64:01:44).
Destination network address	
	A unique Internet Protocol (IP) or Internet Packet Exchange (IPX) address of the destination node.
Differential encoding	Source coding method which is used to code the difference between two samples. Typically used in real-time signals where there is limited change between one sample and the next, such as in audio and speech.
Distance vector routing algorithm	
	Routing algorithms which use the number of hops in a route to find a shortest-path spanning tree. With distance vector routing algorithms, each router to send its entire routing table in each update, but only to its neighbors. They be prone to routing loops, but are relatively simple as compared with link state routing algorithms.
DNS	Domain Naming System. Used on the Internet to translated domain names into IP addresses.
Dot address	Notation for IP addresses in the form <w.x.y.z> where each number represents, in decimal, 1 byte of the 4-byte IP address.
DQDB	Distributed Queue Dual Bus. Data link layer communication protocol, specified in the IEEE 802.6 standard, designed for use in MANs.
DTE	Data terminal equipment. Device at the user end of a user-network interface that is a data source, destination, or both.
Dual homing	Topology where devices connect to the network by two independent access points (points of attachment). One gives the primary connection, and the other is the standby connection that is activated in the event of a failure of the primary connection.
Dynamic address resolution	
	Use of an address resolution protocol to determine and store address information on demand.
DHCP	Dynamic host control protocol. It manages a pool of IP addresses for computers without a known IP address. This allows a finite number of IP addresses to be reused quickly and efficiently by many clients.
Dynamic routing	Routing that adjusts automatically to network topology or traffic changes.
E1	Wide-area digital transmission scheme that is used in Europe to carry data at a rate of 2.048 Mbps.

Early token release	Used in Token Ring networks that allows stations to release the token onto the ring immediately after transmitting, instead of waiting for the first frame to return.
EGP	Exterior Gateway Protocol. Internet protocol for exchanging routing information between autonomous systems (RFC904). Replaced by BGP.
EIA	Electronic Industries Association. Specifies electrical transmission standards.
EIA/TIA-232	Physical layer interface standard that supports unbalanced circuits at signal speeds of up to 64 kbps.
EIA/TIA-449	Physical layer interface for rates up to 2 Mbps.
EIA/TIA-568	Characteristics and applications for UTP cabling.
EIA/TIA-606	Standard for the telecommunications infrastructure of commercial buildings, such as terminations, media, pathways, spaces and grounding.
Encapsulation	Wrapping of data in a particular protocol header.
End system	An end-user device on a network.
Entity	An individual, manageable network device.
Entropy coding	Coding scheme which does not take into account the characteristics of the data and treats all the bits in the same way. It produces lossless coding. Typical methods used are statistical encoding and suppressing repetitive sequences.
Equalization	Used to compensate for communications channel distortions.
Ethernet address	48-bit number that identifies a node on an Ethernet network. Ethernet addresses are assigned by the Xerox Corporation.
Ethernet	A local area network which uses coaxial, twisted-pair or fiber-optic cable as a communication medium. It transmits at a rate of 10 Mbps and was developed by DEC, Intel and Xerox Corporation. The IEEE 802.3 network standard is based upon Ethernet.
ETSI	European Telecommunication Standards Institute. Created by the European PTTs and the European Community (EC) for telecommunications standards in Europe.
Even parity	An error-detection scheme where defined bit-groupings have an even number of 1's.
EBCDIC	Extended Binary Coded Decimal Interchange Code. An 8-bit code alphabet developed by IBM allowing 256 different bit patterns for character definitions.
Exterior gateway protocol	Any internetwork protocol that exchanges routing information between autonomous systems.
Fast Ethernet	See IEEE 802.3u standard.
Fat pipe	Term used to indicate a high level of bandwidth the defined port.

FDDI	Fiber Distributed Data Interface. A standard network technology that uses a dual counter-rotating token-passing fiber ring. It operates at 100 Mbps and provides for reliable backbone connections.
File server	Computer that allows the sharing of files over a network.
FTP	File transfer protocol. A protocol for transmitting files between host computers using the TCP/IP protocol.
Firewall	Device which filters incoming and outgoing traffic.
Flow control	Procedure to regulate the flow of data between two nodes.
Forward adaptive bit allocation	
	This technique is used in audio compression and makes bit allocation decisions adaptively, depending on signal content.
Fragment free cut-through switching	
	A modified cut-through switching technique where a switch or switch module waits until it has received a large enough packet to determine if it is error free.
FCS	Frame check sequence. Standard error detection scheme.
Frame	Normally associated with a packet which has layer 2 information added to it. Packets are thus contained within frames. Frames and packets have variable lengths as opposed to cells which have fixed lengths.
FSK	Frequency-shift Keying. Uses two, or more, frequencies to represent binary digits. Typically used to transmit binary data over speech-limited channels.
Full duplex	Simultaneous, two-way communications.
Gateway	A device that connects networks using different communications protocols, such as between Ethernet and FDDI. It provides protocol translation, in contrast to a bridge which connects two networks that are of the same protocol.
GIF	Standard image compression technique which is copyrighted by CompuServe Incorporated. It uses LZW compression and supports a palette of 256 24-bit colors (16.7M colors). GIF support local and global color tables and animated images.
Half-duplex (HDX)	Two-way communications, one at a time.
Handshake	Messages or signals exchanged between two or more network devices to ensure transmission synchronization.
Handshaking	A reliable method for two devices to pass data.
HCC	Horizontal cross-connect. Wiring closet where the horizontal cabling connects to a patch panel which is connected by backbone cabling to the main distribution facility.
HDLC	ISO standard for the data link layer.
Hello packet	Message transmitted from a root bridge to all other bridges in the network to constantly verify the Spanning Tree setup.

Heterogeneous network	Network consisting of dissimilar devices that run dissimilar protocols.
Hierarchical routing	Routing based on a hierarchical addressing system. IP has a hierarchical structure as they use network numbers, subnet numbers, and host numbers.
Holddown	A router state where they will not advertise information on a specific route, nor accept advertisements about the route for a specific length of time (the hold-down period). This time is used to flush bad information about a route from all routers in the network, or when a fault occurs on a route.
Hop count	Used by the RIP routing protocol to measure the distance between a source and a destination.
Hop	The number of gateways and routers in a transmission path.
Host number	Part of an IP address which identifies the node on a subnetwork.
Host	A computer that communicates over a network. A host can both initiate communications and respond to communications that are addressed to it.
Hub	A hub is a concentration point for data and repeats data from one node to all other connected nodes. Hubs can be active (where they repeat signals sent through them) or passive (where they do not repeat, but merely split, signals sent through them).
Huffman coding	Uses a variable length code for each of the elements within the data. It normally analyses the probability of the element in the data and codes the most probable with fewer bits than the least probable.
Hybrid network	Internetwork made up of more than one type of network technology.
HTML	Hypertext markup language. Standard language that allows the integration of text and images over a distributed network.
IAB	Internet Architecture Board. A group that discusses important matters relating to the Internet.
IANA	Internet Assigned Numbers Authority. Organization which delegates authority for IP address-space allocation and domain-name assignment to the NIC and other organizations.
ICMP	Internet Control Message Protocol. Used to report errors and provides other information relevant to IP packet processing.
IETF	Internet Engineering Task Force. Consists of a number of working groups which are responsible for developing Internet standards.
IGP	Interior Gateway Protocol. Used to exchange routing information within an autonomous system.
IGRP	Interior Gateway Routing Protocol. Developed by Cisco for large and heterogeneous networks.
ISDN	Integrated systems digital network. Communication technology

	that contains two data channels (2B) and a control channel (H). It supports two 64 kbps data channels and sets up a circuit-switched connection.
ITU-TSS	International Telegraph Union Telecommunications Standards Sector. Organization which has replaced the CCITT.
Internet address	An address that conforms to the DARPA-defined Internet protocol. A unique, four byte number identifies a host or gateway on the Internet. This consists of a network number followed by a host number. The host number can be further divided into a subnet number.
IETF	Internet Engineering Task Force. A committee that reviews and supports Internet protocol proposals.
Internet	Connection of nodes on a global network which use a DARPA-defined Internet address.
internet	Two or more connected networks that may, or may not, use the same communication protocol.
Intranet	A company specific network which has additional security against external users.
Inverse ARP	Inverse Address Resolution Protocol. This is a method of building dynamic routes in a network, and allows an access server to discover the network address of a device associated with a virtual circuit.
IP (Internet Protocol)	Part of the TCP/IP which provides for node addressing.
IP address	An address which is used to identify a node on the Internet.
IP multicast	Addressing technique that allows IP traffic to be propagated from one source to a group of destinations.
IPX	Internet Packet Exchange. Novell NetWare communications protocol which is similar to the IP protocol. The packets include network addresses and can be routed from one network to another.
IPX address	Station address on a Novell NetWare network. It consists of two fields: a network number field and a node number field. The node number is the station address of the device and the network number is assigned to the network when the network is started up. It is written in the form: NNNNNNNN:XXXXXX-XXXXXX, where N's represent the network number and X's represent the station address. An example of an IPX address is: DC105333:542C10-FF1432.
ISO	International Standards Organization.
Isochronous transmission	Asynchronous transmission over a synchronous data link. Isochronous signals require a constant bit rate for reliable transport.
ITU-T	The Consultative Committee for International Telephone and Telegraph (now known at the ITU-TSS) is an advisory committee established by the United Nations. It attempts to establish

standards for inter-country data transmission on a worldwide basis.

Jabber	Occurs when the transmission of network signals exceeds the maximum allowable transmission time (20 ms to 150 ms). The medium becomes overrun with data packets. This is caused by a faulty node or wiring connection.
Jitter	Movement of the edges of pulse over time, that may introduce error and loss of synchronization.
JPEG	Image compression technique defined by the Joint Photographic Expert Group (JPEG), a subcommittee of the ISO/IEC. It uses a DCT, quantization, run-length and Huffman coding.
Keep alive interval	Time period between each keep alive message.
Latency	Defines the amount of time between a device receiving data and it being forwarded on. Hubs have the lowest latency (less than $10\,\mu s$), switches the next lowest (between $40\,\mu s$ and $60\,\mu s$), then bridges ($200\,\mu s$ to $300\,\mu s$) and routers have the highest latency (around $1000\,\mu s$).
Learning bridge	Bridge which learns the connected nodes to it. It uses this information to forward or drop frames.
Leased line	A permanent telephone line connection reserved exclusively by the leased customer. There is no need for any connection and disconnection procedures.
Lempel-Ziv coding	Coding method which takes into account repetition in phases, words or parts of words. It uses pointers to refer to previously defined sequences.
LZW coding	Lempel-Ziv Welsh coding. Coding method which takes into account repetition in phases, words or parts of words. It builds up a dictionary of previously sent (or stored) sequences.
Line driver	A device which converts an electrical signal to a form that is transmit-table over a transmission line. Typically, it provides the required power, current and timing characteristics.
Link layer	Layer 2 of the OSI model.
Link segment	A point-to-point link terminated on either side by a repeater. Nodes cannot be attached to a link segment.

Link state routing algorithm

	Routing algorithm where each router broadcasts or multicasts information regarding the cost of reaching each of its neighbors to all nodes in the internetwork. These algorithms create a consistent view of the network but are much more complete that distance vector routing algorithms).
Little-endian	Storage method in which the least byte is stored first.
LLC	Logical Link Control. Higher of the two data link layer sublayers defined by the IEEE, which provides error control, flow control, framing, and MAC-sublayer addressing (IEEE 802.2).

Lossless compression	Where information, once uncompressed, is identical to the original uncompressed data.
Lossy compression	Where information, once uncompressed, cannot be fully recovered.
LSA	Link-state advertisement. Used by link-state protocols to advertise information about neighbors and path costs.
MAC address	A 6-byte data unique data-link layer address. It is normally quoted as a 12-digit hexadecimal number (such as A5:B2:10:64:01:44).
Masking effect	Where noise is only heard by a person when there are no other sounds to mask it.
MDI	Medium Dependent Interface. The IEEE standard for the twisted-pair interface to 10Base-T (or 100Base-TX).
MAC	Media Access Control. Media-specific access-control for Token Ring and Ethernet.
MIC	Media Interface Controller. Media-specific access-control for Token Ring and Ethernet.
MAU	Medium Attachment Unit. Method of converting digital data into a form which can be transmitted over a band-limited channel. Methods use either ASK, FSK, PSK or a mixture of ASK, FSK and PSK.
Microsegmentation	Division of a network into smaller segments. This helps to increase aggregate bandwidth to network devices.
Modem	Modulator-Demodulator. A device which converts binary digits into a form which can be transmitted over a speech-limited transmission channel.
MTU	Maximum Transmission Unit. The largest packet that the IP protocol will send through the selected interface or segment.
Multicast	Packets which are sent to all nodes on a subnet of a group within a network. This differs from a broadcast which forwards packet to all users on the network.
Multimode fiber	Fiber-optic cable that has the ability to carry more than one frequency (mode) of light at a time.
NDIS	Network driver interface specification. Software specification for network adapter drivers. It supports multiple protocols and multiple adapters, and is used in many operating systems, such as Windows.
Network layer	Third layer of the OSI model, which is responsible for ensuring that data passed to it from the transport layer is routed and delivered through the network. It provides end-to-end addressing and routing. It provides support for a number of protocols, including IP, IPX, CLNP, X.25, or DDP.
NT1	Network termination. Network termination for ISDN.
NFS	Network File System. Standard defined by Sun Microsystems for

	accessing remote file systems over a network.
NIS	Network Information Service. Standard defined by Sun Micro-systems for the administration of network-wide databases.
NLM	NetWare Loadable Module. Program that can be loaded into the NetWare NOS.
Node	Any point in a network which provides communications services or where devices interconnect.
N-series connectors	Connector used with thick coaxial cable.
Octet	Same as a byte, a group of eight bits (typically used in communications terminology).
Odd parity	An error-detection scheme where a defined bit-grouping has an odd number of 1's.
ODLI	Open Data-Link Interface. Software specification for network adapter drivers used in NetWare and Apple networks. It supports multiple protocols and multiple adapters.
Optical repeater	A device that receives, restores, and re-times signals from one optical-fiber segment to another.
Packet switching	Network switching in which data is processed in units of whole packets rather than attempting to process data by dividing packets into fixed-length cells.
Packet	A sequence of binary digits that is transmitted as a unit in a computer network. A packet usually contains control information and data. They normally are contained with data link frames.
PAP	Password authentication protocol. Protocol which checks a user's password.
Patch panel	An assembly of pin locations and ports which are typically mounted on a rack or wall bracket in the wiring closet.
PLL	Phase-Locked Loop. Tunes into a small range of frequencies in a signal and follows any variations in them.
PSK	Phase-Shift Keying. Uses two, or more, phase-shifts to represent binary digits. Typically used to transmit binary data over speech-limited channels.
Physical layer	Lowest layer of the OSI model which is responsible for the electrical, mechanical, and handshaking procedures over the interface that connects a device to a transmission medium
Ping	Standard protocol used to determine if TCP/IP nodes are alive. Initially a node sends an ICMP (Internet Control Message Protocol) echo request packet to the remote node with the specified IP address and waits for echo response packets to return.
POP	Point of presence. Physical access point to a long distance carrier interchange.
PPP	Point-to-point protocol. Standard protocol to transfer data over the Internet asynchronously or synchronously.

Port	Physical connection on a bridge or hub that connects to a network, node or other device.
POST	Power-on self test. Hardware diagnostics that runs on a hardware device when that device is powered up.
Protocol	Specification for coding of messages exchanged between two communications processes.
Quantization	Involves converting an analogue level into a discrete quantized level. The number of bits used in the quantization process determines the number of quantization levels.
Quartet signaling	Signaling technique used in 100VG-AnyLAN networks that allows data transmission at 100 Mbps over frame pairs of UTP cabling.
Repeater	A device that receives, restores, and re-times signals from one segment of a network and passes them on to another. Both segments must have the same type of transmission medium and share the same set of protocols. A repeater cannot translate protocols.
RARP	Reverse address resolution protocol. The opposite of ARP which maps an IP address to a MAC address.
RJ-45	Connector used with US telephones and with twisted-pair cables. It is also used in ISDN networks, hubs and switches.
RMON	An SNMP MIB that specifies the types of information listed in a number of special MIB groups that are commonly used for traffic management. Some of the popular groups used are Statistics, History, Alarms, Hosts, Hosts Top N, Matrix, Filters, Events, and Packet Capture.
Routing node	A node that transmits packets between similar networks. A node that transmits packets between dissimilar networks is called a gateway.
RS-232C	EIA-defined standard for serial communications.
RS-422, 423	EIA-defined standard which uses higher transmission rates and cable lengths than RS-232.
RS-449	EIA-defined standard for the interface between a DTE and DCE for 9- and 37-way D-type connectors.
RS-485	EIA-defined standard which is similar to RS-422 but uses a balanced connection.
RLE	Run-length encoding. Coding technique which represents long runs of a certain bit sequence with a special character.
SAP	Service Access Point. Field defined by the IEEE 802.2 specification that is part of the address specification.
SAP	Service Advertisement Protocol. Used by the IPX protocol to provide a means of informing network clients, via routers and servers of available network resources and services.
Segment	A segment is any length of LAN cable terminated at both ends.

	In a bus network, segments are electrically continuous pieces of the bus, connected by repeaters. It can also be bounded by bridges and routers.
SLIP	Serial line internet protocol. A standard used for the point-to-point serial connections running TCP/IP.
Simplex	One-way communication.
SNMP	Simple Network Management Protocol. Standard protocol for managing network devices, such as hubs, bridges, and switches.
Source encoding	Coding method which takes into account the characteristics of the information. Typically used in motion video and still image compression.
Statistical encoding	Where the coding analyses the statistical pattern of the data. Commonly occurring data is coded with a few bits and uncommon data by a large number of bits.

Suppressing repetitive sequences

	Compression technique where long sequences of the same data is compressed with a short code.
Switch	A very fast, low-latency, multiport bridge that is used to segment local area networks.
Synchronous	Data which is synchronized by a clock.
T1	Digital WAN carrier facility for 1.544 Mbps transmission.
TCP	Part of the TCP/IP protocol which provides an error-free connection between two cooperating programs.
TCP/IP Internet	An Internet is made up of networks of nodes that can communicate with each other using TCP/IP protocols.
Telnet	Standard program which allows remote users to log into a station using the TCP/IP protocol.
TIFF	Graphics format that supports many different types of images in a number of modes. It is supported by most packages and, in one mode, provides for enhanced high-resolution images with 48-bit color.
Time to live	A field in the IP header which defines the number of routers that a packet is allowed to traverse before being discarded.
Token	A token transmits data around a token ring network.
Topology	The physical and logical geometry governing placement of nodes on a network.
Transceiver	A device that transmits and receives signals.
Transform encoding	Source-encoding scheme where the data is transformed by a mathematical transform in order to reduce the transmitted (or stored) data. A typical technique is the discrete cosine transform (DCT) and the fast Fourier transform (FFT).
Transport layer	Fourth layer of the OSI model. It allows end-to-end control of transmitted data and the optimized use of network resources.

UART	Universal asynchronous receiver transmitter. Device which converts parallel data into a serial form, which can be transmitted over a serial line, and vice-versa.
V.24	ITU-T-defined specification, similar to RS-232C.
V.25bis	ITU-T specification describing procedures for call set-up and disconnection over the DTE-DCE interface in a PSDN.
V.32/V.32bis	ITU-T standard serial communication for bi-directional data transmissions at speeds of 4.8 or 9.6 Kbps, or 14.4 Kbps for V.32bis.
V.34	Improved v.32 specification with higher transmission rates (28.8 Kbps) and enhanced data compression.
V.35	ITU-T standard describing a synchronous, physical layer protocol used for communications between a network access device and a packet network.
V.42	ITU-T standard protocol for error correction.
VLC-LZW code	Variable-length-code LZW code. Uses a variation of LZW coding where variable-length codes are used to replace patterns detected in the original data.
Vertical cabling	Backbone cabling.
Virtual circuit	Logical circuit which connects two networked devices together.
Workgroup	Collection of nodes on a LAN which exchange data with each other.
X.121	ITU-T standard for an addressing scheme used in X.25 networks.
X.21	ITU-T-defined specification for the interconnection of DTEs and DCEs for synchronous communications.
X.21bis	ITU-T standard for the physical layer protocol for communication between DCE and DTE in an X.25 network.
X.25	ITU-T-defined for packet-switched network connections.
X.28	ITU-T recommendation for terminal-to-PAD interface in X.25 networks.
X.29	ITU-T recommendation for control information in the terminal-to-PAD interface used in X.25 networks.
X.3	ITU-T recommendation for PAD parameters used in X.25 networks.
X.400	ITU-T recommendation for electronic mail transfer.
X.500	ITU-T recommendation for distributed maintenance of files and directories.
X3T9.5	ANSI Task Group definition of FDDI.
X-ON/ X-OFF	The Transmitter On/ Transmitter Off characters are used to control the flow of information between two nodes.

Ap5   Abbreviations

AA	auto-answer
AAL	ATM adaptation layer
AAN	autonomously attached network
ABM	asynchronous balanced mode
AbMAN	Aberdeen MAN
ABNF	augmented BNF
AC	access control
ACAP	application configuration access protocol
ACK	acknowledge
ACL	access control list
ADC	analogue-to-digital converter
ADPCM	adaptive delta pulse code modulation
ADPCM	adaptive differential pulse code modulation
AEP	AppleTalk Echo Protocol
AES	audio engineering society
AFI	authority and format identifier
AGENTX	agent extensibility protocol
AGP	accelerated graphics port
AM	amplitude modulation
AMI	alternative mark inversion
ANSI	American National Standards Institute
APCM	adaptive pulse code modulation
API	application program interface
ARM	asynchronous response mode
ARP	address resolution protocol
ARPA	Advanced Research Projects Agency
AS	Autonomous system
ASCII	American standard code for information exchange
ASK	amplitude-shift keying
AT	attention
ATM	asynchronous transfer mode
AUI	attachment unit interface
BCC	blind carbon copy
BCD	binary coded decimal
BGP	border gateway protocol
BIOS	basic input/output system
B-ISDN	broadband ISDN
BMP	bitmapped
BNC	British Naval Connector
BOM	beginning of message
BOOTP	bootstrap protocol
BPDU	bridge protocol data units
bps	bits per second
BVCP	Banyan Vines control protocol

CAD	computer-aided design
CAN	concentrated area network
CASE	common applications service elements
CATNIP	common architecture for the Internet
CC	carbon copy
CCITT	International Telegraph and Telephone Consultative
CD	carrier detect
CD	compact disk
CDE	common desktop environment
CDFS	CD file system
CD-R	CD-recordable
CD-ROM	compact disk – read-only memory
CF	control field
CGI	common gateway interface
CGM	computer graphics metafile
CHAP	challenge handshake authentication protocol
CHAP	Challenge Handshake Authentication Protocol
CHARGEN	character generator protocol
CIF	common interface format
CMC	common mail call
CMOS	complementary MOS
CN	common name
COM	continuation of message
CON-MD5	content-MD5 header field
CPCS	convergence protocol communications sublayer
CPI	common part indicator
CPSR	computer professionals for social responsibility
CPU	central processing unit
CRC	cyclic redundancy check
CRLF	carriage return, line feed
CRT	cathode ray tube
CSDN	circuit-switched data network
CSMA	carrier sense multiple access
CSMA/CA	CSMA with collision avoidance
CSMA/CD	CSMA with collision detection
CS-MUX	circuit-switched multiplexer
CSPDN	circuit-switched public data network
CTS	clear to send
DA	destination address
DAA	digest access authentication
DAC	digital-to-analogue converter
DAC	dual attachment concentrator
DARPA	Defense Advanced Research Projects Agency
DAS	dual attachment station
DASS	distributed authentication security
DAT	digital audio tape
DAYTIME	daytime protocol
dB	decibel

DBF	NetBEUI frame
DC	direct current
DCC	digital compact cassette
DCD	data carrier detect
DCE	data circuit-terminating equipment
DC-MIB	dial control MIB
DCT	discrete cosine transform
DD	double density
DDE	dynamic data exchange
DENI	Department of Education for Northern Ireland
DES	data encryption standard
DHCP	dynamic host configuration program
DIB	device-independent bitmaps
DIB	directory information base
DISC	disconnect
DISCARD	discard protocol
DLC	data link control
DLL	dynamic link library
DM	disconnect mode
DMA	direct memory access
DNS	domain name server
DNS-SEC	domain name system security extensions
DOS	disk operating system
DPCM	differential PCM
DPSK	differential phase-shift keying
DQDB	distributed queue dual bus
DR	dynamic range
DRAM	dynamic RAM
DSN	delivery status notifications
DSP	domain specific part
DSS	digital signature standard
DTE	data terminal equipment
DTR	data terminal ready
EASE	embedded advanced sampling environment
EaStMAN	Edinburgh/Stirling MAN
EBCDIC	extended binary coded decimal interchange code
EBU	European Broadcast Union
ECHO	echo protocol
ECP	extended communications port
EEPROM	electrically erasable PROM
EF	empty flag
EFF	electronic frontier foundation
EFM	eight-to-fourteen modulation
EGP	exterior gateway protocol
EIA	Electrical Industries Association
EISA	extended international standard interface
EMF	enhanced metafile
ENQ	inquiry

EOM	end of message
EOT	end of transmission
EPP	enhanced parallel port
EPROM	erasable PROM
EPS	encapsulated postscript
ESP	IP encapsulating security payload
ETB	end of transmitted block
ETHER-MIB	ethernet MIB
ETX	end of text
FAT	file allocation table
FATMAN	Fife and Tayside MAN
FAX	facsimile
FC	frame control
FCS	frame check sequence
FDDI	fiber distributed data interface
FDDI-MIB	FDDI management information base
FDM	frequency division multiplexing
FDX	full duplex
FEC	forward error correction
FF	full flag
FFIF	file format for internet fax
FIFO	first in, first out
FINGER	finger protocol
FM	frequency modulation
FRMR	frame reject
FS	frame status
FSK	frequency-shift keying
FTP	file transfer protocol
FYI	for your information
GFI	group format identifier
GGP	gateway-gateway protocol
GIF	graphics interface format
GQOS	guaranteed quality of service
GSSAP	generic security service application
GUI	graphical user interface
HAL	hardware abstraction layer
HD	high density
HDB3	high-density bipolar code no. 3
HDLC	high-level data link control
HDTV	high-definition television
HDX	half duplex
HEFCE	Higher Education Funding Councils of England
HEFCW	Higher Education Funding Councils of Wales
HF	high frequency
HMUX	hybrid multiplexer
HPFS	high performance file system
HTML	Hypertext Mark-up Language
HTTP	Hypertext Transfer Protocol

Hz	Hertz
I/O	input/output
IA5	international alphabet no. 5
IAB	Internet Advisory Board
IAP	internet access provider
IARP	inverse ARP
IBM	International Business Machines
ICMP	internet control message protocol
ICP	internet connectivity provider
IDEA	international data encryption algorithm
IDENT	identification Protocol
IDI	initial domain identifier
IDP	initial domain part
IDPR	inter-domain policy routing
IEEE	Institute of Electrical and Electronic Engineers
IEFF	Internet Engineering Task Force
IFS	installable file system
IGMP	Internet group management protocol
IGMP	Internet group multicast protocol
IGP	interior gateway protocol
ILD	injector laser diode
IMAC	isochronous MAC
IMAP	Internet message access protocol
IOS	input/output supervisor
IP	Internet protocol
IP-ARC	IP over ARCNET networks
IP-ARPA	IP over ARPANET
IP-ATM	IP over ATM
IP-CMPRS	IP with compressed headers
IP-DC	IP over DC Networks
IP-E	IP over ethernet networks
IP-EE	IP over experimental ethernet networks
IP-FDDI	IP over FDDI networks
IP-FR	IP over frame relay
IP-HC	IP over hyperchannel
IP-HIPPI	IP over HIPPI
IP-IEEE	IP over IEEE 802
IP-IPX	IP over IPX networks
IP-MTU	path MTU discovery
IP-NETBIOS	IP over NETBIOS
IPNG	IP next generation
IPP	internet presence provider
IP-SLIP	IP over serial lines
IP-SMDS	IP datagrams over SMDS
IP-TR-MC	IP Multicast over token-ring LANs
IPV6-FDDI	IPv6 over FDDI
IPv6-Jumbo	IPv6 Jumbograms
IPV6-PPP	IPv6 over PPP

IP-WB	IP over wideband network
IPX	Internet packet exchange
IP-X.25	IP over ISDN
IPX-IP	IPX over IP
IRQ	interrupt request
ISA	international standard interface
ISDN	integrated services digital network
IS-IS	immediate system to intermediate system
ISO	International Standards Organization
ISP	internet service provider
ITOT	ISO transport service on top of TCP
ITU	International Telecommunications Union
JANET	joint academic network
JFIF	JPEG file interchange format
JISC	Joint Information Systems Committee
JPEG	Joint Photographic Expert Group
KDC	key distribution centre
KERBEROS	Kerberos network authentication service
LAN	local area network
LAPB	link access procedure balanced
LAPD	link access procedure
LCN	logical channel number
LDAP-URL	LDAP URL Format
LD-CELP	low-delay code excited linear prediction
LED	light emitting diode
LGN	logical group number
LIP	large IPX packets
LLC	logical link control
LRC	longitudinal redundancy check
LSL	link support level
LSP	link state protocol
LSRR	loose source and record route
LZ	Lempel-Ziv
LZW	LZ-Welsh
MAC	media access control
MAIL-MIB	mail monitoring MIB
MAN	metropolitan area network
MAP	messaging API
MAU	multi-station access unit
MD	message digest
MDCT	modified discrete cosine transform
MDI	media dependent interface
MHS	message handling service
MIB-II	management information base-II
MIC	media interface connector
MIME	multi-purpose internet mail extension
MLID	multi-link interface driver
MODEM	modulation/demodulator

MOS	metal oxide semiconductor
MPEG	Motion Picture Experts Group
MPI	multi-precision integer
MSL	maximum segment lifetime
MTP	multicast transport protocol
NAK	negative acknowledge
NCP	NetWare control protocols
NCSA	National Center for Supercomputer Applications
NDIS	network device interface standard
NDS	Novell Directory Services
NETBEUI	NetBIOS extended user interface
NETFAX	network file format for the exchange of images
NHRP	next hop resolution protocol
NIC	network interface card
NICNAME	whois protocol
NIS	network information system
NLSP	netware link-state routing protocol
NNTP	network news transfer protocol
NRZI	non-return to zero with inversion
NSAP	network service access point
NSCA	National Center for Supercomputing Applications
NSM-MIB	network services monitoring MIB
NSS	named service server
NTE	network terminal equipment
NTFS	NT file system
NTP	network time protocol
NTSC	National Television Standards Committee
ODI	open data-link interface
OH	off-hook
ONE-PASS	one-time password system
OSI	open systems interconnection
OSI-UDP	OSI TS on UDP
OSPF	open shortest path first
OUI	originator's unique identifier
PA	point of attachment
PAL	phase alternation line
PAP	password authentication protocol
PC	personal computer
PCM	pulse code modulation
PCT	personal communications technology
PDN	public data network
PGP	pretty good privacy
PHY	physical layer protocol
PING	packet Internet gopher
PISO	parallel-in-serial-out
PKP	public-key partners
PLL	phase-locked loop
PLS	physical signaling

PMA	physical medium attachment
PMD	physical medium dependent
POP3	post office protocol, Version 3
POP-URL	POP URL Scheme
PPP	point-to-point protocol
PPP-AAL	PPP over AAL
PPP-CCP	PPP compression control protocol
PPP-CHAP	PPP challenge handshake authentication
PPP-EAP	PPP extensible authentication protocol
PPP-HDLC	PPP in HDLC framing
PPP-IPCP	PPP control protocol
PPP-ISDN	PPP over ISDN
PPP-LINK	PPP link quality monitoring
PPP-MP	PPP multilink protocol
PPP-NBFCP	PPP NetBIOS frames control protocol
PPP-SNACP	PPP SNA control protocol
PPP-SONET	PPP over SONET/SDH
PPP-X25	PPP in X.25
PPSDN	public packet-switched data network
PS	postscript
PSDN	packet-switched data network
PSE	packet switched exchange
PSK	phase-shift keying
PSTN	public-switched telephone network
QAM	quadrature amplitude modulation
QCIF	quarter common interface format
QIC	quarter inch cartridge
QoS	quality of service
QT	quicktime
QUOTE	quote of the day protocol
RADIUS	remote authentication dial-in service
RAID	redundant array of inexpensive disks
RAM	random-access memory
RD	receive data
REJ	reject
RFC	request for comment
RGB	red, green and blue
RI	ring in
RIF	routing information field
RIP	routing information protocol
RIP2-MD5	RIP-2 MD5 Authentication
RIP2-MIB	RIP Version 2 MIB Extension
RIPNG-IPV6	RIPng for IPv6
RIP-TRIG	Trigger RIP
RLE	run-length encoding
RMON	remote monitoring
RMON-MIB	remote network monitoring MIB
RNR	receiver not ready

RO	ring out
ROM	read-only memory
RPC	remote procedure call
RPSL	routing policy specification language
RR	receiver ready
RSA	Rivest, Shamir and Adleman
RSVP	resource reservation protocol
RTF	rich text format
RTMP	routing table maintenance protocol
RTP	real-time transport protocol
RTSP	real-time streaming protocol
S/PDIF	Sony/Philips digital interface format
SA	source address
SABME	set asynchronous balanced mode extended
SAC	single attachment concentrator
SAP	service advertising protocol
SAPI	service access point identifier
SAR	segment and reassemble
SARPDU	segmentation and reassembly protocol data unit
SAS	single attachment station
SASL	simple authentication and security layer
SASL-ANON	anonymous SASL mechanism
SB-ADCMP	sub-band ADPCM
SCMS	serial copy management system
SCSI	small computer systems interface
SCSP	server cache synchronization protocol
SD	sending data
SD	start delimiter
SDH	synchronous digital hierarchy
SDIF	Sony digital interface
SDLC	synchronous data link control
SDNSDU	secure domain name system dynamic update
SDP	session description protocol
SECAM	séquential couleur à mémoire
SEL	selector/extension local address
SHEFC	Scottish Higher Education Funding Council
SIPO	serial-in parallel-out
SIPP	simple Internet protocol plus
SLM-APP	system-level managed objects for applications
SLP	service location protocol
SMDS	switched multi-bit data stream
SMI	structure of management information
SMP	symmetrical multiprocessing
SMT	station management
SMTP	simple mail transfer protocol
SNA	serial number arithmetic
SNA	systems network architecture (IBM)
SND	send

SNMP	simple network management protocol
SNMP-AT	SNMP over AppleTalk
SNMP-IPX	SNMP over IPX
SNMP-OSI	SNMP over OSI
SNR	signal-to-noise ratio
SONET	synchronous optical network
SPKM	simple public-key GSS-API mechanism
SPX	sequenced packet exchange
SQTV	studio-quality television
SRAM	static RAM
SSL	secure socket layer
SSM	single sequence message
SSRR	strict source and record route
STA	spanning-tree architecture
STM	synchronous transfer mode
STP	shielded twisted-pair
SVGA	super VGA
TCB	transmission control block
TCC	transmission control code
TCP	transmission control protocol
TDAC	time-division aliasing cancellation
TDM	time-division multiplexing
TEI	terminal equipment identifier
TELNET	telnet protocol
TFTP	trivial file transfer protocol
TIFF	tag image file format
TIFF	tagged input file format
TIME	time server protocol
TIP	transaction internet protocol
TMUX	transport multiplexing protocol
TOS	type of service
TP-TCP	ISO transport service on top of the TCP
TR	transmit data
TSR	terminate and stay resident
TTL	time-to-live
TUBA	TCP and UDP with bigger addresses
UDP	user datagram protocol
UI	unnumbered information
UNI	universal network interface
UNI	user network interface
UPS	uninterruptable power supplies
URI	universal resource identifier
URL	uniform resource locator
USB	universal serial bus
USERS	active users protocol
UTF-8	UTF-8 transformation format of ISO 10646
UTP	unshielded twisted pair
UV	ultra violet

VCI	virtual circuit identifier
VCO	voltage controller oscillator
VCR	video cassette recorder
VDD	virtual device driver
VGA	variable graphics adapter
VIM	vendor-independent messaging
VLC-LZW	variable-length-code LZW
VLM	virtual loadable modules
VMM	virtual machine manager
VRC	vertical redundancy check
VRRP	virtual router redundancy protocol
WAIS	wide area information servers
WAN	wide area network
WIMPs	Windows, icons, menus and pointers
WINS	Windows Internet name service
WINSOCK	windows sockets
WORM	write-once read many
WWW	World Wide Web
XDR	external data representation
XOR	exclusive-OR
ZIP	Zone Information Protocol

Ap6   Quick reference

Ap6.1   Miscellaneous

NetBIOS name types

Microsoft networks identify computers by their NetBIOS name. Each is 16 characters long, and the 16th character represents the purpose of the name. An example list of a WINS database is:

```
Name                      Type     Status
FRED             <00>     UNIQUE   Registered
BERT             <00>     UNIQUE   Registered
STAFF            <1C>     GROUP    Registered
STAFF            <1E>     GROUP    Registered
```

The values for the 16th byte are:

00	Workstation	03	Message service
06	RAS server service	1B	Domain master browser
1C	Domain group name	1D	Master browser's name
1E	Normal group name (workgroup)	1F	NetDDE service
20	Server service	21	RAS client
BE	Network Monitor Agent	BF	Network Monitor Utility

On Microsoft Windows, the names in the WINS database can be shown with the `nbstat` command.

Windows NT TCP/IP setup

Microsoft Windows uses the files LMHOSTS, HOSTS and NETWORKS to map TCP/IP names and network addresses. These are stored in the *<winNT root>*\SYSTEM32\DRIVERS\ETC. LMHOSTS maps IP addresses to a computer name. An example format is:

```
#IP-address          host-name
146.176.1.3          bills_pc
146.176.144.10       fred_pc    #DOM:STAFF
```

where comments have a preceding '#' symbol. To preserve compatibility with previous versions of Microsoft LAN Manager, special commands have been included after the comment symbol. These include:

```
#PRE
#DOM:domain
#INCLUDE  fname
#BEGIN_ALTERNATE
#END_ALTERNATE
```

where

#PRE	specifies that the name is preloaded into the memory of the computer and no further references to the LMHOSTS file will be made.
#DOM:*domain*	specifies the name of the domain that the node belongs to.

#BEGIN_ALTERNATE and #END_ALTERNATE are used to group multiple #include's
#include *fname*   specifies other LMHOST files to include.

The HOSTS file format is IP address followed by the fully qualified name (FQDN) and then any aliases. Comments have a preceding '#' symbol. For example:

```
#IP Address        FQDN           Aliases
146.176.1.3        superjanet     janet
146.176.144.10     hp
146.176.145.21     mimas
146.176.144.11     mwave
146.176.144.13     vax
146.176.146.23     oberon
146.176.145.23     oberon
```

Microsoft Windows TCP/IP commands (quick reference)

Command	Description	Examples

arp	Modifies Address Resolution Protocol tables.
	
	-s *IP-address* [*MAC-address*]
	    ; manually modify
	-a [*IP-address*] ; display ARP entry
	-d *IP-address* ; delete entry
		arp -s 146.176.151.10
		    FF-AA-10-3F-A1-3F

finger	Queries users on a remote computer. @*hostname* ; name of remote computer -l ; extend list	finger -l fred@miranda finger @moon
ftp	Remote file transfer. After connection the following commands can be used: ascii binary bye cd dir get hash help lcd ls mget mput open prompt pwd quit remote help user	ftp intel.com
hostname	Displays the TCP/IP hostname of the local node.	hostname
ipconfig	Displays the TCP/IP settings on the local computer. /all ; show all settings	ipconfig /all

`lpq`	Sends a query to a TCP/IP host or printer.	`lpq -p lp_laser` `lpq -s mirands -p dot_matrix`
	-S *print_server* -P *printer*	
`lpr`	Prints to a TCP/IP-based printer.	`lpr -p lp_laser file.ps`
	-S *print_server* -P *printer*	
`nbstat`	Displays mapping of NetBIOS names to IP addresses.	`nbstat -A freds`

-a *NetBIOS-name* ; display name table for
                  ; computer
-A *IP-address*   ; display name table for
                  ; computer
-n   ; display NetBIOS table
of
                   ; local computer

`netstat`	Displays status of TCP/IP connections.	*See Section 5.9.5*

-p *protocol*   ; display for given protocol
-r   ; show routing tables
-s   ; display statistics
-R   ; reload HMHOSTS
-S   ; display NetBIOS sessions
by
                    ; NetBIOS names
-s   ; display NetBIOS sessions
by
                    ; IP addresses

`nslookup`	Queries DNS servers. After connection the following commands can be used:	*See Section 5.9.3*

```
help
finger  [username]
port=port
querytype=type
; type can be A (address),
; CNAME (canonical name which is an alias
for
; another host), MX (mail exchanger which
; handles mail for a given host), NS (name
server
; for the domain), PTR (pointer record
```

which
; maps an IP address to a hostname), SOA
(start
; of authority record) or ANY.

`ping`   Test TCP/IP connectivity.

    `-a`   ; resolve IP addresses to host-
names
    `-n` *count* ; set number of echo packets
    `-l` *size* ; specify packet size
    `-t`   ; continuously ping
    `-i` *ttl* ; set time-to-live field
    `-w` *timeout* ; specify timeout in ms

`rcp`   Remote copy.   `rcp -r \*.txt`
                       `miranda.bill/home`

    [*hostname*[. *username*]]
    `-a` ; ASCII copy
    `-b` ; binary copy
    `-h` ; also hidden files
    `-r` ; recursively copy

`rexec`   Execute remote command.   `rexec miranda -l bill "ls -l"`

`route`   Manipulates TCP/IP routing table. `route gateway 146.151.176.12`
    `-f`   ; delete all routes
    `-p`   ; make a permanent route
    `add`   ; add a route
    `change` ; modify an existing route
    `delete` ; delete a route
    `gateway` ; specifies gateway
    `mask` *netmask* ; define subnet mask
    `print`   ; print current table

`rsh`   Executes remote shell.   `rsh -l bill "ls -l"`

    `-l` *username* ; user name
    `command` ; command to execute

`telnet`   Remote login.   `telnet www.intel.com`

`tftp`   Trivial FTP (uses UDP).

`tracert`   Trace route.

`-d`	; do not resolve IP addresses	
`-h` *max_hops*	; maximum number of hops	
`-w` *timeout*	; specify timeout	

Windows NT system administration commands (quick reference)

Com-mand	Description	Examples
`at`	Runs commands at a specified time. Options include:	`at 14:00 \\freds` `"cmd ping miranda > log"`

	`\\computer-name`
	`time`
	`/every:date` ; such as day of the week such
	    ; as M/T/W/Th/F/S/Su or day
	    ; of the month
		`at 00:00 /every:M/W/F`
		    `"cmd lpr log.txt"`

`attrib`	Displays or changes file attributes. Attributes include:	`attrib +h test.txt`
	`+r, -r,` (read) `+a, -a,` (archive) `+s, -s,` (system) `+h, -h,` (hidden) `/s` (include sub-directories)	
`backup`	Backup program.	
`cacls`	Command-line Access Control Lists (ACLs).	`calcs list.txt /g fred:cf` `calcs *.* /r bill /t`

	`/g` *username* : *right* ; grant user the following
	    ; rights: r (read), c (change),
	    ; f (full control).
	`/p` *username* ; replace rights, these are as
	    ; above, but n (none) is added
	`/r` *username* ; delete all rights
	`/t` ; recursive change	

`chkdsk`	Checks disk. Options include:	`chkdsk c: /f`
	`/f` ; automatically fix errors	
`cmd`	Run command-line shell.	

`convert`	Converts drive partition from FAT to NTFS.	`convert d: /fs:ntfs`
`convlog`	Converts files from Microsoft Information Server, FTP server and Gopher servers, and produces log files in NSCA or EMWAC format.	`convlog -sg -ncsa -o c:\temp *.log`
	`-t` [*emwave* | *ncsa*] ; specify EMWAC or ; NCSA `-s` [*f* | *w* | *g*] ; specify FTP (f), WWW (w) or ; Gopher (g) `-o` *outdir* ; specify output directory	
`diskperf`	Toggles the disk performance counter.	
`ipxroute`	IPX routing.	`ipxsroute servers`
	`servers` ; list NetWare servers	

`jetpack`	Compacts WINS databases.	`net stop wins`
		`jetpack win.mdb tmp.mdb`
		`net start wins`

`netmon`	Network monitoring tool.	
`ntbackup`	Backup file system.	
`rasadmin`	Remote Access Server (RAS) administration.	
`rasautou`	Remote Access Server (RAS) debugging.	
`rasdial`	Remote Access Server (RAS) dial-up.	`rasdial miranda /phone:1112222`
	`/phone` *tel*; telephone number	
`rasphone`	Edit RAS phonebook.	
`rdisk`	Create emergency repair disk.	
`regedit`	Edit registry.	
`restore`	Restores files after a backup.	
`start`	Starts applications from the command line.	

`winnt`	16-bit Window NT installation program.

/r dir ; specify install directory
/s dir ; installation source files

`winnt32`	32-bit Window NT installation program.

Microsoft Windows control services commands (quick reference)

Command	Description	Example
`net accounts`	Controls account settings	
	`/domain` *dom* ; specify default domain	
`net computer`	Adds or deletes computers from current domain.	`net computer \\freds /add` `net computer \\bills /del`
	`\\`*computer-name* `/add`; add computer `/del`; delete computer	
`net config server`	Configure server.	
`net config workstation`	Configure workstation.	
`net continue`	Unpauses a command that was paused with `net pause`.	
`net file`	Closes an opened file. When used on its own without arguments it gives the ID of all opened files. The `/close` option is used with the ID number to close a given file.	
	`/close` ; close file	
`net group`	Creates, edits or deletes groups.	`net group "Staff" /add` `net group "Staff" /add fred`
	`/add` ; add new group or users to the named group ; specified group `/delete` ; delete group or users to the named group ; specified group	
`net help`	Help messages for net.	

`net helpmsg`	Detailed help for a given error message.	
`net local-group`	Create or deletes local groups or local users.	
`net name`	Administers list of names for the Messenger service.	
`net pause`	Pauses a service.	`net pause lpdsvc` *; pause print service*
`net print`	Administers print queues. `\\`*computer-name* `/delete` ; delete job	
`net send`	Sends a text message to users or computers.	`net send bill "Hello"`
`net session`	Displays information of a current session.	
`net share`	Administers networks sharing.	
`net start`	Starts a service.	`net start snmp` *; start SNMP*
`net statistics`	Displays service statistics.	
`net stop`	Stops a service.	`net stop lpdsvc` *; stop print server*
`net time`	Sets or queries time on a remote computer.	
`net use`	Administers networked resources.	
`net user`	Administers user accounts. `password` ; prompts for password `/active:[y/n]` ; active status `/add` ; add user `/delete` ; delete user `/expires:[`*date*`|NEVER]` ; expire time `/fullname: "`*name*`"` ; full name `/homedir:` *homedirpath* ; home directory `/passwdchg: [y |n ]` ; password change `/times: [`*times* `| ALL]` ; login times	`net user bill_c /add` `net user bill_c /active:y`

`net view`	Displays networked resources.	`net view \\freds`
		`net view /domain`

computer-name
/domain [*domain*]   ; list of domain or
                                    ; computers within
the
                                    ; specified domain

Ap6.2 Windows NT architecture

Windows NT/2000 uses two modes:

- Kernel mode. This is a privileged mode of operation and allows all code direct access to the hardware and memory, including memory allocated to user mode processes. Kernel mode processes also have a higher priority over user mode processes.
- User mode. This is a lower privileged mode than kernel mode. It has no direct access to the hardware or to memory. It interfaces to the operating system through well-defined API (Application Program Interface) calls.

Figure B.1 shows an outline of the architecture of NT/2000. It can be seen that only the kernel mode has access to the hardware. This kernel includes executive services which include managers (for I/O, interprocess communications, and so on) and device drivers (which control the hardware). Its parts include:

- Microkernel. Controls basic operating system services, such as interrupt handling and scheduling.
- HAL (Hardware Abstraction Layer). This is a library of hardware-specific programs which give a standard interface between the hardware and software. This can either be Microsoft-written or manufacturer-provided. They have the advantage of allowing for transportability of programs across different hardware platforms.
- Win32 Window Manager. Supports Win32, MS-DOS and Windows 3.*x* applications.

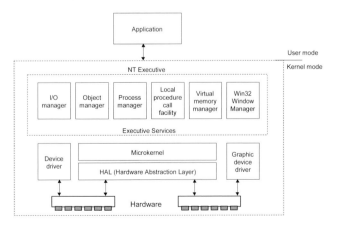

Figure Ap6.1   Windows architecture

Ap7 Quick questions

Question: *I would like some discipline in the design of my network. Thus, what are the main design steps?*

It is important to properly design your network, as incorrect planning can cause problems in the future. The basic steps are:

- **Analyze requirements.** This involves understanding and specifying the requirements of the network, especially its major uses. If possible, future plans should be incorporated. One of the key features is the bandwidth requirements and the size of the network.
- **Develop LAN structure.** This step involves developing a LAN structure for these re-quirements. Typically in organizational networks this will be based on a star topology using Ethernet hubs/switches.
- **Set up addressing and routing.** The final step involves setting up IP addresses and subnets to add structure.

The most important information that is required is the structure of the organization and how information flows between the units, as the designed network is likely to reflect this structure. The information will include:

- Understand the current network (if one exists) especially its strengths and weaknesses.
- Gather information on geographical locations.
- Determine current applications, and future plans for each site and for the organization.
- Develop organizational contacts. These will be the important people who will be in-volved in the development of the network. A mixture of technical and business skills always helps. Technical people tend to be driven by technology ('it should transfer files faster', 'it's easier to install', and so on), whereas business people tend to be driven by applications ('I just want access to a good spreadsheet', 'I want to be able to send e-mails to anyone in the company', and so on). It is also important to get someone in-volved who has experience of legal matters, and/or someone involved in Personnel matters.
- Determine the requirements for external network connections. This is an important decision as the security of the whole network may depend on the choices made on the external connections. Many large companies have a single point of connection to the external Internet as this allows organizations to properly manage internal and external connections to the Internet.
- Determine key objectives of the organization, especially related to mission-critical data and mission-critical operations. These should have top priority over other parts of the network. For example, a hospital would declare its ambulance service as a mission-critical unit, whereas the cuts and bruises unit (if there was one) would not be.
- Determine who is in control of information services. This may be distributed over the organization or over centralized in an MIS (Management Information Service) unit.

Question: *What are the main requirements in designing a network?*

- **Business requirements.**
- **Technical requirements.** The main issues are media contention, reducing excessive broadcasts (routing tables, ARP requests, and so on), backbone requirements, support

for real-time traffic and addressing issues.
- **Performance requirements.** This is likely to involve a network load requirement analysis for the typical loading on the network, and also for the worst-case traffic loading. This will determine the requirement for client/server architectures. An analysis should also be made for the impact of new workstations being added to the network. It should also involve an analysis of the requirements for application software, especially in its bandwidth requirements. Multimedia applications tend to have a large bandwidth requirement, along with centralized database applications and file servers.
- **New application requirements.**
- **Availability requirements.** This defines the usefulness of the network, such as response time, resource availability, and so on.

•

Question: *How do I try to limit the number of collisions on an Ethernet segment?*

Ethernet collisions occur when two nodes try and transmit onto a network segment at the same time. When the transmitting nodes detect this, they transmit a jamming signal to the rest of the network. All the other nodes on the network detect this, and wait for one of the two colliding nodes to get access onto the network segment. These collisions reduce the overall bandwidth of the network segment. An important concept is the collision domain, which defines the physical distance by which a collision is propagated. Repeaters and hubs propagate collisions, but switches, bridges and routers do not. Thus if you want to reduce the amount of collision insert either a switch, a router or a bridge in a network segment.

Question: *I've analyzed the traffic on the network, and I've found that a large portion of the network traffic is related to broadcasts. How can I reduce their effect?*

Broadcasts are sent out when a node wants help from other nodes. Typically, this happens when a node requires the MAC address for a known network address. The broadcast domain defines the physical distance by which a broadcast will be propagated. Hub, bridges and switches all propagate broadcasts, but routers do not. Thus, if you want to reduce the number of broadcasts on a network segment, insert a router, and it will intelligently route data packets into and out of a network segment without too many broadcasts (as the router handles external data routing).

Question: *Can I use the OSI model to design my network?*

Yes. The OSI model can split the network up into identifiable areas. These are:

- **Physical layer.** Network media (typically Cat-5 cable or fiber-optic cable), hubs and repeaters. Cables are normally run conforming to the EIA/TIA-568A standard. This layer should allow for future expansion.
- **Data link layer.** Switches and bridges. These devices will define the size of the collision and broadcast domains.
- **Network layer.** Routers, addressing. This layer filters data packets between network segments.

Question: *I have a local Ethernet hub which I connect to. How far can I run a cable from the hub to my computer?*

If you use Cat-5 horizontal cable, you can get a maximum distance of 100 m (if you were to use fiber cable you could get up to 400 m). A hub can thus cover an area of 200 meters square (assuming that the hub is located in the center of the area).

Question: *Did you mention something about a cat?*

Yes. There are five categories of UTP cables defined in EIA/TIA-568A. Cat-1 is only suitable for telephone communications, Cat-2 supports up to 4 Mbps, Cat-3 supports up to 10 Mbps, Cat-4 supports up to 16 Mbps and Cat-5 supports up to 100 Mbps.

Question: *Which is best, enterprise servers or workgroup servers?*

Well it all depends on your organization. Enterprise servers are typically used when all the users within an organization require access to a single resource, such as with electronic mail. Workgroup servers provide local access to data and application programs, and isolate traffic around these servers. Workgroup servers should be physically located where they are most required. Typically, enterprise servers require to be more centralized in their location, and are more robust than workgroup servers, as the whole organization depends on them. Mirror servers (servers which have exact copies of the main enterprise server) can be used with an enterprise in order to reduce data traffic to the main server.

Question: *Will I do damage if I connect using incorrectly wired cable, also how do I know that I've connected everything correctly? For example, I have a fiber cable which has two connectors and both are the same, how do I get the TX to the RX, and vice-versa?*

It is unlikely that you will do any damage if you connect your cables round the wrong way, as all the inputs and outputs are electrically buffered. This allows them to sustain short-circuits, and incorrect wiring. The key of knowing if your connection is working is to look at the 'keep-alive' signal, which is typically a green LED on the NIC, hub, switch or router. If it is active, or flashing, you have made a proper connection.

With fiber-optic connections, the transceiver unit will activate two green LEDs when you have made a correct connection. If they are not active, swap the connections round and reconnect.

Question: *You have said that Ethernet connections have a cross-over, but when I look at my patch cable, there isn't a cross-over, and pin 1 wires to pin 1, pin 2 to pin 2, and so on? Where's the crossover?*

You are totally correct, and so am I. The standard Ethernet connection must have a cross-over to connect the transmit to the receive, and vice-versa, but most hubs implement the cross-over inside the hub. Thus, all you need is a straight-through cable. I've listed the standard cross-over connections in Section 12.18 (and Figure 11.24), but most of the time you do not need a cross-over when you're connecting to the front of a hub or a switch. It is only at the back of the hub that you may need a cross-over cable. If in doubt look at the 'keep-alive' LED. If it is off after you connect, it is likely that you've got the wrong cable (or the power isn't on, or you've not connected the other end, or the power isn't on the computer, and so on).

Question: *If IP has been such a success, why do we need a new address scheme?*

IP has been a victim of its own success. No one could have imagined how popular it would be. As it has a 32-bit address it can only support up to 4 billion addresses. Unfortunately, not all these addresses can be used, as network addresses are allocated to organizations for their maximum requirement. Also, if an organization uses subnets, then it is unlikely that every subnet has its maximum capacity of hosts.

There are possibly enough IP addresses for all the computers in the world, but the next big wave is going to come from granting IP addresses to virtually every electronic device, such as mobile phones, faxes, printers, traffic lights, telephones, and so on. The stage after this is to grant every object in the world an IP address. This could include cars, trains, people, and even our pets.

Question: *Apart from increasing the number of IP addresses, why change the format, The Internet works, doesn't it, so why change it?*

Ah. Your perception of the Internet is based on what's available now. Few technologies have expanded so fast, and without virtually any inputs from the governments of the world. Look at the worldwide telephone system infrastructure, if it was based on the system that we had thirty years ago there's no way we could communicate as efficiently as we do. The Internet must do the same, if it is to keep pace with the increase in users, devices and the amount of information that can be transferred. At present, you possibly imagine that the Internet is an infrastructure of computers that have big boxes and sit on your desk, and are congregated around servers, and ISPs. In ten or twenty years this perception will change, and computers will almost become invisible, as will the Internet. To cope with this change we need a different infrastructure. To do this we need to identify its weaknesses:

- The Internet and its addressing structure was never really designed to be a global infrastructure and is constraining the access to resources and information.
- Information and databases tend to be static, and fixed to location.
- Difficult to group individual objects into larger objects.
- Difficult to add resources to the Internet (requires an ISP and a valid IP address).
- Search engines are not very good at gathering relevant information. On the WWW, typically users get pages of irrelevant information, which just happens to have the keyword which they are searching for.
- Resources are gathered around local servers.
- Resources are tied to locations with an IP address.
- IP addresses are not logically organized. The IP address given does not give any information about the geographical location of the destination. This then requires complex routing protocols in which routers pass on information about how to get to remote networks.

Question: *Can devices have more than one IP address?*

Yes. Many devices have more than one IP address. In fact each port that connects to a network must have an IP address. A good example of this is with routers, as they connect to two or more networks. Each of the ports of the router must have an IP address which relates to the network to which it connects to. For example if a router connects to three networks of:

146.176.151.0
146.176.152.0
146.176.140.0

then one IP address from each of the networks must be assigned to the router. Thus, it could be assigned the following addresses for its ports:

146.176.151.1
146.176.152.1
146.176.140.1

Question: *Can these addresses be used again for one of the hosts on the connected networks?*

No way. No two ports on the Internet can have the same address.

Question: *Okay, sorry I asked. So what addresses cannot be used for the ports, or the hosts?*

All zeros in the host field, as this identifies the network, and all 1's in the host field as this identifies the broadcast address. Thus in the example above, 146.176.151.0 and 146.176.151.255 could not be used (these addresses use a Class B address with a subnet in the third field).

Question: *Sometimes when I connect to the Internet everything seems fine, but I cannot access WWW sites, and it seems to load pages from a WWW cache?*

This is a common problem, and it is likely that you are connected to the Internet, but the Domain Name Server is not reachable. This means that you cannot resolve domain names into IP addresses. The way to check this is to use the IP address in the URL. For example:

http://www.mypage.com/index.html

could be accessed with:

http://199.199.140.10/index.html

If you can get access with this, you should investigate your DNS. Remember you can normally specify several DNS's, thus find out the address of a remote DNS, just in case your local one goes off-line.

Question: *When I connect to an ISP, what is my IP address, and my domain name? Can I have the same IP address each time, and the same domain name?*

When you connect to your ISP you will be granted an IP address from a pool of assigned IP addresses. There is no guarantee that this will be the same each time you connect. Your domain name will also change, as it is bound to the IP address. It is possible to be allocated a static IP address, but you would have to pay some money to your ISP for the privilege. The advantage of this is that remote computers could connect to you when you connected via your ISP.

You can determine your current IP address if you use the command WINIPCFG (or IPCONFIG). This is particularly useful if you are playing games over the Internet.

Question: *If I move my computer from one network to another, does the IP and MAC address stay the same, and what do I need to change?*

The MAC address will not change as the network card stays with the computer. If the computer is moved to a different subnet or onto a completely different network, the IP address must change, or the data will be routed back to the wrong network. Data would leave the relocated computer, and would arrive at the destination, but any data coming back would be routed to the previously attached network (and thus get lost). Another thing that is likely to change is the gateway. Nodes cannot communicate with the hosts outside their network if they do not know the IP address of the gateway (normally a router), thus if the network changes then the gateway is likely to be different.

The user may also have to set a new Domain Name Server (although a host can have several DNS entries). The first one listed in the DNS entries should be the one that is the most reliable and, possibly, the fastest.

Other changes may be to change the subnet mask (on a Class B network, with a subnet this is typically 255.255.255.0).

Question: *So why do you only have to specify the IP address of the gateway?*

Because the host uses an ARP request to determine the MAC address of the gateway.

Question. *If a computer has no permanent storage, how does it know its own IP address?*

Diskless hosts use the RARP protocol, which broadcasts a message to a RARP server. The RARP server looks-up the MAC address in the source address field in the data frame and sends back its IP address in a reply to the host.

Question. *How is it possible to simply connect a computer to an Ethernet network, and all the computers on the network are able to communicate with it, and how do they know when a computer has been disconnected?*

Computers use the ARP protocol, which allows nodes to determine the MAC address of computers on the network, from given IP addresses. Once they discover the destination MAC address, they update their ARP cache. After a given time, the entries in the table are updated (known as aging the entry).

Question: *How does a node broadcast to the network?*

There are two types of broadcasts. The first is a flooded broadcast, which has 1's in all parts of the IP address (255.255.255.255). The other it a directed broadcast, which has all 1's in the host part of a IP address. For example, to broadcast to the 146.176.151.0 network, the broadcast address is 146.176.151. 255, as all 1's in the host part of the address specifies a broadcast. Routers forward directed broadcasts, but not flooded addresses (as these are local). All hosts and routers must thus know what the subnet mask is.

Question: *Okay. I understand that both the MAC address and the IP address need to be specified for a node to receive data, but how does a node know the MAC address of the remote destination?*

1. A host looks up its local ARP cache (which is in its own RAM, and not stored to the permanent storage) to see if it knows the MAC address for a known IP address.
2. If it does not find the MAC address, it transmits an ARP request to the whole of the network (ARP requests do not travel over routers). The host who matches the transmitted IP address then responds with an ARP reply with its own MAC address in the source address field in the data frame. This is received by the originator of the request, which updates its local ARP cache, and then transmits with the required MAC address.

Question: *Oh, yes. I think I see it now, but what if the destination is on another network, possibly in another country, how does it determine the address of the destination?*

1. The host knows the IP address of the gateway for the network (normally a router). It then uses the MAC address of the gateway, but with the destination IP address of the host that the data is destined for. The gateway senses that the data frame is addressed to itself, and forwards it to the next gateway, and so on.
2. If the node does not know the MAC address of the gateway it will send out an ARP request to the network with the IP address of the gateway.

Question: *Does it matter which port I connect my workstation to the hub with? Do I have to start from port 1, then port 2, and so on.*

No. Hubs and switches are autosensing and automatically use the port that you connect to. You should hopefully see an LED become active when you connect to the port. You can also connect to a cascaded hub/switch to any one of the ports.

Question: *I've got a dual 10/100 switching hub. Can I communicate at 100 Mbps, even though I only have a 10 Mbps networking card?*

No. The switching hub will automatically sense the speed of your networking card, and use that rate. The great advantage of buying a dual speed switch is that you can upgrade your network card over time.

Question: *What's the difference between a data segment and a data packet?*

The transport layer uses data segments, whereas the network layer uses data packets. Data segments allow two or more applications to share the same transport connection. These segments are then split into data packets which have a given maximum size (typically for IP packets this is 64 KB) and each are tagged with a source and destination network address. Different applications can send data segments on a first-come, first-served basis.

Question: *How does a router know that it is getting routing information, and not an IP data packet?*

A routing packet is identified in the protocol field in the IP header. For example the OSPF routing protocol is defined by an 89 in the IP protocol field of the IP header (TCP is defined as 6, and UDP as 17). Example protocol numbers are:

1   Internet Control Message (ICMP)
3   Gateway-to-Gateway (GGP)
8   Exterior Gateway Protocol (EGP)
9   Any private interior gateway (IGP)
45   Inter-Domain Routing Protocol (IDRP)
86   Dissimilar Gateway Protocol (DGP)
88   Interior GRP (IGRP)
89   OSPF

Question: *Some people talk about gateways, and I've got a gateway option in my settings for my network connection. So what's the difference between a gateway and a router?*

A gateway is an old fashioned way of defining the entry and exit point of a network. Most of the time a gateway is a router. You need to define the IP address of the gateway (the router) before you can communicate with external networks.

Question: *So isn't a gateway a better definition for it?*

Well I suppose it is, but it's a router, really. In the past computers were sometimes set up to run a routing protocol and had two or more network cards. These systems acted as gateways.

Question: *Most of the systems I have worked with use the RIP routing protocol. If it is so popular, why should I use anything else?*

RIP is a distance-vector routing protocol which uses a metric to determine the best route to a network. A metric-based system is not really a problem, but RIP uses a very simple method to define the metric: the hop count. This in no way defines the bandwidth on any of the interconnected networks, or the delay, or really anything, apart from the number of routers that it encounters. Another major problem is that the maximum hop count is set at 15, thus if a destination is further than 15 routers away, it cannot be reached.

I could go on all day talking about the problems of RIP, but I will not because it's what makes a lot of networks work. A major problem, though, is that, unlike link-state protocols, each router transmits the complete contents of its routing table to all of its neighbors (even if there have been no changes to its connected networks). This occurs every 30 seconds, and is thus wasteful of bandwidth.

Routing loops can also occur, but these can be overcome with hold-down timers, which do not allow any updates to the metric for a network which is known to be down, for a given time (the hold-down time).

If you really must have a distance-vector approach, choose IGRP, as it better defines the best route, as it uses things like bandwidth, delay, and so on, to define the metric. It also only has an update time period of once every 90 seconds, rather that once every 30 seconds for RIP. Typically routers can run one of many routing protocols, and you can choose the one that fits your network.

Question: *So which is better distance-vector or link-state?*

Well there are advantages and disadvantages with both types. With a distance-vector approach each router sends their complete routing table to their neighbors, at given time intervals. If the network interconnections are not varying this can be wasteful of bandwidth. Another problem is that updates to the network is done on a step-by-step basis (ripple effect), and networks may take some time to converge (that is, to have a consistent view of the complete network).

Link-state routing protocols have the advantage in that they only transmit updates to the rest of the interconnected network when they sense a change in the interconnected parameters. These changes are then broadcast to the rest of the interconnected network. This is thus more efficient in its use of bandwidth, but suffers from initial flooding when the network is first switched on. The convergence is faster than distance-vector, as each router should have the same routing table.

Question: *What's an autonomous system and how does it help with routing?*

An autonomous system (AS) simplifies the structure of the Internet, and is a logical grouping of routers within one or more organizations. InterNIC assigns unique 16-bit AS addresses to organizations. A typical protocol that uses ASs is IGRP (Interior Gateway Routing Protocol).

Question: *So what's the difference between interior and exterior routing protocols?*

Exterior routing protocols route between AS's, whereas interior routing protocols route with a single AS. Typical interior routing protocols are IGRP (distance-vector), Enhanced IGRP (balanced hybrid), RIP (distance-vector) and OSPF (link state).

Question: *You say that high-quality audio uses 16 bits for each sample, but my CD player says that it uses 1- **bit** conversion. Is this right?*

Yes. It is. It uses one bit at a time, as this is thought to give a smoother response. A major problem with CD recordings is that they sometimes lack warmth, and are a little sharp (as they are too perfect). One bit tracking tries to follow the movement of the audio signal. So your CD still uses 16-bit coding.

Question: *I can't understand it. I've just bought a brand-new, state-of-the-art 56 kbps modem, and all I ever get is a maximum transfer speed of 4.19 KB/s. Where am I going wrong, do I need a new ISP?*

No. Your ISP is providing an excellent service, as 56 kbps is split between sending and receiving. As users who access the Internet from modems typically need to receive more data than they send, the bandwidth for receiving is greater than the bandwidth for sending. You can thus receive at a faster rate than you can send. The maximum receiving rate is 33 kbps, which relates to a maximum transfer rate of 4.125 KB/s (there are 8 bits in a byte). If you need a higher-rate you should try ISDN which gives a total transfer rate of 128 kbps (16 KB/s). Otherwise, consider ADSL (Asymmetric Digital Subscriber Line), which gives up to 9 Mbps receiving and 1.1 Mbps sending, over standard telephone lines.

Question: *Everyone seems to be talking about MP-3, but what's so good about it?*

MP-3 audio is set to revolutionize the way that music is distributed and licensed. A typical audio track is sampled at 44 100 times per second, for two channels at 16 bits per sample. Thus the data rate is 1.411 Mbps (176 400 B/s), giving a total of 52 920 000 B (50.47 MB) for a five-minute song. As the storage of a CD is around 650 MB, it is possible to get 64 minutes from the CD.

Obviously it would take too long, with present bandwidths to download a five-minute audio file from the Internet in its raw form (over 3 hours with a 56 kbps modem). If the audio file was compressed with MP-3, it can be reduced to one-tenth of its original size, without losing much of its original content.

So, it is now possible, with MP-3, to get over 10 hours of hi-fi quality music on a CD. But the big change is likely to occur with songs being sampled, and downloaded over the Internet. Users would then pay for the license to play the music, and not for purchasing the CD.

Question: *Why, with video and images, do you convert from RGB into something else?*

Video cameras have sensors for Red, Green and Blue (the primary colors for video information). In TV, before color TV, these colors where converted into luminance (Y). When color TV arrived they had to hide the extra color information and then send it as U and V (Redness and Blueness). Thus for TV, RGB is converted into YUV. With images, the human eye is very sensitive to changes in brightness in any object, and not so sensitive to color changes. Thus color changes can be compressed more than the luminance. This is why RGB is converted in YC_bC_r. For example, 4:2:2 uses twice as many samples for luminance than redness and blueness, and 4:1:1 uses four times as many samples.

Question: *Why when I watch digital TV, or a DVD movie, does the screen sometimes display large rectangular blocks, or objects which seem to move incorrectly across the screen?*

MPEG splits images up into blocks. As part of the compression process, MPEG splits each frame into a series of blocks. These blocks are then transformed. To increase compression, MPEG sends the complete picture every so often, and then just sends updates in the differences between the frames. Thus if your reception is not very good then you may fail to get the complete update of the picture, and only receive parts for the update. Also MPEG tries to track moving objects, it will then group the moving object, and transmit how the object moves. Sometimes this has not been encoded very well, and the object seems to move incorrectly across the screen. Normally this is because there are not enough updates to the complete frame.

Question: *Why does MPEG have to send/store the complete picture every few frames. Would it not be possible to send/store one complete frame, and then just send/store the changes from frame to frame?*

This would work fine, and would give excellent compression, but the user would not be able to move quickly through the MPEG film, as the decoder would have to read the initial frame, and then all the updates to determine how the frames changed. Also if there were corrupt data, it would propagate through the whole film. Thus there is a compromise between the number of intermediate frames between each complete frame.

Question: *All music seems to be becoming digital, but what's the great advantage when you lose something in the conversion?*

Yes. Something is lost in the conversion (the quantization error), but this stays constant, whereas the analogue value is likely to change. The benefits of converting to digital audio outweigh the drawbacks, such as:

- The quality of the digital audio system only depends on the conversion process, whereas the quality of an analogue audio system depends on the component parts of the system.
- Digital components tend to be easier and cheaper to produce than high-specification analogue components.
- Copying digital information is relatively easy and does not lead to a degradation of the signal.
- Digital storage tends to use less physical space than equivalent analogue forms.
- It is easier to transmit digital data.
- Information can be added to digital data so that errors can be corrected.
- Improved signal-to-noise ratios and dynamic ranges are possible with a digital audio system.

Question: *I've been told that I should not use copper cables to connect networks between two buildings. Why?*

Networks use digital signals. These digital signals are referenced to a local ground level (which eventually connects to the earth connection). The ground level can vary between different buildings (and can be large enough to give someone an electrical shock). Thus the ground connection between the two buildings must be broken. If possible for safety, and for reliable digital transmission, you should use a fiber-optic connection.

Also, copper cables can carry electrical surges (such as from lightning strikes), and airborne electrical noise. Electrical surges can cause great damage, and noise can cause the network performance to degrade (as it can cause bit errors).

If possible use fiber-optic cables for any long run of networking media. They tend to produce fewer problems, and allow for easy upgrades (as they have a much greater bandwidth than copper-based cables).

Question: *I thought that Ethernet was a bus-type network, but you have said that it has a star connection.*

Ethernet networks use a bus-type network, but when it connects to a hub the network can be seen as a physical star topology as the hub can be seen as a central point. If it were to fail, then the whole network may fail. Inside the hub the Ethernet connection still uses a bus network.

This is also the case for a ring network which uses MAU (Multistation Access Units) which is like a hub but creates a virtual ring. The MAU can be seen as a physical star, although the actual network is a ring topology.

Question: *What do I need to create a basic network?*

All you really need is two computers, two Ethernet NICs, a hub, and some patch cables. The patch cables connect the computers to the hub, and the hub creates the network. The computers can then simply make a peer-to-peer connection with each.

UNIX/Linux will allow you to access one computer from another, using TELNET, FTP, NDS, and so on, but you would have to assign each computer a unique IP address. As long as you do not connect onto the Internet, you can choose any IP address.

Microsoft Windows uses its own protocol (NetBEUI) to make a peer-to-peer connection (with file/printer sharing).

Question: *Everywhere I read, it says that Ethernet has so many problems, and isn't really a very good networking technique. So why is it so popular?*

Local area networks have evolved over the years. At one time, the big contest was between Token Ring, and Ethernet. Which was best? Well Token Ring was always better at coping with network traffic than Ethernet, especially when the network traffic was heavy. But, remember these were the days before hubs. Thus, most network connections were made from computer to computer with coaxial cable. The big problem with Token Ring was when there was a bad connection or when a computer was disconnected from the network, as this brought the whole network down. Ethernet (10BASE) proved much easier to add and delete computers to and from the network. Thus it triumphed over Token Ring. Soon Ethernet NICs cost much less than Token Ring cards, and were available from many sources (typically, these days, Token Ring cards will cost up to over five times as much as Ethernet ones).

Ethernet has coped well with the evolving networks, and the new hubs made it even easier to connect computers to a network. It faced a big problem, though, when the number of users of a network increased by a large factor. Its answer to this was 100BASE, which ramped up the bit rate by a factor of ten. This worked well, but it suffered when handling traffic over wide areas. Ethernet had a final trump card: 1000BASE, which gives a bit rate of 1 Gbps.

Thus, whatever we throw at Ethernet, it fights back by either ramping up the bit rate (from 10 Mbps to 100 Mbps to 1 Gbps) or it allows multiple simultaneous network connections (through Ethernet switches). So, don't dismiss the King, he's going to be around for a while yet.

Question: *How do you connect a fiber-optic cable to a connector?*

It takes a little bit of skill, but it is just glued onto the end.

Question: *And, how do you get an RJ-45 connector onto twisted-pair cable?*

You strip about 0.5 inch of the outer jacket and fan-out the wires in the correct order. Next you push them fully into the RJ-45 connector, and finally use the special crimping tool to clamp the cable, and make the required contacts. No soldering is involved.

Question: *What's so good about routers?*

Routers are the key components of the Internet. They communicate with each other and try and determine the best way to get to a remote network. As every computer which connects to the Internet must have an IP address, they use these addresses to route data around the Internet. Without routers we would not have an Internet. Routers are generally the best device to isolate traffic from one network and another, as they will only forward data packets if the destination is not on the current network.

Advantages of routers:
- Intelligently route data to find the best path using the network address. A bridge will route if the MAC address is not on the originating segment, whereas a router will intelligently decide whether to forward, or not.
- They do not forward broadcasts, thus they reduce the effect of broadcast storms.

Disadvantages of routers:
- Slower than bridges, as they must process the data packet at a higher level. The data frame is then forwarded in a modified form.
- They are network protocol dependent, whereas bridges will forward any high-level protocol as it is operating on the level 2 (as long as it connects two networks of the same types, such as Ethernet-to-Ethernet). Routers interpret the network level data using the required protocol, such as IP or IPX.

Question: *I live in Edinburgh, and my friend lives in London. How long does it take for a digital pulse to travel from Edinburgh to London?*

Well, there are a lot of assumptions to be made. First we'll assume that there are no intermediate devices in the cable that connects Edinburgh and London, and we'll assume that it is fiber-optic cable, which propagates light pulses at one-third the speed of light (10^8 m/s). Thus for a distance of 500 miles (804.65km,) the time will be:

$$T = \frac{Distance}{Speed} = \frac{804.65 \times 10^3}{1 \times 10^8} = 0.0080465$$
$$= 8.05 \text{ ms}$$

Question: *What are the main rules that I should use when I install network cables?*

Well, the initial installation is important as well installed cable will reduce the likelihood of problems in the future. Cabling problems tend to be one of the top causes of network problems. The rules can be summarized as:

- **Untwisting cables.** The maximum amount of untwisted in a Cat-5 cable is ½ in; this is to maximize the cancellation effect.
- **Cable bend.** The maximum cable bend is 90°.
- **Staples** should never be used as these pierce the outer jacket of the cable. Attach cable ties to cables going on the same path, but never secure them too tightly. If possible secure the cable with cable ties, cable support bars, wire management panels and releasable Velcro straps.
- **Try and minimize outer cable twists and stretching the cable**, and never allow the cable to become kinked, as this changes the characteristic impedance of the cable. The cables within can untwist when stretched.
- **Leave enough cable at each end** so that it can be properly terminated. It is less expensive to add an extra few meters onto the length at either end, than it is to have to re-run the whole cable. Typically, the cable run will have an extra few meters hidden below in the floor, or above in the ceiling, in order to compensate for extra lengths.

Question: *I use a Dial-up connection from home and an Ethernet connection at work. Is there any difference in the way that my applications operate?*

None at all (when you use TCP/IP communications). TCP/IP provides the interface between the networking technology and the application program, and has been designed so that the networking type is transparent to the application program, so, for example, it doesn't matter to a WWW browser that you connect to a modem or over a LAN.

Question: *I'm a user administrator. What are good practices for user accounts, so that I can secure my network?*

1. **GUEST ACCOUNT.** A guest account should always have a password, and should only be used in low-security domains.
2. **RENAME ADMIN.** If the network connects to the Internet, the administrator account should be renamed to deter   hackers.
3. **LIMIT ADMINISTRATOR.** Only log on as an administrator when required. This stops the administrator from accidentally making changes which are incorrect, as the administrator has the right to do anything (every user, no matter how good they are, has deleted something that they didn't intend to).
4. **PASSWORDS FOR ALL.** User accounts should always have a password. On medium-security and high-security domains, the password should expire after a given time, and will require a completely new password (not just the same one as given previously). Some systems remember the best few passwords, and bar the user from using any of them.
5. **CHANGE WHEN FIRST.** New users should change their password after they first log onto a domain. This forces users to protect their own account.
6. **RANDOM NEW PASSWORDS.** In medium-security and high-security networks, initial passwords should be random assigned.

7. **BAD LOCK-OUTS.** User accounts should be locked-out after a given number of bad logins. In low-security domains this should be a simple time out for a number of minutes, but on medium-security and high-security domains this should set to forever (that is, until the system administrator has reset the account, possibly after investigating the cause).

8. **PASSWORD SIZE.** On medium-security and high-security domains, passwords should be at least a given number of characters, and should typically not include words from a standard dictionary, and also include a number. Typically passwords are at least six characters long.

9. **GROUPS.** The user must be assigned to a well-defined group, as members of their group tend to have a high-privilege to the user's resources as any other user.

10. **DELETE OLD ACCOUNTS.** User accounts should have a defined time limit before they become inactive. Users who leave an organization should be deleted as quickly as possible.

Question: *And what other techniques can I apply to my network?*

1. **REGULAR BACKUPS.** No network is   secure from loss of data, either through hardware/software failure, accidental deletion, and external hackers. The only sure way to recover the data on a network is to backup the system, and restore it, if required.

2. **PROPERLY DEFINE AUDIT POLICY.** This should relate to security policies, resource usage, and so on.

3. **PROPERLY DEFINE USERS AND GROUPS.** Domains which split into proper groups are often easier to administer and control than domains which have a few loosely defined groups.

4. **SECURE THE SERVER.** The server is likely to be the most important computer within the domain, as any downtime can affect the whole domain. The server should thus be secure against attack or accidental damage.

5. **MAKE SERVERS ROBUST.** Servers should be protected against failure, especially through mains spikes, and power outages. This typically requires UPS and RAID technology.

6. **DEFINE DOMAINS.** Each domain has at least one server. The larger the domain becomes the more difficult it is to administer it, and the slower it becomes. If possible, define the limits of the domain for effective sharing of information.

7. **DEFINE HOW RESOURCES ARE SHARED.** It is important that resources are shared properly, and certain users should be restricted from certain resources.

8. **SETUP BACKUP RESOURCES.** Key resources should have a backup which will guard against failure. Typically this will involve a backup server, which contains a mirror of the data on the main server.

9. **MAKE NETWORK ROBUST.** The network should be designed so that failures are confined to small areas. Typically, routers and bridges are used to segment the network, and contain faults.

10. **LIMIT EXTERNAL CONNECTIONS.** On secure domains the number of external connections should be limited. Many organizations do not allow modems to be used to connect to a computer, as this could be used by an external user to gain access to the network, without first going through the organizational firewall.

Question: *What are best practices for a secure network?*

1. **BAN EXTERNAL CONNECTIONS.** In a highly secure network, all external traffic should go through a strong firewall. There should be no other external connections on the network. If possible, telephone lines should be monitored to stop data being transferred over without going through firewall.

2. **BAN FLOPPY DISKS AND DATA STORAGE DEVICES.** Employees should not be able to

enter or leave the organization with any data on disk. Some organizations remove floppy disk drives from their computers to try and limit the possibility of transferring data.
3. **NO USER CAN INSTALL SOFTWARE.** Viruses can be easily spread if users are allowed to install their own software.
4. **SECURE ACCESS TO RESOURCES.** Typically users must use swipe cards, or some biometric technique to gain access to a restricted domain.
5. **LIMIT INTERNET ACCESS.** Only key personnel should be given rights to access the external Internet. If possible the computers which access the Internet should be well protected against malicious programs.
6. **FIREWALLS USED BETWEEN DOMAINS.** Internal hackers can be as big a problem as external hackers. Thus firewalls should be used between domains to limit access.
7. **BASE AUTHENTICATION ON MAC ADDRESSES.** Network addresses do not offer good authentication of a user, as they can be easily spoofed. An improved method is to check the MAC address of the computer (as no two computers have the same MAC address).
8. **EVERY FILE AND OBJECT SHOULD HAVE UNIQUELY DEFINED PRIVILEGES.** Every file and resource should have uniquely setup for user privileges which can limit access.
9. **EMPLOY SECURITY MANAGER.** The security manager will be responsible for the design of the initial security model, and any changes to it.
10. **LOG EVERY EVENT.** All the important   security related events should be monitored within each domain. If possible they should be recorded over a long period of time. Software should be used to try and determine incorrect usage.

Question: *How secure is Microsoft Windows?*

The US Government defines certain security levels: D, C1, C2, B1, B2, B3 and A1, which are published in the *Trusted Computer Security Evaluation Criteria* books (each which have different colored cover to define their function), these include:

- **Orange Book.** Describes system security.
- **Red Book.** Interpretation of the Orange book in a network context.
- **Blue Book.** Application of Orange book to systems not covered in the original book.

Microsoft Windows NT/2000 uses the C2 security level. It has the following features:

- **Object control.** Users own certain objects and they have control over how they are accessed.
- **User names and passwords.**
- **No object reuse.** Once a user or a group has been deleted, the user and group numerical IDs are not used again. New users or groups are granted a new ID number.
- **Security auditing system.** This allows the system administrator to trace security aspects, such as user login, bad logins, program access, file access, and so on.
- **Defined keystroke for system access.** In Windows NT/2000, the CNTRL-ALT-DEL keystroke is used by a user to log into the system.

Question: *What does the orange book define?*

The Orange Book produced by the US Department of Defense (DOD) defines levels of security for systems. There are four main divisions, which split into seven main security ratings. Division D is the lowest security level and Division A is the highest. The ratings are:

- **Division D.** This rating provides no protection on files or for users. For example, a DOS-based computer has no real security on files and users, thus it has a Division D rating.
- **Division C.** This rating splits into two groups: C1 rating and C2 rating. C1 contains a trust computing base (TCB) which separates users and data. It suffers from the fact that all the data on the system has the same security level. Thus, users cannot make distinctions between highly secure data and not-so secure data. A C1 system has user names and passwords, as well as some form of control of users and objects. C2 has a higher level of security and provides for some form of accountability and audit. This allows events to be logged and traced, for example, it might contain a list of user logins, network address logins, resource accesses, bad logins, and so on.
- **Division B.** This rating splits into three groups: B1, B2 and B3. Division B rated systems have all the security of a C2 rating, but have more security because they have a different level of security for all system accesses. For example, each computer can have a different security level, each printer can also have different security levels, and so on. Each object (such as a computer, printer, and so on) has a label associated with it. It is with this label that the security is set by. Non-labeled resources cannot be connected to the system. In a B2 rated system, users are notified of any changes of an object that they are using. The TCB also includes separate operator and administrator functions. In a B3 rated system the TCB excludes information which is not related to security. The system should also be designed to be simple to trace, but also well tested to prevent external hackers. It should also have a full-time administrator, audit trails and system recovery methods.
- **Division A.** This is the highest level of security. It is similar to B3, but has formal methods for the systems security policy. The system should also have a security manager, who should document the installation of the system, and any changes to the security model.

Question: *What are the standard groups defined in Microsoft Windows?*

Standard NT accounts

- **Administrator.** Used for administration of a domain.
- **Guest.** Designed for limited-time or occasional user. On medium-security and high-security
- domains, this account should be disabled. Guests should be given unique accounts.
- **System.** Used to run many of the server pro-cesses and for assigning file access permission.

Standard NT domain groups

- **Domain Admins.** Used to assign the administrators group within the domain.
- **Domain Users.** Used to assign the users accounts in the domain.
- **Domain Guests.** Used to assign the guest accounts in the domain.

Standard NT local groups

- **Administrators.** Contains the Administrators account and the Domain Admins domain group.
- **Account Operators**, **Backup Operators**, **Print Operators** and **Server Operators.** Less privileged than the Administrators but more than user accounts. Each perform a specific task for an administrative function.
- **Replicators.** Used by the Directory Replicator Service, which allows for automatic copying of files between systems within a domain.
- **Users.** A group which holds ordinary users.
- **Guests.** A group which holds guest accounts for the local domain.

Ap8 Ethernet monitoring system

The schematic below shows an Ethernet monitoring system. Its component values are:

R1 = 1 kΩ   R2 = 500 Ω   R3 = 10 MΩ   R4 = 39 Ω   R5 = 1.5 kΩ
R6 = 10 Ω   L1 = 1:1, 200 μH   C1 = 100 mF   C2 = 0.1 μF   C3 = 1.5 pF
XTAL = 20 MHz

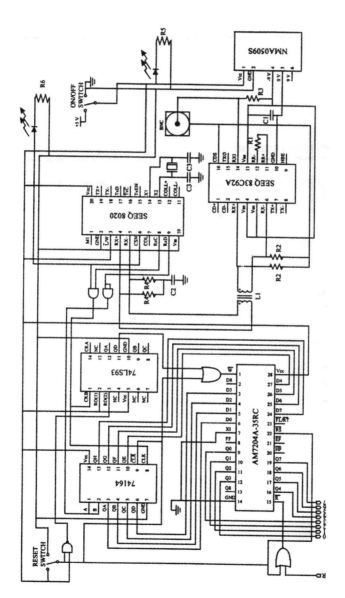

Ap6.1

Ap9   Java reference

Ap9.1   Package java.applet

Ap9.1.1   Class **java.applet.Applet**

The `Applet` class is a superclass of any applet. It provides a standard interface between applets and their environment. The following are defined:

```
// Constructors
public Applet();

// Methods
public void destroy();
public AppletContext getAppletContext();
public String getAppletInfo();
public AudioClip getAudioClip(URL url);
public AudioClip getAudioClip(URL url, String name);
public URL getCodeBase();
public URL getDocumentBase();
public Image getImage(URL url);
public Image getImage(URL url, String name);
public String getLocale();    // Java 1.1
public String getParameter(String name);
public String[][] getParameterInfo();
public void init();
public boolean isActive();
public void play(URL url);
public void play(URL url, String name);
public void resize(Dimension d);
public void resize(int width, int height);
public final void setStub(AppletStub stub);
public void showStatus(String msg);
public void start();
public void stop();
```

Ap9.1.2   Interface **java.applet.AppletContext**

The `AppletContext` interface corresponds to the applet's environment. The following are defined:

```
// Methods
public abstract Applet getApplet(String name);
public abstract Enumeration getApplets();
public abstract AudioClip getAudioClip(URL url);
public abstract Image getImage(URL url);
public abstract void showDocument(URL url);
public abstract void showDocument(URL url, String target);
public abstract void showStatus(String status);
```

Ap9.1.3   Interface **java.applet.AppletStub**

The `AppletStub` interface acts as the interface between the applet and the browser environment or applet viewer environment. The following are defined:

```
// Methods
public abstract void appletResize(int width, int height);
```

```
public abstract AppletContext getAppletContext();
public abstract URL getCodeBase();
public abstract URL getDocumentBase();
public abstract String getParameter(String name);
public abstract boolean isActive();
```

Ap9.1.4 Interface java.applet.AudioClip

The AudioClip interface is a simple abstraction for playing a sound clip. Multiple Audio-Clip items can be playing at the same time, and the resulting sound is mixed together to produce a composite. The following are defined:

```
// Methods
public abstract void loop();
public abstract void play();
public abstract void stop();
```

Ap9.2 Package java.awt

Ap9.2.1 Class java.awt.BorderLayout

The BorderLayout class contains members named "North", "South", "East", "West", and "Center". These are laid out with a given size and constraints. The "North" and "South" components can be stretched horizontally and the "East" and "West" components can be stretched vertically. The "Center" component can be stretched horizontally and vertically. The following are defined:

```
// Constructors
public BorderLayout();
public BorderLayout(int hgap, int vgap);
// Constants
public static final String CENTER;       // Java 1.1
public static final String EAST;         // Java 1.1
public static final String NORTH;        // Java 1.1
public static final String SOUTH;        // Java 1.1
public static final String WEST;         // Java 1.1
// Methods
public void addLayoutComponent(Component comp, Object obj);   // Java 1.1
public void addLayoutComponent(String name, Component comp);  // Java 1.0
public int getHgap();                                  // Java 1.1
public float getLayoutAlignmentX(Container parent);    // Java 1.1
public float getLayoutAlignmentY(Container parent);    // Java 1.1
public int getVgap();                                  // Java 1.1
public void invalidateLayout(Container target);        // Java 1.1
public void layoutContainer(Container target);
public Dimension maximumLayoutSize(Container target);// Java 1.1
public Dimension minimumLayoutSize(Container target);
public Dimension preferredLayoutSize(Container target);
public void removeLayoutComponent(Component comp);
public int setHgap();                                  // Java 1.1
public int setVgap();                                  // Java 1.1
public String toString();
```

Ap9.2.2 Class java.awt.Button

The Button class creates labelled buttons, which can have an associated action when pushed. Three typical actions are: normal, when it has the input focus (the darkening of the outline lets the user know that this is an active object) and when the user clicks the mouse over the button. The following are defined:

```
// Constructors
public Button();
public Button(String label);

// Methods
public synchronized void addActionListener(ActionListern l);   // Java 1.1
public void addNotify();
public String getActionCommand();                              // Java 1.1
public String getLabel();
protected String paramString();
public synchronized void removeActionListener(ActionListener l);
                                                               // Java 1.1
public setActionCommand(String command);                       // Java 1.1
public void setLabel(String label);
```

Ap9.2.3 Class java.awt.Checkbox

The Checkbox class contains a checkbox which has an on/off state. The following are defined:

```
// Constructors
public Checkbox();
public Checkbox(String label);
public Checkbox(String label, boolean state);                  // Java 1.1
public Checkbox(String label, boolean state, Checkbox group);  // Java 1.1
public Checkbox(String label, CheckboxGroup group, boolean state);

// Methods
public synchronized void addItemListener(ItemListener l);      // Java 1.1
public void addNotify();
public CheckboxGroup getCheckboxGroup();
public String getLabel();
public boolean getState();
public Object[] getSelectedObject();                           // Java 1.1
protected String paramString();
public synchronized void removeItemListener(ItemListener l);   // Java 1.1
public void setCheckboxGroup(CheckboxGroup g);
public void setLabel(String label);
public void setState(boolean state);
```

Ap9.2.4 Class java.awt.CheckboxGroup

The CheckGroup class groups a number of checkbox buttons. Only one of the checkboxes can be true (on) at a time. When one button is made true (on) the others will become false (off). The following are defined:

```
// Constructors
public CheckboxGroup();

// Methods
public Checkbox getCurrent();                     // Java 1.0
public Checkbox getSelectedCurrent();             // Java 1.1
public void setCurrent(Checkbox box);             // Java 1.0
public void setSelectedCheckbox(Checkbox box);    // Java 1.1
public String toString();
```

Ap9.2.5 Class java.awt.CheckboxMenuItem

The `CheckboxMenuItem` class allows for a checkbox that can be included in a menu. The following are defined:

```
// Constructors
public CheckboxMenuItem();                                    // Java 1.1
public CheckboxMenuItem(String label);
public CheckboxMenuItem(String label, boolean state);         // Java 1.1

// Methods
public synchronized void addItemListener(ItemListener l);     // Java 1.1
public void addNotify();
public boolean getState();
public synchronized Object[] getSelectObjects();              // Java 1.1
public String paramString();
public synchronized void removeItemListener(ItemListener l);  // Java 1.1
public void setState(boolean t);
```

Ap9.2.6 Class java.awt.Choice

The `Choice` class allows for a pop-up menu. The following are defined:

```
// Constructors
public Choice();

// Methods
public synchronized add(String item);                         // Java 1.1
public void addItem(String item);
public synchronized void addItemListener(ItemListener l);     // Java 1.1
public void addNotify();
public int countItems();                                      // Java 1.0
public String getItem(int index);
public String getItemCount();                                 // Java 1.1
public int getSelectedIndex();
public String getSelectedItem();
protected String paramString();
public synchronized Object[] getSelectedObjects();            // Java 1.1
public synchronized void insert(String item, int index);     // Java 1.1
public synchronized void remove(String item);                // Java 1.1
public synchronized void remove(int position);               // Java 1.1
public synchronized void removeAll();                         // Java 1.1
public synchronized void removeItemListener(ItemListener l);  // Java 1.1
public void select(int pos);
public void select(String str);
```

Ap9.2.7 Class java.awt.Color

This `Color` class supports the RGB colour format. A colour is represented by a 24-bit value of which the red, green and blue components are represented by an 8-bit value (0 to 255). The minimum intensity is 0, and the maximum is 255. The following are defined:

```
// Constants
public final static Color black, blue, cyan, darkGray, gray, green;
public final static Color lightGray, magenta, orange, pink, red;
public final static Color white, yellow;

// Constructors
public Color(float r, float g, float b);
public Color(int rgb);
public Color(int r, int g, int b);
```

```
// Methods
public Color brighter();
public Color darker();
public static Color decode (Strimg nm);                    // Java 1.1
public boolean equals(Object obj);
public int getBlue();
public static Color getColor(String nm);
public static Color getColor(String nm, Color v);
public static Color getColor(String nm, int v);
public int getGreen();
public static Color getHSBColor(float h, float s, float b);
public int getRed();
public int getRGB();
public int hashCode();
public static int HSBtoRGB(float hue, float saturation, float brightness);
public static float[] RGBtoHSB(int r, int g, int b, float hsbvals[]);
public String toString();
```

Ap9.2.8 Class **java.awt.Component**

The Component class is the abstract superclass for many of the Abstract Window Toolkit classes. The following are defined:

```
// Constants
public static final float BOTTOM_ALIGNMENT, CENTER_ALIGNMENT;
public static final float LEFT_ALIGNMENT, RIGHT_ALIGNMENT;
public static final float TOP_ALIGNMENT;

// Methods
public boolean action(Event evt, Object what); // Java 1.0
public synchronized void add(PopupMenu popup); // Java 1.1
public synchronized void addComponentListener(ComponentListener l);
      // Java 1.1
public synchronized void addFocusListener(FocusListener l);     // Java 1.1
public synchronized void addKeyListener(KeyListener l);         // Java 1.1
public synchronized void addMouseListener(MouseListener l);     // Java 1.1
public synchronized void addMouseMotionListener(MouseMotionListener l);
                                                                // Java 1.1
public void addNotify();
public Rectangle bounds();                                      // Java 1.0
public int checkImage(Image image, ImageObserver observer);
public int checkImage(Image image, int width, int height,
        ImageObserver observer);
public boolean contains(int x, int y);                         // Java 1.1
public boolean contains(Point p);                              // Java 1.1
public Image createImage(ImageProducer producer);
public Image createImage(int width, int height);
public void deliverEvent(Event evt);                           // Java 1.0
public void disable();                                         // Java 1.0
public final void displayEvent(AWTEvent e);                    // Java 1.1
public void doLayout();                                        // Java 1.1
public void enable();                                          // Java 1.0
public void enable(boolean cond);                              // Java 1.0
public float getAlignmentX();                                  // Java 1.1
public float getAlignmentY();                                  // Java 1.1
public Color getBackground();
public Rectangle getBounds();                                  // Java 1.1
public ColorModel getColorModel();
public Component getComponentAt(int x, int y);                 // Java 1.1
public Component getComponentAt(Point p);                      // Java 1.1
public Cursor getCursor();                                     // Java 1.1
public Font getFont();
```

```
public FontMetrics getFontMetrics(Font font);
public Color getForeground();
public Graphics getGraphics();
public Locale getLocale();                      // Java 1.1
public Point getLocation();                     // Java 1.1
public Point getLocationOnScreen();             // Java 1.1
public Dimension getMaximumSize();              // Java 1.1
public Dimension getMinimumSize();              // Java 1.1
public Container getParent();
public ComponentPeer getPeer();                 // Java 1.0
public Dimension getPreferredSize();            // Java 1.1
public Dimension getSize();                     // Java 1.1
public Toolkit getToolkit();
public final Object getTreeLock();              // Java 1.1
public boolean gotFocus(Event evt, Object what);  // Java 1.0
public boolean handleEvent(Event evt);          // Java 1.0
public void hide(); // Java 1.0
public boolean imageUpdate(Image img, int flags, int x, int y, int w, int h);
public boolean inside(int x, int y);            // Java 1.0
public void invalidate();
public boolean isEnabled();
public boolean isFocusTransversable();          // Java 1.1
public boolean isShowing();
public boolean isValid();
public boolean isVisible();
public boolean keyDown(Event evt, int key);  // Java 1.0
public boolean keyUp(Event evt, int key);       // Java 1.0
public void layout();                           // Java 1.0
public void list();
public void list(PrintStream out);
public void list(PrintStream out, int indent);
public void list(PrintStream out);              // Java 1.1
public Component locate(int x, int y);          // Java 1.0
public Point location();                        // Java 1.0
public boolean lostFocus(Event evt, Object what); // Java 1.0
public Dimension minimumSize();  // Java 1.0
public boolean mouseDown(Event evt, int x, int y);    // Java 1.0
public boolean mouseDrag(Event evt, int x, int y);    // Java 1.0
public boolean mouseEnter(Event evt, int x, int y);   // Java 1.0
public boolean mouseExit(Event evt, int x, int y);    // Java 1.0
public boolean mouseMove(Event evt, int x, int y);    // Java 1.0
public boolean mouseUp(Event evt, int x, int y);   // Java 1.0
public void move(int x, int y); // Java 1.0
public void nextFocus();    // Java 1.0
public void paint(Graphics g);
public void paintAll(Graphics g);
protected String paramString();
public boolean postEvent(Event evt);   // Java 1.0
public Dimension preferredSize();   // Java 1.0
public boolean prepareImage(Image image, ImageObserver observer);
public prepareImage(Image image, int width, int height, ImageObserver ob-
server);
public void print(Graphics g);
public void printAll(Graphics g);
public synchronized void remove(MenuComponent popup);    // Java 1.1
public synchronized void removeComponentListener(ComponentListener l);
    // Java 1.1
public synchronized void removeFocusListener(FocusListener l);// Java 1.1
public synchronized void removeKeyListener(KeyListener l);  // Java 1.1
public synchronized void removeMouseListener(MouseListener l);// Java 1.1
public synchronized void removeMouseMotionListener(MouseMotionListener l);

    // Java 1.1
public void removeNotify();
```

```
public void repaint();
public void repaint(int x, int y, int width, int height);
public void repaint(long tm);
public void repaint(long tm, int x, int y, int width, int height);
public void requestFocus();
public void reshape(int x, int y, int width, int height);  // Java 1.0
public void resize(Dimension d);   // Java 1.0
public void resize(int width, int height);  // Java 1.0
public void setBackground(Color c);
public void setBounds(int x, int y, int width, int height);   // Java 1.1
public void setBounds(Rectangle r);   // Java 1.1
public synchronized void setCursor(Cursor cursor);   // Java 1.1
public void setEnabled(boolean b);  // Java 1.1
public void setFont(Font f);
public void setForeground(Color c);
public void setLocale(Locale l);   // Java 1.1
public void setLocation(int x, int y);   // Java 1.1
public void setLocation(Point p);   // Java 1.1
public void setName(String name);   // Java 1.1
public void setSize(int width, int height);  // Java 1.1
public void setSize(Dimension d);   // Java 1.1
public void setVisible(boolean b);   // Java 1.1
public void show();  // Java 1.0
public void show(boolean cond);  // Java 1.0
public Dimension size();   // Java 1.0
public String toString();
public void transferFocus();  // Java 1.1
public void update(Graphics g);
public void validate();
```

Ap9.2.9 Class java.awt.Container

The Container class is the abstract superclass representing all components that can hold other components. The following are defined:

```
// Methods
public Component add(Component comp);
public Component add(Component comp, int pos);
public Component add(String name, Component comp);
public void add(Component comp, Object constraints); // Java 1.1
public void add(Component comp, Object constraints, int index);  // Java 1.1
public void addContainerListener(ContainerListener l);   // Java 1.1
public void addNotify();
public int countComponents(); // Java 1.0
public void deliverEvent(Event evt);   // Java 1.0
public void doLayout();     // Java 1.1
public void getAlignmentX();  // Java 1.1
public void getAlignmentY();  // Java 1.1
public Component getComponent(int n);
public Component getComponentAt(int x, int y); // Java 1.1
public Component getComponentAt(Point p);   // Java 1.1
public int getComponentCount();  // Java 1.1
public Component[] getComponents();
public getInsets();  // Java 1.1
public LayoutManager getLayout();
public Dimension getMaximumSize();  // Java 1.1
public Dimension getMinimumSize();  // Java 1.1
public Dimension getPreferredSize();   // Java 1.1
public Insets insets();     // Java 1.0
public void invalidate();  // Java 1.1
pubic boolean isAncestorOf(Component c);  // Java 1.1
public void layout();    // Java 1.0
public void list(PrintStream out, int indent);
```

```
public void list(PrintWriter out, int indent);  // Java 1.1
public Component locate(int x, int y);      // Java 1.0
public Dimension minimumSize();  // Java 1.0
public void paintComponents(Graphics g);
protected String paramString();
public Dimension preferredSize();   // Java 1.0
public void print(Graphics g);   // Java 1.1
public void printComponents(Graphics g);
public void remove(int index);    // Java 1.1
public void remove(Component comp);
public void removeAll();
public void removeContainerListener(ContainerListener l);   // Java 1.1
public void removeNotify();
public void setLayout(LayoutManager mgr);
public void validate();
```

Ap9.2.10   Class java.awt.Cursor

The Cursor class represents a mouse cursor. The following are defined:

```
// Constructors
public Cursor(int type);    // Java 1.1

// Constants
public static final int DEFAULT_CURSOR;    // Java 1.1
public static final int CROSSHAIR_CURSOR, HAND_CURSOR;   // Java 1.1
public static final int MOVE_CURSOR;    // Java 1.1
public static final int TEXT_CURSOR, WAIT_CURSOR;  // Java 1.1
public static final int N_RESIZE_CURSOR, S_RESIZE_CURSOR;   // Java 1.1
public static final int E_RESIZE_CURSOR, W_RESIZE_CURSOR;   // Java 1.1
public static final int NE_RESIZE_CURSOR, NW_RESIZE_CURSOR;    // Java 1.1
public static final int SE_RESIZE_CURSOR, SW_RESIZE_CURSOR;    // Java 1.1

// Methods
public static Cursor getDefaultCursor();  // Java 1.1
public static Cursor getPredefinedCursor();  // Java 1.1
```

Ap9.2.11   Class java.awt.Dialog

The Dialog class supports a dialog window, in which a user can enter data. Dialog windows are invisible until the show method is used. The following are defined:

```
// Constructors
public Dialog(Frame parent);  // Java 1.1
public Dialog(Frame parent, boolean modal);
public Dialog(Frame parent, String title);   // Java 1.1
public Dialog(Frame parent, String title, boolean modal);

// Methods
public void addNotify();
public String getTitle();
public boolean isModal();
public boolean isResizable();
public void setModal(boolean b);    // Java 1.1
protected String paramString();
public void setResizable(boolean resizable);
public void setTitle(String title);
public void show();  // Java 1.1
```

Ap9.2.12 Class java.awt.Dimension

The Dimension class contains the width and height of a component in an object. The following are defined:

```
// Fields
public int height;
public int width;

// Constructors
public Dimension();
public Dimension(Dimension d);
public Dimension(int width, int height);

// Methods
public boolean equals(Object obj); // Java 1.1
public Dimension getSize();   // Java 1.1
public void setSize(Dimension d);   // Java 1.1
public void setSize(int width, int height); // Java 1.1
public String toString();
```

Ap9.2.13 Class java.awt.Event

The Event class encapsulates user events from the GUI. The following are defined:

```
// Fields
public Object arg;
public int clickCount;
public Event evt;
public int id;
public int key;
public int modifiers;
public Object target;
public long when;
public int x;
public int y;

// possible values for the id field
public final static int ACTION_EVENT, GOT_FOCUS;
public final static int KEY_ACTION, KEY_ACTION_RELEASE;
public final static int KEY_PRESS, KEY_RELEASE;
public final static int LIST_DESELECT, LIST_SELECT;
public final static int LOAD_FILE, LOST_FOCUS;
public final static int MOUSE_DOWN, MOUSE_DRAG;
public final static int MOUSE_ENTER, MOUSE_EXIT;
public final static int MOUSE_MOVE, MOUSE_UP;
public final static int SAVE_FILE, SCROLL_ABSOLUTE;
public final static int SCROLL_BEGIN, SCROLL_END; // Java 1.1
public final static int SCROLL_LINE_DOWN, SCROLL_LINE_UP;
public final static int SCROLL_PAGE_DOWN, SCROLL_PAGE_UP;
public final static int WINDOW_DEICONIFY, WINDOW_DESTROY;
public final static int WINDOW_EXPOSE, WINDOW_ICONIFY;
public final static int WINDOW_MOVED;

// possible values for the key field when the
// action is KEY_ACTION or KEY_ACTION_RELEASE
public final static int DOWN, END;
public final static int F1, F2, F3, F4, F5, F6, F7, F8, F9, F10, F11, F12
public final static int HOME, LEFT, PGDN, PGUP, RIGHT, UP;
public final static int INSERT, DELETE;   // Java 1.1
public final static int BACK_SPACE, ENTER;   // Java 1.1
public final static int TAB, ESCAPE;   // Java 1.1
```

```
public final static int CAPS_LOCK, NUM_LOCK;    // Java 1.1
public final static int SCROLL_LOCK, PAUSE;  // Java 1.1
public final static int PRINT_SCREEN;  // Java 1.1

// possible masks for the modifiers field
public final static int ALT_MASK;
public final static int CTRL_MASK;
public final static int META_MASK;
public final static int SHIFT_MASK;

// Constructors
public Event(Object target, int id, Object arg);
public Event(Object target, long when, int id,
    int x, int y, int key, int modifiers);
public Event(Object target, long when, int id,
    int x, int y, int key, int modifiers, Object arg);

// Methods
public boolean controlDown();
public boolean metaDown();
protected String paramString();
public boolean shiftDown();
public String toString();
public void translate(int dX, int dY);
```

Ap9.2.14   Class java.awt.FileDialog

The FileDialog class displays a dialog window. The following are defined:

```
// Fields
public final static int LOAD, SAVE;

// Constructors
public FileDialog(Frame parent); // Java 1.1
public FileDialog(Frame parent, String title);
public FileDialog(Frame parent, String title, int mode);
// Methods
public void addNotify();
public String getDirectory();
public String getFile();
public FilenameFilter getFilenameFilter();
public int getMode();
protected String paramString();
public void setDirectory(String dir);
public void setFile(String file);
public void setFilenameFilter(FilenameFilter filter);
```

Ap9.2.15   Class java.awt.FlowLayout

The FlowLayout class arranges components from left to right. The following are defined:

```
// Fields
public final static int CENTER, LEFT, RIGHT;

// Constructors
public FlowLayout();
public FlowLayout(int align);
public FlowLayout(int align, int hgap, int vgap);

// Methods
public void addLayoutComponent(String name, Component comp);
public int getAlignment();    // Java 1.1
```

```
public int getHgap();    // Java 1.1
public int getVgap();    // Java 1.1
public void layoutContainer(Container target);
public Dimension minimumLayoutSize(Container target);
public Dimension preferredLayoutSize(Container target);
public void removeLayoutComponent(Component comp);
public void setAlignment(int align);    // Java 1.1
public void setHgap(int hgap);    // Java 1.1
public void setVgap(int vgap);    // Java 1.1
public String toString();
```

Ap9.2.16   Class java.awt.Font

The Font class represents fonts. The following are defined:

```
// Fields
protected String name;
protected int size;
protected int style;

// style has the following bit masks
public final static int BOLD, ITALIC, PLAIN;

// Constructors
public Font(String name, int style, int size);

// Methods
public static Font decode(String str);    // Java 1.1
public boolean equals(Object obj);
public String getFamily();
public static Font getFont(String nm);
public static Font getFont(String nm, Font font);
public String getName();
public int getSize();
public int getStyle();
public FontPeer getPeer();    // Java 1.1
public int hashCode();
public boolean isBold();
public boolean isItalic();
public boolean isPlain();
public String toString();
```

Ap9.2.17   Class java.awt.FontMetrics

The FontMetrics class provides information about the rendering of a particular font. The following are defined:

```
// Fields
protected Font font;

// Constructors
protected FontMetrics(Font font);

// Methods
public int bytesWidth(byte data[], int off, int len);
public int charsWidth(char data[], int off, int len);
public int charWidth(char ch);
public int charWidth(int ch);
public int getAscent();
public int getDescent();
public Font getFont();
public int getHeight();
```

```
public int getLeading();
public int getMaxAdvance();
public int getMaxAscent();
public int getMaxDescent();    // Java 1.0
public int[] getWidths();
public int stringWidth(String str);
public String toString();
```

Ap9.2.18   Class java.awt.Frame

The Frame class contains information on the top-level window. The following are defined:

```
// possible cursor types for the setCursor method
public final static int CROSSHAIR_CURSOR, DEFAULT_CURSOR;
public final static int E_RESIZE_CURSOR, HAND_CURSOR;
public final static int MOVE_CURSOR, N_RESIZE_CURSOR;
public final static int NE_RESIZE_CURSOR, NW_RESIZE_CURSOR;
public final static int S_RESIZE_CURSOR, SE_RESIZE_CURSOR;
public final static int SW_RESIZE_CURSOR, TEXT_CURSOR;
public final static int W_RESIZE_CURSOR, WAIT_CURSOR;
// Constructors
public Frame();
public Frame(String title);
// Methods
public void addNotify();
public void dispose();
public int getCursorType();   // Java 1.0
public Image getIconImage();
public MenuBar getMenuBar();
public String getTitle();
public boolean isResizable();
protected String paramString();
public void remove(MenuComponent m);
public void setCursor(int cursorType); // Java 1.0
public void setIconImage(Image image);
public void setMenuBar(MenuBar mb);
public void setResizable(boolean resizable);
public void setTitle(String title);
```

Ap9.2.19   Class java.awt.Graphics

The Graphics class is an abstract class for all graphics contexts. This allows an application to draw onto components or onto off-screen images. The following are defined:

```
// Constructors
protected Graphics();

// Methods
public abstract void clearRect(int x, int y, int width, int height);
public abstract void clipRect(int x, int y, int width, int height);
public abstract void copyArea(int x, int y, int width, int height,
      int dx, int dy);
public abstract Graphics create();
public Graphics create(int x, int y, int width, int height);
public abstract void dispose();
public void draw3DRect(int x, int y, int width, int height, boolean raised);
public abstract void drawArc(int x, int y, int width, int height,
      int startAngle, int arcAngle);
public void drawBytes(byte data[], int offset, int length, int x, int y);
public void drawChars(char data[], int offset, int length, int x, int y);
public abstract boolean drawImage(Image img, int x, int y, Color bgcolor,
      ImageObserver observer);
```

```
public abstract boolean drawImage(Image img, int x, int y,
      ImageObserver observer);
public abstract boolean drawImage(Image img, int x, int y, int width,
      int height, Color bgcolor, ImageObserver observer);
public abstract boolean drawImage(Image img, int x, int y, int width,
      int height, ImageObserver observer);
public abstract boolean drawImage(Image img, int x, int y, int width,
      int height, Color bgcolor, ImageObserver observer); // Java 1.1
public abstract void drawLine(int x1, int y1, int x2, int y2);
public abstract void drawOval(int x, int y,int width, int height);
public abstract void drawPolygon(int xPoints[], int yPoints[], int nPoints);
public void drawPolygon(Polygon p);
public abstract void drawPolyline(int xPoints[], int yPoints[], int nPoints);

    // Java 1.1
public void drawRect(int x, int y, int width, int height);
public abstract void drawRoundRect(int x, int y, int width,
      int height, int arcWidth, int arcHeight);
public abstract void drawString(String str, int x, int y);
public void fill3DRect(int x, int y, int width, int height, boolean raised);
public abstract void fillArc(int x, int y, int width, int height,
      int startAngle int arcAngle);
public abstract void fillOval(int x, int y, int width, int height);
public abstract void fillPolygon(int xPoints[], int yPoints[], int nPoints);
public void fillPolygon(Polygon p);
public abstract void fillRect(int x, int y, int width, int height);
public abstract void fillRoundRect(int x, int y, int width, int height,
      int arcWidth, int arcHeight);
public void finalize();
public abstract Shape getClip();    // Java 1.1
public abstract Rectangle getClipBounds();   // Java 1.1
public abstract Rectangle getClipRect(); // Java 1.0
public abstract Color getColor();
public abstract Font getFont();
public FontMetrics getFontMetrics();
public abstract FontMetrics getFontMetrics(Font f);
public abstract void setClip(int x, int y, int width, int height);  // Java 1.1
public abstract void setClip(Shape clip);    // Java 1.1
public abstract void setColor(Color c);
public abstract void setFont(Font font);
public abstract void setPaintMode();
public abstract void setXORMode(Color c1);
public String toString();
public abstract void translate(int x, int y);
```

Ap9.2.20   Class java.awt.Image

The Image abstract class is the superclass of all classes that represents graphical images.

```
// Constants
public static final int SCALE_AREA_AVERAGING, SCALE_DEFAULT;
public static final int SCALE_FAST, SCALE_REPLICATE;
public static final int SCALE_SMOOTH;

// Fields
public final static Object UndefinedProperty;

// Constructors
public Image();

// Methods
public abstract void flush();
```

```
public abstract Graphics getGraphics();
public abstract int getHeight(ImageObserver observer);
public abstract Object getProperty(String name, ImageObserver observer);
public Image getScaledInstance(int width, int height, int hints);   // Java 1.1
public abstract ImageProducer getSource();
public abstract int getWidth(ImageObserver observer)
```

Ap9.2.21   Class java.awt.Insets

The Insets object represents borders of a container and specifies the space that should be left around the edges of a container. The following are defined:

```
// Fields
public int bottom, left;
public int right, top;
// Constructors
public Insets(int top, int left, int bottom, int right);

// Methods
public Object clone();
public boolean equals(Object obj);  // Java 1.1
public String toString();
```

Ap9.2.22   Class java.awt.Label

The label class is a component for placing text in a container. The following are defined:
```
// Fields
public final static int CENTER, LEFT, RIGHT;

// Constructors
public Label();
public Label(String label);
public Label(String label, int alignment);

// Methods
public void addNotify();
public int getAlignment();
public String getText();
protected String paramString();
public void setAlignment(int alignment);
public void setText(String label);
```

Ap9.2.23   Class java.awt.List

The List object can be used to produce a scrolling list of text items. It can be set up so that the user can either pick one or many items. The following are defined:

```
// Constructors
public List();
public List(int rows);  // Java 1.1
public List(int rows, boolean multipleSelections);

// Methods
public void add(String item); // Java 1.1
public void addActionListener(ActionListener l);   // Java 1.1
public void addItem(String item);
public void addItem(String item, int index);
public synchronized void addItemListener(ItemListener l);   // Java 1.1
public void addNotify();
public boolean allowsMultipleSelections();   // Java 1.0
public void clear();     // Java 1.0
```

```
public int countItems();    // Java 1.0
public void delItem(int position);
public void delItems(int start, int end); // Java 1.0
public void deselect(int index);
public String getItem(int index);
public int getItemCount();    // Java 1.1
public synchronized String[] getItems(); // Java 1.1
public Dimension getMinimumSize(int rows);    // Java 1.1
public Dimension getMinimumSize();   // Java 1.1
public Dimension getPreferredSize(int rows);    // Java 1.1
public Dimension getPreferredSize();   // Java 1.1
public int getRows();
public int getSelectedIndex();
public int[] getSelectedIndexes();
public String getSelectedItem();
public String[] getSelectedItems();
public Object[] getSelectedObjects();  // Java 1.1
public int getVisibleIndex();
public boolean isIndexSelected(int index);   // Java 1.1
public MultipleMode();   // Java 1.1
public boolean isSelected(int index);  // Java 1.0
public void makeVisible(int index);
public Dimension minimumSize();  // Java 1.0
public Dimension minimumSize(int rows);    // Java 1.0
protected String paramString();
public Dimension preferredSize();   // Java 1.0
public Dimension preferredSize(int rows); // Java 1.0
public synchronized void remove(String item);   // Java 1.1
public synchronized void remove(int position); // Java 1.1
public synchronized void removeActionListener(ActionListener l);    // Java 1.1
public synchronized void removeAll(); // Java 1.1
public synchronized void removeItemListener(ItemListener l);  // Java 1.1
public void removeNotify();
public void replaceItem(String newValue, int index);
public void select(int index);
public synchronized void setMultipleMode(boolean b); // Java 1.1
public void setMultipleSelections(boolean v);
```

Ap9.2.24   *Class* **java.awt.MediaTracker**

The `MediaTracker` class contains a number of media objects, such as images and audio.
The following are defined:

```
// Fields
public final static int ABORTED, COMPLETE;
public final static int ERRORED, LOADING;

// Constructors
public MediaTracker(Component comp);

// Methods
public void addImage(Image image, int id);
public void addImage(Image image, int id, int w, int h);
public boolean checkAll();
public boolean checkAll(boolean load);
public boolean checkID(int id);
public boolean checkID(int id, boolean load);
public Object[] getErrorsAny();
public Object[] getErrorsID(int id);
public boolean isErrorAny();
public boolean isErrorID(int id);
public synchronized removeImage(Image image);   // Java 1.1
public synchronized removeImage(Image image, int id);    // Java 1.1
```

```
public synchronized removeImage(Image image, int id, int width, int height);
      // Java 1.1
public int statusAll(boolean load);
public int statusID(int id, boolean load);
public void waitForAll();
public boolean waitForAll(long ms);
public void waitForID(int id);
public boolean waitForID(int id, long ms);
```

Ap9.2.25   Class java.awt.Menu

The Menu object contains a pull-down component for a menu bar. The following are defined:

```
// Constructors
public Menu(); // Java 1.1
public Menu(String label);
public Menu(String label, boolean tearOff);

// Methods
public MenuItem add(MenuItem mi);
public void add(String label);
public void addNotify();
public void addSeparator();
public int countItems();
public MenuItem getItem(int index);
public int getItemCount();    // Java 1.1
public synchronized void Insert(MenuItem menuitem, int index);// Java 1.1
public void InsertSepatator(int index);    // Java 1.1
public boolean isTearOff();
public void remove(int index);
public void remove(MenuComponent item);
public synchronized void removeAll();  // Java 1.1
public void removeNotify();
```

Ap9.2.26   Class java.awt.MenuBar

The MenuBar object contains a menu bar which is bound to a frame. The following are defined:

```
// Constructors
public MenuBar();

// Methods
public Menu add(Menu m);
public void addNotify();
public int countMenus();
public void deleteShortCut(MenuShortCut s);  // Java 1.1
public Menu getHelpMenu();
public Menu getMenu(int i);
public int getMenuCount();    // Java 1.1
public MenuItem getShortcutMenuItem(MenuShortcut s); // Java 1.1
public void remove(int index);
public void remove(MenuComponent m);
public void removeNotify();
public void setHelpMenu(Menu m);
public synchronized Enumeration shortcuts();    // Java 1.1
```

Ap9.2.27   Class java.awt.MenuComponent

The MenuComponent abstract class is the superclass of all menu-related components. The following are defined:

```
// Constructors
public MenuComponent();

// Methods
public final void dispatchEvent(AWTEvent e);    // Java 1.1
public Font getFont();
public String getName();   // Java 1.1
public MenuContainer getParent();
public MenuComponentPeer getPeer(); // Java 1.0
protected String paramString();
public boolean postEvent(Event evt);
public void removeNotify();
public void setFont(Font f);
public void setName(String name);   // Java 1.1
public String toString();
```

Ap9.2.28   Class java.awt.MenuItem

The `MenuItem` class contains all menu items. The following are defined:

```
// Constructors
public MenuItem();   // Java 1.1
public MenuItem(String label);
public MenuItem(String label, MenuShortcut s); // Java 1.1

// Methods
public void addActionListener(ActionListener l);   // Java 1.1
public void addNotify();
public void deleteShortcut();    // Java 1.1
public void disable();  // Java 1.0
public void enable();   // Java 1.0
public void enable(boolean cond);   // Java 1.0
public String getLabel();
public MenuShortcut getShortcut();  // Java 1.1
public boolean isEnabled();
public String paramString();
public synchronized void removeActionListener(ActionListener l);
     // Java 1.1
public void setActionCommand(String command);   // Java 1.1
public synchronized void setEnabled(boolean b);    // Java 1.1
public void setLabel(String label);
public void setShortcut(MenuShortcut s); // Java 1.1
```

Ap9.2.29   Class java.awt.MenuShortcut

The `MenuShortcut` class has been added with Java 1.1. It represents a keystroke used to select a `MenuItem`. The following are defined:

```
// Constructors
public MenuShortcut(int key);    // Java 1.1
public MenuShortcut(int key, boolean useShiftModifier); // Java 1.1

// Methods
public boolean equals(MenuShortcut s);    // Java 1.1
public int getKey();    // Java 1.1
public String toString(); // Java 1.1
public boolean usesShiftModifier();    // Java 1.1
```

Ap9.2.30   Class java.awt.Panel

The Panel class provides space into which an application can attach a component. The following are defined:

```
// Constructors
public Panel();
public Panel(LayoutManger layout);  // Java 1.1

// Methods
public void addNotify();
```

Ap9.2.31   Class java.awt.Point

The Point class represents an (x, y) co-ordinate. The following are defined:

```
// Fields
public int x;
public int y;

// Constructors
public Point();    // Java 1.1
public Point(Point p);  // Java 1.1
public Point(int x, int y);

// Methods
public boolean equals(Object obj);
public Point getLocation();   // Java 1.1
public int hashCode();
public void move(int x, int y);
public void setLocation(Point p);   // Java 1.1
public void setLocation(int x, int y);    // Java 1.1
public String toString();
public void translate(int dx, int dy);
```

Ap9.2.32   Class java.awt.Polygon

The Polygon class consists of an array of (x, y), which define the sides of a polygon. The following are defined:

```
// Fields
public int npoints, xpoints[],ypoints[];

// Constructors
public Polygon();
public Polygon(int xpoints[], int ypoints[], int npoints);

// Methods
public void addPoint(int x, int y);
public boolean contains(Point p);   // Java 1.1
public boolean contains(int x, int y);    // Java 1.1
public Rectangle getBoundingBox();  // Java 1.0
public Rectangle getBounds();    // Java 1.1
public boolean inside(int x, int y);   // Java 1.0
```

Ap9.2.33   Class java.awt.PopupMenu

The PopupMenu class has been added with Java 1.1. It represetns a pop-up menu rather than a pull-down menu. The following are defined:

```
// Constructors
public PopupMenu();  // Java 1.1
public PopupMenu(String label);  // Java 1.1

// Methods
public synchronized void addNotify();  // Java 1.1
public void show(Component origin, int x, int y);  // Java 1.1
```

Ap9.2.34   *Class* java.awt.Rectangle

The Rectangle class defines an area defined by its top-left (*x, y*) co-ordinate, its width and
its height. The following are defined:

```
// Fields
public int height, width, x, y;

// Constructors
public Rectangle();
public Rectangle(Rectangle r);  // Java 1.1
public Rectangle(Dimension d);
public Rectangle(int width, int height);
public Rectangle(int x, int y, int width, int height);
public Rectangle(Point p);
public Rectangle(Point p, Dimension d);
// Methods
public void add(int newx, int newy);
public void add(Point pt);
public void add(Rectangle r);
public boolean contains(Point p);  // Java 1.1
public boolean contains(int x, int y);   // Java 1.1
public boolean equals(Object obj);
public Rectangle getBounds();   // Java 1.1
public Point getLocation();   // Java 1.1
public Dimension getSize();   // Java 1.1
public void grow(int h, int v);
public int hashCode();
public boolean inside(int x, int y);   // Java 1.0
public Rectangle intersection(Rectangle r);
public boolean intersects(Rectangle r);
public boolean isEmpty();
public void move(int x, int y);  // Java 1.0
public void reshape(int x, int y, int width, int height);  // Java 1.0
public void resize(int width, int height);   // Java 1.0
public void setBounds(Rectangle r);    // Java 1.1
public void setBounds(int x, int y, int width, int height);    // Java 1.1
public void setLocation(Point p);   // Java 1.1
public void setLocation(int x, int y);    // Java 1.1
public void setSize(Dimension d);   // Java 1.1
public void setSize(int x, int y);  // Java 1.1
public String toString();
public void translate(int dx, int dy);
public Rectangle union(Rectangle r);
```

Ap9.2.35   *Class* java.awt.Scrollbar

The Scrollbar class is a convenient means of allowing a user to select from a range of values. The following are defined:

```
// Fields
public final static int HORIZONTAL, VERTICAL;

// Constructors
```

```
public Scrollbar();
public Scrollbar(int orientation);
public Scrollbar(int orientation, int value, int visible, int minimum,
        int maximum);

// Methods
public synchronized void addAdjustmenuListener(AdjustmentListener l);
    // Java 1.1
public void addNotify();
public int getBlockIncrement();  // Java 1.1
public int getLineIncrement();   // Java 1.0
public int getMaximum();
public int getMinimum();
public int getOrientation();
public int getPageIncrement();   // Java 1.0
public int getUnitIncrement();   // Java 1.1
public int getValue();
public int getVisible();   // Java 1.0
protected String paramString();
public void setLineIncrement(int l);   // Java 1.0
public synchronized void setMaximum(int max);   // Java 1.1
public synchronized void setMinimum(int min);   // Java 1.1
public synchronized void setOrientation(int orien);   // Java 1.1
public void setPageIncrement(int l);   // Java 1.0
public void setValue(int value);
public void setValues(int value, int visible, int minimum, int maximum);
public void setVisibleAmount(int am);   // Java 1.1
```

Ap9.2.36   Class java.awt.TextArea

The TextArea class allows for a multi-line area for displaying text. The following are defined:

```
// Constructors
public TextArea();
public TextArea(int rows, int cols);
public TextArea(String text);
public TextArea(String text, int rows, int cols);
public TextArea(String text, int rows, int cols, int scrollbars);
        // Java 1.1
// Constants
public static final int SCROLLBARS_BOTH;  // Java 1.1
public static final int SCROLLBARS_HORIZONTAL_ONLY;   // Java 1.1
public static final int SCROLLBARS_NONE;  // Java 1.1
public static final int SCROLLBARS_VERTICAL_ONLY;  // Java 1.1

// Methods
public void addNotify();
public synchronized void append(String str);   // Java 1.1
public void appendText(String str);// Java 1.0
public int getColumns();
public Dimension getMinimumSize(int rows, int cols); // Java 1.1
public Dimension getMinimumSize();  // Java 1.1
public Dimension getPreferredSize(int rows, int cols);   // Java 1.1
public Dimension getPreferredSize();   // Java 1.1
public int getRows();
public int getScrollbarVisibility();   // Java 1.1
public void insertText(String str, int pos);// Java 1.1
public Dimension minimumSize();  // Java 1.0
public Dimension minimumSize(int rows, int cols); // Java 1.0
protected String paramString();
public Dimension preferredSize();   // Java 1.0
public Dimension preferredSize(int rows, int cols);   // Java 1.0
```

```
public void replaceText(String str, int start, int end);   // Java 1.0
public void setColumns(int cols);   // Java 1.1
public void setRows(int rows);   // Java 1.1
```

Ap9.2.37   Class java.awt.TextComponent

The TextComponent class is the superclass of any component that allows the editing of
some text. The following are defined:

```
// Methods
public void addTextListener(TextListener l);   // Java 1.1
public int getCaretPosition();   // Java 1.1
public String getSelectedText();
public int getSelectionEnd();
public int getSelectionStart();
public String getText();
public boolean isEditable();
protected String paramString();
public void removeNotify();
public void removeTextListener(TextListener l);   // Java 1.1
public void select(int selStart, int selEnd);
public void selectAll();
public void setCaretPosition(int position);  // Java 1.1
public void setEditable(boolean t);
public synchronized setSelectionEnd(int selectionEnd);   // Java 1.1
public synchronized setSelectionStart(int selectionStart); // Java 1.1
public void setText(String t);
```

Ap9.2.38   Class java.awt.TextField

The TextField class is a component that presents the user with a single editable line of
text. The following are defined:

```
// Constructors
public TextField();
public TextField(int cols);
public TextField(String text);
public TextField(String text, int cols);

// Methods
public synchronized void addActionListener(ActionListener l); // Java 1.1
public void addNotify();
public boolean echoCharIsSet();
public int getColumns();
public char getEchoChar();
public Dimension getMinimumSize(int cols);   // Java 1.1
public Dimension getMinimumSize();  // Java 1.1
public Dimension getPreferredSize(int cols);   // Java 1.1
public Dimension getPreferredSize();   // Java 1.1
public Dimension minimumSize();  // Java 1.0
public Dimension minimumSize(int cols);   // Java 1.0
protected String paramString();
public Dimension preferredSize();   // Java 1.0
public Dimension preferredSize(int cols);   // Java 1.0
public void setColumns(int cols);   // Java 1.1
public void setEchoChar(char c);   // Java 1.1
public void setEchoCharacter(char c); // Java 1.0
```

Ap9.2.39   Class java.awt.Toolkit

The Toolkit class is the abstract superclass of all actual implementations of the Abstract

Window Toolkit. The following are defined:

```
// Constructors
public Toolkit();

// Methods
public abstract int beep();    // Java 1.1
public abstract int checkImage(Image image, int width,
    int height, ImageObserver observer);
public abstract Image createImage(ImageProducer producer);
public Image createImage(byte[] imagedatea);    // Java 1.1
public Image createImage(byte[] imagedata, int imageoffset,
        int imagelength);    // Java 1.1
public abstract ColorModel getColorModel();
public static Toolkit getDefaultToolkit();
public abstract String[] getFontList();
public abstract FontMetrics getFontMetrics(Font font);
public abstract Image getImage(String filename);
public abstract Image getImage(URL url);
public int getMenuShortcutKeyMask();    // Java 1.1
public abstract PrintJob getPrintJob(Frame frame, String jobtitle,
        Properties props);  // Java 1.1
public abstract int getScreenResolution();
public abstract Dimension getScreenSize();
public abstract Clipboard getSystemClipbaord();    // Java 1.1
public abstract EventQueue getSystemEventQueue();  // Java 1.1
public abstract boolean prepareImage(Image image, int width,
        int height, ImageObserver observer);
public abstract void sync();
```

Ap9.2.40   Class java.awt.Window

The Window class is the top-level window; it has no borders and no menu bar. The following are defined:

```
// Constructors
public Window(Frame parent);
// Methods
public void addNotify();
public synchronized void addWindowListener(WindowListener l); // Java 1.1
public void dispose();
public Component getFocusOwner();   // Java 1.1
public Locale getLocale();    // Java 1.1
public Toolkit getToolkit();
public final String getWarningString();
public boolean isShowing();    // Java 1.1
public void pack();
public postEvent(Event e);    // Java 1.1
public synchronized void removeWindowListener(WindowListener l);
public void show();
public void toBack();
public void toFront();
```

Ap9.3   Package java.awt.datatransfer
Ap9.3.1 Class java.awt.datatransfer.Clipboard

The Clipboard class has been added with Java 1.1. It represents a clipboard onto which data can be transferred using cut-and-paste techniques. The following are defined:

```
// Constructors
public Clipboard(String name);   // Java 1.1

// Methods
public synchronized Transferable getContents(Object requestor);
    // Java 1.1
public String getName();   // Java 1.1
public synchronized void setContents(Transferable contents,
        Clipboard owner);   // Java 1.1
```

Ap9.4   Package java.awt.event

Ap9.4.1 *Class* java.awt.event.ActionEvent

The ActionEvent class has been added with Java 1.1. It occurs when a event happens for a Button, List, MenuItem or TextField. The following are defined:

```
// Constructors
public ActionEvent(Object src, String cmd); // Java 1.1

// Methods
public String getActionCommand();   // Java 1.1
public int getModifiers();    // Java 1.1
public int paramString();  // Java 1.1
```

Ap9.4.2 *Interface* java.awt.event.ActionListener

The ActionListener interface has been added with Java 1.1. It defines the method which is called by an ActionEvent. The following is defined:

```
public void actionPerformed(ActionEvent e); // Java 1.1
```

Ap9.4.3 *Class* java.awt.event.AdjustmentEvent

The AdjustmentEvent class has been added with Java 1.1. It occurs when a event happens for a Scrollbar. The following are defined:

```
// Constructors
public AdjustmentEvent(Object src, int id, int type, int value); // Java 1.1

// Methods
public Adjustable getAdjustable(); // Java 1.1
public int getAdjustmentType(); // Java 1.1
public int getValue(); // Java 1.1
public String paramString(); // Java 1.1
```

Ap9.4.4 *Class* java.awt.event.AdjustmentListener

The AdjustmentListener interface has been added with Java 1.1. It defines the method which is called by an AdjustmentEvent. The following is defined:

```
public void adjustmentValueChanged(AdjustmentEvent e);   // Java 1.1
```

Ap9.4.5 *Class* java.awt.event.ComponentEvent

The ComponentEvent class has been added with Java 1.1. It occurs when a event happens for a Component. The following are defined:

```
// Constructors
```

```
public ComponentEvent(Object src, int id, int type, int value);

// Methods
public Component getComponent(); // Java 1.1
public String paramString();  // Java 1.1
```

Ap9.4.6 *Class* java.awt.event.ComponentListener

The ComponentListener interface has been added with Java 1.1. It defines the method which is called by a ComponentEvent. The following are defined:

```
public void componentHidden(ComponentEvent e);  // Java 1.1
public void componentMoved(ComponentEvent e);   // Java 1.1
public void componentResized(ComponentEvent e); // Java 1.1
public void componentShown(ComponentEvent e);   // Java 1.1
```

Ap9.4.7 *Class* java.awt.event.ContainerEvent

The ComponentEvent class has been added with Java 1.1. It occurs when a event happens for a Container. The following are defined:

```
// Constructors
public ContainerEvent(Component src, int id, Compoent child);

// Methods
public Component getChild();  // Java 1.1
public Component getContainer(); // Java 1.1
public String paramString();  // Java 1.1
```

Ap9.4.8 *Class* java.awt.event.ContainerListener

The ContainerListener interface has been added with Java 1.1. It defines the method which is called by a ContainerEvent. The following are defined:

```
public void componentAdded(ComponentEvent e);   // Java 1.1
public void componentRemoved(ComponentEvent e); // Java 1.1
```

Ap9.4.9 *Class* java.awt.event.ItemEvent

The ItemEvent class has been added with Java 1.1. It occurs when a event happens for a Container. The following are defined:

```
// Constructors
public ItemEvent(ItemSelectable src, int id, Object item, int stateChanged);

   // Java 1.1

// Methods
public Object getItem();   // Java 1.1
public ItemSelectable getItemSelectable();   // Java 1.1
public int getStateChange();  // Java 1.1
public String paramString();  // Java 1.1
```

Ap9.4.10   *Class* java.awt.event.ItemListener

The ItemListener interface has been added with Java 1.1. It defines the method which is called by an ItemEvent. The following is defined:

```
public void itemStateChanged(ItemEvent e);   // Java 1.1
```

Ap9.4.11   *Class* **java.awt.event.KeyEvent**

The KeyEvent class has been added with Java 1.1. It occurs when a event happens for a keypress. The following are defined:

```
// Constructors
public KeyEvent(Component src, int id, long when, int modifiers,
       int keyCode, char keyChar);  // Java 1.1

// Constants
public static final int KEY_LAST, KEY_PRESSED, KEY_RELEASED, KEY_TYPED;
    // Undefined Key and Character (Java 1.1)
public static final int VK_UNDEFINED, CHAR_UNDEFINED;
    // Alphanumeric keys (Java 1.1)
public static final int VK_A, VK_B, VK_C, VK_D, VK_E, VK_F, VK_G, VK_H;
public static final int VK_I, VK_J, VK_K, VK_L, VK_M, VK_N, VK_O, VK_P;
public static final int VK_Q, VK_R, VK_S, VK_T, VK_U, VK_V, VK_W, VK_X;
public static final int VK_Y, VK_Z;
public static final int VK_SPACE;
public static final int VK_0, VK_1, VK_2, VK_3, VK_4, VK_5, VK_6, VK_7;
public static final int VK_8, VK_9;
public static final int VK_NUMPAD0, VK_NUMPAD1, VK_NUMPAD2, VK_NUMPAD3;
public static final int VK_NUMPAD4, VK_NUMPAD5, VK_NUMPAD6, VK_NUMPAD7;
public static final int VK_NUMPAD8, VK_NUMPAD9;
    // Control keys (Java 1.1)
public static final int VK_BACK_SPACE, VK_ENTER, VK_ESCAPE, VK_TAB;
    // Modifier keys (Java 1.1)
public static final int VK_ALT, VK_CAPS_LOCK, VK_CONTROL, VK_META, VK_SHIFT;
    // Function keys (Java 1.1)
public static final int VK_F0, VK_F1, VK_F2, VK_F3, VK_F4, VK_F5, VK_F6;
public static final int VK_F7, VK_F8, VK_F9;
public static final int VK_PRINTSCREEN, VK_SCROLL_LOCK, VK_PAUSE;
public static final int VK_PAGE_DOWN, VK_PAGE_UP;
public static final int VK_DOWN, VK_UP, VK_RIGHT, VK_LEFT;
public static final int VK_END, VK_HOME, VK_ACCEPT, VK_NUM_LOCK, VK_CANCEL;
public static final int VK_CLEAR, VK_CONVERT, VK_FINAL, VK_HELP;
public static final int VK_KANA, VK_KANJI, VK_MODECHANGE, VK_NONCONVERT;
    // Punctuation keys (Java 1.1)
public static final int VK_ADD, VK_BACK_QUOTE, VK_BACK_SLASH;
public static final int VK_CLOSE_BRACKET, VK_COMMA, VK_DECIMAL;
public static final int VK_DIVIDE, VK_EQUALS, VK_MULTIPLY;
public static final int VK_OPEN_BRACKET, VK_PERIOD, VK_QUOTE;
public static final int VK_SEMICOLON, VK_SEPARATOR, VK_SLASH;
public static final int VK_SUBTRACT;

// Methods
public void getKeyChar();  // Java 1.1
public int getKeyCode();   // Java 1.1
public boolean isActionKey(); // Java 1.1
public String paramString(); // Java 1.1
public void setKeyChar(char keyChar); // Java 1.1
public void setKeyCode(int keyCode);  // Java 1.1
public void setModifiers(int modifiers); // Java 1.1
```

Ap9.4.12   *Class* **java.awt.event.KeyListener**

The KeyListener interface has been added with Java 1.1. It defines the method which is called by a KeyEvent. The following is defined:

```
public void keyPressed(KeyEvent e); // Java 1.1
public void keyReleased(KeyEvent e);  // Java 1.1
public void keyTyped(KeyEvent e);   // Java 1.1
```

Ap9.4.13   *Class* **java.awt.event.MouseEvent**

The MouseEvent class has been added with Java 1.1. It occurs when a event happens for a MouseEvent. The following are defined:

```
// Constructors
public MouseEvent(Component src, int id, long when, int modifiers, int x,
      int y, intclickCount, boolean popupTrigger);   // Java 1.1

// Constants
public static final int MOUSE_CLICKED, MOUSE_DRAGGED;
public static final int MOUSE_ENTERED, MOUSE_EXITED;
public static final int MOUSE_FIRST, MOUSE_LAST;
public static final int MOUSE_MOVED, MOUSE_PRESSED;
public static final int MOUSE_RELEASED;

// Methods
public int getClickCount();   // Java 1.1
public Point getPoint();   // Java 1.1
public int getX();   // Java 1.1
public int getY();   // Java 1.1
public boolean isPopupTrigger(); // Java 1.1
public String paramString();   // Java 1.1
public synchronized void translatePoint(int x, int y);   // Java 1.1
```

Ap9.4.14   *Class* **java.awt.event.MouseListener**

The MouseListener interface has been added with Java 1.1. It defines the method which is called by a mouse click event. The following are defined:
```
public void mouseClicked(MouseEvent e);   // Java 1.1
public void mouseEntered(MouseEvent e);   // Java 1.1
public void mouseExited(MouseEvent e); // Java 1.1
public void mousePressed(MouseEvent e);   // Java 1.1
public void mouseReleased(MouseEvent e);   // Java 1.1
```

Ap9.4.15   *Class* **java.awt.event.MouseMouseListener**

The MouseMouseListener interface has been added with Java 1.1. It defines the method which is called by a mouse drag or move event. The following are defined:

```
public void mouseDragged(MouseEvent e);   // Java 1.1
public void mouseMoved(MouseEvent e);  // Java 1.1
```

Ap9.4.16   *Class* **java.awt.eventTextEvent**

The TextEvent class has been added with Java 1.1. It occurs when a event happens for an event within TextField, TextArea or other TextComponent. The following are defined:

```
// Constructors
public TextEvent(Object src, int id);  // Java 1.1

// Constants
public static final int TEXT_FIRST, TEXT_LAST;
public static final int TEXT_VALUE_CHANGED;

// Methods
public String paramString();   // Java 1.1
```

Ap9.4.17   *Class* **java.awt.event.TextListener**

The `TextListener` interface has been added with Java 1.1. It defines the method which is called by a `TextEvent`. The following is defined:

```
public void textValueChanged(TextEvent e);   // Java 1.1
```

Ap9.4.18   *Class* **java.awt.eventWindowEvent**

The `WindowEvent` class has been added with Java 1.1. It occurs when an event happens within a `Window` object. The following are defined:

```
// Constructors
public WindowEvent(Window src, int id);   // Java 1.1

// Constants
public static final int WINDOW_ACTIVATED, WINDOW_CLOSED;
public static final int WINDOW_CLOSING, WINDOW_DEACTIVATED;
public static final int WINDOW_DEICONIFIED, WINDOW_FIRST;
public static final int WINDOW_ICONIFIED, WINDOW_LAST;
public static final int WINDOW_OPENED;

// Methods
public Window getWindow(); // Java 1.1
public String paramString();  // Java 1.1
```

Ap9.4.19   *Class* **java.awt.event.WindowListener**

The `WindowListener` interface has been added with Java 1.1. It defines the method which is called by an `WindowEvent`. The following are defined:

```
public void windowActivated(WindowEvent e);  // Java 1.1
public void windowClosed(WindowEvent e); // Java 1.1
public void windowDeactivated(WindowEvent e);   // Java 1.1
public void windowDeiconified(WindowEvent e);   // Java 1.1
public void windowIconified(WindowEvent e); // Java 1.1
public void windowOpened(WindowEvent e); // Java 1.1
```

Ap9.5   Package **java.awt.image**

This package has been added with Java 1.1 and supports image processing classes.

Ap9.6   Package **java.io**

Ap9.6.1 *Class* **java.io.BufferedOutputStream**

The `BufferedOutputStream` implements a buffered output stream. These streams allow the program to write to an input device without having to worry about the interfacing method. The following are defined:

```
// Fields
protected byte buf[];
protected int count;

// Constructors
```

```
public BufferedOutputStream(OutputStream out);
public BufferedOutputStream(OutputStream out, int size);

// Methods
public void flush();
public void write(byte b[], int off, int len);
public void write(int b);
```

Ap9.6.2 *Class* java.io.BufferedReader

The BufferReader class has been added with Java 1.1. It represents a buffered character input stream. The following are defined:

```
// Constructors
public BufferedReader(Reader in, int sz); // Java 1.1
public BufferedReader(Reader in);    // Java 1.1

// Methods
public void close() throws IOException;   // Java 1.1
public void mark(int readAheadLimit) throws IOException;// Java 1.1
public boolean markSupported() throws IOException;// Java 1.1
public int read() throws IOException;  // Java 1.1
public int read(char [] cbuf, int off, int len) throws IOException; // Java 1.1
public String readLine() throws IOException;// Java 1.1
public boolean ready() throws IOException;   // Java 1.1
public void reset() throws IOException;   // Java 1.1
public long skip(long n) throws IOException;// Java 1.1
```

Ap9.6.3 *Class* java.io.BufferedWriter

The BufferWriter class has been added with Java 1.1. It represents a buffered character output stream. The following are defined:

```
// Constrsuctors
public BufferedWriter(Writer out, int sz);   // Java 1.1
public BufferedWriter(Writer in);   // Java 1.1

// Methods
public void close() throws IOException;   // Java 1.1
public void flush() throws IOException;   // Java 1.1
public void newLine() throws IOException;// Java 1.1
public void write(int c) throws IOException;// Java 1.1
public void write(char [] cbuf, int off, int len) throws IOException;
   // Java 1.1
```

Ap9.6.4 *Class* java.io.ByteArrayInputStream

The ByteArrayInputStream class supports input from a byte array. The following are defined:

```
// Fields
protected byte buf[];
protected int count;
protected int mark; // Java 1.1
protected int pos;

// Constructors
public ByteArrayInputStream(byte buf[]);
public ByteArrayInputStream(byte buf[], int offset, int length);
```

```
// Methods
public int available();
public void mark(int markpos);    // Java 1.1
public boolean markSupported();   // Java 1.1
public int read();
public int read(byte b[], int off, int len);
public void reset();
public long skip(long n);
```

Ap9.6.5 *Class* java.io.ByteArrayOutputStream

The ByteArrayOutputStream class allows supports output to a byte array. The following are defined:

```
// Fields
protected byte buf[];
protected int count;

// Constructors
public ByteArrayOutputStream();
public ByteArrayOutputStream(int size);

// Methods
public void reset();
public int size();
public byte[] toByteArray();
public String toString();
public String toString(int hibyte); // Java 1.0
public String toString(String enc); // Java 1.1
public void write(byte b[], int off, int len);
public void write(int b);
public void writeTo(OutputStream out);
```

Ap9.6.6 *Interface* java.io.DataInput

The DataInput interface gives support for streams to read in a machine-independent way. The following are defined:

```
// Methods
public abstract boolean readBoolean();
public abstract byte readByte();
public abstract char readChar();
public abstract double readDouble();
public abstract float readFloat();
public abstract void readFully(byte b[]);
public abstract void readFully(byte b[], int off, int len);
public abstract int readInt();
public abstract String readLine();
public abstract long readLong();
public abstract short readShort();
public abstract int readUnsignedByte();
public abstract int readUnsignedShort();
public abstract String readUTF();
public abstract int skipBytes(int n);
```

Ap9.6.7 *Class* java.io.DataInputStream

The DataInputStream class allows an application to read data in a machine-independent way. It uses standard Unicode strings which conforms to the UTF-81 specification. The following are defined:

```
// Constructors
public DataInputStream(InputStream in);

// Methods
public final int read(byte b[]);
public final int read(byte b[], int off, int len);
public final boolean readBoolean();
public final byte readByte();
public final char readChar();
public final double readDouble();
public final float readFloat();
public final void readFully(byte b[]);
public final void readFully(byte b[], int off, int len);
public final int readInt();
public final String readLine();  // Java 1.0
public final long readLong();
public final short readShort();
public final int readUnsignedByte();
public final int readUnsignedShort();
public final String readUTF();
public final static String readUTF(DataInput in);
public final int skipBytes(int n);
```

Ap9.6.8 *Interface* java.io.DataOutput

The DataOutput interface gives support for streams to write in a machine-independent way. The following are defined:

```
// Methods
public abstract void write(byte b[]);
public abstract void write(byte b[], int off, int len);
public abstract void write(int b);
public abstract void writeBoolean(boolean v);
public abstract void writeByte(int v);
public abstract void writeBytes(String s);
public abstract void writeChar(int v);
public abstract void writeChars(String s);
public abstract void writeDouble(double v);
public abstract void writeFloat(float v);
public abstract void writeInt(int v);
public abstract void writeLong(long v);
public abstract void writeShort(int v);
public abstract void writeUTF(String str);
```

Ap9.6.9 *Class* java.io.DataOutputStream

The DataOutputStream class allows an application to write data in a machine-independent way. It uses standard Unicode strings which conforms to the UTF-81 specification. The following are defined:

```
// Fields
protected int written;
// Constructors
public DataOutputStream(OutputStream out);

// Methods
public void flush();
public final int size();
public void write(byte b[], int off, int len);
public void write(int b);
```

```
public final void writeBoolean(boolean v);
public final void writeByte(int v);
public final void writeBytes(String s);
public final void writeChar(int v);
public final void writeChars(String s);
public final void writeDouble(double v);
public final void writeFloat(float v);
public final void writeInt(int v);
public final void writeLong(long v);
public final void writeShort(int v);
public final void writeUTF(String str);
```

Ap9.6.10   Class java.io.EOFException

Exception that identifies that the end-of-file has been reached unexpectedly during input. The following are defined:

```
// Constructors
public EOFException();
public EOFException(String s);
```

Ap9.6.11   Class java.io.File

The File class implements the file manipulation operations in an operating system independent way. The following are defined:

```
// Fields
public final static String pathSeparator;
public final static char pathSeparatorChar;
public final static String separator;
public final static char separatorChar;

// Constructors
public File(File dir, String name);
public File(String path);
public File(String path, String name);

// Methods
public boolean canRead();
public boolean canWrite();
public boolean delete();
public boolean equals(Object obj);
public boolean exists();
public String getAbsolutePath();
public String getCanonicalPath();   // Java 1.1
public String getName();
public String getParent();
public String getPath();
public int hashCode();
public boolean isAbsolute();
public boolean isDirectory();
public boolean isFile();
public long lastModified();
public long length();
public String[] list();
public String[] list(FilenameFilter filter);
public boolean mkdir();
public boolean mkdirs();
public boolean renameTo(File dest);
public String toString();
```

Ap9.6.12   *Class* **java.io.FileDescriptor**

The `FileDescriptor` class provides a way to cope with opening files or sockets. The following are defined:

```
// Fields
public final static FileDescriptor err, in, out;

// Constructors
public FileDescriptor();

// Methods
public void sync();  // Java 1.1
public boolean valid();
```

Ap9.6.13   *Class* **java.io.FileInputStream**

The `FileInputStream` class provides supports for an input file. The following are defined:

```
// Constructors
public FileInputStream(File file);
public FileInputStream(FileDescriptor fdObj);
public FileInputStream(String name);

// Methods
public int available();
public void close();
protected void finalize();
public final FileDescriptor getFD();
public int read();
public int read(byte b[]);
public int read(byte b[], int off, int len);
public long skip(long n);
```

Ap9.6.14   *Interface* **java.io.FilenameFilter**

The `FilenameFile` interface is used to filter filenames. The following is defined:

```
// Methods
public abstract boolean accept(File dir, String name);
```

Ap9.6.15   *Class* **java.io.FileNotFoundException**

Exception that identifies that a file could not be found. The following are defined:

```
// Constructors
public FileNotFoundException();
public FileNotFoundException(String s);
```

Ap9.6.16   *Class* **java.io.FileOutputStream**

The `FileOutputStream` class provides supports for an output file. The following are defined:

```
// Constructors
public FileOutputStream(File file);
public FileOutputStream(String name, boolean append);// Java 1.1
public FileOutputStream(FileDescriptor fdObj);
public FileOutputStream(String name);
```

```
// Methods
public void close();
protected void finalize();
public final FileDescriptor getFD();
public void write(byte b[]);
public void write(byte b[], int off, int len);
public void write(int b);
```

Ap9.6.17   *Class* java.io.FilterInputStream

The `FilterInputStream` class is the superclass of all classes that filter input streams. The following are defined:

```
// Fields
protected InputStream in;

// Constructors
protected FilterInputStream(InputStream in);

// Methods
public int available();
public void close();
public void mark(int readlimit);
public boolean markSupported();
public int read();
public int read(byte b[]);
public int read(byte b[], int off, int len);
public void reset();
public long skip(long n);
```

Ap9.6.18   *Class* java.io.FilterOutputStream

The `FilterOutputStream` class is the superclass of all classes that filter output streams. The following are defined:

```
// Fields
protected OutputStream out;

// Constructors
public FilterOutputStream(OutputStream out);

// Methods
public void close();
public void flush();
public void write(byte b[]);
public void write(byte b[], int off, int len);
public void write(int b);
```

Ap9.6.19   *Class* java.io.InputStream

The `InputStream` class is the superclass of all classes representing an input stream of bytes. The following are defined:

```
// Constructors
public InputStream();

// Methods
public int available();
public void close();
public void mark(int readlimit);
```

```
public boolean markSupported();
public abstract int read();
public int read(byte b[]);
public int read(byte b[], int off, int len);
public void reset();
public long skip(long n);
```

Ap9.6.20   *Class* **java.io.InterruptedIOException**

Exception that identifies that an I/O operation has been interrupted. The following are defined:

```
// Fields
public int bytesTransferred;

// Constructors
public InterruptedIOException();
public InterruptedIOException(String s);
```

Ap9.6.21   *Class* **java.io.IOException**

Exception that identifies that an I/O exception has occurred. The following are defined:

```
// Constructors
public IOException();
public IOException(String s);
```

Ap9.6.22   *Class* **java.io.LineNumberInputStream**

The LineNumberInputStream class provides support for the current line number in an input stream. Each line is delimited by either a carriage return character ('\r'), new-line character ('\n') or both together. The following are defined:

```
// Constructors
public LineNumberInputStream(InputStream in);

// Methods
public int available();
public int getLineNumber();
public void mark(int readlimit);
public int read();
public int read(byte b[], int off, int len);
public void reset();
public void setLineNumber(int lineNumber);
public long skip(long n);
```

Ap9.6.23   *Class* **java.io.OutputStream**

The InputStream class is the superclass of all classes representing an output stream of bytes. The following are defined:

```
// Constructors
public OutputStream();

// Methods
public void close();
public void flush();
public void write(byte b[]);
public void write(byte b[], int off, int len);
```

```
public abstract void write(int b);
```

Ap9.6.24   Class java.io.PipedInputStream

The `PipedInputStream` class provides support for pipelined input communications. The following are defined:

```
// Constructors
public PipedInputStream();
public PipedInputStream(PipedOutputStream src);

// Methods
public void close();
public void connect(PipedOutputStream src);
public int read();
public int read(byte b[], int off, int len);
```

Ap9.6.25   Class java.io.PipedOutputStream

The `PipedOutputStream` class provides support for pipelined output communications. The following are defined:

```
// Constructors
public PipedOutputStream();
public PipedOutputStream(PipedInputStream snk);

// Methods
public void close();
public void connect(PipedInputStream snk);
public void write(byte b[], int off, int len);
public void write(int b);
```

Ap9.6.26   Class java.io.PrintStream

The `PrintStream` class provides support for output print streams. The following are defined:

```
// Constructors
public PrintStream(OutputStream out);  // Java 1.0
public PrintStream(OutputStream out, boolean autoflush);// Java 1.0

// Methods
public boolean checkError();
public void close();
public void flush();
public void print(boolean b);
public void print(char c);
public void print(char s[]);
public void print(double d);
public void print(float f);
public void print(int i);
public void print(long l);
public void print(Object obj);
public void print(String s);
public void println();
public void println(boolean b);
public void println(char c);
public void println(char s[]);
public void println(double d);
public void println(float f);
```

```
public void println(int i);
public void println(long l);
public void println(Object obj);
public void println(String s);
public void write(byte b[], int off, int len);
public void write(int b);
```

Ap9.6.27   *Class* **java.io.PushbackInputStream**

The `PushbackInputStream` class provides support to put bytes back into an input stream. The following are defined:

```
// Fields
protected int pushBack;

// Constructors
public PushbackInputStream(InputStream in);

// Methods
public int available();
public boolean markSupported();
public int read();
public int read(byte bytes[], int offset, int length);
public void unread(int ch);
```

Ap9.6.28   *Class* **java.io.RandomAccessFile**

The `RandomAccessFile` class support reading and writing from a random access file. The following are defined:

```
// Constructors
public RandomAccessFile(File file, String mode);
public RandomAccessFile(String name, String mode);

// Methods
public void close();
public final FileDescriptor getFD();
public long getFilePointer();
public long length();
public int read();
public int read(byte b[]);
public int read(byte b[], int off, int len);
public final boolean readBoolean();
public final byte readByte();
public final char readChar();
public final double readDouble();
public final float readFloat();
public final void readFully(byte b[]);
public final void readFully(byte b[], int off, int len);
public final int readInt();
public final String readLine();
public final long readLong();
public final short readShort();
public final int readUnsignedByte();
public final int readUnsignedShort();
public final String readUTF();
public void seek(long pos);
public int skipBytes(int n);
public void write(byte b[]);
public void write(byte b[], int off, int len);
public void write(int b);
public final void writeBoolean(boolean v);
public final void writeByte(int v);
```

```
public final void writeBytes(String s);
public final void writeChar(int v);
public final void writeChars(String s);
public final void writeDouble(double v);
public final void writeFloat(float v);
public final void writeInt(int v);
public final void writeLong(long v);
public final void writeShort(int v);
public final void writeUTF(String str);
```

Ap9.6.29   *Class* java.io.SequenceInputStream

The SequenceInputStream supports the combination of several input streams into a single input stream. The following are defined:

```
// Constructors
public SequenceInputStream(Enumeration e);
public SequenceInputStream(InputStream s1, InputStream s2);

// Methods
public void avialable();    // Java 1.1
public void close();
public int read();
public int read(byte buf[], int pos, int len);
```

Ap9.6.30   *Class* java.io.StreamTokenizer

The StreamTokenizer class splits an input stream into tokens. These tokens can be defined by number, quotes strings or comment styles. The following are defined:

```
// Fields
public double nval;
public String sval;
public int ttype;

// possible values for the ttype field
public final static int TT_EOF, TT_EOL, TT_NUMBER, TT_WORD;

// Constructors
public StreamTokenizer(InputStream I);

// Methods
public void commentChar(int ch);
public void eolIsSignificant(boolean flag);
public int lineno();
public void lowerCaseMode(boolean fl);
public int nextToken();
public void ordinaryChar(int ch);
public void ordinaryChars(int low, int hi);
public void parseNumbers();
public void pushBack();
public void quoteChar(int ch);
public void resetSyntax();
public void whitespaceChars(int low, int hi);
public void slashStarComments(boolean flag);
public String toString();
public void whitespaceChars(int low, int hi);
public void wordChars(int low, int hi);
```

Ap9.6.31　*Class* **java.io.StringBufferInputStream**

The `StringBufferInputStream` class supports stream input buffers. The following are defined:

```
// Fields
protected String buffer;
protected int count, pos;

// Constructors
public StringBufferInputStream(String s);

// Methods
public int available();
public int read();
public int read(byte b[], int off, int len);
public void reset();
public long skip(long n);
```

Ap9.6.32　*Class* **java.io.UTFDataFormatException**

Exception that identifies that a malformed UTF-8 string has been read in a data input stream. The following are defined:

```
// Constructors
public UTFDataFormatException();
public UTFDataFormatException(String s);
```

Ap9.7　Package **java.lang**

Ap9.7.1 *Class* **java.lang.ArithmeticException**

Exception that is thrown when an exceptional arithmetic condition has occurred, such as a division-by-zero or a square root of a negative number. The following are defined:

```
// Constructors
public ArithmeticException();
public ArithmeticException(String s);
```

Ap9.7.2 *Class* **java.lang.ArrayIndexOutOfBoundsException**

Exception that is thrown when an illegal index term in an array has been accessed. The following are defined:

```
// Constructors
public ArrayIndexOutOfBoundsException();
public ArrayIndexOutOfBoundsException(int index);
public ArrayIndexOutOfBoundsException(String s);
```

Ap9.7.3 *Class* **java.lang.ArrayStoreException**

Exception that is thrown when the wrong type of object is stored in an array of objects. The following are defined:

```
// Constructors
public ArrayStoreException();
```

```
public ArrayStoreException(String s);
```

Ap9.7.4 *Class* java.lang.Boolean

The `Boolean` class implements the primitive type boolean of an object. Other methods are included for a converting a boolean to a String and vice versa. The following are defined:

```
public final static Boolean FALSE, TRUE;
public final static Boolean TYPE;   // Java 1.1


// Constructors
public Boolean(boolean value);
public Boolean(String s);

// Methods
public boolean booleanValue();
public boolean equals(Object obj);
public static boolean getBoolean(String name);
public int hashCode();
public String toString();
public static Boolean valueOf(String s);
```

Ap9.7.5 *Class* java.lang.Character

The `Character` class implements the primitive type character of an object. Other methods are defined for determining the type of a character, and converting characters from upper-case to lowercase and vice versa. The following are defined:

```
// Constants
public final static int MAX_RADIX, MAX_VALUE;
public final static int MIN_RADIX, MIN_VALUE;
public final static int TYPE; // Java 1.1
// Character type constants
public final static byte COMBINING_SPACE_MARK; // Java 1.1
public final static byte CONNECTOR_PUNCUATION, CONTROL; // Java 1.1
public final static byte CURRENCY_SYMBOL, DASH_PUNCTUATION;// Java 1.1
public final static byte DIGIT_NUMBER, ENCLOSING_MARK;  // Java 1.1
public final static byte END_PUNCTUATION, FORMAT; // Java 1.1
public final static byte LETTER_NUMBER, LINE_SEPERATOR; // Java 1.1
public final static byte LOWERCASE_LETTER, MATH_SYMBOL; // Java 1.1
public final static byte MODIFIER_LETTER, MODIFIER_SYMBOL; // Java 1.1
public final static byte NON_SPACING_MARK, OTHER_LETTER;// Java 1.1
public final static byte OTHER_NUMBER, OTHER_PUNCTUATION;  // Java 1.1
public final static byte OTHER_SYMBOL, PARAGRAPH_SEPARATOR;// Java 1.1
public final static byte PRIVATE_USE, SPACE_SEPARATOR;  // Java 1.1
public final static byte START_PUNCTUATION, SURROGATE;  // Java 1.1
public final static byte TITLECASE_LETTER, UNASSIGNED;  // Java 1.1
public final static byte UPPERCASE_LETTER;  // Java 1.1


// Constructors
public Character(char value);

// Methods
public char charValue();
public static int digit(char ch, int radix);
public boolean equals(Object obj);
public static char forDigit(int digit, int radix);
public static char getNumericValue(char ch);// Java 1.1
public static char getType(char ch);   // Java 1.1
public static boolean isDefined(char ch);
```

```
public static boolean isDigit(char ch);
public static boolean isISOControl(char ch); // Java 1.1
public static boolean isIdentifierIgnoreable(char ch);  // Java 1.1
public static boolean isJavaIndentierPart(char ch);  // Java 1.1
public static boolean isJavaIndentierStart(char ch); // Java 1.1
public static boolean isJavaLetter(char ch); // Java 1.0
public static boolean isJavaLetterOrDigit(char ch);  // Java 1.0
public static boolean isLetter(char ch);
public static boolean isLetterOrDigit(char ch);
public static boolean isLowerCase(char ch);
public static boolean isSpace(char ch);  // Java 1.0
public static boolean isSpaceChar(char ch);  // Java 1.0
public static boolean isTitleCase(char ch);
public static boolean isUnicodeIdentifierPart(char ch); // Java 1.1
public static boolean isUnicodeIdentifierStart(char ch); // Java 1.1
public static boolean isUpperCase(char ch);
public static boolean isWhitespace(char ch); // Java 1.1
public static char toLowerCase(char ch);
public String toString();
public static char toTitleCase(char ch);
public static char toUpperCase(char ch);
```

Ap9.7.6 *Class* java.lang.*Class*

The Class class implements the class Class and interfaces in a running Java application.
The following are defined:

```
// Methods
public static Class forName(String className);
public ClassLoader getClassLoader();
public Class[] getInterfaces();
public String getName();
public Class getSuperclass();
public boolean isInterface();
public Object newInstance();
public String toString();
```

Ap9.7.7 *Class* java.lang.*Class*CastException

Exception that is thrown when an object is casted to a subclass which it is not an instance.
The following are defined:

```
// Constructors
public ClassCastException();
public ClassCastException(String s);
```

Ap9.7.8 *Class* java.lang.Compiler

The Compiler class supports Java-to-native-code compilers and related services. The following are defined:

```
// Methods
public static Object command(Object any);
public static boolean compileClass(Class clazz);
public static boolean compileClasses(String string);
public static void disable();
public static void enable();
```

Ap9.7.9 Class java.lang.Double

The Double class implements the primitive type double of an object. Other methods are included for a converting a double to a String and vice versa. The following are defined:

```
// Fields
public final static double MAX_VALUE, MIN_VALUE;
public final static double NaN, NEGATIVE_INFINITY, POSITIVE_INFINITY;
public final static double TYPE; // Java 1.1

// Constructors
public Double(double value);
public Double(String s);

// Methods
public static long doubleToLongBits(double value);
public double doubleValue();
public boolean equals(Object obj);
public float floatValue();
public int hashCode();
public int intValue();
public boolean isInfinite();
public static boolean isInfinite(double v);
public boolean isNaN();
public static boolean isNaN(double v);
public static double longBitsToDouble(long bits);
public long longValue();
public String toString();
public static String toString(double d);
public static Double valueOf(String s);
```

Ap9.7.10   Class java.lang.Error

Exception that is thrown when there are serious problems that a reasonable application should not try to catch. The following are defined:

```
// Constructors
public Error();
public Error(String s);
```

Ap9.7.11   Class java.lang.Exception

Exception that is thrown that indicates conditions that a reasonable application might want to catch.

```
// Constructors
public Exception();
public Exception(String s);
```

Ap9.7.12   Class java.lang.Float

The Float class implements the primitive type float of an object. Other methods are included for a converting a float to a String and vice versa. The following are defined:

```
// Fields
public final static float MAX_VALUE MIN_VALUE;
public final static float NaN, NEGATIVE_INFINITY, POSITIVE_INFINITY;
public final static float TYPE;  // Java 1.1

// Constructors
```

```
public Float(double value);
public Float(float value);
public Float(String s);

// Methods
public double doubleValue();
public boolean equals(Object obj);
public static int floatToIntBits(float value);
public float floatValue();
public int hashCode();
public static float intBitsToFloat(int bits);
public int intValue();
public boolean isInfinite();
public static boolean isInfinite(float v);
public boolean isNaN();
public static boolean isNaN(float v);
public long longValue();
public String toString();
public static String toString(float f);
public static Float valueOf(String s);
```

Ap9.7.13   Class java.lang.IllegalAccessError

Exception that is thrown when an application attempts to access or modify a field, or to call a method that it does not have access to. The following are defined:

```
// Constructors
public IllegalAccessError();
public IllegalAccessError(String s);
```

Ap9.7.14   Class java.lang.IllegalArgumentException

Exception that is thrown when a method has been passed an illegal or inappropriate argument. The following are defined:

```
// Constructors
public IllegalArgumentException();
public IllegalArgumentException(String s);
```

Ap9.7.15   Class java.lang.IllegalThreadStateException

Exception that is thrown to indicate that a thread is not in an appropriate state for the requested operation. The following are defined:

```
// Constructors
public IllegalThreadStateException();
public IllegalThreadStateException(String s);
```

Ap9.7.16   Class java.lang.IndexOutOfBoundsException

Exception that is thrown to indicate that an index term is out of range. The following are defined:

```
// Constructors
public IndexOutOfBoundsException();
public IndexOutOfBoundsException(String s);
```

Ap9.7.17 Class java.lang.Integer

The `Integer` class implements the primitive type integer of an object. Other methods are included for a converting a integer to a String and vice versa. The following are defined:

```
// Fields
public final static int MAX_VALUE, MIN_VALUE;
public final static int TYPE; // Java 1.1

// Constructors
public Integer(int value);
public Integer(String s);

// Methods
public Integer decode(String nm);    // Java 1.1
public double doubleValue();
public boolean equals(Object obj);
public float floatValue();
public static Integer getInteger(String nm);
public static Integer getInteger(String nm, int val);
public static Integer getInteger(String nm, Integer val);
public int hashCode();
public int intValue();
public long longValue();
public static int parseInt(String s);
public static int parseInt(String s, int radix);
public static String toBinaryString(int i);
public static String toHexString(int i);
public static String toOctalString(int i);
public String toString();
public static String toString(int i);
public static String toString(int i, int radix);
public static Integer valueOf(String s);
public static Integer valueOf(String s, int radix);
```

Ap9.7.18 Class java.lang.InternalError

Exception that is thrown when an unexpected internal error has occurs. The following are defined:

```
// Constructors
public InternalError();
public InternalError(String s);
```

Ap9.7.19 Class java.lang.InterruptedException

Exception that is thrown when a thread is waiting, sleeping, or otherwise paused for a long time and another thread interrupts it using the interrupt method in class Thread. The following are defined:

```
// Constructors
public InterruptedException();
public InterruptedException(String s);
```

Ap9.7.20 Class java.lang.Long

The `Long` class implements the primitive type long of an object. Other methods are included for a converting a long to a String and vice versa. The following are defined:

```
// Fields
```

```
public final static long MAX_VALUE, MIN_VALUE;
public final static long TYPE;    // Java 1.1

// Constructors
public Long(long value);
public Long(String s);

// Methods
public double doubleValue();
public boolean equals(Object obj);
public float floatValue();
public static Long getLong(String nm);
public static Long getLong(String nm, long val);
public static Long getLong(String nm, Long val);
public int hashCode();
public int intValue();
public long longValue();
public static long parseLong(String s);
public static long parseLong(String s, int radix);
public static String toBinaryString(long i);
public static String toHexString(long i);
public static String toOctalString(long i);
public String toString();
public static String toString(long i);
public static String toString(long i, int radix);
public static Long valueOf(String s);
public static Long valueOf(String s, int radix);
```

Ap9.7.21   Class java.lang.Math

The Math class contains methods to perform basic mathematical operations. The following are defined:

```
// Fields
public final static double E;
public final static double PI;

// Methods
public static double abs(double a);
public static float abs(float a);
public static int abs(int a);
public static long abs(long a);
public static double acos(double a);
public static double asin(double a);
public static double atan(double a);
public static double atan2(double a, double b);
public static double ceil(double a);
public static double cos(double a);
public static double exp(double a);
public static double floor(double a);
public static double IEEEremainder(double f1, double f2);
public static double log(double a);
public static double max(double a, double b);
public static float max(float a, float b);
public static int max(int a, int b);
public static long max(long a, long b);
public static double min(double a, double b);
public static float min(float a, float b);
public static int min(int a, int b);
public static long min(long a, long b);
public static double pow(double a, double b);
public static double random();
public static double rint(double a);
```

```
public static long round(double a);
public static int round(float a);
public static double sin(double a);
public static double sqrt(double a);
public static double tan(double a);
```

Ap9.7.22   *Class* **java.lang.NegativeArraySizeException**

Exception that is thrown when an array is created with a negative size.

```
// Constructors
public NegativeArraySizeException();
public NegativeArraySizeException(String s);
```

Ap9.7.23   *Class* **java.lang.NullPointerException**

Exception that is thrown when an application attempts to use a null pointer. The following are defined:

```
// Constructors
public NullPointerException();
public NullPointerException(String s);
```

Ap9.7.24   *Class* **java.lang.Number**

The Number class contains the superclass of classes for float, double, integer and long. It can be used to convert values into int, long, float or double. The following are defined:

```
// Methods
public abstract double doubleValue();
public abstract float floatValue();
public abstract int intValue();
public abstract long longValue();
```

Ap9.7.25   *Class* **java.lang.NumberFormatException**

Exception that is thrown when an application attempts to convert a string to one of the numeric types, but that the string does not have the appropriate format.

```
// Constructors
public NumberFormatException();
public NumberFormatException(String s);
```

Ap9.7.26   *Class* **java.lang.Object**

The Object class contains the root of the class hierarchy. The following are defined:

```
// Constructors
public Object();

// Methods
protected Object clone();
public boolean equals(Object obj);
protected void finalize();
public final Class getClass();
public int hashCode();
public final void notify();
public final void notifyAll();
public String toString();
```

```
public final void wait();
public final void wait(long timeout);
public final void wait(long timeout, int nanos);
```

Ap9.7.27   Class java.lang.OutOfMemoryError

Exception that is thrown when an application runs out of memory. The following are defined:

```
// Constructors
public OutOfMemoryError();
public OutOfMemoryError(String s);
```

Ap9.7.28   Class java.lang.Process

The Process class contains methods which are used to control the process. The following are defined:

```
// Constructors
public Process();
// Methods
public abstract void destroy();
public abstract int exitValue();
public abstract InputStream getErrorStream();
public abstract InputStream getInputStream();
public abstract OutputStream getOutputStream();
public abstract int waitFor();
```

Ap9.7.29   Class java.lang.Runtime

The Runtime class allows the application to interface with the environment in which it is running. The following are defined:

```
// Methods
public Process exec(String command);
public Process exec(String command, String envp[]);
public Process exec(String cmdarray[]);
public Process exec(String cmdarray[], String envp[]);
public void exit(int status);
public long freeMemory();
public void gc();
public InputStream getLocalizedInputStream(InputStream in);    // Java 1.0
public OutputStream getLocalizedOutputStream(OutputStream out);  // Java 1.0
public static Runtime getRuntime();
public void load(String filename);
public void loadLibrary(String libname);
public void runFinalization();
public long totalMemory();
public void traceInstructions(boolean on);
public void traceMethodCalls(boolean on);
```

Ap9.7.30   Class java.lang.SecurityManager

The SecurityManager class is an abstract class that allows applications to determine if it is safe to execute a given operation. The following are defined:

```
// Fields
 protected boolean inCheck;

// Constructors
```

```
  protected SecurityManager();

// Methods
public void checkAccept(String host, int port);
public void checkAccess(Thread g);
public void checkAccess(ThreadGroup g);
public void checkConnect(String host, int port);
public void checkConnect(String host, int port, Object context);
public void checkCreateClassLoader();
public void checkDelete(String file);
public void checkExec(String cmd);
public void checkExit(int status);
public void checkLink(String lib);
public void checkListen(int port);
public void checkPackageAccess(String pkg);
public void checkPackageDefinition(String pkg);
public void checkPropertiesAccess();
public void checkPropertyAccess(String key);
public void checkRead(FileDescriptor fd);
public void checkRead(String file);
public void checkRead(String file, Object context);
public void checkSetFactory();
public boolean checkTopLevelWindow(Object window);
public void checkWrite(FileDescriptor fd);
public void checkWrite(String file);
protected int classDepth(String name);
protected int classLoaderDepth();
protected ClassLoader currentClassLoader();
protected Class[] getClassContext();
public boolean getInCheck();
public Object getSecurityContext();
protected boolean inClass(String name);
protected boolean inClassLoader();
```

Ap9.7.31   *Class* java.lang.StackOverflowError

Exception that is thrown when a stack overflow occurs. The following are defined:

```
// Constructors
public StackOverflowError();
public StackOverflowError(String s);
```

Ap9.7.32   *Class* java.lang.String

The String class represents character strings. As in C, a string is delimted by inverted commas. It contains string manipulation methods, such as concat (string concatenation), equals (if string is equal to), toLowCase (to convert a string to lowercase), and so on. The following are defined:

```
// Constructors
public String();
public String(byte ascii[], int hibyte); // Java 1.0
public String(byte ascii[], int hibyte, int offset, int count);  // Java 1.0
public String(char value[]);
public String(char value[], int offset, int count);
public String(String value);
public String(StringBuffer buffer);
public String(byte ascii[], int offset, int length, String enc); // Java 1.1

// Methods
```

```
public char charAt(int index);
public int compareTo(String anotherString);
public String concat(String str);
public static String copyValueOf(char data[]);
public static String copyValueOf(char data[], int offset, unt count);
public boolean endsWith(String suffix);
public boolean equals(Object anObject);
public boolean equalsIgnoreCase(String anotherString);
public void getBytes(int srcBegin, int srcEnd, byte dst[], int dstBegin);
public void getChars(int srcBegin, int srcEnd, char dst[], int dstBegin);
public int hashCode();
public int indexOf(int ch);
public int indexOf(int ch, int fromIndex);
public int indexOf(String str);
public int indexOf(String str, int fromIndex);
public String intern();
public int lastIndexOf(int ch);
public int lastIndexOf(int ch, int fromIndex);
public int lastIndexOf(String str);
public int lastIndexOf(String str, int fromIndex);
public int length();
public boolean regionMatches(boolean ignoreCase, int toffset,
   String other, int ooffset, int len);
public boolean regionMatches(int toffset, String other, int offset, int len);
public String replace(char oldChar, char newChar);
public boolean startsWith(String prefix);
public boolean startsWith(String prefix, int toffset);
public String substring(int beginIndex);
public String substring(int beginIndex, int endIndex);
public char[] toCharArray();
public String toLowerCase();
public String toLowerCase(Locale locale); // Java 1.1

public String toString();
public String toUpperCase();
public String toUpperCase(Locale locale); // Java 1.1
public String trim();
public static String valueOf(boolean b);
public static String valueOf(char c);
public static String valueOf(char data[]);
public static String valueOf(char data[], int offset, int count);
public static String valueOf(double d);
public static String valueOf(float f);
public static String valueOf(int i);
public static String valueOf(long l);
public static String valueOf(Object obj);
```

Ap9.7.33   Class java.lang.StringBuffer

The StringBuffer class implements a string buffer. The following are defined:

```
// Constructors
public StringBuffer();
public StringBuffer(int length);
public StringBuffer(String str);
// Methods
public StringBuffer append(boolean b);
public StringBuffer append(char c);
public StringBuffer append(char str[]);
public StringBuffer append(char str[], int offset, int len);
public StringBuffer append(double d);
public StringBuffer append(float f);
public StringBuffer append(int i);
```

```
public StringBuffer append(long l);
public StringBuffer append(Object obj);
public StringBuffer append(String str);
public int capacity();
public char charAt(int index);
public void ensureCapacity(int minimumCapacity);
public void getChars(int srcBegin, int srcEnd, char dst[], int dstBegin);
public StringBuffer insert(int offset, boolean b);
public StringBuffer insert(int offset, char c);
public StringBuffer insert(int offset, char str[]);
public StringBuffer insert(int offset, double d);
public StringBuffer insert(int offset, float f);
public StringBuffer insert(int offset, int i);
public StringBuffer insert(int offset, long l);
public StringBuffer insert(int offset, Object obj);
public StringBuffer insert(int offset, String str);
public int length();
public StringBuffer reverse();
public void setCharAt(int index, char ch);
public void setLength(int newLength);
public String toString();
```

Ap9.7.34   Class java.lang.StringIndexOutOfBoundsException

Exception that is thrown when a string is indexed with a negative value or a value which is greater than or equal to the size of the string. The following are defined:

```
// Constructors
public StringIndexOutOfBoundsException();
public StringIndexOutOfBoundsException(int index);
public StringIndexOutOfBoundsException(String s)
```

Ap9.7.35   Class java.lang.System

The System class implements a number of system methods. The following are defined:

```
// Fields
public static PrintStream err, in, out;
// Methods
public static void arraycopy(Object src, int src_position,
       Object dst, int dst_position, int length);
public static long currentTimeMillis();
public static void exit(int status);
public static void gc();
public static Properties getProperties();
public static String getProperty(String key);
public static String getProperty(String key, String def);
public static SecurityManager getSecurityManager();
public static void load(String filename);
public static void loadLibrary(String libname);
public static void runFinalization();
public static void setProperties(Properties props);
public static void setSecurityManager(SecurityManager s);
```

Ap9.7.36   Class java.lang.Thread

The Thread class implements one or more threads. The following are defined:

```
// Fields
public final static int MAX_PRIORITY, MIN_PRIORITY, NORM_PRIORITY;
```

```
// Constructors
public Thread();
public Thread(Runnable target);
public Thread(Runnable target, String name);
public Thread(String name);
public Thread(ThreadGroup group, Runnable target);
public Thread(ThreadGroup group,Runnable target, String name);
public Thread(ThreadGroup group, String name);

// Methods
public static int activeCount();
public void checkAccess();
public int countStackFrames();
public static Thread currentThread();
public void destroy();
public static void dumpStack();
public static int enumerate(Thread tarray[]);
public final String getName();
public final int getPriority();
public final ThreadGroup getThreadGroup();
public void interrupt();
public static boolean interrupted();
public final boolean isAlive();
public final boolean isDaemon();
public boolean isInterrupted();
public final void join();
public final void join(long millis);
public final void join(long millis, int nanos)
public final void resume();
public void run();
public final void setDaemon(boolean on);
public final void setName(String name);
public final void setPriority(int newPriority);
public static void sleep(long millis);
public static void sleep(long millis, int nanos)
public void start();
public final void stop();
public final void stop(Throwable obj);
public final void suspend();
public String toString();
public static void yield();
```

Ap9.7.37   *Class* **java.lang.ThreadGroup**

The ThreadGroup class implements a set of threads. The following are defined:

```
// Constructors
public ThreadGroup(String name);
public ThreadGroup(ThreadGroup parent, String name);

// Methods
public int activeCount();
public int activeGroupCount();
public final void checkAccess();
public final void destroy();
public int enumerate(Thread list[]);
public int enumerate(Thread list[], boolean recurse);
public int enumerate(ThreadGroup list[]);
public int enumerate(ThreadGroup list[], boolean recurse);
public final int getMaxPriority();
public final String getName();
public final ThreadGroup getParent();
public final boolean isDaemon();
```

```
public void list();
public final boolean parentOf(ThreadGroup g);
public final void resume();
public final void setDaemon(boolean daemon);
public final void setMaxPriority(int pri);
public final void stop();
public final void suspend();
public String toString();
public void uncaughtException(Thread t, Throwable e);
```

Ap9.7.38   *Class* java.lang.Throwable

The `Throwable` class is the superclass of all errors and exceptions in the Java language. The following are defined:

```
// Constructors
public Throwable();
public Throwable(String message);

// Methods
public Throwable fillInStackTrace();
public String getMessage();
public void printStackTrace();
public void printStackTrace(PrintStream s);
public String toString();
```

Ap9.7.39   *Class* java.lang.UnknownError

Exception that is thrown when an unknown error occurs. The following are defined:

```
// Constructors
public UnknownError();
public UnknownError(String s);
```

Ap9.8   Package *java.net*

Ap9.8.1 *Class* java.net.DatagramPacket

The `DatagramPacket` class implements datagram packets. The following are defined:

```
// Constructors
public DatagramPacket(byte[] ibuf, int ilength);
public DatagraamPacket(byte[] ibuf, int ilength, inetAddress iadd, int iport);

// Methods
public synchronized InetAddress getAddress();
public synchronized byte[] getData();
public synchronized int getLength();
public synchronized int getPort();
public synchronized void setAddress(InetAddress iaddr); // Java 1.1
public synchronized void setDate(byte[] ibuf); // Java 1.1
public synchronized void setLength(int ilength);  // Java 1.1
public synchronized void setPort(int iport); // Java 1.1
```

Ap9.8.2 *Class* java.net.InetAddress

The `InetAddress` class represents Internet addresses. The following are defined:

```
// Methods
public InetAddress[] getAllByName(String host);
public InetAddress getByName(String host);
public InetAddress getLocalHost(String host);
public boolean equals(Object obj);
public byte[] getAddress();
public String getHostAddress();
public String getHostName();
public int hashCode();
public boolean isMulticastAddress();   // Java 1.1
public String toString();
```

Ap9.8.3 *Class* java.net.ServerSocket

The ServerSocket class represents servers which listen for a connection from clients. The following are defined:

```
// Constructors
public ServerSocket(int port);
public ServerSocket(int port, int backlog);
public ServerSocket(int port, int backlog, InetAddress bindAddr);
    // Java 1.1
// Methods
public Socket accept();
public void close();
public InetAddress getInetAddress();
public synchronized int getSoTimeout();   // Java 1.1
public String toString();
```

Ap9.8.4 *Class* java.net.Socket

The Socket class represents socket connections over a network. The following are defined:

```
// Constructors
public Socket(String host, int port);
public Socket(InetAddress addr, int port);
public Socket(InetAddress addr, int port, boolean stream); // Java 1.0
public Socket(String host, int port, InetAddress addr, int localport);
   // Java 1.1
public Socket(InetAddress addr, int port, InetAddress localAddress,
       int localport);  // Java 1.1

// Methods
public synchronized void close();
public InetAddress getInetAddress();
public InputStream getInputStream();
public InetAddress getLocalAddress();  // Java 1.1
public int getLocalPort();
public OutputStream getOutputStream();
public int getPort();
public int getSoLinger();  // Java 1.1
public synchronized int getSoTimed();  // Java 1.1
public boolean getTcpNoDelay();  // Java 1.1
public void setSoLinger(boolean on, int val);   // Java 1.1
public synchronized void setSoTimed(int timeout); // Java 1.1
public void setTcpNoDelay(boolean on); // Java 1.1
public String toString();
```

Ap9.8.5 *Class* **java.net.SocketImpl**

The `SocketImpl` class represents socket connections over a network. The following are defined:

```
// Methods
public abstract void accept(SocketImpl s);
public abstract int available();
public abstract void bind(InetAddress host, int port);
public abstract void close();
public abstract void connect(String host, int port);
public abstract void connect(InetAddress addr, int port);
public abstract void create(boolean stream);
public FileDescriptor getFileDescriptor();
public InetAddress getInetAddress();
public abstract InetAddress getInputStream();
```

Ap9.8.6 *Class* **java.net.URL**

The `URL` class represents Uniform Resource Locators. The following are defined:

```
// Constructors
public URL(String protocol, String host, int port, String file);
public URL(String protocol, String host, String file);
public URL(String spec);
public URL(URL context, String spec);

// Methods
public boolean equals(Object obj);
public final Object getContent();
public String getFile();
public String getHost();
public int getPort();
public String getProtocol();
public String getRef();
public int hashcode();
public URLConnection openConnection();
public final InputStream openStream();
public boolean sameFile(URL other);
public String toExternalForm();
public String toString();
```

Ap9.9   Package **java.utils**

Ap9.9.1 *Class* **java.utils.BitSet**

The `BitSet` class implements boolean operations. The following are defined:

```
// Constructors
public BitSet();
public BitSet(int nbits);

// Methods
public void and(BitSet set);
public void clear(int bit);
public Object clone();
public boolean equals(Object obj);
public boolean get(int bit);
public int hashCode();
```

```
public void or(BitSet set);
public void set(int bit);
public int size();
public String toString();
public void xor(BitSet set);
```

Ap9.9.2 Class java.utils.Calender

The Calender class has been added with Java 1.1. It supports dates and times.

Ap9.9.3 Class java.utils.Date

The Date class supports dates and times. The following are defined:

```
// Constructors
public Date();
public Date(int year, int month, int date);            // Java 1.0
public Date(int year, int month, int date, int hrs, int min); // Java 1.0
public Date(int year, int month, int date, int hrs, int min, int sec);
    // Java 1.0
public Date(long date); // Java 1.0
public Date(String s);  // Java 1.0

// Methods
public boolean after(Date when);
public boolean before(Date when);
public boolean equals(Object obj);
public int getDate();    // Java 1.0
public int getDay(); // Java 1.0
public int getHours();   // Java 1.0
public int getMinutes();    // Java 1.0
public int getMonth();   // Java 1.0
public int getSeconds();    // Java 1.0
public long getTime();
public int getTimezoneOffset();  // Java 1.0
public int getYear();    // Java 1.0
public int hashCode();
public static long parse(String s);
public void setDate(int date);   // Java 1.0
public void setHours(int hours); // Java 1.0
public void setMinutes(int minutes);   // Java 1.0
public void setMonth(int month); // Java 1.0
public void setSeconds(int seconds);   // Java 1.0
public void setTime(long time);
public void setYear(int year);   // Java 1.0
public String toGMTString();  // Java 1.0
public String toLocaleString();  // Java 1.0
public String toString();
public static long UTC(int year, int month, int date, int hrs, int min,
       int sec);  // Java 1.0
```

Ap9.9.4 Class java.utils.Dictionary

The Dictionary class is the abstract parent of any class which maps keys to values. The following are defined:

```
// Constructors
public Dictionary();

// Methods
public abstract Enumeration elements();
```

```
public abstract Object get(Object key);
public abstract boolean isEmpty();
public abstract Enumeration keys();
public abstract Object put(Object key, Object value);
public abstract Object remove(Object key);
public abstract int size();
```

Ap9.9.5 *Class* java.utils.EmptyStackException

The `EmptyStackException` is thrown when the stack is empty. The following is defined:

```
// Constructors
public EmptyStackException();
```

Ap9.9.6 *Class* java.utils.Hashtable

This `Hashtable` class supports a hashtable which maps keys to values. The following are defined:

```
// Constructors
public Hashtable();
public Hashtable(int initialCapacity);
public Hashtable(int initialCapacity, float loadFactor);
// Methods
public void clear();
public Object clone();
public boolean contains(Object value);
public boolean containsKey(Object key);
public Enumeration elements();
public Object get(Object key);
public boolean isEmpty();
public Enumeration keys();
public Object put(Object key, Object value);
protected void rehash();
public Object remove(Object key);
public int size();
public String toString();
```

Ap9.9.7 *Class* java.utils.NoSuchElementException

The `NoSuchElementException` is thrown when there are no more elements in the enumeration. The following are defined:

```
// Constructors
public NoSuchElementException();
public NoSuchElementException(String s);
```

Ap9.9.8 *Class* java.utils.Observable

The `Observable` class represents an observable object. The following are defined:

```
// Constructors
public Observable();
// Methods
public void addObserver(Observer o);
protected void clearChanged();
public int countObservers();
public void deleteObserver(Observer o);
public void deleteObservers();
public boolean hasChanged();
```

```
public void notifyObservers();
public void notifyObservers(Object arg);
protected void setChanged();
```

Ap9.9.9 Class java.utils.Properties

The Properties class represents a persistent set of properties. The following are defined:

```
// Fields
protected Properties defaults;

// Constructors
public Properties();
public Properties(Properties defaults);

// Methods
public String getProperty(String key);
public String getProperty(String key, String defaultValue);
public void list(PrintStream out);
public void load(InputStream in);
public Enumeration propertyNames();
public void save(OutputStream out, String header);
```

Ap9.9.10   Class java.utils.Random

The Random class implements pseudo-random generator functions. The following are defined:

```
// Constructors
public Random();
public Random(long seed);

// Methods
public double nextDouble();
public float nextFloat();
public double nextGaussian();
public int nextInt();
public long nextLong();
public void setSeed(long seed);
```

Ap9.9.11   Class java.utils.Stack

The Stack class implements a last-in-first-out (LIFO) stack.

```
// Constructors
public Stack();

// Methods
public boolean empty();
public Object peek();
public Object pop();
public Object push(Object item);
public int search(Object o);
```

Ap9.9.12   Class java.utils.StringTokenizer

The StringTokenizer class allows strings to be split into tokens. The following are defined:

```
// Constructors
public StringTokenizer(String str);
```

```
public StringTokenizer(String str, String delim);
public StringTokenizer(String str, String delim, boolean returnTokens);

// Methods
public int countTokens();
public boolean hasMoreElements();
public boolean hasMoreTokens();
public Object nextElement();
public String nextToken();
public String nextToken(String delim);
```

Ap9.9.13   Class java.utils.Vector

The Vector class implements a growable array of objects. The following are defined:

```
// Fields
protected int capacityIncrement;
protected int elementCount;
protected Object elementData[];

// Constructors
public Vector();
public Vector(int initialCapacity);
public Vector(int initialCapacity, int capacityIncrement);

// Methods
public final void addElement(Object obj);
public final int capacity();
public Object clone();
public final boolean contains(Object elem);
public final void copyInto(Object anArray[]);
public final Object elementAt(int index);
public final Enumeration elements();
public final void ensureCapacity(int minCapacity)
public final Object firstElement();
public final int indexOf(Object elem);
public final int indexOf(Object elem, int index);
public final void insertElementAt(Object obj, int index);
public final boolean isEmpty();
public final Object lastElement();
public final int lastIndexOf(Object elem);
public final int lastIndexOf(Object elem, int index);
public final void removeAllElements();
public final boolean removeElement(Object obj);
public final void removeElementAt(int index);
public final void setElementAt(Object obj, int index);
public final void setSize(int newSize);
public final int size();
public final String toString();
public final void trimToSize();
```

Ap10 NIS, NFS, RC, FTP and DNS

Ap10.1 Example Internet domain name server files

In the following example setup, there are two name servers (ees99 and eepc02) within the eece.napier.ac.uk domain. The Internet domain naming process is run with the named program and reads from the named.boot file (to use a file other than /etc/named.boot the -b option is used). Its contents are given next and it lists six main subnet (146.176.144.x to 146.176.151.x). The files net/net144 to net/net151 contain the definition of the hosts that connect to these subnets.

```
;   @(#)named.boot.slave 1.13      (Berkeley)   87/07/21
;   boot file for secondary name server
; Note that there should be one primary entry for each SOA record.
;
directory       /usr/local/adm/named

; type     domain                        source host/file       backup file

primary    eece.napier.ac.uk             eece.napier.ac.uk
primary    144.176.146.in-addr.arpa      net/net144
primary    145.176.146.in-addr.arpa      net/net145
primary    146.176.146.in-addr.arpa      net/net146
primary    147.176.146.in-addr.arpa      net/net147
primary    150.176.146.in-addr.arpa      net/net150
primary    151.176.146.in-addr.arpa      net/net151
primary    0.0.127.IN-ADDR.ARPA          named.local
primary    0.0.127.IN-ADDR.ARPA          named.local
cache      .                             root.cache
```

The first line (after the comments, which begin with a semi-colon) defines that the master file (eece.napier.ac.uk) contains authoritative data for the eece.napier.ac.uk domain. All domain names are then relative to this domain. For example, a computer within this domain which has name pc444 will have the full domain name of:

pc444.eece.napier.ac.uk

The second line of the file defines that the file net/net144 contains the authoritative data on the 144.176.146.in-addr.arpa domain, and so on. The cache line specifies that data in the root.cache file is to be place in the backup cache.

The following shows the contents of the eece.napier.ac.uk file on the ees99 computer. Each master zone should begin with an SOA record for the zone. The A entry defines an address, NS defines a name server, CNAME defines an alias and MX a mail server. It can be seen that ees99 has the mw alias, thus ees99.eece.napier.ac.uk is the same as mw.eece.napier.ac.uk.

```
@       IN    SOA    ees99.eece.napier.ac.uk.  mike.ees99.eece.napier.ac.uk. (
                     199806171        ; Serial
                     10800            ; Refresh every 3 hrs
                     1800             ; Retry every 1/2 hr
                     604800           ; Expire (seconds)
                     259200 )         ; Minimum time-to-live
        IN    NS     ees99.eece.napier.ac.uk.
```

```
                   IN    NS      eepc02.eece.napier.ac.uk.
localhost          IN    A       127.0.0.1
@                  IN    MX      11        146.176.151.139.
hp350              IN    A       146.176.144.10
mwave              IN    A       146.176.144.11
hplb69             IN    CNAME   mwave
vax                IN    A       146.176.144.13
miranda            IN    A       146.176.144.14
triton             IN    A       146.176.144.20
mimas              IN    A       146.176.146.21
ees99              IN    A       146.176.151.99
mw                 IN    CNAME   ees99
```

The SOA lists a serial number, which has to be increased each time the master file is changed. This is because secondary servers check the serial number at an interval specified by the refresh time (Refresh). If the serial number increases then a zone transfer is done to load the new data. If the master server cannot be contacted when a refresh is due then the retry time (Retry) specifies the interval at which refreshes occur. If the master server cannot be contacted within the expire time interval (Expire) then all data from the zone is discard by secondary servers.

The following file lists some of the contents of the net/net151 file. The NS entry defines the two name servers (ees99 and eepc02) and the PTR entry maps an IP address to a domain name.

```
@     IN    SOA     ees99.eece.napier.ac.uk.  mike.ees99.eece.napier.ac.uk. (
                         199706091          ; Serial
                         10800              ; Refresh
                         1800               ; Retry
                         604800             ; Expire
                         259200 )           ; Minimum
      IN    NS      ees99.eece.napier.ac.uk.
      IN    NS      eepc02.eece.napier.ac.uk.
50    IN    PTR     ee50.eece.napier.ac.uk.
61    IN    PTR     eepc01.eece.napier.ac.uk.
62    IN    PTR     eepc02.eece.napier.ac.uk.
222   IN    PTR     pctest.eece.napier.ac.uk.
2     IN    PTR     pc345.eece.napier.ac.uk.
3     IN    PTR     pc307.eece.napier.ac.uk.
4     IN    PTR     pc320.eece.napier.ac.uk.
5     IN    PTR     pc331.eece.napier.ac.uk.
6     IN    PTR     pc401.eece.napier.ac.uk.
7     IN    PTR     pc404.eece.napier.ac.uk.
```

and for the net/net151 file:

```
@  IN    SOA     ees99.eece.napier.ac.uk.  mike.ees99.eece.napier.ac.uk. (
                      199806171          ; Serial
                      10800              ; Refresh
                      1800               ; Retry
                      604800             ; Expire
                      259200 )           ; Minimum
   IN    NS      ees99.eece.napier.ac.uk.
   IN    NS      eepc02.eece.napier.ac.uk.
10 IN    PTR     ees10.eece.napier.ac.uk.
11 IN    PTR     ees11.eece.napier.ac.uk.
12 IN    PTR     ees12.eece.napier.ac.uk.
13 IN    PTR     ees13.eece.napier.ac.uk.
14 IN    PTR     ees14.eece.napier.ac.uk.
15 IN    PTR     ees15.eece.napier.ac.uk.
```

The entries take the form:

<domain>   *<op_ttl>*   *<opt_class>*   *<type><resource_record_data>*

where

domain	either a . which defines the root domain, a @ which defines the current origin, or a standard domain name. If it is a standard domain and it does not end with a ., then current origin is appended to the domain, else the domain names unmodified.
op_ttl	is an optional number for the time to live.
opt_class	is the object address type. This can be IN (for DARPA Internet) or HS (for Hesiod class).
resource_record	This contains one of the following definitions:

- A (address).
- CNAME (canonical name which is an alias for another host).
- GID (group ID).
- HINFO (host information)
- MB (mailbox domain name).
- MG (mailbox domain name).
- MIFO (mailbox or mail list information).
- MR (mail rename domain name).
- MX (mail exchanger which handles mail for a given host).
- NS (name server for the domain).
- PTR (pointer record which maps an IP address to a hostname).
- SOA (start of authority record). The domain of originating host, domain address of maintainer, a serial and the other parameters (refresh, retry time, expire time and minimum TTL) are also defined.
- TXT (text string).
- UID (user information).
- WKS (well known service). This defines an IP address followed by a list of services.

The contents of the `sobasefile` is given next. This defines the two domain name servers.

```
@  IN      SOA     ees99.eece.napier.ac.uk.   mike.ees99.eece.napier.ac.uk. (
                        19970307         ; Serial
                        10800            ; Refresh
                        1800             ; Retry
                        604800           ; Expire
                        259200 )         ; Minimum
   IN      NS      ees99.eece.napier.ac.uk.
   IN      NS      eepc02.eece.napier.ac.uk.
```

Ap10.2 TCP/IP services

Port	Protocol	Service	Comment
1	TCP	TCPmux	
7	TCP/UDP	echo	
9	TCP/UDP	discard	Null

11	TCP	systat	Users
13	TCP/UDP	daytime	
15	TCP	netstat	
17	TCP	qotd	Quote
18	TCP/UDP	msp	Message send protocol
19	TCP/UDP	chargen	ttytst source
21	TCP	ftp	
23	TCP	telnet	
25	TCP	smtp	Mail
37	TCP/UDP	time	Timserver
39	UDP	rlp	Resource location
42	TCP	nameserver	IEN 116
43	TCP	whois	Nicname
53	TCP/UDP	domain	Domain name server
57	TCP	mtp	Deprecated
67	TCP	bootps	BOOTP server
67	UDP	bootps	
68	TCP/UDP	bootpc	BOOTP client
69	UDP	tftp	
70	TCP/UDP	gopher	Internet Gopher
77	TCP	rje	Netrjs
79	TCP	finger	
80	TCP/UDP	www	WWW HTTP
87	TCP	link	Ttylink
88	TCP/UDP	kerberos	Kerberos v5
95	TCP	supdup	
101	TCP	hostnames	
102	TCP	iso-tsap	ISODE.
105	TCP/UDP	csnet-ns	CSO name server
107	TCP/UDP	rtelnet	Remote Telnet
109	TCP/UDP	pop2	POP version 2
110	TCP/UDP	pop3	POP version 3
111	TCP/UDP	sunrpc	
113	TCP	auth	Rap identity authentication
115	TCP	sftp	
117	TCP	uucp-path	
119	TCP	nntp	USENET News Transfer Protocol
123	TCP/UDP	ntp	Network Time Protocol
137	TCP/UDP	netbios-ns	NETBIOS Name Service
138	TCP/UDP	netbios-dgm	NETBIOS Datagram Service
139	TCP/UDP	netbios-ssn	NETBIOS session service
143	TCP/UDP	imap2	Interim Mail Access Protocol Ver2
161	UDP	snmp	Simple Net Management Protocol
162	UDP	snmp-trap	SNMP trap
163	TCP/UDP	cmip-man	ISO management over IP (CMOT)
164	TCP/UDP	cmip-agent	
177	TCP/UDP	xdmcp	X Display Manager
178	TCP/UDP	nextstep	NeXTStep NextStep
179	TCP/UDP	bgp	BGP
191	TCP/UDP	prospero	
194	TCP/UDP	irc	Internet Relay Chat
199	TCP/UDP	smux	SNMP Unix Multiplexer
201	TCP/UDP	at-rtmp	AppleTalk routing
202	TCP/UDP	at-nbp	AppleTalk name binding
204	TCP/UDP	at-echo	AppleTalk echo
206	TCP/UDP	at-zis	AppleTalk zone information

210	TCP/UDP	z3950	NISO Z39.50 database
213	TCP/UDP	ipx	IPX
220	TCP/UDP	imap3	Interactive Mail Access
372	TCP/UDP	ulistserv	UNIX Listserv
512	TCP/UDP	exec	Comsat
513	TCP	login	
513	UDP	who	Whod
514	TCP	shell	No passwords used
514	UDP	syslog	
515	TCP	printer	Line printer spooler
517	UDP	talk	
518	UDP	ntalk	
520	UDP	route	RIP
525	UDP	timed	Timeserver
526	TCP	tempo	Newdate
530	TCP	courier	Rpc
531	TCP	conference	Chat
532	TCP	netnews	Readnews
533	UDP	netwall	Emergency broadcasts
540	TCP	uucp	Uucp daemon
543	TCP	klogin	Kerberized 'rlogin' (v5)
544	TCP	kshell	Kerberized 'rsh' (v5)
556	TCP	remotefs	Brunhoff remote filesystem
749	TCP	kerberos-adm	Kerberos 'kadmin' (v5)
750	UDP	#kerberos	Kerberos (server) UDP
750	TCP	#kerberos	Kerberos (server) TCP
760	TCP	krbupdate	Kerberos registration
761	TCP	kpasswd	Kerberos "passwd"
765	TCP	webster	Network dictionary
871	TCP	supfilesrv	SUP server
1127	TCP	supfiledbg	SUP debugging
1524	TCP	ingreslock	
1524	UDP	ingreslock	
1525	TCP	prospero-np	Prospero non-privileged
1525	UDP	prospero-np	
2105	TCP	eklogin	Kerberos encrypted rlogin
5002	TCP	rfe	Radio Free Ethernet

Ap10.3 netnfsrc file

This sections outlines an example netnfsrc (NFS startup file) file. In the script portion given below the NFS_CLIENT is set to a 1 if the host is set to a client (else it will be 0) and the NFS_SERVER parameter is set to a 1 if the host is set to a server (else it will be 0). Initially the NFS clients and servers are started. Note that a host can be a client, a server, both or neither.

Next the mountd daemon is started, after which the NFS daemons (nfsd) are started (only on servers). After this the biod daemon is run.

```
NFS_CLIENT=1
NFS_SERVER=1
START_MOUNTD=0
#       Read in /etc/exports
if [ $LFS -eq 0 -a $NFS_SERVER -ne 0 -a -f /etc/exports ] ; then
    > /etc/xtab
    /usr/etc/exportfs -a  && echo "    Reading in /etc/exports"
    set_return
```

```
fi

if [ $NFS_SERVER -ne 0 -a $START_MOUNTD -ne 0 -a -f /usr/etc/rpc.mountd ] ;
then
    /usr/etc/rpc.mountd && echo "starting up the mountd" && echo
                             "\t/usr/etc/rpc.mountd"
    set_return
fi
##
if [ $LFS -eq 0 -a $NFS_SERVER -ne 0 -a -f /etc/nfsd ] ; then
    /etc/nfsd 4 && echo "starting up the NFS daemons" && echo "\t/etc/nfsd 4"
    set_return
fi
##
if [ $NFS_CLIENT -ne 0 ] ; then
    if [ -f /etc/biod ] ; then
        /etc/biod 4 && echo
            "starting up the BIO daemons" && echo "\t/etc/biod 4"
        set_return
fi
    /bin/cat /dev/null > /etc/nfs.up
fi
```

The next part of the netnfsrc file deals with the NIS services. There are three states:
NIS_MASTER_SERVER, NIS_SLAVE_SERVER and NIS_CLIENT. A host can either be a master server or a slave server, but cannot be both. All NIS servers must also be NIS clients, so
the NIS_MASTER_SERVER or NIS_SLAVE_SERVER parameters should be set to 1. Initially
the domain name is set using the command domainname (in this case it is eece).

```
NIS_MASTER_SERVER=1
NIS_SLAVE_SERVER=0
NIS_CLIENT=1
NISDOMAIN=eece
NISDOMAIN_ERR=""

if [ "$NISDOMAIN" -a -f /bin/domainname ] ; then
    echo "\t/bin/domainname $NISDOMAIN"
    /bin/domainname $NISDOMAIN
    if [ $? -ne 0 ] ; then
    echo "Error:  NIS domain name not set" >&2
    NISDOMAIN_ERR=TRUE
    fi
else
    echo "\tNIS domain name not set"
    NISDOMAIN_ERR=TRUE
fi
```

Next portmap is started for ARPA clients.

```
if [ -f /etc/portmap ] ; then
    echo "\t/etc/portmap"
    /etc/portmap
    if [ $? -ne 0 ] ; then
    echo  "Error:  NFS portmapper NOT powered up"   >&2
    exit 1
    fi
fi
```

Next the NIS is started.

```
if [ "$NISDOMAIN_ERR" -o \( $NIS_MASTER_SERVER -eq 0 -a $NIS_SLAVE_SERVER -eq
0\
    -a $NIS_CLIENT -eq 0 \) ] ; then
    echo "    Network Information Service not started."
else
    echo "    starting up the Network Information Service"

    HOSTNAME=`hostname`

    if [ $NIS_MASTER_SERVER -ne 0 -o $NIS_SLAVE_SERVER -ne 0 ]; then
    NIS_SERVER=TRUE
    fi

    if [ $NIS_MASTER_SERVER -ne 0 -a $NIS_SLAVE_SERVER -ne 0 ]; then
     echo "NOTICE:both NIS_MASTER_SERVER and NIS_SLAVE_SERVER variables set;"
     echo "\t$HOSTNAME will be only a NIS slave server."
     NIS_MASTER_SERVER=0
    fi

 if [ $NIS_CLIENT -eq 0 ]; then
 echo "NOTICE:$HOSTNAME will be a NIS server, but the NIS_CLIENT variable is"
 echo "\tnot set; $HOSTNAME will also be a NIS client."
 NIS_CLIENT=1
 fi
```

Next the yp services are started.

```
#  The verify_ypserv function determines if it is OK to start ypserv(1M)
#  (and yppasswdd(1M) for the master NIS server).  It returns its result
#  in the variable NISSERV_OK - if non-null, it is OK to start ypserv(1M);
#  if it is null, ypserv(1M) will not be started.
#
#  First, the filesystem containing /usr/etc/yp is examined to see if it
#  supports long or short filenames.  Once this is known, the proper list
#  of standard NIS map filenames is examined to verify that each map exists
#  in the NIS domain subdirectory.  If any map is missing, verify_ypserv
#  sets NISSERV_OK to null and returns.
##

verify_ypserv() {
    ##
    #  LONGNAMES are the names of the NIS maps on a filesystem that
    #  supports long filenames.
    ##

    LONGNAMES="group.bygid.dir group.bygid.pag group.byname.dir \
        group.byname.pag hosts.byaddr.dir hosts.byaddr.pag \
        hosts.byname.dir hosts.byname.pag networks.byaddr.dir \
        networks.byaddr.pag networks.byname.dir networks.byname.pag \
        passwd.byname.dir passwd.byname.pag passwd.byuid.dir \
        passwd.byuid.pag protocols.byname.dir protocols.byname.pag \
        protocols.bynumber.dir protocols.bynumber.pag \
        rpc.bynumber.dir rpc.bynumber.pag services.byname.dir \
        services.byname.pag ypservers.dir ypservers.pag"
    ##
    #  SHORTNAMES are the names of the NIS maps on a filesystem that
    #  supports only short filenames (14 characters or less).
    ##
```

```
SHORTNAMES="group.bygi.dir group.bygi.pag group.byna.dir \
        group.byna.pag hosts.byad.dir hosts.byad.pag \
        hosts.byna.dir hosts.byna.pag netwk.byad.dir \
        netwk.byad.pag netwk.byna.dir netwk.byna.pag \
        passw.byna.dir passw.byna.pag passw.byui.dir \
        passw.byui.pag proto.byna.dir proto.byna.pag \
        proto.bynu.dir proto.bynu.pag rpc.bynu.dir \
        rpc.bynu.pag servi.byna.dir servi.byna.pag \
        ypservers.dir ypservers.pag"

NISSERV_OK=TRUE

if `/usr/etc/yp/longfiles`; then
    NAMES=$LONGNAMES
else
    NAMES=$SHORTNAMES
fi

for NAME in $NAMES ; do
    if [ ! -f /usr/etc/yp/$NISDOMAIN/$NAME ] ; then
        NISSERV_OK=
        return
    fi
done
}
```

Next ypserv and ypbind are started.

```
    if [ "$NIS_SERVER" -a -f /usr/etc/ypserv ] ; then
verify_ypserv
if [ "$NISSERV_OK" ] ; then
/usr/etc/ypserv && echo "\t/usr/etc/ypserv"
            set_return
else
    echo "\tWARNING:  /usr/etc/ypserv not started:  either"
    echo "\t          - the directory /usr/etc/yp/$NISDOMAIN does not exist
or"
    echo "\t          - some or all of the $NISDOMAIN NIS domain's"
    echo "\t            maps are missing."
    echo "\tTo initialize $HOSTNAME as a NIS server, see ypinit(1M)."
            returnstatus=1
fi
 fi
 if [ $NIS_CLIENT -ne 0 -a -f /etc/ypbind ] ; then
/etc/ypbind  && echo "\t/etc/ypbind "
     set_return

     ##
     #   check if the NIS domain is bound. If not disable NIS
     ##
     CNT=0;
     MAX_NISCHECKS=2
     NIS_CHECK=YES
     echo " Checking NIS binding."
     while [ ${CNT} -le ${MAX_NISCHECKS} -a "${NIS_CHECK}" = "YES" ]; do
/usr/bin/ypwhich 2>&1 | /bin/fgrep 'not bound ypwhich' > /dev/null

     if [ $? -eq 0 ]; then
         CNT=`expr $CNT + 1`
         if [ ${CNT} -le 2 ]; then
         sleep 5
```

```
           else
             echo "  Unable to bind to NIS server using domain ${NISDOMAIN}."
             echo "  Disabling NIS"
             /bin/domainname ""
             /bin/ps -e | /bin/grep ypbind | \
               kill -15 `/usr/bin/awk '{ print $1 }'`
             NIS_CHECK=NO
             returnstatus=1
             break;
               fi
           else
               echo " Bound to NIS server using domain ${NISDOMAIN}."
               NIS_CHECK=NO
           fi
             done
       fi

       ##
       if [ $NIS_MASTER_SERVER -ne 0 -a -f /usr/etc/rpc.yppasswdd ] ; then
       if [ "$NISSERV_OK" ] ; then
             echo "\t/usr/etc/rpc.yppasswdd"
             /usr/etc/rpc.yppasswdd /etc/passwd -m passwd PWFILE=/etc/passwd
         set_return
       else
           echo "\tWARNING:  /usr/etc/rpc.yppasswdd not started:  refer to the"
           echo "\t          reasons listed in the WARNING above."
               returnstatus=1
       fi
        fi
fi
```

Finally the PC-NFS daemons (pcnfsd) and the lock manager daemon (rpc.lockd) status monitor daemon (rpc.statd) are started.

```
PCNFS_SERVER=1
if [ $LFS -eq 0 -a $PCNFS_SERVER -ne 0 -a -f /etc/pcnfsd ] ; then
    /etc/pcnfsd && echo "starting up the PC-NFS daemon" && echo "\t/etc/pcnfsd"
    set_return
fi

if [ $NFS_CLIENT -ne 0 -o $NFS_SERVER -ne 0 ] ; then
    if [ -f /usr/etc/rpc.statd ] ; then
    /usr/etc/rpc.statd && echo "starting up the Status Monitor daemon" && echo
"\t/usr/etc/rpc.statd"
        set_return
    fi
    if [ -f /usr/etc/rpc.lockd ] ; then
    /usr/etc/rpc.lockd && echo "starting up the Lock Manager daemon" && echo
"\t/usr/etc/rpc.lockd"
        set_return
    fi
fi
exit $returnstatus
```

Ap10.4 rc file

The rc file is executed when the UNIX node starts. It contains a number of functions (such as localrc(), hfsmount(), and so on) which are called from a main section. The example script given next contains some of the functions defined in Table Ap10.1.

Table Ap10.1   Sample rc functions

Function	Description
localrc()	Add local configuration to the node. In the example script the Bones-Licensing 2.4 is started locally on the node. This part of the script will probably be the only function which is different on different nodes.
hfsmount()	Mounts local disk drives
map_keyboard()	Loads appropriate keymap
syncer_start()	The syncer helps to minimize file damage when this is a power failure or a system crash
lp_start()	Starts the lp (line printer) scheduler
net_start()	Starts networking through netlinkrc
swap_start()	Starts swapping on alternate swap devices

```
initialize()
{
   if [ "$SYSTEM_NAME" = "" ]
   then
   SYSTEM_NAME=pollux
      export SYSTEM_NAME
   fi
}

localrc()
{

#%%CSIBeginFeature: Bones-Licensing 2.4
   DESIGNERHOME=/win/designer-2.0
   export DESIGNERHOME

   echo -n "Starting Bones-Licensing 2.4 ..."
   if [ -f ${DESIGNERHOME}/bin/start-lmgrd ]; then
      ${DESIGNERHOME}/bin/start-lmgrd
      echo " lmgrd."
   else
      echo " failed."
   fi
}

set_date()
{
  if [ $SET_PARMS_RUN -eq 0 ] ; then
   if [ $TIMEOUT -ne 0 ] ; then
      echo "\007Is the date `date` correct? (y or n, default: y) \c"
      reply=`line -t $TIMEOUT`
      echo ""

      if [ "$reply" = y -o "$reply" = "" -o "$reply" = Y ]
```

```
        then
            return
        else
            if [ -x /etc/set_parms ]; then
                /etc/set_parms time_only
            fi
        fi
    fi

    fi # if SET_PARMS_RUN
}
hfsmount()
{
    # create /etc/mnttab with valid root entry
    /etc/mount -u >/dev/null

    # enable quotas on the root file system
    # (others are enabled by mount)
    [ -f /quotas -a -x /etc/quotaon ] && /etc/quotaon -v /

    # Mount the HFS volumes listed in /etc/checklist:
    /etc/mount -a -t hfs -v
    # (NFS volumes are mounted via net_start() function)

    # Uncomment the following mount command to mount CDFS's
    /etc/mount -a -t cdfs -v

    # Preen quota statistics
    [ -x /etc/quotacheck ] && echo checking quotas && /etc/quotacheck -aP
}
map_keyboard()
{
#
itemap_option=""
if [ -f /etc/kbdlang ]
then
    read MAP_NAME filler < /etc/kbdlang
    if [ $MAP_NAME ]
    then
        itemap_option="-l $MAP_NAME"
    fi
fi
if [ -x /etc/itemap ]
then
    itemap -i -L $itemap_option -w /etc/kbdlang
fi
}

syncer_start()
{
    if /usr/bin/rtprio 127 /etc/syncer
    then
        echo syncer started
    fi
}
lp_start()
{
    if [ -s /usr/spool/lp/pstatus ]
    then
        lpshut > /dev/null 2>&1
        rm -f /usr/spool/lp/SCHEDLOCK
        lpsched
        echo line printer scheduler started
    fi
```

```
}
clean_ex()
{
    if [ -x /usr/bin/ex ]
    then
        echo "preserving editor files (if any)"
        ( cd /tmp; expreserve -a )
    fi
}

clean_uucp()
{
    if [ -x /usr/lib/uucp/uuclean ]
    then
        echo "cleaning up uucp"
        /usr/lib/uucp/uuclean -pSTST -pLCK -n0
    fi
}
net_start()
{
    if [ -x /etc/netlinkrc ] && /etc/netlinkrc
    then
        echo NETWORKING started.
    fi
}
swap_start()
{
    if /etc/swapon -a
    then
        echo 'swap device(s) active'
    fi
}
cron_start()
{
    if [ -x /etc/cron ]
    then
        if [ -f /usr/lib/cron/log ]
        then
            mv /usr/lib/cron/log /usr/lib/cron/OLDlog
        fi
        /etc/cron && echo cron started
    fi
}

audio_start ()
{
    # Start up the audio server
    if [ -x /etc/audiorc ] && /etc/audiorc
    then
        echo "Audio server started"
    fi
}

#
# The main section of the rc script
#

# Where to find commands:
PATH=/bin:/usr/bin:/usr/lib:/etc

# Set termio configuration for output device.
stty clocal icanon echo opost onlcr ixon icrnl ignpar

if [ ! -f /etc/rcflag ]    # Boot time invocation only
```

```
then
    # /etc/rcflag is removed by /etc/brc at boot and by shutdown
    touch /etc/rcflag

    hfsmount
    map_keyboard
    setparms
    initialize
    switch_over
    uname -S $SYSTEM_NAME
    hostname $SYSTEM_NAME

    swap_start
    syncer_start
    lp_start
    clean_ex
    clean_uucp
    net_start
    audio_start
    localrc
fi
```

Ap10.5 FTP commands

ABOR	Abort previous command	**ACCT**	Specify account
ALLO	Allocate storage	**APPE**	Append to a file
CDUP	Go to directory above	**CWD**	Change working directory
DELE	Delete a file	**HELP**	Show help information
LIST	List directory (ls -l)	**MKD**	Make directory
MDTM	Show last modification time	**MODE**	Specify data transfer mode
NLST	Give name of list of files	**NOOP**	No operation (to prevent discon tion)
PASS	Specify password	**PASV**	Prepare for server-to-server tran
PORT	Specify port	**PWD**	Display current working directo
QUIT	Quit session	**REST**	Restart incomplete session
RETR	Retrieve a file	**RMD**	Remove a directory
RNFR	Specify rename-from filename	**RNTO**	Spread rename-to filename
SITE	Non-standard commands	**SIZE**	Return size of file
STOR	Store a file	**STOU**	Store a file with a unique name
STRU	Specify data transfer structure	**SYST**	Show operation system type
TYPE	Specify data transfer type	**USER**	Specify user name
XCUP	Change of parent of current working directory	**XCWD**	Change working directory
XMKD	Make a directory	**XPWD**	Print a directory
XRMD	Remove a directory		

The ftpd daemon is run from the Internet daemon (inetd and inetd.conf). It is automatically run when there is a request from the ftp port which is specified in the /etc/services file (typically port 21). Users who use ftp must have an account in the /etc/password file and any users who are barred from ftp access should be listed in the /etc/ftpusers file.

Anonymous FTP logins are where the user logs in as anonymous (typically using their e-mail address as the password). The user then uses the ~ftp directory for all transfers. Typically the structure is:

~ftp/bin	Contains a copy of the /bin/ls file.
~ftp/etc	Contains the passwd, group and logingroup files for the users which own files within ~ftp.
~ftp/etc/passwd	Defines users who own files within ~ftp.
~ftp/etc/group	Defines groups who own files within ~ftp.
~ftp/pub	General area where files can be uploaded to or downloaded from.

Note that anonymous FTP is inherently dangerous to system security. To protect against damage the -l option in the ftpd daemon can be used to log all accesses to the system log. The -t option in the ftpd daemon defines the timeout time for a session.

In order to permit anonymous FTP, a line similar to the following must be added to the /etc/password file:

```
ftp:*:400:10:anonymousFTP:/user/ftp:/bin/false
```

where, in this case, 400 is the unique user ID for the ftp login, 10 is the group ID number for the guest group and /user/ftp specifies the home directory for the anonymous ftp account.

Ap10.6 Telnet

The Internet daemon (inetd) starts the telnetd daemon when there is a request from the telnet port which is specified in the /etc/services files (typically port 23). To start the telnetd the /etc/inetd.conf file must contain the line:

```
telnet stream tcp nowait root /etc/telnetd telnetd -b/etc/issue
```

Ap11 RFC's

The IAB (Internet Advisor Board) has published many documents on the TCP/IP protocol family. They are known as RFC (request for comment) and can be obtained using FTP from the following:

- Internet Network Information Center (NIC) at `nic ddn mil`, or one of several other FTP sites, such as from the InterNIC Directory and Database Services server at `ds.internic.net`
- Through electronic mail from the automated InterNIC Directory and Database Services mail server at `mailserv@ds.internic.net` The main body of the message should contain the command:

```
document-by-name rfcNNNN
```

where NNNN is the number of the RFC Multiple requests can be made by sending a single message with each specified document separated by comma-separated list.

The main RFC documents are:

RFC768	**User Datagram Protocol**
RFC775	Directory-Oriented FTP Commands
RFC781	Specification of the Internet Protocol Timestamp Option
RFC783	TFTP Protocol
RFC786	User Datagram Protocol (UDP)
RFC791	**Internet Protocol (IP)**
RFC792	**Internet Control Message Protocol (ICMP)**
RFC793	**Transmission Control Protocol (TCP)**
RFC799	Internet Name Domains
RFC813	Window and Acknowledgment in TCP
RFC815	IP Datagram Reassembly Algorithms
RFC821	**Simple Mail-Transfer Protocol (SMTP)**
RFC822	**Standard for the Format of ARPA Internet Text Messages**
RFC823	DARPA Internet Gateway
RFC827	Exterior Gateway Protocol (EGP)
RFC877	**Standard for the Transmission of IP Datagrams over Public Data Networks**
RFC879	TCP Maximum Segment Size and Related Topics
RFC886	Proposed Standard for Message Header Munging
RFC893	Trailer Encapsulations
RFC894	**Standard for the Transmission of IP Datagrams over Ethernet Networks**
RFC895	**Standard for the Transmission of IP Datagrams over Experimental Ethernet Networks**
RFC896	Congestion Control in TCP/IP Internetworks
RFC903	Reverse Address Resolution Protocol
RFC904	Exterior Gateway Protocol Formal Specifications
RFC906	Bootstrap Loading Using TFTP
RFC919	**Broadcast Internet Datagram**
RFC920	Domain Requirements
RFC932	Subnetwork Addressing Schema
RFC949	FTP Unique-Named Store Command
RFC950	Internet Standard Subnetting Procedure
RFC951	Bootstrap Protocol

RFC959	**File Transfer Protocol**
RFC974	**Mail Routing and the Domain System**
RFC980	Protocol Document Order Information
RFC1009	Requirements for Internet Gateways
RFC1011	**Official Internet Protocol**
RFC1013	X Windows System Protocol
RFC1014	XDR: External Data Representation Standard
RFC1027	Using ARP to Implement Transparent Subnet Gateways
RFC1032	Domain Administrators Guide
RFC1033	Domain Administrators Operation Guide
RFC1034	**Domain Names - Concepts and Facilities**
RFC1035	Domain Names - Implementation and Specifications
RFC1041	Telnet 3270 Regime Option
RFC1042	**Standard for the Transmission of IP Datagrams over IEEE 802 Networks**
RFC1043	Telnet Data Entry Terminal Option
RFC1044	**Internet Protocol on Network System's HYPERchannel**
RFC1053	**Telnet X 3 PAD Option**
RFC1055	**Nonstandard for Transmission of IP Datagrams over Serial Lines**
RFC1056	PCMAIL: A Distributed Mail System for Personal Computers
RFC1058	**Routing Information Protocol**
RFC1068	Background File Transfer Program (BFTP)
RFC1072	TCP Extensions of Long-Delay Paths
RFC1073	Telnet Window Size Option
RFC1074	NSFNET Backbone SPF-based Interior Gateway Protocol
RFC1079	Telnet Terminal Speed Option
RFC1080	Telnet Remote Flow Control Option
RFC1084	BOOTP Vendor Information Extensions
RFC1088	**Standard for the Transmission of IP Datagrams over NetBIOS Network**
RFC1089	SNMP over Ethernet
RFC1091	Telnet Terminal-Type Option
RFC1094	NFS: Network File System Protocol Specification
RFC1101	DNS Encoding of Network Names and Other Types
RFC1102	Policy Routing in Internet Protocols
RFC1104	Models of Policy-Based Routing
RFC1112	**Host Extension for IP Multicasting**
RFC1122	**Requirement for Internet Hosts - Communication Layers**
RFC1123	**Requirement for Internet Hosts - Application and Support**
RFC1124	Policy Issues in Interconnecting Networks
RFC1125	Policy Requirements for Inter-Administrative Domain Routing
RFC1127	Perspective on the Host Requirements RFC
RFC1129	Internet Time Protocol
RFC1143	Q Method of Implementing Telnet Option Negotiation
RFC1147	FYI on a Network Management Tool Catalog
RFC1149	Standard for the Transmission of IP Datagrams over Avian Carriers
RFC1155	**Structure and Identification of Management Information for TCP/IP-Based Internets**
RFC1156	**Management Information Base for Network Management of TCP/IP-Based Internets**
RFC1157	**Simple Network Management Protocol (SNMP)**
RFC1163	Border Gateway Protocol (BGP)
RFC1164	Application of the Border Gateway Protocol in the Internet
RFC1166	Internet Numbers
RFC1171	Point-to-Point Protocol for the Transmission of Multi-Protocol Datagrams
RFC1172	Point-to-Point Protocol Initial Configuration Options
RFC1173	Responsibilities of Host and Network Managers
RFC1175	FYI on Where to Start: A Bibliography of Internetworking Information

RFC1178	Choosing a Name For Your Computer
RFC1179	Line Printer Daemon Protocol
RFC1184	Telnet Linemode Option
RFC1187	Bulk Table Retrieval with the SNMP
RFC1188	Proposed Standard for the Transmission of TP Datagrams over FDDI Networks
RFC1195	Use of OSI IS-IS for Routing in TCP/IP and Dual Environments
RFC1196	Finger User Information Protocol
RFC1198	FYI on the X Windows System
RFC1201	Transmitting IP Traffic over ARCNET Networks
RFC1205	520 Telnet Interface
RFC1208	Glossary of Networking Terms
RFC1209	Transmission of IP Datagrams over the SMDS Service
RFC1212	**Concise MIB Definitions**
RFC1213	**MIB for Network Management of TCP/IP-Based Internets**
RFC1214	OSI Internet Management: Management Information Base
RFC1215	Convention for Defining Traps for Use with the SNMP
RFC1219	On the Assignment of Subnet Numbers
RFC1220	Point-to-Point Protocol Extensions for Bridges
RFC1224	Techniques for Managing Asynchronous Generated Alerts
RFC1227	SNMP MUX Protocol and MIB
RFC1228	SNMP-DPI: Simple Network Management Protocol Distributed Program Interface
RFC1229	Extensions to the Generic-interface MIB
RFC1230	IEEE 802 4 Token Bus MIB
RFC1231	IEEE 802 5 Token Ring MIB
RFC1232	Definitions of Managed Objects for the DS1 Interface Type
RFC1233	Definitions of Managed Objects for the DS3 Interface Type
RFC1236	IP to X 121 Address Mapping for DDN IP
RFC1238	CLNS MIB for Use with Connectionless Network Protocol
RFC1239	Reassignment of Experiment MIBs to Standard MIBs
RFC1243	Appletalk Management Information Base
RFC1245	OSPF Protocol Analysis
RFC1246	Experience with the OSPF Protocol
RFC1247	OSPF Version2
RFC1253	OSPF Version2: Management Information Base
RFC1254	Gateway Congestion Control Survey
RFC1267	A Border Gateway Protocol (BGP-3)
RFC1271	Remote Network Monitoring Management Information Base
RFC1321	The MD5 Message-Digest Algorithm
RFC1340	**Assigned Numbers**
RFC1341	MIME Mechanism for Specifying and Describing the Format of Internet Message Bodies
RFC1360	**IAB Official Protocol Standards**
RFC1522	MIME (Multipurpose Internet Mail Extensions) Part Two : Message Header Extensions for Non-ASCII Text
RFC1521	MIME (Multipurpose Internet Mail Extensions) Part One : Mechanisms for Specifying and Describing the Format of Internet Mail Message Bodies)
RFC1583	OSPF Version2
RFC1630	Universal Resource Identifiers in WWW
RFC1738	Uniform Resource Identifiers (URL)
RFC1752	The Recommendation for the IP Next-Generation Protocol
RFC1771	A Border Gateway Protocol 4 (BGP-4)
RFC1808	Relative Uniform Resource Identifiers
RFC1809	Using the Flow Label in IPv6
RFC1825	Security Architecture for the Internet Protocol
RFC1826	IP Authentication Header
RFC1827	IP Encapsulating Security Payload (ESP)
RFC1828	IP Authentication Using Keyed MD5

RFC1948	Defending Against Sequence Number Attacks
RFC1949	Scalable Multicast Key Distribution
RFC1950	ZLIB Compressed Data Format Specification version 3 3
RFC1951	DEFLATE Compressed Data Format Specification version 1 3
RFC1952	GZIP file format specification version 4 3
RFC1953	Ipsilon Flow Management Protocol Specification for IPv4 Version 1 0
RFC1954	Transmission of Flow Labelled IPv4 on ATM Data Links Ipsilon Version 1 0
RFC1955	New Scheme for Internet Routing and Addressing (ENCAPS) for IPNG
RFC1956	Registration in the MIL Domain
RFC1957	Some Observations on Implementations of the Post Office Protocol (POP3)
RFC1958	Architectural Principles of the Internet
RFC1959	An LDAP URL Format
RFC1960	A String Representation of LDAP Search Filters
RFC1961	GSS-API Authentication Method for SOCKS Version 5
RFC1962	The PPP Compression Control Protocol (CCP)
RFC1963	PPP Serial Data Transport Protocol (SDTP)
RFC1964	The Kerberos Version 5 GSS-API Mechanism
RFC1965	Autonomous System Confederations for BGP
RFC1966	BGP Route Reflection An alternative to full mesh IBGP
RFC1967	PPP LZS-DCP Compression Protocol (LZS-DCP)
RFC1968	The PPP Encryption Control Protocol (ECP)
RFC1969	The PPP DES Encryption Protocol (DESE)
RFC1970	Neighbor Discovery for IP Version 6 (IPv6)
RFC1971	IPv6 Stateless Address Autoconfiguration
RFC1972	A Method for the Transmission of IPv6 Packets over Ethernet Networks
RFC1973	PPP in Frame Relay
RFC1974	PPP Stac LZS Compression Protocol
RFC1975	PPP Magnalink Variable Resource Compression
RFC1976	PPP for Data Compression in Data Circuit-Terminating Equipment (DCE)
RFC1977	PPP BSD Compression Protocol
RFC1978	PPP Predictor Compression Protocol
RFC1979	PPP Deflate Protocol
RFC1980	A Proposed Extension to HTML : Client-Side Image Maps
RFC1981	Path MTU Discovery for IP version 6
RFC1982	Serial Number Arithmetic
RFC1983	Internet Users' Glossary
RFC1984	IAB and IESG Statement on Cryptographic Technology and the Internet
RFC1985	SMTP Service Extension for Remote Message Queue Starting
RFC1986	Experiments with a Simple File Transfer Protocol for Radio Links using Enhanced Trivial File Transfer Protocol (ETFTP)
RFC1987	Ipsilon's General Switch Management Protocol Specification Version 1 1
RFC1988	Conditional Grant of Rights to Specific Hewlett-Packard Patents In Conjunction With the Internet Engineering Task Force's Internet-Standard Network Management Framework
RFC1989	PPP Link Quality Monitoring
RFC1990	The PPP Multilink Protocol
RFC1991	PGP Message Exchange Formats
RFC1992	The Nimrod Routing Architecture
RFC1993	PPP Gandalf FZA Compression Protocol
RFC1994	PPP Challenge Handshake Authentication Protocol (CHAP)
RFC1995	Incremental Zone Transfer in DNS
RFC1996	A Mechanism for Prompt Notification of Zone Changes
RFC1997	BGP Communities Attribute
RFC1998	An Application of the BGP Community Attribute in Multi-home Routing
RFC1999	Request for Comments Summary RFC Numbers 1900-1999
RFC2000	**INTERNET OFFICIAL PROTOCOL STANDARDS**
RFC2001	TCP Slow Start, Congestion Avoidance, Fast Retransmit, and Fast

RFC2053	The AM (Armenia) Domain
RFC2054	WebNFS Client Specification
RFC2055	WebNFS Server Specification
RFC2056	Uniform Resource Locators for Z39 50
RFC2057	Source Directed Access Control on the Internet
RFC2058	Remote Authentication Dial In User Service (RADIUS)
RFC2059	RADIUS Accounting
RFC2060	INTERNET MESSAGE ACCESS PROTOCOL - VERSION 4rev1
RFC2061	IMAP4 COMPATIBILITY WITH IMAP2BIS
RFC2062	Internet Message Access Protocol - Obsolete Syntax
RFC2063	Traffic Flow Measurement: Architecture
RFC2064	Traffic Flow Measurement: Meter MIB
RFC2065	Domain Name System Security Extensions
RFC2066	TELNET CHARSET Option
RFC2067	IP over HIPPI
RFC2068	Hypertext Transfer Protocol -- HTTP/1 1
RFC2069	An Extension to HTTP: Digest Access Authentication
RFC2070	Internationalization of the Hypertext Markup Language
RFC2071	Network Renumbering Overview: Why would I want it and what is it anyway?
RFC2072	Router Renumbering Guide
RFC2073	An IPv6 Provider-Based Unicast Address Format
RFC2074	Remote Network Monitoring MIB Protocol Identifiers
RFC2075	IP Echo Host Service
RFC2076	Common Internet Message Headers
RFC2077	The Model Primary Content Type for Multipurpose Internet Mail Extensions
RFC2078	Generic Security Service Application Program Interface, Version2
RFC2079	Definition of an X 500 Attribute Type and an Object Class to Hold Uniform Resource Identifiers (URIs)
RFC2080	RIPng for IPv6
RFC2081	RIPng Protocol Applicability Statement
RFC2082	RIP-2 MD5 Authentication
RFC2083	PNG (Portable Network Graphics) Specification
RFC2084	Considerations for Web Transaction Security
RFC2085	HMAC-MD5 IP Authentication with Replay Prevention
RFC2086	IMAP4 ACL extension
RFC2087	IMAP4 QUOTA extension
RFC2088	IMAP4 non-synchronizing literals
RFC2089	V2ToV1 Mapping SNMPv2 onto SNMPv1 within a bi-lingual SNMP agent
RFC2090	TFTP Multicast Option
RFC2091	Triggered Extensions to RIP to Support Demand Circuits
RFC2092	Protocol Analysis for Triggered RIP
RFC2093	Group Key Management Protocol (GKMP) Specification
RFC2094	Group Key Management Protocol (GKMP) Architecture
RFC2095	IMAP/POP AUTHorize Extension for Simple Challenge/Response
RFC2096	IP Forwarding Table MIB
RFC2097	The PPP NetBIOS Frames Control Protocol (NBFCP)
RFC2098	Toshiba's Router Architecture Extensions for ATM : Overview
RFC2099	Request for Comments Summary RFC Numbers2000-2099
RFC2100	The Naming of Hosts
RFC2101	IPv4 Address Behavior Today
RFC2102	Multicast Support for Nimrod : Requirements and Solution Approaches
RFC2103	Mobility Support for Nimrod : Challenges and Solution Approaches
RFC2104	HMAC: Keyed-Hashing for Message Authentication
RFC2105	Cisco Systems' Tag Switching Architecture Overview
RFC2106	Data Link Switching Remote Access Protocol
RFC2107	Ascend Tunnel Management Protocol - ATMP

RFC2108	Definitions of Managed Objects for IEEE 802 3 Repeater Devices using SMIv2
RFC2109	HTTP State Management Mechanism
RFC2110	MIME E-mail Encapsulation of Aggregate Documents, such as HTML (MHTML)
RFC2111	Content-ID and Message-ID Uniform Resource Locators
RFC2112	The MIME Multipart/Related Content-type
RFC2113	IP Router Alert Option
RFC2114	Data Link Switching Client Access Protocol
RFC2115	Management Information Base for Frame Relay DTEs Using SMIv2
RFC2116	X 500 Implementations Catalog-96
RFC2117	Protocol Independent Multicast-Sparse Mode (PIM-SM): Protocol
RFC2118	Microsoft Point-To-Point Compression (MPPC) Protocol
RFC2119	Key words for use in RFCs to Indicate Requirement Level
RFC2120	Managing the X 500 Root Naming Context
RFC2121	Issues affecting MARS Cluster Size
RFC2122	VEMMI URL Specification
RFC2123	Traffic Flow Measurement: Experiences with NeTraMet
RFC2124	Cabletron's Light-weight Flow Admission Protocol Specification
RFC2125	The PPP Bandwidth Allocation Protocol (BAP) / The PPP Bandwidth Allocation Control Protocol (BACP)
RFC2126	ISO Transport Service on top of TCP (ITOT)
RFC2127	ISDN Management Information Base using SMIv2
RFC2128	Dial Control Management Information Base using SMIv2
RFC2129	Toshiba's Flow Attribute Notification Protocol (FANP)
RFC2130	The Report of the IAB Character Set Workshop held29 February - 1 March, 1996
RFC2131	Dynamic Host Configuration Protocol
RFC2132	DHCP Options and BOOTP Vendor Extensions
RFC2133	Basic Socket Interface Extensions for Ipv6
RFC2134	Articles of Incorporation of Internet Society
RFC2135	Internet Society By-Laws ISOC Board of Trustees
RFC2136	Dynamic Updates in the Domain Name System (DNS UPDATE)
RFC2137	Secure Domain Name System Dynamic Update
RFC2138	Remote Authentication Dial In User Service (RADIUS)
RFC2139	RADIUS Accounting
RFC2140	TCP Control Block Interdependence
RFC2141	URN Syntax
RFC2142	Mailbox Names for Common Services, Roles and Functions
RFC2143	Encapsulating IP with the Small Computer System Interface
RFC2145	Use and Interpretation of HTTP Version Numbers
RFC2146	U S Government Internet Domain Names Federal Networking
RFC2147	TCP and UDP over IPv6 Jumbograms
RFC2148	Deployment of the Internet White Pages Service
RFC2149	Multicast Server Architectures for MARS-based ATM multicasting
RFC2150	Humanities and Arts: Sharing Center Stage on the Internet
RFC2151	A Primer On Internet and TCP/IP Tools and Utilities
RFC2152	UTF-7 A Mail-Safe Transformation Format of Unicode
RFC2153	PPP Vendor Extensions
RFC2154	OSPF with Digital Signatures
RFC2155	Definitions of Managed Objects for APPN using SMIv2
RFC2165	Service Location Protocol
RFC2166	APPN Implementer's Workshop Closed Pages Document DLSw v2 0 Enhancements
RFC2167	Referral Whois (RWhois) Protocol V1 5
RFC2168	Resolution of Uniform Resource Identifiers using the Domain Name System
RFC2169	A Trivial Convention for using HTTP in URN Resolution
RFC2170	Application REQuested IP over ATM (AREQUIPA)
RFC2171	MAPOS - Multiple Access Protocol over SONET/SDH Version 1
RFC2172	MAPOS Version 1 Assigned Numbers

RFC2173	A MAPOS version 1 Extension - Node Switch Protocol
RFC2174	A MAPOS version 1 Extension - Switch-Switch Protocol
RFC2175	MAPOS 16 - Multiple Access Protocol over SONET/SDH with 16 Bit Addressing
RFC2176	IPv4 over MAPOS Version 1
RFC2177	IMAP4 IDLE command
RFC2178	OSPF Version2
RFC2179	Network Security For Trade Shows
RFC2180	IMAP4 Multi-Accessed Mailbox Practice
RFC2181	Clarifications to the DNS Specification
RFC2182	Selection and Operation of Secondary DNS Servers
RFC2183	Communicating Presentation Information in Internet Messages: The Content-Disposition Header Field
RFC2184	MIME Parameter Value and Encoded Word Extensions: Character Sets, Languages, and Continuations
RFC2185	Routing Aspects of IPv6 Transition
RFC2186	Internet Cache Protocol (ICP), version2
RFC2187	Application of Internet Cache Protocol (ICP), version2
RFC2188	AT&T/Neda's Efficient Short Remote Operations (ESRO) Protocol Specification Version 1 2
RFC2189	Core Based Trees (CBT version2) Multicast Routing
RFC2190	RTP Payload Format for H 263 Video Streams
RFC2191	VENUS - Very Extensive Non-Unicast Service
RFC2192	IMAP URL Scheme
RFC2193	IMAP4 Mailbox Referrals
RFC2194	Review of Roaming Implementations
RFC2195	IMAP/POP AUTHorize Extension for Simple Challenge/Response
RFC2196	Site Security Handbook
RFC2197	SMTP Service Extension for Command Pipelining
RFC2198	RTP Payload for Redundant Audio Data
RFC2200	INTERNET OFFICIAL PROTOCOL STANDARDS
RFC2201	Core Based Trees (CBT) Multicast Routing Architecture
RFC2202	Test Cases for HMAC-MD5 and HMAC-SHA-1
RFC2203	RPCSEC_GSS Protocol Specification
RFC2204	ODETTE File Transfer Protocol
RFC2205	Resource ReSerVation Protocol (RSVP) -- Version 1 Functional Specification
RFC2206	RSVP Management Information Base using SMIv2
RFC2207	RSVP Extensions for IPSEC Data Flows
RFC2208	Resource ReSerVation Protocol (RSVP) -- Version 1 Applicability Statement Some Guidelines on Deployment
RFC2209	Resource ReSerVation Protocol (RSVP) -- Version 1 Message Processing Rules
RFC2210	The Use of RSVP with IETF Integrated Services
RFC2211	Specification of the Controlled-Load Network Element Service
RFC2212	Specification of Guaranteed Quality of Service
RFC2213	Integrated Services Management Information Base using SMIv2
RFC2214	Integrated Services Management Information Base Guaranteed Service Extensions using SMIv2
RFC2215	General Characterization Parameters for Integrated Service Network Elements
RFC2216	Network Element Service Specification Template
RFC2217	Telnet Com Port Control Option
RFC2218	A Common Schema for the Internet White Pages Service
RFC2219	Use of DNS Aliases for Network Services
RFC2220	The Application/MARC Content-type
RFC2221	IMAP4 Login Referrals
RFC2222	Simple Authentication and Security Layer (SASL)
RFC2223	Instructions to RFC Authors
RFC2224	NFS URL Scheme

RFC2226	IP Broadcast over ATM Networks
RFC2227	Simple Hit-Metering and Usage-Limiting for HTTP
RFC2228	FTP Security Extensions
RFC2229	A Dictionary Server Protocol
RFC2230	Key Exchange Delegation Record for the DNS
RFC2231	MIME Parameter Value and Encoded Word Extensions: Character Sets, Languages, and Continuations
RFC2232	Definitions of Managed Objects for DLUR using SMIv2
RFC2233	The Interfaces Group MIB using SMIv2
RFC2234	Augmented BNF for Syntax Specifications: ABNF
RFC2235	Hobbes' Internet Timeline
RFC2236	Internet Group Management Protocol, Version2
RFC2237	Japanese Character Encoding for Internet Messages
RFC2238	Definitions of Managed Objects for HPR using SMIv2
RFC2239	Definitions of Managed Objects for IEEE 802 3 Medium Attachment Units (MAUs) using SMIv2
RFC2240	A Legal Basis for Domain Name Allocation
RFC2241	DHCP Options for Novell Directory Services
RFC2242	NetWare/IP Domain Name and Information
RFC2243	OTP Extended Responses
RFC2244	ACAP -- Application Configuration Access Protocol
RFC2245	Anonymous SASL Mechanism
RFC2247	Using Domains in LDAP/X 500 Distinguished Names
RFC2248	Network Services Monitoring MIB
RFC2249	Mail Monitoring MIB
RFC2250	RTP Payload Format for MPEG1/MPEG2 Video
RFC2251	Lightweight Directory Access Protocol (v3)
RFC2252	Lightweight Directory Access Protocol (v3): Attribute Syntax Definitions
RFC2253	Lightweight Directory Access Protocol (v3): UTF-8 String Representation of Distinguished Names
RFC2254	The String Representation of LDAP Search Filters
RFC2255	The LDAP URL Format
RFC2256	A Summary of the X 500(96) User Schema for use with LDAPv3
RFC2257	Agent Extensibility (AgentX) Protocol Version 1
RFC2258	Internet Nomenclator Project
RFC2259	Simple Nomenclator Query Protocol (SNQP)
RFC2260	Scalable Support for Multi-homed Multi-provider Connectivity
RFC2261	An Architecture for Describing SNMP Management Frameworks
RFC2262	Message Processing and Dispatching for the Simple Network Management Protocol (SNMP)
RFC2263	SNMPv3 Applications
RFC2264	User-based Security Model (USM) for version 3 of the Simple Network Management Protocol (SNMPv3)
RFC2265	View-based Access Control Model (VACM) for the Simple Network Management Protocol (SNMP)
RFC2266	Definitions of Managed Objects for IEEE 802 12 Repeater Devices
RFC2267	Network Ingress Filtering: Defeating Denial of Service Attacks which employ IP Source Address Spoofing
RFC2268	A Description of the RC2(r) Encryption Algorithm
RFC2269	Using the MARS model in non-ATM NBMA networks
RFC2270	Using a Dedicated AS for Sites Homed to a Single Provider
RFC2271	An Architecture for Describing SNMP Management Frameworks
RFC2272	Message Processing and Dispatching for the Simple Network Management Protocol (SNMP)
RFC2273	SNMPv3 Applications
RFC2274	User-based Security Model (USM) for version 3 of the Simple Network Management

	Protocol (SNMPv3)
RFC2275	View-based Access Control Model (VACM) for the Simple Network Management Protocol (SNMP)
RFC2276	Architectural Principles of Uniform Resource Name Resolution
RFC2277	IETF Policy on Character Sets and Languages
RFC2278	IANA Charset Registration Procedures
RFC2279	UTF-8, a transformation format of ISO 10646
RFC2280	Routing Policy Specification Language (RPSL)
RFC2281	Cisco Hot Standby Router Protocol (HSRP)
RFC2282	IAB and IESG Selection, Confirmation, and Recall Process: Operation of the Nominating and Recall Committees
RFC2283	Multiprotocol Extensions for BGP-4
RFC2284	PPP Extensible Authentication Protocol (EAP)
RFC2285	Benchmarking Terminology for LAN Switching Devices
RFC2286	Test Cases for HMAC-RIPEMD160 and HMAC-RIPEMD128
RFC2287	Definitions of System-Level Managed Objects for Applications
RFC2288	Using Existing Bibliographic Identifiers as Uniform Resource Names
RFC2289	A One-Time Password System
RFC2290	Mobile-IPv4 Configuration Option for PPP IPCP
RFC2291	Requirements for a Distributed Authoring and Versioning Protocol for the World Wide Web
RFC2292	Advanced Sockets API for IPv6
RFC2293	Representing Tables and Subtrees in the X 500 Directory
RFC2294	Representing the O/R Address hierarchy in the X 500 Directory Information Tree
RFC2295	Transparent Content Negotiation in HTTP
RFC2296	HTTP Remote Variant Selection Algorithm -- RVSA/1
RFC2297	Ipsilon's General Switch Management Protocol Specification Version2 0
RFC2298	An Extensible Message Format for Message Disposition Notifications
RFC2300	**INTERNET OFFICIAL PROTOCOL STANDARDS**
RFC2301	File Format for Internet Fax
RFC2302	Tag Image File Format (TIFF) - image/tiff MIME Sub-type Registration
RFC2303	Minimal PSTN address format in Internet Mail
RFC2304	Minimal FAX address format in Internet Mail
RFC2305	A Simple Mode of Facsimile Using Internet Mail
RFC2306	Tag Image File Format (TIFF) - F Profile for Facsimile
RFC2307	An Approach for Using LDAP as a Network Information Service
RFC2308	Negative Caching of DNS Queries (DNS NCACHE)
RFC2309	Recommendations on Queue Management and Congestion Avoidance in the Internet
RFC2310	The Safe Response Header Field
RFC2311	S/MIME Version2 Message Specification
RFC2312	S/MIME Version2 Certificate Handling
RFC2313	PKCS #1: RSA Encryption Version 1 5
RFC2314	PKCS #10: Certification Request Syntax Version 1 5
RFC2315	PKCS #7: Cryptographic Message Syntax Version 1 5
RFC2316	Report of the IAB Security Architecture Workshop
RFC2317	Classless IN-ADDR ARPA delegation
RFC2318	The text/css Media Type
RFC2319	Ukrainian Character Set KOI8-U
RFC2320	Definitions of Managed Objects for Classical IP and ARP Over ATM Using SMIv2 (IPOA-MIB)
RFC2321	RITA -- The Reliable Internetwork Troubleshooting Agent
RFC2322	Management of IP numbers by peg-dhcp
RFC2323	IETF Identification and Security Guidelines
RFC2324	Hyper Text Coffee Pot Control Protocol (HTCPCP/1 0)
RFC2325	Definitions of Managed Objects for Drip-Type Heated Beverage Hardware Devices using SMIv2

RFC2380	RSVP over ATM Implementation Requirements
RFC2381	Interoperation of Controlled-Load Service and Guaranteed Service with ATM
RFC2382	A Framework for Integrated Services and RSVP over ATM
RFC2383	ST2+ over ATM Protocol Specification - UNI 3 1 Version
RFC2384	POP URL Scheme
RFC2385	Protection of BGP Sessions via the TCP MD5 Signature Option
RFC2386	A Framework for QoS-based Routing in the Internet
RFC2387	The MIME Multipart/Related Content-type
RFC2388	Returning Values from Forms: multipart/form-data
RFC2389	Feature negotiation mechanism for the File Transfer Protocol
RFC2390	Inverse Address Resolution Protocol
RFC2391	Load Sharing using IP Network Address Translation (LSNAT)
RFC2392	Content-ID and Message-ID Uniform Resource Locators
RFC2396	Uniform Resource Identifiers (URI): Generic Syntax
RFC2397	The 'data' URL scheme
RFC2398	Some Testing Tools for TCP Implementors
RFC2400	**INTERNET OFFICIAL PROTOCOL STANDARDS**
RFC2401	Security Architecture for the Internet Protocol
RFC2402	IP Authentication Header
RFC2410	The NULL Encryption Algorithm and Its Use With IPsec
RFC2411	IP Security Document Roadmap
RFC2413	Dublin Core Metadata for Resource Discovery
RFC2414	Increasing TCP's Initial Window
RFC2415	Simulation Studies of Increased Initial TCP Window Size
RFC2416	When TCP Starts Up With Four Packets Into Only Three Buffers
RFC2417	Definitions of Managed Objects for Multicast over UNI 3 0/3 1 based ATM Networks
RFC2418	IETF Working Group Guidelines and Procedures
RFC2419	The PPP DES Encryption Protocol, Version2 (DESE-bis)
RFC2420	The PPP Triple-DES Encryption Protocol (3DESE)
RFC2421	Voice Profile for Internet Mail - version2
RFC2422	Toll Quality Voice - 32 kbit/s ADPCM MIME Sub-type Registration
RFC2423	VPIM Voice Message MIME Sub-type Registration
RFC2424	Content Duration MIME Header Definition
RFC2425	A MIME Content-Type for Directory Information
RFC2426	vCard MIME Directory Profile
RFC2427	**Multiprotocol Interconnect over Frame Relay**
RFC2428	FTP Extensions for IPv6 and NATs
RFC2429	RTP Payload Format for the 1998 Version of ITU-T Rec H 263 Video (H 263+)
RFC2430	A Provider Architecture for Differentiated Services and Traffic Engineering (PASTE)
RFC2431	RTP Payload Format for BT 656 Video Encoding
RFC2432	Terminology for IP Multicast Benchmarking
RFC2433	Microsoft PPP CHAP Extensions
RFC2434	Guidelines for Writing an IANA Considerations Section in RFCs
RFC2435	RTP Payload Format for JPEG-compressed Video
RFC2436	Collaboration between ISOC/IETF and ITU-T
RFC2437	PKCS #1: RSA Cryptography Specifications Version2 0
RFC2438	Advancement of MIB specifications on the IETF Standards Track
RFC2439	BGP Route Flap Damping
RFC2440	OpenPGP Message Format
RFC2441	Working with Jon Tribute delivered at UCLA
RFC2442	The Batch SMTP Media Type
RFC2443	A Distributed MARS Service Using SCSP
RFC2444	The One-Time-Password SASL Mechanism
RFC2445	Internet Calendaring and Scheduling Core Object Specification (iCalendar)
RFC2446	iCalendar Transport-Independent Interoperability Protocol (iTIP) Scheduling Events, BusyTime, To-dos and Journal Entries

RFC2447   iCalendar Message-based Interoperability Protocol (iMIP)
RFC2448   AT&T's Error Resilient Video Transmission Technique
RFC2449   POP3 Extension Mechanism",
RFC2453   RIP Version2 Carrying Additional Information",
RFC2455   Definitions of Managed Objects for APPN",
RFC2456   Definitions of Managed Objects for APPN TRAPS
RFC2457   Definitions of Managed Objects for Extended Border Node
RFC2458   Toward the PSTN/Internet Inter-Networking --Pre-PINT Implementations
RFC2468   I REMEMBER IANA

Quick Guide

802.12-MIB	RFC2020
802.3-MIB	RFC2108
802.5-MIB	RFC1748
ABNF	RFC2234
ACAP	RFC2244
AGENTX	RFC2257
APPN-MIB	RFC2155
ARCH-SNMP	RFC2271
ARP	RFC26
ATM-ENCAP	RFC83/1695/1755
BGP	RFC1771/1745/1772/1657/1997/1269/1403
BOOTP	RFC951/2132
CLDAP	RFC1798
CON-MD5	RFC1864
CONTENT	RFC1049
DAA	RFC2069
DASS	RFC1507
DAYTIME	RFC867
DC-MIB	RFC2128
DECNET-MIB	RFC1559
DHCP	RFC2131/1534/2132/2241
DISCARD	RFC863
DNS	RFC2181/1886/1995/2163/974/2308/1996/1612/2065/1611/2136
DOMAIN	RFC1034/1035
DSN	RFC1894
ECHO	RFC862
ENTITY-MIB	RFC2037
ESP	RFC1827
ETHER-MIB	RFC1643
FDDI-MIB	RFC1285/1512
FFIF	RFC2301
FINGER	RFC1288
FRAME-MIB	RFC2115
FTP	RFC959/2389/1415/2228
GQOS	RFC2212
GSSAP	RFC2078/1509/1964/1961
HOST-MIB	RFC1514
HTML	RFC1866/2070
HTTP-1.1	RFC2068/2109
IARP	RFC2390
ICMP	RFC792/1256/1885
IDENT	RFC1413/1414
IGMP	RFC2236/1112
IMAP	RFC2086/1731/2177/2088/2221/2193/2342/2087 2359/2195/2192/2060

IP-ARC	RFC1
IP-ARPA	RFC22
IP-ATM	RFC25
IP-FDDI	RFC90
IP-FR	RFC2427
IP-IEEE	RFC42
IP-IPX	RFC32
IP-NETBIOS	RFC88
IPNG	RFC1752
IP-SLIP	RFC55
IP-SMDS	RFC1209
IPV6	RFC1883/1826/1971/1972/2019/2147/1970/2023
IP	RFC7/56/1552/1234
ISDN-MIB	RFC2127
IS-IS	RFC1195
KERBEROS	RFC1510
LDAP	RFC2252/2253/1960/1959/2255/2251
MAIL	RFC822/2249/2142
MHTML	RFC2110
MIB	RFC1212/1213/2011/2012/2013/1239
MIME	RFC2045/2422/2049/1767/1847/2231/2046/2077
	2047/2015/2387/1892/1848/2426/2421/2423
MOBILEIP	RFC2005/2006/2002/2344
MODEM-MIB	RFC1696
NETBIOS	RFC1001/1002
NETFAX	RFC1314
NETWAREIP	RFC2242
NHRP	RFC2332/2333/2335
NICNAME	RFC954
NNTP	RFC977
NTP	RFC1119/1305
ONE-PASS	RFC2289
OSI-NSAP	RFC1629
OSI-UDP	RFC1240
OSPF	RFC2328/1793/2370/1850/1584/1587
PEM	RFC1423/1422/1421/1424
POP3	RFC1939/1734/2384
PPP	RFC1661/1662/1474/1473/1471/1472/ 2364
	1378/1638/1962/1994/1762/2284/1968/1973
	2363/1332/1618/1570/1989/1990/2097/1377
	2043/1619/1663/1598
QUOTE	RFC865
RADIUS	RFC2138
RARP	RFC3
RIP	RFC1723/1722/2082/1724/1582
RIPNG	RFC2080/2091
RMON-MIB	RFC2021/2074/1757
RPC	RFC1831/ 2203
RPSL	RFC2280
RREQ	RFC1812
RSVP	RFC2205/2208/2207/2210/2206/2209
RTP	RFC1889/1890/2029/2032/2035/2250/2198
RTSP	RFC2326/2222
SDP	RFC2327
SIP-MIB	RFC1694
SLM-APP	RFC2287
SLP	RFC2165

SMFAX-IM	RFC2305
SMI	RFC1155/1902
SMTP	RFC821/1870/1869/2197/1652/1891/2034/1985
SNA	RFC1982/2051/1666
SNMP	RFC1157/1351/1419/1420/1381/1418/1353 1352/1441/1907/2273/1382/2274
SOCKSV5	RFC1928
SONET-MIB	RFC1595
STR-LDAP	RFC2254
TABLE-MIB	RFC2096
TCP	RFC793/2018/1323/2001
TELNET	RFC854/855
TFTP	RFC1350/2347/2348/2349
TIFF	RFC2302
TIME	RFC868
TIP	RFC2371
TMUX	RFC1692
TOS	RFC1349
TP-TCP	RFC1006
TRANS-IPV6	RFC1933
TRANS-MIB	RFC1906
TXT-DIR	RFC2425
UDP	RFC768
UPS-MIB	RFC1628
URI	RFC2079/2396
URL	RFC1738/1808/2017/2368/ 2056
USERS	RFC866
UTF-8	RFC2279
VRRP	RFC2338
WHOIS++	RFC1835/1913/1914
X.500	RFC1777/1778/1567
X25-MIB	RFC1461
XDR	RFC1832

Ap12   Assigned number values

This section contains information extracted from RFC1700 [Reynolds and Postel] on assigned number values.

Ap12.1 IP Special addresses

The main forms of IP addresses are:

```
IP-address ::=  { <Network-number>, <Host-number> }
```

   and

```
IP-address ::=  { <Network-number>, <Subnet-number>, <Host-number> }
```

Special addresses are:

{0, 0}.	Host on this network. This address can only be used as a source address
{0, <Host-number>}	Host on this network
{−1, −1}.	Limited broadcast. This address can only be used as a destination address, and should not be forwarded outside the current subnet.
{<Network-number>, −1}	Directed broadcast to specified network. This address can only be used as a destination address.
{<Network-number>, <Subnet-number>, −1}	Directed broadcast to specified subnet. This address can only be used as a destination address.
{<Network-number>, -1, -1}	Directed broadcast to all subnets of specified subnetted network. This address can only be used as a destination address.
{127, <any>}	Internal host loopback address. This address should never appear outside a host.

where −1 represents an address of all 1's.

IP Versions

```
Decimal   Keyword    Version
   0                 Reserved
  1-3                Unassigned
   4       IP        Internet Protocol
   5       ST        ST Datagram Mode
   6       SIP       Simple Internet Protocol
   7       TP/IX     TP/IX: The Next Internet
   8       PIP       The P Internet Protocol
   9       TUBA      TUBA
 10-14               Unassigned
  15                 Reserved
```

IP protocol numbers

Decimal	Keyword	Protocol
0		Reserved
1	ICMP	Internet Control Message
2	IGMP	Internet Group Management
3	GGP	Gateway-to-Gateway
4	IP	IP in IP (encasulation)
5	ST	Stream
6	TCP	Transmission Control
7	UCL	UCL
8	EGP	Exterior Gateway Protocol
9	IGP	any private interior gateway
10	BBN-RCC-MON	BBN RCC Monitoring
11	NVP-II	Network Voice Protocol
12	PUP	PUP
13	ARGUS	ARGUS
14	EMCON	EMCON
15	XNET	Cross Net Debugger
16	CHAOS	Chaos
17	UDP	User Datagram
18	MUX	Multiplexing
19	DCN-MEAS	DCN Measurement Subsystems
20	HMP	Host Monitoring
21	PRM	Packet Radio Measurement
22	XNS-IDP	XEROX NS IDP
23	TRUNK-1	Trunk-1
24	TRUNK-2	Trunk-2
25	LEAF-1	Leaf-1
26	LEAF-2	Leaf-2
27	RDP	Reliable Data Protocol
28	IRTP	Internet Reliable Transaction
29	ISO-TP4	ISO Transport Protocol Class 4
30	NETBLT	Bulk Data Transfer Protocol
31	MFE-NSP	MFE Network Services Protocol
32	MERIT-INP	MERIT Internodal Protocol
33	SEP	Sequential Exchange Protocol
34	3PC	Third Party Connect Protocol
35	IDPR	Inter-Domain Policy Routing Protocol
36	XTP	XTP
37	DDP	Datagram Delivery Protocol
38	IDPR-CMTP	IDPR Control Message Transport Proto
39	TP++	TP++ Transport Protocol
40	IL	IL Transport Protocol
41	SIP	Simple Internet Protocol
42	SDRP	Source Demand Routing Protocol
43	SIP-SR	SIP Source Route
44	SIP-FRAG	SIP Fragment
45	IDRP	Inter-Domain Routing Protocol
46	RSVP	Reservation Protocol
47	GRE	General Routing Encapsulation
48	MHRP	Mobile Host Routing Protocol
49	BNA	BNA
50	SIPP-ESP	SIPP Encap Security Payload
51	SIPP-AH	SIPP Authentication Header
52	I-NLSP	Integrated Net Layer Security TUBA
53	SWIPE	IP with Encryption
54	NHRP	NBMA Next Hop Resolution Protocol
61		any host internal protocol
62	CFTP	CFTP
63		any local network
64	SAT-EXPAK	SATNET and Backroom EXPAK
65	KRYPTOLAN	Kryptolan
66	RVD	MIT Remote Virtual Disk Protocol

```
 67    IPPC         Internet Pluribus Packet Core
 68                 any distributed file system
 69    SAT-MON      SATNET Monitoring
 70    VISA         VISA Protocol
 71    IPCV         Internet Packet Core Utility
 72    CPNX         Computer Protocol Network Executive
 73    CPHB         Computer Protocol Heart Beat
 74    WSN          Wang Span Network
 75    PVP          Packet Video Protocol
 76    BR-SAT-MON   Backroom SATNET Monitoring
 77    SUN-ND       SUN ND PROTOCOL-Temporary
 78    WB-MON       WIDEBAND Monitoring
 79    WB-EXPAK     WIDEBAND EXPAK
 80    ISO-IP       ISO Internet Protocol
 81    VMTP         VMTP
 82    SECURE-VMTP  SECURE-VMTP
 83    VINES        VINES
 84    TTP          TTP
 85    NSFNET-IGP   NSFNET-IGP
 86    DGP          Dissimilar Gateway Protocol
 87    TCF          TCF
 88    IGRP         IGRP
 89    OSPFIGP      OSPFIGP
 90    Sprite-RPC   Sprite RPC Protocol
 91    LARP         Locus Address Resolution Protocol
 92    MTP          Multicast Transport Protocol
 93    AX.25        AX.25 Frames
 94    IPIP         IP-within-IP Encapsulation Protocol
 95    MICP         Mobile Internetworking Control Pro.
 96    SCC-SP       Semaphore Communications Sec. Pro.
 97    ETHERIP      Ethernet-within-IP Encapsulation
 98    ENCAP        Encapsulation Header
 99                 any private encryption scheme
100    GMTP         GMTP
```

Ports

```
0                   Reserved
1     tcpmux        TCP Port Service Multiplexer
2     compressnet   Management Utility
3     compressnet   Compression Process
5     rje           Remote Job Entry
7     echo          Echo
11    discard       Discard
13    systat        Active Users
15    daytime       Daytime
17    qotd          Quote of the Day
18    msp           Message Send Protocol
19    chargen       Character Generator
20    ftp-data      File Transfer [Default Data]
21    ftp           File Transfer [Control]
23    telnet        Telnet
25    smtp          Simple Mail Transfer
27    nsw-fe        NSW User System FE
29    msg-icp       MSG ICP
31    msg-auth      MSG Authentication
33    dsp           Display Support Protocol
37    time          Time
38    rap           Route Access Protocol
39    rlp           Resource Location Protocol
41    graphics      Graphics
42    nameserver    Host Name Server
43    nicname       Who Is
44    mpm-flags     MPM FLAGS Protocol
```

```
45     mpm            Message Processing Module
46     mpm-snd        MPM [default send]
47     ni-ftp         NI FTP
48     auditd         Digital Audit Daemon
49     login          Login Host Protocol
50     re-mail-ck     Remote Mail Checking Protocol
51     la-maint       IMP Logical Address Maintenance
52     xns-time       XNS Time Protocol
53     domain         Domain Name Server
54     xns-ch         XNS Clearinghouse
55     isi-gl         ISI Graphics Language
56     xns-auth       XNS Authentication
58     xns-mail       XNS Mail
61     ni-mail        NI MAIL
62     acas           ACA Services
64     covia          Communications Integrator (CI)
65     tacacs-ds      TACACS-Database Service
66     sql*net        Oracle SQL*NET
67     bootps         Bootstrap Protocol Server
68     bootpc         Bootstrap Protocol Client
69     tftp           Trivial File Transfer
70     gopher         Gopher
71     netrjs-1       Remote Job Service
72     netrjs-2       Remote Job Service
73     netrjs-3       Remote Job Service
74     netrjs-4       Remote Job Service
76     deos           Distributed External Object St
78     vettcp         vettcp
79     finger         Finger
80     www-http       World Wide Web HTTP
81     hosts2-ns      HOSTS2 Name Server
82     xfer           XFER Utility
83     mit-ml-dev     MIT ML Device
84     ctf            Common Trace Facility
85     mit-ml-dev     MIT ML Device
86     mfcobol        Micro Focus Cobol
88     kerberos       Kerberos
89     su-mit-tg      SU/MIT Telnet Gateway
90     dnsix          DNSIX Securit Attribute Token
91     mit-dov        MIT Dover Spooler
92     npp            Network Printing Protocol
93     dcp            Device Control Protocol
94     objcall        Tivoli Object Dispatcher
95     supdup         SUPDUP
96     ixie           DIXIE Protocol Specification
97     swift-rvf      Swift Remote Vitural File Prot
98     tacnews        TAC News
99     metagram       Metagram Relay
101    hostname       NIC Host Name Server
102    iso-tsap       ISO-TSAP
103    gppitnp        Genesis Point-to-Point Trans N
104    acr-nema       ACR-NEMA Digital Imag. & Comm.
105    csnet-ns       Mailbox Name Nameserver
106    3com-tsmux     3COM-TSMUX
107    rtelnet        Remote Telnet Service
108    snagas         SNA Gateway Access Server
109    pop2           Post Office Protocol - Version 2
110    pop3           Post Office Protocol - Version 3
111    sunrpc         SUN Remote Procedure Call
112    mcidas         McIDAS Data Transmission Proto
113    auth           Authentication Service
114    audionews      Audio News Multicast
115    sftp           Simple File Transfer Protocol
116    ansanotify     ANSA REX Notify
```

```
117   uucp-path      UUCP Path Service
118   sqlserv        SQL Services
119   nntp           Network News Transfer Protocol
120   cfdptkt        CFDPTKT
121   erpc           Encore Expedited Remote Pro.Ca
122   smakynet       SMAKYNET
123   ntp            Network Time Protocol
124   ansatrader     ANSA REX Trader
125   locus-map      Locus PC-Interface Net Map Ser
126   unitary        Unisys Unitary Login
127   locus-con      Locus PC-Interface Conn Server
128   gss-xlicen     GSS X License Verification
129   pwdgen         Password Generator Protocol
130   cisco-fna      cisco FNATIVE
131   cisco-tna      cisco TNATIVE
132   cisco-sys      cisco SYSMAINT
133   statsrv        Statistics Service
134   ingres-net     INGRES-NET Service
135   loc-srv        Location Service
136   profile        PROFILE Naming System
137   netbios-ns     NETBIOS Name Service
138   netbios-dgm    NETBIOS Datagram Service
139   netbios-ssn    NETBIOS Session Service
140   emfis-data     EMFIS Data Service
141   emfis-cntl     EMFIS Control Service
142   bl-idm         Britton-Lee IDM
143   imap2          Interim Mail Access Protocol
144   news           NewS
145   uaac           UAAC Protocol
146   iso-tp0        ISO-IP0
147   iso-ip         ISO-IP
148   cronus         CRONUS-SUPPORT
149   aed-512        AED 512 Emulation Service
150   sql-net        SQL-NET
151   hems           HEMS
152   bftp           Background File Transfer Program
153   sgmp SGMP
154   netsc-prod     NETSC
155   netsc-dev      NETSC
156   sqlsrv         SQL Service
157   knet-cmp       KNET/VM Command/Message Protocol
158   pcmail-srv     PCMail Server
159   nss-routing    NSS-Routing
160   sgmp-traps     SGMP-TRAPS
161   snmp           SNMP
162   snmptrap       SNMPTRAP
163   cmip-man       CMIP Manager
164   cmip-agent     CMIP Agent
165   xns-courier    Xerox
166   s-net          Sirius Systems
167   namp           NAMP
168   rsvd           RSVD
169   send           SEND
170   print-srv      Network PostScript
171   multiplex      Network Innovations Multiplex
172   cl/1           Network Innovations CL/1
173   xyplex-mux     Xyplex
174   mailq          MAILQ
175   vmnet          VMNET
176   genrad-mux     GENRAD-MUX
177   xdmcp          X Display Manager Control Protocol
178   nextstep       NextStep Window Server
179   bgp            Border Gateway Protocol
180   ris            Intergraph
```

```
181    unify            Unify
182    audit            Unisys Audit SITP
183    ocbinder         OCBinder
184    ocserver         OCServer
185    remote-kis       Remote-KIS
186    kis              KIS Protocol
187    aci              Application Communication Inte
188    mumps            Plus Five's MUMPS
189    qft              Queued File Transport
190    gacp             Gateway Access Control Protoco
191    prospero         Prospero Directory Service
192    osu-nms          OSU Network Monitoring System
193    srmp             Spider Remote Monitoring Proto
194    irc              Internet Relay Chat Protocol
195    dn6-nlm-aud      DNSIX Network Level Module Aud
196    dn6-smm-red      DNSIX Session Mgt Module Audit
197    dls              Directory Location Service
198    dls-mon          Directory Location Service Mon
199    smux             SMUX
200    src              IBM System Resource Controller
201    at-rtmp          AppleTalk Routing Maintenance
202    at-nbp           AppleTalk Name Binding
203    at-3             AppleTalk Unused
204    at-echo          AppleTalk Echo
205    at-5             AppleTalk Unused
206    at-zis           AppleTalk Zone Information
207    at-7             AppleTalk Unused
208    at-8             AppleTalk Unused
209    tam              Trivial Authenticated Mail Pro
210    z39.50           ANSI Z39.50
211    914c/g           Texas Instruments 914C/G Termi
212    anet             ATEXSSTR
213    ipx              IPX
214    vmpwscs          VM PWSCS
215    softpc           Insignia Solutions
216    atls             Access Technology License Serv
217    dbase            dBASE Unix
218    mpp              Netix Message Posting Protocol
219    uarps            Unisys ARPs
220    imap3            Interactive Mail Access Protocol
221    fln-spx          Berkeley rlogind with SPX auth
222    rsh-spx          Berkeley rshd with SPX auth
223    cdc              Certificate Distribution Center
243    sur-meas         Survey Measurement
245    link             LINK
246    dsp3270          Display Systems Protocol
344    pdap             Prospero Data Access Protocol
345    wserv            Perf Analysis Workbench
346    zserv            Zebra server
347    fatserv          Fatmen Server
348    csi-sgwp         Cabletron Management Protocol
371    clearcase        Clearcase
372    ulistserv        Unix Listserv
373    legent-1         Legent Corporation
374    legent-2         Legent Corporation
375    hassle           Hassle
376    nip              Amiga Envoy Network Inquiry Pr
377    tnETOS           NEC Corporation
378    dsETOS           NEC Corporation
379    is99c            TIA/EIA/IS-99 modem client
380    is99s            TIA/EIA/IS-99 modem server
381    hp-collector     hp performance data collector
382    hp-managed-node  hp performance data managed no
383    hp-alarm-mgr     hp performance data alarm mana
```

```
384    arns          A Remote Network Server System
385    ibm-app       IBM Application
386    asa           ASA Message Router Object Def.
387    aurp          Appletalk Update-Based Routing
388    unidata-ldm   Unidata LDM Version 4
389    ldap          Lightweight Directory Access P
390    uis           UIS
391    synotics-relay SynOptics SNMP Relay Port
392    synotics-brokerSynOptics Port Broker Port
393    dis           Data Interpretation System
394    embl-ndt      EMBL Nucleic Data Transfer
395    netcp         NETscout Control Protocol
396    netware-ip    Novell Netware over IP
397    mptn          Multi Protocol Trans. Net.
398    kryptolan     Kryptolan
400    work-sol      Workstation Solutions
401    ups           Uninterruptible Power Supply
402    genie         Genie Protocol
403    decap         decap
404    nced nced
405    ncld ncld
406    imsp Interactive Mail Support Proto
407    timbuktu      Timbuktu
408    prm-sm        Prospero Resource Manager Sys.
409    prm-nm        Prospero Resource Manager Node
410    decladebug    DECLadebug Remote Debug Protoc
411    rmt           Remote MT Protocol
412    synoptics-trap Trap Convention Port
413    smsp SMSP
414    infoseek      InfoSeek
415    bnet BNet
416    silverplatter Silverplatter
417    onmux         Onmux
418    hyper-g       Hyper-G
419    ariel1        Ariel
420    smpte         SMPTE
421    ariel2        Ariel
422    ariel3        Ariel
423    opc-job-start IBM Operations Planning and Co
424    opc-job-track IBM Operations Planning and Co
425    icad-el       ICAD
426    smartsdp      smartsdp
427    svrloc        Server Location
428    ocs_cmu       OCS_CMU
429    ocs_amu       OCS_AMU
430    utmpsd        UTMPSD
431    utmpcd        UTMPCD
432    iasd IASD
433    nnsp NNSP
434    mobileip-agent MobileIP-Agent
435    mobilip-mn    MobilIP-MN
436    dna-cml       DNA-CML
437    comscm        comscm
438    dsfgw         dsfgw
439    dasp          dasp
440    sgcp          sgcp
441    decvms-sysmgt decvms-sysmgt
442    cvc_hostd     cvc_hostd
443    https         https   MCom
444    snpp          Simple Network Paging Protocol
445    microsoft-ds  Microsoft-DS
446    ddm-rdb       DDM-RDB
447    ddm-dfm       DDM-RFM
448    ddm-byte      DDM-BYTE
```

```
449   as-servermap    AS Server Mapper
450   tserver         TServer
512   exec            remote process execution;
513   login            remote login
514   cmd             like exec, but automatic
515   printer         spooler
517   talk            like tenex link, but across
518   ntalk
519   utime           unixtime
520   efs             extended file name server
525   timed           timeserver
526   tempo           newdate
530   courier         rpc
531   conference      chat
532   netnews         readnews
533   netwall         for emergency broadcasts
539   apertus-ldp     Apertus Technologies Load Dete
540   uucp uucpd
541   uucp-rlogin     uucp-rlogin  Stuart Lynne
543   klogin
544   kshell          krcmd
550   new-rwho        new-who
555   dsf
556   remotefs        rfs server
560   rmonitor        rmonitord
561   monitor
562   chshell         chcmd
564   9pfs            plan 9 file service
565   whoami          whoami
570   meter           demon
571   meter           udemon
600   ipcserver       Sun IPC server
607   nqs  nqs
606   urm             Cray Unified Resource Manager
608   sift-uft        Sender-Initiated/Unsolicited F
609   npmp-trap       npmp-trap
610   npmp-local      npmp-local
611   npmp-gui        npmp-gui
634   ginad           ginad
666   mdqs
666   doom            doom Id Software
704   elcsd           errlog copy/server daemon
709   entrustmanager  EntrustManager
729   netviewdm1      IBM NetView DM/6000 Server/Cli
730   netviewdm2      IBM NetView DM/6000 send
731   netviewdm3      IBM NetView DM/6000 receive/tc
741   netgw           netGW
742   netrcs          Network based Rev. Cont. Sys.
744   flexlm          Flexible License Manager
747   fujitsu-dev     Fujitsu Device Control
748   ris-cm          Russell Info Sci Calendar Mana
749   kerberos-adm    kerberos administration
750   rfile
751   pump
752   qrh
753   rrh
754   tell send
758   nlogin
759   con
760   ns
761   rxe
762   quotad
763   cycleserv
764   omserv
```

```
765   webster
767   phonebook       phone
769   vid
770   cadlock
771   rtip
772   cycleserv2
773   submit
774   rpasswd
775   entomb
776   wpages
780   wpgs
786   concert         Concert
800   mdbs_daemon
801   device
996   xtreelic        Central Point Software
997   maitrd
998   busboy
999   garcon
1000  cadlock
```

Multicast

```
224.0.0.0          Base Address (Reserved)
224.0.0.1          All Systems on this Subnet
224.0.0.2          All Routers on this Subnet
224.0.0.3          Unassigned
224.0.0.4          DVMRP    Routers
224.0.0.5          OSPFIGP  OSPFIGP All Routers
224.0.0.6          OSPFIGP  OSPFIGP Designated Routers
224.0.0.7          ST Routers
224.0.0.8          ST Hosts
224.0.0.9          RIP2 Routers
224.0.0.10         IGRP Routers
224.0.0.11         Mobile-Agents
224.0.0.12-224.0.0.255     Unassigned
224.0.1.0          VMTP Managers Group
224.0.1.1          NTP      Network Time Protocol
224.0.1.2          SGI-Dogfight
224.0.1.3          Rwhod
224.0.1.4          VNP
224.0.1.5          Artificial Horizons - Aviator
224.0.1.6          NSS - Name Service Server
224.0.1.7          AUDIONEWS - Audio News Multicast
224.0.1.8          SUN NIS+ Information Service
224.0.1.9          MTP Multicast Transport Protocol
224.0.1.10         IETF-1-LOW-AUDIO
224.0.1.11         IETF-1-AUDIO
224.0.1.12         IETF-1-VIDEO
224.0.1.13         IETF-2-LOW-AUDIO
224.0.1.14         IETF-2-AUDIO
224.0.1.15         IETF-2-VIDEO
224.0.1.16         MUSIC-SERVICE
224.0.1.17         SEANET-TELEMETRY
224.0.1.18         SEANET-IMAGE
224.0.1.19         MLOADD
224.0.1.20         any private experiment
224.0.1.21         DVMRP on MOSPF
224.0.1.22         SVRLOC
224.0.1.23         XINGTV
224.0.1.24         microsoft-ds
224.0.1.25         nbc-pro
224.0.1.26         nbc-pfn
224.0.1.27-224.0.1.255     Unassigned
224.0.2.1          "rwho" Group (BSD) (unofficial)
```

```
224.0.2.2                     SUN RPC PMAPPROC_CALLIT
224.0.3.000-224.0.3.255       RFE Generic Service
224.0.4.000-224.0.4.255       RFE Individual Conferences
224.0.5.000-224.0.5.127       CDPD Groups
224.0.5.128-224.0.5.255       Unassigned
224.0.6.000-224.0.6.127       Cornell ISIS Project
224.0.6.128-224.0.6.255       Unassigned
224.1.0.0-224.1.255.255       ST Multicast Groups
224.2.0.0-224.2.255.255       Multimedia Conference Calls
224.252.0.0-224.255.255.255   DIS transient groups
232.0.0.0-232.255.255.255     VMTP transient groups
```

IP type of service

```
TOS Value        Description
   0000          Default
   0001          Minimize Monetary Cost
   0010          Maximize Reliability
   0100          Maximize Throughput
   1000          Minimize Delay
   1111          Maximize Security


Type of Service recommended values:


Protocol             TOS Value
TELNET (1)           1000                    (minimize delay)
FTP
   Control           1000                    (minimize delay)
   Data (2)          0100                    (maximize throughput)
TFTP                 1000                    (minimize delay)
SMTP (3)
   Command phase     1000                    (minimize delay)
   DATA phase        0100                    (maximize throughput)
Domain Name Service
   UDP Query         1000                    (minimize delay)
   TCP Query         0000
   Zone Transfer     0100                    (maximize throughput)
NNTP                 0001                    (minimize monetary cost)
ICMP
   Errors            0000
   Requests          0000 (4)
   Responses         <same as request> (4)
Any IGP              0010                    (maximize reliability)
EGP                  0000
SNMP                 0010                    (maximize reliability)
BOOTP                0000
```

ICMP type numbers

```
Type    Name
   0    Echo Reply
   1    Unassigned
   2    Unassigned
   3    Destination Unreachable
   4    Source Quench
   5    Redirect
   6    Alternate Host Address
   7    Unassigned
   8    Echo
   9    Router Advertisement
  10    Router Selection
  11    Time Exceeded
  12    Parameter Problem
```

```
13      Timestamp
14      Timestamp Reply
15      Information Request
16      Information Reply
17      Address Mask Request
18      Address Mask Reply
19      Reserved (for Security)
20-29   Reserved (for Robustness Experiment)
30      Traceroute
31      Datagram Conversion Error
32      Mobile Host Redirect
33      IPv6 Where-Are-You
34      IPv6 I-Am-Here
35      Mobile Registration Request
36      Mobile Registration Reply
37-255  Reserved


Type    Name
  0       Echo Reply
          Codes
              0  No Code
  3       Destination Unreachable
          Codes
              0  Net Unreachable
              1  Host Unreachable
              2  Protocol Unreachable
              3  Port Unreachable
              4  Fragmentation Needed and Don't Fragment was Set
              5  Source Route Failed
              6  Destination Network Unknown
              7  Destination Host Unknown
              8  Source Host Isolated
              9  Communication with Destination Network is
                 Administratively Prohibited
             10  Communication with Destination Host is
                 Administratively Prohibited
             11  Destination Network Unreachable for Type of Service
             12  Destination Host Unreachable for Type of Service
  4       Source Quench
          Codes
              0  No Code
  5       Redirect
          Codes
              0  Redirect Datagram for the Network (or subnet)
              1  Redirect Datagram for the Host
              2  Redirect Datagram for the Type of Service and Network
              3  Redirect Datagram for the Type of Service and Host
  6       Alternate Host Address
          Codes
              0  Alternate Address for Host
  7       Unassigned
  8       Echo
          Codes
              0  No Code
  9       Router Advertisement
          Codes
          0  No Code
 10       Router Selection
          Codes
              0  No Code
 11       Time Exceeded
          Codes
              0  Time to Live exceeded in Transit
              1  Fragment Reassembly Time Exceeded
```

```
12       Parameter Problem
         Codes
             0   Pointer indicates the error
             1   Missing a Required Option
             2   Bad Length
13       Timestamp
         Codes
             0   No Code
14       Timestamp Reply
         Codes
             0   No Code
15       Information Request
         Codes
             0   No Code
16       Information Reply
         Codes
             0   No Code
17       Address Mask Request
         Codes
             0   No Code
18       Address Mask Reply
         Codes
             0   No Code
30       Traceroute
31       Datagram Conversion Error
32       Mobile Host Redirect
33       IPv6 Where-Are-You
34       IPv6 I-Am-Here
35       Mobile Registration Request
36       Mobile Registration Reply
```

TCP options

```
Type      Length         Description
  0    -   End of Option List
  1    -   No-Operation
  2    4   Maximum Segment Lifetime
  3    3   WSOPT - Window Scale
  4    2   SACK Permitted
  5    N   SACK
  6    6   Echo (obsoleted by option 8)
  7    6   Echo Reply (obsoleted by option by 8)
  8   10   TSOPT - Time Stamp Option
  9    2   Partial Order Connection Permited
 10    5   Partial Order Service Profile
 11        CC
 12        CC.NEW
 13        CC.ECHO
 14    3   TCP Alternate Checksum Request
 15    N   TCP Alternate Checksum Data
 16        Skeeter
 17        Bubba
 18    3   Trailer Checksum Option
```

Domain Names

For the Internet (IN) class the following are defined:

```
TYPE   Value Description
A      1     Host address
NS     2     Authoritative name server
MD     3     Mail destination (Obsolete - use MX)
MF     4     Mail forwarder (Obsolete - use MX)
```

```
CNAME   5    Canonical name for an alias
SOA     6    Start of a zone of authority
MB      7    Mailbox domain name
MG      8    Mail group member
MR      9    Mail rename domain name
NULL    10   Null RR
WKS     11   Well-known service description
PTR     12   Domain name pointer
HINFO   13   Host information
MINFO   14   Mailbox or mail list information
MX      15   Mail exchange
TXT     16   Text strings
RP      17   For Responsible Person
AFSDB   18   For AFS Data Base location
```

Mail encoder header types

```
Keyword    Description
EDIFACT    EDIFACT format
EDI-X12    EDI X12 format
EVFU       FORTRAN format
FS         File System format
Hex        Hex binary format
LZJU90     LZJU90 format
LZW        LZW format
Message    Encapsulated Message
PEM        Privacy Enhanced Mail
PGP        Pretty Good Privacy
Postscript Postscript format
Shar       Shell Archive format
Signature  Signature
Tar        Tar format
Text       Text
uuencode   uuencode format
URL        external URL-reference
```

BOOTP and DHCP parameters

Tag	Name	Data Length	Meaning
0	Pad	0	None
1	Subnet Mask	4	Subnet Mask Value
2	Time Offset	4	Time Offset in Seconds from UTC
3	Gateways	N	N/4 Gateway addresses
4	Time Server	N	N/4 Timeserver addresses
5	Name Server	N	N/4 IEN-116 Server addresses
6	Domain Server	N	N/4 DNS Server addresses
7	Log Server	N	N/4 Logging Server addresses
8	Quotes Server	N	N/4 Quotes Server addresses
9	LPR Server	N	N/4 Printer Server addresses
10	Impress Server	N	N/4 Impress Server addresses
11	RLP Server	N	N/4 RLP Server addresses
12	Hostname	N	Hostname string
13	Boot File Size	2	Size of boot file in 512 byte chunks
14	Merit Dump File		Client to dump and name the file to dump it to
15	Domain Name	N	The DNS domain name of the client
16	Swap Server	N	Swap Server addeess
17	Root Path	N	Path name for root disk
18	Extension File	N	Path name for more BOOTP info
19	Forward On/Off	1	Enable/Disable IP Forwarding
20	SrcRte On/Off	1	Enable/Disable Source Routing
21	Policy Filter	N	Routing Policy Filters
22	Max DG Assembly	2	Max Datagram Reassembly Size
23	Default IP TTL	1	Default IP Time to Live
24	MTU Timeout	4	Path MTU Aging Timeout

```
25       MTU Plateau         N      Path MTU  Plateau Table
26       MTU Interface       2      Interface MTU Size
27       MTU Subnet          1      All Subnets are Local
28       Broadcast Address   4      Broadcast Address
29       Mask Discovery      1      Perform Mask Discovery
30       Mask Supplier       1      Provide Mask to Others
31       Router Discovery    1      Perform Router Discovery
32       Router Request      4      Router Solicitation Address
33       Static Route        N      Static Routing Table
34       Trailers            1      Trailer Encapsulation
35       ARP Timeout         4      ARP Cache Timeout
36       Ethernet            1      Ethernet Encapsulation
37       Default TCP TTL     1      Default TCP Time to Live
38       Keepalive Time      4      TCP Keepalive Interval
39       Keepalive Data      1      TCP Keepalive Garbage
40       NIS Domain          N      NIS Domain Name
41       NIS Servers         N      NIS Server Addresses
42       NTP Servers         N      NTP Server Addresses
43       Vendor Specific     N      Vendor Specific Information
44       NETBIOS Name Srv    N      NETBIOS Name Servers
45       NETBIOS Dist Srv    N      NETBIOS Datagram Distribution
46       NETBIOS Note Type   1      NETBIOS Note Type
47       NETBIOS Scope       N      NETBIOS Scope
48       X Window Font       N      X Window Font Server
49       X Window Manmager   N      X Window Display Manager
50       Address Request     4      Requested IP Address
51       Address Time        4      IP Address Lease Time
52       Overload            1      Overloaf "sname" or "file"
53       DHCP Msg Type       1      DHCP Message Type
54       DHCP Server Id      4      DHCP Server Identification
55       Parameter List      N      Parameter Request List
56       DHCP Message        N      DHCP Error Message
57       DHCP Max Msg Size   2      DHCP Maximum Message Size
58       Renewal Time        4      DHCP Renewal (T1) Time
59       Rebinding Time      4      DHCP Rebinding (T2) Time
60       Class Id            N      Class Identifier
61       Client Id           N      Client Identifier
62       Netware/IP Domain   N      Netware/IP Domain Name
63       Netware/IP Option   N      Netware/IP sub Options
128-154  Reserved
255      End                 0      None
```

Directory system names

```
Keyword   Attribute (X.520 keys)
 CN       CommonName
 L        LocalityName
 ST       StateOrProvinceName
 O        OrganizationName
 OU       OrganizationalUnitName
 C        CountryName
```

Content types and subtypes

```
Type   Subtype
text   plain
   richtext
   tab-separated-val
multipart   mixed
   alternative
   digest
   parallel
   appledouble
   header-set
```

```
message  rfc822
   partial
   external-body
   news
application octet-stream
   postscript
   oda
   atomicmail
   andrew-inset
   slate
   wita
   dec-dx
   dca-rft
   activemessage
   rtf
   applefile
   mac-binhex40
   news-message-id
   news-transmission
   wordperfect5.1
   pdf
   zip
   macwriteii
   msword
   remote-printing
image jpeg
   gif
   ief
   tiff
audio basic
video mpeg
   quicktime
```

Character Sets

```
US-ASCII       ISO-8859-1     ISO-8859-2     ISO-8859-3
ISO-8859-4     ISO-8859-5     ISO-8859-6     ISO-8859-7
ISO-8859-8     ISO-8859-9
```

Access Types

```
FTP            ANON-FTP       TFTP           AFS
LOCAL-FILE     MAIL-SERVER
```

Conversion Values

```
7BIT           8BIT           BASE64         BINARY
QUOTED-PRINTABLE
```

MIME / X.400 mapping table

MIME content-type	X.400 Body Part
text/plain	
charset=us-ascii	ia5-text
charset=iso-8859-x	Extended Body Part - GeneralText
text/richtext	no mapping defined
application/oda	Extended Body Part - ODA
application/octet-stream	bilaterally-defined
application/postscript	Extended Body Part - mime-postscript-body
image/g3fax	g3-facsimile
image/jpeg	Extended Body Part - mime-jpeg-body
image/gif	Extended Body Part - mime-gif-body
audio/basic	no mapping defined
video/mpeg	no mapping defined

X.400 to MIME Table

X.400 Basic Body Part	MIME content-type
ia5-text	text/plain;charset=us-ascii
voice	No Mapping Defined
g3-facsimile	image/g3fax
g4-class1	no mapping defined
teletex	no mapping defined
videotex	no mapping defined
encrypted	no mapping defined
bilaterally-defined	application/octet-stream
nationally-defined	no mapping defined
externally-defined	See Extended Body Parts

X.400 Extended body part conversion

X.400 Extended Body Part	MIME content-type
GeneralText	text/plain;charset=iso-8859-x
ODA	application/oda
mime-postscript-body	application/postscript
mime-jpeg-body	image/jpeg
mime-gif-body	image/gif

Inverse ARP

Number	Operation Code (op)
1	REQUEST
2	REPLY
3	request Reverse
4	reply Reverse
5	DRARP-Request
6	DRARP-Reply
7	DRARP-Error
8	InARP-Request
9	InARP-Reply
10	ARP-NAK

Number	Hardware Type (hrd)
1	Ethernet (10Mb)
2	Experimental Ethernet (3Mb)
3	Amateur Radio AX.25
4	Proteon ProNET Token Ring
5	Chaos
6	IEEE 802 Networks
7	ARCNET
8	Hyperchannel
9	Lanstar
10	Autonet Short Address
11	LocalTalk
12	LocalNET
13	Ultra link
14	SMDS
15	Frame Relay
16	Asynchronous Transmission Mode
17	HDLC
18	Fibre Channel
19	Asynchronous Transmission Mode
20	Serial Line
21	Asynchronous Transmission Mode

IEEE 802 numbers of interest

```
   Link Service Access Point
   IEEE      Internet
   binary    binary    decimal   Description
   00000000 00000000       0     Null LSAP
   01000000 00000010       2     Indiv LLC Sublayer Mgt
   11000000 00000011       3     Group LLC Sublayer Mgt
   00100000 00000100       4     SNA Path Control
   01100000 00000110       6     Reserved (DOD IP)
   01110000 00001110      14     PROWAY-LAN
   01110010 01001110      78     EIA-RS 511
   01111010 01011110      94     ISI IP
   01110001 10001110     142     PROWAY-LAN
   01010101 10101010     170     SNAP
   01111111 11111110     254     ISO CLNS IS 8473
   11111111 11111111     255     Global DSAP
```

IANA Ethernet address block

The Internet Assigning Numbers Authority (IANA) owns the starting Ethernet address of:

0000 0000 0000 0000 0111 1010 (which is 00-00-5E)

This address can be used with the multicast bit (which is the first bit to the address) to create an Internet Multicast. It has the form:

```
1000 0000 0000 0000 0111 1010 xxxx xxx0 xxxx xxxx xxxx xxxx

|                                      |
Multicast Bit                          0 = Internet Multicast
                                       1 = Assigned by IANA for
                                               other uses
```

This gives an address range from 01-00-5E-00-00-00 to 01-00-5E-7F-FF-FF .

Ap6.1.2   Ethernet vendor address

An Ethernet address is 48 bits. The first 24 bits identifies the manufacturer and the next 24 bits identifies the serial number. The manufacturer codes include:

```
00000C  Cisco
00000E  Fujitsu
00000F  NeXT
000010  Sytek
00001D  Cabletron
000020  DIAB
000022  Visual Technology
00002A  TRW
000032  GEC Computers Ltd
00005A  S & Koch
00005E  IANA
000065  Network General
00006B  MIPS
000077  MIPS
00007A  Ardent
000089  Cayman Systems
000093  Proteon
00009F  Ameristar Technology
```

```
0000A2   Wellfleet
0000A3   NAT
0000A6   Network General
0000A7   NCD
0000A9   Network Systems
0000AA   Xerox
0000B3   CIMLinc
0000B7   Dove
0000BC   Allen-Bradley
0000C0   Western Digital
0000C5   Farallon phone net card
0000C6   HP INO
0000C8   Altos
0000C9   Emulex
0000D7   Dartmouth College
0000DD   Gould
0000DE   Unigraph
0000E2   Acer Counterpoint
0000EF   Alantec
0000FD   High Level Hardvare
000102   BBN
001700   Kabel
008064   Wyse Technology
00802D   Xylogics, Inc.
00808C   Frontier Software Development
0080C2   IEEE 802.1 Committee
0080D3   Shiva
00AA00   Intel
00DD00   Ungermann-Bass
00DD01   Ungermann-Bass
020701   Racal InterLan
020406   BBN
026086   Satelcom MegaPac
02608C   3Com
02CF1F   CMC
080002   3Com
080003   ACC
080005   Symbolics
080008   BBN
080009   Hewlett-Packard
08000A   Nestar Systems
08000B   Unisys
080011   Tektronix, Inc.
080014   Excelan
080017   NSC
08001A   Data General
08001B   Data General
08001E   Apollo
080020   Sun
080022   NBI
080025   CDC
080026   Norsk Data (Nord)
080027   PCS Computer Systems
080028   TI
08002B   DEC
08002E   Metaphor
08002F   Prime Computer
080036   Intergraph
080037   Fujitsu-Xerox
080038   Bull
080039   Spider Systems
080041   DCA
080046   Sony
080047   Sequent
```

```
080049  Univation
08004C  Encore
08004E  BICC
080056  Stanford University
08005A  IBM
080067  Comdesign
080068  Ridge
080069  Silicon Graphics
08006E  Concurrent
080075  DDE
08007C  Vitalink
080080  XIOS
080086  Imagen/QMS
080087  Xyplex
080089  Kinetics
08008B  Pyramid
08008D  XyVision
080090  Retix Inc
800010  AT&T
```

Ethernet multicast addresses

An Ethernet multicast address has a multicast bit, a 23-bit vendor identifier part and a 24-bit vendor assigned part.

```
Ethernet                Type
Address                 Field   Usage
01-00-5E-00-00-00-      0800    Internet Multicast
01-00-5E-7F-FF-FF
01-00-5E-80-00-00-      ????    Internet reserved by IANA
01-00-5E-FF-FF-FF
01-80-C2-00-00-00       -802-   Spanning tree (for bridges)
09-00-02-04-00-01?      8080?   Vitalink printer
09-00-02-04-00-02?      8080?   Vitalink management
09-00-09-00-00-01       8005    HP Probe
09-00-09-00-00-01       -802-   HP Probe
09-00-09-00-00-04       8005?   HP DTC
09-00-1E-00-00-00       8019?   Apollo DOMAIN
09-00-2B-00-00-00       6009?   DEC MUMPS?
09-00-2B-00-00-01       8039?   DEC DSM/DTP?
09-00-2B-00-00-02       803B?   DEC VAXELN?
09-00-2B-00-00-03       8038    DEC Lanbridge Traffic Monitor (LTM)
09-00-2B-00-00-04       ????    DEC MAP End System Hello
09-00-2B-00-00-05       ????    DEC MAP Intermediate System Hello
09-00-2B-00-00-06       803D?   DEC CSMA/CD Encryption?
09-00-2B-00-00-07       8040?   DEC NetBios Emulator?
09-00-2B-00-00-0F       6004    DEC Local Area Transport (LAT)
09-00-2B-00-00-1x       ????    DEC Experimental
09-00-2B-01-00-00       8038    DEC LanBridge Copy packets
09-00-2B-01-00-01       8038    DEC LanBridge Hello packets
09-00-4E-00-00-02?      8137?   Novell IPX
09-00-56-00-00-00-      ????    Stanford reserved
09-00-56-FE-FF-FF
09-00-56-FF-00-00-      805C    Stanford V Kernel, version 6.0
09-00-56-FF-FF-FF
09-00-77-00-00-01       ????    Retix spanning tree bridges
09-00-7C-02-00-05       8080?   Vitalink diagnostics
0D-1E-15-BA-DD-06       ????    HP
AB-00-00-01-00-00       6001    DEC Maintenance Operation Protocol
AB-00-00-02-00-00       6002    DEC Maintenance Operation Protocol
AB-00-00-03-00-00       6003    DECNET Phase IV end node Hello
AB-00-00-04-00-00       6003    DECNET Phase IV Router Hello packets
AB-00-00-05-00-00       ????    Reserved DEC through
```

```
AB-00-03-FF-FF-FF
AB-00-03-00-00-00        6004    DEC Local Area Transport (LAT) - old
AB-00-04-00-xx-xx        ????    Reserved DEC customer private use
AB-00-04-01-xx-yy        6007    DEC Local Area VAX Cluster groups
                                 Sys. Communication Architecture (SCA)
CF-00-00-00-00-00        9000    Ethernet Configuration Test protocol
                                 (Loopback)
```

Ethernet broadcast address

```
FF-FF-FF-FF-FF-FF        0600    XNS packets, Hello or gateway search?
FF-FF-FF-FF-FF-FF        0800    IP (e.g. RWHOD via UDP) as needed
FF-FF-FF-FF-FF-FF        0804    CHAOS
FF-FF-FF-FF-FF-FF        0806    ARP (for IP and CHAOS) as needed
FF-FF-FF-FF-FF-FF        0BAD    Banyan
FF-FF-FF-FF-FF-FF        1600    VALID packets, Hello or gateway search?
FF-FF-FF-FF-FF-FF        8035    Reverse ARP
FF-FF-FF-FF-FF-FF        807C    Merit Internodal (INP)
FF-FF-FF-FF-FF-FF        809B    EtherTalk
```

Index

adaptive dictionary data compression, 184
Adaptive Huffman, 183, 184, 1443
ADC, 23, 198, 1461
address
    bus, 10, 12, 14–16
    field, 324, 325, 357, 362, 377, 380, 423, 435,
        453, 465, 466, 485, 499, 522, 527, 684
    filtering, 699
    resolution, 601, 1443
addressable memory, 15, 16, 401
addressing, 58, 94, 97, 152, 360, 405, 437, 495,
    501, 502, 516, 531, 536, 556, 674, 796, 815,
    892, 922, 1449, 1453–1456, 1460
ADPCM, 442, 471, 1461, 1469, 1587
AES, 1461
AFI, 485, 486, 1461
AGP, 1461
AIX, 56
alias, 902
alphabet shifting, 738
ALT, 987, 1188, 1191, 1409, 1421, 1512, 1527
AM, 24, 150, 161–163, 167, 168, 401, 1444, 1461,
    1581
AMI, 463, 464, 1461
amplitude modulation, 150, 161, 164, 208,
    1461, 1468
amplitude-shift keying, 163
anchors, 989
AND, 227, 228, 258, 1141–1144, 1146
angle, 343, 424, 767, 1168, 1170, 1416
animation, 23, 176, 697, 815, 820, 1181, 1249,
    1325
anonymous, 821, 822, 863, 864, 1469, 1573,
    1574
ANSI, 20, 151, 274, 373, 375, 418, 425, 428, 431,
    434, 983, 1437, 1444, 1445, 1460, 1461
API, 50, 57, 81, 605, 796, 797, 804, 889, 1180,
    1461, 1466, 1470, 1481, 1585, 1586
Apple, 56, 57, 59, 564, 796, 952, 1317, 1319,
    1330, 1444, 1457
applet viewer, 1132
AppleTalk, 59, 319, 607, 660, 668, 671, 876, 877,
    1444, 1461, 1470
application layer, 313, 314, 316, 320, 536, 595,
    1444
application level gateway, 700, 701
ARC, 1465
architecture, 2–5, 9, 10, 110, 308, 337, 436, 516,

520, 551, 565, 687, 796, 818, 875, 919, 926,
    1441, 1462, 1469, 1470, 1481
archive, 885, 1477
arithmetic operator, 1139, 1140
arp, 325, 376–380, 529, 601, 658, 660, 662, 663,
    666, 671, 855, 856, 893, 983, 1444, 1445,
    1454, 1458, 1461, 1465, 1474, 1576, 1585,
    1588
arrowkeys, 1197
ASCII, 17, 20, 151, 185, 239, 244, 261–264, 267,
    292, 296, 297, 598, 742, 744, 745, 747, 765,
    766, 768–771, 797, 798, 803, 805–809, 901,
    916, 983, 1136, 1137, 1142, 1151, 1437,
    1439, 1444, 1461, 1476
    BEL, 962, 1437
    bit stream timings, 263
    CR, 242, 299, 799, 800, 801, 811, 1437
    DC1, 265, 1437
    DC2, 1437
    DC3, 1437
    DC4, 265, 1437
    EOT, 451, 801, 813, 1437, 1464
    FF, 325, 376–378, 381, 386, 411, 422, 529,
        808, 984, 1437, 1440, 1464, 1474
    HT, 1437
    LF, 799, 800, 801, 811, 1437
    NUL, 1437
    SUB, 970, 1437
    VT, 1437
ASK, 163, 164, 1444, 1456, 1461
ASP, 1085-1130
aspect ratio, 215, 217
asymmetric and symmetric switches, 398
asymmetrical compression, 195
asynchronous, 47, 121, 261, 263, 295, 296, 303,
    422, 423, 452, 455, 457, 468, 476, 1407,
    1445, 1460, 1461, 1469
asynchronous modem, 296
AT, 56, 291, 292, 297, 298, 301–305, 352, 367,
    757, 962, 1405, 1408, 1461, 1470, 1583, 1588
at (execute commands at later date), 74
ATDT, 291, 297, 298, 300, 301
ATH, 292, 298–301
ATM, 152, 227, 240, 259, 295, 355, 372, 390,
    398, 401, 429, 431–442, 444–447, 451, 461,
    473, 487, 532, 575, 595, 653, 673, 990, 997,
    1441, 1442, 1445, 1447, 1448, 1461, 1465,
    1578–1582, 1584–1587

companding, 1444

compatibility, 57, 297, 313, 355, 368, 372, 404, 567, 605, 780, 877, 928, 939, 1180,1321, 1473

compilation, 1168

compiler, 942, 943, 1131–1133, 1167, 1171, 1177, 1199, 1226

components, 958

composite video, 210

compression, 164, 174–176, 179–182, 184–193, 195, 196, 198–202, 214, 222, 224, 295, 297, 471, 671, 764, 765, 828, 832, 834, 835, 884, 897, 905, 907, 952, 986, 999, 1330, 1331, 1409, 1452, 1455, 1456, 1459, 1460, 1468

    images, 815

    TV, 214

    methods, 179

    ratio, 189, 190, 202, 214

    time, 191

computational Difficulty, 734

concatenated, 765, 902, 1137

concentrator, 328, 329, 334, 425, 1462, 1469

connection-oriented, 320, 321, 442, 443, 533, 537, 558, 567, 877, 922, 1442, 1448

connectors, 7, 26, 28, 153, 260, 317, 323, 333, 338, 352, 355, 364, 365, 371, 409, 413, 414, 1457, 1458

consecutive zeros, 418, 420, 421

console, 323, 656, 658, 661, 664, 866, 1320

constants, 1163, 1170, 1504, 1506, 1507, 1510, 1515, 1522, 1527–1529, 1541

constructors, 1156, 1159, 1503–1506, 1510–1559

content, 14, 157, 158, 160, 401, 689, 765, 784–786, 802, 803, 805–807, 810, 813, 827, 828, 830, 832, 834, 835, 933, 1319–1325, 1330, 1452, 1462

    advisor, 784, 785

contention, 53, 333, 355, 370–372, 398

continuous, 235, 250, 598, 1330, 1459

control

    field, 359–361, 410, 411, 421, 422, 434, 435, 451, 453–455, 457, 458, 465, 467, 468, 831, 1445, 1462

    token, 331, 332, 409–411

convolutional code

    coding tree, 251

    k/n code, 250

    maximim likelihood, 253

    most favored route, 257

    rate code, 235

    Trellis diagram, 165, 251–258

    Viteribi decoder, 253

co-operative multitasking, 42

cookies, 1063

core system components, 45

correction, 165, 227, 235, 236, 239, 244, 249, 297, 314, 451, 458, 1406, 1460, 1464

cosine, 190, 191, 197, 1168, 1459, 1463, 1466

counting to Infinity, 681

CR, 242, 299, 799–801

CR character, 299, 800

CRC, 234, 239–242, 250, 357, 358, 372, 410, 423, 443, 444, 456, 469, 667, 1443, 1449, 1462

    decoding, 241

    -CCITT, 239, 240, 241, 456

    -8, 10,12,16, 32, 239, 240, 241

crossed-pair, 352

crosstalk,21, 26, 28, 29, 159, 236–338, 339, 351, 375, 1449

cross-talk, 21, 26, 159, 345, 375

    near-end, 351

CRT, 1462

cryptographic keys, 736

cryptographics, 731

CSDN, 170, 473, 1462

CSMA, 333, 334, 356, 362, 371, 372, 390, 398, 1441, 1449, 1462

    /CA, 1462

    /CD, 333, 334, 356, 362, 371, 372, 390, 398, 1441, 1449, 1462

CSS, 1291–1299

Crtl, 75, 602, 1188, 1190, 1512

Ctrl-Alt-Del, 75

CTS, 261, 265, 268, 269, 282–285, 1407, 1412, 1413, 1462

current, 72, 75, 896, 897, 909, 1182, 1192–1194, 1199

cut sheet, 350, 1449

cut-through switching, 400, 1449

cyclic redundancy check, 234, 357, 358, 410, 456, 469, 1462

cyclic redundancy check, 234, 1449

cylinders, 342

DA, 410, 422, 423, 1440, 1462

DAC, 23, 177, 425, 1462

intranets, 697, 759, 815

IP, 31, 56, 90, 113, 115, 117, 152, 314, 315, 318–
320, 322, 333, 335, 357, 359, 360, 376, 377,
378–380, 382, 404, 432, 437, 440, 447, 495–
505, 512, 513, 515–528, 529, 531, 532, 536–
538, 540, 550, 552, 553, 555, 560, 565, 567,
595, 597, 598, 600–603, 605, 608, 614, 617,
619, 632, 633, 635, 637, 653, 656, 660, 662–
666, 668, 669, 671, 672, 674, 684, 693, 697,
698–704, 706, 707, 731, 780, 785, 794, 797,
815, 842, 852– 854, 855–858, 860, 861, 876,
877, 881, 889, 892, 893, 919, 921, 922, 924,
926, 938, 939, 983, 1131, 1442–1444, 1446,
1449, 1450, 1452–1454, 1456–1459, 1464–
1466, 1473–1476, 1575–1589

address allocation, 519

address format, 501

address range, 503

address, 31, 113, 117, 152, 318, 320, 322,
359, 376–380, 382, 432, 437, 440, 495,
496, 498, 499–505, 512, 513, 515–524,
526, 528, 532, 537, 595, 597, 598, 600,
601, 603, 608, 614, 617, 619, 632, 633,
635, 637, 656, 660, 662–666, 669, 675,
684, 693, 698–700, 702–704, 706, 785,
852–861, 881, 893, 983, 1131, 1443, 1444,
1446, 1450, 1453, 1454, 1457, 1458, 1473–
1476

addressing, 152, 432, 495, 501, 502

class A, 442, 501–505, 1580

class B, 442, 501–505, 506, 530

class C, 442, 501– 506, 656, 660

creating subnets, 504

function, 497

group addresses, 515

header, 377, 499, 516–518, 521–25, 532, 537,
540, 1459

multicasting, 515

protocol, 359, 360, 440, 497– 500, 536, 598,
794, 797, 892, 1446, 1452, 1454, 1456,
1459, 1575

spoofing, 703, 706

subnet masks, 505

time-to-live, 499, 523, 524, 556, 598, 599,
601, 860, 922, 1470, 1476

v6 header format, 517

v6, 516–518, 1465, 1468

Ver4, 516, 517

Ver6, 516–518, 532, 1578–1580, 1586

IPX, 37, 59, 314, 318, 319, 335, 357, 516, 529,
552–559, 563, 565, 567, 607, 660, 672, 674,
875, 876, 877, 919, 921, 922, 923, 925, 926,
934, 938, 939, 1450, 1454, 1456, 1458, 1465,
1466, 1470, 1478

.COM, 876

/SPX, 37, 59, 357, 553, 876, 877, 919

AppleTalk, 876

IPX.COM, 876

IPXODI, 564, 565, 876

ODI, 564, 565, 876

packet format, 922

IRQ, 53, 55, 265, 279, 1466

IRQ0, 53, 54

IRQ1, 47, 53, 54

IRQ12, 54

IRQ13, 54

IRQ14, 54

IRQ15, 54

IRQ2, 53, 54

IRQ3, 53, 54

IRQ4, 53, 54

IRQ5, 53, 54

IRQ6, 54

IRQ7, 53, 54

IRQ8, 54

IRQ9, 54

ISA, 155, 1466

ISDN, 1, 152, 170, 201, 295, 307, 433, 461–470,
532, 703, 817, 818, 1446, 1453, 1456, 1458,
1461, 1466, 1468, 1582

basic rate, 461, 462, 464

B-channels, 462, 465, 469

B-ISDN, 461, 462, 1461

broadband, 461

call clearing, 470

call establish, 470, 471

channels, 462

data link layer, 465

D-channel, 459, 462–469, 1446

D-channel contention, 468

dial-up, 818

frame format, 464, 465

H0, 462, 1405

H11, 462, 463

H12, 462, 463

information messages, 470

919, 921–926, 939, 1444–1447, 1449, 1452,
1453, 1456–1460, 1468, 1470, 1476
filters, 699, 702
Internet Gopher, 597
sniffing, 706
switched, 170, 428, 473, 474, 479, 480, 483,
484, 1460, 1468
PAL, 174, 193, 203–214, 1317, 1467
palette, 188, 190, 1452
PAM, 375
paragraph, 970, 1420, 1421
parallel port, 53, 54, 153, 260, 1464
parameter list, 1170
parameter passing, 1131
parameters, 947, 988, 992, 1175, 1177, 1187,
1193, 1195
PARC, 57, 115
parity, 235, 238, 262, 284, 285, 878
even, 238, 244, 248, 262, 275–277, 280
odd, 238, 244, 261, 262, 749
passive, 110, 329, 413, 542, 547, 1453
password, 30, 31, 36, 95, 113, 114, 116, 119,
312, 659, 660, 664–668, 685, 686, 702, 703,
705, –711, 767, 786, 811, 820–822, 834, 863,
864, 881, 911, 926, 935, 996, 997, 1223,
1457, 1467, 1480, 1573, 1574
patch, 347, 348, 350, 352, 373, 1452
patch panels, 350
PATH, 314, 693, 1131, 1572
PCM, 150, 166, 198, 420, 431, 433, 442, 463,
464, 471, 1443, 1444, 1449, 1463, 1467
adaptive delta modulation, 1443
delta modulation, 471, 1449
low-delay CELP, 471
TDM, 166, 431, 433, 463
PCMCIA, 359
pcnfsd, 121, 1569
PCX, 188, 189, 190
PDN, 170, 473, 1467
PDUs, 326, 496
peer-to-peer, 29, 30, 31, 59, 81, 311, 542, 875,
881
perceived, 190, 199, 200
permanent connection, 170, 296, 462, 473
permutations, 1153
PGP, 733, 764 –770, 777, 778, 1467, 1579, 1580
example encryption, 766
authentication, 777

key management options, 766
phase
modulation (PM), 163
quadrature, 208
shift keying, 163
phases, 163, 165, 184, 439, 1455
phone, 5, 6, 147, 292, 295, 298, 512, 702, 1478
photographic, 23
PHY, 418, 428, 441, 1467
physical, 314, 316, 318, 361, 362, 383, 418, 420,
428, 495, 603, 705, 876, 1451, 1457, 1458
addresses, 318
layer, 313–317, 322, 361, 366, 373, 427, 441,
462, 463, 474, 476, 876, 1451, 1457, 1460,
1467
media dependent, 418
signaling (PLS) and physical medium attachment (PMA), 362
PIN numbers, 735
ping, 495, 521, 595, 597, 598, 601, 670, 671,
1467, 1476, 1477
pipeline, 98
pipes, 69, 70, 81
PISO, 1467
pixel aspect ratio, 217
pixel ratio, 217
pixels, 174, 175, 180, 188, 191–194, 197, 201,
203, 207, 213, 214, 217, 221, 224, 987, 988,
991, 992, 1175, 1317
PKP, 733, 1467
plaintext, 223, 224, 733, 736, 740, 741, 748, 754,
759, 765, 766, 774, 824
plastic cable, 339
Platform for Internet Content Selection, 784
playing cards, 1172
PLL, 162, 198, 385, 386, 1457, 1467
PMD, 418, 428, 1468
pointer, 57, 65, 269, 270, 386, 523, 527, 528,
540, 548, 806, 819, 910, 1131, 1137, 1475
point-to-point protocol, 411, 498, 603, 670,
671, 672, 702, 1448, 1457, 1465, 1468, 1578–
1582, 1585– 1589
polarization, 817
poll/final bit, 467
polygons, 1195
polynomial, 227, 228, 239–243, 436, 456, 469
port number, 121, 279, 280, 287, 402, 537, 538–
540, 544, 602, 607, 614, 634, 639, 698, 705,

set asynchronous balance mode extended, 468

shared memory, 81

shared secret-key authentication, 771

shared-file approach versus client/server
approach, 794

sharing disk resources (network file servers),
310

sharing information, 309, 310

shielded twisted pair, 409, 414, 1447

shielding, 338

shift registers, 228, 234

shortest-job-first, 66

S-HTTP, 779, 783

signal frequency content, 157

signal-to-noise ratio, 159, 196, 375, 1470

simplex, 153, 1459

sine, 163, 1168, 1170

single-tasking, 37

SIPO, 198, 1469

SIPP, 516, 1469

SKIPJACK, 749

slave in, 425

slave out, 425

slices and macroblocks, 193

SMA, 346, 364, 1462

SMDS, 599, 672, 1442, 1465, 1469, 1577

SMT, 418, 420, 428, 1469

SMTP, 32, 538, 540, 595, 632, 698, 699, 704,
780, 794, 796–804, 809–811, 894, 1469,
1575, 1579, 1580, 1583, 1587, 1590
    example transmission, 801, 802
    MIME, 797
    operation, 797
    overview, 798
    responses, 801
    transfer, 799

SNA, 308, 359–361, 553, 560, 876, 919, 924,
1468, 1469

SNMP, 32, 518, 538, 540, 550, 841, 842, 844,
845, 851, 894, 1458, 1459, 1470, 1480, 1576,
1577, 1581, 1584, 1585, 1590

SNR, 159, 1470

socket, 81, 560, 607–611, 613, 614, 629, 630–
633, 634, 700, 779, 924, 1167, 1554, 1582
    connection, 629
    creating, 631
    number, 533, 538, 731
    Windows, 877

software handshaking, 265, 267

software interrupts, 51

SONET, 441, 1468, 1470, 1582, 1583, 1590

source
    address, 357, 377, 401, 410, 412, 422, 527,
        698, 699, 1449, 1469
    destination address, 330, 331, 333, 356, 357,
        409, 412, 731
    compression, 187
    route bridging, 323
    encoding, 190, 1459

SPACE, 239, 738, 743, 744, 833, 1134, 1136,
    1437, 1511, 1527, 1541

spanning tree, 323, 324, 381, 672

SPARC, 57, 889

speech, 21, 23, 147, 149, 152, 157, 160, 174, 176,
    177, 295, 311, 370, 427, 431–433, 446, 461,
    471, 785, 793, 794, 817, 1330, 1444, 1450,
    1452, 1456, 1457
    compression, 471

split horizon, 681

SPX, 90, 314, 355, 357, 532, 536, 552, 553, 555,
    556, 558, 559, 565, 567, 607, 668, 875–877,
    919, 921–923, 926, 938, 1470
    IPX, 90, 355, 532, 536, 551–553, 565, 567,
        607, 668, 875–877, 919, 926, 938
    packet format, 559, 923

SQDV, 203

SQL, 1333–1350

square root, 1148, 1170, 1240, 1241, 1243, 1540

SRAM, 10, 1470

SREJ, 236, 455

SSL, 748, 779, 780, 784, 1470

ST connector, 364

standalone, 307, 398, 952, 1132, 1133, 1216

standard input/output, 902, 905, 909

star network, 328, 330, 331, 367

start and end delimiter, 410, 421, 466

start bit, 261, 262, 263, 296, 422

start delimiter, 357, 411, 412, 421–423, 1469

startup files and scripts, 933

starvation, 87

stateless protocol, 822, 824

static interference, 345

static methods, 1162

station management, 418

statistical
    encoding, 180, 186, 1451, 1459

multiplexing, 438
stereo audio, 198
STM, 433, 434, 438, 441, 447, 1470
stop bit, 261–263, 265, 271, 275–277, 280, 286, 288, 295, 296, 1445
store-and-forward switching, 400
STP, 337, 339, 366, 381, 382, 413–415, 1470
streaming, 1330, 1331
stream-oriented, 537
string manipulation, 1549
striping with parity, 878
strowger, 150
STS-1, 441
SUB, 970
sub-band, 1469
subcarrier, 204, 208, 209, 211
subnet, 404, 484, 495, 504–506, 511, 513, 517, 521, 524, 530, 656, 663, 664, 667, 684, 853, 855, 856, 859, 1453–1456, 1476
    masks, 505, 684
subsampling, 191, 212
subscript, 970
Sun Microsystems, 92, 110, 952, 1330, 1456, 1457, 1586
SuperJANET, 429, 447, 599
supervisory frames, 454–456, 467
suppressing repetitive sequences, 180, 1459
SVGA, 215, 1470
switch, 322, 333, 372, 374, 381, 397–402, 404, 405, 413, 434, 437–440, 598, 600, 656, 662, 668, 669, 938, 1134, 1149, 1150, 1413, 1443–1446, 1452, 1573
    cut-through, 400, 401, 1449
    store-and-forward, 401, 1443
    switching hubs, 397
sync pulse, 204, 208, 209, 211
synchronization, 37, 42, 97, 166, 184, 533, 555, 691, 893, 921, 926, 936, 937, 1319, 1452, 1455, 1469, 1586
synchronization bits, 462, 464
synchronized, 107, 296, 385, 420, 441, 465, 630, 635, 927, 938, 1134, 1325, 1445, 1459, 1505–1509, 1516–1525, 1528, 1553, 1554
synchronous, 111, 295, 422, 423, 428, 433, 441, 451, 1407, 1454, 1460, 1469, 1470
synchronous modems, 296
syndrome, 247–249
system timer, 54

tab, 1137, 1415, 1511, 1527
task manager, 75
task switching, 69
TCP, 31, 35, 37, 46, 56, 59, 90, 91, 94, 115, 120, 308, 314, 315, 320, 333, 355, 357, 359, 360, 432, 440, 495, 496, 498–500, 516, 518, 520, 523, 524, 531, 532, 535–549, 552, 553, 558, 560, 565, 567, 595, 597, 598, 601–603, 605, 607, 614, 619, 620, 630, 634, 668, 672, 697, 698, 704, 706, 731, 780, 794, 797–800, 815, 824, 831, 842, 854, 856, 860, 865, 876, 877, 889, 892, 893, 919, 922, 924, 926, 938, 939, 983, 1131, 1446, 1452, 1454, 1457, 1459, 1466, 1470, 1473–1476, 1575–1577, 1579, 1580, 1582, 1587, 1590
    connection, 541
    connection states, 543
    header format, 538, 539
    internets, 500
    ISN selection, 545
    opening and closing a connection, 546
    ports and sockets, 538
    protocol data unit, 496, 538
    sequence numbers, 537, 541, 544
    specification, 541
    TCB parameters, 544, 545
    UDP, 536
    user commands, 547
TCP user commands
    ABORT, 543, 549
    CLOSE, 541, 543, 544, 546–548, 602, 603
    OPEN, 541–543, 547, 691, 692, 693, 694
    RECEIVE, 69, 70, 382, 541–543, 546, 548
    SEND, 69, 70, 541–543, 548, 799
    STATUS, 542, 543, 549
TCP/IP, 31, 35, 37, 46, 56, 59, 90, 91, 308, 314, 320, 333, 355, 357, 359, 360, 440, 495, 496, 498, 500, 520, 531, 532, 536, 549, 552, 553, 560, 565, 567, 595, 597, 598, 601, 602, 605, 634, 697, 698, 704, 706, 780, 794, 797, 815, 824, 842, 854, 856, 860, 876, 877, 889, 892, 919, 924, 926, 938, 939, 983, 1131, 1446, 1452, 1454, 1457, 1459, 1473–1577, 1582
    Class A, 501, 505
    Class B, 442, 501, 502, 505
    Class C, 442, 501, 505
    gateway, 496, 500, 560, 924
    implementation, 500